a concept dictionary of english

a
concept
dictionary
of english

Julius Laffal

GALLERY PRESS   Essex   Connecticut

and

HALSTED PRESS, A DIVISION OF

JOHN WILEY & SONS
New York   London   Sydney   Toronto

Other books by Julius Laffal:
Pathological and Normal Language (1965)

Published by:
Gallery Press
and
Halsted Press, a Division of John Wiley & Sons, Inc., New York

Gallery Press
North Main Street
Essex, Connecticut 06426

Library of Congress Catalog Card Number 72-97927

ISBN 0 470-51160-5

Printed in the United States of America
by Halliday Lithograph Corporation
West Hanover, Massachusetts 02339

"Every other author may aspire to praise; the lexicographer can only hope to escape reproach."

-Samuel Johnson
A Dictionary of the English Language (1755)

preface

Fifteen years ago I began to explore a new approach to understanding the anomalous speech of psychotic patients then in psychotherapeutic treatment with me at the Veterans Administration Hospital in West Haven. It seemed to me that if one had a broad sample of a patient's language, it might be possible to shed light on his more obscure statements by observing how the words in these passages were used in other contexts. I chose one patient whose language was both intriguing and difficult to follow and had thirty of his interviews, ranging over a two year period, transcribed from tape recordings.
As I tried to apply this method, it became clear that some way would have to be found of equating different words with substantially the same reference. That was the beginning of the present dictionary. I think it is important to mention this particular origin of the dictionary because it reveals an implicit orientation toward understanding the psychology of individual speakers.

I began to group words into categories, using at first the criterion of synonymity, and subsequently the additional criteria of similarity and relatedness. *Auto* and *car* are synonyms, *auto* and *truck* are similar, and *auto* and *train* are related. As word categories evolved, I applied what I called the method of "contextual associates" to a theoretical issue in the interpretation of symbolism in the memoirs of Daniel Paul Schreber (1903). In this method the kinds of

words occurring in the contexts of separate key words are compared
to determine the similarity of contexts, and by implication the cognitive similarity of the key words. Schreber's work had been made
famous by Sigmund Freud's use of it to show the development of paranoia (Freud, 1911). But two English psychiatrists, Ida Macalpine
and Richard A. Hunter (1955) disputed Freud's interpretations, and
in particular his assumption that the sun and God represented father
figures in Schreber's writing. My study (Laffal, 1960) attempted to
determine objectively whether the contexts of *sun* and *God* in Schreber's writing were more similar to his contexts for typically male
or typically female words.

How this kind of analysis evolved further is described in my book,
Pathological and Normal Language (1965). The method seemed pro-
mising, and I turned my attention to development of a dictionary of
word concepts which would permit one to explore content without
tripping endlessly over problems of word equivalence. Once a dictionary of word concepts was available, applying computer methods
went hand in hand, always with an eye toward application in studies
of the language of individual speakers.

George Sadowsky wrote a computer text analysis program for me
in 1963 at Yale, for use on the IBM 709. The program was designed
to accept a cardpunched text, with each word edited into root form
similar to the dictionary entries, and to output a profile showing how
frequently the various dictionary concepts were used in the text. This
program was used in several studies (Laffal, 1969; Hartsough and
Laffal, 1970). Subsequently Lawrence MacNaughton III wrote a similar program for use on the IBM 1130 at Wesleyan University, incor-
porating a novel "fallback" procedure which permitted a text to be
analyzed without prior editing into root words. The fallback procedure defined a dictionary equivalent of a text word as the first dictionary entry which matched most initial letters of the text word.

Whenever I thought of publishing the dictionary, it seemed that
word definitions, a usual ingredient of dictionaries, would call for an
unduly large book with much superfluous material. In considering
ways of shortening the whole work to include only what was essential, I happened on the idea of mnemonic code names for the conceptual categories. Up to that moment the concept categories had been
identified by numbers, with word names attached to the numbers
(Laffal, 1965). The original word names were simply words chosen
from the categories, not to be taken as core words or as defining
words for the concepts. No matter how hard I stressed this, it seemed difficult to convey that the concept name word was simply a sample
word from the category and not representative of all words in the
category. I finally realized that the concept name did inevitably cre-

ate a meaning expectation for the category as a whole. It was then that I thought of mnemonic names and brief word names for the categories, the challenge being to find ones that would hit closely at a central component of the category meaning. A certain degree of freedom in conveying meanings is created by a mnemonic neologism. Thus, SIML may be read as *similar, similarity, simulate* and *assimilate*; MOTV may be read as *motive, motivate* and *emotive;* and MECH may be read as *mechanism, mechanic* and *mechanical*. This little increase in generality has made illustrative sentences or definitions less necessary. The brief word or mnemonic neologism does not always fill the bill, particularly for categories which encompass several somewhat different meanings. But this reflects the larger problem of placement of words in categories of optimal fit. While each word has been examined and reexamined for best placement, the dictionary user will undoubtedly differ with me in many instances over the concepts assigned to a word.

The concept dictionary provides a means of looking through a speaker's language to the concepts which lie behind them. In this respect it is like an interlingual dictionary, translating words into the the more general language of concepts. The concept language consists of 118 content categories empirically derived by grouping words related in meaning. Of these, one is a "no score" (NSCR) category, in which such function words as articles and relative pronouns are placed, and one is a "hand score" (HSCR) category indicating that an editor's judgment is required as to appropriate content. Personal pronouns are in the HSCR category. Around 23,500 words of English are categorized.

The 118 categories are not a best or a final group of categories. It is possible to expand the number by redefining some categories, or to reduce it by merging categories. If someone who had never seen this dictionary undertook to divide the language into 118 concepts, it is highly likely that he would come up with a group which resembled the present one. This assertion is based on the fact that there are many similarities between the content categories in apparently unrelated studies. Such, for example, are Carl D. Buck's *A Dictionary of Selected Synonyms in the Principal Indo-European Languages* (1949) and Caroline Spurgeon's *Shakespeare's Imagery and What It Tells Us* (1935).

Part 1 presents the rationale of the dictionary and illustrates its application. Part 2 contains brief descriptions of each category. Part 3 is an alphabetical listing of all the words in the dictionary. Each word is followed by a letter indicating part of speech, and one or two mnemonic code names, representing the appropriate concepts for the word. The mnemonic names are four or fewer letters. The letters identifying part of speech are defined in footnotes at intervals throughout the dictionary proper.

Part 4 is a listing of the dictionary words by category. If the reader wishes to note the words in a category or in some combination of categories, he may look up the category in its alphabetical place. For category combinations, he may scan the words of a category and pick out those which receive the relevant second category. This part provides an overview of the content of each category, and words for specific categories if the reader wishes to focus upon limited areas of content.

Words derivable from the dictionary entries by adding or subtracting a suffix are not listed unless the suffix alters the meaning substantially. A computer oriented fallback procedure is described on page 12 which identifies the appropriate dictionary entry for a word not listed in its exact textual form. What may appear to be redundant entries in the dictionary are made necessary by this fallback procedure. The redundancy is amply compensated for by economy in the total number of words listed.

The present dictionary is in the tradition of the thesaurus or analogic dictionary represented by Peter Mark Roget (1852), Prudence Boissière (1882), Franz Dornseiff (1933), and Julio Casares (1959). The earlier dictionaries were designed primarily to help the reader find a word for what he had in mind, while incidentally embodying a philosophical viewpoint about the relationship between experience and language. The first of these concerns has disappeared as a serious reason for preparing a conceptual dictionary. The second is now part of a growing interest in semantic theory, that is, the theory of how we conceptualize our world in words (Katz and Postal, 1964; Fillenbaum and Rapoport, 1972; Miller, 1972).

A Concept Dictionary of English is, as far as I know, the first to organize the vocabulary of a language with concepts rather than specific words as practical target elements. The dictionary has been applied in a number of automatic computer analyses of conceptual content, and it is possible to incorporate it directly into a program for computerized content analysis. However, the simplicity of the dictionary makes hand analysis of content eminently feasible.

The range of possible applications of a concept dictionary is broad. Practical experience alone will tell whether some of the possibilities are workable. Psychological studies with earlier forms of the present concept dictionary applied it in a variety of ways: comparing segments within a single individual's speech and writing (Laffal, 1960, 1961, 1965); comparing the speech content of separate speakers as topic changed (Laffal and Feldman, 1962, 1963; Laffal, 1967); tracing developmental changes in children's language (Laffal, 1969);

comparing the language content of psychotherapists with that of their patients (Watson and Laffal, 1963); and comparing the language content of scientists from different disciplines (Hartsough and Laffal, 1970). The dictionary may be used in comparative literature, in the manner of Caroline Spurgeon's analysis of Shakespeare's imagery (1935): examination of selections from separate authors shows a striking predilection for different contents (Laffal, 1970). The dictionary could become a tool in effective language use, since it offers the opportunity to discover one's preferences and deficiencies in language for the available conceptual areas. The dictionary may also be used in the analysis of political documents. On pages 16 and 17 a segment of the *Declaration of Independence* is analyzed. The categories weighted most heavily in this segment are LEAD, LAW, GRUP, MOTV, MALE, SIML, WHOL, TRUE, END, AID, BGIN, DAMG and EVER. LEAD, LAW, GRUP, MALE and WHOL stem from references to government, king, people and mankind: the issue and the contending forces. MOTV and TRUE reflect references to rights and causes. SIML is high in frequency because of words like *accordingly, equal, same* and *such.* END refers primarily to abolishing and suspending, and BGIN to creating and instituting, the first characteristic of the king, the second of the Creator. Similiarly, DAMG refers to injuries, usurpations and dangers to which the states are exposed, and AID to safety, security and exercise of powers which they seek. EVER refers to tradition, custom and patience.

During the many years in which the dictionary evolved, numerous colleagues, assistants and students helped its growth in various ways. I wish especially to acknowledge the contributions of Sheldon Feldman and Ross Hartsough in collaborative research using the dictionary; of George Sadowsky, Lawrence MacNaughton III, Linda Metz, James M. Macfarlane and Alex R. Strong in programming the dictionary for computer analysis of texts; of Rae Bartozzi, Michael Perle and Paul Laffal in helping organize the dictionary and differentiate word meanings in its early stages; of Mary Berloni and Jean Flood in so patiently typing the manuscript. I owe a great debt to Wesleyan University for making its computer facilities available to me. In the year before this book went to press my wife Florence worked intensively with me reviewing every entry for alternative possible classifications and shepherding the work toward publication; without her collaboration the dictionary could not have been published.

Julius Laffal

Middletown, Connecticut

contents

1

structure of
the dictionary

conceptual domains

A conceptual dictionary is a collection of the words of a language organized to show the kinds of content represented in the words. The categories of content are presumed to reflect cognitive-conceptual sets which are evoked whenever a pertinent word is encountered. The evidence for the existence of such sets is substantial, stemming from the work of Weston Bousfield (1953) who showed that if a series of randomly mixed words from several distinct classes were presented to subjects, they would recall the words in an organized fashion by classes (See also Bousfield, Cohen and Whitmarsh, 1958; Bousfield, Puff and Cowan, 1964; Tulving, 1962; Cofer, 1965, 1968; and Mandler, 1967). Like the thesaurus and the synonym dictionary, the concept dictionary has as its major purpose the identification and exploitation of similarities in the meanings of words.

Ordinary speakers are in substantial agreement about the meanings of words, although the words may also carry personal connotations. Commonality of meaning stems from the similarity of our experiences as human beings and from the similarity of the processes by which we learn our language. It is to the commonality of meaning that a concept dictionary addresses itself.

Peter Mark Roget's thesaurus (1852) was designed to supply for the English language "a collection of the words it contains and of the idiomatic combinations peculiar to it, arranged, not in alphabetical

order as they are in a dictionary, but according to the *ideas* which
they express." Roget wished to provide his readers with a practical
device for finding words to fit what they wished to say. Regarding the
organization of his work, he said, "I have taken as my guide the more
obvious characters of the ideas for which expressions were to be tabu-
lated, arranging them under such classes and categories as reflec-
tion and experience had taught me would conduct the inquirer most
readily and quickly to the object of his search. Commencing with the
ideas expressing abstract relations, I proceeded to those which relate to space and to the phenomena of the material world, and lastly
to those in which the mind is concerned, and which comprehend intellect, volition, and feeling."

In Roget's thesaurus, groups of words are lodged in a hierarchy
based on logical relations to each other and to superordinate and subordinate ideas. It was not Roget's intention to create a conceptual
scheme of language, but to help the logically minded man find words
for his thoughts. Nevertheless he provided the earliest model of a
conceptual scheme of language. That his scheme has not been used in
scientific studies of language and concepts underlying language is
attributable to two facts: that its 1,000 headings represent too fine a
division of language for practical research purposes, and that it is an
abstract scheme, relatively removed from common, everyday experience. This latter touchstone has been eagerly sought by the modern
concept dictionary maker as the basis for a *catalogus mundi*.

Prudence Boissière (1882) provided a conceptual scheme similar
to Roget's for the French language, and in more recent years Franz
Dornseiff (1933) and Julio Casares (1959) have prepared analogic dictionaries of German and Spanish. The work of Dornseiff and Casares
is of special interest. Both exceed Roget in number of categories,
Dornseiff having around 1,500 and Casares 2,000. In each case there
is a grand design for the categorization of the subject matter of the
lexicon, and subdivisions under which words with similar and related
meanings are grouped. But within each category the reader is addressed to intersecting and related categories based on associative
relationships. Thus the schemes have not only a logical structure,
but a psychological one as well, stemming from the experiential association of otherwise dissimilar things. We are as yet a long way from
a combined logical-psychological conceptual picture of language, but
Dornseiff and Casares have, I believe, provided a glimpse of a pro-
mising direction. The present conceptual dictionary does not pursue
this lead directly, but some applications of it have explored the relationship of apparently unrelated words and concepts by examining
the associated textual material appearing in close contiguity with
these words and concepts (Laffal, 1960, 1965).

How is a concept dictionary derived? Linguistic models of research call for an informant speaker of the language to make judgments about particular usages; psychological models use group responses to derive norms of individual use. Analogic or conceptual dictionaries, however, are generally derived from written examples, from search of other dictionaries, and from the dictionary maker himself as a knowledgeable speaker of the language. The possibility of error due to subjectivity is thus fairly strong in conceptual dictionaries and it behooves the dictionary maker to introduce controls wherever possible.

The present concept dictionary relied for such controls on interaction with colleagues, reliability checks, and empirical tests. Particularly in the earlier stages of development of the dictionary, while only core groups of words and general category descriptions existed, reliability checks were part of all empirical studies performed. In one study (Watson and Laffal, 1963) recategorization of an interview segment by a single scorer after five weeks gave an 85.4 percent agreement between the two sets of scores, and in another (Laffal and Feldman, 1962) three scorers had 90 percent, 83 percent, and 82 percent agreement in categorizing individual words. Another form of reliability test was applied to speech samples from several psychiatric patients. The samples were divided in two by taking alternate lines of the typed texts, and content profiles of the separate texts were prepared. The profiles had Pearson correlation coefficients ranging from $r=.932$ to $r=.956$ when all 94 of the categories in existence at that time were employed. When very high and very low frequency categories were eliminated from the profiles, leaving only 34 middle frequency categories, reliability correlation coefficients ranged from .801 to .935. While these reliability coefficients apply to profiles as wholes rather than to specific categories, they nevertheless show that the categories tend to be quite stable. In one of the earliest studies applying the concept dictionary (Laffal, 1960) reliabilities for samples of text surrounding key words under study, ranged from Pearson correlation coefficient $r=.566$ to $r=.737$. Other inter-scorer reliability tests gave uniformly high indices of agreement when judges were required to place words into categories based on category descriptions alone (Laffal, 1963). These checks and tests provide limited evidence of objectivity of the categories. However, the author's own judgments were a major factor in the evolution of the category system, and the dictionary in its present form is best viewed as a product of subjective intuitions, interactions with others, and empirical applications.

Roget, Boissière, Dornseiff, Casares and others who have made analogic dictionaries were primarily interested in words rather than categories. A word might fit rather poorly in a particular category with no harm done, as long as it had some affinity with other words in the category; and it made little difference whether the thesaurus had 1,000 or 2,000 categories. For conceptual content analysis, accurate placement of a word within a category is a crucial matter. Furthermore, the number of categories must be limited for practical reasons. With a category system of 118, around 500 words seems to be a minimum sample size for producing a usable content profile, while a 2,000 word sample gives a fairly good profile as far as stability and reliability are concerned. If one derives thus a rough rule of thumb that sample size must be around 4 times the category number as a minimum and 15 times the category number for a good content profile, a system of 1,000 categories would require 4,000 words minimally and 15,000 words preferably. The larger the required sample, the more cumbersome and costly the analysis.

One modern effort at a concept dictionary is the conceptual scheme of the French language devised by Rudolf Hallig and Walther von Wartburg (1963). These authors hold that the meaning of a word is made up of several components, of which one is a logical universal or general conception. In addition there are secondary meanings, which they seek to exclude from their analysis, involving subjective associations, feeling tones, and transient connections which accrue because of some context in which the word is used. While the meaning of a word may vary with the particular circumstances of its use, Hallig and Wartburg believe the logical universal is a durable conceptual presentation, implicit in the word, which is not altered by its context.

Like older field theorists of language (Trier, 1934; Weisgerber, 1938), Hallig and Wartburg set upon their scheme of concepts the requirement that it be internally logical according to a unitary viewpoint and guiding plan, and that the arrangement succeed in joining everything together into an integrated whole. However, in classifying words, Hallig and Wartburg seek to assume the standpoint of the gifted average individual observing the world with a pre-scientific, naive realism. Their plan of concepts begins with the postulation of three superordinate domains, THE UNIVERSE, MAN, and MAN AND UNIVERSE. Under THE UNIVERSE there follow such subdivisions as Heaven and Atmosphere, Earth, Plants, and Animals. Under MAN the subdivisions are Man as a Physical Being, Spirit and Intellect, Man as a Social Being, and The Social Organization. MAN AND UNIVERSE is subdivided into The *A Priori,* and Science and Technique. Within each of the subdivisions there are further branches.

Despite its desired naiveté, the Hallig and Wartburg scheme is, like Roget's, highly logical in outlook. The stress upon a logical system is related to the authors' interest in a conceptual structure applicable to languages as such rather than to particular speakers. In contrast, the psychologist is primarily interested in speakers and in comparisons between speakers.

The difference between a logical and a psychological viewpoint may be illustrated by how Hallig and Wartburg handle words of physical violence and harm. Almost all such words appear under the superordinate rubric MAN and its various subdivisions, dispersed among non-violent words. Thus, *gash, bruise, sprain* and *fracture* are taken as expressions of "Health and illness," itself under the major subdivision Man as a Physical Being. Words like *torment, torture, misfortune* and *catastrophe* are taken as expressions of "Feelings," under the major subdivision Spirit and Intellect. Words like *assassinate, punish, ambush* and *fight* are under The Social Organization, and its subordinate divisions, "Judiciary organization," and "War."

The Hallig and Wartburg system gives each word a fixed place in a hierarchical structure of concepts, implying in this instance that violence is strictly a human activity under MAN, and that its various manifestations are otherwise conceptually quite distinct, falling into different domains. With respect to weather and animals, which are under the superordinate heading THE UNIVERSE, the only word with an overtone of violence is *wild* for animals. Whether this accords with a naive view of the world is open to question, since tornadoes and tempests are experienced by us as destructive events and animals are readily identified with violent actions. The contrasting view in the present dictionary is that violence itself is a distinct conceptual domain evoked equally in a variety of experiences involving the human, the animate generally, and the inanimate. Whatever its form, it is categorized under the heading DAMG.

Whether something is in or out is psychologically a significant experience, represented by many tokens in the language. In the system of Hallig and Wartburg, words referring to in-ness and out-ness are lumped under the subdivision Space, within the large domain MAN AND UNIVERSE. Words like *up* and *down* and *forward* and *back* are likewise under Space. While the general rubric is undoubtedly applicable, the specific spatial experiences have psychological implications which may be lost if the words are not conceptually discriminated from each other.

The word *start* in *We will start the project shortly,* and the word *born* in *He was born on July first,* have a significant common experiential component - "beginning." There is also a common element in *plane, roof* and *high* in the sentences, *The plane will soon be in Chicago, He stood on the roof of the house,* and *The wall is high.* The common content has to do with experiences of "up-ness" and things which are "up" with respect to us. The knowledge that human cognition operates with such identities across varieties of reference has been of great importance in understanding the symptoms, fantasies and behavior of disturbed individuals, as well as in understanding dreams and symbols. Logical schemes lack most from the point of view of psychological analysis, in overlooking such experiential similarities in apparently discrete references.

In setting out to develop a system of concepts Hallig and Wartburg, as did Roget, began with superordinate ideas, dividing the words of the language according to these ideas, while progressively refining the subdivisions by logical considerations. An empirical, psychologically oriented approach is to bundle words by experientially common meanings without pre-defined concepts, allowing these bundles of meaning to grow until concepts emerge. The present dictionary evolved from this approach. The process may be described as a sequence of steps in which increasingly general criteria for commonality of experience were used to group words.

The initial step in the process was to list synonymous words. Some authors (Ogden, 1932) have suggested that opposition in meaning is a fundamental psychological phenomenon and a unifying device by which vocabulary may be organized. This is an important observation, supported by the fact that polar experiences, for example of up and down, are often implicit in single words (*descend, climb, elevator*). Casares (1959) made judicious use of the principle in organizing the subject matter of his ideological dictionary. However, there are many uni-dimensional areas of meaning in language. Good and bad, big and little, helping and hurting, are experiential opposites, but there are no substantial oppositions to time, number, religion and a host of other dimensions.

Synonymy alone, or with antonymy, is not a practical basis for arriving at domains of experiential meaning, because the number of separate meanings each represented by a few synonyms is extremely large. However, if one applies the question, "What words are similar in meaning, even if not synonymous?" the size of each grouping grows larger and the number of separate domains shrinks. Words like *walk, run, ride* and *go* readily group themselves as experientially similar, although not synonymous. Application of the criterion of similarity in addition to that of synonymy leads to broader and more inclusive bundles. Nevertheless even this expansion leaves one with a scheme of impractical variety.

Beyond synonymy and similarity, relatedness of experience referred to may be taken as a basis for organizing words. If a group of words such as *chair, stool, bench, seat* and *couch* evolves from

the application of synonymy and similarity, considerations of relatedness may draw *table* into the same domain of reference. The merging of *table* and *chair* into a single cluster also immediately projects
the outlines of a category which could include other words like *bed,
dresser, bureau* and *chest,* all of which also refer to ordinary household furnishings. The principle of relatedness begins to bring into
view the outlines of a system of manageable proportions.

A great deal of work may be done with the three principles of synonymy, similarity and relatedness. Each new word considered in
constructing such a scheme of experiential concepts will either fit a
growing group of other words or suggest a new arrangement of groups.
At some point in this process of grouping words, instead of asking
whether a new word suggests a new concept or requires a reorganiza-
tion of the existing concepts, it is possible to ask to which of the
existing concepts the new word is closest.

Assume that one domain encompassed such words as *walk, run*
and *go*, and another domain encompassed such words as *weak, helpless* and *impotent*. The word *soar* would seem better related to
the first than to the second group, where *fail* would seem more pertinent to the second. However, such a word as *stumble* might share
both domains. Asking to which already existent group a new word
might belong (once the groupings had become substantial) extends
the relatedness criterion and places a word in a group because it is
closer in meaning to the words in that group than to the words in any
other group. This does not preclude changing the system, but weighs
prior judgments against each new judgment to be made and accepts
change only on compelling grounds. Once the system has progressed
to this point, alterations in it are likely to occur mainly because existing categories are found to overlap and to require redefinition of
boundaries and differences.

In a conceptual dictionary with psychological objectives, the conceptual scheme must provide an adequate basis for discriminating the
language of one speaker from another, and each entity in the scheme
must contribute to such potential. This militates against the use of
concepts which, although experientially valid, have many tokens in
everyone's speech or which draw few tokens in the language at large.
Such global categories as "nature," "man," "animate" and "inanimate" do not discriminate between separate speakers since they contribute large numbers of tokens to everyone's speech. On the other
hand, there are few words which refer to spatial "right" and "left,"
and comparatively few occurrences of such references. This argues
against setting up separate categories for such a distinction. Obvi-
ously, then, there are possible and valid experiential concepts which
will have little utility in a scheme oriented toward exploring individual

differences in language content.

One criterion for acceptability of a category is that it not encompass too many or too few tokens (more precisely, that it not occur too often or too infrequently), lest it fail to contribute toward discrimination of individual differences. Where, in the present dictionary, a category turned out to be unduly large, what was also readily apparent was some basis for splitting it to produce more limited categories. And where a category seemed too narrow, it readily melted into another category whose domain of reference then swelled to include the new meaning. The area of aggression was one which required subdivision along lines differentiating physical violence, anger and simple disagreement. In the area of sex, homosexual and heterosexual references were at first separated. However, relatively few references to homosexuality as such occur, and all sexual references were therefore combined into one domain. Some disproportions in numbers of word tokens within categories will be evident; however, categories with more words will not necessarily occur more frequently since rate of occurrence of a category is also dependent on relative frequency of use of its particular tokens. For example, the category of negation (NO) has few tokens, but these tokens are used quite frequently.

Another criterion for acceptability of a category, related to well known ideas of reliability and validity, has to do with its distinctiveness. The domains of reference in a scheme of language must be sufficiently discriminable from each other so that judges considering a word will be in agreement as to which concepts are involved. If the domains of meaning are too closely related, this will be a difficult judgment and an unreliable one. To the extent that judgment about the presence of a concept is unreliable, the pertinence of the concept to other aspects of behavior may be dubious. Distinctiveness of each concept category is therefore an important desideratum.

In the present dictionary many words are defined, for a given usage, by two concepts. For example, categories referring to religion and to language both apply to *scriptures*; for *bird*, both animality and ability to fly are important. At the same time, numerous words may, in their various uses, refer to more than two dimensions of experience. To deal with this, additional entries for a particular word are included which contain the different meanings. Thus, the word *murder* involves death, violence and criminality. In the dictionary, *murder* is given two sets of meanings, the first CRIM DEAD, and the second DAMG DEAD. The first set includes criminality and death, the second violence and death. In any particular usage, one or the other combination may be more applicable.

An effort has been made to identify the most important concepts in a word in its various usages, but it would have been futile to attempt to capture, conceptually, all the finer possible meanings. Arne Naess (1957) described synonymy as follows: "the relation is one of identity, but only identity in one respect among others. Nothing is intuited about the degree of strictness of identity required. Considerable laxness is permitted." His description of synonymy is apt equally to the idea of a concept, which is defined here as a cognitive response common to a set of words because of an underlying commonality in the experiences referred to by the words. There is no assumption that concepts assigned to a word reflect totality of word meaning. For a word to be classified within a given concept, it must contain as a component of its meaning, the experiential phenomena addressed by the concept. The object, action or quality referred to by a word may be different from the reference of its companion words within a concept. This will not prohibit its being in the concept, as long as it contains an experiential component in common with the other words in the concept.

There is at present no evidence concerning the relative strength of evocation of the various cognitive concepts for given words; the assumption is therefore made that all words which evoke a concept evoke it in equal strength. Thus, frequency of occurrence of words within a concept is taken as a linear measure of relative strength of the concept for a speaker.

Further experience will undoubtedly dictate further changes in the category structure. Some of these changes may be anticipated. The category GO is the largest of the 118. There are over 900 entries in it, some of them fairly commonly used, and this category will therefore tend to be scored high in many protocols. However, up to the present, the category has resisted efforts to cleave it along clearly ascertainable lines. One possibility would be to make a distinction between travel of persons and movement of things. This would separate out words like *walk* and *throw*, the one referring to human and animal movement, the other usually referring to objects. But words like *carry, bring* and *roll* would pose many problems and the effect of separating along these lines might be to require alternative categorizations for many words depending on animal or object context. Movement in a small compass might also be contrasted with extended movement. Thus, words like *dance, gyrate, rotate* and *budge* might be separated out of the large category. Further possibilities are suggested by George Miller's (1972) discussion of the many options faced in dividing motion verbs into experiential groups.

Other categories seem to invite division. In the case of FORM, plans, models and organizations might reasonably be separated from physical shapes and structures. Words referring to giving (*bestow,*

bequeath, offer) are at present scored under AID, somewhat uncom-
fortably. They do not, however, form a sizable contingent of their
own and therefore no effort has been made to break them out. It is
possible that they might combine with some words from the GO category (*toss, throw, send*) to form a new grouping.

These are a few of the problems which remain unsolved as the dictionary is published. Questions of misclassification will also undoubtedly arise. Some tokens seem forced into the category system; the
unacceptable alternative was to create new categories with small numbers of tokens. Perhaps with a more precise analysis of their possible
meanings, these items might find a better fit. However, by far most
of the items are readily assignable to categories. This gives promise
that ultimately a balanced category structure may develop which will
closely reflect the content of the vocabulary while remaining practical enough for application to small samples of language.

The fact that concepts are conceived of as experiential responses
universally made by members of the speaking community whenever
given words are used, does not mean that the system cannot characterize idiosyncratic usages of particular words. Eugen Bleuler (1950,
p. 153) quotes a schizophrenic patient as saying, ''As a child I was an
apartment.'' Further discussion with the patient revealed that *apartment* meant for him apart or different. A concept analysis of the
patient's language might discover many words related to *child* (such
as *youth, infant, young*), and to *apartment* (such as *room, house,
cubicle*), but nowhere would there be a cue as to the special meaning
attributed by him to *apartment*. However, if a search were made of
words that came in close context with *apartment* type words, such
sentences might be found as: *As a youth I lived alone in a room;
The infant was left by himself in the house;* and *Each student had
a separate cubicle.*

The word groupings in such sentences would reveal that the concept which subsumes *apartment* (HOME) occurred closely with concepts which subsume *child* (YNG) and *apart* (SEP). Such an associa-
tional analysis of concepts might reveal the elements of a central fantasy which could account for the patient's odd distortion in the meaning of *apartment*. Actual applications of this technique of ''contextual associates'' may be seen in Laffal (1960, 1965, p. 125ff).

analyzing texts

Below are rules for special situations in word categorization.
1. Compound words. Words like *nonpartisan, longlived, loud-*

mouthed and *ladylike* may be broken apart into constituent words with each constituent getting the concept scorings appropriate to it. Some common compound words have been included in the dictionary as if they were single units; but if a compound word does not appear in the dictionary, treating the parts as separate words will usually result in most appropriate categorization.

2. Idiomatic expressions. In expressions like *hit the sack* and *kick the bucket* an idiomatic meaning is conveyed, often contained in a special meaning of one of the words. An effort has been made to capture the special sense in expressions by scoring one of the words with the appropriate meaning. Thus *sack* is categorized in one case HOLW REST, giving it an affinity with *bed* (FURN REST); *hit* in one of its meanings, is categorized GO; *kick* is in one instance categorized DEAD.

3. Proper names, place names and titles. Proper names, place names and titles are replaced by a categorizable word which most aptly designates the individual or thing named. Thus if the text says, *Margaret was a housewife* wherever the name *Margaret* appears, the word *housewife* is substituted for it and the scoring for the name becomes the scoring for *housewife* (LADY HOME). There may be two parts to a proper name (*Bill Jones*) but the name is scored as a single unit, being replaced by the noun which most aptly designates the person. Sometimes the title attached to a name is the most apt designation: *Captain Jones commanded a minesweeper.* Wherever *Jones* appears alone, the word *captain* is substituted for scoring purposes. Names of countries may be replaced by *nation* or, if the reference in the name is to the language of the country, *language* may be substituted. If reference is made to a people (*The English*) an appropriate substitute would be *group*. Other examples of categorization of place names, languages and nationals are shown on page 28. Names of cities may be replaced by *city*, titles by an appropriate reference (*book, song*). If the title contains categorizable words, these may be categorized along with a word added to identify the nature of the reference.

4. Pronouns. Wherever possible, nouns to which personal pronouns refer are substituted for the pronouns, and then categorized accordingly. However, relative pronouns, interrogative pronouns, demonstrative pronouns and indefinite pronouns are not scored or replaced by scorable words. The relative pronoun (*who, which, that*) is most often a formal device for referring to an immediately precedent noun, and to score it with the categories of its referent noun would merely entail duplication. The referents of interrogative pronouns (*who, what*) are usually unknown until later, and it would therefore not be appropriate to give these pronouns the contents of their

ultimate referents. Indefinite pronouns (*any, each, neither, some*) are given category scorings of their own despite the fact that they may refer to some noun referent.

A separate category (WE) has been established for reference to the self (*I, me, we, us*). Where the first person pronoun occurs in a text, the WE category, rather than the referent noun categories is applied, although one could decide to apply the noun referent alone, or as well. The reason for giving a separate category to first person pronouns is that frequency of self reference is sometimes a significant cue in understanding an individual through his language. However, this would also be a high frequency category in a first person narrative. Other personal pronouns (*he, it, they, you, she*) are replaced by the nouns to which they refer. Reflexive personal pronouns such as *myself* and *himself* are treated in the one case as self reference and in the other as replaceable by a noun referent.

5. Abbreviations, apostrophes, accents and phrases. Where abbreviations are encountered, the full title should be spelled out and categorized word by word, or some word equivalent should be provided which may be categorized. Thus *VFW* may be spelled out as *Veterans of Foreign Wars* or the words *veterans' group* may be substituted for the abbreviation.

Where apostrophes represent abbreviation, the words should be spelled out. Thus, *don't* should become *do not* and *won't* should become *will not* for purposes of categorization. In other instances, apostrophes may be treated as if they were non-existent, *o'clock* becoming *oclock* in the dictionary, or as if they terminated a word, *man's* being read as *man* for categorization purposes.

Accents are disregarded in the dictionary (*agapé, curé, distingué*), since computers do not make provision for accented letters.

Where phrases appear in the dictionary, they are spelled without word spacing (*aswellas, matteroffact, uptodate*). This too is a computer oriented convention, applied to the relatively few phrases included in the dictionary. Ultimately, if feasible, the dictionary may expand to include common phrases whose meanings are not contained in their individual word components.

6. Fallback procedure. The dictionary is designed for computer analyses of texts with minimal editorial participation. If the dictionary is used as a stored comparison source for computer content analyses, a program may be written to categorize a text word not in the dictionary by selecting as the appropriate equivalent, the first dictionary entry matching the greatest number of initial letters of the text word. Thus, *blurred* and *blurring* are not in the dictionary, but if they occurred in a text, they would match with the dictionary entry *blur* as the first entry maximally similar in initial letters. *Recognize*

is not in the dictionary, but *recognition* is. Any form of the verb
recognize would match with *recognition* on the letters *recogni-*,
and *recognition* would therefore be selected as the appropriate dictionary entry.

The fallback procedure requires certain entries in the dictionary
which may seem redundant. This is necessary lest the wrong entry
be selected for text words not perfectly matched in the dictionary.
The following series of entries will illustrate the redundancy and the
reasons for it.

Muse v IDEA	Mushroom v LARG QUIK
Museum n HOME	Mushroomed v LARG QUIK
Mush n EASY FOOD	Mushrooming v LARG QUIK
Mush n FOOL	Music n MUSC
Mushroom n FOOD VEGT	Musing v IDEA

Musing is included, but *mused* is not. If the word *mused* occurred
in a text to be computer-analyzed, it would match with *muse* as the
first maximally similar word. However, if *musing* occurred in a text
and *musing* were not in the dictionary, it would match with *music*.
Mushroomed and *mushrooming* are in the dictionary, since these words
will almost always have the LARG QUIK meaning where unsuffixed
mushroom might mean either FOOD VEGT or LARG QUIK. If *mushroomed* and *mushrooming* were not in the dictionary, whenever these
words occurred in a text, they would match as first choice with
Mushroom n FOOD VEGT.

7. Editing. Earlier versions of the dictionary have already served
extensively in computer analyses of language content (Laffal, 1965,
1967, 1968, 1969; Hartsough and Laffal, 1970). The kinds of problems
which face any interlingual translation program with respect to homo-
graphs also face the researcher who wishes to translate an English
sample automatically by means of computer into the categories of the
concept dictionary. Thus the noun *father* would in some instances refer to a male parent, and in other instances to a priest. The adjective
some would in certain occurrences mean "a few" (*Give the elephant
some peanuts.*); on other occasions it would have no more than the
force of an article (*Some student asked for you.*); and it might also
suggest emphasis (*That was some party!*). These are distinctions
that, for the most part, can best be made by an editor. Where the
noun *father* or the adjective *some* were used in a text, a machine
program which contained the dictionary as a comparison source would
find several homographic entries, i.e. an ambiguity, sequenced in
order of judged frequency of occurrence.

Several options are available for dealing with such cases. One is
to select only the first meaning; this results in accurate categorization in most but not all instances. With this option, when *father* mean-

ing "priest" occurred in a text it would be categorized as if it referred to a male parent. In the same manner, by use of this option, the adjective *some* would always be categorized as if it meant "a few." Another option is to instruct the computer to include categorizations of the first two, the first three, the first four, or all of the set of meanings for a word in the dictionary. This, however, may introduce irrelevant meanings and obscure the content picture. Another option which will deal with some homographic ambiguities discriminable by part of speech is for an editor to indicate part of speech beside the word. A similar approach would be to note by number in parentheses which meaning among the several for a given word is appropriate. A computer program may then make the correct dictionary choice.

An even simpler way of dealing with the problem is for the editor to change an ambiguous word to an unambiguous one that has a similar value in the dictionary. Thus *fly* (noun) could be changed to *moth* which receives the same categorization (BUG UP), and *fly* (verb) could be changed to *soar* which is categorized GO UP. Although the actual content is changed by these alterations, the dictionary concept choices become unambiguous.

Some familiarity with the contents of the dictionary will permit an editor to avoid certain ambiguities. For example, where the word *in* refers to physical presence in something, the category IN is scored. Where *in* is used with another sense, as *in case of, in my opinion*, no score (NSCR) is applied. In preparing a text for IBM card punching, an editor may eliminate all *ins* but those referring to physical location. The same applies to the article *a*, also a NSCR item. Other words like the "no score" auxiliary verb *have* may be deleted by an editor in order to avoid conflict with the categorized verb of possession, *to have*. However, where such editorial procedures are used, care must be exercised either to exclude the NSCR item from the dictionary or to remove it from a primary position.

8. Grammatical part of speech. Syntactic part of speech is of relatively minor importance in the dictionary. Where a word may be used as noun, verb or adjective, with substantially the same conceptual meaning, the choice of part of speech has been arbitrary, usually reflecting a usage encountered when the dictionary was being constructed. The dictionary token thus stands for that word no matter what its syntactic use in any particular context may be. Hallig and Wartburg (1963, p. 96) develop the idea that since the words in a conceptual dictionary are linguistic signs which represent concepts, it does not matter what grammatical form the signs have. However, grammatical part of speech may distinguish between homographic words, hence in some instances contributes significant semantic information. For this reason it is included in the dictionary, even

though often not crucial.

9. Some general points. The order in which the categories associated with a word appear in the alphabetic part of the dictionary is of no importance. The mnemonic concept names are linked to numbers for convenience in computer use. Thus the category FOOL has the number 001, the category AGRE has the number 003, the category AFAR 044, and so on. Wherever two concept names appear for a word, they will be ordered by number, rather than alphabetically, but this ordering is of no importance and does not reflect priority of meaning. The numbers assigned to concepts are not relevant in any way, and are not shown in the present dictionary.

The dictionary is oriented toward a general vocabulary, although some rarely used and technical words are included. If the dictionary is to be applied to special fields, care should be exercised to identify technical meanings of common words, and possibly to include these technical meanings in the dictionary as well.

In most instances the categorizations shown in the dictionary will capture a significant component of the meaning of a word. However, rare meanings of some words may not be categorized. What appear to be puzzling categorizations will often make sense if the reader thinks of (or looks up in a standard dictionary) some less common applications of the words.

sample text

To illustrate the analysis of a text, a selection from the *Declaration of Independence* is shown with appropriate categories below each scorable word. Text words which are not in the dictionary are replaced, for purposes of categorization, by words shown beside them in parentheses. Where a word is understood but not in the text, it is also inserted in parentheses. If no category appears beneath a word, the word is not scored (NSCR). Personal pronouns, which appear in the dictionary as HSCR (hand score) items, are in the example given the categories of their noun referents.

Following the selection is a tabulation of the various concept categories, ordered by frequency of occurrence. For a suggestion as to interpretation of some aspects of the profile, see PREFACE, xi.

We hold these truths to be self evident, that all men are
WE IDEA TRUE SOLE OPEN SHRP WHOL MALE

created equal, that they are endowed by their Creator
BGIN SIML WHOL MALE AID HAVE WHOL MALE BGIN HOLY

with certain unalienable (inalienable) rights, that among these (rights)
SHRP EVER TRUE MOTV JOIN TRUE MOTV

are life, liberty and the pursuit of happiness. That to secure these
LIVE OPEN GO MOTV GLAD AID

rights, governments are instituted among men, deriving their
TRUE MOTV LEAD LAW BGIN JOIN MALE BGIN LEAD LAW

just powers from the consent of the governed, that whenever any
GOOD TRUE POWR AGRE LEAD LAW TIME

form of government becomes destructive of these ends, it is the
FORM LEAD LAW EVNT DAMG END MOTV

right of the people to alter or to abolish it, and to institute new
TRUE MOTV GRUP VARY END LEAD LAW BGIN NEW

government, laying its foundation on such principles and
LEAD LAW BGIN LEAD LAW CRUX FORM SIML CRUX IDEA

organizing its powers in such form, as to them shall seem
FORM LEAD LAW POWR SIML FORM GRUP IDEA VIEW

most likely to effect their safety and happiness. Prudence, indeed, will
MUCH MUCH END GRUP AID GLAD GOOD EMPH

dictate that governments long established should not be changed for
LEAD TALK LEAD LAW EVER BGIN EVER NO VARY

light and transient causes; and accordingly all experience hath
GLAD TRIV VARY SEP MOTV SIML WHOL EVNT

shown, that mankind are more disposed to suffer, while evils are
VIEW WHOL GRUP MUCH MOTV PANG TIME BAD

sufferable, than to right themselves by abolishing the forms to
AGRE GOOD TRUE WHOL GRUP END FORM

which they are accustomed. But when a long train of abuses
WHOL GRUP SIML EVER OPPO TIME AFAR FORW DAMG

and usurpations, pursuing invariably the same object evinces
DAMG HAVE GO MOTV EVER SIML END MOTV OPEN VIEW

a design to reduce them under absolute despotism,
MOTV LITL WHOL GRUP DOWN SUB WHOL EMPH AGGR LEAD

it is their right, it is their duty, to
WHOL GRUP TRUE MOTV WHOL GRUP MOTV WORK

throw off such government, and to provide new guards for their
GO SEP SIML LEAD LAW AID NEW BLOK AID WHOL GRUP

future security. Such has been the patient sufferance of these
FORW TIME AID SIML EVER REST PANG

Colonies; and such is now the necessity which constrains them
GRUP SUB SIML NEW CRUX MOTV BLOK GRUP SUB

to alter their former systems of government. The history of the
VARY GRUP SUB PAST FORM LEAD LAW IDEA PAST

present   King   of Great Britain (country) is a   history   of repeated
NEW   LEAD MALE   PLAC   IDEA PAST   SIML

injuries and usurpations,   all   having in direct   object   the establishment
DAMG   DAMG HAVE WHOL HAVE   SHRP   END MOTV   BGIN EVER

of an   absolute   tyranny   over these States. To prove this,   let   facts
WHOL EMPH AGGR LEAD   UP   PLAC   TRUE   AGRE TRUE

be submitted to a   candid   world.   He   has refused   his   assent
AID   OPEN TRUE WHOL LEAD MALE   OPPO LEAD MALE AGRE

to laws, the most wholesome and necessary for the public good.   He
LAW   MUCH   GOOD   CRUX MOTV   GRUP GOOD LEAD MALE

has forbidden   his   governors to pass laws of immediate and
BLOK   LEAD MALE LEAD LAW AGRE LAW   QUIK

pressing importance, unless suspended in their operations till   his
CRUX   CRUX   OPPO BLOK END   LAW WORK   TIME LEAD MALE

assent should be obtained; and when so   suspended,   he   has
AGRE   HAVE   SIML   BLOK END LEAD MALE

utterly neglected to attend to them.   He   has refused to pass
EMPH   AGGR LACK MOTV   LAW LEAD MALE   OPPO   AGRE

other laws for the accommodation of large districts of people, unless
OPPO LAW   SIML AID   LARG PLAC   GRUP   OPPO

those people would relinquish the   right   of representation in the
GRUP   SEP LACK   TRUE MOTV   SIML LAW   IN

legislature, a   right   inestimable to them, and formidable to   tyrants
LEAD LAW   TRUE MOTV LARG IDEA   GRUP   POWR   AGGR LEAD

only.   He   has   called   together legislative bodies at places
SOLE LEAD MALE HEAR TALK   JOIN LEAD LAW GRUP   PLAC

unusual, uncomfortable, and distant from the depository of   their
AFAR   PANG   AFAR SEP   HOLW   LEAD LAW GRUP

public records, for the sole   purpose of fatiguing   them   into
GRUP WRIT   SOLE   MOTV   WEAK   LEAD LAW GRUP IN

compliance with   his   measures.   He   has dissolved
AGRE   LEAD MALE   LAW LEAD MALE   END SEP

representative   houses   repeatedly, for opposing with manly firmness
SIML LAW   GRUP LAW   SIML   OPPO   MALE POWR

his   invasions on the   rights   of the people.   He   has
LEAD MALE DAMG IN   TRUE MOTV   GRUP LEAD MALE

refused for a long time, after such dissolutions, to cause others to be
OPPO   EVER TIME BACK SIML END SEP   BGIN SOLE

elected; whereby the legislative powers, incapable of annihilation, have
MOTV   LEAD LAW POWR   WEAK   DAMG END

returned to the people at   large   for their exercise; the State
BACK GO   GRUP   LARG OPEN   GRUP AID   PLAC

remaining in the meantime exposed to   all   the dangers of invasion from
EVER   TIME   OPEN WHOL   DAMG   DAMG IN

without, and convulsions within.
OUT   VARY PANG   IN

Tabulation of Category Frequencies
in Sample from *Declaration of Independence*

LEAD 34	AGRE 8	POWR 5	LARG 3	HEAR 1
LAW 26	OPPO 8	VARY 5	PAST 3	HOLW 1
GRUP 25	TIME 7	AGGR 4	SHRP 3	HOLY 1
MOTV 22	CRUX 6	EMPH 4	VIEW 3	LITL 1
MALE 18	FORM 6	GO 4	BACK 2	LIVE 1
SIML 16	IDEA 6	MUCH 4	EVNT 2	NO 1
WHOL 16	OPEN 6	NEW 4	FORW 2	OUT 1
TRUE 14	SEP 6	PANG 4	LACK 2	QUIK 1
END 11	BLOK 5	SOLE 4	TALK 2	REST 1
AID 9	GOOD 5	SUB 4	WEAK 2	TRIV 1
BGIN 9	HAVE 5	AFAR 3	WORK 2	UP 1
DAMG 9	IN 5	GLAD 3	BAD 1	WE 1
EVER 9	PLAC 5	JOIN 3	DOWN 1	WRIT 1

2

category
descriptions

category names

AFAR	DAMG	GARB	LAW	OPEN	SUB
AGGR	DEAD	GLAD	LEAD	OPPO	TALK
AGRE	DIRT	GO	LITL	OUT	TIME
AID	DOWN	GOOD	LIVE	PANG	TRIV
ANML	EASY	GRUP	MALE	PAST	TRUE
ASTR	EDUC	HAVE	MART	PATH	UP
BACK	EMPH	HEAR	MECH	PLAC	VAPR
BAD	END	HEAT	MEDC	PLAY	VARY
BGIN	ERTH	HOLW	MONY	POWR	VEGT
BLOK	EVER	HOLY	MOTV	QUIK	VEHC
BLUR	EVNT	HOME	MSMT	REST	VIEW
BODY	FABR	HSCR	MTRL	SEP	WE
BUG	FALS	IDEA	MUCH	SEX	WEA
BULG	FLOW	IN	MUSC	SHRP	WEAK
CLEN	FOND	ION	MYTH	SICK	WHOL
COLD	FOOD	JOIN	NEAR	SIML	WORK
COLR	FOOL	KIN	NEW	SIP	WRIT
COVR	FORM	LACK	NO	SOLE	YNG
CRIM	FORW	LADY	NSCR	SOMA	
CRUX	FURN	LARG	NUMR	SOME	

the categories

AFAR - Words relating to the unusual, the unexpected and the distant. AFAR words are in contrast with the "familiar and usual" meaning in SIML. The kinds of ideas in AFAR are: distance and remoteness; abnormality and unnaturalness; unusualness and infrequency; chance and unpredictability.

AGGR - Words relating to disadvantages, detriment, dislike and anger. AGGR words have stronger affective connotations than those in OPPO but do not have the implication of physical harm which is present in DAMG words. The kinds of ideas in AGGR are: criticism and derision; rejection and disrespect; clashes and friction; complaint and anger; harshness and austerity.

AGRE - Words relating to cooperation, consent, approval and agreement. Words in AGRE have stronger affective overtones than those in SIML but less than those in FOND. The kinds of ideas in AGRE are: allowing and permitting; agreeing and accepting; praising and commending; cooperation and collaboration.

AID - The underlying ideas are those of help, advantage and support. Words in AID are in contrast with those in AGGR and DAMG. The kinds of ideas included are: assistance and help; protection and support; usefulness and benefit; guidance and advice; offering and giving; benevolence and nurturance; services and agencies.

ANML - References to animals other than insects (which are scored BUG) are included here. For sea animals the category FLOW is also applied; for flying animals the second category is UP. Animal skins have FABR as a second score. If the reference is to the animal as food or to a food product derived from animals, the word is scored ANML FOOD. No distinction in categorization is made between wild and domestic animals. Human references are not included in ANML although general terms referring to the animal kingdom are (*vertebrate, mammal*).

ASTR - Words relating to astronomical bodies, space and astrology. The additional category UP is used in some instances, since in a naive geocentric view the heavenly bodies are "above."

BACK - References to physical location or direction back or behind, but not to temporal past. BACK contrasts with FORW, and includes references to returning, following and being rearward.

BAD - Words with negative moral or ethical connotations. Contrasting words are in GOOD. The kinds of ideas in BAD are: evil and sin; profanity and blasphemy; baseness and debauchery; roguishness and scurrilousness; dishonesty and insincerity.

BGIN - Words referring to birth, creation and beginning. The kinds of ideas included are: initiating and starting; reproduction and pro-creation; causes and origins; innovation and originality.

BLOK - Words referring to blocking, obstruction and confinement, either physical or in an abstract sense. Included are ideas of curb-ing and barring; seizing and apprehending; censoring and prohibit-ing; binding and tying; constraint and constriction.

BLUR - Words referring to obscurity and vagueness. Included are ideas of doubt and uncertainty; questioning and guessing; confusion and chaos; dimness and shadowiness; mystery and unintelligibility. Words in SHRP and FORM contrast with the words in BLUR.

BODY - References to visible or external limbs and features of hu-man bodies, animal bodies and plants. Internal bodily and vegeta-tive processes and parts are included in SOMA.

BUG - References to insects and microscopic animals and organisms such as ants, worms, butterflies, bacteria and germs.

BULG - Words referring to fullness, mounds and protrusions. Included are such ideas as: accumulation and piling; stuffing and bloating; jutting and sticking out; mountains and hills.

CLEN - References to cleanliness, grooming and purification. The contrasting category is DIRT. Included are ideas of washing and bathing; laundering and ironing; currying and pruning; sterilization and decontamination; scrubbing and polishing.

COLD - References to coldness, winter and polar regions.

COLR - References to color, including black and white. COLR words are implicitly visual and this category therefore implies the VIEW category as well. The separation of a COLR category and a VIEW category is based primarily on the idea that while color words fit together naturally, inclusion of other visual words would create a jarring conglomerate. A parallel case is that of MUSC words ver-sus words referring more generally to sounds and hearing.

COVR - Words referring to being covered, secret or hidden. Included are such ideas as: veil and lid; blanket and burying; camouflage and hiding; secret and spying; mask and disguise. Ideas opposed to these are in the category OPEN.

CRIM - References to illicitness, lawbreaking, crime and criminals.

CRUX - References to what is crucial and essential, and to impor-tance, worth and seriousness. The kinds of ideas included are: significance and necessity; qualifications and attributes; heart and core; fundamentals and foundation; substantive and vital.

DAMG - References to violence, harm and danger. DAMG words re-flect violent hostility and physical damage, where AGGR words re-late to disadvantages and non-physical hostility. Ideas included in DAMG are: annihilation and destruction; war and fighting; instruments and events of harmful potential; risks and emergencies; cruelty and injury. Where a word may carry either a DAMG or an AGGR connotation, the more likely meaning is applied, even though in some contexts the other meaning would hold. In instances where a DAMG or AGGR meaning is equally likely, both choices are included (*abuse, aggression*). Words like *admiral, captain* and *general* are not included in DAMG, although *soldier* is, since the idea of war is not as immediate and pressing in them as in *soldier*.

DEAD - Words relating to death. Included are such ideas as: suicide and murder; funerals and widowhood; epitaphs and obituaries.

DIRT - References to uncleanliness, filth and deterioration. Opposing ideas are in the category CLEN. Included are such ideas as: dirt and excrement; erosion and decay; adulteration and pollution; soiling and sullying; dowdiness and sloppiness.

DOWN - References to the direction downward and to being below or under. The opposing category is UP. Included are such ideas as: descent and fall; floor and bottom; base and foot; depth and profundity; prostration and bowing.

EASY - References to lightness of weight, smoothness and easiness. Included are such ideas as: flexibility and resilience; spontaneity and informality; softness and smoothness; simplicity and effortlessness; lightness and airiness.

EDUC - References to education, learning and teaching. Included are such ideas as: schools and students; scholarship and erudition; teaching and training.

EMPH - References to emphasis and accentuation, as well as words themselves conveying emphasis. Included are emphatic interjections such as *darn* and *fiddlesticks*; adverbs like *very* and *positively*; and content words like *accent* and *emphasis*.

END - Words referring to halting, finishing and outcomes. Included are such ideas as: abolishing and ending; terminals and limits; ultimates and extremes; goals and conclusions.

ERTH - References to terra firma. Size of the reference to earth is not a consideration; thus *continent* and *clod* are both in ERTH. Included are such ideas as: materials drawn from the earth; hills, valleys and fields; soil and stones.

EVER - References to constancy, habituation and duration. Included are such ideas as: everlasting and continuous; rigidity and hardness; custom and habit; the usual and the conventional; consistency and stability; preservation and permanence.

EVNT - References, usually of a somewhat abstract and non-specific nature, to events, behavior and circumstance. Included are such ideas as: mien and bearing; happening and occurring; state and situation; being and doing.

FABR - References to fabrics and cloth-like products. Included are: cloth and yard goods; animal skins and furs; synthetic fabrics; fiber and rope.

FALS - References to deception, falseness and affectation. Included are such ideas as: dishonesty and lying; errors and mistakes; artificiality and sham.

FLOW - References to water, bodies of water, things and activities related to water, and liquidity. FLOW is not applied automatically to all liquids, but in those cases where the liquid quality is of primary importance. Words in the category SIP (*drink, coffee*) are by and large not in the FLOW category, some other second significant score having been given priority. Included in FLOW are such ideas as: water and moisture; rivers, lakes and seas; sea animals and ships; rain and hail; swimming and diving; flowing and draining.

FOND - References to loving, cherishing and friendship. The opposing category is AGGR. Words in FOND are affectively more positive and stronger than words in AGRE. Included in FOND are such ideas as: admiration and adoration; camaraderie and fellowship; devotion and compassion; fondling and petting.

FOOD - References to eating and to food. Foods usually have a second scoring showing their nature (VEGT, ANML, etc.). References to potables are in the category SIP; FOOD and SIP should therefore cover the range of eating and drinking. Included in FOOD are such ideas as: biting and chewing; foodstuffs and nourishment; restaurants and utensils; ingestion and digestion; smoking and tobacco.

FOOL - References to foolishness and stupidity. Included are such ideas as: silliness and ridiculousness; ignorance and nonsense; buffoonery and asininity; vanity and foppery.

FORM - References to structures and configurations both of a concrete and an abstract nature. Where organized knowledge or symbolic representations are involved (e.g., *ideology, diagram*) the additional category IDEA will apply. The kinds of ideas in FORM are: shapes and forms; plans and policies; doctrine and theory; construction and configuration; maps and charts; rituals and ceremonies; grammar and syntax (with the additional category TALK).

FORW - References to front, forward and sequences. Words of future time are included with the added scoring TIME, but future tense of verbs is not categorized as such. The kinds of ideas included are: forward and toward; preceding and before; series and lists.

FURN - References to furniture and household furnishings and implements. Some words which might be expected to appear here do not, because other categories are more prominent and displace FURN in their meanings (*bookcase* HOLW WRIT, *highchair* YNG REST).

GARB - References to wearing apparel, activities such as sewing and darning, and adornments worn with clothing.

GLAD - References to comfort, happiness and humor. The contrasting psychological state is represented by the category PANG. Included are such ideas as: cheerfulness and buoyancy; smiling and laughing; joking and wit; pleasure and joy; serenity and peace; contentment and composure.

GO - References to travel and movement. Movement is implicit in many words, but GO is scored only when it is prominent in the meaning. Words relating to roads and directions are under PATH. The kinds of ideas included in GO are: traveling and going; gyrating and dancing; sending and throwing.

GOOD - References to morality, propriety, goodness and beauty. The opposing category is BAD. Included in GOOD are such ideas as: moral and ethical; civility and conscientiousness; integrity and purity; adornment and ornamentation; splendor and luster.

GRUP - References to groups and bunches. Included are such ideas as: class and division; race and nation; collecting and gathering.

HAVE - References to having, holding and possessing. Included are such ideas as: owning and belonging; frugality and possessiveness; taking and getting; maintaining and keeping.

HEAR - References to sound and noise. Words referring to musical sounds and instruments are categorized MUSC. Where hearing is not a central component of meaning, as in many references to speech, HEAR is not applied. The kinds of ideas included in HEAR are: loudness and audibility; acoustics and listening; silence.

HEAT - References to heat and warmth. Ideas included are: fire and fuel; cooking and boiling; sun and summer.

HOLW - References to containers and hollow objects, and to encompassing and surrounding. The kinds of ideas included are: bottles and boxes; pots and cups; orifices and recesses; tubes and pipes; circumscribing and enveloping.

HOLY - References to religious figures, activities and objects.

HOME - References to dwellings and enclosures within which men and animals live and work. Included are such ideas as: home and house; nest and cave; room and office.

HSCR - A non-content "hand score" category indicating that an editor must substitute appropriate words to be categorized. Personal pronouns other than the first person pronoun are included in this category. The first person pronoun is given its own category score (WE). Relative pronouns (*who, which, that*) are given the "no score" (NSCR) category.

IDEA - References to rational processes, thinking and knowledge. Included are: understanding and intelligence; memory and awareness; analyzing and interpreting; symbolic representations such as maps and diagrams; doctrines and ideas. The category IDEA is also applied to disciplines and bodies of scientific knowledge such as Biology and Physics, but this is regarded as a relatively weak meaning displaceable by other more important meanings.

IN - References to being physically inside, to entering, and to being directed inward. The preposition *in* is categorized IN only when there is clear allusion to being physically in. Otherwise, for such usages as *in case of*, it is categorized NSCR ("no score").

ION - References to electricity, atoms and molecules. Ideas included are those relating to radio, to electrical phenomena and measurement, and to molecular structure. The category ION contains common words in what could become a number of subcategories dealing with molecular structure and its manifestations.

JOIN - References to coming together and uniting. Included are such ideas as: allegiance and ally; meeting and joining; touch and contact.

KIN - References to kinship, marriage, family and clan.

LACK - Words referring to lack or absence. Included are such ideas as: void and emptiness; loss and want; expenditure and waste.

LADY - References to femininity. Only those words are categorized LADY in which the female reference is prominent. Included are references to women, female body features and female clothing.

LARG - References to largeness, increase in size and distance, and weightiness. Included are such ideas as: bigness and thickness; excessive and overdone; blossom and grow; add and extend.

LAW - References to law, law enforcement and government. Included are such ideas as: attorney and court; police and law; political party and governing body.

LEAD - References to authority, leading and controlling. A related category is POWR which has to do with achievement and strength, and an opposing category is SUB which contains words of subjugation and submission. Included are such ideas as: administration and ruling; dominance and supremacy; managing and directing.

LITL - References to smallness, brevity and diminution. The opposing category is LARG. Included in LITL are such ideas as: abatement and contraction; devaluation and reduction; little and few; thin and slight; particle and mite.

LIVE - References to living and abiding. Included are such ideas as: existence and life; residing and inhabiting; organism and animate.

MALE - References to maleness and features and activities distinctively male. Where maleness is implicit but not a significant component of meaning, MALE is not applied (*soldier, hoodlum*). Words with *-man* or *-men* as suffix are categorized MALE.

MART - References to business, commerce and trade. Included are references to shopkeepers and shops, accounting and bookkeeping, credit and finance. References to labor and employment are categorized WORK. Professions such as lawyer, physician and teacher are categorized only within their relevant areas and are not categorized MART or WORK.

MECH - References to machinery, instruments and mechanical devices, other than vehicles and simple tools. Included are such references as: device and contraption; engine and mechanism; telescope and microscope; telephone and dictaphone.

MEDC - References to medical matters, health and cure. Included are such ideas as: physician and hospital; drugs and medicine; healing and therapy.

MONY - References to money, buying and selling. Included are such ideas as: finance and fee; cost and expense; betting and gambling; salary and earnings; bond and security.

MOTV - References to motivational and feeling states, predilections and responsibilities. The underlying ideas relate to: wishing and wanting; preferring and choosing; risks and attempts; obligations and commitments; basic motivations such as hunger and thirst; concern and attention; attitudes and sensitivities.

MSMT - References to measurements and instruments of measurement. Included are measurement terms of time, distance, temperature and weight.

MTRL - References to basic materials other than fabrics, and to substances out of which other products are made. If it is possible to identify the origin of the material, a second category may so indicate. Such materials as woods, metals, chemicals, oils and plastics are included in MTRL.

MUCH - References to large amounts, abundance and plentifulness. Included are such ideas as: much and sufficient; sumptuous and lavish; copious and rich; many and frequent.

MUSC - References to music, musical sounds and musical instruments. HEAR contains references to sounds not of a musical nature. Some words (*ring, resonant, whistle*) which could validly be placed in HEAR, are in MUSC because of the musical quality in their reference. Included in MUSC are allusions to musical devices and notes, songs and dances, and melodious sounds.

MYTH - References to the supernatural, the mythical and the magical. Included are such ideas as: fantasy and dreams; sorcery and miracles; unreality and superstition.

NEAR - References to nearness, native and familiarity. Included are such ideas as: approach and closeness; recognition and acquaintance; indigenous and endemic; almost and approximate.

NEW - References to newness, novelty and the present. Included are such ideas as: modern and present-day; fresh and fashionable; refurbished and rejuvenated; virgin and unused.

NO - Words of negation and denial are in this category, basically including the various forms of *no* and *not*.

NSCR - "No score" words. Included in the NSCR category are grammatical function words such as articles and auxiliary verbs, and a variety of prepositions, conjunctions and relative pronouns which have little independent content reference.

NUMR - References to numbers and mathematical operations. Included are such ideas as: geometry and trigonometry; numerical quantities; ratios and scores; statistical and actuarial.

OPEN - References to freedom, discovery and metaphorical or physical opening. Opposing ideas are in the categories BLOK and COVR. Included in OPEN are such ideas as: unfastening and loosening; liberty and spontaneity; doors and openings; exposing and exhibiting; exploring and reconnoitering.

OPPO - References to dissimilarities, differences and contests. Included are such ideas as: unconventional and deviant; conflict and opposition; inopportune and irregular.

OUT - References to being outside, to discharging and to emanation. Included are such ideas as: emitting and expelling; external and outward; extraction and extirpation; erasing and eroding.

PANG - References to upset states of mind including such affects as anxiety, fear and guilt. The kinds of ideas in PANG are: agony and pain; moodiness and depression; distraction and consternation; gruesomeness and horror; shame and trouble.

PAST - References to the past and to age. Included are such ideas as: ancient and historical; bygone and old; former and prior; old-fashioned and outmoded. Past time represented by the past tense of verbs is not categorized.

PATH - References to roads, passageways and directions. Included are such ideas as: thoroughfare and highway; duct and channel; route and direction.

PLAC - References to locations and areas, and to placing and locating. Included are such ideas as: town and country; place and site; region and locale; right and left. Inclusion of place names in the dictionary, with homonyms referring to language and inhabitants, would have required an inordinately large number of entries. Therefore only a few place names are included, along with a few language names and names of nationals, as paradigms for categorizing such words. Some of these entries are shown below:

Place Reference	Language Reference	Reference to National
America n PLAC		
American j PLAC		American n GRUP
Dutch j PLAC	Dutch n TALK	Dutch n GRUP
Holland n PLAC		
England n PLAC		
English j PLAC	English n TALK	English n GRUP
	Hebrew n TALK	Hebrew n GRUP
	Sanskrit n TALK	

In a text to be categorized, the words *place, language* or *group* may be substituted for place, language or national names, to provide for proper categorization.

PLAY - References to recreation and entertainment. Included are such ideas as: theater and sports; party and fiesta; toys and playing.

POWR - References to ability, achievement, strength and bravery. Included are such ideas as: adeptness and skill; fearlessness and hardiness; success and accomplishment; force and power. The opposing category is WEAK. A number of words are categorized POWR WEAK (*defeat, overwhelm, subdue*) since the ideas of overcoming and of someone or something overcome are intertwined.

QUIK - References to speed, suddenness and alertness. Included are such ideas as: running and darting; rapidity and haste; awake and active; bustling and liveliness.

REST - References to slowness, immobility and resting. Included are such ideas as: sitting and lying; numbness and unconsciousness; stillness and quiescence; inactivity and waiting.

SEP - References to separation, splitting and cutting. Included are such ideas as: detaching and divesting; solitude and isolation; tearing and parting; expunging and expelling; fugitive and refugee.

SEX - Words with prominent sexual implications, including such ideas as: romance and love; courting and marriage; genitalia and intercourse.

SHRP - References to sharp edges, points and precision. Included are such ideas as: knives and cutting; accuracy and clarity; concentrating and focussing.

SICK - References to illness, infection and malady. Included are such ideas as: virus and disease; aberration and disorder; medical illness and physical abnormality. While the category SOMA is implicit in many illnesses, it is applied as an additional score only when there is specific reference to body processes or organs.

SIML - References to similarity, equality and suitability. Included are such ideas as: approximation and agreement; applicability and appropriateness; repeating and retracing; sign and symbol; consistency and evenness.

SIP - References to drinking, sucking and potables.

SOLE - References to self, singleness and egocentricity. Included are such ideas as: only and lone; individual and private; case and instance; idiosyncrasy and autonomy.

SOMA - References to bodily and vegetative processes and internal body parts. Included are such ideas as: odor and smell; ingesting and excreting; anatomical and physiological.

SOME - References to a segment, a few, and to possibility. Included are such ideas as: portion and piece; aspect and facet; phase and stage; occasional and sometimes.

SUB - References to subordination, dependence and subjection. The opposing category is LEAD. Included are such ideas as: accessory and secondary; servant and vassal; deference and obedience; demotion and downgrading; minor and junior.

TALK - References to language and vocal communication. WRIT also includes language words, but where there is a distinct reference to writing as such. Where a word may refer either to speech or to writing, the TALK category is applied. Typical animal cries are categorized ANML TALK. Language names are categorized TALK (See examples under PLAC, page 28). References to syntax and grammar are categorized TALK FORM. While words in TALK have an implicit HEAR quality, this second category is applied only when the "sound and hearing" aspect is as important as the "communication" aspect (*call, loudspeaker*).

TIME - References to time and periods of time. References to future time are categorized FORW TIME. References to past time are under the category PAST. Included in this category are references to seasons, months, days, time of day and clock time.

TRIV - References to triviality, vapidity and valuelessness. Included are such ideas as: uselessness and obsolescence; humdrum and boredom; hackneyed and superficial; unimportant and inessential.

TRUE - References to truth and proof. Included are such ideas as: right and correct; candor and sincerity; testing and validating.

UP - References to being up and above, to climbing and flight, and to flying creatures. Included are such ideas as: height and top; winged insect and bird; airplane and kite; mounting and rising; ladder and stairs.

VAPR - References to vapors, gases and mist. Included are such ideas as: cloud and fog; aroma and odor; breath and respiration.

VARY - References to alteration of form or position, deviation, instability and transience. Included are such ideas as: modification and evolution; plasticity and flexibility; oscillating and vibrating; avoiding and replacing; bending and circling.

VEGT - References to vegetation and to plant products. Included are fruits, grains, vegetables, flowers, trees and wood, as well as cloth derived from vegetation.

VEHC - References to vehicles of transportation, characteristic parts of vehicles, and conductors of vehicles.

VIEW - References to vision and light. Included are such ideas as: sight and seeing; exhibition and display; window and eyeglass; flag and decal; picture and photograph. Color words receive their own special scoring (COLR) and are not included here.

WE - All uses of the first person pronoun. The singular first person pronoun is given the additional score SOLE.

WEA - References to weather and climate.

WEAK - References to weakness, failure and inexpertness. Where the idea of a servile or subordinate relationship is prominent, the category SUB is applied. Certain words which include connotations both of defeat and of victory are categorized POWR WEAK (*defeat, beat*). Included in WEAK are such ideas as: awkwardness and insecurity; immaturity and imperfection; exhaustion and fatigue; inability and impotence.

WHOL - References to totality, entirety, generality and universality. Included are such ideas as: all and whole; amount and total; comprehensive and exhaustive; humanity and world.

WORK - References to work and to activities requiring considerable expenditure of energy. Included are such ideas as: construction and manufacture; hand tools and jobs; effort and labor. Trades which are typically manual and blue-collar are included in WORK (*blacksmith, carpenter*), while small merchant and sales type trades are included in MART. Other professions (*doctor, lawyer*) are categorized within their own domains of activity rather than as WORK or MART.

WRIT - References to written language, to writing instruments and to documents. If a word may be categorized either WRIT or TALK depending on context, TALK has been applied as the preferred category. Words like *statement* and *prologue* will therefore appear in TALK but not in WRIT.

YNG - References to infancy, youth and immaturity. Included are such ideas as: callow and young; boy and girl; fledgling and suckling; precocity and adolescence.

3

alphabetic listing
of words
with categories

Each word in the dictionary is listed alphabetically in this section, followed by a letter symbol indicating part of speech, and by code names of one or two categories. Footnotes at intervals throughout the listing explain the letter symbols for parts of speech. For a word with several different meanings, the meaning judged most common is placed first. Phrases are presented as if they were a single word (*UnitedStates*), a convention applied for computer analyses. If a word is truncated for the sake of the column format, the reader will have little difficulty in providing the completion (*Electrocardiogr/ -am* or *-aphy*).

A a NSCR
A n WRIT
A n WRIT EDUC
A n WRIT MUSC
Aback d BACK
Aback d BACK PANG
Abacus n NUMR
Abaft d BACK FLOW
Abandon v SEP
Abandon n OPEN
Abandon n BAD
Abase v BAD WEAK
Abash v PANG
Abate v LITL
Abbe n LEAD HOLY
Abbess n LADY HOLY
Abbey n HOME HOLY
Abbot n LEAD HOLY
Abbreviate v LITL
ABC n WRIT
ABC n CRUX WRIT
Abdicate v SEP LACK
Abdomen n BODY HOLW
Abduct v CRIM SEP
Aberrant j VARY OPPO
Aberration n VARY OPPO
Aberration n VARY SICK
Abet v AID
Abeyance n BLOK REST
Abhor v AGGR
Abide v AGRE EVER
Abide v EVER LIVE
Abiding j EVER
Ability n POWR
Abject j WEAK
Abjure v AGGR LACK
Ablaze j HEAT VIEW
Able j POWR
Ablebodied j POWR BODY
Abloom j VEGT
Ablution n CLEN FLOW
Ably d POWR
Abnegate v NO LACK
Abnormal j OPPO AFAR
Abnormal j OPPO SICK
Abnormity n BAD AFAR
Aboard b IN VEHC
Abode n HOME LIVE
Abolish v END
Abominable j AGGR
Aborigine n BGIN NEAR
Abortion n BGIN BLOK
Abound v MUCH
About b NSCR
About b NEAR
About b VARY
Above b UP
Above b LEAD UP
Aboveboard j OPEN UP
Abracadabra n FOOL TALK
Abrade v DAMG
Abrasion n DAMG

Abrasive j DAMG
Abrasive n AGGR MTRL
Abreaction n MEDC OUT
Abreast d SIML NEAR
Abridge v LITL
Abroad d AFAR
Abroad d LARG
Abrogate v END
Abrupt j QUIK
Abrupt j AGGR QUIK
Abscess n DIRT SICK
Abscissa n FORM
Abscond v CRIM GO
Absence n SEP
Absence n SEP LACK
Absent v SEP
Absentminded j FOOL IDEA
Absinthe n SIP VEGT
Absolute j WHOL EMPH
Absolution n AGRE OPEN
Absolution n AGRE HOLY
Absolutism n WHOL LEAD
Absolve v AGRE OPEN
Absorb v IN
Absorb v MOTV
Abstain v BLOK LACK
Abstemious j BLOK LACK
Abstention n BLOK LACK
Abstinence n BLOK LACK
Abstract j IDEA
Abstract n OUT
Abstract n LITL IDEA
Abstruse j BLUR COVR
Absurd j FOOL
Abundant j MUCH
Abuse n DAMG
Abuse n AGGR
Abut v JOIN
Abutment n AID FORM
Abutment n JOIN
Abuzz j HEAR
Abyss n DOWN HOLW
Academic j EDUC
Academies n GRUP EDUC
Academies n HOME EDUC
Academy n GRUP EDUC
Academy n HOME EDUC
Accede v AGRE
Accede v POWR
Accelerate v QUIK GO
Accelerator n QUIK MECH
Accent n EMPH
Accent n TALK EMPH
Accentuate v EMPH
Accept v AGRE
Accept v HAVE
Access n GO
Access n LARG
Accessible j GO
Accessible j OPEN
Accession n AGRE
Accession n POWR GO

Accession n LARG JOIN
Accessory n AID SUB
Accident n DAMG
Accident n AFAR EVNT
Accidental j AFAR EVNT
Accidental j TRIV
Acclaim v AGRE POWR
Acclimate v SIML EVER
Accolade n AGRE POWR
Accommodate v SIML AID
Accompany v JOIN
Accompany v JOIN MUSC
Accomplice n CRIM AID
Accomplish v POWR
Accord n SIML
Accord v AGRE AID
According c SIML
According v AGRE AID
Accordion n MUSC
Accost v TALK
Accost v TALK SEX
Accouchement n BGIN REST
Account n IDEA
Account n MART MONY
Account n MOTV
Accountable j MOTV
Accountant n MART NUMR
Accouterment n GARB AID
Accredit v AGRE
Accretion n LARG JOIN
Accrue v LARG
Acculturation n GRUP IDEA
Accumulate v LARG BULG
Accumulate v LARG HAVE
Accurate j SHRP TRUE
Accursed j BAD AGGR
Accuse v AGGR
Accustom v SIML EVER
Ace n POWR PLAY
Ace n DAMG POWR
Acetate n MTRL
Acetylene n HEAT MTRL
Ache n PANG
Ache n PANG MOTV
Achieve v POWR
Acid j FOOD SOMA
Acid j AGGR
Acid n MTRL
Acknowledge v AGRE
Acme n UP
Acne n DIRT BODY
Acolyte n AID HOLY
Acorn n FOOD VEGT
Acoustic j HEAR
Acquaint v NEAR IDEA
Acquiesce v AGRE
Acquire v HAVE
Acquisition n HAVE
Acquit v OPEN
Acquit v EVNT
Acre n ERTH MSMT
Acrid j AGGR

Parts of speech: a article; b preposition; c conjunction; d adverb; f prefix; i interjection;
j adjective; n noun; p pronoun; r phrase; v verb.

Acrid j AGGR SOMA
Acrimony n AGGR
Acrobat n PLAY
Acropolis n POWR PLAC
Across b AFAR
Across b EVER
Across b JOIN
Across b LARG
Acrostic n WRIT
Acrylic n MTRL
Acrylic n COLR
Act n EVNT
Act n PLAY
Act n LAW
Acting j SIML EVNT
Acting n PLAY
Acting v EVNT
Action n EVNT
Action n DAMG
Action n MECH
Action n LAW
Action n QUIK EVNT
Activate v BGIN
Active j EVNT
Active j QUIK EVNT
Activity n EVNT
Activity n QUIK EVNT
Actor n MALE PLAY
Actress n LADY PLAY
Actual j TRUE
Actuarial j NUMR
Actuaries n MART WRIT
Actuary n MART WRIT
Actuate v BGIN
Acuity n SHRP
Acumen n POWR IDEA
Acute j EMPH
Acute j SHRP
Ad n OPEN
Ad n AID PLAY
Adage n TALK IDEA
Adagio n REST MUSC
Adamant j EVER
Adamant n ERTH MTRL
Adapt v SIML VARY
Add v LARG NUMR
Add v LARG JOIN
Added v LARG NUMR
Added v LARG JOIN
Addendum n LARG JOIN
Adder n ANML
Adder n LARG NUMR
Addict n SICK MOTV
Adding v LARG NUMR
Adding v LARG JOIN
Addition n LARG JOIN
Addition n LARG NUMR
Additive n LARG JOIN
Addle v BLUR
Addle v DIRT
Address n WRIT PLAC
Address n TALK
Address n POWR
Address v MOTV
Adduce v IDEA

Adenoids n SOMA
Adept j POWR
Adequate j MUCH
Adequate j MUCH POWR
Adhere v JOIN
Adhere v AGRE JOIN
Adhesion n JOIN
Adhesion n AGRE JOIN
Adhesive j JOIN
Adhoc j VARY
Adieu n SEP
Adinfinitum d EVER
Adios i SEP
Adjacent j NEAR
Adjective n TALK FORM
Adjoin v JOIN
Adjourn v END
Adjudge v IDEA
Adjudge v LAW IDEA
Adjudicate v LAW IDEA
Adjunct n JOIN
Adjust v SIML VARY
Adjutant n AID
Adjutant n LEAD
Adlib v EASY TALK
Administer v LEAD
Administer v AID
Administration n LEAD
Admirable j GOOD
Admiral n LEAD FLOW
Admire v FOND
Admissible j AGRE
Admission n GO IN
Admission n AGRE
Admit v AGRE
Admit v GO IN
Admixture n JOIN
Admonish v AGGR TALK
Ado n PANG
Adobe j ERTH MTRL
Adolescent j YNG
Adonis n GOOD MALE
Adopt v AGRE HAVE
Adopt v AGRE
Adore v FOND
Adorn v GOOD
Adrenalin n SOMA MTRL
Adrift d GO FLOW
Adroit j POWR
Adulate v FOND SUB
Adult n POWR
Adulterate v DIRT
Adulterer n BAD SEX
Adulterous j BAD SEX
Adultery n BAD SEX
Adulthood n POWR
Adumbrate v BLUR FORW
Advance n FORW GO
Advance n FORW
Advance n FORW SEX
Advance v FORW AID
Advantage n AID
Advent n GO
Advent n HOLY
Adventist n HOLY

Adventitious j TRIV
Adventure n DAMG
Adverb n TALK FORM
Adversary n OPPO
Adverse j OPPO
Advertise v OPEN
Advice n AID IDEA
Advise v AID IDEA
Advocate v LAW
Advocate n AGRE
Adze n SHRP
Aegis n AID
Aeon n EVER TIME
Aerate v VAPR CLEN
Aerial j VAPR UP
Aerial n BULG UP
Aerialist n PLAY UP
Aerie n ANML HOME
Aero j VEHC UP
Aerodynamics n VAPR POWR
Aeronaut n VEHC UP
Aeroplane n VEHC UP
Aesthetic j GOOD
Aether n VAPR
Aetiology n BGIN IDEA
Afar d AFAR
Affable j FOND
Affair n EVNT
Affair n JOIN SEX
Affaire n JOIN SEX
Affect n MOTV
Affect v FALS
Affectation n FALS
Affection n FOND
Affianced j SEX KIN
Affidavit n WRIT TRUE
Affiliate n JOIN
Affinity n SIML JOIN
Affinity n FOND JOIN
Affirm v TRUE
Affirmative j AGRE
Affix v JOIN
Afflict v DAMG
Affluence n MUCH MONY
Afford v AID
Afford v MONY
Affray n DAMG
Affront v AGGR
Afghan n GARB
Afire j HEAT VIEW
Aflame j HEAT VIEW
Afloat j GO FLOW
Aforementioned j FORW TALK
Aforesaid j FORW TALK
Aforethought n FORW IDEA
Afoul d BLOK
Afraid j PANG
Afresh d NEW
Aft j BACK FLOW
After b BACK
After b MOTV
Aftermath n DAMG END
Afternoon n TIME
Afterward d BACK
Again d SIML

Against b OPPO
Against b NEAR
Agape j HOLW OPEN
Agape n FOND HOLY
Agate n ERTH MTRL
Agate n WRIT
Age n TIME
Age v PAST
Aged j PAST
Ageless j EVER TIME
Agency n AID
Agenda n WRIT
Agent n AID
Agglutinate v JOIN
Aggrandize v LARG
Aggravate v AGGR PANG
Aggregate j WHOL GRUP
Aggression n DAMG
Aggression n AGGR
Aggrieve v PANG
Aghast j PANG
Agile j POWR
Aging j PAST
Agitate v PANG
Agitate v VARY
Aglow j VIEW
Agnostic j OPPO HOLY
Ago j PAST
Agog j PANG MOTV
Agony n PANG
Agrarian j ERTH VEGT
Agree v AGRE
Agree v SIML
Agreeable j AGRE
Agriculture n ERTH VEGT
Agronomy n ERTH VEGT
Aground d BLOK ERTH
Ahead d FORW
Ahoy i TALK FLOW
Aid v AID
Aide n AID
Ail v SICK
Aim n SHRP
Aim n MOTV
Aimless j BLUR
Air n VAPR WEA
Air n VAPR UP
Air n MUSC
Air v VAPR OPEN
Aircraft n VEHC UP
Aired v VAPR WEA
Aired v VAPR OPEN
Airedale n ANML
Airing v VAPR WEA
Airing v VAPR OPEN
Airless j VAPR LACK
Airline n VEHC UP
Airplane n VEHC UP
Airport n HOME UP
Airs n VAPR WEA
Airs n VAPR FALS
Airs n MUSC
Airs v VAPR OPEN
Airy j VAPR WEA
Airy j VAPR EASY

Aisle n PATH
Ajar j OPEN
Akimbo j VARY BODY
Akin j SIML
Alabaster n ERTH MTRL
Alacarte j FOOD WRIT
Alack i PANG
Alacrity n QUIK
Aladdin n MYTH YNG
Alamode j FOOD
Alamode j SIML NEW
Alarm n PANG
Alarm n HEAR PANG
Alas i PANG
Alb n GARB HOLY
Albatross n ANML UP
Albino n COLR LACK
Album n WRIT
Album n MUSC
Alchemist n MYTH
Alcohol n MTRL VEGT
Alcohol n SIP VEGT
Alcoholic j SIP VEGT
Alcoholic n SIP SICK
Alcoholism n SIP SICK
Alcove n HOME
Alderman n LEAD LAW
Ale n SIP VEGT
Alert j QUIK MOTV
Alfalfa n VEGT
Algae n FLOW VEGT
Algebra n NUMR
Algorithm n NUMR
Alias n FALS TALK
Alibi n IDEA
Alien j OPPO SEP
Alienate v OPPO SEP
Alienation n OPPO SEP
Alienation n SICK SEP
Alienist n SICK SEP
Alight j VIEW
Alight v DOWN GO
Align v SIML
Alike j SIML
Aliment n FOOD AID
Alimentary j FOOD SOMA
Alimentary j FOOD AID
Alimony n MONY SEP
Aline v SIML
Alive j LIVE
Alkali n MTRL
All j WHOL
Allay v GLAD
Allegation n TALK
Allege v TALK
Allegiance n AGRE JOIN
Alleging v TALK
Allegory n MYTH
Allegro j QUIK MUSC
Allergy n SICK
Alleviate v AID
Alley n PATH
Alliance n AGRE JOIN
Allied j AGRE JOIN
Allies n AGRE JOIN

Alligator n ANML FLOW
Alligator n ANML FABR
Alliterate v SIML TALK
Allocate v AID SOME
Allot v AID SOME
Allow v AGRE
Allowance n AGRE
Allowance n MONY
Alloy n JOIN MTRL
Alloy n JOIN TRIV
Allright d AGRE
Allude v TALK
Allure n FOND
Allusion n TALK
Alluvial j ERTH FLOW
Ally n AGRE JOIN
Almamater n HOME EDUC
Almanac n WRIT
Almighty j WHOL POWR
Almighty n LEAD HOLY
Almond n FOOD VEGT
Almost d NEAR
Alms n AID
Aloft d UP
Alone j SOLE SEP
Along b NEAR
Along d JOIN
Along d FORW
Alongside d NEAR
Aloof j AFAR SEP
Aloud d HEAR
Alpaca n ANML
Alpaca n ANML FABR
Alpha n WRIT
Alpha n ASTR VIEW
Alpha n MTRL ION
Alpha n BGIN
Alphabet n FORW WRIT
Alpine j BULG PLAC
Alps n BULG PLAC
Already d PAST
Alright d AGRE
Also d SIML
Alsoran n GO WEAK
Altar n HOLY FORM
Alter v VARY
Altercation n DAMG
Alternate v VARY
Alternating v VARY
Alternative n MOTV
Although c OPPO
Altimeter n MSMT UP
Altitude n MSMT UP
Alto j MUSC
Altogether d WHOL
Altruism n GOOD AID
Alum n MTRL
Aluminum n MTRL
Alumna n LADY EDUC
Alumni n MALE EDUC
Alumnus n MALE EDUC
Always d EVER
Am v NSCR
Am v EVNT
Amalgam n JOIN

Amanuensis n WRIT
Amass v LARG HAVE
Amass v LARG
Amateur j WEAK
Amatory j FOND SEX
Amaze v PANG
Amazingly d EMPH PANG
Amazon n PLAC FLOW
Amazon n POWR LADY
Ambassador n LEAD
Amber n COLR
Amber n ERTH MTRL
Ambergris n ANML MTRL
Ambidextrous j POWR BODY
Ambiguous j BLUR
Ambition n POWR MOTV
Ambivalent j BLUR MOTV
Amble v GO
Ambrosia n SOMA GOOD
Ambulance n MEDC VEHC
Ambulant j GO
Ambulatory j GO
Ambush n DAMG COVR
Amebic j BUG
Ameliorate v AID
Amen i AGRE HOLY
Amenable j AGRE
Amend n AID
Amend v VARY
Amenity n GOOD
America n PLAC
American j PLAC
American n GRUP
Amethyst n ERTH MTRL
Amethyst n COLR
Amiable j FOND
Amicable j FOND
Amid b IN JOIN
Amiss j FALS
Amity n FOND
Ammeter n ION MSMT
Ammonia n MTRL
Ammunition n DAMG
Amnesia n BLUR SICK
Amnesty n AGRE OPEN
Amoeba n BUG
Among b JOIN
Amoral j BAD
Amorous j FOND SEX
Amorphous j BLUR
Amortize v MART MONY
Amount n WHOL
Amount n SOME
Amour n FOND SEX
Ampere n ION MSMT
Amphibious j ERTH FLOW
Amphitheater n HOME PLAY
Ample j MUCH LARG
Amplify v LARG
Amplitude n MSMT
Amply d MUCH LARG
Amputate v BODY SEP
Amuck j DAMG PANG
Amulet n AID MYTH
Amuse v GLAD

An a NSCR
Anachronism n FALS PAST
Anaclitic j AID
Anaconda n ANML
Anaemic j SICK
Anaemic j WEAK
Anaesthesia n REST
Anagram n VARY WRIT
Anal j DIRT SOMA
Analgesic n GLAD MEDC
Analogy n SIML
Analyze v IDEA
Anarchy n BLUR LAW
Anathema n AGGR
Anatomy n SOMA IDEA
Ancestor n PAST KIN
Anchor v BLOK
Anchorage n BLOK
Anchorite n SOLE SEP
Anchovy n FOOD FLOW
Anchovy n ANML FLOW
Ancient j PAST
Ancillary j AID SUB
And c NSCR
Andante j REST MUSC
Andes n BULG PLAC
Andiron n HEAT FURN
Androgynous j LADY MALE
Anecdote n TALK
Anemic j SICK
Anemic j WEAK
Anemometer n VAPR MSMT
Anemone n VEGT
Anesthesia n REST
Anew d NEW
Angel n GOOD HOLY
Angel n FOOD
Anger n AGGR
Angle n FORM
Angle n MOTV
Angle v VARY
Angle v FLOW SHRP
Angler n FLOW SHRP
Anglican j PLAC
Anglican j GRUP HOLY
Anglicize v PLAC
Angling v MOTV
Angling v VARY
Angling v FLOW SHRP
Anglophile n FOND PLAC
Anglophobe n AGGR PLAC
Anglosaxon j GRUP
Angora n ANML FABR
Angry j AGGR
Angstrom n ION MSMT
Anguish n PANG
Angular j FORM
Animadversion n AGGR TALK
Animal n ANML
Animate v QUIK LIVE
Animism n IDEA MYTH
Animosity n AGGR
Anise n FOOD VEGT
Ankle n BODY
Anklet n GARB

Annals n WRIT PAST
Anneal v HEAT FORM
Annex n JOIN
Annex v JOIN HAVE
Annihilate v DAMG END
Anniversary n TIME
Annotate v WRIT
Announce v TALK
Annoy v AGGR PANG
Annual j TIME
Annual n WRIT TIME
Annuity n MONY TIME
Annul v END NO
Anode n ION
Anodyne n GLAD AID
Anoint v MTRL FLOW
Anoint v HOLY FLOW
Anomaly n OPPO
Anonymous j TALK COVR
Another j NSCR
Another j OPPO
Another p SOLE
Answer n TALK
Answer n TALK IDEA
Ant n BUG
Antagonize v AGGR
Antarctic n COLD PLAC
Ante f FORW
Ante f PAST
Ante n MONY
Anteater n ANML
Antebellum j DAMG PAST
Antecede v FORW PAST
Antechamber n FORW HOME
Antedate v FORW PAST
Antediluvian j FLOW PAST
Antelope n ANML
Antemortem j DEAD FORW
Antenna n BULG UP
Antenna n ANML BODY
Anterior j FORW
Anteroom n FORW HOME
Anthem n MUSC
Anthology n GRUP WRIT
Anthracite n HEAT MTRL
Anthropoid n ANML
Anthropology n GRUP IDEA
Anti b OPPO
Antibiotic n MEDC
Antibody n MEDC
Antic n FOOL
Anticipate v FORW MOTV
Anticlimax n TRIV
Antidote n MEDC
Antimacassar n CLEN FURN
Antinomy n OPPO
Antipasto n FOOD
Antipathy n AGGR
Antiphony n VARY MUSC
Antipodes n OPPO PLAC
Antiquity n PAST
Antiseptic j MEDC
Antithesis n OPPO IDEA
Antitoxin n MEDC
Antitype n OPPO

Antler n ANML BODY	Appease v GLAD AID	Approve v AGRE
Antonym n OPPO TALK	Appellate j LAW	Approximate j NEAR
Anus n DIRT SOMA	Appellation n TALK	Approximate v SIML NEAR
Anvil n FORM WORK	Append v JOIN	Approximately d NEAR
Anxiety n PANG	Appendage n JOIN	Apricot n FOOD VEGT
Any j NSCR	Appendectomy n MEDC SOMA	Apricot n COLR
Any j SOME	Appendices n JOIN WRIT	April n TIME
Anybody p SOLE	Appendices n SOMA JOIN	Apriori j IDEA
Anyhow d NSCR	Appendicitis n SOMA SICK	Apron n GARB
Anyone p SOLE	Appending v JOIN	Apron n FORW
Anything p NSCR	Appetite n FOOD MOTV	Apron n COVR
Anyway d NSCR	Appetite n MOTV	Apropos d SIML
Anywhere d PLAC	Applause n AGRE HEAR	Apse n HOME HOLY
Aorta n SOMA	Apple n FOOD VEGT	Apt j SIML
Apache n GRUP	Applejack n SIP VEGT	Apt j MOTV
Apache n CRIM GRUP	Applesauce n FOOD VEGT	Apt j POWR
Apart d SEP	Applesauce n FOOL FOOD	Aptitude n POWR
Apartheid n GRUP SEP	Appliance n FURN MECH	Aqua n FLOW
Apartment n HOME	Appliance n MECH	Aquacade n PLAY FLOW
Apathy n PANG LACK	Applicable j SIML	Aquamarine n ERTH MTRL
Ape n ANML	Applicant n MOTV	Aquamarine n COLR
Ape v FOOL ANML	Application n SIML	Aquarium n HOME FLOW
Aperture n HOLW OPEN	Application n JOIN	Aquarius n ASTR MYTH
Apex n UP	Application n MOTV	Aquatic j FLOW
Aphasia n SICK TALK	Application n WRIT MOTV	Aquatint n COLR
Aphid n BUG DIRT	Applicator n JOIN	Aqueduct n FLOW PATH
Aphorism n TALK IDEA	Applied v SIML	Aquiline j ANML UP
Aphrodisiac n SEX MOTV	Applied v JOIN	Arabesque n VARY FORM
Aphrodite n LADY HOLY	Applied v MOTV	Arable j ERTH VEGT
Apiary n BUG HOME	Apply v SIML	Arachnid n BUG
Apices n UP	Apply v JOIN	Arbiter n LEAD IDEA
Apiece d SOLE	Apply v MOTV	Arbitrary j EVER MOTV
Apish j ANML	Appoint v MOTV	Arbitrate v LEAD IDEA
Apish j FOOL ANML	Appointed v MOTV	Arbor n HOME VEGT
Aplomb n POWR	Appointed v FURN	Arbor n VEGT
Apocalypse n WRIT HOLY	Appointee n MOTV	Arbor n MECH
Apocalypse n DAMG FORW	Appointment n JOIN	Arc n FORM
Apocrypha n WRIT HOLY	Appointment n MOTV	Arcade n HOME
Apocryphal j FALS	Appointment n FURN	Arcane j COVR
Apogee n UP	Apportion v AID SOME	Arch n FORM
Apollo n MALE MYTH	Apposition n SIML	Arch n BODY
Apollo n GOOD MALE	Appraise v CRUX IDEA	Arch j POWR
Apology n AGRE IDEA	Appreciable j LARG	Archaeology n ERTH PAST
Apoplectic j SICK PANG	Appreciate v FOND IDEA	Archaic j PAST
Apoplexy n SICK	Appreciate v FOND	Archangel n LEAD HOLY
Apostasy n OPPO IDEA	Appreciate v LARG	Archbishop n LEAD HOLY
Apostle n LEAD HOLY	Apprehension n PANG	Arched v FORM
Apostolic j LEAD HOLY	Apprehension n IDEA	Archeology n ERTH PAST
Apostrophe n WRIT	Apprehension n BLOK	Archer n DAMG SHRP
Apostrophe n TALK	Apprentice n SUB WORK	Arches n FORM
Apothecary n MEDC	Apprise v IDEA	Arches n BODY
Appalachian j BULG PLAC	Approach v GO NEAR	Archetype n SIML CRUX
Appall v PANG	Approbation n AGRE	Arching v FORM
Apparatus n MECH	Appropriate j SIML	Archipelago n ERTH FLOW
Apparel n GARB	Appropriate v MONY HAVE	Architect n IDEA FORM
Apparent j OPEN	Appropriate v HAVE	Archives n WRIT
Apparition n VIEW MYTH	Appropriated v MONY HAVE	Archives n HOME WRIT
Appeal n AID MOTV	Appropriated v HAVE	Arctic n COLD PLAC
Appeal n FOND	Appropriates v MONY HAVE	Arctics n GARB
Appear v VIEW	Appropriates v HAVE	Ardent j FOND
Appear v IDEA VIEW	Appropriation n MONY HAVE	Arduous j PANG MOTV
Appearance n VIEW	Appropriation n HAVE	Are v NSCR

Parts of speech: a article; b preposition; c conjunction; d adverb; f prefix; i interjection;
j adjective; n noun; p pronoun; r phrase; v verb.

Are v EVNT
Area n PLAC
Area n MSMT
Area n HOLW
Arena n HOME PLAY
Argosy n FLOW VEHC
Argot n CRIM TALK
Argue v AGGR TALK
Argue v OPPO TALK
Aria n MUSC
Arid j FLOW LACK
Arid j TRIV LACK
Aries n ASTR MYTH
Arise v GO UP
Arise v BGIN UP
Aristocracy n LEAD LAW
Aristocracy n LEAD GRUP
Aristocrat n LEAD GRUP
Arithmetic n NUMR
Ark n FLOW VEHC
Ark n HOLW HOLY
Arm n BODY
Arm n DAMG MECH
Arm n POWR
Armada n DAMG VEHC
Armadillo n ANML
Armageddon n DAMG PLAC
Armament n DAMG MECH
Armature n FORM
Armature n MECH
Armature n DAMG AID
Armchair n FURN REST
Armed v DAMG MECH
Armed j BODY
Armful n BODY BULG
Armies n DAMG GRUP
Armies n MUCH GRUP
Arming v DAMG MECH
Armistice n DAMG END
Armor n DAMG AID
Armories n DAMG HOME
Armory n DAMG HOME
Armory n VIEW
Armpit n BODY HOLW
Arms n BODY
Arms n DAMG MECH
Arms n VIEW
Army n DAMG GRUP
Army n MUCH GRUP
Aroma n VAPR SOMA
Arose v GO UP
Arose v BGIN UP
Around b VARY
Around b HOLW
Around b NEAR
Arouse v MOTV
Arouse v QUIK
Arpeggio n QUIK MUSC
Arraign v AGGR LAW
Arrange v FORM
Arrange v AGRE
Arrant j BAD
Array n FOR W
Array n GARB
Arrears n MONY MOTV

Arrest v BLOK LAW
Arrest v BLOK
Arrive v GO
Arrive v POWR GO
Arrogant j AGGR POWR
Arrogate v HAVE
Arrow n SHRP
Arrow n DAMG SHRP
Arroyo n ERTH HOLW
Arsenal n DAMG HOLW
Arsenic n DAMG MTRL
Arson n CRIM HEAT
Art n POWR
Artery n SOMA
Artery n JOIN PATH
Artesian j DOWN ERTH
Artful j POWR
Arthritis n SICK
Artichoke n FOOD VEGT
Article n WRIT
Article n NSCR
Article n TALK FORM
Articular j BODY JOIN
Articulate v TALK SHRP
Articulate v JOIN
Artifact n WORK
Artifice n FALS
Artificial j FALS
Artillery n DAMG MECH
Artisan n POWR WORK
Artist n POWR
Artiste n POWR PLAY
Artless j EASY
Artless j WEAK
Arts n POWR
Arts n POWR EDUC
Aryan j GRUP
As c NSCR
As c SIML
Asbestos n ERTH MTRL
Ascend v GO UP
Ascendancy n LEAD UP
Ascension n GO UP
Ascertain v IDEA SHRP
Ascetic j LACK
Ascot n GARB
Ascribe v IDEA MOTV
Aseptic j CLEN MEDC
Asexual j SEX LACK
Ash n HEAT MTRL
Ash n COLR
Ash n MTRL VEGT
Ash n VEGT
Ashamed j PANG
Ashen j COLR
Ashes n HEAT MTRL
Ashes n VEGT
Ashore d ERTH FLOW
AshWednesday n HOLY TIME
Aside d NEAR SEP
Aside n TALK SEP
Asinine j FOOL ANML
Ask v TALK
Askance d VARY AGGR
Asked v TALK

Askew d VARY
Aslant d VARY
Asleep d REST
Asocial j GRUP SEP
Asp n ANML DAMG
Asparagus n FOOD VEGT
Aspect n VIEW
Aspect n VIEW SOME
Aspen n VEGT
Asperity n AGGR
Aspersion n AGGR TALK
Asphalt n ERTH MTRL
Asphyxiate v DAMG DEAD
Aspirant n MOTV
Aspirate v HEAR TALK
Aspirate v VAPR OUT
Aspirating v HEAR TALK
Aspirating v VAPR OUT
Aspiration n MOTV
Aspiration n VAPR OUT
Aspiration n HEAR TALK
Aspirator n MECH OUT
Aspire v MOTV
Aspirin n MEDC
Aspiring j MOTV
Ass n BACK BODY
Ass n ANML
Ass n FOOL ANML
Assail v DAMG
Assassinate v DAMG DEAD
Assault n DAMG
Assay n MSMT
Assay v IDEA
Assed j BACK BODY
Assemble v GRUP JOIN
Assemble v JOIN
Assembly n GRUP JOIN
Assembly n JOIN
Assent v AGRE
Assert v TALK
Assert v POWR
Assertive j POWR
Asses n BACK BODY
Asses n ANML
Asses n FOOL ANML
Assess v CRUX IDEA
Assess v MONY
Asset n HAVE
Asset n CRUX AID
Assiduous j EVER MOTV
Assign v MOTV
Assignable j MOTV
Assignation n JOIN SEX
Assimilate v SIML SOMA
Assimilate v SIML
Assist v AID
Associate v GRUP JOIN
Associate v JOIN IDEA
Assonance n SIML HEAR
Assort v GRUP SEP
Assort v SIML
Assort v JOIN
Assortment n OPPO
Assortment n GRUP SEP
Assuage v GLAD AID

Assume v HAVE
Assume v IDEA
Assume v FALS HAVE
Assumption n IDEA
Assumption n HAVE
Assumption n POWR HOLY
Assure v AID
Assure v SHRP
Aster n VEGT
Asterisk n WRIT EMPH
Astern d BACK FLOW
Asthma n SICK
Astigmatism n SICK VIEW
Astonish v PANG
Astound v PANG
Astray d FALS GO
Astride j BODY SEP
Astringent j AGGR
Astringent j BLOK
Astringent n MEDC
Astrology n ASTR MYTH
Astronaut n ASTR VEHC
Astronomical j ASTR IDEA
Astronomical j ASTR LARG
Astronomy n ASTR IDEA
Astrophysics n ASTR IDEA
Astute j POWR IDEA
Asunder d SEP
Aswellas r SIML
Asylum n AID
Asylum n MEDC HOME
Asymmetry n VARY FORM
At b NSCR
At b NEAR
Atavism n PAST
Ate v FOOD SOMA
Ate v FOOD PANG
Ate v DAMG FOOD
Atheism n OPPO HOLY
Athlete n POWR PLAY
Athwart b OPPO
Athwart b JOIN
Atlantic n PLAC FLOW
Atlas n IDEA FORM
Atlas n POWR MYTH
Atmosphere n VAPR ASTR
Atmosphere n VAPR HOLW
Atmosphere n VAPR MSMT
Atmospheric j VAPR ASTR
Atmospheric j VAPR HOLW
Atoll n ERTH FLOW
Atom n MTRL ION
Atomic j MTRL ION
Atomizer n VAPR MECH
Atone v AGRE
Atonement n AGRE HOLY
Atonement n AGRE
Atop d UP
Atrocious j BAD
Atrocious j BAD DAMG
Atrocity n BAD DAMG
Atrocity n BAD
Atrophy n WEAK LACK
Atropine n MEDC VEGT
Attach v JOIN

Attach v FOND JOIN
Attach v BLOK LAW
Attache n LEAD LAW
Attached v JOIN
Attached v FOND JOIN
Attached v BLOK LAW
Attaches v JOIN
Attaches v FOND JOIN
Attaches v BLOK LAW
Attack v DAMG
Attack v MOTV
Attain v POWR GO
Attempt n MOTV
Attempt n DAMG
Attend v AID JOIN
Attend v JOIN
Attend v GO JOIN
Attend v MOTV
Attendance n GO JOIN
Attendance n GRUP JOIN
Attendant j JOIN
Attendant n AID
Attendant n AID JOIN
Attention n MOTV
Attentive j MOTV
Attenuate v LITL WEAK
Attest v TRUE
Attic n HOME UP
Attire n GARB
Attitude n MOTV
Attitude n BODY EVNT
Attorney n LAW
Attract v GO JOIN
Attract v MOTV
Attractive j GOOD
Attractive j FOND MOTV
Attribute n CRUX HAVE
Attribute v IDEA MOTV
Attrition n WEAK
Atypical j OPPO
Auburn j COLR
Auction n MART MONY
Audacity n AGGR POWR
Audible j HEAR
Audience n GRUP HEAR
Audience n HEAR JOIN
Audio j HEAR
Audit v NUMR IDEA
Audit v HEAR
Auditor n NUMR IDEA
Auditor n HEAR
Auditorium n HEAR HOME
Auditory j HEAR
Aufwiedersehen i SEP
Auger n SHRP WORK
Augment v LARG
Augur v FORW MYTH
August n TIME
August j POWR
Augustly d POWR
Auk n ANML UP
Aunt n LADY KIN
Aura n VAPR HOLW
Aura n HOLW
Aura n SICK PANG

Aural j HEAR
Aureole n HOLW VIEW
Aurevoir i SEP
Auricle n SOMA
Aurora n ASTR VIEW
Auscultation n MEDC HEAR
Auspice n LEAD AID
Auspicious j AID
Austere j PANG
Austere j AGGR
Authentic j TRUE
Author n WRIT
Authoring v WRIT
Authority n LEAD
Authorize v AGRE LEAD
Autism n SICK SOLE
Auto n VEHC
Auto v GO VEHC
Autobahn n VEHC PATH
Autobiography n SOLE PAST
Autochthonous j BGIN NEAR
Autoclave n CLEN HEAT
Autocracy n LEAD LAW
Autocracy n LEAD SOLE
Autoed v GO VEHC
Autoerotic j SOLE SEX
Autograph v WRIT
Autohypnosis n SOLE REST
Automat n MART FOOD
Automate v MECH
Automatic j MECH
Automatic n DAMG MECH
Automatism n MECH
Automobile n VEHC
Automotive j VEHC
Autonomic j SOMA
Autonomy n SOLE OPEN
Autopsy n DEAD IDEA
Autumn n TIME
Auxiliary j AID SUB
Auxiliary n GRUP AID
Avail v AID
Avail v HAVE
Avalanche n DOWN BULG
Avantgarde n FORW NEW
Avarice n MOTV
Avenge v DAMG
Avenue n PATH
Aver v TALK
Average j EASY
Average j NUMR
Avers v TALK
Averse j AGGR
Aversion n AGGR
Aversion n VARY
Avert v VARY BLOK
Avert v VARY
Aviary n ANML HOME
Aviation n VEHC UP
Avid j MOTV
Avocado n FOOD VEGT
Avocation n PLAY
Avoid v VARY
Avow v AGRE TALK
Await v REST

Awake j QUIK
Award n POWR AID
Award n AID
Aware j IDEA
Away d SEP
Awe n PANG
Awesome j PANG
Awestricken j PANG
Awful j BAD
Awful j PANG
Awfully d EMPH

Awfully d BAD
Awhile d TIME
Awing v PANG
Awkward j WEAK
Awl n SHRP WORK
Awning n UP COVR
Awoke v QUIK
Awry j VARY FALS
Ax n SHRP WORK
Axe n SHRP WORK
Axed v SHRP WORK

Axes n SHRP WORK
Axes n FORM
Axing v SHRP WORK
Axiom n IDEA TRUE
Axis n FORM
Axis n AGRE JOIN
Axle n MECH VEHC
Aye d AGRE
Azalea n VEGT
Aztec j GRUP
Azure j COLR

B

B n WRIT
B n WRIT EDUC
B n WRIT MUSC
Baa n ANML TALK
Babble v HEAR TALK
Babied v AID YNG
Babies n YNG
Babies v AID YNG
Baby n YNG
Baby v AID YNG
Babying v AID YNG
Bachelor n SOLE MALE
Bachelor n POWR EDUC
Back n BACK
Back n BACK BODY
Back n BACK PLAY
Back v BACK GO
Back v BACK AID
Backbone n POWR BODY
Backbone n BACK BODY
Backfield n BACK PLAY
Background n BACK
Background n BACK CRUX
Backward d BACK
Backward j BACK WEAK
Backwood j BACK VEGT
Bacon n ANML FOOD
Bacteria n BUG
Bad j BAD
Bad j BAD DAMG
Bad j BAD DIRT
Bad j BAD FALS
Bad j BAD PANG
Bade v TALK
Badge n VIEW
Badge n POWR VIEW
Baffle n BLOK
Baffle v BLUR
Bag n HOLW
Bag n GARB HOLW
Bag n LADY HOLW
Bag v BLOK HOLW
Baggage n HOLW HAVE
Bagged v HOLW
Bagged v BLOK HOLW
Bagging v HOLW
Bagging v BLOK HOLW
Baggy j HOLW
Bagpipe n MUSC
Bail n LAW OPEN
Bail n HOLW

Bail v HOLW FLOW
Bail v GO
Bait v AGGR
Bait v MOTV
Bake v FOOD HEAT
Bake v HEAT
Bakelite n MTRL
Bakery n MART FOOD
Balance n SOME
Balance n SIML
Balance n MECH MSMT
Balcony n HOME UP
Bald j BODY LACK
Bald j OPEN
Bale n GRUP
Baleful j AGGR
Baling v GRUP
Balk v AGGR
Balk v BLOK
Balk v FALS PLAY
Ball n FORM
Ball n PLAY FORM
Ball n PLAY MUSC
Ball n DAMG FORM
Ball n MALE SEX
Ball v BLUR
Ballad n TALK MUSC
Balled v FORM
Balled v BLUR
Ballerina n LADY PLAY
Ballet n GO MUSC
Balloon n VAPR PLAY
Balloon n VAPR VEHC
Balloon v BULG
Ballot n MOTV
Ballroom n HOME PLAY
Baloney n ANML FOOD
Baloney n FOOL FOOD
Balsa n VEGT
Balsa n MTRL VEGT
Balsam n VEGT
Balsam n MTRL VEGT
Bamboozle v BLUR FALS
Ban n BLOK
Banana n FOOD VEGT
Band n MUSC
Band n JOIN
Band n GRUP JOIN
Band n GARB
Band n FORM
Bandage v AID COVR

Bandana n GARB
Banded v GRUP JOIN
Banded v FORM
Bandied v TALK
Bandied v VARY
Banding v GRUP JOIN
Banding v FORM
Bandit n CRIM
Bands n GRUP JOIN
Bands n MUSC
Bands n GARB HOLW
Bands n JOIN
Bands n FORM
Bandstand n MUSC
Bandy v TALK
Bandy v VARY
Bang n HEAR
Bang n BODY
Bang v DAMG
Banish v BLOK SEP
Bank n MART MONY
Bank n ERTH FLOW
Bank n ERTH BULG
Bank n FORW
Bank v AID
Bank v BLOK BULG
Bank v VARY GO
Bank v BULG
Banknote n MONY
Bankroll n MONY
Bankrupt j MONY LACK
Banned v BLOK
Banner j POWR VIEW
Banner n VIEW
Banns n SEX KIN
Banquet n FOOD
Bans n BLOK
Banshee n LADY MYTH
Banter v FOOL TALK
Baptize v HOLY FLOW
Bar n FORM
Bar n BLOK
Bar n SIP FORM
Bar n GRUP LAW
Bar n MART SIP
Bar n MUSC
Barb n SHRP
Barbarian n DAMG
Barbaric j DAMG
Barbecue n FOOD HEAT
Barbed j SHRP

Barbell n FORM WORK
Barber n MART SHRP
Bare j BODY OPEN
Bare j TRIV
Bare j LACK
Bare j OPEN
Barefoot j BODY OPEN
Bareheaded j BODY OPEN
Barely d NEAR
Bargain n AGRE MART
Bargain n MART TRIV
Barge n FLOW VEHC
Barge v POWR GO
Barged v POWR GO
Barges n FLOW VEHC
Barges v POWR GO
Barging v POWR GO
Bark n BODY VEGT
Bark n FLOW VEHC
Bark n ANML TALK
Barker n HEAR TALK
Barn n ANML HOME
Barns n ANML HOME
Barnstorm v GO TALK
Barnstorm v GO UP
Barnyard n ANML HOME
Barometer n VAPR MSMT
Baroque j VARY FORM
Baroque j FORM PAST
Barracks n HOME
Barrage n DAMG GRUP
Barred v BLOK
Barred v FORM
Barrel n HOLW
Barrel v QUIK GO
Barren j LACK
Barricade n BLOK
Barrier n BLOK
Barring v BLOK
Barring v FORM
Bartender n SIP AID
Barter v MART
Base n DOWN FORM
Base n CRUX HOME
Base n CRUX
Base n MTRL
Base j BAD
Base n PLAY
Baseball n PLAY
Baseboard n MTRL FORM
Based v CRUX
Based v CRUX HOME
Baseless j FALS
Basely d BAD
Basement n DOWN HOME
Baseness n BAD
Baser j BAD
Bases n DOWN FORM
Bases n CRUX HOME
Bases n CRUX
Bases n PLAY
Basest j BAD
Bash v DAMG
Bashful j WEAK
Basic j CRUX

Basin n HOLW
Basing v CRUX
Basing v DOWN FORM
Basis n CRUX
Bask v GLAD REST
Basked v GLAD REST
Basket n HOLW
Basketball n HOLW PLAY
Basketry n HOLW FORM
Bass n MUSC
Bass n ANML FLOW
Bass n FOOD FLOW
Bassinet n REST YNG
Bastard n BAD
Bastard n BAD KIN
Baste v FOOD
Baste v GARB JOIN
Bat n FORM
Bat n ANML UP
Bat n PLAY FORM
Bat v VARY
Bat v DAMG
Batch n SOME
Bath n CLEN FLOW
Bath n CLEN HOME
Bathe v CLEN FLOW
Bathrobe n CLEN GARB
Bathroom n CLEN HOME
Bathtub n CLEN HOLW
Batik n COLR FABR
Baton n LEAD FORM
Battalion n DAMG GRUP
Batted v PLAY FORM
Batted v DAMG
Batter n FOOD
Batter n PLAY FORM
Batter v DAMG
Batteries n MECH ION
Batteries n GRUP
Batteries n PLAY
Batteries n DAMG GRUP
Battering v DAMG
Batters n PLAY FORM
Batters v DAMG
Battery n MECH ION
Battery n DAMG
Battery n GRUP
Battery n PLAY
Battier j FOOL SICK
Batting v PLAY FORM
Batting v DAMG
Battle n DAMG
Battlefield n DAMG ERTH
Battleship n DAMG FLOW
Batty j FOOL SICK
Bauble n TRIV
Bawdy j BAD SEX
Bawl v SOMA PANG
Bay n BLOK
Bay n VEGT
Bay n COLR
Bay n HOLW FLOW
Bay n BULG
Bay v ANML TALK
Bayed v ANML TALK

Baying v ANML TALK
Bayonet n DAMG SHRP
Bays n HOLW FLOW
Bays n BULG
Bays v ANML TALK
Bazaar n MART
Be v NSCR
Be v EVNT
Beach n ERTH FLOW
Beachcomber n FLOW REST
Beacon n VIEW
Bead n GARB FORM
Bead n SHRP
Bead n LITL FORM
Bead n HOLY FORM
Beagle n ANML
Beak n ANML BODY
Beaked j ANML BODY
Beaker n HOLW
Beam n FORM
Beam n VIEW
Beam v SHRP
Beam v GLAD
Bean n FOOD VEGT
Bean n BODY
Bean n DAMG BODY
Bear n ANML
Bear v HAVE
Bear v BGIN
Bear v GO
Bear v AGRE
Bear v EVNT
Bear v POWR
Beard n BODY
Beard v POWR WEAK
Bearer n HAVE
Bearer n BGIN
Bearing v HAVE
Bearing v BGIN
Bearing v GO
Bearing v AGRE
Bearing n EASY MECH
Bearing v POWR
Bearing n EVNT
Bearing n PATH
Bearings n EASY MECH
Bearings n PATH
Beast n ANML
Beast n ANML BAD
Beat v DAMG
Beat v POWR WEAK
Beat n VARY MUSC
Beat n LAW PATH
Beat v QUIK GO
Beat j WEAK
Beaten j POWR WEAK
Beaten j DAMG
Beaten j EVER
Beaten j WORK
Beatnik n OPPO GRUP
Beau n FOND MALE
Beautician n BODY GOOD
Beauties n GOOD
Beautiful j GOOD
Beauty n GOOD

Beaver n ANML
Beaver n ANML FABR
Becalm v FLOW REST
Became v NSCR
Became v EVNT
Became v SIML
Because c IDEA
Beck n MOTV
Beckon v MOTV
Become v NSCR
Become v EVNT
Become v SIML
Bed n FORM
Bed n FURN REST
Bed n ERTH
Bedeck v GOOD
Bedevil v BAD PANG
Bedlam n BLUR HEAR
Bedridden j SICK REST
Bedroom n HOME REST
Beds n FORM
Beds n FURN REST
Beds n ERTH
Bedside j NEAR REST
Bedspread n FURN COVR
Bedstead n FURN REST
Bedtime n REST TIME
Bee n BUG UP
Bee n PLAY
Beech n VEGT
Beech n MTRL VEGT
Beef n ANML FOOD
Beef v AGGR TALK
Beefed v AGGR TALK
Beefier j ANML FOOD
Beefing v AGGR TALK
Beefs v AGGR TALK
Beefsteak n ANML FOOD
Beefy j ANML FOOD
Beefy j LARG BODY
Beehive n BUG HOME
Been v NSCR
Been v EVNT
Beer n SIP VEGT
Beetle n BUG UP
Beetle n MECH WORK
Before c FORW
Before d PAST
Befriend v FOND
Befuddle v BLUR
Beg v MOTV LACK
Beg v VARY
Began v BGIN
Beggar n MOTV LACK
Begged v MOTV LACK
Begged v VARY
Begin v BGIN
Begrudge v AGGR
Beguile v FALS
Beguile v GLAD
Begun v BGIN
Behalf n AID

Behave v EVNT
Behave v GOOD
Behavior n EVNT
Behead v DEAD BODY
Beheld v VIEW
Behind b BACK
Behind b BACK AID
Behind n BACK BODY
Behinds n BACK BODY
Behold v VIEW
Beholden j MOTV
Beholder n VIEW
Beige j COLR
Beige n ANML FABR
Being v NSCR
Being n LIVE
Being v EVNT
Belch v SOMA HEAR
Belch v DAMG OUT
Belfry n UP MUSC
Belie v FALS
Belief n AGRE IDEA
Believe v AGRE IDEA
Belittle v AGGR LITL
Bell n MUSC
Bell n TIME MUSC
Belle n LADY GOOD
Bellied v BODY BULG
Bellies n BODY SOMA
Bellies v BODY BULG
Belligerent j DAMG
Bellow v HEAR TALK
Belly n BODY SOMA
Belly v BODY BULG
Bellying v BODY BULG
Belong v SIML
Belong v HAVE
Belong v JOIN
Below b DOWN
Below b DOWN SUB
Belt n GARB
Belt n FORM
Belt v DAMG
Bench n FORM
Bench n POWR LAW
Bench n FURN REST
Bend n VARY
Bend v VARY WEAK
Bender n VARY
Bender n GLAD SIP
Bends n VARY
Bends n VARY SICK
Bends v VARY WEAK
Beneath b DOWN
Beneath b DOWN SUB
Benediction n AID HOLY
Beneficial j AID
Beneficiary n AID HAVE
Benefit n AID
Benevolent j GOOD AID
Benighted j FOOL
Benign j GOOD AID

Bent j VARY
Bent v VARY WEAK
Bequeath v AID
Berate v AGGR TALK
Bereave v DEAD LACK
Bereave v LACK
Bereft v LACK
Beret n GARB
Berg n BULG
Bermudas n GARB PLAC
Berry n FOOD VEGT
Berserk j SICK PANG
Berth n FLOW REST
Berth n OPEN
Berth n REST
Beseech v MOTV
Beset v PANG
Beset v DAMG
Beside b NEAR
Beside b PANG
Beside b NSCR
Besides d NSCR
Besiege v DAMG
Besmirch v DIRT
Besought v MOTV
Best j GOOD
Best v POWR WEAK
Bested v POWR WEAK
Bestial j ANML BAD
Besting v POWR WEAK
Bestow v AID
Bet v MONY MOTV
Beta n WRIT
Beta n ASTR VIEW
Beta n MTRL ION
Betray v AGGR FALS
Betray v FALS OPEN
Betrothed j SEX KIN
Better j GOOD
Better j MEDC
Better n MONY MOTV
Better v POWR WEAK
Better v AID
Betterment n AID
Betting v MONY MOTV
Bettor n MONY MOTV
Between b JOIN
Between b SEP
Bevel v VARY
Beverage n SIP FLOW
Bewail v TALK PANG
Beware v DAMG MOTV
Bewilder v BLUR
Bewitch v FOND MYTH
Bewitch v BAD MYTH
Beyond b AFAR
Beyond n DEAD AFAR
Bias n FALS MOTV
Bias n VARY
Bib n GARB YNG
Bib n GARB
Bible n WRIT HOLY

Parts of speech: a article; b preposition; c conjunction; d adverb; f prefix; i interjection;
j adjective; n noun; p pronoun; r phrase; v verb.

Biblical j HOLY PAST
Biblical j WRIT HOLY
Bibliography n WRIT
Bicameral j LEAD LAW
Bicarbonate n MTRL
Bicentennial n TIME
Bicep n BODY
Bicker v AGGR TALK
Bicycle n VEHC
Bicycle v GO VEHC
Bid v TALK
Bid v MOTV
Bide v REST
Biding v REST
Bier n DEAD HOLW
Bifocal j AID VIEW
Big j LARG
Big j LARG POWR
Big LARG AID
Big j LARG BULG
Bigamy n SEX KIN
Bigot n FALS MOTV
Bigtop n HOME PLAY
Bike n VEHC
Bike v GO VEHC
Biked v GO VEHC
Biking v GO VEHC
Bikini n GARB LADY
Bilateral j SIML PLAC
Bile n SOMA
Bile n AGGR SOMA
Bilge n DIRT FLOW
Bilge n HOLW FLOW
Bilge n BULG
Bilk v FALS
Bill n MONY
Bill n WRIT
Bill n ANML BODY
Bill n WRIT LAW
Bill v BODY SEX
Billboard n WRIT FORM
Billed v MONY
Billed v WRIT
Billed v BODY SEX
Billet v HOME
Billfold n HOLW MONY
Billiard n PLAY
Billies n DAMG FORM
Billing v MONY
Billing v WRIT
Billing v BODY SEX
Billion n NUMR
Billionaire n MUCH MONY
Billow n BULG FLOW
Billow n BULG
Billy n DAMG FORM
Billygoat n ANML MALE
Bimonthly d NUMR TIME
Bin n HOLW
Binary j NUMR
Bind v BLOK
Bind v JOIN
Binge n GLAD SIP
Bingo n PLAY
Binocular j BODY VIEW

Binoculars n MECH VIEW
Bio f SOMA
Biochemist n SOMA IDEA
Biography n WRIT PAST
Biology n SOMA IDEA
Biopsy n MEDC SOMA
Bipartisan j AGRE MOTV
Birch n VEGT
Birch n MTRL VEGT
Bird n ANML UP
Bird n AGGR TALK
Birdie n NUMR PLAY
Birds n ANML UP
Birdseye j LITL VIEW
Birdseye j FORM FABR
Birdseye n VEGT
Birth n BGIN
Birthday n BGIN TIME
Birthmark n BGIN VIEW
Biscuit n FOOD
Biscuit n ERTH MTRL
Biscuit n COLR
Bisect v SEP SHRP
Bishop n LEAD HOLY
Bishop n PLAY HOLY
Bistro n FOOD HOME
Bit n LITL SOME
Bit n BLOK
Bit n OPEN
Bit n LITL MONY
Bit n SHRP WORK
Bit v FOOD SOMA
Bit v DAMG
Bitch n ANML LADY
Bitch n BAD LADY
Bitch v AGGR TALK
Bitched v AGGR TALK
Bitches n ANML LADY
Bitches n BAD LADY
Bitches v AGGR TALK
Bitching v AGGR TALK
Bite n FOOD SOMA
Bite n BLOK
Bite n DAMG
Biting v FOOD SOMA
Biting v DAMG
Bitten v FOOD SOMA
Bitten v DAMG
Bitter j FOOD SOMA
Bitter j AGGR PANG
Bitterly d AGGR PANG
Bivouac n HOME
Blab v TALK OPEN
Black j COLR
Black j BAD COLR
Black j COLR AGGR
Black j COLR CRIM
Black j COLR DIRT
Black n COLR AID
Black n COLR GRUP
Blackball v COLR AGGR
Blackbird n ANML UP
Blackboard n COLR FORM
Blacken v COLR
Blacken v COLR DIRT

Blackjack n COLR DAMG
Blackjack n COLR PLAY
Blackjack n COLR VIEW
Blackjack n COLR VEGT
Blackmail v CRIM MONY
Blackout n BLUR COLR
Blackout n BLUR REST
Blacksmith n HEAT WORK
Blackwidow n BUG LADY
Blade n SHRP
Blade n BODY VEGT
Blade n BODY
Blade n POWR MALE
Blame v AGGR MOTV
Blameless j GOOD
Blanch v COLR
Bland j EASY
Blandish v FALS
Blank n LACK
Blank n WRIT LACK
Blank n DAMG LACK
Blanked v LACK
Blanked v WRIT LACK
Blanket n FURN REST
Blanket n COVR
Blare v HEAR
Blarney n FALS TALK
Blasphemy n BAD TALK
Blast n DAMG HEAR
Blast n HEAR
Blast n WEA DAMG
Blasted v DAMG HEAR
Blasted v HEAR
Blasted j BAD
Blastoff n DAMG SEP
Blatant j OPEN
Blather n FOOL TALK
Blaze n HEAT VIEW
Blaze v VIEW
Blaze v BGIN VIEW
Blazer n GARB
Blazon n VIEW
Bleach v COLR
Bleached v COLR
Bleachers n PLAY REST
Bleak j PANG
Bleary j BLUR
Bleat v ANML TALK
Bled v SOMA OUT
Bled v COLR OUT
Bleed v SOMA OUT
Bleed v COLR OUT
Blemish n DIRT
Blend v JOIN
Bless v AID HOLY
Blew v LARG
Blew v DAMG
Blew v SOMA
Blew v VAPR GO
Blew v MUSC
Blight n DAMG SICK
Blimp n VEHC UP
Blind j SICK VIEW
Blind j VIEW COVR
Blindfold n VIEW COVR

Blink v VARY VIEW
Blip n VIEW
Bliss n GLAD
Blister n DIRT BULG
Blister n BULG HOLW
Blithe j GLAD
Blithering j FOOL TALK
Blizzard n WEA DAMG
Bloat v BULG
Blob n BLUR
Bloc n GRUP
Block n FORM
Block n BLOK
Block n PLAY FORM
Block n DEAD FORM
Block n PATH
Block n MECH
Block n GRUP
Blockade n BLOK DAMG
Blockhead n FOOL
Blonde j COLR
Blonde n COLR BODY
Blood n SOMA
Bloodhound n ANML SOMA
Bloodied v DAMG SOMA
Bloods n SOMA
Bloodshed n DAMG SOMA
Bloodshot j SICK VIEW
Bloodthirsty j DAMG SOMA
Bloody j SOMA
Bloody j DAMG SOMA
Bloody j BAD SOMA
Bloodying v DAMG SOMA
Bloom v BODY VEGT
Bloom v LARG POWR
Bloomed v BODY VEGT
Bloomed v LARG POWR
Bloomers n GARB LADY
Blossom v BODY VEGT
Blossom v LARG POWR
Blot n DIRT
Blot v BLOK FLOW
Blot v VIEW COVR
Blotch n DIRT
Blotted v DIRT
Blotted v BLOK FLOW
Blotted v VIEW COVR
Blotter n WRIT
Blotter n BLOK FLOW
Blouse n GARB LADY
Blow n DAMG
Blow v VAPR GO
Blow v LARG
Blow v SOMA
Blow v MUSC
Blow v POWR TALK
Blower n VAPR MECH
Blubber n ANML SOMA
Blubber v TALK PANG
Blue j COLR
Blue j COLR PANG
Bluebeard n DAMG MYTH
Bluebell n VEGT
Blueberry n FOOD VEGT
Bluebird n ANML UP

Blueblood n POWR
Bluecollar j WORK
Bluefish n ANML FLOW
Bluefish n FOOD FLOW
Bluejay n ANML UP
Bluelaw n BLOK LAW
Blueprint n IDEA FORM
Blues n COLR PANG
Blues n PANG MUSC
Blues n COLR
Bluest j COLR
Bluest j COLR PANG
Bluff n FALS
Bluff n ERTH BULG
Bluff j OPEN
Bluffed v FALS
Bluffing v FALS
Blunder n FALS WEAK
Blunderbuss n DAMG MECH
Blunt j BLUR
Blunt j AGGR OPEN
Blur v BLUR
Blurb n TALK
Blurt v TALK
Blush v COLR BODY
Bluster v WEA AGGR
Bluster v AGGR TALK
Boar n ANML
Board n VEHC
Board n MTRL VEGT
Board n FOOD LIVE
Board n LEAD GRUP
Board n FORM
Board v MTRL COVR
Board v IN VEHC
Boarded v FOOD LIVE
Boarded v MTRL COVR
Boarded v IN VEHC
Boarder n FOOD LIVE
Boarder n IN VEHC
Boarding v FOOD LIVE
Boarding v MTRL COVR
Boarding v IN VEHC
Boardinghouse n FOOD HOME
Boards n MTRL VEGT
Boards n LEAD GRUP
Boards n FORM
Boards v MTRL COVR
Boards v FOOD LIVE
Boards v IN VEHC
Boast n POWR TALK
Boat n FLOW VEHC
Boat n HOLW
Bob v VARY
Bob n MONY
Bob n FORM
Bob v BODY SHRP
Bobbed v VARY
Bobbed v BODY SHRP
Bobbies n LAW
Bobbin n FORM
Bobbing v VARY
Bobbing v BODY SHRP
Bobble v WEAK
Bobby n LAW

Bobbypin n BODY JOIN
Bobbysox n GARB YNG
Bobcat n ANML
Bobolink n ANML UP
Bobs v VARY
Bobs v BODY SHRP
Bobsled n COLD VEHC
Bobwhite n ANML UP
Bode v FORW
Bode v REST
Bodice n GARB LADY
Bodies n BODY
Bodies n DEAD BODY
Bodies n GRUP
Bodies n LARG
Bodily j BODY
Boding v FORW
Body n BODY
Body n DEAD BODY
Body n GRUP
Body n BODY SOLE
Body n LARG
Body n CRUX
Bodyguard n DAMG AID
Bog n ERTH FLOW
Bog v BLOK
Bogey n NUMR PLAY
Bogged v BLOK
Bogus j FALS
Bohemian j OPPO GRUP
Boil v HEAT
Boil v AGGR HEAT
Boil n DIRT BODY
Boiled v HEAT
Boiled v AGGR HEAT
Boiler n HEAT MECH
Boisterous j AGGR HEAR
Bold j POWR
Bolero n GO MUSC
Bolero n GARB
Bolster n EASY FURN
Bolster v AID
Bolstered v AID
Bolstering v AID
Bolt n BLOK MECH
Bolt n JOIN MECH
Bolt n FABR
Bolt n DAMG
Bolt v QUIK GO
Bolt v FOOD QUIK
Bomb n DAMG
Bombard v DAMG
Bombardier n DAMG
Bombast n FOOL TALK
Bomber n DAMG
Bomber n DAMG VEHC
Bonafide j TRUE
Bonanza n MUCH MONY
Bonbon n FOOD
Bond n JOIN
Bond n MART MONY
Bond n MTRL
Bond n BLOK JOIN
Bondage n BLOK SUB
Bonded v JOIN

Bonded v MART MONY
Bonding v JOIN
Bonding v MART MONY
Bone n SOMA
Bone n SOMA MTRL
Bone v SOMA SEP
Bone v IDEA
Bonehead n FOOL BODY
Boner n FOOL FALS
Bonfire n HEAT
Bonier j SOMA
Boning v SOMA SEP
Boning v IDEA
Bonnet n GARB
Bonnet n MECH COVR
Bonus n AID MONEY
Bonvoyage i GO SEP
Bony j SOMA
Boo v AGGR TALK
Book n WRIT
Book v MOTV
Book v WRIT LAW
Bookcase n HOLW WRIT
Booked v MOTV
Booked v WRIT LAW
Bookie n MONY MOTV
Booking v MOTV
Booking v WRIT LAW
Bookish j WRIT
Bookkeeper n MART WRIT
Booklet n WRIT
Books n WRIT
Books v MOTV
Books v WRIT LAW
Bookseller n MART WRIT
Bookstore n MART WRIT
Boom n HEAR
Boom n LARG
Boom n FORM
Boomed v HEAR
Boomed v LARG
Boomerang v VARY GO
Boos n AGGR TALK
Boost v AID
Boot n GARB
Boot n GARB GO
Boot n GARB SEP
Boot v GARB WEAK
Booted v GARB
Booted v GARB GO
Booted v GARB WEAK
Bootee n GARB YNG
Bootery n GARB MART
Booth n HOME
Bootleg j CRIM
Bootless j WEAK TRIV
Booty n HAVE
Booze n SIP VEGT
Border v END
Border v END NEAR
Bore n TRIV PANG
Bore v HAVE
Bore v HOLW IN
Bore v BGIN
Bore v GO

Bore v AGRE
Bore v EVNT
Bore n HOLW
Bore v POWR
Bored v TRIV PANG
Bored v HOLW IN
Boredom n TRIV PANG
Boring v TRIV PANG
Boring v HOLW IN
Born v BGIN
Borne v AGRE
Borne v BGIN
Borne v GO
Borne v HAVE
Borne v EVNT
Borough n PLAC
Borrow v HAVE
Borsch n SIP FOOD
Bosom n BODY LADY
Bosom j FOND BODY
Boss n LEAD
Bossy j LEAD
Bossy n ANML LADY
Botany n IDEA VEGT
Botch v WEAK
Both j NUMR
Bother v AGGR PANG
Bottle n HOLW
Bottle n SIP HOLW
Bottleneck n BLOK
Bottom n DOWN
Bottom n DOWN BODY
Bottomless j DOWN
Botulism n SICK
Boudoir n LADY HOME
Bough n BODY VEGT
Bought v MONY HAVE
Bouillon n SIP FOOD
Boulder n ERTH
Boulevard n PATH
Bounce v VARY GO
Bounce v DAMG GO
Bouncer n DAMG GO
Bound j BLOK
Bound j JOIN
Bound j GO
Bound j MOTV
Bound n QUIK GO
Bound n END NEAR
Boundary n END
Bounded v QUIK GO
Bounded v END NEAR
Bounding v QUIK GO
Bounding v END NEAR
Boundless j LARG
Bounds n BLOK
Bounds v QUIK GO
Bounds v END NEAR
Bounty n MUCH AID
Bouquet n GRUP VEGT
Bourbon n SIP VEGT
Bourgeois n GRUP
Boutique n MART
Boutonniere n GARB VEGT
Bovine j ANML

Bow n VARY DOWN
Bow n FORW
Bow n VARY
Bow n FORM
Bow n GARB
Bow n DAMG
Bow n MUSC
Bow v DOWN SUB
Bowed v VARY DOWN
Bowed v VARY
Bowed v DOWN SUB
Bowed v MUSC
Bowel n DIRT SOMA
Bower n HOME VEGT
Bower n VARY
Bower n MUSC
Bowing v VARY DOWN
Bowing v VARY
Bowing v DOWN SUB
Bowing v MUSC
Bowl n HOLW
Bowl n HOME PLAY
Bowl v PLAY
Bowl v DAMG
Bowled v PLAY
Bowled v DAMG
Bowler n GARB
Bowler n PLAY
Bowling n PLAY
Bowling v DAMG
Bowwow n ANML TALK
Box n HOLW FORM
Box n PLAY REST
Box v DAMG
Box v DAMG PLAY
Box v BLOK
Boxcar n HOLW VEHC
Boxed v HOLW FORM
Boxed v DAMG
Boxed v DAMG PLAY
Boxed v BLOK
Boxer n ANML
Boxer n DAMG PLAY
Boxing v HOLW FORM
Boxing v DAMG
Boxing v DAMG PLAY
Boxing v BLOK
Boxwood n VEGT
Boy n MALE YNG
Boycott v BLOK SEP
Boyfriend n FOND MALE
Bra n GARB LADY
Brace n GRUP
Brace n WORK
Brace n AID
Bracelet n GARB HOLW
Bracket n FORM
Bracket n HOLW
Brad n JOIN SHRP
Brag v POWR TALK
Braggart n POWR TALK
Braid n FORM
Braille n WRIT
Brain n SOMA IDEA
Brain v DAMG SOMA

Brainless j FOOL
Brainwash v CLEN IDEA
Braise v HEAT
Brake n BLOK MECH
Branch n BODY VEGT
Branch n SOME
Branch v SEP
Brand n HEAT
Brand n HEAT VIEW
Brand n MART VIEW
Brandies n SIP VEGT
Branding v HEAT
Branding v HEAT VIEW
Brandish v DAMG
Brandy n SIP VEGT
Bras n GARB LADY
Brash j FOOL POWR
Brass n ERTH MTRL
Brass n COLR
Brass n LEAD
Brass n MUSC
Brass n FOOL POWR
Brassiere n GARB LADY
Brassy j ERTH MTRL
Brassy j COLR
Brassy j MUSC
Brassy j FOOL POWR
Brat n AGGR YNG
Brave j POWR
Brave n POWR MALE
Bravo i POWR
Brawl n DAMG
Bray n ANML TALK
Braze v HEAT JOIN
Brazen j ERTH MTRL
Brazen j FOOL POWR
Breach n DAMG SEP
Bread n FOOD VEGT
Breadbasket n FOOD SOMA
Breadth n LARG
Breadwinner n MONY WORK
Break n DAMG SEP
Break n AID
Break n SEP
Break n DAMG CRIM
Break v WEAK
Breakdown n WEAK
Breakdown n SICK PANG
Breakdown n SEP
Breaker n DAMG FLOW
Breaker n SEP
Breakfast n FOOD
Breakwater n BLOK FLOW
Breast n BODY
Breast n BODY LADY
Breath n VAPR SOMA
Breathe v VAPR SOMA
Breather n SOMA REST
Breathless j SOMA PANG
Breathtaking j SOMA PANG
Bred v BGIN
Breech n BACK BODY
Breech n MECH
Breeches n GARB MALE
Breed n BGIN GRUP

Breed v BGIN
Breeding n BGIN
Breeding n BGIN GOOD
Breeze n VAPR WEA
Breeze n VAPR EASY
Brethren n MALE KIN
Brevity n LITL
Brew n SIP
Brew v BGIN SIP
Bribe n CRIM MONY
Bricabrac n FURN TRIV
Brick n MTRL FORM
Brick n GOOD
Bricklayer n FORM WORK
Bride n LADY KIN
Bride n LADY SEX
Bridegroom n MALE KIN
Bridegroom n MALE SEX
Brides n LADY KIN
Brides n LADY SEX
Bridesmaid n LADY AID
Bridge n JOIN PATH
Bridge n PLAY
Bridge n FORM
Bridge n BODY
Bridge n FLOW VEHC
Bridle v BLOK
Bridle v AGGR
Brief j LITL
Brief n TALK LITL
Brief v TALK IDEA
Briefed v TALK IDEA
Briefing v TALK IDEA
Briefs n TALK LITL
Briefs n TALK IDEA
Briefs n GARB LITL
Brig n BLOK HOME
Brig n FLOW VEHC
Brigade n GRUP
Brigadier n LEAD
Bright j VIEW
Bright j POWR
Bright j POWR IDEA
Brilliant j POWR IDEA
Brilliant j VIEW
Brilliant j POWR
Brim n END
Brim v BULG
Bring v GO
Brink n END
Brisk j QUIK
Bristle n ANML MTRL
Bristle v AGGR
Brittle j WEAK
Broach v TALK OPEN
Broach v OPEN
Broach n SHRP
Broad j LARG
Broad n LADY
Broadcast n LARG TALK
Broadcloth n FABR
Broads n LADY
Broadside n LARG FORM
Broadside n DAMG
Brocade n FABR

Broccoli n FOOD VEGT
Brochure n WRIT
Brogue n TALK
Brogue n GARB
Broil v HEAT
Broiler n HEAT
Broiler n ANML FOOD
Broke v DAMG SEP
Broke v SEP
Broke v WEAK
Broke j MONY LACK
Broken j DAMG SEP
Broken j SEP
Broken j WEAK
Brokenhearted j SOMA PANG
Broker n MART MONY
Bromide n MEDC
Bronchial j SOMA
Bronchitis n SOMA SICK
Bronco n ANML
Bronze j COLR
Bronze n ERTH MTRL
Brooch n GARB
Brood v PANG
Brood n GRUP YNG
Brood j BGIN YNG
Brooded v PANG
Brooding v PANG
Brook n FLOW
Brook v AGRE
Brooked v AGRE
Brooking v AGRE
Broom n CLEN
Broomstick n CLEN FORM
Broth n SIP FOOD
Brothel n MART SEX
Brother n MALE KIN
Brother n MALE HOLY
Brotherhood n MALE KIN
Brotherinlaw n MALE KIN
Brought v GO
Brow n BODY
Brow n END UP
Browbeat v AGGR
Brown n COLR
Brown v COLR HEAT
Brownie n AID MYTH
Brownie n LADY YNG
Brownie n COLR FOOD
Browning v COLR
Browning v COLR HEAT
Brownstone j COLR ERTH
Browse v VIEW
Browse v FOOD VEGT
Bruise v DAMG BODY
Bruise v DAMG
Brunette j COLR
Brunette n COLR BODY
Brunt n DAMG
Brush n CLEN
Brush n EASY JOIN
Brush n VEGT
Brush n ANML BODY
Brush n DAMG JOIN
Brusque j AGGR

Brute n DAMG
Bubble n HOLW FLOW
Bubble n HEAR FLOW
Buccaneer n CRIM FLOW
Buck n MONY
Buck n ANML MALE
Buck n MALE
Buck n MOTV
Buck v OPPO
Bucked v OPPO
Bucket n HOLW
Bucking v OPPO
Buckle n GARB JOIN
Buckle v VARY WEAK
Buckle v POWR
Bucolic j ERTH
Bud v BGIN VEGT
Budded v BGIN VEGT
Buddhism n GRUP HOLY
Buddies n FOND
Budding v BGIN VEGT
Buddy n FOND
Budge v GO
Budget n MONY
Buff n COLR
Buff v CLEN
Buff n ANML FABR
Buff n FOND MOTV
Buffalo n ANML
Buffalo v ANML FALS
Buffed v CLEN
Buffer n AID
Buffet n HOLW FURN
Buffet n FOOD
Buffoon n FOOL GLAD
Bug n BUG
Bug n BUG SICK
Bug n BUG FALS
Bug v AGGR PANG
Bug v HEAR COVR
Bugaboo n MYTH PANG
Bugbear n MYTH PANG
Bugged v AGGR PANG
Bugged v HEAR COVR
Buggies n VEHC
Bugging v AGGR PANG
Bugging v HEAR COVR
Buggy n VEHC
Bugle n MUSC
Build v FORM WORK
Build n BODY FORM
Building n HOME FORM
Building v FORM WORK
Bulb n VIEW
Bulb n BGIN VEGT
Bulb n HOLW
Bulge v BULG
Bulk n LARG
Bulk n MUCH
Bulkhead n BLOK FORM
Bulkier j LARG
Bulky j LARG

Bull n ANML MALE
Bull n FOOL TALK
Bull n WRIT HOLY
Bull n LAW
Bull v ANML POWR
Bulldog n ANML
Bulldoze v VEHC WORK
Bulldoze v DAMG
Bulldozer n VEHC WORK
Bulled v ANML POWR
Bullet n DAMG
Bulletin n WRIT
Bullfight n ANML DAMG
Bullheaded j AGGR BODY
Bullies n DAMG
Bulling v ANML POWR
Bulls n ANML MALE
Bulls n WRIT HOLY
Bulls v ANML POWR
Bulls n LAW
Bullseye n BODY SHRP
Bully n DAMG
Bully j GOOD
Bulwark n AID FORM
Bum n BAD WEAK
Bumblebee n BUG UP
Bump n BULG
Bump v DAMG JOIN
Bump v JOIN
Bump v DAMG DEAD
Bumped v DAMG JOIN
Bumped v JOIN
Bumped v DAMG DEAD
Bumper n DAMG AID
Bumper j LARG
Bumpier j BULG
Bumping v DAMG JOIN
Bumping v JOIN
Bumping v DAMG DEAD
Bumpkin n WEAK
Bumptious j AGGR
Bumpy j BULG
Bun n FOOD
Bun n BODY
Bunch n GRUP
Bunco n CRIM FALS
Bundle n GRUP
Bundle n BULG
Bungalow n HOME
Bungle v WEAK
Bunion n BULG SICK
Bunk n FOOL FALS
Bunk n FURN REST
Bunked v FURN REST
Bunker n HOLW
Bunker n DAMG HOME
Bunker n BLOK ERTH
Bunking v FURN REST
Bunko n CRIM FALS
Bunny n ANML
Buoy n FLOW VIEW
Buoy v FLOW UP

Buoy v GLAD
Buoyant j FLOW UP
Buoyant j GLAD
Burble v HEAR TALK
Burden n HAVE PANG
Burden n IDEA
Bureau n HOLW FURN
Bureau n GRUP
Bureaucracy n LEAD LAW
Burgeon v BGIN
Burglar n CRIM
Burgundy n SIP VEGT
Burgundy n COLR
Buried v COVR
Buried v DEAD COVR
Burlap n VEGT FABR
Burlesque n FOOL
Burlesque n FOOL PLAY
Burlier j LARG
Burly j LARG
Burn v HEAT
Burn v AGGR HEAT
Burn v DAMG HEAT
Burning j HEAT
Burning j AGGR HEAT
Burning j DAMG HEAT
Burnish v CLEN VIEW
Burp v SOMA HEAR
Burro n ANML
Burrow n ERTH HOME
Burrow v ERTH IN
Burrow v COVR
Bursary n MONY
Bursitis n SICK
Burst n DAMG HEAR
Burst n DAMG SEP
Burst n QUIK
Burst v QUIK GO
Bury v COVR
Bury v DEAD COVR
Bus n VEHC
Bus v GO VEHC
Busboy n AID MALE
Bush n VEGT
Bush n ERTH VEGT
Bush n ANML BODY
Bushed j WEAK
Bushel n MSMT
Bushel n HOLW MSMT
Bushes n VEGT
Bushes n ERTH VEGT
Bushier j VEGT
Bushing n BLOK MECH
Bushwhacker n DAMG VEGT
Bushy j VEGT
Bushy j BULG
Busier j WORK
Business n MART
Business n EVNT
Business n MOTV
Businessman n MART MALE
Busing v GO VEHC

Parts of speech: a article; b preposition; c conjunction; d adverb; f prefix; i interjection;
j adjective; n noun; p pronoun; r phrase; v verb.

Buss n FOND SEX
Bussed v GO VEHC
Bussed v FOND SEX
Busses n VEHC
Busses v GO VEHC
Busses v FOND SEX
Bussing v GO VEHC
Bussing v FOND SEX
Bust n BODY FORM
Bust n BODY LADY
Bust n WEAK
Bust n DAMG
Bust n GLAD
Busted v WEAK
Busted v DAMG
Buster n MALE
Buster n DAMG
Busting v WEAK
Busting v DAMG
Bustle n QUIK GO
Bustle n GARB LADY
Busy j WORK
Busybody n AGGR MOTV
But c OPPO
But d TRIV

Butane n VAPR
Butcher n DAMG DEAD
Butcher n MART FOOD
Butler n AID MALE
Butt n BACK
Butt n DAMG
Butt n FOOD HEAT
Butt n WEAK
Butt n MSMT
Butt n HOLW
Butt v JOIN
Butte n ERTH BULG
Butted v DAMG
Butted v JOIN
Butter n ANML FOOD
Butter v FOOD FALS
Buttercup n VEGT
Butterfinger n BODY WEAK
Butterflies n BUG UP
Butterflies n BUG PANG
Butterfly n BUG UP
Butterfly n BUG FORM
Buttermilk n ANML SIP
Butting v DAMG
Butting v JOIN

Buttock n BACK BODY
Button n BULG
Button n GARB JOIN
Buttonhole n GARB HOLW
Buttonhole v GARB BLOK
Buttress n AID FORM
Buxom j BODY LADY
Buy v MART MONY
Buzz v HEAR
Buzzard n ANML UP
Buzzard n ANML AGGR
By b NSCR
By b NEAR
By b NEAR TIME
By i SEP
By n FORW PLAY
Byby i SEP
Bye i SEP
Bye n FORW PLAY
Byebye i SEP
Bygone j PAST
Bypass v GO SEP
Byproduct n END NEAR
Bystander n NEAR REST
Byword n TALK

C

C n WRIT
C n WRIT EDUC
C n WRIT MUSC
Cab n VEHC
Cabal n GRUP COVR
Cabala n HOLY COVR
Cabana n HOME FLOW
Cabaret n MART PLAY
Cabbage n FOOD VEGT
Cabbies n VEHC
Cabby n VEHC
Cabin n HOME
Cabinet n LEAD GRUP
Cabinet n HOME
Cabinet n HOLW FURN
Cable n MTRL
Cable n WRIT
Cable n MTRL MSMT
Cablegram n WRIT
Cabob n ANML FOOD
Caboose n HOME VEHC
Cache n HOLW COVR
Cackle n ANML TALK
Cacophony n OPPO HEAR
Cactus n VEGT
Cad n BAD
Cadaver n DEAD BODY
Caddy n AID PLAY
Caddy n AID FURN
Cadence n VARY MUSC
Cadet n MALE YNG
Cadet n EDUC
Cadge v MOTV
Cadmium n MTRL
Cadmus n LEAD MYTH
Cadre n GRUP FORM
Caesar n LEAD

Caesarian j BGIN SHRP
Cafe n MART FOOD
Cafeaulait n SIP
Cafeteria n MART FOOD
Caffeine n FOOD MTRL
Cage n BLOK HOME
Cagey j POWR IDEA
Cagier j POWR IDEA
Caginess n POWR IDEA
Caging v BLOK HOME
Cahier n WRIT
Cain n PANG
Caisson n DAMG HOLW
Caisson n DAMG VEHC
Caisson n HOLW FLOW
Cajole v FOND FALS
Cake n FORM
Cake n FOOD
Calaboose n BLOK HOME
Calamity n DAMG
Calcium n MTRL
Calculate v IDEA
Calculate v NUMR IDEA
Calculator n MECH NUMR
Calculus n NUMR
Caldron n HOLW HEAT
Calendar n WRIT TIME
Calender v EASY MECH
Calf n ANML YNG
Calf n BODY
Calf n ANML FABR
Caliber n POWR
Caliber n MSMT
Calibrate v MSMT
Calibre n POWR
Calibre n MSMT
Calico j VEGT FABR

Caliper n MECH MSMT
Caliph n LEAD HOLY
Calisthenic j PLAY WORK
Calk v BLOK MTRL
Call n HEAR TALK
Call n GO JOIN
Call n MOTV
Callgirl n BAD SEX
Calling v HEAR TALK
Calling v GO JOIN
Calling n MOTV
Calling n WORK
Callous j AGGR
Callous j BODY
Callow j WEAK YNG
Callus n BODY
Calm j GLAD EASY
Calory n HEAT MSMT
Calory n FOOD MSMT
Calumny n AGGR FALS
Calve v ANML BGIN
Calved v ANML BGIN
Calves n ANML YNG
Calves n BODY
Calves v ANML BGIN
Calving v ANML BGIN
Calvinism n GRUP HOLY
Calypso n TALK MUSC
Calyx n BODY VEGT
Cam n MECH
Camaraderie n FOND JOIN
Came v GO
Camel n ANML
Camelot n PLAC MYTH
Cameo n GARB FORM
Camera n MECH VIEW
Camera n HOME COVR

Camion n VEHC
Camouflage v FALS COVR
Camp n GRUP HOME
Camp n HOME
Campaign n MOTV
Campaign n DAMG
Camporee n GRUP HOME
Campus n HOME EDUC
Camshaft n MECH
Can v NSCR
Can n HOLW
Can n BACK BODY
Can n CLEN HOME
Can v END
Canal n FLOW PATH
Canape n FOOD
Canary n ANML UP
Canary n COLR
Canasta n PLAY
Cancan n GO MUSC
Cancel v END
Cancer n SICK
Cancer n ASTR MYTH
Candelabrum n VIEW FORM
Candescence n VIEW
Candid j OPEN TRUE
Candidate n MOTV
Candies n FOOD
Candle n HEAT VIEW
Candle n VIEW MSMT
Candlelight n HEAT VIEW
Candor n OPEN TRUE
Candy n FOOD
Candy n FOOD
Cane n AID FORM
Cane n FOOD VEGT
Cane n MTRL VEGT
Cane v DAMG FORM
Caned v DAMG FORM
Caned v MTRL VEGT
Canine n ANML
Canine n FOOD BODY
Caning v DAMG FORM
Caning v MTRL VEGT
Canister n HOLW
Canker n SICK
Canned v HOLW
Canned v END
Cannery n HOME HOLW
Cannibal n DAMG FOOD
Cannibalize v DAMG SEP
Cannier j POWR IDEA
Cannily d POWR IDEA
Canning v HOLW
Canning v END
Cannon n DAMG MECH
Cannot v NO
Canny j POWR IDEA
Canoe n FLOW VEHC
Canon n WRIT HOLY
Canon n LEAD HOLY
Canon n MUSC
Canon n IDEA FORM
Canonical j WRIT HOLY
Canonical j LEAD HOLY
Canonical j MUSC

Canonical j IDEA FORM
Canonize v LEAD HOLY
Canopy n UP COVR
Cans n HOLW
Cans n BACK BODY
Cans v END
Cant n VARY
Cant n TALK COVR
Cant n FALS TALK
Cantaloupe n FOOD VEGT
Cantankerous j AGGR
Cantata n TALK MUSC
Canted v VARY
Canted v FALS TALK
Canteen n SIP HOLW
Canteen n MART FOOD
Canter v GO
Canto n WRIT SOME
Canton n PLAC
Cantor n TALK HOLY
Canvas n FABR
Canvas n FLOW FABR
Canvass n IDEA MOTV
Canyon n ERTH HOLW
Cap n GARB
Cap n COVR
Cap n DAMG PLAY
Cap v END
Cap v POWR
Capable j POWR
Capacious j LARG
Capacitance n ION MSMT
Capacities n POWR
Capacity n POWR
Capacity n LARG
Cape n GARB
Cape n ERTH FLOW
Caper n FOOD VEGT
Caper n CRIM
Caper n GLAD GO
Capillary j HOLW LITL
Capillary n SOMA HOLW
Capital j LEAD PLAC
Capital j LARG WRIT
Capital j GOOD
Capital j CRUX
Capital j DEAD
Capital j MART MONY
Capital n FORM UP
Capitalism n MART MONY
Capitalize v LARG WRIT
Capitalize v AID
Capitalize v MART MONY
Capitol n LEAD HOME
Capitulate v WEAK
Capon n ANML FOOD
Capote n GARB
Caprice n VARY MOTV
Capricorn n ASTR MYTH
Caps n GARB
Caps n DAMG PLAY
Caps v COVR
Caps v POWR
Caps v END
Capsize v VARY DAMG

Capstan n MECH FLOW
Capsule n HOLW LITL
Captain n LEAD
Caption n WRIT
Captious j AGGR
Captivate v MOTV
Captive j BLOK
Captor n BLOK
Capture v BLOK
Car n VEHC
Caramel n FOOD VEGT
Carat n MSMT
Caravan n GRUP VEHC
Caravan n VEHC
Carbine n DAMG MECH
Carbohydrate n FOOD MTRL
Carbon n MTRL
Carbon n SIML WRIT
Carbonate n MTRL
Carbondioxide n MTRL
Carbuncle n ERTH MTRL
Carbuncle n COLR
Carbuncle n DIRT BODY
Carburetor n MECH
Carcass n DEAD BODY
Card n WRIT
Card n PLAY
Card n MTRL
Card n GLAD
Card v CLEN SEP
Cardboard n MTRL
Carded v WRIT
Carded v CLEN SEP
Cardiac j SOMA
Cardigan n GARB
Cardinal j CRUX
Cardinal j COLR
Cardinal j CRUX NUMR
Cardinal n LEAD HOLY
Cardinal n ANML UP
Cardinal n GARB LADY
Cardinals n LEAD HOLY
Cardinals n ANML UP
Cardinals n GARB LADY
Carding v WRIT
Carding v CLEN SEP
Cardiograph n SOMA MECH
Cardiology n MEDC SOMA
Care n MOTV
Care n AID
Care n PANG
Cared v MOTV
Cared v AID
Careen v VARY
Career n WORK
Career v QUIK GO
Carefree j GLAD
Careful j AID MOTV
Careless j MOTV LACK
Cares n MOTV
Cares n PANG
Cares v AID
Caress v FOND JOIN
Caress v EASY JOIN
Caret n WRIT

Caretaker n AID WORK
Careworn j PANG
Cargo n MART VEHC
Carhop n AID VEHC
Caribbean j PLAC FLOW
Caribou n ANML
Caricature n FOOL SIML
Caring v MOTV
Caring v AID
Carload n BULG VEHC
Carmine n COLR
Carnage n DAMG DEAD
Carnal j BODY
Carnal j BODY SEX
Carnassial j ANML BODY
Carnation n VEGT
Carnation n COLR
Carnival n PLAY
Carnivorous j ANML FOOD
Carol n TALK MUSC
Carom n VARY GO
Carouse v SIP PLAY
Caroused v SIP PLAY
Carousel n PLAY
Carp n ANML FLOW
Carp n FOOD FLOW
Carp v AGGR TALK
Carped v AGGR TALK
Carpenter n FORM WORK
Carpet n DOWN FURN
Carping v AGGR TALK
Carport n HOME VEHC
Carps v AGGR TALK
Carriage n VEHC
Carriage n EVNT
Carriage n MECH
Carried v GO HAVE
Carried v HAVE
Carried v POWR
Carried v AID
Carried v EVNT
Carrier n GO HAVE
Carrier n MART VEHC
Carrier n FLOW VEHC
Carrot n FOOD VEGT
Carrousel n PLAY
Carry v GO HAVE
Carry v HAVE
Carry v POWR
Carry v AID
Carry v EVNT
Carryall n VEHC
Cart n VEHC
Cart v GO VEHC
Cartage n MONY VEHC
Cartage n GO VEHC
Carteblanche n MOTV
Carted v GO VEHC
Carter n GO VEHC
Cartilage n SOMA
Carting v GO VEHC
Cartographer n IDEA FORM
Carton n HOLW
Cartoon n FOOL VIEW
Cartridge n DAMG

Cartwheel n VARY GO
Cartwheel n MONY
Carve v SHRP FORM
Cascade n DOWN FLOW
Case n IDEA
Case n LAW
Case n SICK SOLE
Case n HOLW
Case n TALK FORM
Case n SOLE EVNT
Case v CRIM IDEA
Cased v HOLW
Cased v CRIM IDEA
Casement n VIEW FORM
Casement n HOLW
Cash v MONY
Cashed v MONY
Cashew n FOOD VEGT
Cashier n MART MONY
Cashier v SEP
Cashing n MONY
Cashmere n ANML FABR
Casing v HOLW
Casing v CRIM IDEA
Casino n MART PLAY
Cask n HOLW
Casket n DEAD HOLW
Casket n HOLW
Casserole n FOOD HOLW
Cassino n PLAY
Cassock n GARB HOLY
Cast n GRUP PLAY
Cast n GO
Cast n FORM
Cast n COLR
Castanet n MUSC
Castaway j FLOW SEP
Castaway j GO SEP
Caste n GRUP
Caster n HOLW FURN
Caster n GO MECH
Castigate v AGGR
Casting n GRUP PLAY
Casting n FORM
Casting v GO
Castiron j ERTH MTRL
Castle n HOME
Castle n HOME PLAY
Castling v HOME PLAY
Castoff j SEP WEAK
Castor n ANML GARB
Castor n VEGT
Castor n ANML MTRL
Castor n HOLW FURN
Castor n GO MECH
Castoroil n MTRL VEGT
Castrate v SEX LACK
Casual j EASY
Casual j GARB EASY
Casualty n DAMG
Casuistry n FALS IDEA
Cat n ANML
Cataclysm n DAMG
Catacomb n DEAD HOLW
Catalepsy n SICK

Catalogue n FORW WRIT
Catamaran n FLOW VEHC
Catapult n GO MECH
Catapult n DAMG MECH
Cataract n DOWN FLOW
Cataract n SICK VIEW
Catastrophe n DAMG
Catatonia n SICK
Catbird n ANML UP
Catcall n ANML TALK
Catch v HAVE
Catch v BLOK
Catch v GO JOIN
Catcher n PLAY HAVE
Catches v HAVE
Catches v BLOK
Catches v GO JOIN
Catechism n WRIT HOLY
Categorical j GRUP
Category n GRUP
Cater v AID
Cater v FOOD AID
Caterpillar n BUG
Catfish n ANML FLOW
Catfish n FOOD FLOW
Catgut n ANML MTRL
Catharsis n CLEN OUT
Cathedral n HOME HOLY
Catholic j GRUP HOLY
Catholic j WHOL
Cattail n VEGT
Cattier j ANML AGGR
Cattle n ANML
Catty j ANML AGGR
Caucasian j GRUP
Caucus n GRUP LAW
Caught v HAVE
Caught v BLOK
Caught v GO JOIN
Cauldron n HOLW HEAT
Cauliflower n FOOD VEGT
Caulk v BLOK MTRL
Cause n BGIN
Cause n MOTV
Causeway n PATH
Caustic j AGGR
Caustic n DAMG MTRL
Cauterize v HEAT
Caution n AID MOTV
Cavalcade n GO GRUP
Cavalier j AGGR POWR
Cavalier j TRIV
Cavalier n ANML DAMG
Cavalry n ANML DAMG
Cave n ERTH HOME
Cave v DAMG WEAK
Caveat n AGGR
Cavern n ERTH HOME
Caviar n FOOD FLOW
Cavil n AGGR TRIV
Caving v DAMG WEAK
Cavity n HOLW
Caw n ANML TALK
Cease v END
Ceaseless j EVER

Cedar n VEGT
Cedar n MTRL VEGT
Cede v WEAK
Cede v AGRE AID
Ceding v WEAK
Ceding v AGRE AID
Ceiling n UP COVR
Celebrant n GLAD PLAY
Celebrate v GLAD PLAY
Celebrated v GLAD PLAY
Celebrated j POWR
Celebrity n POWR
Celerity n QUIK
Celery n FOOD VEGT
Celestial j ASTR UP
Celestial j LEAD HOLY
Celibacy n SEX LACK
Cell n BLOK HOME
Cell n HOLW
Cell n GRUP
Cell n SOMA
Cellar n DOWN HOME
Cellist n MUSC
Cello n MUSC
Cellophane n MTRL
Cellular j SOMA HOLW
Celluloid n MTRL
Celtic n TALK
Cement n JOIN MTRL
Cemetery n DEAD HOLW
Cenotaph n DEAD FORM
Cenozoic j PAST
Censor v BLOK IDEA
Censoring v BLOK IDEA
Censorious j AGGR
Censure v AGGR
Census n GRUP NUMR
Cent n MONY
Centaur n ANML MYTH
Centavo n MONY
Centenarian n PAST
Centenaries n TIME
Centenary j TIME
Centennial j TIME
Center n PLAC SHRP
Centerpiece n GOOD FURN
Centigrade j HEAT MSMT
Centipede n BUG
Central j CRUX SHRP
Central j PLAC SHRP
Centrifugal j GO SEP
Centrifuge n MECH SEP
Centripetal j GO IN
Centuries n TIME
Centurion n LEAD
Century n TIME
Ceramic j ERTH MTRL
Cereal n FOOD VEGT
Cerebral j SOMA IDEA
Cerebrate v IDEA
Cerecloth n DEAD FABR
Cerement n DEAD GARB
Ceremony n HOLY FORM
Ceremony n EVER FORM
Certain j SHRP

Certainly d EMPH
Certificate n WRIT TRUE
Certify v TRUE
Certitude n SHRP
Cervine j ANML
Cessation n END
Cesspool n DIRT HOLW
Chafe v HEAT
Chafe v PANG
Chafe v DAMG
Chafe v AGGR JOIN
Chaff n VEGT
Chaff n GLAD TALK
Chaff n TRIV
Chagrin n PANG
Chain n BLOK JOIN
Chain n FORW JOIN
Chair n FURN REST
Chair n LEAD
Chair n DAMG DEAD
Chairman n LEAD
Chaise n VEHC
Chaise n FURN REST
Chalet n HOME
Chalice n SIP HOLW
Chalk n WRIT MTRL
Challenge v OPPO
Chamber n HOME
Chamber n HOLW
Chamber n GRUP LAW
Chambermaid n LADY AID
Champ n POWR
Champ v AGGR FOOD
Champagne n SIP VEGT
Champed v AGGR FOOD
Champing v AGGR FOOD
Champion n POWR
Champion n POWR AID
Chance n MOTV
Chance n AFAR EVNT
Chancellery n LEAD HOME
Chancellery n LEAD LAW
Chancellor n LEAD LAW
Chancery n LEAD LAW
Chancery n LEAD HOME
Chandelier n FURN VIEW
Change n VARY
Change n MONY
Changeless j EVER
Channel n FLOW PATH
Channel n HOLW
Channel n HEAR VIEW
Chanson n TALK MUSC
Chant v TALK MUSC
Chanticleer n ANML MALE
Chanting v TALK MUSC
Chaos n BLUR
Chaotic j BLUR
Chap n MALE
Chap n DAMG BODY
Chap n ANML BODY
Chapeau n GARB
Chapel n HOME HOLY
Chaperone n AID JOIN
Chaplain n LEAD HOLY

Chapped v DAMG BODY
Chapter n WRIT SOME
Chapter n GRUP SOME
Char v DAMG HEAT
Character n SOLE
Character n GOOD
Character n WRIT
Character n CRUX
Characteristic j CRUX
Characterize v CRUX
Charade n BLUR PLAY
Charcoal n HEAT MTRL
Charcoal n COLR MTRL
Charge n MONY
Charge n AGGR
Charge n LEAD MOTV
Charge n ION
Charge n QUIK GO
Charge n DAMG
Charger n ANML
Charger n MECH ION
Chariot n VEHC
Charisma n LEAD MOTV
Charity n GOOD AID
Charlatan n FALS
Charleyhorse n SOMA PANG
Charm n MYTH
Charm n FOND GOOD
Charnel j DEAD HOLW
Chart n IDEA FORM
Charter n WRIT LAW
Charter v MART MONY
Chartreuse n COLR
Chase n BACK GO
Chase n DAMG GO
Chased v BACK GO
Chaser n SIP
Chaser n BACK GO
Chasm n ERTH HOLW
Chassis n MECH FORM
Chaste j GOOD
Chasten v DAMG
Chastise v DAMG
Chastity n GOOD
Chat n TALK
Chat n ANML UP
Chateau n HOME
Chatted v TALK
Chattel n HAVE
Chattel n SUB
Chatter v TALK
Chatter v VARY HEAR
Chatterbox n MUCH TALK
Chauffeur n AID VEHC
Chauvinism n FOND GRUP
Cheap j MONY TRIV
Cheap j TRIV
Cheapskate n MONY TRIV
Cheat v CRIM FALS
Check n WRIT
Check n WRIT MONY
Check n BLOK
Check n TRUE
Checked v WRIT
Checked v BLOK

Checked v TRUE
Checker n PLAY
Checker n TRUE
Checker v VARY
Checkerboard n PLAY FORM
Checkered j VARY
Checkmate v BLOK PLAY
Cheddar n ANML FOOD
Cheek n BODY
Cheek n AGGR BODY
Cheekbone n BODY
Cheep n ANML TALK
Cheer n GLAD
Cheer n AGRE TALK
Cheer n GLAD FOOD
Cheerful j GLAD
Cheering v GLAD
Cheering v AGRE TALK
Cheerio i SEP
Cheerless j PANG
Cheese n ANML FOOD
Cheeseburger n ANML FOOD
Cheesecake n FOOD
Cheesecake n LADY VIEW
Cheesecloth n VEGT FABR
Cheetah n ANML
Chef n LEAD FOOD
Chefdoeuvre n POWR
Chemical n MTRL
Chemise n GARB LADY
Chemist n MTRL IDEA
Cherish v FOND
Cherokee n GRUP
Cheroot n FOOD HEAT
Cherry n FOOD VEGT
Cherry n MTRL VEGT
Cherry n COLR
Chess n PLAY
Chest n BODY
Chest n HOLW FURN
Chesterfield n GARB
Chesterfield n FURN REST
Chestnut n FOOD VEGT
Chestnut n MTRL VEGT
Chestnut n COLR
Chevies n DAMG GO
Chevron n VIEW
Chevy n DAMG GO
Chew v FOOD SOMA
Cheyenne n GRUP
Chianti n SIP VEGT
Chiaroscuro n COLR
Chic j GOOD
Chicanery n FALS
Chick n ANML YNG
Chick n LADY YNG
Chicken n ANML UP
Chicken n ANML FOOD
Chicken n ANML WEAK
Chickened v ANML WEAK
Chickening v ANML WEAK
Chickenpox n SICK

Chicle n FOOD VEGT
Chicory n FOOD VEGT
Chide v AGGR TALK
Chief j LEAD
Chieftain n LEAD
Chiffon n GARB LADY
Chiffon n FABR
Chihuahua n ANML
Child n YNG
Child n KIN YNG
Childbirth n BGIN YNG
Childhood n TIME YNG
Childish j FOOL YNG
Childless j LACK YNG
Childlike j SIML YNG
Children n YNG
Children n KIN YNG
Chili n FOOD VEGT
Chill n COLD
Chime v MUSC
Chimney n HOLW HEAT
Chimneysweep n CLEN WORK
Chimpanzee n ANML
Chin n BODY
China n FOOD FURN
Chinchilla n ANML
Chinchilla n ANML FABR
Chink n HOLW SEP
Chink n MUSC
Chintz n VEGT FABR
Chip n MONY PLAY
Chip n LITL SEP
Chip n FOOD LITL
Chip n SIML LITL
Chip v SEP SHRP
Chip v AID
Chip v GO PLAY
Chipmunk n ANML
Chipped v SEP SHRP
Chipped v LITL SEP
Chipped v AID
Chipped v GO PLAY
Chippendale j FURN
Chipper j GLAD
Chipper n SEP SHRP
Chipping v LITL SEP
Chipping v AID
Chipping v GO PLAY
Chirography n WRIT
Chiropractor n MEDC BODY
Chirp v ANML TALK
Chisel v SHRP WORK
Chisel v CRIM FALS
Chit n YNG
Chit n WRIT MONY
Chitchat n TALK TRIV
Chivalry n GOOD
Chive n FOOD VEGT
Chlorinate v VAPR CLEN
Chlorine n VAPR
Chloroform n VAPR REST
Chlorophyll n MTRL VEGT

Chlorophyll n COLR VEGT
Chock n BLOK FORM
Chocolate n FOOD VEGT
Chocolate n SIP VEGT
Chocolate n COLR
Choice n MOTV
Choice j GOOD
Choir n GRUP MUSC
Choke v BLOK DAMG
Choke v BLOK
Choker n GARB
Choker n BLOK
Cholera n SICK
Choleric j AGGR PANG
Cholesterol n SOMA MTRL
Choose v MOTV
Chop n DAMG SHRP
Chop n ANML FOOD
Chop n VARY
Chop n BODY
Chop v SHRP
Chopped v DAMG SHRP
Chopped v SHRP
Chopper n SHRP
Chopper n VEHC UP
Choppy j VARY
Chops n ANML FOOD
Chops n DAMG SHRP
Chops n BODY
Chops v SHRP
Chopstick n FOOD
Chopsuey n FOOD
Choral j GRUP MUSC
Chord n MUSC
Chord n FORM
Chore n WORK
Choreography n GO MUSC
Chorography n IDEA FORM
Chorus n GRUP MUSC
Chorus n GRUP PLAY
Chosen j MOTV
Chow n FOOD
Chow n ANML
Chowder n SIP FOOD
Chowmein n FOOD
Christ n LEAD HOLY
Christen v HOLY
Christian j GRUP HOLY
Christmas n HOLY TIME
Chromatic j COLR
Chromatic j MUSC
Chrome n COLR
Chrome n MTRL
Chromium n MTRL
Chromosome n SOMA
Chronic j EVER
Chronicle n WRIT PAST
Chronicle n WRIT
Chronology n FORW TIME
Chronometer n MSMT TIME
Chrysanthemum n VEGT
Chubby j LARG BODY

Parts of speech: a article; b preposition; c conjunction; d adverb; f prefix; i interjection;
j adjective; n noun; p pronoun; r phrase; v verb.

Chuck n ANML FOOD
Chuck n BLOK MECH
Chuck v GO
Chuck n FOND JOIN
Chucked v GO
Chucked v FOND JOIN
Chucking v GO
Chucking v FOND JOIN
Chuckle v GLAD
Chucks v GO
Chucks v FOND JOIN
Chug n HEAR
Chug v GO HEAR
Chum n FOND
Chum n FOOD FLOW
Chummy j FOND
Chump n FOOL
Chump v FOOD SOMA
Chunk n LARG SOME
Church n HOME HOLY
Church n GRUP HOLY
Churchyard n PLAC HOLY
Churl n AGGR
Churn n VARY HOLW
Churn v VARY
Chute n DOWN GO
Cicada n BUG UP
Ciceronian j POWR TALK
Cider n SIP VEG
Cigar n FOOD HEAT
Cigarette n FOOD HEAT
Cilia n BODY
Cinch n EASY
Cinch n ANML GARB
Cinch n BLOK HAVE
Cinched v BLOK HAVE
Cinching v BLOK HAVE
Cinder n HEAT MTRL
Cinderella n LADY MYTH
Cinema n HOME PLAY
Cinerator n HOLW HEAT
Cinnamon n FOOD VEGT
Cinque n NUMR
Cipher n NUMR
Cipher n WRIT COVR
Circa b NEAR TIME
Circle n HOLW FORM
Circle n GRUP
Circle v VARY GO
Circlet n GARB HOLW
Circuit n VARY GO
Circuit n ION PATH
Circular j FORM
Circular n WRIT
Circulate v VARY GO
Circulating v VARY GO
Circulation n SOMA GO
Circulation n VARY WRIT
Circulation n VARY GO
Circulatory j SOMA GO
Circumcise v SEX SHRP
Circumference n HOLW OUT
Circumflex n WRIT EMPH
Circumlocution n VARY TALK
Circumnavigate v VARY GO

Circumscribe v BLOK HOLW
Circumscribe v HOLW WRIT
Circumspect j AID MOTV
Circumstance n EVNT
Circumstantial j EVNT
Circumvent v VARY FALS
Circus n HOME PLAY
Cistern n HOLW FLOW
Citadel n POWR HOME
Citation n TALK
Cite v TALK
Cities n PLAC
Citing v TALK
Citizen n SOLE
Citizenry n GRUP
Citric j FOOD VEGT
Citron n FOOD VEGT
Citronella n VEGT
Citrus j FOOD VEGT
City n PLAC
Civic j GRUP
Civics n GRUP LAW
Civil j GRUP LAW
Civil j GRUP
Civil j GOOD
Civilian n SOLE
Civility n GOOD
Civilize v GOOD
Clack v HEAR
Clad v GARB
Claim v MOTV
Claim v HAVE
Clairvoyant j VIEW MYTH
Clam n ANML FLOW
Clam n FOOD FLOW
Clam v ANML BLOK
Clamber v GO
Clammed v ANML FLOW
Clammed v ANML BLOK
Clammier j FLOW
Clamming v ANML FLOW
Clamming v ANML BLOK
Clammy j FLOW
Clamor v HEAR PANG
Clamp v BLOK
Clamp v BLOK JOIN
Clan n GRUP KIN
Clandestine j COVR
Clang v MUSC
Clangor n MUSC
Clank n HEAR
Clap n HEAR
Clap n AGRE HEAR
Clap n SICK SEX
Clapboard n MTRL VEGT
Clapped v HEAR
Clapped v AGRE HEAR
Claptrap n FOOL FALS
Claque n AGRE GRUP
Claret n SIP VEGT
Claret n COLR
Clarify v OPEN SHRP
Clarify v CLEN SHRP
Clarinet n MUSC
Clarion j SHRP MUSC

Clarity n OPEN SHRP
Clash v OPPO
Clash v HEAR
Clasp n BLOK JOIN
Clasp n BLOK HAVE
Class n GRUP
Class n GRUP EDUC
Class n POWR
Classic j POWR EVER
Classic j EVER PAST
Classify v GRUP
Classify v GRUP COVR
Classing v GRUP
Classmate n JOIN EDUC
Classroom n HOME EDUC
Classy j POWR
Clatter v HEAR
Clatter v GO HEAR
Clause n TALK FORM
Claustrophobia n BLOK PANG
Clavichord n MUSC
Clavicle n SOMA
Claw n BODY SHRP
Claw v DAMG SHRP
Clay n ERTH MTRL
Clean j CLEN
Clean j WHOL CLEN
Cleanliness n CLEN
Cleanse v CLEN
Clear j CLEN
Clear j OPEN
Clear j SHRP
Clear v OPEN HAVE
Clear v GO OPEN
Clear v AGRE OPEN
Clearly d OPEN
Cleat n BLOK FORM
Cleavage n SEP
Cleave v SEP SHRP
Cleave v JOIN
Cleaver n SEP SHRP
Clef n WRIT MUSC
Cleft n SEP
Clemency n GLAD
Clemency n GOOD AID
Clement j GLAD
Clench v BLOK JOIN
Clench v BLOK HAVE
Clerestory n VIEW UP
Clergy n GRUP HOLY
Clergyman n HOLY
Cleric n HOLY
Clerical j HOLY
Clerical j MART WRIT
Clerk n HOLY
Clerk n MART WRIT
Clever j POWR IDEA
Clew n AID OPEN
Clew n FORM
Cliche n TALK TRIV
Click v HEAR
Click v POWR
Client n MART MONY
Cliff n ERTH BULG
Climacteric n CRUX TIME

Climactic j CRUX UP
Climate n WEA
Climax n CRUX UP
Climb v GO UP
Clime n WEA
Clinch v BLOK JOIN
Clinch v POWR
Cling v JOIN
Cling v EVER JOIN
Clinic n MEDC
Clinic n MEDC HOME
Clink n MUSC
Clink n BLOK HOME
Clip n SEP SHRP
Clip n DAMG
Clip n QUIK GO
Clip n JOIN
Clip n HOLW
Clip n SOME
Clip n GARB
Clipped v SEP SHRP
Clipped v DAMG
Clipped v JOIN
Clipper n FLOW VEHC
Clipper n SEP SHRP
Clique n GRUP
Clitoris n LADY SEX
Cloaca n DIRT SOMA
Cloak n GARB
Cloak n COVR
Clock n MECH TIME
Clockwise j FORW TIME
Clockwork n MECH TIME
Clod n ERTH
Clod n FOOL
Clod n ANML FOOD
Clodhopper n FOOL ERTH
Clodhopper n GARB ERTH
Clog n GARB
Clog n BLOK
Cloisonne n COLR FORM
Cloister n HOME HOLY
Cloister n HOME
Cloister v HOME SEP
Close d NEAR
Close v COVR
Close j FOND NEAR
Close n END
Close v GO NEAR
Closed v COVR
Closed v END
Closed v GO NEAR
Closet n HOLW
Closet n CLEN HOME
Closeup n NEAR VIEW
Closing v COVR
Closing v END
Closing v GO NEAR
Closure n END
Clot v VARY FORM
Clot n BLOK SOMA
Cloth n FABR
Clothe v GARB
Clothes n GARB
Clothespin n GARB BLOK

Clothier n GARB MART
Clothing n GARB
Cloture n END LAW
Cloud n WEA BLUR
Cloud v BLUR
Cloud n VAPR BLUR
Cloudburst n WEA FLOW
Cloudless j VAPR WEA
Clove n FOOD VEGT
Clover n VEGT
Cloverleaf j FORM VEGT
Clown n FOOL GLAD
Cloy v BULG
Club n FORM
Club n GRUP
Club n GRUP HOME
Club n PLAY
Club v DAMG
Clubbed j FORM
Clubbed v DAMG
Clubbing v DAMG
Clubfoot n BODY SICK
Clubhouse n GRUP HOME
Cluck v ANML TALK
Clue n AID OPEN
Clue n FORM
Clump n BULG
Clump n GRUP
Clump n GO HEAR
Clumsy j WEAK
Clung v JOIN
Clung v EVER JOIN
Cluster n GRUP
Clutch n BLOK HAVE
Clutch n BLOK MECH
Clutch n ANML BGIN
Clutch n BLOK CRUX
Clutter n BLUR DIRT
Clutter n BLUR HEAR
Coach n VEHC
Coach n LEAD PLAY
Coagulate v VARY FORM
Coal n HEAT MTRL
Coalesce v JOIN
Coalition n JOIN
Coarse j VARY
Coarse j LARG
Coarse j BAD
Coarse j AGGR
Coast n ERTH FLOW
Coast v EASY GO
Coastal j ERTH FLOW
Coasted v EASY GO
Coaster n FLOW VEHC
Coaster n HOLW FURN
Coaster n VEHC
Coasting v EASY GO
Coastward d ERTH FLOW
Coastwise d ERTH FLOW
Coat n GARB
Coat n COVR
Coat n ANML BODY
Coauthor n JOIN WRIT

Coax v FOND MOTV
Cob n BODY VEGT
Cob n SOME
Cobalt n MTRL
Cobble v ERTH FORM
Cobble v GARB
Cobbled v ERTH FORM
Cobbled v GARB
Cobbler n SIP VEGT
Cobbler n FOOD VEGT
Cobbler n GARB
Cobbles v ERTH FORM
Cobbles v GARB
Cobblestone n ERTH FORM
Cobra n ANML
Cobweb n BUG HOME
Cocaine n MEDC VEGT
Cock n ANML MALE
Cock n LEAD
Cock n BLOK MECH
Cock v VARY
Cockandbull j FOOL ANML
Cocked v VARY
Cockeyed j FOOL BODY
Cockeyed j VARY BODY
Cockier j POWR
Cocking v VARY
Cockle n ANML FLOW
Cockle n VEGT
Cockle n FOOD VEGT
Cockpit n HOME VEHC
Cockpit n ANML DAMG
Cockroach n BUG
Cocks n ANML MALE
Cocks n LEAD
Cocks n BLOK MECH
Cocks v VARY
Cocksure j POWR SHRP
Cockswain n LEAD VEHC
Cocktail n SIP
Cocktail n FOOD
Cocktail n ANML
Cocky j POWR
Cocoa n SIP VEGT
Cocoa n VEGT
Cocoa n COLR
Cocoanut n FOOD VEGT
Coconut n FOOD VEGT
Cocoon n BUG HOME
Cod n ANML FLOW
Cod n FOOD FLOW
Coddle v FOND AID
Coddle v FOOD HEAT
Code n IDEA FORM
Code n IDEA COVR
Codefendant n SIML LAW
Codeine n MEDC
Codger n AGGR WEAK
Codify v IDEA FORM
Coding v IDEA FORM
Coding v IDEA COVR
Coed n LADY EDUC
Coeducation n JOIN EDUC
Coefficient n NUMR
Coequal j SIML

Coerce v AGGR POWR
Coeval j SIML TIME
Coexist v JOIN LIVE
Coffee n SIP VEGT
Coffee n COLR
Coffer n HOLW
Coffin n DEAD HOLW
Cog n MECH
Cog n FALS
Cog v BULG JOIN
Cogent j IDEA TRUE
Cogitate v IDEA
Cognac n SIP VEGT
Cognate j SIML KIN
Cognition n IDEA
Cognizance n IDEA
Cognomen n TALK
Cohabit v JOIN LIVE
Cohere v JOIN
Cohere v JOIN IDEA
Cohesion n JOIN
Cohort n GRUP
Coiffure n GARB BODY
Coil v VARY FORM
Coin n MONY
Coin v BGIN
Coincide v SIML EVNT
Coitus n JOIN SEX
Coke n HEAT MTRL
Coke n SIP VEGT
Col n ERTH PATH
Cola n SIP VEGT
Colander n HOLW SEP
Cold j COLD
Cold j COLD AGGR
Cold n SICK
Coldcuts n COLD FOOD
Coleslaw n FOOD VEGT
Colic n SICK PANG
Coliseum n HOME PLAY
Collaborate v AGRE JOIN
Collage n JOIN FORM
Collapse v WEAK
Collapse v VARY LITL
Collapsible j VARY LITL
Collar n GARB
Collar n GARB BLOK
Collarbone n BODY SOMA
Collard n FOOD VEGT
Collate v SIML
Collateral n SIML JOIN
Collateral n MART AID
Colleague n JOIN
Collect v GRUP HAVE
Collect v GRUP JOIN
Collect v MONY HAVE
Collect v LARG BULG
Collect v GLAD
Collector n GRUP HAVE
Colleen n LADY YNG
College n HOME EDUC
College n GRUP
Collide v DAMG JOIN
Collie n ANML
Collier n ERTH WORK

Collier n FLOW VEHC
Colligate v JOIN
Collimate v MECH VIEW
Collinear j SIML FORM
Collision n DAMG JOIN
Collocate v JOIN FORM
Colloid n MTRL
Colloquy n JOIN TALK
Collude v BAD JOIN
Collusion n BAD JOIN
Cologne n SOMA GOOD
Colon n WRIT
Colon n DIRT SOMA
Colonel n LEAD
Colonial j GRUP
Colonialism n GRUP SUB
Colonize v GRUP
Colonize v GRUP SUB
Colonnade n FORM
Colony n GRUP
Colony n GRUP SUB
Color n COLR
Colorless j COLR LACK
Colorless j COLR TRIV
Colossal j LARG
Colosseum n HOME PLAY
Colossus n LARG FORM
Colt n ANML YNG
Column n FORM
Column n FORW FORM
Column n WRIT
Columnist n WRIT
Coma n SICK REST
Coma n BLUR REST
Comanche n GRUP
Comb n CLEN
Comb n ANML BODY
Comb v OPEN VIEW
Comb v VARY FLOW
Combat n DAMG
Combed v CLEN
Combed v OPEN VIEW
Combed v VARY FLOW
Comber n VARY FLOW
Comber n OPEN VIEW
Combination n JOIN
Combination n JOIN NUMR
Combine v JOIN
Combine n MECH VEGT
Combing v CLEN
Combing v OPEN VIEW
Combing v VARY FLOW
Combustion n HEAT
Come v GO
Comeback n POWR GO
Comeback n AGGR TALK
Comedian n GLAD PLAY
Comedown n GO WEAK
Comedy n GLAD PLAY
Comely j GOOD
Comer n GO
Comer n POWR GO
Comes v GO
Comestible n FOOD
Comet n ASTR

Comfit n FOOD VEGT
Comfort v GLAD AID
Comfortable j GLAD
Comforted v GLAD AID
Comforter n GARB
Comforter n FURN REST
Comfortless j PANG
Comic j GLAD
Comics n GLAD WRIT
Coming v GO
Comity n FOND GOOD
Comma n WRIT
Command v LEAD
Commanded v LEAD
Commandeer v LEAD HAVE
Commandment n LEAD
Commandment n LEAD HOLY
Commando n DAMG
Commemorate v IDEA PAST
Commence v BGIN
Commencement n BGIN EDUC
Commencement n BGIN
Commend v AGRE
Commensurate j SIML
Comment v TALK
Commerce n MART
Commerce n JOIN
Commerce n JOIN SEX
Commercial j MART
Commingle v JOIN
Commiserate v FOND PANG
Commissar n LEAD
Commissariat n LEAD GRUP
Commissaries n LEAD
Commissaries n MART HOME
Commissary n LEAD
Commissary n MART HOME
Commission n POWR
Commission n GRUP
Commission n EVNT
Commission n LEAD
Commissioned v POWR
Commissioned v LEAD
Commissioner n LEAD
Commit v EVNT
Commit v BLOK
Commit v AGRE MOTV
Commit v GRUP LAW
Committed v EVNT
Committed v BLOK
Committed v AGRE MOTV
Committed v GRUP LAW
Committee n GRUP
Commix v JOIN
Commixture n JOIN
Commode n HOLW FURN
Commode n CLEN HOLW
Commode n GARB LADY
Commodious j LARG AID
Commodity n MART
Commodity n AID
Commodore n LEAD FLOW
Common j WHOL
Common j SIML
Common j TRIV

Common j EVER
Common n WHOL PLAC
Commoned v WHOL
Commoner n GRUP WEAK
Commonplace j MUCH TRIV
Commons n GRUP LAW
Commons n GRUP HOME
Commonweal n WHOL AID
Commonwealth n GRUP
Commotion n PANG
Communal j WHOL GRUP
Commune n GRUP JOIN
Commune v JOIN TALK
Communed v JOIN TALK
Communicable j JOIN
Communicant n GRUP HOLY
Communicant n TALK
Communicate v TALK
Communicate v JOIN
Communing v JOIN TALK
Communion n GRUP JOIN
Communion n GRUP HOLY
Communion n JOIN TALK
Communion n FOOD HOLY
Communique n TALK
Communism n GRUP
Community n WHOL GRUP
Communize v GRUP
Commutator n MECH ION
Commute v GO VEHC
Commute v VARY
Commuter n GO VEHC
Commuting v GO VEHC
Commuting v VARY
Compact j LITL
Compact n GARB LADY
Compact n AGRE
Companies n GRUP
Companies n MART GRUP
Companion n FOND JOIN
Companion n SIML JOIN
Company n GRUP
Company n MART GRUP
Company n FOND JOIN
Compare v SIML
Compartment n HOME
Compartment n HOLW
Compass n MSMT PATH
Compass n END
Compass v VARY GO
Compass v POWR
Compass v BLOK HOLW
Compassed v VARY GO
Compassed v POWR
Compassed v BLOK HOLW
Compassing v VARY GO
Compassing v POWR
Compassing v BLOK HOLW
Compassion n FOND
Compatible j SIML
Compatriot n SIML GRUP
Compeer n SIML
Compel v POWR
Compendium n WRIT LITL
Compensate v SIML

Compensate v MONY
Compete v OPPO
Competence n POWR
Compile v JOIN
Complacence n GLAD
Complain v AGGR PANG
Complaint n AGGR PANG
Complaint n SICK PANG
Complaisance n FOND
Complect v JOIN FORM
Complected j COLR BODY
Complected v JOIN FORM
Complement n SIML
Complement n WHOL
Complete v WHOL END
Completely d WHOL EMPH
Complex j BLUR
Complex n PANG
Complex n FORM
Complexion n COLR BODY
Compliance n AGRE
Complicate v BLUR
Complicity n JOIN MOTV
Complied v AGRE
Compliment n AGRE
Comply v AGRE
Component n SOME
Comport v EVNT
Comport v SIML
Compose v BGIN FORM
Compose v GLAD
Compose v FORM
Composing v BGIN FORM
Composing v GLAD
Composing v FORM
Composition n WRIT FORM
Composition n FORM
Composition n BGIN FORM
Compost n AID MTRL
Compost n JOIN
Composure n GLAD
Compound n JOIN
Compound n HOME
Compound v LARG JOIN
Compound v AGRE
Comprehend v IDEA
Comprehend v WHOL
Compress v BLOK LITL
Compressor n BLOK MECH
Comprise v WHOL JOIN
Compromise v AGRE
Compromise v WEAK
Comptroller n LEAD MONY
Compulsion n POWR MOTV
Compulsory j POWR MOTV
Compunction n PANG
Compute v NUMR IDEA
Computed v NUMR IDEA
Computer n MECH NUMR
Computer n NUMR IDEA
Comrade n FOND JOIN
Con d OPPO
Con j CRIM FALS
Con n BLOK CRIM
Con v IDEA

Concatenate v FORW JOIN
Concave j HOLW FORM
Conceal v COVR
Concede v AGRE
Concede v AGRE WEAK
Concede v AGRE AID
Conceit n FOOL POWR
Conceit n FOOL IDEA
Conceited j FOOL POWR
Conceive v IDEA
Conceive v BGIN YNG
Concentrate v IDEA SHRP
Concentrate v SHRP
Concentration n IDEA SHRP
Concentration n SHRP
Concentration n BLOK
Concentric j SIML SHRP
Concept n IDEA
Conception n BGIN YNG
Concern n PANG MOTV
Concern n MART GRUP
Concerned v PANG MOTV
Concerning b NSCR
Concerning v PANG MOTV
Concert n MUSC
Concert n AGRE
Concerted j AGRE
Concerto n MUSC
Concession n AGRE
Concession n MART AID
Concession n AGRE WEAK
Concession n AGRE AID
Conch n HOLW FLOW
Concierge n AID OPEN
Conciliate v AGRE
Concise j LITL
Conclave n HOME COVR
Conclave n JOIN COVR
Conclude v END IDEA
Conclusion n END IDEA
Concoct v FORM
Concomitant n JOIN
Concord n AGRE
Concordance n FORW WRIT
Concourse n JOIN PATH
Concrete j MTRL
Concrete j ERTH MTRL
Concubine n LADY SEX
Concupiscent j SEX MOTV
Concur v AGRE
Concur v JOIN
Concussion n DAMG
Condemn v AGGR
Condense v LITL
Condense v VARY FLOW
Condenser n ION
Condescend v AGRE LEAD
Condign j SIML
Condiment n FOOD
Condition n EVNT
Condition n AGRE CRUX
Condition v AID
Conditional j AGRE CRUX
Conditioned v AID
Conditioning v AID

Condole v FOND PANG
Condominium n GRUP HAVE
Condominium n LEAD GRUP
Condone v AGRE
Condor n ANML UP
Conduce v AID
Conduct v LEAD
Conduct v EVNT
Conduct v GO
Conductance n ION PATH
Conducting v LEAD
Conducting v EVNT
Conducting v GO
Conduction n GO
Conductivity n PATH
Conduit n HOLW PATH
Cone n FORM
Cone n BODY VEGT
Cone n FOOD FORM
Confab n TALK
Confabulate v TALK
Confabulate v FALS TALK
Confect v FORM
Confecting v FORM
Confection n FOOD
Confederacy n GRUP JOIN
Confederate n CRIM JOIN
Confederate n GRUP JOIN
Confer v JOIN TALK
Confer v AID
Conference n JOIN TALK
Conference n AID
Conference n GRUP JOIN
Confess v AGRE
Confess v AGRE HOLY
Confessing v AGRE
Confessing v AGRE HOLY
Confessional n HOME HOLY
Confessional n FOND HOLY
Confetti n MTRL PLAY
Confidant n FOND COVR
Confide v FOND COVR
Confidence n FOND COVR
Confidence n POWR MOTV
Confident j FOND COVR
Confident j POWR MOTV
Confidential j FOND COVR
Confidential j COVR
Configuration n FORM
Confine v BLOK
Confirm v AGRE TRUE
Confirm v HOLY
Confiscate v BLOK HAVE
Confiture n FOOD
Conflagration n DAMG HEAT
Conflict n AGGR
Conflict n DAMG
Conflict v OPPO
Confluence n JOIN PATH
Conform v SIML
Confound v BLUR
Confound v BAD

Confrere n JOIN MALE
Confront v FORW JOIN
Confuse v BLUR
Confute v OPPO
Conga n GO MUSC
Congeal v VARY FORM
Congenial j AGRE
Congenital j BGIN SOMA
Conger n ANML FLOW
Conger n FOOD FLOW
Congest v BLOK BULG
Conglomerate n GRUP JOIN
Congratulate v FOND
Congregate v GRUP JOIN
Congregating v GRUP JOIN
Congregation n GRUP HOLY
Congregation n GRUP JOIN
Congregational j GRUP HOLY
Congress n LEAD LAW
Congress n GRUP JOIN
Congress n JOIN SEX
Congressional j LEAD LAW
Congressman n LEAD LAW
Congruent j SIML
Congruity n SIML
Conic j FORM
Coniferous j BODY VEGT
Conjecture n BLUR IDEA
Conjoin v JOIN
Conjugal j SEX KIN
Conjugate v SEX KIN
Conjugate v SIML JOIN
Conjugate v TALK FORM
Conjunction n JOIN
Conjunction n TALK FORM
Conjunctive j JOIN
Conjure v MYTH
Conjure v MOTV
Connect v JOIN
Conned v CRIM FALS
Conning n FLOW VEHC
Conning v CRIM FALS
Conniption n PANG
Connive v AGRE BAD
Connoisseur n POWR IDEA
Connote v IDEA
Connubial j SEX KIN
Conquer v POWR WEAK
Conquest n POWR WEAK
Conquistador n DAMG POWR
Cons n OPPO
Cons v CRIM FALS
Cons v IDEA
Consanguine j JOIN KIN
Conscience n GOOD IDEA
Conscienceless j BAD IDEA
Conscientious j GOOD IDEA
Conscious j IDEA
Conscript v JOIN MOTV
Consecrate v HOLY MOTV
Consecutive j FORW
Consensus n AGRE

Consent v AGRE
Consequence n CRUX
Consequence n END
Conservation n EVER AID
Conservatism n EVER
Conservative j EVER
Conservator n EVER AID
Conservatories n HOME IDEA
Conservatories n HOME VEGT
Conservatory n HOME IDEA
Conservatory n HOME VEGT
Conserve v EVER AID
Conserve v EVER
Conserve n FOOD
Consider v IDEA
Considerable j MUCH LARG
Considerate j GOOD AID
Consideration n IDEA
Consideration n GOOD AID
Consign v AGRE AID
Consist v WHOL
Consisted v WHOL
Consistency n SIML FORM
Consistency n SIML EVER
Consistent j SIML EVER
Consistent j SIML FORM
Console v GLAD AID
Console n MUSC
Console n HOLW FURN
Consoled v GLAD AID
Consolidate v POWR
Consolidate v JOIN
Consoling v GLAD AID
Consomme n SIP FOOD
Consonance n SIML
Consonant j SIML
Consonant n TALK FORM
Consort n JOIN SEX
Consort n JOIN
Consort n SEX KIN
Consort v SIML JOIN
Conspicuous j OPEN VIEW
Conspire v BAD JOIN
Conspire v AGRE JOIN
Constable n LEAD LAW
Constabulary n LEAD LAW
Constant j EVER
Constellation n ASTR GRUP
Consternation n PANG
Constipate v BLOK SOMA
Constituency n GRUP LAW
Constituent n GRUP LAW
Constituent n SOME
Constitute v BGIN FORM
Constitute v FORM
Constituting v BGIN FORM
Constituting v FORM
Constitution n BGIN FORM
Constitution n FORM
Constitution n LAW
Constitution n SOMA
Constrain v BLOK

Parts of speech: a article; b preposition; c conjunction; d adverb; f prefix; i interjection;
j adjective; n noun; p pronoun; r phrase; v verb.

Constrict v BLOK
Constrictor n ANML BLOK
Constrictor n BLOK
Construct v FORM WORK
Construct n IDEA FORM
Constructing v FORM WORK
Constructive j AID
Construe v IDEA
Consul n LEAD LAW
Consult v AID IDEA
Consume v FOOD SOMA
Consume v END LACK
Consume v DAMG
Consume v MOTV
Consummate v END
Consummate v JOIN SEX
Consumption n END LACK
Consumption n FOOD SOMA
Consumption n SICK
Consumption n DAMG
Contact v JOIN
Contact v JOIN TALK
Contagion n SICK JOIN
Contagion n JOIN
Contain v HOLW IN
Contain v BLOK IN
Contaminate v DIRT
Contemn v AGGR
Contemplate v IDEA
Contemporary j SIML TIME
Contempt n AGGR
Contend v OPPO
Contend v IDEA
Content j GLAD
Content n HOLW IN
Content n IN IDEA
Contention n OPPO
Contention n IDEA
Contentious j AGGR
Contest n OPPO
Context n HOLW WRIT
Contiguity n JOIN
Continence n BLOK LACK
Continent j BLOK LACK
Continent n ERTH PLAC
Continental j ERTH PLAC
Continently d BLOK LACK
Contingency n EVNT
Contingent n EVNT
Contingent n GRUP
Continual j EVER
Continuation n EVER
Continuation n EVER GO
Continue v EVER
Continue v EVER GO
Continuing v EVER
Continuing v EVER GO
Continuity n EVER
Continuous j EVER
Continuum n EVER
Contort v VARY
Contorting v VARY
Contortionist n VARY BODY
Contour n FORM
Contraband j MART CRIM

Contrabass n MUSC
Contraceptive j BGIN BLOK
Contract n AGRE
Contract n AGRE WRIT
Contract v HAVE
Contract v LITL
Contracting v AGRE
Contracting v LITL
Contracting v HAVE
Contraction n LITL
Contractive j LITL
Contractor n AGRE WORK
Contractor n AGRE
Contractor n LITL
Contractual j AGRE
Contradict v OPPO
Contraindicate v OPPO
Contralto n MUSC
Contraption n MECH
Contrary j OPPO
Contrast v OPPO
Contravene v OPPO
Contribute v AID
Contribute v AID MONY
Contrite j PANG
Contrive v IDEA FORM
Control v LEAD
Controlled v LEAD
Controller n LEAD MONY
Controller n LEAD
Controversy n OPPO
Contumacy n AGGR
Contuse v DAMG BODY
Convalesce v MEDC
Convection n GO HEAT
Convene v GRUP JOIN
Convenience n AID
Convening v GRUP JOIN
Convent n HOME HOLY
Convention n GRUP JOIN
Convention n EVER
Convention n AGRE GRUP
Conventional j EVER
Conventional j EVER TRIV
Conventional j AGRE GRUP
Converge v GO JOIN
Converge v SIML
Conversant j NEAR IDEA
Conversation n TALK
Converse v TALK
Converse n OPPO
Conversed v TALK
Converses v TALK
Conversing v TALK
Conversion n VARY
Convert v VARY
Convertible j VARY
Convertible n VARY VEHC
Convex j FORM
Convey v GO
Conveyance n VEHC
Conveyance n GO
Convict v BLOK CRIM
Convicting v BLOK CRIM
Conviction n AGRE IDEA

Conviction n BLOK CRIM
Convince v AGRE IDEA
Convivial j GLAD
Convocation n GRUP JOIN
Convocation n GRUP EDUC
Convoke v GRUP JOIN
Convolute v VARY
Convoy v GO JOIN
Convulse v VARY PANG
Coo v FOND TALK
Coo v ANML TALK
Cook v FOOD HEAT
Cook v HEAT
Cookbook n FOOD WRIT
Cookie n FOOD
Cooking v FOOD HEAT
Cooking v HEAT
Cool j COLD
Cool j GLAD COLD
Cool j COLD GOOD
Cool j COLD AGGR
Coolant n COLD
Cooler j COLD
Cooler j GLAD COLD
Cooler n COLD HOLW
Cooler n COLD BLOK
Coolie n WORK
Cooling v COLD
Cooling v GLAD COLD
Coon n ANML
Coop n ANML HOME
Coop v BLOK HOME
Coop n AGRE AID
Cooped v BLOK HOME
Cooper n HOLW WORK
Cooperate v AGRE AID
Cooping v BLOK HOME
Coopt v GRUP MOTV
Coordinate n SIML
Coordinate n MSMT
Coordinate v LEAD
Cop n LAW
Cop v HAVE
Cop v WEAK
Cop n FORM FABR
Copartner n JOIN
Cope v POWR
Cope v FORM COVR
Copernican j ASTR
Copied v SIML
Copied v SIML WRIT
Coping n FORM COVR
Coping v POWR
Copious j MUCH
Copped v HAVE
Copped v WEAK
Copper n ERTH MTRL
Copper n MTRL MONY
Copper n COLR
Copperhead n ANML
Coppersmith n MTRL WORK
Copping v HAVE
Copping v WEAK
Copra n FOOD VEGT
Copulate v JOIN SEX

Copulating v JOIN SEX
Copulative j JOIN
Copulative n TALK FORM
Copy n SIML
Copy n SIML WRIT
Copyright v LAW HAVE
Coquetry n SEX TRIV
Coral n MTRL FLOW
Coral n COLR
Coral n ANML FLOW
Cord n FABR
Cord n SOMA
Cord n MSMT
Cord n JOIN
Cordial j FOND
Cordial n SIP VEGT
Cording n FABR
Cordon n BLOK
Cordon n GARB FABR
Cordovan j PLAC FABR
Corduroy j VEGT FABR
Corduroys n GARB FABR
Core n CRUX SHRP
Core n CRUX VEGT
Corelative j JOIN
Coring v CRUX VEGT
Cork n BLOK MTRL
Cork n MTRL VEGT
Corkscrew n VARY MECH
Corn n FOOD VEGT
Corn n BODY
Corn n FOOL TRIV
Corn v EVER FOOD
Cornea n SOMA VIEW
Corned j EVER FOOD
Corner n FORM
Corner n JOIN PATH
Corner n HOLW
Corner v BLOK
Corners n FORM
Corners n JOIN PATH
Corners v BLOK
Cornerstone n ERTH CRUX
Cornet n MUSC
Cornier j FOOL TRIV
Cornstarch n FOOD VEGT
Cornu n ANML BODY
Cornucopia n MUCH HOLW
Corny j FOOL TRIV
Corny j FOOD VEGT
Corny j BODY
Corollary j JOIN IDEA
Corona n SOMA UP
Corona n ASTR VIEW
Corona n FOOD HEAT
Corona n VIEW
Coronary j SOMA
Coronary j GARB LEAD
Coronation n GARB LEAD
Coroner n DEAD LEAD
Coronet n GARB LEAD
Coronet n GARB
Coronet n ANML BODY
Corpora n WHOL
Corpora n DEAD BODY

Corporal j BODY
Corporal n SUB
Corporally d BODY
Corporals n SUB
Corporate j GRUP JOIN
Corporation n MART GRUP
Corporation n LEAD GRUP
Corporation n BODY BULG
Corporative j GRUP JOIN
Corporeal j BODY
Corps n GRUP
Corpse n DEAD BODY
Corpsman n DAMG MEDC
Corpulence n LARG BODY
Corpus n WHOL
Corpuscle n SOMA
Corral v BLOK HOME
Corral n ANML HOME
Correct v TRUE
Correlate v JOIN
Correspond v WRIT
Correspond v SIML
Corridor n PATH
Corrigible j TRUE
Corroborate v TRUE
Corrode v DIRT WEAK
Corrosion n DIRT WEAK
Corrugate v VARY FORM
Corrupt j BAD DIRT
Corsage n GARB VEGT
Corsage n GARB LADY
Corsair n CRIM FLOW
Corselet n GARB LADY
Corset n GARB LADY
Cortege n GRUP JOIN
Cortex n SOMA
Cortex n BODY VEGT
Cortical j SOMA
Cortices n SOMA
Cortices n BODY VEGT
Cosecant n NUMR FORM
Cosey j GLAD
Cosey n FOOD HOLW
Cosie j GLAD
Cosily d GLAD
Cosine n NUMR FORM
Cosines n NUMR FORM
Cosiness n GLAD
Cosmetic j BODY GOOD
Cosmic j WHOL FORM
Cosmology n WHOL IDEA
Cosmonaut n ASTR VEHC
Cosmopolitan j WHOL PLAC
Cosmos n WHOL FORM
Cosmos n VEGT
Cossack n ANML DAMG
Cost n MONY
Cost n LACK
Costermonger n MART FOOD
Costly j MUCH MONY
Costly j LACK
Costume n GARB
Cosy j GLAD
Cosy n FOOD HOLW
Cot n FURN REST

Cot n HOME
Cot n COVR
Cotangent n NUMR FORM
Cote n ANML HOME
Cotenant n SIML LIVE
Coterie n GRUP
Coterminous j SIML END
Cotillion n GO MUSC
Cottage n HOME
Cotton n VEGT FABR
Cotton v FOND
Cottontail n ANML
Couch n FURN REST
Couch v REST
Couch v DOWN
Couch v TALK
Couchant j REST
Couched v TALK
Couched v REST
Couches n FURN REST
Couches v TALK
Couches v REST
Couching v TALK
Couching v REST
Cougar n ANML
Cough n SOMA HEAR
Could v NSCR
Coulomb n ION MSMT
Council n LEAD GRUP
Council n GRUP IDEA
Councilor n LEAD GRUP
Counsel n AID IDEA
Counsel n AID LAW
Count n NUMR
Count n LEAD MALE
Count v CRUX AID
Countdown n NUMR
Counted v NUMR
Counted v CRUX AID
Countenance n BODY
Countenance v AGRE BODY
Counter d OPPO
Counter n NUMR
Counter n MART FORM
Counter v OPPO
Counteract v OPPO
Counterbalance v SIML OPPO
Countered v OPPO
Counterfeit j FALS
Countering v OPPO
Countermand v OPPO
Countermarch n BACK GO
Counterpane n FURN COVR
Counterpart n SIML
Counterpoise v SIML OPPO
Counters n NUMR
Counters n MART FORM
Counters v OPPO
Countersank v DOWN HOLW
Countersign n SIML VIEW
Countersign v WRIT
Countersink v DOWN HOLW
Countersunk v DOWN HOLW
Counterweight n OPPO
Countess n LEAD LADY

Counties n PLAC
Counting v NUMR
Counting v CRUX AID
Countless j MUCH NUMR
Country n PLAC
Country n ERTH PLAC
Countryside n ERTH PLAC
County n PLAC
Coup n DAMG POWR
Coupe n VEHC
Couple n NUMR
Couple n JOIN NUMR
Couple n JOIN
Couple v JOIN SEX
Coupled v JOIN
Coupled v JOIN SEX
Couplet n JOIN WRIT
Coupling v JOIN
Coupling v JOIN SEX
Coupon n WRIT
Courage n POWR
Courier n GO WRIT
Course n PATH
Course n ERTH PATH
Course n EDUC
Course n FOOD
Course n FORM
Course n EVER
Course v QUIK GO
Coursed v QUIK GO
Courser n ANML QUIK
Courser n ANML UP
Court n HOME LAW
Court n HOME PLAY
Court n GRUP
Court n HOME PLAC
Court v FOND SEX
Court v MOTV
Courted v FOND SEX
Courted v MOTV
Courteous j GOOD
Courtesan n LADY SEX
Courtesies n GOOD
Courtesy n GOOD
Courthouse n HOME LAW
Courtier n SUB
Courting v FOND SEX
Courting v MOTV
Courtly j GOOD
Courtmartial n LAW
Courtroom n HOME LAW
Courts HOME LAW
Courts n HOME PLAY
Courts n HOME PLAC
Courts v FOND SEX
Courts v MOTV
Courtship n FOND SEX
Courtyard n HOME PLAC
Cousin n KIN
Covalence n JOIN ION
Covary v SIML VARY
Cove n HOLW FORM
Cove n HOLW FLOW
Cove n ERTH HOLW
Covenant n AGRE

Coventry n PLAC SEP
Cover n COVR
Cover n HOLW WRIT
Cover v GO
Cover v JOIN SEX
Cover v AID
Cover v SIML
Coverage n COVR
Coverage n AID
Coverage n GO
Coverall n GARB
Coverlet n FURN COVR
Covert j COVR
Covert n AID COVR
Covert n FABR
Covet v MOTV
Covey n ANML GRUP
Cow n ANML LADY
Cow v WEAK PANG
Coward n WEAK
Cowbird n ANML UP
Cowboy n ANML MALE
Cowcatcher n ANML BLOK
Cowed v WEAK PANG
Cower n WEAK PANG
Cowgirl n ANML LADY
Cowhide n ANML FABR
Cowing v WEAK PANG
Coworker n SIML WORK
Cowpuncher n ANML MALE
Coxswain n LEAD VEHC
Coy j WEAK
Coyote n ANML
Cozy j GLAD
Cozy n FOOD HOLW
Crab n ANML FLOW
Crab n FOOD FLOW
Crab n AGGR PANG
Crab n ANML ASTR
Crabapple n FOOD VEGT
Crabbed v ANML FLOW
Crabbed v AGGR PANG
Crabbier j AGGR PANG
Crabbing v ANML FLOW
Crabbing v AGGR PANG
Crabby j AGGR PANG
Crack n SEP
Crack n HEAR
Crack n DAMG
Crack n MOTV
Crack j POWR
Crack n GLAD TALK
Crack v WEAK
Cracked v SEP
Cracked v HEAR
Cracked v DAMG
Cracked v WEAK
Cracked v GLAD TALK
Cracker n FOOD
Cracker n WEAK
Crackerjack n POWR
Crackerjack n FOOD
Crackle v HEAR
Crackle v SEP
Crackling n HEAR

Crackling n ANML FOOD
Crackpot n FOOL
Cradle n REST YNG
Cradle n AID FORM
Craft n POWR WORK
Craft n POWR FALS
Craft n GRUP WORK
Craft n VEHC
Crafted v POWR WORK
Craftier j POWR FALS
Crafting v POWR WORK
Crafty j POWR FALS
Crag n ERTH BULG
Cram v BULG
Cram v BULG IDEA
Cramp n BLOK SOMA
Cramp n BLOK
Cranberry n FOOD VEGT
Crane n MECH UP
Crane n ANML UP
Crane v LARG
Craned v LARG
Cranial j SOMA
Craning v LARG
Craniology n SOMA MSMT
Cranium n SOMA
Crank n MECH
Crank n AGGR PANG
Crankcase n HOLW MECH
Crankiness n AGGR PANG
Cranking v MECH
Cranks n MECH
Cranks n AGGR PANG
Crankshaft n MECH FORM
Cranky j AGGR PANG
Cranny n HOLW
Crap n DIRT SOMA
Crap n PLAY
Crape n GARB PANG
Craps v DIRT SOMA
Craps n PLAY
Crash n DAMG HEAR
Crash n VEGT FABR
Crass j FOOL
Crate n HOLW
Crater n HOLW
Cravat n GARB
Crave v MOTV
Craven j WEAK
Craving v MOTV
Crawfish n ANML FLOW
Crawl n GO REST
Crawl n GO FLOW
Crawl n HOLW FLOW
Crawl v BODY PANG
Crayfish n ANML FLOW
Crayon n COLR WRIT
Craze n SEP
Craze n NEW MOTV
Craze v SICK PANG
Crazed j SICK PANG
Crazed j SEP
Crazier j FOOL
Crazier j SICK PANG
Crazier j FOND

Crazily d FOOL
Craziness n FOOL
Craziness n SICK PANG
Crazing n SEP
Crazy j FOOL
Crazy j SICK PANG
Crazy j FOND
Creak v HEAR
Cream n FOOD
Cream n ANML SIP
Cream n POWR GOOD
Cream n COLR
Cream n EASY
Cream v POWR WEAK
Cream v FOOD SEP
Creamed v FOOD
Creamed v POWR WEAK
Creamed v EASY
Creamed v FOOD SEP
Creamer n SIP HOLW
Creamer n FOOD SEP
Creamery n ANML FOOD
Crease n VARY
Crease n HOLW PLAY
Create v BGIN
Creator n BGIN
Creator n BGIN HOLY
Creature n SOLE
Creature n ANML
Creche n HOME HOLY
Creche n AID YNG
Credence n AGRE IDEA
Credence n HOLW FURN
Credential n WRIT TRUE
Credenza n HOLW FURN
Credible j TRUE
Credit n AGRE
Credit n MART MONY
Credit n EDUC
Creditor n MART MONY
Credo n AGRE IDEA
Credulous j AGRE IDEA
Creed n AGRE IDEA
Creek n FLOW
Creep v GO REST
Creep v BODY PANG
Creeper n GO VEGT
Creeper n GO REST
Creeper n ANML UP
Creeper n BLOK GO
Cremate v DEAD HEAT
Creole n GRUP
Crepe n FABR
Crept v GO REST
Crescendo n LARG MUSC
Crescent j FORM
Crescent j LARG
Crescent n ASTR FORM
Cress n FOOD VEGT
Crest n UP
Crest n ANML BODY
Crest n VIEW
Crestfallen j PANG
Cresting v UP
Cretin n FOOL SICK

Crevasse n HOLW SEP
Crevice n HOLW SEP
Crew n GRUP
Crib n HOLW
Crib n HOME
Crib n PLAY
Crib n REST YNG
Crib n CRIM WRIT
Cribbage n PLAY
Cribbed v HOLW
Cribbed v REST YNG
Cribbed v CRIM WRIT
Cribbing v HOLW
Cribbing v REST YNG
Cribbing v CRIM WRIT
Crick n SOMA PANG
Cricket n BUG
Cricket n PLAY
Cricket n GOOD PLAY
Cried v SOMA PANG
Cried v HEAR TALK
Crier n HEAR TALK
Crime n CRIM
Criminal j CRIM
Criminology n CRIM LAW
Crimp v VARY
Crimp v BLOK
Crimson j COLR
Cringe v WEAK PANG
Crinkle v VARY
Cripple v SICK WEAK
Cripple v DAMG WEAK
Crisis n DAMG CRUX
Crisp j NEW
Crisp j SHRP
Crisp v VARY
Crisscross v VARY JOIN
Crisscross v VARY GO
Criterion n TRUE
Critic n AGGR IDEA
Critical j AGGR IDEA
Critical j CRUX
Criticism n AGGR IDEA
Critique n IDEA
Croak v ANML TALK
Croak v DEAD
Croaked v ANML TALK
Croaked v DEAD
Croaker n ANML TALK
Crochet v GARB JOIN
Crocodile n ANML FLOW
Cromagnon j PAST
Crony n FOND
Crook n CRIM
Crook n VARY
Crooking v VARY
Croon v TALK MUSC
Crop n VEGT
Crop n BODY SHRP
Crop n ANML BODY
Crop n FORM
Crop n ANML FABR
Cropped v BODY SHRP
Cropper n VEGT WORK
Cropper n DOWN WEAK

Croquet n PLAY
Cross v GO
Cross v JOIN
Cross n FORM
Cross j AGGR PANG
Cross j OPPO
Cross n HOLY FORM
Cross v WRIT SEP
Crosscountry j ERTH GO
Crossexamine v BLUR TALK
Crosshatch n WRIT FORM
Crossover n JOIN PATH
Crossroad n JOIN PATH
Crossways d FORM
Crosswise d FORM
Crosswise d OPPO
Crossword n JOIN WRIT
Crotch n SEP FORM
Crotch n BODY SEP
Crotched j SEP FORM
Crotchety j OPPO PANG
Crouch v VARY DOWN
Croup n BACK BODY
Croup n SICK
Croupier n LEAD PLAY
Crow n ANML UP
Crow v ANML TALK
Crow v POWR TALK
Crowbar n FORM WORK
Crowd n GRUP
Crown n GARB LEAD
Crown n BODY UP
Crown n MONY
Crown n UP
Crown v DAMG BODY
Crown v GOOD
Crucial j CRUX
Crucible n HOLW HEAT
Crucified v DAMG
Crucifix n HOLY FORM
Crucifixion n DAMG HOLY
Crucify v DAMG
Crude j WEAK
Crude j BAD AGGR
Cruel j BAD DAMG
Cruet n HOLW
Cruise v GO FLOW
Cruise v GO VEHC
Cruller n FOOD
Crumb n FOOD LITL
Crumb n LITL SOME
Crumble v SEP WEAK
Crumpet n FOOD
Crumple v VARY
Crunch n HEAR
Crusade v DAMG HOLY
Crush n DAMG
Crush n FOND SEX
Crust n FOOD COVR
Crust n COVR
Crust n AGGR
Crustacean n ANML FLOW
Crutch n AID FORM
Crux n CRUX
Crux n FORM

Cry n SOMA PANG
Cry n HEAR TALK
Crypt n DEAD HOLW
Cryptic j BLUR COVR
Cryptogram n WRIT COVR
Crystal n MTRL VIEW
Crystal n MTRL FORM
Crystallize v MTRL FORM
Crystallize v SHRP FORM
Cub n ANML YNG
Cub n WEAK YNG
Cubbed v ANML YNG
Cubbyhole n HOME
Cube n FORM
Cube n NUMR
Cubic j FORM
Cubic j NUMR
Cubicle n HOME
Cubism n FORM
Cubit n MSMT
Cuckoo n ANML UP
Cuckoo n FOOL
Cuckoo n ANML TALK
Cucumber n FOOD VEGT
Cud n FOOD
Cuddle v FOND JOIN
Cudgel n DAMG
Cue n AID IDEA
Cue n PLAY
Cuff n GARB
Cuff n DAMG
Cuisine n FOOD
Culdesac n END PATH
Culinary j FOOD
Cull v SEP
Culminate v END
Culottes n GARB LADY
Culpable j AGGR MOTV
Culprit n BAD CRIM
Cult n FOND HOLY
Cult n GRUP HOLY
Cultivate v GOOD IDEA
Cultivate v ERTH WORK
Cultivate v MOTV
Culture n GOOD IDEA
Culture n AID
Culvert n HOLW
Cumbersome n WEAK
Cumulate v LARG HAVE
Cumulate v LARG BULG
Cumuli n VAPR WEA
Cumuli n LARG BULG
Cumulus n VAPR WEA
Cumulus n LARG BULG
Cunning j POWR
Cunning j POWR FALS
Cunning j GOOD
Cup n SIP HOLW
Cup n HOLW
Cup n POWR HOLW
Cupboard n FOOD HOLW
Cupcake n FOOD

Cupful n BULG HOLW
Cupid n FOND MYTH
Cupidity n MOTV
Cupped v HOLW
Cupping v HOLW
Cur n ANML AGGR
Curable j MEDC AID
Curable j EVER
Curative j MEDC AID
Curator n LEAD AID
Curb n BLOK
Curb n MART
Curd n LARG SIP
Curdle v LARG SIP
Cure n MEDC AID
Cure n EVER
Cure n LEAD HOLY
Curfew n BLOK TIME
Curie n MSMT
Curing v MEDC AID
Curing v EVER
Curio n AFAR
Curios n AFAR
Curiosity n MOTV
Curious j MOTV
Curious j AFAR
Curl n VARY
Curl n VARY BODY
Curler n VARY
Curler n PLAY
Curlicue n VARY
Curling v VARY
Curling n PLAY
Curr v ANML TALK
Currant n FOOD VEGT
Currency n MONY
Currency n NEW
Current j NEW
Current n FLOW
Current n ION
Curriculum n EDUC
Curried v FOOD VEGT
Curried v CLEN
Curried v MOTV
Curried v DAMG
Curry n FOOD VEGT
Curry v CLEN
Curry v MOTV
Curry v DAMG
Currycomb v CLEN
Curs n ANML AGGR
Curse n BAD TALK
Curse n BAD AGGR
Cursing v BAD TALK
Cursive j EASY WRIT
Cursory j QUIK TRIV
Curt j AGGR LITL
Curtail v BLOK LITL
Curtain n FURN COVR
Curtain n COVR
Curtain n PLAY COVR
Curtsy n FOND

Curvaceous j VARY LADY
Curve n VARY
Curving v VARY
Cushier j EASY
Cushion n EASY
Cushy j EASY
Cusp n BULG SHRP
Cuspid n FOOD BODY
Cuspidor n SOMA HOLW
Cuss n BAD TALK
Cuss n FOOL
Custard n FOOD
Custodian n AID WORK
Custodian n AID HAVE
Custodian n BLOK HAVE
Custody n AID HAVE
Custody n BLOK HAVE
Custom n EVER
Custom j MART
Custom n LAW
Customary j EVER
Customer n MART MONY
Customer n SOLE
Cut v SEP SHRP
Cut v LITL SHRP
Cut v VARY GO
Cut v DAMG SHRP
Cut v BLOK SHRP
Cutaneous j BODY
Cutaway j SEP SHRP
Cutaway n GARB
Cute j GOOD
Cuticle n BODY
Cutlass n DAMG SHRP
Cutlery n FOOD FURN
Cutlet n ANML FOOD
Cutoff n VARY PATH
Cutoff n BLOK SHRP
Cutout n BLOK SHRP
Cutpurse n CRIM
Cutter n SEP SHRP
Cutter n FLOW VEHC
Cutthroat n DAMG CRIM
Cutting v SEP SHRP
Cutting v LITL SHRP
Cutting v VARY GO
Cutting v DAMG SHRP
Cutting v BLOK SHRP
Cutworm n BUG
Cyanide n MTRL
Cybernetic j LEAD MECH
Cycle n VARY FORW
Cycle n VARY GO
Cycle n VEHC
Cycle v GO VEHC
Cycled v VARY GO
Cycled v GO VEHC
Cyclic j VARY FORW
Cycling v VARY GO
Cycling v GO VEHC
Cyclist n VEHC
Cyclone n WEA DAMG

Parts of speech: a article; b preposition; c conjunction; d adverb; f prefix; i interjection;
          j adjective; n noun; p pronoun; r phrase; v verb.

Cyclops n MYTH
Cyclotron n MECH ION
Cylinder n HOLW FORM
Cylindrical j HOLW FORM
Cymbal n MUSC

Cynic n AGGR
Cypher n NUMR
Cypher n WRIT COVR
Cypress n VEGT
Cypress n MTRL VEGT

Cyprian n BAD SEX
Cyst n SOMA HOLW
Cytology n SOMA IDEA
Cytoplasm n SOMA MTRL

D

D n WRIT
D n WRIT EDUC
D n WRIT MUSC
Dab n JOIN SOME
Dabbed v JOIN SOME
Dabble v FLOW
Dabble v TRIV
Dace n ANML FLOW
Dachshund n ANML
Dacron n FABR
Dactyl n WRIT
Dad n MALE KIN
Dad n LEAD MALE
Dada n OPPO FORM
Dada n MALE KIN
Dada n LEAD MALE
Daddy n MALE KIN
Daddy n LEAD MALE
Daddylonglegs n BUG BODY
Dado n FORM
Daedal j POWR
Daemon n BAD MYTH
Daffier j FOOL
Daffodil n VEGT
Daffodil n COLR
Daffy j FOOL
Daft j FOOL
Dagger n SHRP
Daggle v DIRT
Daglock n DIRT BODY
Daguerreotype n VIEW
Dahlia n VEGT
Daily j EVER TIME
Daily n WRIT TIME
Dainty j GOOD
Daiquiri n SIP
Dairy j ANML FOOD
Dais n POWR FORM
Daisies n VEGT
Daisy n VEGT
DalaiLama n LEAD HOLY
Dale n ERTH HOLW
Dally v REST TRIV
Dally v SEX TRIV
Dalmatian n ANML PLAC
Dalmatic n GARB
Dam n BLOK FLOW
Dam n ANML LADY
Damage n DAMG
Damask n PLAC FABR
Damask n ERTH MTRL
Damask n COLR
Dame n LEAD LADY
Dame n LADY
Damn v BAD AGGR
Damp v FLOW
Damp v BLOK

Dams n BLOK FLOW
Dams n ANML LADY
Damsel n LADY
Dance n GO MUSC
Dandelion n VEGT
Dander n AGGR
Dandies n FOOL GARB
Dandle v FOND JOIN
Dandruff n DIRT BODY
Dandy j GOOD
Dandy n FOOL GARB
Dane n ANML PLAC
Danger n DAMG
Dangle v DOWN
Danish n FOOD PLAC
Dank j FLOW
Danube n PLAC FLOW
Daphne n VEGT
Dapper j GARB GOOD
Dapple n ANML COLR
Dapple v COLR
Dare v POWR MOTV
Dark j COLR
Dark j BLUR COLR
Dark j BAD BLUR
Darling j FOND
Darn i EMPH
Darn v GARB JOIN
Darned j EMPH
Darned v GARB JOIN
Darnel n VEGT
Darning v GARB JOIN
Darningneedle n BUG UP
Dart n SHRP
Dart n QUIK GO
Dart n GARB JOIN
Darted v QUIK GO
Darter n ANML FLOW
Darting v QUIK GO
Dash n QUIK GO
Dash n SOME
Dash n WRIT FORM
Dash n POWR
Dash n MECH VIEW
Dash v DAMG GO
Dashboard n MECH VIEW
Dashing j POWR
Dashing v QUIK GO
Dashing v DAMG GO
Dastard n BAD WEAK
Data n TRUE
Date n TIME
Date n JOIN TIME
Date n FOOD VEGT
Dateless j BLUR TIME
Dating v TIME
Dating v JOIN TIME

Dative j TALK FORM
Datum n TRUE
Daub v BLUR
Daughter n LADY KIN
Daunt v WEAK
Dauntless j POWR
Dauphin n LEAD MALE
Dauphine n LEAD LADY
Davenport n FURN REST
Davit n MECH UP
DavyJones n DOWN FLOW
Daw n ANML UP
Dawdle v REST TRIV
Dawn v BGIN TIME
Day n TIME
Daybreak n BGIN TIME
Daydream n TIME MYTH
Daylight n VIEW TIME
Daytime n TIME
Daze v BLUR PANG
Dazzle v BLUR VIEW
Dazzle v FOND MOTV
DDT n MTRL
Deacon n HOLY
Deacon v TALK HOLY
Deacon v FALS
Deaconess n LADY HOLY
Deactivate v REST
Dead j DEAD
Dead j DEAD TRIV
Dead d EMPH
Deadbeat n DEAD WEAK
Deaden v DEAD REST
Deaden v DEAD TRIV
Deadeye n MECH FLOW
Deadline n END TIME
Deadlock n BLOK
Deadwood n DEAD TRIV
Deaf j HEAR SICK
Deaf j AGGR HEAR
Deafen v HEAR SICK
Deal n PLAY SEP
Deal n AGRE
Deal n SOME
Deal n MTRL VEGT
Deal v EVNT
Deal v MART
Dealer n MART
Dealer n PLAY SEP
Dealing v PLAY SEP
Dealing v EVNT
Dealing v MART
Deals v PLAY SEP
Deals n AGRE
Deals v EVNT
Deals v MART
Dealt v PLAY SEP

Dealt v EVNT
Dealt v MART
Dean n LEAD
Dean n LEAD EDUC
Dear j FOND
Dear j MUCH MONY
Dearth n LACK
Death n DEAD
Deathbed n DEAD REST
Deathless j DEAD EVER
Debacle n DAMG WEAK
Debar v BLOK
Debark v FLOW SEP
Debase v BAD
Debate n OPPO TALK
Debauch v BAD MOTV
Debenture n MART MONY
Debility n WEAK
Debit n MART MONY
Debonaire j GLAD
Debouch v GO OUT
Debride v SEP SHRP
Debris n DIRT
Debt n MART MONY
Debt n MOTV
Debut n BGIN
Debutante n BGIN LADY
Decade n TIME
Decadence n BAD
Decagonal j FORM
Decal n JOIN VIEW
Decamp v GO SEP
Decanter n HOLW
Decapitate v BODY SEP
Decathlon n PLAY
Decay n DIRT WEAK
Decease v DEAD
Decedent n DEAD
Deceit n FALS
Deceive v FALS
Decelerate v GO REST
December n TIME
Decency n GOOD
Decennial n TIME
Decennium n TIME
Decent j GOOD
Decenter v VARY SHRP
Decentralize v VARY SHRP
Deception n FALS
Decibel n HEAR MSMT
Decide v IDEA
Decided v IDEA
Decided j EMPH
Decidedly d EMPH
Deciduous j VARY BODY
Decimal n NUMR
Decimate v DAMG
Decipher v WRIT OPEN
Decision n IDEA
Decisive j POWR IDEA
Deck n FORM
Deck n GRUP PLAY
Deck v GOOD
Deck v GARB GOOD
Decked v GOOD

Decked v GARB GOOD
Decked v FORM
Decking v GOOD
Decking v GARB GOOD
Decking v FORM
Declaim v TALK
Declamation n TALK
Declare v TALK
Declension n DOWN GO
Declension n OPPO
Declension n TALK FORM
Decline v OPPO
Decline v DOWN GO
Decline v TALK FORM
Declivity n DOWN
Decoct v HEAT FLOW
Decode v WRIT OPEN
Decollate v BODY SEP
Decolletage n GARB LADY
Decolor v COLR
Decompensate v WEAK
Decompose v DIRT SEP
Decompose v SEP
Decompress v VARY POWR
Decontaminate v CLEN
Decontrol v OPEN
Decor n GOOD
Decorate v GOOD
Decorate v POWR GOOD
Decorous j GOOD
Decorum n GOOD
Decoy n FALS
Decrease n LITL
Decree n LEAD TALK
Decrement n LITL
Decrepit j DIRT WEAK
Decrepitate v HEAR
Decrepitude n DIRT WEAK
Decrescendo n LITL MUSC
Decrescent j LITL WEAK
Decretal n WRIT HOLY
Decried v AGGR TALK
Decry v AGGR TALK
Dedicate v AGRE
Deduce v IDEA
Deduct v SEP
Deducting v SEP
Deductive j IDEA
Deed n WRIT LAW
Deed n EVNT
Deem v IDEA
Deep j DOWN
Deep j DOWN CRUX
Deep j DOWN EMPH
Deep n DOWN FLOW
Deepsea j DOWN FLOW
Deer n ANML
Deface v DAMG DIRT
Defacto j TRUE
Defalcate v CRIM MONY
Defame v AGGR FALS
Default n WEAK
Defeat v POWR WEAK
Defeating v POWR WEAK
Defeatist n WEAK

Defecate v DIRT SOMA
Defect n WEAK
Defect v SEP WEAK
Defend v AID
Defendant n LAW
Defense n AID
Defenseless j WEAK
Defer v BLOK REST
Defer v AGRE SUB
Deference n AGRE SUB
Deficiency n LACK
Deficit n LACK
Defied v AGGR OPPO
Defile v AGGR DIRT
Defile n PATH
Defile v FORW GO
Define v IDEA
Defining v IDEA
Definite j SHRP
Definitely d EMPH
Definition n IDEA
Definition n SHRP
Definitive j IDEA SHRP
Deflate v VAPR LITL
Deflect v VARY GO
Deflower v DAMG SEX
Deflower v SEP VEGT
Defoliate v SEP VEGT
Deform v VARY DIRT
Deform v BAD VARY
Deform v VARY FORM
Defraud v CRIM FALS
Defray v MONY
Defrost v VARY COLD
Deft j POWR
Defunct j DEAD END
Defy v AGGR OPPO
Degeneracy n BAD
Degenerate j BAD
Degenerate v DIRT
Degrade v BAD
Degrade v AGGR SUB
Degree n MSMT
Degree n EDUC
Degree n SOME
Dehumanize v BAD AGGR
Dehumidify v OUT FLOW
Dehydrate v FLOW LACK
Deicide n DEAD HOLY
Deify v LEAD HOLY
Deign v AGRE LEAD
Deism n LEAD HOLY
Deity n LEAD HOLY
Deject v PANG
Dejure j LAW
Delay n BLOK REST
Delectable j GOOD
Delegate n MOTV
Delegating v MOTV
Delegation n GRUP MOTV
Delegation n MOTV
Delete v OUT SEP
Deleterious j DAMG
Deliberate v IDEA MOTV
Delicacy n WEAK

Delicacy n FOOD GOOD
Delicacy n MOTV
Delicate j WEAK
Delicate j GOOD
Delicate j MOTV
Delicatessen n MART FOOD
Delicious j GOOD
Delight v FOND GLAD
Delimit v BLOK
Delineate v SHRP FORM
Delinquency n CRIM
Delinquency n WEAK
Deliquesce v VARY FLOW
Delirious j SICK PANG
Deliver v GO
Deliver v TALK
Deliver v AID OPEN
Deliver v BGIN
Deliverance n AID OPEN
Deliveries n GO
Deliveries n BGIN
Delivery n GO
Delivery n TALK
Delivery n BGIN
Dell n ERTH HOLW
Delouse v BUG CLEN
Delphinium n VEGT
Delta n ERTH FLOW
Delta n WRIT
Delude v FALS
Deluge n BULG FLOW
Deluge n BULG
Delusion n FALS
Delve v OPEN
Demagogue n LEAD FALS
Demand v MOTV
Demarcate v BLOK SEP
Demean v EVNT
Demean v BAD
Demeanor n EVNT
Dementia n SICK IDEA
Demerit n BAD
Demerit n BAD FALS
Demigod n LEAD HOLY
Demijohn n HOLW
Demilitarize v DAMG END
Demise n DEAD
Demitasse n SIP VEGT
Demitasse n SIP HOLW
Demobilize v DAMG END
Democracy n GRUP LAW
Democrat n GRUP LAW
Democrat n GRUP
Demography n GRUP IDEA
Demolish v DAMG
Demolition n DAMG
Demon n BAD MYTH
Demoniac j BAD MYTH
Demonology n MYTH
Demonstrate v IDEA TRUE
Demonstrate v VIEW
Demoralize v WEAK
Demote v SUB
Demur v OPPO
Demure j WEAK

Den n HOME
Denature v VARY CRUX
Denied v OPPO NO
Denier n OPPO NO
Denier n MSMT FABR
Denier n MONY
Denigrate v BAD
Denim n VEGT FABR
Denizen n LIVE
Denomination n GRUP
Denomination n TALK
Denominator n CRUX NUMR
Denominator n NUMR
Denote v IDEA
Denouement n END OPEN
Denounce v AGGR TALK
Dens n HOME
Dense j LARG
Dense j FOOL
Density n MSMT
Density n FOOL
Dent v HOLW
Dental j FOOD BODY
Dentate j FOOD BODY
Dentifrice n CLEN BODY
Dentist n MEDC BODY
Dentition n FOOD BODY
Denture n FOOD BODY
Denude v SEP
Denunciation n AGGR TALK
Deny v OPPO NO
Deodorant n CLEN SOMA
Deodorize v CLEN SOMA
Depart v GO SEP
Departed v GO SEP
Departed j DEAD SEP
Department n GRUP SOME
Depend v AID
Depend v AID SUB
Dependability n AID
Depict v VIEW
Deplete v LACK
Deplore v PANG
Deploy v LARG GO
Depopulate v DAMG GRUP
Deport v GO SEP
Deport v EVNT
Depose v SEP WEAK
Depose v TALK LAW
Deposing v SEP WEAK
Deposing v TALK LAW
Deposit n MONY
Deposit n NSCR
Depositing v MONY
Depositing v NSCR
Deposition n TALK LAW
Depository n HOLW
Depot n HOME
Deprave v BAD
Deprecate v AGGR
Depreciable j CRUX LITL
Depreciate v AGGR
Depreciate v CRUX LITL
Depredate v DAMG CRIM
Depress v DOWN

Depress v PANG
Depression n PANG
Depression n DOWN HOLW
Depression n DOWN
Deprive v LACK
Depth n DOWN
Deputation n GRUP
Deputies n MOTV
Deputy n MOTV
Derail v VARY GO
Derange v VARY
Derange v SICK
Derby n QUIK GO
Derby n GARB MALE
Derelict j BAD WEAK
Derelict n SEP
Deride v FOOL AGGR
Derision n FOOL AGGR
Derive v BGIN
Derive v HAVE
Dermal j BODY
Dermatitis n BODY SICK
Dermatologist n MEDC BODY
Derogate v AGGR
Derrick n MECH
Derriere n BACK BODY
Derringdo n POWR MOTV
Derringer n DAMG MECH
Dervish n GRUP HOLY
Descant n MUSC
Descant v TALK
Descend v DOWN GO
Descendant n BGIN KIN
Descended v DOWN GO
Descendent n BGIN KIN
Descent n DOWN GO
Describe v SIML TALK
Describe v SIML GO
Descried v OPEN VIEW
Description n SIML TALK
Descry v OPEN VIEW
Desecrate v DAMG HOLY
Desegregate v JOIN
Desensitize v GLAD
Desensitize v REST
Desert n ERTH HEAT
Desert n MOTV
Desert v SEP
Deserted v SEP
Deserting v SEP
Deserve v MOTV
Desiccate v FLOW LACK
Design n IDEA FORM
Design n MOTV
Designate v MOTV
Desirable j GOOD MOTV
Desire n MOTV
Desire n SEX MOTV
Desiring v MOTV
Desiring v SEX MOTV
Desist v END
Desk n FURN WRIT
Desolate j SEP PANG
Desolate v DAMG
Despair n PANG

Desperado n CRIM
Desperate j PANG
Despicable j BAD AGGR
Despise v AGGR
Despite b OPPO
Despite n AGGR
Despoil v DAMG CRIM
Despondent j PANG
Despot n AGGR LEAD
Dessert n FOOD
Destine v END
Destitute j LACK
Destroy v DAMG
Destroyer n DAMG
Destroyer n DAMG FLOW
Destruction n DAMG
Desultory j VARY
Detach v SEP
Detachment n GRUP SOME
Detachment n SEP
Detail n SOME
Detail n GRUP SOME
Detail v MOTV
Detain v BLOK
Detect v OPEN
Detecting v OPEN
Detective n LAW
Detention n BLOK
Deter v BLOK
Detergent n CLEN
Deteriorate v DIRT WEAK
Determine v IDEA
Determine v EVER MOTV
Detest v AGGR
Dethrone v SEP WEAK
Detonate v DAMG HEAR
Detour n VARY GO
Detract v AGGR
Detrain v SEP VEHC
Detriment n AGGR
Deuce n NUMR PLAY
Deuce n BAD
Deuteron n MTRL ION
Deuteronomy n WRIT HOLY
Devaluate v LITL
Devaluate v LITL WEAK
Devastate v DAMG
Develop v LARG VARY
Develop v VARY
Develop v VARY AID
Deviate v VARY
Deviate v VARY OPPO
Device n MECH
Device n FALS
Device n VIEW
Devil n BAD LEAD
Devil n BAD
Devil n SUB
Devil v FOOD
Devil v BAD AGGR
Devious j VARY
Devise v IDEA FORM
Devise v LAW MOTV
Devoid j LACK
Devolve v GO

Devote v FOND
Devotion n FOND
Devotion n FOND HOLY
Devour v FOOD SOMA
Devour v DAMG
Devour v MOTV
Devout j HOLY MOTV
Dew n FLOW
Dexedrine n MEDC
Dexterity n POWR
Dextrous j POWR
Dextrose n FOOD MTRL
Dhow n FLOW VEHC
Diabetes n SICK
Diabolic j BAD
Diacritic n WRIT EMPH
Diadem n GARB LEAD
Diagnosis n IDEA
Diagonal j FORM
Diagram n IDEA FORM
Dial n VIEW FORM
Dialect n TALK
Dialectic n IDEA
Dialed v VIEW FORM
Dialing v VIEW FORM
Dialogue n TALK
Dialysis n SEP
Diameter n MSMT
Diametrically d OPPO
Diamond n ERTH MTRL
Diamond n PLAY
Diamond n FORM
Diapason n MUSC
Diaper n GARB YNG
Diaphanous j VIEW
Diaphragm n BLOK SOMA
Diaphragm n BLOK
Diaries n WRIT
Diarrhea n DIRT SICK
Diary n WRIT
Diathermy n MEDC HEAT
Diatribe n AGGR TALK
Dice n PLAY
Dice v LITL SHRP
Dichotomy n SEP
Dichromatic j COLR
Dicker v MART TALK
Dickey n GARB
Dickey n ANML
Dictaphone n TALK MECH
Dictate v TALK
Dictate v LEAD TALK
Dictator n LEAD
Diction n TALK
Dictionary n FORW WRIT
Dictum n TALK IDEA
Did v NSCR
Did v EVNT
Didactic j EDUC
Diddle v TRIV
Die v DEAD
Die n PLAY
Die n MECH
Diehard n OPPO DEAD
Dielectric n ION

Diet n FOOD
Diet n LEAD LAW
Differ v OPPO
Difference n OPPO
Different j OPPO
Differential n OPPO
Differential n MECH
Difficult j BLUR BLOK
Diffident j WEAK
Diffract v VARY
Diffuse j BLUR
Diffuse j LARG
Diffuse v LARG GO
Dig v OPEN
Dig n AGGR
Dig v FOND IDEA
Digest v FOOD SOMA
Digest n TALK LITL
Digestion n FOOD SOMA
Digit n NUMR
Digit n BODY
Dignify v POWR GOOD
Dignitary n POWR
Dignity n POWR GOOD
Digress v VARY TALK
Dihedral n FORM
Dike n BLOK FLOW
Dilapidate v DIRT
Dilate v LARG
Dilatory j BLOK REST
Dilemma n BLUR PANG
Dilettante n WEAK TRIV
Diligence n EVER MOTV
Diligent j EVER MOTV
Dill j FOOD VEGT
Dillydally v REST
Dilute v WEAK
Diluvial j BULG FLOW
Dim v BLUR
Dime n MONY
Dimension n FORM
Dimension n MSMT
Dimension n LARG
Diminish v LITL
Diminutive j LITL
Dimity n VEGT FABR
Dimorphic j OPPO FORM
Dimple n BODY HOLW
Din n HEAR
Dine v FOOD SOMA
Diner n FOOD SOMA
Diner n MART FOOD
Dinette n FOOD HOME
Ding n MUSC
Dinghy n FLOW VEHC
Dingier j DIRT
Dingy j DIRT
Dinky j TRIV
Dinned v HEAR
Dinner n FOOD
Dinnerware n FOOD FURN
Dinning v HEAR
Dinosaur n ANML
Dint n POWR
Diocese n LEAD HOLY

Diode n MECH ION
Dioxide n MTRL
Dip n DOWN
Dip n IN FLOW
Dip n FOOD IN
Diphtheria n SICK
Diphthong n TALK FORM
Diploma n POWR WRIT
Diplomacy n POWR LAW
Diplomat n LEAD LAW
Dipped v DOWN
Dipped v IN FLOW
Dipper n HOLW FLOW
Dipper n ASTR HOLW
Dipsomaniac n SIP SICK
Dire j DAMG
Direct j SHRP
Direct v LEAD
Direction n LEAD
Direction n PATH
Directive n LEAD
Director n LEAD
Directory n FORW WRIT
Dirge n PANG MUSC
Dirigible n VEHC UP
Dirk n DAMG SHRP
Dirt n DIRT
Dirt n BAD DIRT
Dirt n DIRT ERTH
Disability n WEAK
Disadvantage n WEAK
Disagree v OPPO
Disagreeable j AGGR
Disallow v OPPO
Disappear v VIEW SEP
Disappoint v PANG
Disapprove v OPPO
Disarm v DAMG WEAK
Disarm v AGRE
Disarray n DIRT
Disassociate v SEP
Disaster n DAMG
Disavow v OPPO
Disband v END SEP
Disbar v LAW SEP
Disbar v BLOK SEP
Disbelief n OPPO IDEA
Disburse v MONY
Disc n FORM
Disc n TALK MUSC
Disc n SOMA
Discard v SEP
Discern v IDEA
Discern v VIEW
Discharge v SEP
Discharge v OUT SEP
Discharge v DAMG OUT
Disciple n HOLY SUB
Disciple n SUB
Disciplinarian n LEAD
Discipline n LEAD
Discipline n EDUC

Discipline v DAMG LEAD
Disclaim v OPPO
Disclose v OPEN
Discolor v COLR DIRT
Discomfit v PANG
Discomfort v PANG
Discompose v PANG
Disconcert v PANG
Disconnect v SEP
Disconsolate j PANG
Discontent j PANG
Discontinue v END
Discord n AGGR
Discount v LITL MONY
Discount v FALS
Discounted v LITL MONY
Discounted v FALS
Discountenance v AGGR PANG
Discourage v AGGR PANG
Discourse n TALK
Discourteous j AGGR
Discover v OPEN
Discredit v BAD AGGR
Discredit v FALS
Discreet j GOOD
Discrepancy n OPPO
Discrete j SEP
Discretion n GOOD IDEA
Discretion n MOTV
Discriminate v OPPO IDEA
Discriminate v AGGR
Discursive j VARY
Discus n PLAY FORM
Discuss v TALK
Disdain n AGGR
Disease n SICK
Disembark v SEP VEHC
Disembowel v SOMA SEP
Disenchant v PANG
Disengage v OPEN SEP
Disentangle v OPEN SEP
Disfavor n AGGR
Disfigure v DIRT BODY
Disgrace v BAD
Disgruntle v AGGR PANG
Disguise n FALS COVR
Disgust v PANG
Dish n FOOD HOLW
Dish n HOLW FORM
Dishabille n GARB EASY
Disharmony n AGGR
Dishcloth n CLEN
Dishearten v PANG
Dished v FOOD HOLW
Dished v HOLW FORM
Dishevel v BLUR
Dishonest j BAD FALS
Dishonor n BAD AGGR
Dishwasher n CLEN FURN
Disillusion v PANG
Disinfect v CLEN MEDC
Disinherit v AGGR SEP

Disintegrate v DAMG SEP
Disinter v ERTH OUT
Disjointed j BLUR SEP
Disk n FORM
Disk n TALK MUSC
Disk n SOMA
Dislike v AGGR
Dislocate v VARY
Dislodge v OPEN SEP
Disloyal j AGGR FALS
Dismal j PANG
Dismantle v SEP
Dismay n PANG
Dismember v BODY SEP
Dismiss v SEP
Dismount v DOWN SEP
Disobedient j AGGR
Disorder n BLUR
Disorder n DAMG
Disorder n SICK
Disorderly j BLUR
Disorderly j DAMG
Disorderly j BAD SEX
Disorganize v BLUR
Disown v AGGR SEP
Disparage v AGGR
Disparate j OPPO
Dispassionate j GLAD
Dispatch n WRIT
Dispatch n QUIK
Dispatch v GO
Dispatch v DEAD
Dispatched v GO
Dispatched v DEAD
Dispatching v GO
Dispatching v DEAD
Dispel v SEP
Dispensary n MEDC
Dispensation n AID
Dispensation n AID OPEN
Dispense v AID
Dispense v LACK
Dispensing v AID
Dispensing v LACK
Disperse v GO SEP
Dispirit v PANG
Displace v VARY
Display v OPEN VIEW
Displease v AGGR
Dispose v SEP
Dispose v MOTV
Dispose v FORM
Dispossess v SEP
Disproportion n OPPO
Disprove v FALS
Dispute n AGGR
Disqualify v WEAK
Disquiet v PANG
Disquisition n TALK
Disregard v OPPO
Disrepair n DIRT
Disreputable j BAD

Parts of speech: a article; b preposition; c conjunction; d adverb; f prefix; i interjection;
j adjective; n noun; p pronoun; r phrase; v verb.

Disrespect n AGGR
Disrobe v GARB SEP
Disrupt v BLOK AGGR
Dissatisfy v AGGR
Dissect v SEP SHRP
Disseminate v LARG OPEN
Dissension n OPPO
Dissent v OPPO
Dissertation n WRIT IDEA
Disservice n AGGR
Dissident n OPPO
Dissimilar j OPPO
Dissipate v SEP
Dissipate v WEAK
Dissociate v SEP
Dissolute j BAD
Dissolution n END SEP
Dissolve v VARY FLOW
Dissolve v END SEP
Dissolve v BLUR
Dissonance n OPPO HEAR
Dissuade v VARY IDEA
Distaff j LADY
Distance n AFAR
Distance n MSMT
Distant j AFAR
Distasteful j AGGR
Distemper n SICK
Distemper n AGGR PANG
Distemper n COLR
Distend v LARG
Distill v FLOW
Distillate n FLOW
Distilled v FLOW
Distillery n SIP WORK
Distinct j OPPO
Distinct j SHRP
Distinction n OPPO
Distinction n SHRP
Distinction n POWR
Distingue j POWR
Distinguish v OPPO
Distinguish v SHRP
Distinguish v POWR
Distort v VARY FALS
Distract v VARY IDEA
Distract v PANG
Distraught j PANG
Distress n PANG
Distribute v AID
Distribute v SEP
Distributor n AID
Distributor n MECH
Distributor n SEP
District n PLAC
Distrust v AGGR
Disturb v PANG
Disunion n SEP
Disunite v SEP
Disuse n END
Ditch n ERTH HOLW
Ditch v DOWN FLOW
Ditch v SEP
Ditties n TALK MUSC
Ditto n SIML WRIT

Ditto n SIML
Ditty n TALK MUSC
Diva n POWR LADY
Divan n FURN REST
Dive n DOWN GO
Dive n DOWN FLOW
Dive n MART SIP
Diver n DOWN GO
Diver n DOWN FLOW
Diverge v VARY OPPO
Divers n DOWN GO
Divers n DOWN FLOW
Diverse j OPPO
Diversify v OPPO
Diversion n VARY
Diversion n VARY IDEA
Divert v VARY
Divert v VARY IDEA
Divest v SEP
Divide v SEP
Divide v NUMR SEP
Dividend n MART MONY
Dividend n NUMR SEP
Divine j LEAD HOLY
Divine j GOOD
Divine v IDEA
Diving v DOWN GO
Diving v DOWN FLOW
Divining v IDEA
Divinity n LEAD HOLY
Division n SEP
Division n NUMR SEP
Division n GRUP SOME
Division n DAMG GRUP
Divisive j OPPO SEP
Divisor n NUMR SEP
Divorce n SEP
Divot n ERTH LITL
Divulge v OPEN
Dizzy j BLUR PANG
Do v NSCR
Do v EVNT
Dobbin n ANML
Docile j GLAD SUB
Dock n BLOK FLOW
Dock n LAW REST
Dock v LITL
Docked v BLOK FLOW
Docked v LITL
Docket n WRIT LAW
Doctor n MEDC
Doctor n POWR EDUC
Doctor v FALS
Doctorate n POWR EDUC
Doctrine n IDEA FORM
Document n WRIT
Document v WRIT TRUE
Documentary n WRIT TRUE
Dodge v VARY GO
Doe n ANML LADY
Does v NSCR
Does v EVNT
Does n ANML LADY
Doff v SEP
Dog n ANML

Dog n ANML BAD
Dog v ANML AGGR
Dog n MECH
Dogfight n DAMG UP
Dogged j EVER
Dogged v ANML AGGR
Doggerel n WRIT TRIV
Dogging v ANML AGGR
Doghouse n ANML HOME
Dogleg n ANML VARY
Dogma n IDEA FORM
Dogtired j EMPH WEAK
Dogwood n VEGT
Doily n FURN FABR
Doing v NSCR
Doing v EVNT
Doldrums n PANG
Doldrums n FLOW REST
Dole v AID
Doleful j PANG
Doling v AID
Doll n PLAY
Doll n LADY GOOD
Doll v GARB GOOD
Dollar n MONY
Dolled v GARB GOOD
Dollies n PLAY
Dollies n VEHC
Dolling v GARB GOOD
Dolly n PLAY
Dolly n VEHC
Dolphin n ANML FLOW
Dolt n FOOL
Domain n LEAD HAVE
Domain n LEAD
Dome n UP COVR
Domestic j NEAR
Domestic n AID HOME
Domicile n HOME LIVE
Dominant j LEAD
Dominate v LEAD
Domineer v LEAD
Dominican j GRUP HOLY
Dominion n LEAD HAVE
Domino n PLAY
Domino n GARB COVR
Don v GARB
Don n LEAD
Donate v AID
Done v NSCR
Done v END
Done v EVNT
Donkey n ANML
Donkey n FOOL ANML
Donned v GARB
Donor n AID
Donut n FOOD
Doodad n MECH TRIV
Doodle v WRIT TRIV
Doom n DEAD END
Door n BLOK OPEN
Doorbell n OPEN MUSC
Doorkeeper n AID OPEN
Doorman n AID MALE
Doorway n OPEN PATH

Dope n FOOL
Dope n MEDC REST
Dope n IDEA
Dope n MTRL
Doped v MEDC REST
Doped v IDEA
Doping v MEDC REST
Doping v IDEA
Dories n FLOW VEHC
Dories n ANML FLOW
Dorm n HOME
Dormant j REST
Dorsal j BACK
Dory n FLOW VEHC
Dory n ANML FLOW
Dose n SOME
Dossier n WRIT
Dot n WRIT LITL
Dot n LITL
Dot n AID MONY
Dotage n FOOL PAST
Dote v FOND
Double j NUMR
Double n NUMR PLAY
Double n SIML
Double j FALS
Double v VARY GO
Doublecross v FALS NUMR
Doubt v BLUR
Doubtless j SHRP
Dough n FOOD VEGT
Dough n MONY
Doughnut n FOOD
Doughty j POWR
Douse v END FLOW
Douse v END
Douse v FLOW
Dove n ANML UP
Dove v DOWN GO
Dove v DOWN FLOW
Dovetail v JOIN FORM
Dowager n LADY PAST
Dowdy j GARB DIRT
Dowel n JOIN
Down d DOWN
Down d DOWN PANG
Down n DOWN PLAY
Down v POWR WEAK
Down n BODY
Down n ERTH
Downcast j DOWN PANG
Downed v DOWN
Downed v POWR WEAK
Downfall n DOWN WEAK
Downgrade v DOWN SUB
Downgrade n DOWN PATH
Downhill d DOWN BULG
Downing v DOWN
Downing v POWR WEAK
Downpour n WEA FLOW
Downright d EMPH
Downstairs d DOWN UP
Downstream d DOWN FLOW
Downtown d DOWN PLAC
Downtrodden j DOWN SUB

Downward d DOWN
Dowry n AID MONY
Doze v REST
Dozen n NUMR
Dozer n REST
Dozer n ERTH VEHC
Drab j COLR TRIV
Drab n COLR FABR
Draft n WRIT FORM
Draft n VAPR
Draft n FLOW
Draft n WRIT MONY
Draft n JOIN MOTV
Drafted v WRIT FORM
Drafted v JOIN MOTV
Draftee n JOIN MOTV
Drafthorse n ANML WORK
Drag v GO
Dragnet n BLOK
Dragon n ANML MYTH
Dragonfly n BUG UP
Dragoon n DAMG
Drain v OUT FLOW
Drake n ANML UP
Dram n MSMT
Drama n PLAY PANG
Drank v SIP SOMA
Drape n FABR COVR
Drapery n FURN COVR
Drastic j EMPH
Draughts n FLOW
Draughts n WRIT MONY
Draughts n SOME
Draughts n PLAY
Draughtsman n WRIT FORM
Draw v GO
Draw v OUT
Draw v WRIT
Draw v IDEA
Draw v SOMA IN
Draw v FLOW
Draw v SIML PLAY
Drawback n WEAK
Drawbridge n OPEN PATH
Drawer n HOLW FURN
Drawers n HOLW FURN
Drawers n GARB
Drawl n TALK REST
Drawn v GO
Drawn v OUT
Drawn v WRIT
Drawn v IDEA
Drawn v SIML PLAY
Drawn j VARY PANG
Dray n VEHC
Dread v PANG
Dreadnaught n DAMG FLOW
Dream n IDEA MYTH
Dream n MYTH MOTV
Dream n GOOD MYTH
Dreamland n PLAC MYTH
Dreary j PANG
Dreg n DIRT
Drench v FLOW
Dress n GARB LADY

Dress v GARB
Dress v FOOD
Dress v AID
Dress v AGGR TALK
Dress v GOOD
Dressed v GARB
Dressed v FOOD
Dressed v AID
Dressed v AGGR TALK
Dressed v GOOD
Dresser n GARB
Dresser n AID
Dresser n HOLW FURN
Dresser n GOOD
Dresses v GARB
Dresses n GARB LADY
Dresses v FOOD
Dresses v AID
Dresses v AGGR TALK
Dresses v GOOD
Dressier j GARB GOOD
Dressing v GARB
Dressing v FOOD
Dressing v AID
Dressing v AGGR TALK
Dressing v GOOD
Dressmaker n GARB MART
Dressy j GARB GOOD
Drew v GO
Drew v OUT
Drew v WRIT
Drew v IDEA
Drew v SOMA IN
Drew v SIML PLAY
Dribble v FLOW
Dribble v GO PLAY
Drift v GO REST
Driftwood n FLOW VEGT
Drill n MECH SHRP
Drill v EDUC
Drill v SHRP WORK
Drink v SIP SOMA
Drip n FLOW
Drip n FOOL
Drive v GO VEHC
Drive v POWR MOTV
Drivel n FOOL TALK
Driver n LEAD VEHC
Driver n VEHC WORK
Driveway n PATH
Drizzle n WEA FLOW
Droll j GLAD
Dromedary n ANML
Drone n BUG UP
Drone v HEAR
Drone n VEHC UP
Drool v SOMA FLOW
Droop v DOWN WEAK
Drop n LITL FLOW
Drop n DOWN GO
Drop n POWR
Dropped v DOWN GO
Dropping v DOWN GO
Dropsy n SICK
Drosophila n BUG UP

Dross n DIRT
Drought n FLOW LACK
Drove v GO VEHC
Drove v POWR MOTV
Drove n GRUP
Drown v DEAD FLOW
Drowsy j REST
Drub v DAMG
Drudge v TRIV WORK
Drug n MEDC
Drug v MEDC REST
Drugged v MEDC REST
Drugging v MEDC REST
Druggist n MART MEDC
Drugs n MEDC
Drugs v MEDC REST
Drugstore n MART MEDC
Druid n GRUP HOLY
Drum n MUSC
Drum n HOLW
Drum n SOMA HEAR
Drummed v MUSC
Drumstick n ANML FOOD
Drumstick n MUSC
Drunk j SIP PANG
Drunk v SIP SOMA
Dry j FLOW LACK
Dual j SIML NUMR
Dubious j BLUR
Duchess n LEAD LADY
Duck n ANML UP
Duck v VARY
Duck v DOWN FLOW
Duck n VEGT FABR
Duckbill n ANML FLOW
Ducked v VARY
Ducked v DOWN FLOW
Ducking v VARY
Ducking v DOWN FLOW
Duckling n ANML YNG
Duckpin n PLAY
Duct n HOLW PATH
Ductile j VARY EASY
Ductless j HOLW PATH
Dud n WEAK
Dude n FOOL GARB
Duds n GARB
Due j MOTV
Due j TIME
Due j SIML
Duel n DAMG

Dues n MONY
Duet n NUMR MUSC
Duffer n WEAK
Duffle n FABR
Dufflebag n HOLW FABR
Dug v OPEN
Dugout n ERTH HOME
Dugout n FLOW VEHC
Duke n LEAD MALE
Dull j BLUR
Dull j COLR
Dull j TRIV
Dull v REST
Dullard n FOOL
Dulled v BLUR
Dulled v REST
Dulling v BLUR
Dulling v REST
Dulls v BLUR
Dulls v REST
Duly d SIML
Dumb j FOOL
Dumb j TALK LACK
Dumbbell n FOOL
Dumbbell n PLAY WORK
Dumbfound v BLUR PANG
Dumbwaiter n AID MECH
Dummy n FOOL
Dummy n PLAY
Dummy n FALS
Dummy n WRIT
Dump n DIRT HOLW
Dump n DOWN PANG
Dump n DAMG HOLW
Dump v DOWN GO
Dumped v DOWN GO
Dumpier j LARG LITL
Dumping v DOWN GO
Dumpling n FOOD
Dumpy j LARG LITL
Dun j COLR
Dun v MONY MOTV
Dunce n FOOL
Dune n ERTH BULG
Dung n DIRT SOMA
Dungaree n FABR
Dungarees n GARB
Dungeon n BLOK HOME
Dunghill n DIRT BULG
Dunk v IN FLOW
Dunned v MONY MOTV

Duo n NUMR
Duo n NUMR MUSC
Duodecimal j NUMR
Duodenum n SOMA
Dupe n FALS
Duplex j NUMR
Duplex n HOME NUMR
Duplicate v SIML
Duplicator n WRIT MECH
Duplicity n FALS
Durable j EVER
Duration n EVER TIME
Duress n PANG
During b EVER TIME
Dusk j COLR
Dusk n BLUR TIME
Dust n DIRT ERTH
Dust n ERTH
Dust v CLEN ERTH
Dusted v CLEN ERTH
Duster n CLEN ERTH
Duster n GARB
Dusting v CLEN ERTH
Dutch j PLAC
Dutch n TALK
Dutch n GRUP
Duties n MOTV WORK
Duties n MART MONY
Duty n MOTV WORK
Duty n MART MONY
Dwarf v LITL
Dwell v HOME LIVE
Dwell v EVER REST
Dwindle v LITL
Dye n COLR
Dyestuff n COLR MTRL
Dying v DEAD
Dying v DEAD MOTV
Dynamic j POWR
Dynamism n POWR
Dynamite v DAMG MTRL
Dynamo n POWR MECH
Dynasty n LEAD
Dyne n POWR MSMT
Dysentery n SICK
Dysfunction n WEAK
Dyspepsia n SICK
Dysphoria n PANG
Dystrophy n SICK

E

E n WRIT
E n WRIT MUSC
E n WRIT EDUC
Each j SOLE
Eager j MOTV
Eagle n ANML UP
Eagle n NUMR PLAY
Eagle n ANML MONY
Ear n BODY HEAR
Ear n BODY VEGT
Earache n BODY PANG

Eardrum n BODY HEAR
Earl n LEAD MALE
Earldom n LEAD
Earlier j FORW TIME
Earlier j PAST
Early j FORW TIME
Early j PAST
Earmark v SHRP
Earn v MONY WORK
Earned v MONY WORK
Earnest j CRUX MOTV

Earring n GARB BODY
Earshot n BODY HEAR
Earth n ERTH
Earth n ASTR ERTH
Earthbound j BLOK ERTH
Earthenware j ERTH
Earthling n ERTH LIVE
Earthquake n DAMG ERTH
Earthward d ERTH FORW
Earthwork n ERTH BULG
Earthworm n BUG ERTH

Earthy j ERTH
Ease n GLAD EASY
Easel n FORM
Easier j GLAD EASY
East n PLAC PATH
Easter n HOLY TIME
Easterly j PLAC PATH
Easterly n WEA PLAC
Eastern j PLAC PATH
Easy j GLAD EASY
Easygoing j GLAD EASY
Eat v FOOD SOMA
Eat v FOOD PANG
Eat v DAMG FOOD
Eave n FORM UP
Eaves n FORM UP
Eavesdrop v HEAR COVR
Ebb v BACK FLOW
Ebony n COLR
Ebony n MTRL VEGT
Ebony n VEGT
Ecce v VIEW
Eccentric j AFAR
Eccentric j VARY FORM
Eccentric n MECH
Ecclesiastes n WRIT HOLY
Ecclesiastic j HOLY
Echelon n FORW FORM
Echo v SIML HEAR
Eclair n FOOD
Eclat n AGRE
Eclat n BAD OPEN
Eclectic n IDEA MOTV
Eclipse v BLUR COVR
Ecology n WHOL LIVE
Economic j MART MONY
Economical j MONY HAVE
Economist n MART MONY
Economize v MONY HAVE
Economy n MART MONY
Economy n MONY HAVE
Ecstasy n GLAD
Ectomorph n BODY LITL
Ectoplasm n SOMA
Ectoplasm n SOMA MYTH
Ecumenical j WHOL HOLY
Eczema n DIRT BODY
Eddy n VARY FLOW
Edema n SICK
Edge n SHRP
Edge n END SHRP
Edge n POWR SHRP
Edge n SHRP PANG
Edge v GO
Edible j FOOD
Edict n LEAD TALK
Edifice n FORM
Edified v GOOD
Edify v GOOD
Edit v AID WRIT
Editing v AID WRIT
Edition n WRIT
Editor n AID WRIT
Educate v EDUC
Educator n LEAD EDUC

Educe v OUT
Eek i PANG
Eel n ANML FLOW
Eel n FOOD FLOW
Eerie j AFAR PANG
Efface v OUT SEP
Efface v WEAK
Effect n END
Effect n HAVE
Effected v END
Effecting v END
Effective j POWR
Effeminate j LADY
Efferent j GO SEP
Effervesce v HEAR FLOW
Effervesce v GLAD
Effete j WEAK
Efficacy n POWR
Efficiency n POWR
Effigy n SIML
Effluvium n OUT
Effort n WORK
Effortless j EASY
Effrontery n AGGR
Effulgent j VIEW
Effusive j FOND
Effusive j OUT
Egalitarian j SIML
Egg n ANML FOOD
Egg n BGIN SOMA
Egg n SOLE
Egg v MOTV
Egged v MOTV
Egghead n BODY IDEA
Egging v MOTV
Eggnog n ANML SIP
Eggplant n FOOD VEGT
Eggshell n FOOD HOLW
Eggshell n COLR FOOD
Ego n SOLE
Egocentric j SOLE MOTV
Egotism n SOLE MOTV
Egret n ANML UP
Eight n NUMR
Eighteen n NUMR
Eighth n NUMR
Eighth n NUMR MUSC
Eighty n NUMR
Either c NSCR
Ejaculate v QUIK TALK
Ejaculate v SOMA OUT
Eject v OUT SEP
Eke v AID
Elaborate j GOOD
Elaborate v IDEA
Elapse v SEP TIME
Elastic j VARY EASY
Elastic n VARY FABR
Elbow n BODY
Elbow v BODY GO
Elder n PAST
Elder n LEAD PAST
Elderberry n VEGT
Elderly j PAST
Elect v MOTV

Elective j MOTV
Elective n EDUC MOTV
Electorate n GRUP MOTV
Electric j ION
Electric j MOTV
Electrician n ION WORK
Electricity n ION
Electrify v ION
Electrify v MOTV
Electro f ION
Electrocardiogr n SOMA MSMT
Electrocute v DAMG DEAD
Electrode n END ION
Electromagnet n JOIN ION
Electrometer n ION MSMT
Electromotive j POWR ION
Electron n ION
Electroscope n ION MSMT
Electrostatic j ION REST
Elegance n GOOD
Elegy n TALK PANG
Element n MTRL ION
Element n CRUX SOME
Element n NEAR
Elementary j CRUX SOME
Elements n CRUX SOME
Elements n MTRL ION
Elements n WEA
Elephant n ANML
Elephantine j ANML LARG
Elevate v GO UP
Elevate v POWR UP
Elevation n GO UP
Elevation n POWR UP
Elevation n MSMT UP
Elevator n DOWN UP
Eleven n NUMR
Elf n LITL MYTH
Elicit v OPEN OUT
Eligible j SIML MOTV
Eliminate v OUT SEP
Elite j POWR GOOD
Elite j WRIT
Elk n ANML
Elks n ANML
Elks n ANML GRUP
Ellipse n FORM
Ellipsis n TALK LACK
Elliptic j FORM
Elm n VEGT
Elocution n TALK
Elongate v LARG
Elope v GO SEP
Eloquence n POWR TALK
Else j OPPO
Elsewhere d OPPO PLAC
Elucidate v IDEA SHRP
Elude v VARY OPEN
Elusive j VARY OPEN
Elves n LITL MYTH
Emaciate v LITL LACK
Emanate v OUT
Emancipate v OPEN
Emasculate v SEX WEAK
Embalm v DEAD EVER

Embankment n ERTH FORM
Embargo n BLOK LAW
Embark v BGIN GO
Embarrass v PANG
Embassy n LEAD
Embattle v DAMG AID
Embellish v GOOD
Ember n HEAT
Embezzle v CRIM
Embitter v AGGR PANG
Emblazon v COLR VIEW
Emblem n VIEW
Embody v BODY IN
Embolden v POWR
Emboss v GOOD BULG
Embrace n FOND JOIN
Embrace n BLOK JOIN
Embroider v GARB GOOD
Embroider v FALS GOOD
Embroil v AGGR PANG
Embryo n BGIN SOMA
Emcee n LEAD PLAY
Emerald n ERTH MTRL
Emerald n COLR
Emerge v GO OUT
Emergency n DAMG
Emeries n AGGR MTRL
Emeritus j POWR PAST
Emery n AGGR MTRL
Emetic n SOMA OUT
Emigrant j GO SEP
Emigrate v GO SEP
Eminence n POWR
Eminence n BULG UP
Eminent j POWR
Emissary n AID
Emission n OUT
Emit v OUT
Emotion n PANG
Emotion n MOTV
Empathy n FOND
Emperor n LEAD MALE
Emphasis n EMPH
Empire n LEAD
Empirical j EVNT
Employ v AID
Employ v WORK
Employed v AID
Employed v WORK
Employee n WORK
Employer n LEAD WORK
Emporium n MART HOME
Empower v POWR LEAD
Empty j LACK
Empty j TRIV
Empty v OUT LACK
Emulate v SIML
Emulsion n FLOW
Enable v POWR
Enact v LAW
Enact v PLAY
Enamel n MTRL

Enamel n COLR MTRL
Enamor v FOND SEX
Encephalitis n SICK
Enchant v FOND
Enchantress n FOND LADY
Encircle v BLOK HOLW
Enclose v IN COVR
Enclosure n IN COVR
Enclosure n BLOK HOLW
Encode v VARY WRIT
Encompass v BLOK
Encore n SIML PLAY
Encounter n JOIN
Encounter n DAMG JOIN
Encourage v AID
Encroach v AGGR GO
Encrust v DIRT COVR
Encumber v BLOK
Encyclopedia n FORW WRIT
End n END
End n END MOTV
End n END PLAY
End n DEAD END
Endanger v DAMG
Endeavor v MOTV
Ended v END
Endemic j WHOL NEAR
Ending v END
Endive n FOOD VEGT
Endless j EVER
Endogamy n SEX KIN
Endogenous j BGIN IN
Endomorph n LARG BODY
Endomorph n ERTH FORM
Endorse v AGRE WRIT
Endow v AID HAVE
Endure v EVER
Endure v EVER PANG
Enemy n AGGR
Energy n POWR
Enervate v WEAK
Enfant n YNG
Enforce v POWR
Engage v JOIN
Engage v SEX KIN
Engage v MOTV
Engage v DAMG JOIN
Engage v MART MONY
Engender v BGIN
Engine n MECH
Engine n MECH VEHC
Engineer n MECH FORM
Engineer n LEAD VEHC
England n PLAC
English j PLAC
English n GRUP
English n TALK
Engorge v FOOD BULG
Engrave v SHRP
Engross v MOTV
Enhance v LARG GOOD
Enigma n BLUR

Enjoin v LEAD
Enjoin v BLOK
Enjoy v GLAD
Enjoy v GLAD HAVE
Enjoyable j GLAD
Enlarge v LARG
Enlargement n LARG
Enlargement n LARG VIEW
Enlighten v IDEA
Enlist v AID
Enlist v JOIN
Enliven v QUIK LIVE
Enmesh v BLOK JOIN
Enmity n AGGR
Ennoble v LEAD GOOD
Ennui n TRIV PANG
Enormity n LARG
Enormity n BAD LARG
Enormous j LARG
Enough d MUCH
Enquire v BLUR TALK
Enrage v AGGR
Enrapture v GLAD
Enrich v MUCH MONY
Enrich v GOOD AID
Enroll v JOIN WRIT
Enroute j PATH
Ensconce v GLAD REST
Ensconce v COVR
Ensemble n GRUP
Ensemble n GRUP MUSC
Ensemble n GARB GRUP
Enshrine v IN HOLY
Ensign n LEAD FLOW
Ensign n VIEW
Enslave v BLOK SUB
Ensnare v BLOK
Ensue v BACK
Ensure v AID SHRP
Entail v JOIN
Entente n AGRE GRUP
Enter v GO IN
Enter v IN WRIT
Enterprise n POWR MOTV
Entertain v PLAY
Entertain v IDEA
Enthrall v FOND
Enthusiasm n MOTV
Entice v MOTV
Entire j WHOL
Entities n WHOL
Entitle v AGRE MOTV
Entitle v TALK
Entity n WHOL
Entourage n GRUP JOIN
Entrail n SOMA
Entrance n GO IN
Entrance v FOND
Entranced v FOND
Entrancing v FOND
Entreat v MOTV
Entree n FOOD

Parts of speech: a article; b preposition; c conjunction; d adverb; f prefix; i interjection;
j adjective; n noun; p pronoun; r phrase; v verb.

Entree n GO IN
Entrench v AGGR GO
Entrench v ERTH HOLW
Entries n GO IN
Entries n IN WRIT
Entropy n POWR NUMR
Entrust v FOND AID
Entry n GO IN
Entry n IN WRIT
Enucleate v OUT SEP
Enumerate v NUMR IDEA
Enunciate v TALK
Enuresis n SOMA WEAK
Envelop v HOLW COVR
Envelope n HOLW
Enveloped v HOLW COVR
Envious j AGGR MOTV
Environment n WHOL HOLW
Envy v AGGR MOTV
Ephemeral j VARY SEP
Epic j POWR
Epicure n FOOD MOTV
Epicure n GLAD MOTV
Epidemic n WHOL SICK
Epidermis n BODY
Epigram n TALK IDEA
Epigraph n WRIT
Epilepsy n SICK
Epilogue n END TALK
Episcopal j HOLY
Episode n EVNT
Epistle n WRIT
Epistle n WRIT HOLY
Epitaph n DEAD WRIT
Epithet n BAD TALK
Epitome n TALK LITL
Epitome n LITL
Epitomize v LITL
Epoch n TIME
Equable j SIML
Equal j SIML
Equalitarian j SIML
Equanimity n GLAD
Equate v SIML
Equation n SIML NUMR
Equation n SIML
Equator n HEAT PLAC
Equilibrate v SIML
Equilibrium n SIML
Equip v AID
Equipment n AID
Equipment n AID HAVE
Equitable j SIML GOOD
Equities n SIML GOOD
Equities n SIML CRUX
Equity n SIML GOOD
Equity n SIML CRUX
Equivalent j SIML
Equivocal j BLUR
Eradicate v SEP
Erase v SEP
Erect v FORM UP
Erect v UP
Erection n FORM UP
Erection n MALE SEX

Erg n POWR MSMT
Ermine n ANML
Ermine n ANML FABR
Erode v WEAK
Erode v SEP
Eros n SEX MYTH
Erosion n WEAK
Erosion n SEP
Erotic j SEX
Errand n GO AID
Errant j VARY FALS
Errant j VARY GO
Erratic j VARY
Erratic j VARY AFAR
Error n BAD FALS
Error n FALS WEAK
Erstwhile d PAST
Erudite j EDUC
Erupt v DAMG OUT
Erupt v BODY OUT
Escalate v GO UP
Escalate v LARG
Escapade n GO OPEN
Escape n GO OPEN
Escape n VARY OPEN
Escapement n MECH TIME
Escarole n FOOD VEGT
Eschew v VARY
Escort v AID JOIN
Esoteric j AFAR COVR
ESP n IDEA MYTH
Especially d EMPH
Espionage n VIEW COVR
Espouse v AGRE JOIN
Esprit n POWR MOTV
Espritdecorps n POWR GRUP
Esquire n MALE
Essay n WRIT
Essay v MOTV
Essence n CRUX
Essence n MTRL
Essential j CRUX
Establish v BGIN EVER
Establish v IDEA TRUE
Establishment n BGIN EVER
Establishment n EVER GRUP
Establishment n IDEA TRUE
Establishment n MART
Estate n ERTH HAVE
Estate n HAVE
Estate n EVNT
Esteem n FOND IDEA
Esteem n IDEA
Esthetic j GOOD
Estimate v IDEA
Estuary n FLOW
Etcetera n SIML
Etch v VIEW SHRP
Eternal j EVER
Ether n VAPR
Ether n VAPR ASTR
Ethereal j VAPR MYTH
Etherize v VAPR
Ethic n GOOD
Ethnic j GRUP

Ethno f GRUP
Ethnography n GRUP IDEA
Ethnology n GRUP IDEA
Etiology n BGIN IDEA
Etiquette n GOOD
Etude n MUSC
Etymology n BGIN TALK
Eucalyptus n VEGT
Eucalyptus n MTRL VEGT
Eucharist n FOOD HOLY
Euclid n NUMR IDEA
Eugenic j BGIN GOOD
Eulogy n AGRE TALK
Euphemism n GOOD TALK
Euphony n AGRE HEAR
Euphoria n GLAD
Evacuate v OUT SEP
Evade v VARY
Evaluate v CRUX IDEA
Evanesce v VARY SEP
Evangel n HOLY
Evaporate v VAPR FLOW
Evasion n VARY
Eve n FORW TIME
Even d EMPH
Even d SIML
Even n TIME
Evened v SIML
Evening n TIME
Evening v SIML
Evens v SIML
Event n EVNT
Eventual j END
Ever d EVER
Evergreen n VEGT
Everlasting j EVER
Evermore d EVER
Every j WHOL
Everybody p WHOL SOLE
Everyday j EVER
Everyman n WHOL SOLE
Everyone p WHOL SOLE
Everything p WHOL
Everywhere d WHOL PLAC
Evict v OUT SEP
Evidence n TRUE
Evidence v OPEN SHRP
Evident j OPEN SHRP
Evil n BAD
Evince v OPEN VIEW
Evoke v BGIN OUT
Evolve v VARY FORW
Ewe n ANML LADY
Exacerbate v AGGR
Exact j SHRP
Exact v POWR MOTV
Exacted v POWR MOTV
Exacting v POWR MOTV
Exactly d SHRP
Exactly d EMPH
Exacts v POWR MOTV
Exaggerate v LARG FALS
Exalt v POWR GOOD
Examination n OPEN IDEA
Examination n OPEN TRUE

Example n SIML
Exasperate v AGGR PANG
Excavate v HOLW OUT
Exceed v LARG
Exceed v POWR
Exceeding v LARG
Exceeding v POWR
Exceedingly d EMPH
Excel v POWR
Excellence n POWR GOOD
Except b OPPO
Exception n OPPO
Exceptional j AFAR
Excerpt n WRIT SOME
Excess n LARG
Exchange n VARY
Exchange n MART MONY
Excise n MART MONY
Excise v SEP SHRP
Excised v SEP SHRP
Excising v SEP SHRP
Excite v MOTV
Excite v PANG
Exclaim v TALK EMPH
Exclamation n TALK EMPH
Exclude v BLOK SEP
Exclusive j BLOK SEP
Excommunicate v HOLY SEP
Excrement n DIRT OUT
Excrete v DIRT OUT
Excruciating j PANG
Exculpate v AGRE OPEN
Excursion n GO
Excursive j VARY TALK
Excuse v AGRE IDEA
Excuse v AGRE OPEN
Execrable j AGGR
Execute v DAMG DEAD
Execute v EVNT
Executing v DAMG DEAD
Executing v EVNT
Executive n LEAD
Executor n LEAD
Exegesis n IDEA
Exemplary j GOOD
Exemplify v SIML
Exempt v OPEN
Exercise n WORK
Exercise n EDUC
Exercise n PLAY
Exercise v AID
Exercise v PANG
Exert v WORK
Exhale v VAPR SOMA
Exhaust n OUT
Exhaust v END LACK
Exhaust v WEAK
Exhausting v OUT
Exhausting v END LACK
Exhausting v WEAK
Exhaustion n WEAK
Exhaustive j WHOL END
Exhibit n OPEN VIEW
Exhibition n OPEN VIEW
Exhibitionist n VIEW SEX

Exhilarate v GLAD
Exhort v MOTV
Exhume v ERTH OUT
Exigency n LACK
Exile v BLOK SEP
Exist v LIVE
Evist v EVNT
Existence n LIVE
Existence n EVNT
Existentialist n SOLE LIVE
Exit n GO OUT
Exodus n GO OUT
Exogenous j BGIN OUT
Exonerate v AGRE OPEN
Exorbitant j LARG
Exorcise v BAD AID
Exordium n FORW TALK
Exotic j AFAR
Expand v LARG
Expanse n LARG
Expatiate v TALK
Expatriate v SEP
Expect v MOTV
Expectancy n MOTV
Expediency n AID
Expedite v QUIK AID
Expediting v QUIK AID
Expedition n GO
Expedition n GO GRUP
Expedition n QUIK AID
Expel v OUT SEP
Expend v LACK
Expending v LACK
Expenditure n MONY LACK
Expenditure n LACK
Expense n MONY LACK
Expense n LACK
Expensive j MUCH MONY
Expensive j LACK
Experience n EVNT
Experience n POWR
Experiment n TRUE
Expert j POWR
Expiate v AGRE
Expire v END
Expire v DEAD
Expire v VAPR SOMA
Explain v IDEA
Explanation n IDEA
Expletive n TALK EMPH
Explicate v IDEA
Explicit j SHRP
Explode v DAMG HEAR
Exploit n POWR
Exploit v AGGR AID
Exploit v AID
Exploitation n AGGR AID
Exploited v AGGR AID
Exploited v AID
Exploiting v AGGR AID
Exploiting v AID
Explore v GO OPEN
Explore v OPEN IDEA
Explorer n GO OPEN
Explosion n DAMG HEAR

Explosive n DAMG HEAR
Exponent n NUMR
Exponent n AGRE
Export v MART OUT
Expose v OPEN
Expose v OPEN VIEW
Exposing v OPEN
Exposing v OPEN VIEW
Exposition n IDEA
Exposition n OPEN VIEW
Expository j IDEA
Expostulate v AGGR IDEA
Exposure n OPEN VIEW
Exposure n OPEN
Expound v TALK IDEA
Express j QUIK
Express j SHRP
Express n QUIK VEHC
Express v TALK
Expressed v TALK
Expression n MOTV
Expression n TALK
Expressionism n OPEN MOTV
Expunge v SEP
Expurgate v CLEN OUT
Exquisite j GOOD
Exquisite j EMPH
Extant j LIVE
Extemporize v EASY
Extend v LARG
Extend v LARG GO
Extend v AID
Extension n LARG
Extension n LARG GO
Extension n AID
Extensive j MUCH LARG
Extent n LARG
Extenuate v LITL
Exterior n OUT
Exterminate v DAMG DEAD
External j OUT
Extinct j DEAD END
Extinguish v END
Extirpate v DAMG OUT
Extol v AGRE
Extort v CRIM
Extra d MUCH EMPH
Extra j MUCH
Extra n MUCH WRIT
Extra n AID PLAY
Extract v OUT
Extracting v OUT
Extraction n OUT
Extraction n BGIN OUT
Extradite v GO LAW
Extraneous j OUT TRIV
Extraordinary j AFAR GOOD
Extraordinary j AFAR
Extrapolate v IDEA
Extrapolate v NUMR
Extrasensory j AFAR SOMA
Extravagance n MUCH MONY
Extravagance n MUCH GOOD
Extravagant j MUCH MONY
Extravagant j MUCH GOOD

Extravaganza n PLAY
Extreme j LARG EMPH
Extreme j OPPO AFAR
Extreme j AFAR
Extremity n END AFAR
Extremity n END BODY
Extremity n END PANG
Extricate v OPEN

Extrinsic j OUT TRIV
Extrovert n OUT MOTV
Extrude v OUT
Exuberant j GLAD
Exude v OUT
Exult v GLAD
Eye n BODY VIEW
Eye n BODY VEGT

Eye n SHRP
Eye n HOLW OPEN
Eyeball n BODY VIEW
Eyebrow n BODY VIEW
Eyeglass n BODY VIEW
Eyelash n BODY VIEW
Eyelid n BODY COVR

F

F n WRIT
F n WRIT MUSC
F n WRIT EDUC
Fable n TALK MYTH
Fabric n FABR
Fabricate v WORK
Fabricate v FALS
Fabulous j AFAR MYTH
Fabulous j GOOD
Facade n FORW
Face n BODY
Face n FORW
Face v BODY FORW
Facet n SOME
Facetious j GLAD
Facial j BODY
Facile j EASY
Facilitate v AID
Facility n AID
Facility n EASY
Facing v FORW
Facing v BODY FORW
Facsimile n SIML
Fact n TRUE
Faction n OPPO GRUP
Factitious j FALS
Factor n SOME
Factor n NUMR
Factor n MART AID
Factored v NUMR
Factoring v NUMR
Factory n HOME WORK
Faculty n POWR
Faculty n LEAD EDUC
Fad n NEW MOTV
Fade v BLUR COLR
Fade v BLUR
Fade v WEAK
Fading v BLUR COLR
Fading v BLUR
Fading v WEAK
Faeces n DIRT SOMA
Fag v WEAK
Fag n FOOD HEAT
Fag n SIML SEX
Fagged v WEAK
Fahrenheit j HEAT MSMT
Fail v WEAK
Faint v BLUR REST
Faint j WEAK PANG
Faint j BLUR
Fainted v BLUR REST
Fainting v BLUR REST
Fair j GOOD

Fair n PLAY
Fair j COLR
Fairhaired j COLR BODY
Fairies n MYTH
Fairies n SIML SEX
Fairly d EMPH
Fairly d GOOD
Fairs n PLAY
Fairy n MYTH
Fairy n SIML SEX
Fairyland n PLAC MYTH
Faith n AGRE
Faith n AGRE HOLY
Faithless j AGGR
Fake n FALS
Faking v FALS
Fakir n HOLY MYTH
Falcon n ANML UP
Falderol n FOOL
Fall n DOWN GO
Fall n TIME
Fall n BAD DOWN
Fall n DOWN FLOW
Fall v DAMG DOWN
Fall v HAVE
Fall v AGRE
Fallacy n FALS
Fallible j WEAK
Falling v DOWN GO
Falling v DAMG DOWN
Falling v HAVE
Falling v AGRE
Fallow j ERTH REST
False j FALS
Falsetto n FALS MUSC
Falter v VARY WEAK
Fame n POWR
Familiar j NEAR
Family n GRUP KIN
Famine n FOOD LACK
Famine n LACK
Famish v FOOD LACK
Fan n VAPR MECH
Fan v LARG
Fan v VARY COLD
Fan n FOND MOTV
Fan v VARY WEAK
Fanatic n FOOL MOTV
Fancied v IDEA MYTH
Fancied v FOND
Fancier j GOOD
Fancier n FOND
Fancies v IDEA MYTH
Fancies v FOND

Fanciest j GOOD
Fanciful j IDEA MYTH
Fancy j GOOD
Fancy n IDEA MYTH
Fancy n FOND
Fanfare n POWR MUSC
Fang n ANML BODY
Fanned v LARG
Fanned v VARY COLD
Fanned v VARY WEAK
Fantasied v IDEA MYTH
Fantastic j IDEA MYTH
Fantastic j GOOD
Fantasy v IDEA MYTH
Far d AFAR
Farad n ION MSMT
Faraway j AFAR
Farce n FOOL
Fare n MONY VEHC
Fare n FOOD
Fare v GO
Fared v GO
Fares n MONY VEHC
Fares v GO
Farewell n GO SEP
Farfetched j FOOL AFAR
Farina n FOOD VEGT
Faring v GO
Farm n ERTH WORK
Farmhouse n ERTH HOME
Farmyard n HOME PLAC
Farreaching j LARG AFAR
Farsighted j AFAR VIEW
Fart n VAPR SOMA
Farther d AFAR
Farthing n MONY
Fascinate v FOND
Fascism n LEAD GRUP
Fashion n EVNT
Fashion n GARB
Fashion n NEW
Fashion v FORM WORK
Fashionable j NEW
Fashioning v FORM WORK
Fast d QUIK
Fast d BLOK
Fast n FOOD LACK
Fasted v FOOD LACK
Fasten v BLOK
Faster j QUIK
Fastest j QUIK
Fastidious j TRIV MOTV
Fasting v FOOD LACK
Fat j LARG BODY

Fat j LARG
Fat n MTRL
Fatal j DAMG DEAD
Fate n END
Fathead n FOOL BODY
Father n MALE KIN
Father n LEAD MALE
Father n LEAD HOLY
Fatherinlaw n MALE KIN
Fatherinlaw n LEAD MALE
Fatherland n LEAD PLAC
Fatherless j LEAD LACK
Fatherless j KIN LACK
Fathom n FLOW MSMT
Fathom v OPEN IDEA
Fatigue v WEAK
Fatigues n GARB WORK
Fatigues v WEAK
Fatuous j FOOL
Faucet n BLOK MECH
Fault n FALS
Fault n BAD FALS
Fault n ERTH SEP
Faultfinding n AGGR FALS
Faultless j POWR GOOD
Fauna n ANML
Fauxpas n FALS
Favor n FOND AID
Favoring v FOND AID
Favorite j FOND
Fawn n ANML YNG
Fawn n COLR
Fawn v FOND SUB
Fawned v FOND SUB
Fawning v FOND SUB
Faze v PANG
Fear v PANG
Fearless j POWR
Feasibility n AID
Feast n FOOD
Feat n POWR
Feather n ANML BODY
Feather n POWR
Feather v REST
Featherbed v TRIV WORK
Featherbrain n FOOL
Feathercut n BODY SHRP
Featheredge n SHRP
Featherless j BODY LACK
Featherweight n EASY MSMT
Feature n BODY
Feature n CRUX VIEW
Featuring v CRUX VIEW
Febrile j HEAT SICK
February n TIME
Feces n DIRT SOMA
Fecund j MUCH BGIN
Fed v FOOD
Fed v FOOD SOMA
Fed v AID
Fed v PANG
Federal j GRUP LAW
Federation n GRUP JOIN
Fedora n GARB
Fee n MONY

Feeble j WEAK
Feed n FOOD
Feed v FOOD SOMA
Feed v AID
Feedback n BACK AID
Feel v BODY JOIN
Feel v MOTV
Feet n BODY
Feet n MSMT
Feign v FALS
Felicitate v FOND GLAD
Felicitous j AGRE GLAD
Feline j ANML
Fell v DOWN GO
Fell v DAMG DOWN
Fell v GARB JOIN
Fell v HAVE
Fell v AGRE
Fellow n MALE
Fellow n SIML
Fellow n GRUP JOIN
Fellowship n FOND
Fellowship n GRUP
Felony n CRIM
Felt v BODY JOIN
Felt v MOTV
Felt n FABR
Female n LADY
Feminine j LADY
Femur n SOMA
Fence n BLOK
Fence v PLAY SHRP
Fence n CRIM
Fend v BLOK AID
Fender n BLOK AID
Fenestra n SOMA HOLW
Fenestrate j HOLW OPEN
Ferment n VARY
Ferment n VARY PANG
Fern n VEGT
Ferocity n DAMG
Ferret n ANML
Ferret v ANML OPEN
Ferried v GO VEHC
Ferries n FLOW VEHC
Ferries v GO VEHC
Ferro f ERTH MTRL
Ferrule n HOLW COVR
Ferry n FLOW VEHC
Ferry v GO VEHC
Fertilize v BGIN AID
Fervent j MOTV
Fervor n MOTV
Fester v DIRT SICK
Festival n GLAD PLAY
Festive j GLAD PLAY
Festoon v PLAY FORM
Fetal j BGIN SOMA
Fetch v GO
Fetching v GO
Fetching j FOND
Fetid j DIRT SOMA
Fetish n FOND MYTH
Fetlock n ANML BODY
Fetter v BLOK

Fetus n BGIN SOMA
Feud n DAMG
Feudal j LEAD SUB
Fever n HEAT SICK
Few j LITL SOME
Fez n GARB
Fiance n MALE KIN
Fiancee n LADY KIN
Fiasco n WEAK
Fiat n LEAD TALK
Fib n FALS
Fiber n FABR
Fibrous j FABR
Fickle j VARY
Fiction n FALS MYTH
Fictitious j FALS MYTH
Fiddle v MUSC
Fiddle v PLAY
Fiddlesticks i FOOL EMPH
Fidelity n AGRE
Fidelity n SIML SHRP
Fidget v PANG
Fiduciary n MONY
Fiduciary n AID
Fie i BAD
Field n ERTH
Field n GRUP
Field n ERTH PLAY
Field n PLAC
Fielder n ERTH PLAY
Fielding v ERTH PLAY
Fiend n BAD DAMG
Fiend n MOTV
Fierce j DAMG
Fierier j HEAT
Fiery j HEAT
Fiesta n PLAY
Fife n MUSC
Fifteen n NUMR
Fifth n NUMR
Fifth n NUMR MUSC
Fifth n SIP NUMR
Fifthcolumn n DAMG COVR
Fifthwheel n TRIV
Fifty n NUMR
Fig n FOOD VEGT
Fig n TRIV VEGT
Fight n DAMG
Figment n MYTH
Figurative j SIML
Figure n FORM
Figure n NUMR
Figure n SIML
Figure v IDEA
Figure v CRUX
Figured v NUMR
Figured v IDEA
Figured v CRUX
Figurehead n LEAD FALS
Figurehead n BODY FLOW
Figurine n FORM
Figuring v NUMR
Figuring v IDEA
Figuring v CRUX
Filament n LITL FORM

Filbert n FOOD VEGT
Filch v CRIM
File v FORW GO
File v WORK
File v FORW WRIT
Filet n ANML FOOD
Filet n FORM FABR
Filial j KIN YNG
Filibuster v BLOK TALK
Filigree n FORM
Filing v FORW GO
Filing v WORK
Filing v FORW WRIT
Filings n MTRL WORK
Fill n BULG
Filled v BULG
Fillet n ANML FOOD
Fillet n FORM FABR
Fillies n ANML
Filling v BULG
Fillip v QUIK BODY
Fillip v MOTV
Filly n ANML YNG
Film n VIEW
Film n PLAY VIEW
Film n COVR
Film n BLUR
Filter v SEP
Filth n DIRT
Filtrate n SEP
Fin n ANML BODY
Fin n FORM
Fin n MONY NUMR
Finagle v FALS
Final j END
Finance v MART MONY
Finch n ANML UP
Find v OPEN
Fine j GOOD
Fine j LITL
Fine n AGGR MONY
Fined v AGGR MONY
Finer j GOOD
Finer j LITL
Finery n GARB GOOD
Fines v AGGR MONY
Finesse n POWR
Finest j GOOD
Finest j LITL
Finger n BODY
Finger n BODY MSMT
Finger v BODY JOIN
Fingernail n BODY SHRP
Fingerprint n BODY WRIT
Finicky j TRIV MOTV
Fining n AGGR MONY
Finish n END
Finish n POWR END
Finish n EASY END
Finite j END
Fiord n FLOW
Fir n VEGT

Fir n MTRL VEGT
Fire n HEAT VIEW
Fire v DAMG HEAT
Fire v HEAT MOTV
Fire v SEP
Firearm n DAMG MECH
Fireball n HEAT VIEW
Fireboat n HEAT FLOW
Firebox n HOLW HEAT
Firebrand n HEAT MTRL
Firebrand n DAMG
Firebreak n BLOK HEAT
Firebrick n HEAT MTRL
Firebug n CRIM HEAT
Firecracker n HEAR HEAT
Fired v DAMG HEAT
Fired v HEAT MOTV
Fired v HEAT VIEW
Fired v SEP
Firefly n BUG UP
Firelight n HEAT VIEW
Fireman n HEAT MALE
Fireplace n HOLW HEAT
Fireplug n HEAT FLOW
Firepower n DAMG POWR
Fireproof j AID HEAT
Fires n HEAT VIEW
Fires v DAMG HEAT
Fires v HEAT MOTV
Fires v SEP
Fireside j HEAT NEAR
Firetrap n BLOK HEAT
Firewood n HEAT VEGT
Fireworks n HEAT VIEW
Firing v DAMG HEAT
Firing v HEAT MOTV
Firing v HEAT VIEW
Firing v SEP
Firm j POWR
Firm j EVER
Firm n MART
Firmament n ASTR UP
First j FORW NUMR
Firstborn j BGIN FORW
Firstborn n BGIN KIN
Firstclass j POWR FORW
Firsthand d BGIN FORW
Firstrate j POWR FORW
Fiscal j MART MONY
Fish n ANML FLOW
Fish n FOOD FLOW
Fished v ANML FLOW
Fisherman n MALE FLOW
Fishier j ANML FALS
Fishmonger n MART FOOD
Fishwife n AGGR LADY
Fishy j ANML FLOW
Fishy j ANML FALS
Fission n SEP
Fissure n HOLW SEP
Fist n DAMG BODY
Fit v SIML

Fit j POWR
Fit n PANG
Fit n VARY
Fitful j VARY
Fitful j VARY PANG
Five n NUMR
Fiver n MONY NUMR
Fix v AID
Fix v SHRP
Fix v JOIN
Fix v FALS
Fix v AGGR
Fix v EVER
Fixative n EVER
Fixture n FURN
Fixture n EVER
Fizz n SIP HEAR
Fizz n HEAR
Fizzle n WEAK
Fizzle n HEAR
Fjord n FLOW
Flabbergast v PANG
Flabbier j EASY WEAK
Flabby j EASY WEAK
Flaccid j EASY WEAK
Flag n VIEW
Flag n ERTH FORM
Flag v WEAK
Flagellate v DAMG
Flagon n HOLW
Flagrant j BAD OPEN
Flags n VIEW
Flags n ERTH FORM
Flags v WEAK
Flagship n LEAD FLOW
Flagstaff n VIEW FORM
Flagstone n ERTH FORM
Flail v DAMG
Flair n POWR
Flak n DAMG
Flake n SOME
Flaking v SOME
Flaky j SOME
Flamboyant j POWR VIEW
Flame n HEAT VIEW
Flame n HEAT SEX
Flame n COLR HEAT
Flamed v HEAT VIEW
Flamenco n GO MUSC
Flameproof j AID HEAT
Flaming v HEAT VIEW
Flamingo n ANML UP
Flank n ANML BODY
Flank n PLAC
Flank v VARY GO
Flank v NEAR
Flanked v VARY GO
Flanking v VARY GO
Flannel n FABR
Flap n VARY HEAR
Flap n VARY FORM
Flapped v VARY HEAR

Parts of speech: a article; b preposition; c conjunction; d adverb; f prefix; i interjection;
j adjective; n noun; p pronoun; r phrase; v verb.

Flapped v VARY FORM
Flapper n POWR LADY
Flapper n VARY HEAR
Flare v HEAT VIEW
Flare v LARG
Flare v AGGR
Flash v QUIK VIEW
Flashier j POWR VIEW
Flashlight n VIEW
Flashy j POWR VIEW
Flask n HOLW
Flat j FORM
Flat j MUSC
Flat j WEAK
Flat j COLR
Flat j EMPH
Flat n HOME
Flat n ERTH
Flat n WEAK VEHC
Flatboat n FLOW VEHC
Flatcar n FORM VEHC
Flatfish n ANML FLOW
Flatfish n FOOD FLOW
Flatfoot n BODY FORM
Flatfoot n BODY LAW
Flatfooted j EMPH
Flatfooted j BODY FORM
Flatiron n CLEN EASY
Flatly d EMPH
Flats n HOME
Flats n WEAK VEHC
Flats n MUSC
Flats n ERTH
Flatten v FORM
Flatten v MUSC
Flatten v POWR WEAK
Flatter v FOND FALS
Flatus n VAPR SOMA
Flaunt v POWR VIEW
Flavor n FOOD SOMA
Flaw n FALS WEAK
Flawless j POWR GOOD
Flea n BUG
Fleabitten j BUG DIRT
Fleabitten j BUG COLR
Fleck n DIRT SOME
Fleck n SOME
Flection n VARY
Fled v QUIK GO
Fledge v POWR AID
Fledgling n WEAK YNG
Flee v QUIK GO
Fleece n ANML FABR
Fleece v ANML SHRP
Fleece v CRIM
Fleet n GRUP VEHC
Fleet j QUIK
Fleeting j VARY QUIK
Flesh n BODY
Flesh n COLR BODY
Flesh v MOTV
Flew v GO UP
Flew v QUIK GO
Flex v VARY
Flexible j VARY EASY

Flexing v VARY
Flick n VARY QUIK
Flicked v VARY QUIK
Flicker n PLAY VIEW
Flicker n VARY VIEW
Flicker n VARY QUIK
Flicker n ANML UP
Flier n GO UP
Flies n BUG UP
Flies v GO UP
Flies v QUIK GO
Flies n GARB
Flight n GO SEP
Flightier j FOOL VARY
Flighty j FOOL VARY
Flimflam v CRIM FALS
Flimsy j WEAK
Flinch v PANG
Fling n GO MUSC
Fling n QUIK GO
Fling n MOTV
Flint n ERTH MTRL
Flip n VARY QUIK
Flip j GLAD TRIV
Flip n SIP VEGT
Flippancy n GLAD TRIV
Flipped v VARY QUIK
Flipper n ANML BODY
Flipping v VARY QUIK
Flips v VARY QUIK
Flirt v SEX TRIV
Flirt v TRIV
Flit v QUIK GO
Flivver n VEHC
Float v GO FLOW
Float v GO UP
Float n PLAY VEHC
Floated v GO FLOW
Floated v GO UP
Floating v GO FLOW
Floating v GO UP
Flock n GRUP
Flock n ANML GRUP
Flock v GO GRUP
Flocked v GO GRUP
Flocking v GO GRUP
Floe n COLD FLOW
Flog v DAMG
Flood n BULG FLOW
Floodgate n BLOK FLOW
Floodlight n VIEW
Floor n DOWN FORM
Floor n DOWN TALK
Floor v DAMG DOWN
Flop v VARY HEAR
Flop v WEAK
Flop v DOWN
Flophouse n MART HOME
Floral j VEGT
Florid j GOOD TRIV
Florid j COLR
Florist n VEGT
Floss n FABR
Flotilla n GRUP FLOW
Flotsam n FLOW TRIV

Flounce n GARB FORM
Flounce v VARY GO
Flounder n ANML FLOW
Flounder n FOOD FLOW
Flounder v VARY WEAK
Floundered v VARY WEAK
Floundering v VARY WEAK
Flour n FOOD VEGT
Flourish n GOOD
Flourish v LARG POWR
Flourished v LARG POWR
Flourishing v LARG POWR
Flout v AGGR
Flow v FLOW
Flow v EASY
Flowed v FLOW
Flowed v EASY
Flower n VEGT
Flower n POWR VEGT
Flowerpot n HOLW VEGT
Flowery j GOOD TRIV
Flowery j VEGT
Flown v GO UP
Flown v QUIK GO
Flu n SICK
Fluctuate v VARY
Flue n HOLW
Fluent j EASY
Fluent j EASY TALK
Fluff n EASY MTRL
Fluff n WEAK
Fluffy j EASY MTRL
Fluid n FLOW
Fluid j EASY
Fluke n ANML FLOW
Fluke n FOOD FLOW
Fluke n AFAR AID
Fluke n BLOK SHRP
Flung v QUIK GO
Flunk v WEAK
Flunkies n SUB
Flunky n SUB
Fluorescent j VIEW
Flurry n QUIK
Flurry n PANG
Flush v GO FLOW
Flush j SIML
Flush j BULG HAVE
Flush j SHRP
Flush n COLR BODY
Flush n SIML PLAY
Flushed v GO FLOW
Flushed v COLR BODY
Flushing v GO FLOW
Flushing v COLR BODY
Fluster v PANG
Flute n MUSC
Flute n HOLW FORM
Flutter n VARY HEAR
Flutter n VARY QUIK
Flux n FLOW
Fly n BUG UP
Fly v GO UP
Fly n GARB
Fly n VEHC

Fly v QUIK GO
Flyer n GO UP
Flyer n WRIT
Flyer n MOTV
Flyer n QUIK VEHC
Flyleaf n WRIT
Flywheel n MECH
Foal n ANML YNG
Foam n FLOW
Fob n GARB JOIN
Fob n GARB HOLW
Focus n SHRP
Fodder n FOOD
Foe n AGGR
Foetus n BGIN SOMA
Fog n WEA BLUR
Fog n VAPR BLUR
Fogies n PAST
Fogy n PAST
Foible n WEAK
Foil v BLOK WEAK
Foil n MTRL
Foil n PLAY SHRP
Foiled v BLOK WEAK
Foiling v BLOK WEAK
Foist v FALS
Fold n VARY FORM
Fold n ANML GRUP
Fold n GRUP
Fold n ANML HOME
Fold v VARY WEAK
Folded v VARY
Folded v VARY WEAK
Folder n HOLW WRIT
Folder n HOLW
Folder n VARY FORM
Folding v VARY
Folding v VARY WEAK
Foliage n BODY VEGT
Folio n WRIT
Folk j GRUP
Folklore n GRUP MYTH
Folks n GRUP KIN
Folks n GRUP
Follicle n BODY HOLW
Follicle n VEGT
Follow v BACK GO
Follow v AGRE SUB
Folly n FOOL
Foment v BGIN AGGR
Fond j FOND
Fondle v FOND JOIN
Fondle v EASY JOIN
Font n HOLW FLOW
Font n WRIT
Food n FOOD
Fool n FOOL
Fool v FALS
Foolhardy j FOOL POWR
Foolproof j POWR
Foot n BODY
Foot n MSMT
Foot n DOWN BODY
Foot v BODY AID
Foot v BODY GO

Football n BODY PLAY
Foothill n DOWN BULG
Foothold n BODY AID
Footing n BODY AID
Footing v BODY GO
Footlight n DOWN VIEW
Footloose j GO OPEN
Footman n AID MALE
Footnote n DOWN WRIT
Footpath n BODY PATH
Footprint n BODY WRIT
Foots v BODY AID
Foots v BODY GO
Footsore j BODY PANG
Footstep n BODY GO
Footstool n BODY REST
Fop n FOOL GARB
For b NSCR
For b SIML
For b AGRE MOTV
Forage v FOOD OPEN
Foray v DAMG
Forbade v BLOK
Forbear v BLOK LACK
Forbid v BLOK
Forbidding j AGGR
Forbidding v BLOK
Force n POWR
Force n POWR GRUP
Forced v POWR
Forceps n MECH
Forcible j POWR
Ford v GO FLOW
Fore n FORW
Forearm n BODY
Forearm v DAMG FORW
Forearmed v DAMG FORW
Forearming v DAMG FORW
Forebear n PAST KIN
Forebode v BAD FORW
Forecast n FORW TALK
Forecastle n HOME FLOW
Foreclose v BLOK
Forefather n PAST KIN
Forefinger n BODY
Forefront n FORW
Forego v LACK
Forego v FORW GO
Foregone j FORW SHRP
Foreground n ERTH FORW
Forehead n BODY
Foreign j AFAR
Foreknowledge n FORW IDEA
Foreman n LEAD WORK
Foremost j POWR FORW
Foremost j FORW EMPH
Forename n FORW TALK
Forenoon n TIME
Forensic j LAW
Forerunner n FORW GO
Foresee v FORW VIEW
Foreshadow v BLUR FORW
Foresight n FORW VIEW
Forest n VEGT
Forestall v BLOK FORW

Foretaste n FORW SOMA
Foretell v FORW TALK
Forethought n FORW IDEA
Foretold v FORW TALK
Forever d EVER
Forewarn v AGGR FORW
Foreword n FORW TALK
Forfeit v LACK
Forge v FALS WRIT
Forge v HEAT WORK
Forge v GO
Forgery n FALS WRIT
Forgery n FALS
Forget v BLUR IDEA
Forgive v AGRE
Fork n FOOD FURN
Fork n WORK
Fork n MUSC
Fork n SEP
Forlorn j PANG
Form n FORM
Form n WRIT FORM
Form n GRUP EDUC
Formal j EVER FORM
Format n FORM
Formation n FORM
Formative j FORM
Formed v FORM
Former j PAST
Former j FORW
Formerly d PAST
Formidable j POWR
Forming v FORM
Formless j BLUR FORM
Formulate v IDEA FORM
Fornicate v BAD SEX
Foresake v SEP
Forswear v AGGR LACK
Forsythia n VEGT
Fort n POWR HOME
Forte j EMPH MUSC
Forte n POWR
Forth d FORW
Forthcoming j FORW TIME
Forthright j FORW SHRP
Forthwith d QUIK
Forties n NUMR
Fortify v POWR AID
Fortissimo j EMPH MUSC
Fortitude n POWR
Fortnight n TIME
Fortress n POWR HOME
Fortuitous j AFAR EVNT
Fortunate j AID
Fortune n AID
Fortune n END AID
Fortune n MUCH MONY
Forty n NUMR
Forum n TALK OPEN
Forward d FORW
Forward v FORW GO
Forward j POWR FORW
Forward n FORW PLAY
Forward v FORW AID
Forwarded v FORW GO

Forwarded v FORW AID
Forwarding v FORW GO
Forewarding v FORW AID
Forwards v FORW GO
Forwards n FORW PLAY
Forwards v FORW AID
Fossil n PAST
Foster v AID
Fought v DAMG
Foul n FALS PLAY
Foul j DIRT
Foul j BAD
Found v OPEN
Found v BGIN
Foundation n CRUX FORM
Foundation n GRUP
Founded v BGIN
Founded j CRUX
Founder n BGIN
Founder v WEAK
Foundered v WEAK
Foundering v WEAK
Foundling n SEP YNG
Foundry n HEAT WORK
Founds v BGIN
Founds v CRUX FORM
Fountain n HOLW FLOW
Fountain n FLOW
Fountainhead n BGIN FLOW
Four n NUMR
Fourscore j NUMR
Foursome n GRUP NUMR
Fourteen n NUMR
Fourth n NUMR
Fourth n NUMR MUSC
Fowl n ANML UP
Fox n ANML
Fox n ANML FABR
Fox v ANML FALS
Foxed v ANML FALS
Foxglove n VEGT
Foxhole n ERTH HOME
Foxhound n ANML
Foxing v ANML FALS
Foxtrot n GO MUSC
Foyer n HOME
Fracas n DAMG
Fraction n NUMR SOME
Fractious j AGGR
Fracture v DAMG SEP
Fragile j WEAK
Fragment n SOME
Fragrance n VAPR SOMA
Frail j WEAK
Frame n VIEW FORM
Frame n FORM
Frame n PLAY SOME
Frame v FALS
Frameup n CRIM FALS
Framework n FORM
Franc n MONY
Franchise n MART
Franchise n LAW MOTV
Frank j OPEN
Frank n GO OPEN

Frankfurter n ANML FOOD
Frantic j PANG
Fraternal j MALE KIN
Fraternity n MALE KIN
Fraternize v FOND JOIN
Fratricide n DEAD KIN
Frau n LADY KIN
Fraud n CRIM FALS
Fraught j BULG
Fray n DAMG
Fray v TRIV
Frazzle n TRIV
Frazzle n PANG
Freak n AFAR
Freckle n COLR BODY
Free v OPEN
Freedom n OPEN
Freeze v COLD
Freeze v COLD PANG
Freezer n COLD HOLW
Freight n MONY VEHC
Freight n MART VEHC
Freighter n FLOW VEHC
Frenzy n PANG
Frequency n NUMR
Frequency n MUCH
Frequent j MUCH
Frequent v EVER
Frequented v EVER
Frequenting v EVER
Fresco n COLR
Fresh j NEW
Fresh j AGGR
Freshen v NEW
Freshman n EDUC SUB
Fret n FORM
Fret n MUSC
Fret v AGGR PANG
Fretful j PANG
Freudian j MEDC IDEA
Friar n MALE HOLY
Fricasse n ANML FOOD
Friction n OPPO JOIN
Friday n TIME
Fried v FOOD HEAT
Fried v HEAT
Friend n FOND
Fries f FOOD HEAT
Fries v HEAT
Frieze n FORM
Frigate n FLOW VEHC
Fright n PANG
Frigid j COLD
Frigid j COLD SEX
Frill n FORM TRIV
Fringe n END
Frisk v OPEN
Frisk v GLAD
Friskier j GLAD
Frisky j GLAD
Fritter n FOOD VEGT
Fritter v TRIV
Frivolous j GLAD TRIV
Frizz v VARY
Frizz v HEAR HEAT

Frizzle v HEAR HEAT
Frizzle v VARY
Fro d SEP
Frock n GARB HOLY
Frock n GARB
Frog n ANML
Frog n ANML HEAR
Frog n GARB
Frog n JOIN
Frolic v GLAD PLAY
From b NSCR
From b SEP
Frond n BODY VEGT
Front j FORW
Front n FALS FORW
Front n DAMG FORW
Frontier n END FORW
Frontiersman n FORW MALE
Fronting v FORW
Frontispiece n FORW VIEW
Frosh n EDUC SUB
Frost n COLD FLOW
Frost n COLD FOOD
Frosty j COLD FLOW
Frosty j COLD AGGR
Froth v FLOW
Froth v SOMA FLOW
Frown n AGGR
Frowzy j DIRT
Froze v COLD
Froze v COLD PANG
Fructify v BGIN AID
Frugal j LITL HAVE
Fruit n FOOD VEGT
Fruit n END VEGT
Fruit n SEX VEGT
Fruited j FOOD VEGT
Fruiter n VEHC VEGT
Fruiter n FOOD VEGT
Fruitful j FOOD VEGT
Fruitful j AID VEGT
Fruition n END AID
Fruitless j WEAK VEGT
Frustrate v BLOK AGGR
Fry v FOOD HEAT
Fry v HEAT
Fry n TRIV YNG
Fry n FLOW YNG
Fryer n ANML FOOD
Frying v FOOD HEAT
Frying v HEAT
Fuchsia n VEGT
Fuchsia n COLR
Fudge n FOOD
Fudge n FOOL
Fudge v FALS
Fudged v FALS
Fudging v FALS
Fuel n HEAT MTRL
Fugitive n GO SEP
Fugue n MUSC
Fulcrum n AID
Fulfill v AID
Full j BULG
Full j WHOL BULG

Fullfledged j WHOL POWR
Fullgrown j WHOL LARG
Fulllength j WHOL LARG
Fulltime j WHOL TIME
Fulsome j FALS PANG
Fumble v WEAK
Fume n VAPR DIRT
Fume v AGGR PANG
Fumigate v CLEN
Fuming v AGGR PANG
Fun n GLAD
Function n EVNT
Function n WORK
Function n GRUP PLAY
Functional j WORK
Functioned v EVNT
Functioned v WORK
Functioning v EVNT
Functioning v WORK
Fund n MONY
Fund n HAVE
Fundamental n CRUX
Funeral n DEAD
Funereal j DEAD PANG
Fungicide n MEDC SICK
Fungus j SICK VEGT
Fungus n VEGT

Funk n PANG
Funnel n HOLW
Funnier j FOOL GLAD
Funnier j GLAD
Funnies n GLAD VIEW
Funniest j FOOL GLAD
Funniest j GLAD
Funny j FOOL GLAD
Funny j GLAD
Fur n ANML FABR
Furious j AGGR
Furl v VARY
Furlong n MSMT
Furlough n PLAY
Furnace n HOLW HEAT
Furnish v AID
Furnish v FURN
Furniture n FURN
Furor n PANG
Furrier n GARB MART
Furring n MTRL FORM
Furrow v HOLW
Furry j ANML BODY
Further d MUCH
Further d AFAR
Further v AID
Furthered v AID

Furthering v AID
Furthermore d MUCH
Furthers v AID
Furtive j COVR
Fury n AGGR
Fuse n HEAT
Fuse v HEAT FLOW
Fuse v JOIN
Fused v HEAT FLOW
Fused v JOIN
Fuselage n FORM VEHC
Fusible j HEAT FLOW
Fusillade n DAMG
Fusing v HEAT FLOW
Fusing v JOIN
Fusion n JOIN
Fuss n PANG
Futile j WEAK TRIV
Future n FORW TIME
Fuzz n EASY MTRL
Fuzz n LAW
Fuzzier j BLUR
Fuzzier j EASY MTRL
Fuzzy j BLUR
Fuzzy j EASY MTRL

G

G n WRIT
G n WRIT MUSC
Gab n TALK
Gabardine n FABR
Gabbed v TALK
Gabble v ANML TALK
Gabby j TALK
Gaberdine n GARB
Gable n FORM UP
Gad v GO
Gad v AGGR SHRP
Gadabout n GO
Gadfly n BUG AGGR
Gadget n MECH
Gaff n BLOK SHRP
Gaff n AGGR
Gaffed v BLOK SHRP
Gaffed v AGGR
Gaffer n MALE PAST
Gag n GLAD FALS
Gag n BLOK TALK
Gag v SOMA PANG
Gagged v BLOK TALK
Gagged v SOMA PANG
Gagging v BLOK TALK
Gagging v SOMA PANG
Gaiety n GLAD
Gain v LARG HAVE
Gain v HAVE
Gained v LARG HAVE
Gained v HAVE
Gainer n LARG HAVE
Gainer n VARY DOWN
Gainful j HAVE
Gains v LARG HAVE

Gains v HAVE
Gainsay v OPPO TALK
Gait n GO
Gala j GLAD PLAY
Galactic j ASTR GRUP
Galactose n MTRL
Galaxy n ASTR GRUP
Gale n WEA DAMG
Gall n SOMA
Gall n AGGR POWR
Gall n SICK
Gall v AGGR PANG
Gallant j POWR
Galled v AGGR PANG
Galleon n FLOW VEHC
Gallery n HOME
Galley n FOOD HOME
Galley n FLOW VEHC
Galley n WRIT
Galling v AGGR PANG
Gallivant v GO
Gallon n MSMT
Gallop n QUIK GO
Gallow n DEAD FORM
Gallow n GARB
Galls v AGGR PANG
Gallstone n SOMA SICK
Galore j MUCH
Galosh n GARB
Galvanic j ION
Galvanize v MTRL
Galvanize v MOTV
Galvanometer n ION MSMT
Gambit n MOTV
Gambit n PLAY

Gamble v MONY MOTV
Gambol v GLAD GO
Game n PLAY
Game n ANML FOOD
Game j SICK WEAK
Game j POWR MOTV
Gamekeeper n ANML AID
Gamester n MONY MOTV
Gamete n BGIN SOMA
Gamma n WRIT
Gammaglobulin n MEDC SOMA
Gamut n FORW
Gander n ANML UP
Gang n GRUP
Gangling j LARG WEAK
Gangplank n FLOW PATH
Gangrene n SICK
Gangster n CRIM
Gangway n PATH
Gantlet n DAMG
Gantlet n JOIN PATH
Gantry n FORM
Gap n SEP LACK
Gape v BODY OPEN
Gape v HOLW OPEN
Gape v VIEW
Gaping v BODY OPEN
Gaping v HOLW OPEN
Gaping v VIEW
Garage n HOME VEHC
Garb n GARB
Garbage n DIRT
Garble v BLUR FALS
Garden n ERTH VEGT
Gardenia n VEGT

Gargle v CLEN FLOW
Gargoyle n FOOL FORM
Garish j VIEW TRIV
Garland n FORM VEGT
Garlic n FOOD VEGT
Garment n GARB
Garner v HAVE
Garnet n ERTH MTRL
Garnet n COLR
Garnish v FOOD GOOD
Garnish v BLOK LAW
Garnish v GOOD
Garret n HOME UP
Garrison n DAMG HOME
Garrison n DAMG GRUP
Garrulous j TALK TRIV
Garter n GARB
Gas n VAPR
Gas n MTRL FLOW
Gas n VAPR DAMG
Gas v VAPR TALK
Gash n DAMG SHRP
Gash n SHRP
Gasket n BLOK MECH
Gasoline n MTRL FLOW
Gasp v SOMA HEAR
Gastric j SOMA HOLW
Gastronomy n FOOD SOMA
Gat n DAMG MECH
Gate n BLOK OPEN
Gatepost n OPEN FORM
Gateway n OPEN PATH
Gather v HAVE
Gather v JOIN
Gather v IDEA
Gather v GRUP JOIN
Gauche j WEAK
Gaudy j VIEW TRIV
Gauge v MSMT
Gaunt j PANG
Gauntlet n GARB DAMG
Gauze n FABR
Gave v AID
Gave v WEAK
Gave v VARY
Gave v NSCR
Gavel n LEAD HEAR
Gavotte n GO MUSC
Gawk n FOOL WEAK
Gawk v FOOL VIEW
Gawkier j FOOL WEAK
Gawky j FOOL WEAK
Gay j GLAD
Gay j SIML SEX
Gaze v VIEW
Gazelle n ANML
Gazette n WRIT
Gear n AID
Gear n MECH
Gee i NSCR
Geese n ANML UP
Geezer n FOOL PAST

Geisha n LADY PLAY
Gelatine n MTRL
Gelatine n FOOD
Gelding n SEX LACK
Gem n GOOD MTRL
Gemini n ASTR MYTH
Gendarme n LAW
Gender n SEX
Gene n BGIN SOMA
Genealogy n PAST KIN
General n WHOL
General n LEAD
Generate v BGIN
Generating v BGIN
Generation n BGIN GRUP
Generation n BGIN
Generator n MECH ION
Generator n BGIN
Generic j WHOL
Generosity n GOOD AID
Generous j GOOD AID
Genes n BGIN SOMA
Genesis n BGIN
Genetic j BGIN
Genial j GLAD
Genie n POWR MYTH
Genital j BODY SEX
Genitive j TALK FORM
Genius n POWR IDEA
Genocide n DEAD GRUP
Genre n GRUP
Gent n MALE
Genteel j GOOD
Gentian n VEGT
Gentile n GRUP HOLY
Gentility n GOOD
Gentle j GOOD
Gentle j EASY
Gentleman n GOOD MALE
Gentry n LEAD GRUP
Genuflect v VARY BODY
Genuine j TRUE
Genus n GRUP
Geocentric j ERTH SHRP
Geochemist n ERTH IDEA
Geography n ERTH IDEA
Geology n ERTH IDEA
Geometry n NUMR FORM
Geophysics n ERTH IDEA
Geranium n VEGT
Geriatric j MEDC PAST
Germ n BGIN
Germ n BUG SICK
Germ n BGIN VEGT
Germ n BGIN SOMA
Germaine j SIML CRUX
Germicide n MEDC
Germinate v BGIN LARG
Gerrymander v FALS LAW
Gerund n TALK FORM
Gestate v BGIN
Gesticulate v BODY EVNT

Gesture n BODY EVNT
Get v HAVE
Get v GO
Get v DAMG
Get v NSCR
Geyser n HEAT FLOW
Ghastly j PANG
Gherkin n FOOD VEGT
Ghetto n BLOK GRUP
Ghost n MYTH
Ghoul n BAD MYTH
Giant n LARG
Gibberish n FOOL TALK
Gibbon n ANML
Gibe n AGGR TALK
Gibing v AGGR TALK
Giblet n ANML FOOD
Giddy j BLUR PANG
Gift n AID
Gift n POWR AID
Gifted j POWR AID
Gigantic j LARG
Gigantism n LARG SICK
Giggle v GLAD
Gigolo n MALE SEX
Gild v COLR MTRL
Gill n SOMA FLOW
Gill n BODY
Gill n MSMT
Gilt j COLR MTRL
Gimmick n FALS
Gin n SIP VEGT
Gin n MECH
Ginger n FOOD VEGT
Ginger n POWR
Gingerly d REST
Gingham n VEGT FABR
Gink n FOOL
Ginkgo n VEGT
Giraffe n ANML
Gird v GARB
Gird v AID
Gird v BLOK HOLW
Girded v GARB
Girded v AID
Girded v BLOK HOLW
Girder n FORM
Girdle n GARB LADY
Girdle v VARY GO
Girdle v SHRP
Girl n LADY YNG
Girlfriend n FOND LADY
Girth n ANML GARB
Girth n HOLW MSMT
Gist n CRUX
Give v AID
Give v WEAK
Give v VARY
Give v NSCR
Gizzard n ANML SOMA
Glacier n COLD FLOW
Glad j GLAD

Parts of speech: a article; b preposition; c conjunction; d adverb; f prefix; i interjection;
j adjective; n noun; p pronoun; r phrase; v verb.

Glade n VEGT
Gladiator n DAMG
Gladiola n VEGT
Glamor n POWR GOOD
Glance n QUIK VIEW
Glance v VARY GO
Gland n SOMA
Glare n VIEW
Glare n AGGR VIEW
Glass n MTRL
Glass n HOLW MTRL
Glass n AID VIEW
Glassblower n MTRL WORK
Glasses n HOLW MTRL
Glasses n AID VIEW
Glassware n HOLW MTRL
Glassy j EASY
Glassy j BLOK PANG
Glaucoma n SICK VIEW
Glaze n COLR MTRL
Glaze n VIEW
Glaze n FOOD
Glaze n COLD FLOW
Glazier n MART VIEW
Glazing v COLR MTRL
Glazing v VIEW
Glazing v FOOD
Glazing v COLD FLOW
Gleam n VIEW
Glean v HAVE
Glee n GLAD
Glee n GRUP MUSC
Glen n ERTH HOLW
Glib j EASY
Glide v EASY GO
Glider n VEHC UP
Glider n EASY FURN
Glimmer v VIEW
Glimpse n QUIK VIEW
Glissade n EASY GO
Glissando n EASY MUSC
Glisten v VIEW
Glitter n VIEW
Gloat v GLAD
Globe n WHOL ERTH
Globe n FORM
Globule n LITL FORM
Glockenspiel n MUSC
Gloom n BLUR
Gloom n BLUR PANG
Glory n POWR GOOD
Gloss n EASY VIEW
Gloss n FALS VIEW
Gloss n WRIT IDEA
Glossary n FORW WRIT
Glossy j EASY VIEW
Glove n GARB
Glove n GARB PLAY
Glow n HEAT VIEW
Glowed v HEAT VIEW
Glower v AGGR VIEW
Glucose n MTRL
Glucose n FOOD
Glue v JOIN MTRL
Glum j PANG

Glut v FOOD BULG
Glut v BULG
Glutted v FOOD BULG
Glutted v BULG
Glutton n FOOD BULG
Glutton n ANML
Glycerin n MTRL
Gnarl n VARY VEGT
Gnarl v VARY
Gnash v AGGR
Gnat n BUG UP
Gnaw v FOOD SOMA
Gnaw v FOOD PANG
Gnome n LITL MYTH
Gnostic j HOLY
Gnu n ANML
Go v GO
Go v EVNT
Goad v POWR SHRP
Goal n END
Goal n END PLAY
Goalie n END PLAY
Goat n ANML
Goat n ANML WEAK
Goatee n BODY
Goatherd n ANML AID
Gob n SOME
Gob n FLOW
Gobble v FOOD SOMA
Gobble v ANML TALK
Goblet n SIP HOLW
Goblin n BAD MYTH
Gocart n VEHC
God n LEAD HOLY
Godchild n KIN YNG
Goddess n LADY HOLY
Godfather n MALE KIN
Godfather n LEAD MALE
Godmother n LADY KIN
Godmother n LADY AID
Godparent n LEAD KIN
Goggle v VARY VIEW
Goggles n AID VIEW
Goggles v VARY VIEW
Gold n COLR
Gold n ERTH MTRL
Gold n MTRL MONY
Golden j COLR
Golden j COLR GOOD
Goldfish n ANML FLOW
Golf n PLAY
Goliath n LARG
Gonad n SOMA SEX
Gondola n FLOW VEHC
Gone v GO
Gone v EVNT
Gong n MUSC
Gonorrhea n SICK SEX
Goo n BLUR FLOW
Good j GOOD
Good j POWR GOOD
Goodby n SEP
Goodhearted j SOMA GOOD
Goodly j LARG MUCH
Goodly j POWR GOOD

Goodness n GOOD
Goodnight n SEP TIME
Goods n MART FABR
Goof v FOOL WEAK
Goofy j FOOL
Goon n FOOL DAMG
Goon n FOOL
Goose n ANML UP
Goose n ANML FOOD
Goose n FOOL ANML
Goose v GLAD BODY
Goosed v GLAD BODY
Goosing v GLAD BODY
Gopher n ANML
Gore n DAMG SOMA
Gore v DAMG SHRP
Gorge n ERTH HOLW
Gorge n BLOK BULG
Gorge v FOOD BULG
Gorge n SOMA HOLW
Gorged v FOOD BULG
Gorgeous j GOOD
Gorging v FOOD BULG
Gorgon n BAD LADY
Gorgon n LADY MYTH
Gorier j DAMG SOMA
Gorilla n ANML
Gorilla n ANML DAMG
Gory j DAMG SOMA
Gosling n ANML YNG
Gospel n WRIT HOLY
Gossamer j EASY FABR
Gossip n TALK TRIV
Got v HAVE
Got v GO
Got v DAMG
Got v NSCR
Gothic j PAST
Gothic j WRIT
Gouache n COLR
Gouge n HOLW
Gouge v CRIM MONY
Goulash n FOOD
Gourd n BODY VEGT
Gourd n SIP HOLW
Gourmet n FOOD MOTV
Gout n SICK
Govern v LEAD
Govern v LEAD LAW
Governed v LEAD
Governed v LEAD LAW
Governess n LEAD LADY
Government n LEAD LAW
Governor n LEAD LAW
Governor n LEAD MECH
Gown n GARB
Grab v HAVE
Grace n TALK HOLY
Grace n GOOD AID
Grace n LADY MYTH
Graced v GOOD AID
Graceful j GOOD AID
Gracing v GOOD AID
Gracious j GOOD AID
Grackle n ANML UP

Gradation n FORW
Grade n VARY PATH
Grade n FORW MSMT
Grade n FORW EDUC
Gradual j REST
Graduate v POWR EDUC
Graduate v FORW MSMT
Graft n JOIN VEGT
Graft n BODY JOIN
Graft n CRIM
Graham j VEGT
Grail n HOLW HOLY
Grain n VEGT
Grain n LITL
Grain n MSMT
Grained v FORM
Graining v FORM
Gram n MSMT
Grammar n TALK FORM
Gramophone n MECH MUSC
Granary n HOLW VEGT
Grand j POWR GOOD
Grandam n LADY KIN
Grandam n LADY PAST
Grandchild n KIN YNG
Grandeur n POWR
Grandfather n MALE KIN
Grandfather n LEAD MALE
Grandiloquence n POWR TALK
Grandiose j POWR FALS
Grandma n LADY KIN
Grandma n LADY AID
Grandmother n LADY KIN
Grandmother n LADY AID
Grandpa n MALE KIN
Grandpa n LEAD MALE
Grandparent n LEAD KIN
Grandson n MALE KIN
Grandstand n POWR PLAY
Grange n ERTH HOME
Grange n ERTH GRUP
Granite n ERTH
Granny n LADY KIN
Granny n LADY PAST
Grant n AID
Granule n LITL FORM
Grape n FOOD VEGT
Grape n COLR
Grapefruit n FOOD VEGT
Grapevine n FOOD VEGT
Grapevine n TALK COVR
Graph n IDEA FORM
Graphic j VIEW SHRP
Graphic j WRIT
Graphing v IDEA FORM
Graphite n ERTH MTRL
Graphology n WRIT IDEA
Grapnel n BLOK
Grapple v DAMG JOIN
Grapple v BLOK JOIN
Grasp n HAVE
Grass n VEGT
Grasshopper n BUG
Grate n FORM

Grate v HEAR
Grate v VARY LITL
Grate v AGGR PANG
Grateful j AGRE AID
Gratify v AGRE AID
Grating n FORM
Grating v HEAR
Grating v VARY LITL
Grating v AGGR PANG
Gratis d AID
Gratitude n AGRE AID
Gratuities n AID MONY
Gratuitous j TRIV
Gratuitous j AID OPEN
Gratuity n AID MONY
Grave j CRUX PANG
Grave n DEAD HOLW
Gravel n ERTH
Graven j VIEW SHRP
Gravestone n DEAD ERTH
Graveyard n DEAD HOLW
Gravitate v GO JOIN
Gravity n GO JOIN
Gravity n CRUX PANG
Gravy n FOOD
Gravy n AID
Gray j COLR
Graze v FOOD VEGT
Graze v EASY JOIN
Grease v EASY MTRL
Greasepaint n COLR BODY
Greasier j DIRT MTRL
Greasy j DIRT MTRL
Great j LARG
Great j POWR GOOD
Greed n MOTV
Greek n BLUR TALK
Green j COLR
Green j COLR WEAK
Green n COLR VEGT
Greenback n COLR MONY
Greenery n COLR VEGT
Greenhorn n WEAK
Greenhouse n HOME VEGT
Greet v FOND
Gregarious j GRUP
Gremlin n BLOK MYTH
Grenade n DAMG
Grenadier n DAMG
Grenadier n ANML FLOW
Grenadine n SIP VEGT
Grew v LARG VARY
Grew v VARY
Grew v EVNT
Grey j COLR
Grid n FORM
Gridded v FORM
Griddle n FOOD HEAT
Gridiron n HEAT FORM
Gridiron n PLAY FORM
Gridiron n FORM
Grief n PANG
Griffin n ANML MYTH
Grill n FOOD HEAT
Grill n MART FOOD

Grill v BLUR TALK
Grille n FORM
Grilled v FOOD HEAT
Grilled v BLUR TALK
Grim j AGGR PANG
Grimace v PANG
Grime n DIRT
Griminess n DIRT
Grimy j DIRT ‹
Grin n GLAD
Grind v WORK
Grind v VARY LITL
Grind v DAMG
Grinder n WORK
Grinder n VARY LITL
Grinder n FOOD
Grinder n FOOD BODY
Grinds v WORK
Grinds v VARY LITL
Grinds v DAMG
Grindstone n MECH SHRP
Gringo n GRUP
Grip n BLOK
Grip n HOLW
Grip n SICK
Gripe v PANG
Grippe n SICK
Gripped v BLOK
Grisly j BAD PANG
Grist n VEGT
Grist n CRUX SOME
Gristle n SOMA
Grit n POWR
Grit n ERTH
Grit v HEAR
Grits n FOOD VEGT
Grits v HEAR
Grizzly n ANML COLR
Grizzly j COLR
Groan n TALK PANG
Groats n FOOD VEGT
Grocer n MART FOOD
Grog n SIP
Groggy j WEAK PANG
Groin n BODY
Groom v CLEN
Groom n MALE KIN
Groom n MALE SEX
Groom v AID
Groomed v CLEN
Groomed v AID
Grooming v CLEN
Grooming v AID
Groove n HOLW
Grope v BLUR
Gross j LARG
Gross j WHOL
Gross n NUMR
Gross j BAD
Grossed v WHOL
Grossing v WHOL
Grotesque j FOOL
Grotto n ERTH HOME
Grouch n AGGR PANG
Ground n ERTH

Ground n CRUX IDEA
Ground v WORK
Ground v VARY DAMG
Ground v VARY LITL
Groundless j TRIV
Group n GRUP
Grouse n ANML UP
Grouse v AGGR TALK
Grove n VEGT
Grovel v WEAK
Grow v LARG VARY
Grow v VARY
Grow v EVNT
Growl n HEAR
Growl n AGGR TALK
Grown v LARG VARY
Grown v VARY
Grown v EVNT
Grownup n LARG POWR
Growth n LARG VARY
Growth n LARG BODY
Grub n BUG YNG
Grub n FOOD
Grub v TRIV WORK
Grubbed v TRIV WORK
Grubbier j BUG DIRT
Grubbier j DIRT
Grubby j BUG DIRT
Grubby j DIRT
Grudge n AGGR
Gruel n FOOD
Gruel v DAMG
Grueling j DAMG
Gruesome j PANG
Gruff j AGGR
Grumble v AGGR TALK
Grumpy j AGGR PANG
Grunt n HEAR TALK
Guano n ANML MTRL
Guaranty n AGRE AID
Guard n BLOK AID
Guard n BLOK PLAY
Guardhouse n BLOK HOME
Guardian n AID

Guarding v BLOK AID
Guava n FOOD VEGT
Gubernatorial j LEAD LAW
Guerrilla j DAMG
Guess v BLUR IDEA
Guest n AID JOIN
Guff n FALS TALK
Guffaw n GLAD HEAR
Guidance n LEAD AID
Guide n LEAD AID
Guidebook n AID WRIT
Guild n GRUP
Guile n FALS
Guileless j EASY GOOD
Guillotine n DEAD SHRP
Guilt n CRIM PANG
Guiltless j GOOD
Guinea n MONY
Guise n GARB FALS
Guitar n MUSC
Gulch n ERTH HOLW
Gulf n FLOW
Gulf n HOLW
Gulf n ERTH HOLW
Gull n ANML UP
Gull v FALS
Gulled v FALS
Gullet n SOMA HOLW
Gullible j WEAK
Gullies n ERTH HOLW
Gulling v FALS
Gully n ERTH HOLW
Gulp n FOOD SOMA
Gum n SOMA
Gum n FOOD VEGT
Gum n SOMA VEGT
Gum n JOIN MTRL
Gum v BLOK JOIN
Gumbo n SIP FOOD
Gumbo n ERTH
Gumbo n VEGT
Gumdrop n FOOD
Gummed v JOIN MTRL
Gummed v BLOK JOIN

Gummy j JOIN MTRL
Gumption n POWR
Gun n DAMG MECH
Gun n QUIK MECH
Gunboat n DAMG FLOW
Gunman n DAMG MALE
Gunned v DAMG MECH
Gunned v QUIK MECH
Gunny n FABR
Gunpowder n DAMG MTRL
Gunshot n DAMG HEAR
Gunwale n FLOW FORM
Guppy n ANML FLOW
Gurgle v HEAR FLOW
Guru n LEAD HOLY
Gush v FLOW
Gush v FOND
Gust n VAPR WEA
Gustation n FOOD SOMA
Gusto n MOTV
Gut n SOMA HOLW
Gut n POWR SOMA
Gut v SOMA OUT
Gut v DAMG
Gutted v SOMA OUT
Gutted v DAMG
Gutter n HOLW
Gutter n BAD HOLW
Gutteral j HEAR
Guy n MALE
Guy n AID
Guyed v AID
Guying v AID
Guzzle v SIP SOMA
Gym n HOME PLAY
Gymnasium n HOME PLAY
Gymnasium n HOME EDUC
Gymnast n PLAY
Gynecology n MEDC LADY
Gyp v FALS
Gypsum n MTRL
Gypsy n GO GRUP
Gyrate v VARY GO
Gyroscope n VARY MECH

H

H n WRIT
Haberdasher n GARB MART
Habiliment n GARB
Habilitate v GARB
Habilitate v AID
Habit n EVER
Habit n GARB
Habitable j LIVE
Habitant n LIVE
Habitat n LIVE
Habitual j EVER
Habitude n EVER
Hacienda n HOME
Hack v SHRP
Hack v DAMG
Hack n SOMA HEAR
Hack n ANML WEAK
Hack n VEHC

Hackle n ANML BODY
Hackney n ANML
Hackney n VEHC
Hackneyed j TRIV
Had v NSCR
Had v HAVE
Haddock n ANML FLOW
Haddock n FOOD FLOW
Hades n DEAD MYTH
Haft n BULG
Hag n BAD LADY
Hag n LADY MYTH
Hagfish n ANML FLOW
Haggada n WRIT HOLY
Haggard j PANG
Haggard n ANML UP
Haggle v AGGR TALK
Hagiology n WRIT HOLY

Hail v WEA FLOW
Hail v TALK
Hail v GO
Hail v AGRE TALK
Hails v WEA FLOW
Hails v TALK
Hails v GO
Hails v AGRE TALK
Hailstone n WEA FLOW
Hair n BODY
Hairbrush n CLEN BODY
Haircloth n BODY FABR
Haircut n BODY SHRP
Hairdo n BODY AID
Hairdresser n BODY AID
Hairless j BODY LACK
Hairpin n BLOK BODY
Hake n ANML FLOW

Hake n FOOD FLOW
Halakah n LAW HOLY
Halcyon j GLAD
Halcyon n ANML UP
Hale j MEDC POWR
Hale v GO
Haled v GO
Hales v GO
Half n NUMR SOME
Half n PLAY SOME
Halfback n BACK PLAY
Halfbaked j FOOL
Halfcocked j WEAK
Halfhearted j WEAK
Halfpenny n MONY
Halfway j GO SOME
Halfwit n FOOL
Halibut n ANML FLOW
Halibut n FOOD FLOW
Haling v GO
Halitosis n DIRT SOMA
Hall n HOME
Hallelujah i GLAD EMPH
Hallmark n GOOD WRIT
Hallow v HOLY
Hallowed j HOLY
Halloween n PLAY TIME
Hallucinate v IDEA MYTH
Hallucinogen n MEDC MYTH
Hallucinosis n SICK MYTH
Hallway n HOME PATH
Halo n VAPR VIEW
Halo n GOOD VIEW
Halogen n MTRL
Halt n BLOK END
Halt n SICK WEAK
Halted v BLOK END
Halter n BLOK
Halter n BLOK DEAD
Halter n GARB LADY
Halve v SEP SOME
Ham n BODY
Ham n ANML FOOD
Ham n WEAK
Ham v FOOL WEAK
Hamburger n ANML FOOD
Hamlet n PLAC
Hammed v FOOL WEAK
Hammer n WORK
Hammer n DAMG MECH
Hammerhead n ANML FLOW
Hammock n ERTH VEGT
Hammock n FURN REST
Hamper n HOLW
Hamper v BLOK
Hamster n ANML
Hamstring n SOMA
Hamstring v BLOK SOMA
Hand n BODY
Hand n BODY AID
Hand n BODY WRIT
Hand n AGRE BODY
Hand n BODY WORK
Hand n BODY NEAR
Hand n BODY PLAY

Hand n BODY MSMT
Hand n BODY GRUP
Handbag n GARB BODY
Handbook n AID WRIT
Handcuff n BLOK BODY
Handed j BODY
Handed v BODY AID
Handful n BODY SOME
Handicap n BLOK WEAK
Handicraft n BODY WORK
Handier j POWR BODY
Handily d POWR BODY
Handing v BODY AID
Handiwork n BODY WORK
Handkerchief n GARB
Handle n AID BULG
Handle v BODY JOIN
Handle v LEAD BODY
Handmade j BODY FORM
Handmaid n LADY AID
Hands n BODY
Hands v BODY AID
Hands n BODY WORK
Hands n BODY PLAY
Hands n BODY MSMT
Hands n BODY GRUP
Handshake n BODY JOIN
Handsome j GOOD
Handwriting n BODY WRIT
Handy j POWR BODY
Handyman n AID WORK
Hang v DOWN
Hang v DEAD DOWN
Hang v EVER HAVE
Hang v REST
Hangar n HOME VEHC
Hangbird n ANML UP
Hanged v DEAD DOWN
Hanger n DOWN
Hanger n SHRP
Hangman n DEAD MALE
Hangout n REST
Hangover n PANG
Hangover n EVER
Hangup n BLOK
Hank n MSMT
Hanker v MOTV
Hankypanky n FALS
Hansom n VEHC
Hanukkah n HOLY TIME
Hap n AFAR EVNT
Haphazard j BLUR
Haphtarah n WRIT HOLY
Hapless j WEAK
Happen v EVNT
Happier j GLAD
Happily d GLAD
Happy j GLAD
Harakiri n DEAD SHRP
Harangue v BLUR TALK
Harass v AGGR PANG
Harbinger n FORW TIME
Harbor n AID FLOW
Harbor v AID HOME
Hard j EVER

Hard j POWR
Hard j PANG
Hard j AGGR
Hardbitten j AGGR
Hardboiled j AGGR
Hardhead n ANML FLOW
Hardhearted j AGGR SOMA
Hardier j POWR
Hardihood n POWR
Hardily d POWR
Hardly d TRIV
Hardpan n ERTH
Hardship n PANG
Hardtack n FOOD
Hardware n MECH WORK
Hardy j POWR
Hare n ANML
Harebrain j FOOL
Harelip n BODY SICK
Harem n LADY SEX
Hark v HEAR
Harlequin n GLAD PLAY
Harlot n BAD SEX
Harm n DAMG
Harmless j AID TRIV
Harmonic j NUMR
Harmonic j SIML MUSC
Harmonica n MUSC
Harmonious j SIML
Harmonious j SIML MUSC
Harmonize v SIML
Harmonize v SIML MUSC
Harmony n SIML
Harmony n SIML MUSC
Harness n GARB BLOK
Harness n AID
Harness v BLOK
Harp n MUSC
Harp v EVER TALK
Harped v EVER TALK
Harping v EVER TALK
Harpoon n DAMG SHRP
Harpsichord n MUSC
Harried v DAMG PANG
Harrier n QUIK GO
Harrier n ANML
Harrier n DAMG PANG
Harrier n ANML UP
Harrow v DAMG PANG
Harrow v ERTH MECH
Harry v DAMG PANG
Harsh j AGGR
Harumscarum j BLUR DAMG
Harvest n HAVE VEGT
Has v NSCR
Has v HAVE
Hash n FOOD
Hash n BLUR JOIN
Hashed v BLUR JOIN
Hashing v BLUR JOIN
Hasp n BLOK
Hassock n FURN REST
Haste n QUIK
Hasten v QUIK GO
Hasten v QUIK

Hat n GARB
Hatch v BGIN
Hatch n BLOK OPEN
Hatch n WRIT FORM
Hatched v BGIN
Hatched v BLOK OPEN
Hatched v WRIT FORM
Hatchery n ANML BGIN
Hatchet n SHRP WORK
Hate n AGGR
Hating v AGGR
Hatred n AGGR
Haughty j AGGR POWR
Haul v GO
Haul n HAVE
Haunch n BODY
Haunt v EVER MYTH
Hauteur n AGGR POWR
Havana n FOOD PLAC
Have v NSCR
Have v HAVE
Haven n AID HOME
Haversack n GARB HOLW
Haves n HAVE
Having v NSCR
Having v HAVE
Havoc n DAMG
Hawk n ANML UP
Hawk v MART MONY
Hawk v SOMA HEAR
Hawked v MART MONY
Hawked v SOMA HEAR
Hawking v MART MONY
Hawking v SOMA HEAR
Hawthorn n VEGT
Hay n VEGT
Hay n REST VEGT
Haycock n BULG VEGT
Haymaker n DAMG REST
Haymaker n VEGT WORK
Haymow n HOLW VEGT
Haystack n BULG VEGT
Haywire d BLUR
Hazard n DAMG MOTV
Hazard n AFAR EVNT
Haze n WEA BLUR
Haze n VAPR BLUR
Haze v AGGR PANG
Hazed v AGGR PANG
Hazel n VEGT
Hazel n COLR
Hazier j WEA BLUR
Hazier j VAPR BLUR
Hazing v AGGR PANG
Hazy j WEA BLUR
Hazy j VAPR BLUR
Hazzan n HOLY MUSC
He p HSCR
Head n BODY
Head v FORW GO
Head n FORW
Head n LEAD

Head n BODY IDEA
Head n ERTH BULG
Head n CLEN HOME
Headache n BODY PANG
Headed v FORW GO
Headed v FORW
Headed v LEAD
Headed j BODY
Header n FORW
Header n PLAY
Header n MECH VEGT
Header n BODY
Headier j BODY PANG
Heading n FORW WRIT
Heading v FORW GO
Heading v FORW
Heading v LEAD
Headless j BODY LACK
Headless j LEAD LACK
Headlight n FORW VIEW
Headline n FORW WRIT
Headlock n BLOK BODY
Headlong j QUIK BODY
Headlong j BODY FORW
Headmost j FORW EMPH
Headpiece n GARB BODY
Headquarters n LEAD HOME
Heads n BODY
Heads v FORW GO
Heads v FORW
Heads v LEAD
Heads n BODY IDEA
Headsman n DAMG
Headstone n DEAD ERTH
Headstrong j POWR BODY
Headway n FORW GO
Heady j BODY PANG
Heal v MEDC AID
Health n MEDC AID
Heap n BULG
Heap n MUCH BULG
Hear v HEAR
Hearken v HEAR
Hearsay n HEAR TALK
Hearse n DEAD VEHC
Hearse n DEAD FORM
Heart n SOMA
Heart n CRUX
Heart n PLAY
Heart n POWR MOTV
Heartache n SOMA PANG
Heartbreak n SOMA PANG
Heartburn n SOMA SICK
Hearten v POWR AID
Heartfelt j GOOD MOTV
Hearth n HOLW HEAT
Heartier j POWR
Heartless j AGGR
Heartrending j SOMA PANG
Heartsick j SOMA PANG
Heartstring n SOMA MOTV
Hearty j POWR

Heat n HEAT
Heat n HEAT SEX
Heat n PLAY
Heated v HEAT
Heath n ERTH VEGT
Heath n VEGT
Heathen j OPPO HOLY
Heating v HEAT
Heats v HEAT
Heats n PLAY
Heave v GO
Heave v VARY
Heave v SOMA OUT
Heaven n ASTR UP
Heaven n DEAD MYTH
Heaven n GLAD GOOD
Heavenward d ASTR UP
Heavier j LARG
Heavier j MUCH
Heavy j LARG
Heavy j MUCH
Heavyweight n LARG MSMT
Hebephrenic j SICK
Hebrew n TALK
Hebrew n GRUP
Heck i EMPH
Heckle v AGGR TALK
Hectic j PANG
Hectic j SICK
Hector v DAMG
Hedge n BLOK VEGT
Hedge n BLOK
Hedgehog n ANML
Hedgehog n BLOK DAMG
Hedgerow n FORW VEGT
Hedonism n GLAD
Heed v AGRE
Heedless j MOTV LACK
Heehaw n ANML TALK
Heel n BODY
Heel n BACK
Heel n GARB
Heel n BAD AGGR
Heel v VARY
Heeled j BACK
Heeled j GARB
Heeled j MONY
Heeled v VARY
Heeler n SUB
Heeling v VARY
Heeling v GARB
Heeling v BACK
Heelless j GARB LACK
Heft n POWR
Heft n LARG
Heft v GO UP
Heftier j LARG
Hefty j LARG
Heifer n ANML YNG
Height n UP
Height n MSMT UP
Heighten v LARG UP

Parts of speech; a article; b preposition; c conjunction; d adverb; f prefix; i interjection;
j adjective; n noun; p pronoun; r phrase; v verb.

Heinous j BAD DAMG
Heir n HAVE
Heiress n LADY HAVE
Heirloom n EVER HAVE
Held v HAVE
Held v BLOK
Held v JOIN
Held v IDEA
Held v BLOK CRIM
Held v EVER
Held v EVNT
Helical j VARY FORM
Helicoid j VARY FORM
Helicopter n VEHC UP
Heliocentric j ASTR HEAT
Helios n LEAD MYTH
Heliotrope n ERTH MTRL
Heliotrope n COLR
Heliotrope n ASTR VEGT
Heliotropism n ASTR HEAT
Helium n VAPR
Hell n BAD PANG
Hell n DEAD MYTH
Hello i JOIN
Helm n LEAD FORM
Helmet n GARB AID
Help n AID
Help n AID WORK
Helpless j WEAK
Helterskelter j BLUR QUIK
Hem n GARB END
Hem v BLOK
Hem v HEAR TALK
Hemal j SOMA
Hemi f NUMR SOME
Hemic j SOMA
Hemicycle n SOME FORM
Hemisphere n PLAC
Hemisphere n SOME FORM
Hemlock n VEGT
Hemoglobin n SOMA
Hemophilia n SICK
Hemorrhage n SICK
Hemorrhoid n SICK
Hemp n VEGT FABR
Hemp n MEDC VEGT
Hen n ANML LADY
Hence d SEP
Hence d FORW TIME
Hence c NSCR
Hence d NEAR
Henceforth d FORW TIME
Henchman n MALE SUB
Hennery n ANML HOME
Henpeck v AGGR SUB
Hep j IDEA
Hepatitis n SICK
Heptagon n FORM
Her p HSCR
Herald n FORW TALK
Heraldry n VIEW
Herb n FOOD VEGT
Herb n MEDC VEGT
Herbivore n FOOD VEGT
Herculean j POWR

Hercules n ASTRO POWR
Herd n ANML GRUP
Here d NEAR
Hereabout d NEAR PLAC
Hereafter d FORW TIME
Hereby d NSCR
Heredity n BGIN HAVE
Herein d IN NEAR
Hereon d NEAR
Heresy n OPPO HOLY
Heretic n OPPO HOLY
Heretofore d PAST
Herewith d NEAR
Heritage n BGIN HAVE
Hermaphrodite n LADY MALE
Hermeneutic j IDEA
Hermetic j MYTH
Hermetic j BLOK
Hermit n SOLE SEP
Hermit n FOOD
Hermitage n SOLE SEP
Hermitage n SIP VEGT
Hernia n BULG SICK
Hero n POWR MALE
Heroic j POWR
Heroin n MEDC VEGT
Heroine n POWR LADY
Heroism n POWR
Heron n ANML UP
Herring n ANML FLOW
Herring n FOOD FLOW
Herringbone j FORM
Hers p HSCR
Herself p HSCR
Hesitate v BLUR REST
Hessian n VEGT FABR
Heterochromatic j MUCH COLR
Heterodox j OPPO IDEA
Heterogeneous j OPPO
Heteronomy n LAW SUB
Heteronym n OPPO TALK
Heterosexual j SEX
Heterosis n POWR JOIN
Heterozygous j BGIN OPPO
Hew v SHRP
Hex n AGGR MYTH
Hexagon n FORM
Hexameter n TALK
Hey i EMPH
Heyday n POWR TIME
Hi i AGRE
Hiatus n SEP LACK
Hibachi n FOOD HEAT
Hibernal j COLD TIME
Hibernate v REST TIME
Hiccup v SOMA HEAR
Hick n WEAK
Hickory n VEGT
Hickory n MTRL VEGT
Hidden v COVR
Hide v COVR
Hide n BODY
Hide n ANML FABR
Hide v DAMG BODY
Hidebound j BLOK BODY

Hidebound j FOOL BLOK
Hideous j BAD
Hideout n HOME COVR
Hie v QUIK GO
Hied v QUIK GO
Hierarchy n LEAD FORW
Hieratic j HOLY
Hieroglyphic n WRIT
Hieroglyphic n BLUR WRIT
Hies v QUIK GO
Hifi n SHRP MUSC
Higgledypiggledy d BLUR
High j UP
High j GLAD UP
High j POWR UP
High j EMPH
High j MSMT UP
High j GOOD UP
Highball n SIP
Highball v QUIK GO
Highballed v QUIK GO
Highballing v QUIK GO
Highboy n HOLW FURN
Highchair n REST YNG
Highfalutin j FOOL UP
Highland n ERTH UP
Highlight v VIEW SHRP
Highness n UP
Highness n LEAD
Highschool n HOME EDUC
Highstrung j PANG
Hightoned j POWR FALS
Highway n PATH
Highwayman n CRIM MALE
Hijack v CRIM
Hike v GO
Hike v GO UP
Hilarity n GLAD
Hill n ERTH BULG
Hill n BULG
Hillbilly n BULG WEAK
Hillock n ERTH BULG
Hillside n ERTH BULG
Hilt n BULG
Him p HSCR
Himself p HSCR
Hind j BACK
Hind n ANML LADY
Hind n ANML FLOW
Hind n WORK
Hinder v BLOK
Hindermost j BACK
Hindrance n BLOK
Hinge n JOIN
Hint n IDEA SOME
Hinted v IDEA SOME
Hinterland n ERTH AFAR
Hip n BODY
Hip n FORM
Hipped j FORM
Hippie n OPPO GRUP
Hippodrome n HOME PLAY
Hippopotamus n ANML
Hipshot j BODY SICK
Hire v MART MONY

Hireling n MONY SUB
Hirsute j BODY
His p HSCR
Hiss n HEAR
Hiss n AGGR TALK
Hiss n ANML TALK
Hist i HEAR EMPH
Histology n SOMA IDEA
History n IDEA PAST
Hit v DAMG
Hit n POWR
Hit v GO
Hit v JOIN
Hitch n JOIN
Hitch n BLOK
Hitch n VARY GO
Hitch v GO AID
Hitched v JOIN
Hitched v BLOK
Hitched v VARY GO
Hitched v GO AID
Hitchhike v GO AID
Hither d NEAR
Hitherto d EVER NEW
Hitherto d NEAR
Hive n BUG HOME
Hives n BUG HOME
Hives n SICK
Ho i EMPH
Hoar j COLR PAST
Hoard n HAVE COVR
Hoarse j HEAR
Hoax n FALS
Hob n BULG HEAT
Hob n BULG PLAY
Hobbies n PLAY
Hobble v VARY GO
Hobble v GO WEAK
Hobble v BLOK
Hobbled v VARY GO
Hobbled v GO WEAK
Hobbled v BLOK
Hobbledehoy n WEAK YNG
Hobby n PLAY
Hobnail n JOIN SHRP
Hobnob v AGRE NEAR
Hobo n GO OPEN
Hockey n PLAY
Hocus n CRIM FALS
Hocuspocus n FOOL FALS
Hod n HOLW
Hodgepodge n BLUR JOIN
Hoe n WORK
Hog n ANML
Hog n ANML FOOD
Hog v SOLE MOTV
Hogged v SOLE MOTV
Hogging v SOLE MOTV
Hognose n ANML
Hogshead n HOLW MSMT
Hogwash n ANML DIRT
Hohenzollern n LEAD GRUP
Hoist n GO UP
Hold v HAVE
Hold n BLOK

Hold n HOLW
Hold v JOIN
Hold v IDEA
Hold v BLOK CRIM
Hold v EVER
Hold v EVNT
Holdfast n BLOK HAVE
Holdfast n BLOK
Holdover n EVER
Hole n HOLW OPEN
Holiday n PLAY TIME
Holier j HOLY
Holing v HOLW
Holland n PLAC
Holland n PLAC FABR
Hollandaise n FOOD
Holler n HEAR TALK
Hollies n VEGT
Hollow n HOLW
Hollow j LACK
Hollow j HOLW TRIV
Holly n VEGT
Holocaust n DAMG HEAT
Holster n HOLW
Holy j HOLY
Homage n SUB
Homage n AGRE
Home n HOME
Home n HOME PLAY
Home n CRUX
Homeless j HOME LACK
Homelier j WEAK
Homelike j SIML HOME
Homely j WEAK
Homemade j HOME FORM
Homeostasis n EVER SOMA
Homer n HOME PLAY
Homer n ANML UP
Homered v HOME PLAY
Homering v HOME PLAY
Homesick j HOME PANG
Homespun j HOME FABR
Homestead n ERTH HOME
Homeward j FORW HOME
Homicide n CRIM DEAD
Homily n TALK HOLY
Homing v GO HOME
Homo n MALE
Homo n GRUP MALE
Homocentric j SIML SHRP
Homochromatic j SIML COLR
Homogeneous j SIML
Homogenize v SIML
Homonym n SIML TALK
Homosexual n SIML SEX
Homozygous j SIML BGIN
Hone v SHRP
Hones v SHRP
Honest j GOOD TRUE
Honey n BUG FOOD
Honey n FOND GOOD
Honeymoon n FOND SEX
Honeysuckle n VEGT
Honk v HEAR
Honk v ANML TALK

Honkytonk n MART SIP
Honor n POWR GOOD
Hood n COVR
Hood n GARB
Hood n CRIM
Hoodlum n CRIM
Hooey n FOOL
Hoof n ANML BODY
Hoof v BODY GO
Hook n BLOK SHRP
Hook n VARY
Hook n VARY DAMG
Hookah n FOOD HOLW
Hooky n SEP
Hooligan n DAMG
Hoop n HOLW FORM
Hoosegow n BLOK HOME
Hoot n AGGR HEAR
Hoot n ANML TALK
Hooves n ANML BODY
Hop n QUIK GO
Hop n GO MUSC
Hop n VEGT
Hope n MOTV
Hopeless j PANG
Hoping v MOTV
Hopped v QUIK GO
Hopper n HOLW
Horde n GRUP
Horizon n ASTR AFAR
Horizontal j FORM
Hormone n SOMA
Horn n MUSC
Horn n ANML BODY
Horn n HOLW
Horn n BULG
Horn n ANML MTRL
Horned j ANML BODY
Hornet n BUG UP
Horoscope n ASTR MYTH
Horrendous j PANG
Horrible j PANG
Horrid j PANG
Horrify v PANG
Horror n PANG
Horse n ANML
Horse n ANML FORM
Horse v FOOL ANML
Horseback n ANML BODY
Horsepower n POWR MSMT
Horseradish n FOOD VEGT
Horses n ANML
Horses n ANML FORM
Horses v FOOL ANML
Horseshoe n ANML GARB
Horsing v FOOL ANML
Horticulture n VEGT
Hosanna i AGRE HOLY
Hose n HOLW FLOW
Hose n GARB
Hosier n GARB MART
Hosing v HOLW FLOW
Hospitable j GOOD AID
Hospital n MEDC HOME
Hospitality n GOOD AID

Hospitalize v MEDC HOME
Host n AID
Host n MUCH GRUP
Host n FOOD HOLY
Hostage n BLOK
Hosted v AID
Hostel n MART HOME
Hostess n LADY AID
Hostility n AGGR
Hosting v AID
Hot j HEAT
Hot j HEAT MOTV
Hot j POWR HEAT
Hot j HEAT PANG
Hot j HEAT SEX
Hot j CRIM HEAT
Hotdog n ANML FOOD
Hotel n MART HOME
Hothouse n HOME VEGT
Hotrod n QUIK VEHC
Hound n ANML
Hound v AGGR
Hour n MSMT TIME
Hourglass n MSMT TIME
House n HOME
House n GRUP LAW
House n GRUP HOME
Housecoat n GARB LADY
Houseful n BULG HOME
Household j HOME FURN
Housekeeper n AID HOME
Housewife n LADY HOME
Housewife n LADY KIN
Housework n HOME WORK
Housing n HOME
Housing n HOLW
Hovel n HOME
Hover v GO UP
Hover v VARY
How d NSCR
Howdah n REST
However c NSCR
Howitzer n DAMG MECH
Howl n ANML TALK
Hoyden n AGGR LADY
Hub n CRUX SHRP
Hubbub n HEAR PANG
Huckleberry n FOOD VEGT
Huckster n MART MONY
Huddle n GRUP JOIN
Hue n COLR
Huff n AGGR
Huff v VAPR SOMA
Hug v FOND JOIN
Hug v NEAR
Huge j LARG
Hula n GO MUSC
Hulk n FLOW VEHC
Hulk n LARG BODY
Hulk v LARG
Hulked v LARG
Hulking v LARG
Hull n FLOW FORM

Hull n BODY VEGT
Hull v SEP VEGT
Hullabaloo n HEAR PANG
Hum v MUSC
Human j WHOL GRUP
Humane j GOOD AID
Humanism n GOOD AID
Humanitarian n GOOD AID
Humanities n GOOD EDUC
Humanity n WHOL GRUP
Humanity n GOOD AID
Humanize v GOOD AID
Humble j WEAK
Humbug n FOOL FALS
Humdrum j TRIV
Humid j FLOW
Humidify v FLOW
Humidor n HOLW
Humiliate v AGGR WEAK
Humility n WEAK
Hummed v MUSC
Humming v MUSC
Hummingbird n ANML UP
Hummock n BULG
Humor n GLAD
Humor n SOMA FLOW
Humor n MOTV
Humored v MOTV
Humoresque n GLAD MUSC
Humoring v MOTV
Hump n BODY BULG
Hump n BULG
Humus n ERTH MTRL
Hunch n IDEA
Hunch n VARY BULG
Hunchback n VARY BODY
Hunched v VARY BULG
Hunching v VARY BULG
Hundred n NUMR
Hung v DOWN
Hung v DEAD DOWN
Hung v EVER HAVE
Hung v REST
Hung j BLOK
Hunger n FOOD MOTV
Hungry j FOOD MOTV
Hunk n SOME
Hunt v ANML DAMG
Hunt v MOTV
Hurdle n BLOK
Hurdygurdy n MECH MUSC
Hurl v GO
Hurl v DAMG GO
Hurrah i GLAD EMPH
Hurricane n WEA DAMG
Hurried v QUIK
Hurried v QUIK GO
Hurry v QUIK
Hurry v QUIK GO
Hurt v DAMG
Hurt v PANG
Hurtle v QUIK GO
Husband n MALE KIN

Husband n MALE SEX
Husband v AID
Husbanded v AID
Husbanding v AID
Husbandry n AID
Hush n HEAR REST
Husk n BODY VEGT
Huskier j LARG POWR
Huskier j HEAR
Huskies n ANML
Huskies n LARG POWR
Huskiest j LARG POWR
Huskiest j HEAR
Huskily d HEAR
Huskily d SOMA POWR
Husky j LARG POWR
Husky j HEAR
Husky n ANML
Hussy n BAD LADY
Hustle v QUIK GO
Hustle v LADY SEX
Hut n HOME
Hutch n HOME
Huzza i GLAD EMPH
Hyacinth n VEGT
Hyacinth n COLR
Hyacinth n ERTH MTRL
Hybrid j BGIN JOIN
Hybrid j OPPO JOIN
Hydrangea n VEGT
Hydrant n HOLW FLOW
Hydraulic j MECH FLOW
Hydrocarbon n MTRL ION
Hydrodynamic j POWR FLOW
Hydroelectric j ION FLOW
Hydrogen n VAPR
Hydroplane n VEHC UP
Hyena n ANML
Hygiene n CLEN MEDC
Hymen n LADY SEX
Hymn n HOLY MUSC
Hymnal n WRIT HOLY
Hyperactive j QUIK
Hyperbola n FORM
Hyperbole n LARG TALK
Hyperbolic j FORM
Hypercritical j AGGR
Hypersensitive j PANG
Hypertension n SICK
Hyperventilate v LARG SOMA
Hyphen n WRIT SEP
Hypnotism n REST
Hypoactive j REST
Hypochondria n SICK PANG
Hypocrisy n FALS
Hypodermic n MEDC SHRP
Hypotension n SICK
Hypotenuse n FORM
Hypothesis n IDEA
Hypothetical j IDEA
Hysterectomy n MEDC SOMA
Hysteria n SICK PANG

I p SOLE WE
I n WRIT
I n WRIT FORM
Iambic j TALK
Ibex n ANML
Ibis n ANML UP
Ice n COLD FLOW
Ice n COLD FOOD
Iceberg n COLD FLOW
Icebox n COLD HOLW
Icecream n COLD FOOD
Icicle n COLD FLOW
Iciness n COLD FLOW
Icing n COLD FLOW
Icing n COLD FOOD
Icon n FORM
Icon n HOLY FORM
Iconoclast n OPPO HOLY
Icy j COLD FLOW
Icy j COLD AGGR
Id n POWR MOTV
Idea n IDEA
Ideal n GOOD IDEA
Identical j SIML
Identify v IDEA SHRP
Identity n SOLE SHRP
Ideogram n WRIT VIEW
Ideology n IDEA FORM
Idiocy n FOOL
Idiom n TALK
Idiosyncrasy n AFAR SOLE
Idiosyncrasy n CRUX SOLE
Idiot n FOOL
Idle j REST LACK
Idle j TRIV
Idle v REST
Idol n FOND HOLY
Idyl n ERTH TALK
Idyl n ERTH GOOD
If c NSCR
If n BLUR
Igloo n HOME
Igneous j HEAT
Ignition n BGIN HEAT
Ignoble j BAD WEAK
Ignominy n BAD
Ignorance n FOOL
Ignore v OPPO
Ilk n GRUP
Ill j SICK
Ill j BAD
Illegal j CRIM
Illegible j BLUR WRIT
Illegitimate j CRIM
Illegitimate j FALS
Illfated j DAMG END
Illiberal j BLOK
Illicit j BAD CRIM
Illimitable j WHOL LARG
Illiteracy n FOOL WRIT
Illness n SICK
Illogical j FALS IDEA
Illtreat v DAMG
Illuminate v VIEW
Illuminate v IDEA VIEW

Illuminate v WRIT VIEW
Illusion n IDEA MYTH
Illusory j IDEA MYTH
Illustrate v VIEW
Illustrate v IDEA VIEW
Illustrious j POWR
Image n VIEW
Imaginary j IDEA MYTH
Imagine v IDEA
Imagine v IDEA MYTH
Imaging v VIEW
Imbalance n OPPO
Imbecile n FOOL
Imbibe v SIP SOMA
Imbroglio n BLUR OPPO
Imbue v IN HAVE
Imitate v SIML FALS
Immaculate j CLEN
Immanent j EVER IN
Immaterial j TRIV
Immaterial j MYTH
Immature j WEAK YNG
Immeasurable j LARG
Immediate j NEAR
Immediate j QUIK
Immemorial j EVER PAST
Immense j LARG
Immerse v IN
Immigrate v GO IN
Imminence n NEAR TIME
Immobile j REST
Immoderate j BAD
Immodest j BAD
Immoral j BAD
Immortal j EVER LIVE
Immovable j EVER REST
Immune j MEDC AID
Immune j AID OPEN
Immure v BLOK IN
Immutable j EVER
Imp n BAD YNG
Impact n DAMG JOIN
Impact v JOIN
Impair v DAMG WEAK
Impale v SHRP
Impart v AID
Impartial j TRUE
Imparting v AID
Impassable j BLOK
Impasse n BLOK END
Impassioned j MOTV
Impassive j MOTV LACK
Impatience n PANG
Impeach v AGGR LAW
Impeach v AGGR
Impeccable j GOOD
Impecunious j MONY LACK
Impede v BLOK
Impel v MOTV
Impel v GO
Impend v NEAR TIME
Impenetrable j BLOK
Imperative j CRUX MOTV
Imperative j LEAD
Imperceptible j VIEW COVR

Imperfect j WEAK
Imperfect j TALK FORM
Imperial j LEAD
Imperil v DAMG
Imperious j LEAD
Imperious j CRUX MOTV
Imperishable j EVER LIVE
Impermanence n VARY
Impermeable j BLOK
Impersonal j SOLE LACK
Impersonate v SIML FALS
Impertinence n AGGR TRIV
Imperturbable j GLAD
Impervious j BLOK
Impetigo n DIRT SICK
Impetuous j QUIK MOTV
Impetuous j DAMG QUIK
Impetus n BGIN POWR
Impiety n OPPO HOLY
Impinge v AGGR JOIN
Impious j OPPO HOLY
Impish j BAD YNG
Implacable j AGGR EVER
Implant v IN
Implausible j FALS
Implement v AID
Implement n WORK
Implicate v JOIN IDEA
Implicit j IN IDEA
Implicit j IN
Implicit j EMPH
Implied v IDEA
Implode v DAMG IN
Implore v MOTV
Implosion n DAMG IN
Imply v IDEA
Impolite j AGGR
Import n MART IN
Import n CRUX IDEA
Importance n CRUX
Importation n MART IN
Importune v MOTV
Impose v AGGR POWR
Impossible j BLUR BLOK
Impostor n FALS
Impotence n WEAK
Impotence n SEX WEAK
Impound v BLOK HAVE
Impoverish v WEAK LACK
Impractical j WEAK
Impregnable j POWR
Impregnate v IN
Impregnate v BGIN
Impresario n LEAD PLAY
Impress v POWR MOTV
Impress n VIEW
Impression n VIEW
Impression n POWR MOTV
Impressionism n VIEW
Impressive j POWR MOTV
Imprimatur n AGRE WRIT
Imprison v BLOK HOME
Improbable j AFAR
Impromptu j EASY QUIK
Improper j BAD

Improper j FALS
Impropriety n BAD
Improve v GOOD AID
Improvident j LACK
Improving v GOOD AID
Improvise v BGIN EASY
Imprudent j BAD
Impudence n AGGR
Impugn v AGGR
Impulse n QUIK MOTV
Impunity n OPEN
Impure j DIRT
Impute v IDEA MOTV
In b IN
In b NSCR
Inability n WEAK
Inaccessible j BLOK
Inaccuracy n FALS
Inaction n REST
Inadequacy n WEAK
Inadmissible j OPPO
Inadvertent j FALS
Inadvisable j OPPO
Inalienable j EVER
Inane j FOOL TRIV
Inanimate j DEAD
Inapplicable j OPPO
Inappropriate j OPPO
Inarticulate j BLUR TALK
Inattentive j OPPO
Inaudible j HEAR
Inaugurate v BGIN
Incalculable j LARG BLUR
Incandescence n HEAT VIEW
Incantation n TALK MYTH
Incapable j WEAK
Incapacity n WEAK
Incarcerate v BLOK HOME
Incarnate j SIML BODY
Incautious j DAMG
Incendiary n DAMG HEAT
Incense n SOMA HEAT
Incense v AGGR PANG
Incentive n MOTV
Incessant j EVER
Incest n CRIM SEX
Inch n MSMT
Inch v GO REST
Inchoate j BGIN BLUR
Incident n EVNT
Incident j JOIN
Incidental j TRIV
Incinerate v HEAT
Incipient j BGIN
Incise v SHRP
Incisor n BODY SHRP
Incite v BGIN MOTV
Incivility n AGGR
Inclement j AGGR
Incline v VARY
Incline v MOTV
Inclose v IN COVR

Include v WHOL
Incognito d FALS COVR
Incoherence n FOOL BLUR
Income n MONY
Incoming j GO IN
Incommunicado j BLOK TALK
Incomparable j POWR
Incomparable j OPPO
Incompatible j OPPO
Incompetence n WEAK
Incomplete j SOME WEAK
Incomprehensible j BLUR IDEA
Inconceivable j BLUR IDEA
Inconclusive j BLUR
Incongruity n OPPO
Inconsequent j TRIV
Inconsiderate j AGGR
Inconsistency n OPPO
Inconsolable j PANG
Inconsonant j OPPO
Inconspicuous j BLUR VIEW
Inconstant j VARY
Incontestable j POWR TRUE
Incontinence n SOMA WEAK
Incontrovertible j POWR TRUE
Inconvenience v PANG
Incorporate v MART JOIN
Incorporate v IN JOIN
Incorrect j FALS
Incorrigible j BAD
Incorrupt j GOOD
Increase n LARG
Incredible j AFAR
Incredulity n OPPO IDEA
Increment n LARG
Incriminate v CRIM
Incrustation n DIRT COVR
Incubate v BGIN
Inculcate v EDUC
Incumbent n MOTV
Incur v MOTV
Incurable j EVER SICK
Indebted j MOTV
Indecency n BAD
Indecipherable j BLUR
Indecision n BLUR
Indecorous j BAD
Indeed d EMPH
Indefatigable j POWR
Indefensible j FALS
Indefensible j BAD
Indefensible j WEAK
Indefinable j BLUR
Indefinite j BLUR
Indelible j EVER
Indelicate j AGGR
Indemnify v AID MONY
Indemnity n AID
Indemnity n AID MONY
Indent v HOLW
Independence n SOLE OPEN
Indescribable j BLUR

Indestructible j POWR EVER
Indeterminate j BLUR
Index n WRIT
Index n BODY
Index n MSMT
Indicate v SHRP
Indicate v IDEA
Indict v AGGR LAW
Indifference n TRIV LACK
Indigenous j BGIN NEAR
Indigent j LACK
Indigestion n FOOD SICK
Indignation n AGGR
Indignity n AGGR
Indigo n COLR
Indigo n COLR VEGT
Indirect j VARY
Indiscernible j BLUR
Indiscretion n BAD
Indiscriminate j BLUR
Indispensable j CRUX
Indispose v PANG
Indisputable j POWR TRUE
Indissoluble j EVER
Indistinct j BLUR
Indistinguishable j BLUR
Indium n MTRL
Individual n SOLE
Indivisible j WHOL JOIN
Indoctrinate v IDEA FORM
Indolence n REST
Indomitable j POWR
Indoor j IN
Indubitable j TRUE
Induce v IDEA MOTV
Induce v BGIN
Induct v BGIN JOIN
Inductance n POWR ION
Induction n BGIN JOIN
Induction n IDEA
Induction n POWR ION
Induction n BGIN
Indulge v AGRE AID
Indurate j AGGR EVER
Indurate j EVER
Industrial j MART WORK
Industries n MART WORK
Industrious j EVER WORK
Industry n EVER WORK
Industry n MART WORK
Inebriate v SIP PANG
Inedible j OPPO FOOD
Ineffable j BLUR
Ineffaceable j EVER
Ineffectual j WEAK
Inefficacy n WEAK
Inefficiency n WEAK
Inelastic j EVER
Ineligible j WEAK
Ineluctable j POWR EVER
Inept j WEAK
Inequality n OPPO

Parts of speech: a article; b preposition; c conjunction; d adverb; f prefix; i interjection;
          j adjective; n noun; p pronoun; r phrase; v verb.

Inequity n OPPO
Ineradicable j EVER
Inerasable j EVER
Inert j REST
Inertia n REST
Inescapable j POWR EVER
Inessential j TRIV
Inestimable j LARG IDEA
Inevitable j POWR EVER
Inexact j BLUR FALS
Inexcusable j BAD
Inexhaustible j POWR EVER
Inexorable j EVER
Inexpedient j OPPO
Inexpensive j MONY TRIV
Inexperience n WEAK
Inexpert j WEAK
Inexpiable j BAD
Inexplainable j BLUR IDEA
Inexplicable j BLUR IDEA
Inexpressible j BLUR TALK
Inexpressive j BLUR
Inextinguishable j EVER
Inextirpable j EVER
Inextricable j BLOK
Infallible j POWR EVER
Infallible j EVER
Infamy n BAD
Infancy n YNG
Infant n YNG
Infanticide n DEAD YNG
Infantile j YNG
Infantry n DAMG
Infatuate v FOND
Infeasible j BLOK
Infect v DIRT SICK
Infect v MOTV
Infelicitous j OPPO
Infer v IDEA
Inferior j DOWN SUB
Inferior j DOWN
Infernal j BAD
Inferno n BAD DAMG
Infertile j BGIN LACK
Infest v MUCH DAMG
Infidel n OPPO HOLY
Infiltrate v GO IN
Infinite j LARG EVER
Infinitely d EMPH
Infinitesmal j LITL
Infinities n LARG EVER
Infinitive n TALK FORM
Infinity n LARG EVER
Infirm j WEAK
Infirmary n MEDC HOME
Infirmity n WEAK
Inflame v HEAT
Inflame v HEAT MOTV
Inflame v AGGR HEAT
Inflammable j HEAT
Inflammation n HEAT
Inflammatory j AGGR HEAT
Inflate v VAPR BULG
Inflating v VAPR BULG
Inflation n LARG MONY

Inflation n VAPR BULG
Inflect v TALK FORM
Inflexible j EVER
Inflict v DAMG
Influence n POWR
Influential j POWR
Influenza n SICK
Influx n GO IN
Inform v TALK IDEA
Informal j EASY
Informality n EASY
Informant n TALK IDEA
Information n IDEA
Informative j IDEA
Informer n TALK OPEN
Infraction n OPPO
Infrared j COLR
Infrequency n AFAR
Infringe v AGGR
Infuriate v AGGR
Infuse v IN
Ingenious j POWR IDEA
Ingenue n LADY WEAK
Ingenuity n POWR IDEA
Ingenuous j EASY OPEN
Ingest v FOOD SOMA
Inglorious j BAD WEAK
Ingot n FORM
Ingrained j CRUX IN
Ingrate n AGGR
Ingratiate v FOND
Ingratitude n AGGR
Ingredient n SOME
Ingress n GO IN
Inhabit v IN LIVE
Inhale v VAPR SOMA
Inharmonious j OPPO
Inherent j EVER CRUX
Inherit v HAVE
Inhibit v BLOK
Inhospitable j AGGR
Inhuman j DAMG
Inhumane j DAMG
Inhume v DEAD COVR
Inimical j AGGR
Iniquity n BAD
Initial j BGIN
Initial n WRIT
Initiate v BGIN
Inject v IN
Injudicious j BAD
Injunction n BLOK LAW
Injure v DAMG
Injury n DAMG
Injustice n BAD
Ink n COLR WRIT
Inkling n IDEA
Inlaid j IN FORM
Inland j ERTH IN
Inlaw n KIN
Inlay n IN FORM
Inlet n IN FLOW
Inmate n IN LIVE
Inmost j IN EMPH
Inn n MART HOME

Innards n SOMA IN
Innards n IN
Innate j BGIN IN
Inner j IN
Innermost j IN EMPH
Inning n PLAY SOME
Innkeeper n MART HOME
Innocence n GOOD
Innocence n EASY GOOD
Innocuous j AID TRIV
Innovate v BGIN
Innuendo n IDEA
Innumerable j MUCH
Inoculate v MEDC IN
Inoffensive j AID TRIV
Inoperable j WEAK
Inoperative j WEAK
Inopportune j OPPO
Inordinate j LARG
Inorganic j MTRL
Inpatient n SICK IN
Input n GO IN
Inquest n LAW OPEN
Inquire v BLUR TALK
Inquisitive j BLUR TALK
Inroad n DAMG
Insane j SICK PANG
Insane j FOOL
Insanitary j DIRT
Insatiable j LACK
Inscription n WRIT
Inscrutable j BLUR COVR
Insect n BUG
Insecticide n BUG DEAD
Insecure j WEAK
Inseminate v IN SEX
Insensate j REST
Insensate j FOOL
Insensate j AGGR REST
Insensible j REST
Insensitive j REST
Insensitive j AGGR REST
Inseparable j EVER JOIN
Insert v IN
Inset n IN
Inside d IN
Insidious j DAMG
Insight n IDEA VIEW
Insignia n VIEW
Insignificance n TRIV
Insincere j BAD FALS
Insinuate v IDEA
Insipid j TRIV
Insist v MOTV
Insolence n AGGR
Insoluble j EVER
Insolvable j BLOK EVER
Insolvent j MONY LACK
Insomnia n PANG
Insouciance n GLAD
Inspect v OPEN VIEW
Inspector n OPEN VIEW
Inspector n LAW OPEN
Inspire v VAPR SOMA
Inspire v POWR MOTV

Instability n VARY WEAK
Install v FORM
Install v BGIN
Installment n MONY SOME
Installment n SOME
Instance n SIML
Instance n SOLE EVNT
Instant j QUIK
Instant n TIME
Instantaneous j QUIK
Instead d OPPO
Instep n BODY
Instigate v BGIN AGGR
Instill v IN
Instinct n MOTV
Institute n HOME
Institute n GRUP
Institute v BGIN
Instituted v BGIN
Instituting v BGIN
Institution n EVER FORM
Institution n HOME
Institution n GRUP
Institution n BGIN
Instruct v EDUC
Instructive j EDUC
Instructor n LEAD EDUC
Instrument n AID
Instrument n MUSC
Instrument n AID MECH
Insubordinate j AGGR
Insubstantial j WEAK TRIV
Insufferable j PANG
Insufficient j WEAK LACK
Insular j SEP
Insular j ERTH FLOW
Insulate v BLOK SEP
Insulin n MEDC
Insult n AGGR
Insuperable j BLOK EVER
Insure v MART AID
Insure v AID
Insurgence n DAMG
Insurmountable j BLOK EVER
Insusceptible j REST
Intact j WHOL AID
Intake n GO IN
Intangible n MYTH
Integer n NUMR
Integer n WHOL NUMR
Integral j WHOL CRUX
Integral j WHOL NUMR
Integrate v WHOL JOIN
Integrity n GOOD
Intellect n IDEA
Intelligence n IDEA
Ihtemperance n AGGR
Intemperance n AGGR MOTV
Intend v MOTV
Intensity n EMPH
Intent n MOTV
Intentional j MOTV
Inter v DEAD COVR
Interact v JOIN
Interbreed v BGIN KIN

Intercede v AID
Intercept v BLOK
Interchange n SIML VARY
Interchange n VARY PATH
Intercom n JOIN TALK
Interconnect v JOIN
Intercourse n JOIN
Intercourse n JOIN SEX
Interdependence n AID JOIN
Interdict v BLOK
Interest n MOTV
Interest n MART MONY
Interfere v BLOK
Interim n SEP TIME
Interior n IN
Interject v IN SEP
Interjection n TALK EMPH
Interlace v JOIN
Interline v IN FABR
Interlock v BLOK JOIN
Interlocutor n TALK
Interlude n SEP TIME
Intermarry v SEX KIN
Intermediary n AID JOIN
Intermediate j PLAC
Interment n DEAD COVR
Intermezzo n MUSC
Interminable j EVER
Intermission n SEP TIME
Intermittent j VARY
Intern n MEDC
Intern v BLOK
Internal j IN
International j GRUP JOIN
Interne n MEDC
Internecine j DAMG DEAD
Interned v BLOK
Interned v MEDC
Internee n BLOK
Interplay n JOIN
Interpolate v IN SEP
Interpose v IN SEP
Interpret v IDEA
Interred v DEAD COVR
Interrogate v BLUR TALK
Interrupt v BLOK END
Intersect v JOIN SEP
Intersperse v SEP
Interstate j JOIN PLAC
Interstellar j ASTR
Interval n SEP TIME
Interval n SEP
Intervene v AID SEP
Intervene v SEP
Interview n JOIN TALK
Intestate j LAW LACK
Intestine n SOMA HOLW
Intimacy n FOND JOIN
Intimacy n JOIN SEX
Intimate j FOND JOIN
Intimate j JOIN SEX
Intimate v IDEA
Intimidate v WEAK PANG
Into b IN
Intolerable j PANG

Intolerance n AGGR
Intone v TALK MUSC
Intoxicate v SIP PANG
Intractable j AGGR
Intramural j IN
Intramuscular j SOMA IN
Intransigent j AGGR
Intransitive j TALK FORM
Intravenous j SOMA IN
Intrepid j POWR
Intricacy n BLUR
Intrigue v MOTV
Intrigue n FALS COVR
Intrinsic j CRUX IN
Introduce v BGIN NEAR
Introduce v BGIN
Introjection n IN IDEA
Introspect v IN IDEA
Introvert v IN MOTV
Introvert v VARY IN
Intrusion n AGGR IN
Intuition n IDEA MOTV
Inundate v BULG FLOW
Inure v AGGR EVER
Invade v DAMG IN
Invalid j SICK WEAK
Invalid j FALS
Invaluable j CRUX
Invariable j EVER
Invasion n DAMG IN
Invective n AGGR TALK
Inveigh v AGGR TALK
Inveigle v FALS MOTV
Invent v BGIN
Invent v BGIN FALS
Inventory n MART HAVE
Invert v VARY OPPO
Invest v MART MONY
Invest v BGIN LEAD
Investigate v OPEN IDEA
Investing v MART MONY
Investing v BGIN LEAD
Inveterate j EVER
Invidious j AGGR
Invigorate v POWR
Invincible j POWR
Inviolable j POWR
Invisible j VIEW COVR
Invite v MOTV
Invocation n AID MOTV
Invoice n MART WRIT
Invoke v AID MOTV
Involuntary j WEAK
Involve v JOIN
Involved j BLUR
Involved v JOIN
Invulnerable j POWR
Inward d IN
Ion n MTRL ION
Irascible j AGGR PANG
Irate j AGGR
Ire n AGGR
Iridescence n COLR VIEW
Iris n BODY VIEW
Iris n VEGT

Irk v AGGR PANG
Iron n ERTH MTRL
Iron n BLOK MTRL
Iron n CLEN EASY
Ironclad j POWR MTRL
Ironed v CLEN EASY
Ironic j FOOL AGGR
Ironies n FOOL AGGR
Ironing v CLEN EASY
Ironmonger n MART ERTH
Irony n FOOL AGGR
Irradiate v VIEW
Irrational j FOOL
Irreclaimable j LACK
Irreconcilable j OPPO
Irrecoverable j LACK
Irredeemable j LACK
Irredeemable j EVER
Irrefutable j TRUE
Irregular j OPPO
Irregular j VARY
Irrelevance n TRIV
Irreligious j OPPO HOLY
Irremediable j EVER
Irremovable j EVER

Irreparable j EVER
Irreplaceable j LACK
Irrepressible j OPEN
Irreproachable j GOOD
Irresistible j POWR
Irresolute j WEAK
Irresponsible j WEAK
Irreverence n BAD AGGR
Irreversible j EVER
Irrevocable j EVER
Irrigate v FLOW
Irritate v AGGR PANG
Is v NSCR
Is v EVNT
Island n ERTH FLOW
Island n SEP
Isle n ERTH FLOW
Ism n IDEA FORM
Isochromatic j SIML COLR
Isochronous j SIML TIME
Isolate v SOLE SEP
Isomeric j SIML ION
Isometric j SIML MSMT
Isomorphic j SIML FORM
Isosceles j SIML FORM

Isotherm n SIML HEAT
Isotope n SIML ION
Issuance n OUT
Issue n OPPO
Issue n OUT
Issue n WRIT
Issue n BGIN KIN
Issued v OUT
Issuing v OUT
Isthmus n ERTH JOIN
It p HSCR
Italicize v WRIT EMPH
Itch v SOMA PANG
Itch v PANG MOTV
Item n NSCR
Iterate v SIML TALK
Itinerant j GO
Itinerary n PATH
Its p HSCR
Ivies n VEGT
Ivory n ANML MTRL
Ivory j COLR
Ivy n VEGT

J

J n WRIT
Jab n DAMG
Jabbed v DAMG
Jabber v FOOL TALK
Jack n JOIN MECH
Jack n MECH UP
Jack n MALE
Jack n VIEW
Jack n PLAY
Jackal n ANML
Jackal n ANML SUB
Jackass n ANML
Jackass n FOOL ANML
Jacked v MECH UP
Jacket n GARB
Jacket n COVR
JackFrost n WEA COLD
Jacking v MECH UP
Jackknife n SHRP
Jackknife v VARY
Jackknifed v VARY
Jackknifes v VARY
Jackknifing v VARY
Jackpot n WHOL HOLW
Jackrabbit n ANML
Jade n COLR
Jade n ERTH MTRL
Jade n ANML WEAK
Jade n LADY
Jade v WEAK
Jaded v WEAK
Jading v WEAK
Jag n SIP PANG
Jag v VARY SHRP
Jagged j VARY SHRP
Jaguar n ANML
Jail n BLOK HOME

Jalopy n VEHC
Jam n FOOD VEGT
Jam n BLOK
Jam n MUSC
Jamb n FORM
Jamboree n GRUP PLAY
Jammed v BLOK
Janitor n AID WORK
January n TIME
Jar n HOLW
Jar v VARY AGGR
Jar v AGGR PANG
Jargon n FOOL TALK
Jarred v VARY AGGR
Jarred v AGGR PANG
Jasmine n VEGT
Jasper n ERTH MTRL
Jasper n COLR
Jaundice n COLR SICK
Jaundice v AGGR
Jaunt n GO
Jauntily d GLAD EASY
Jaunty j GLAD EASY
Javelin n DAMG SHRP
Jaw n BODY
Jaw n BLOK
Jaw v AGGR TALK
Jawed j BODY
Jawed v AGGR TALK
Jawing v AGGR TALK
Jay n ANML UP
Jaywalk v OPPO GO
Jazz n MUSC
Jealous j AGGR
Jeans n GARB
Jeep n VEHC
Jeer v AGGR TALK

Jehovah n LEAD HOLY
Jell v VARY FORM
Jellies n FOOD
Jellies n MTRL
Jello n FOOD
Jelly n FOOD
Jelly n MTRL
Jellyfish n ANML FLOW
Jellyfish n ANML WEAK
Jeopardy n DAMG
Jerk n VARY QUIK
Jerk n FOOL
Jerked v VARY QUIK
Jerkin n GARB
Jerking v VARY QUIK
Jersey n FABR
Jersey n ANML PLAC
Jersey n GARB
Jest n GLAD
Jest n FOOL GLAD
Jesus n LEAD HOLY
Jet n QUIK FLOW
Jet n VEHC UP
Jet n ERTH MTRL
Jet n COLR
Jetliner n VEHC UP
Jetted v QUIK FLOW
Jetted v VEHC UP
Jetties n BLOK FLOW
Jetting v VEHC UP
Jetting v QUIK FLOW
Jettison v SEP
Jetty n BLOK FLOW
Jew n GRUP HOLY
Jewel n GARB GOOD
Jeweler n MART GOOD
Jezebel n BAD LADY

Jibe v SIML
Jiffy n QUIK TIME
Jig n GO MUSC
Jig n FORM
Jig n VARY MECH
Jig v VARY SHRP
Jigged v GO MUSC
Jigged v VARY SHRP
Jigger n SIP MSMT
Jigging v GO MUSC
Jigging v VARY SHRP
Jiggle n VARY
Jilt v AGGR SEP
Jingle n MUSC
Jingle n TALK
Jinks n FOOL GLAD
Jitterbug n GO MUSC
Jitters n PANG
Jittery j PANG
Job n WORK
Jockey n ANML PLAY
Jockey v FALS
Jog n VARY
Jog v GO REST
Join v JOIN
Joint j JOIN
Joint n HOME
Joint n BODY JOIN
Joke n FOOL GLAD
Joked v FOOL GLAD
Joker n FALS
Joker n PLAY
Jolly j GLAD
Jolt n DAMG
Jolt n VARY DAMG
Jonquil n VEGT
Josh v GLAD TALK
Jostle v VARY JOIN

Jot v WRIT
Jot n LITL
Jounce v VARY GO
Journal n WRIT
Journey n GO
Journeyman n POWR WORK
Jovial j GLAD
Joy n GLAD
Jubilation n GLAD
Jubilee n GLAD TIME
Judge n LEAD IDEA
Judge n LEAD LAW
Judge v IDEA
Judicial j LAW
Judicial j IDEA
Judicious j GOOD IDEA
Jug n HOLW
Jug n BLOK HOME
Juggle v VARY FALS
Juice n SIP VEGT
Juice n FLOW
Juice n POWR
Juicier j SIP VEGT
Juicier j MOTV
Juicy j SIP VEGT
Juicy j MOTV
Juke n MUSC
July n TIME
Jumble n BLUR JOIN
Jumbo j LARG
Jump n QUIK GO
Jump n POWR
Jump v DAMG
Jumped v QUIK GO
Jumped v DAMG
Jumper n GARB
Jumper n QUIK GO
Jumpier j PANG

Jumping v QUIK GO
Jumping v DAMG
Jumpy j PANG
Junction n JOIN PATH
June n TIME
Jungle n VEGT
Junior j EDUC SUB
Junior j SUB YNG
Juniper n VEGT
Junk n DIRT TRIV
Junk n FLOW VEHC
Junket n FOOD VEGT
Junket n GO PLAY
Junta n GRUP LAW
Jupiter n ASTR
Jupiter n LEAD MYTH
Juries n GRUP LAW
Juries v GRUP IDEA
Jurisdiction n LEAD LAW
Jurisprudence n LAW IDEA
Juror n GRUP LAW
Juror n GRUP IDEA
Jury n GRUP LAW
Jury n GRUP IDEA
Just d NEAR
Just d EMPH
Just d TRIV
Just j GOOD TRUE
Justice n GOOD TRUE
Justice n LEAD LAW
Justify v GOOD IDEA
Justify v SIML WRIT
Justly d GOOD TRUE
Justness n GOOD TRUE
Jut v BULG
Jute n VEGT FABR
Juvenile j YNG
Juxtapose v JOIN

K

K n WRIT
Kabob n ANML FOOD
Kaiser n LEAD MALE
Kale n FOOD VEGT
Kaleidoscope n VARY VIEW
Kangaroo n ANML
Kangaroo n FALS LAW
Kaput j END WEAK
Katydid n BUG
Kayak n FLOW VEHC
Kazoo n MUSC
Keel n FLOW FORM
Keel v VARY DAMG
Keen j SHRP
Keen j SHRP MOTV
Keen v TALK PANG
Keened v TALK PANG
Keening v TALK PANG
Keens v TALK PANG
Keep v EVER
Keep v EVER AID
Keep v EVER HAVE
Keeps v EVER
Keeps v EVER AID

Keeps v EVER HAVE
Keepsake n FOND HAVE
Keg n HOLW
Kelp n FLOW VEGT
Ken n IDEA
Kennel n ANML HOME
Kennel n ANML GRUP
Kept v EVER
Kept v EVER AID
Kept v EVER HAVE
Kerchief n GARB
Kernel n BGIN VEGT
Kernel n CRUX
Kerosene n ERTH MTRL
Kerygma n WRIT HOLY
Ketch n FLOW VEHC
Ketchup n FOOD VEGT
Kettle n HOLW
Key n OPEN
Key n CRUX
Key n MUSC
Key n ERTH FLOW
Key v PANG
Keyboard n FORW MUSC

Keyboard n FORW FORM
Keyed v CRUX
Keyed v MUSC
Keyed v PANG
Keyhole n HOLW OPEN
Keying v CRUX
Keying v MUSC
Keying v PANG
Keynote n CRUX
Keys n OPEN
Keys n CRUX
Keys n MUSC
Keys n ERTH FLOW
Keys v PANG
Keystone n CRUX FORM
Khaki n VEGT FABR
Khaki n COLR
Khaki n GARB COLR
Khakis n GARB COLR
Kibitz v AGGR TALK
Kick n BODY GO
Kick n DAMG BODY
Kick n GLAD
Kick v DEAD

Kickback n BACK MONY
Kid n ANML YNG
Kid n YNG
Kid n ANML FABR
Kid v FOOL GLAD
Kidded v FOOL GLAD
Kidnap v CRIM SEP
Kidney n SOMA
Kidney n ANML FOOD
Kill v DAMG DEAD
Kill v BLOK DEAD
Kiln n HOLW HEAT
Kilogram n MSMT
Kilometer n MSMT
Kilowatt n ION MSMT
Kilt n GARB MALE
Kilter n WEAK
Kimono n GARB
Kin n KIN
Kind j GOOD AID
Kind n SIML GRUP
Kinder j GOOD AID
Kindergarten n EDUC YNG
Kindest j GOOD AID
Kindhearted j GOOD AID
Kindle v HEAT
Kindliness n GOOD AID
Kindling n HEAT MTRL
Kindly d GOOD AID
Kindred j SIML JOIN
Kindred j KIN
Kinematic j GO MECH
Kinetic j GO
King n LEAD MALE
King n LEAD PLAY

Kingdom n GRUP PLAC
Kink n VARY
Kipper n ANML FLOW
Kipper n FOOD FLOW
Kiss v FOND SEX
Kit n AID
Kitchen n FOOD HOME
Kite n PLAY UP
Kite n ANML UP
Kiting v PLAY UP
Kitten n ANML YNG
Kitties n ANML YNG
Kitties n MONY
Kitty n ANML YNG
Kitty n MONY
Klan n GRUP
Kleenex n CLEN
Knack n POWR
Knapsack n GARB HOLW
Knave n BAD
Knave n PLAY
Knead v VARY
Knee n BODY
Kneecap n BODY
Kneel v DOWN BODY
Knell n MUSC
Knell n DEAD MUSC
Knew v IDEA
Knew v NEAR IDEA
Knickknack n FURN TRIV
Knife n SHRP
Knife v DAMG SHRP
Knight n DAMG
Knight n PLAY
Knit v GARB JOIN

Knit v JOIN
Knives n SHRP
Knob n BULG
Knock v HEAR
Knock v DAMG
Knock v AGGR
Knock v END
Knock v BGIN SEX
Knockkneed j VARY BODY
Knockout n DAMG REST
Knockout n GOOD
Knot n BLOK JOIN
Knot n BULG JOIN
Knot n GRUP JOIN
Knot n BODY VEGT
Knot n QUIK MSMT
Knothole n HOLW VEGT
Know v IDEA
Know v NEAR IDEA
Knowhow n POWR IDEA
Knowledge n IDEA
Knowledge n IDEA SEX
Knuckle n BODY
Koala n ANML
Kohlrabi n FOOD VEGT
Kolkohz n ERTH WORK
Koran n WRIT HOLY
Kosher j FOOD HOLY
Kosher j GOOD
Kowtow v DOWN SUB
Kremlin n LEAD PLAC
Krishna n LEAD HOLY
Krypton n VAPR
Kudos n POWR
Kumquat n FOOD VEGT

L

L n WRIT
L n WRIT FORM
Label n WRIT
Labor n WORK
Laboratory n HOME WORK
Labyrinth n BLUR PATH
Lace n FORM FABR
Lace v JOIN
Lace v FORM
Lace v DAMG
Laceration n DAMG BODY
Lack n LACK
Lackadaisical j REST
Lacked v LACK
Lackey n SUB
Laconic j TALK LITL
Lacquer v COLR MTRL
Lacrosse n PLAY
Lacrymose j SOMA PANG
Lactation n SIP SOMA
Lacuna n LACK
Lad n MALE YNG
Ladder n DOWN UP
Laden j BULG

Ladies n LADY
Ladies n LEAD LADY
Lading n BULG
Ladle n HOLW
Lady n LADY
Lady n LEAD LADY
Lag n REST
Laggard j REST
Lagoon n FLOW
Laid v REST
Laid v BGIN
Laid v JOIN SEX
Laid v NSCR
Lair n ANML HOME
Laissezfaire n OPEN
Laity n GRUP
Lake n FLOW
Lam v GO
Lam v DAMG
Lamb n ANML YNG
Lamb n ANML FOOD
Lamb n ANML FABR
Lambent j EASY VIEW
Lame j SICK WEAK

Lame j WEAK
Lament n TALK PANG
Laming v SICK WEAK
Lamp n VIEW
Lampoon v FOOL AGGR
Lance n DAMG SHRP
Land n ERTH
Land n ERTH PLAC
Land v ERTH GO
Land v BLOK HAVE
Landed j ERTH
Landed v ERTH GO
Landed v BLOK HAVE
Landing v ERTH GO
Landing v BLOK HAVE
Landing n HOME
Landlord n MART HOME
Landmark n ERTH VIEW
Landowner n ERTH HAVE
Landscape v ERTH VEGT
Landward d ERTH
Lane n PATH
Language n TALK
Languid j REST

Parts of speech; a article; b preposition; c conjunction; d adverb; f prefix; i interjection; j adjective; n noun; p pronoun; r phrase; v verb.

Languish v REST WEAK
Languor n REST
Lank j LARG LITL
Lank j EASY
Lanolin n ANML MTRL
Lantern n VIEW
Lanyard n BLOK FABR
Lap n BODY
Lap n MSMT PATH
Lap v SIP SOMA
Lap v FLOW
Lap v JOIN
Lapel n GARB
Lapful n BODY BULG
Lapped v SIP SOMA
Lapped v FLOW
Lapped v JOIN
Lapse v END
Lapse v WEAK
Larboard n PLAC FLOW
Larceny n CRIM
Lard n ANML MTRL
Lard v JOIN
Larded v ANML MTRL
Larded v JOIN
Larder n FOOD HOLW
Large j LARG
Large j MSMT
Large n LARGE OPEN
Largo j REST MUSC
Lariat n BLOK FABR
Lark n ANML UP
Lark n GLAD
Larva n BUG YNG
Laryngitis n SOMA SICK
Larynx n SOMA TALK
Lascivious j BAD SEX
Lash n DAMG
Lash n BODY
Lash v BLOK
Lashing v DAMG
Lashing v BLOK
Lass n LADY YNG
Lassitude n REST PANG
Lasso n BLOK FABR
Last v EVER
Last j BACK END
Last j PAST
Last n END
Last n FORM
Lasting j EVER
Lasting n FABR
Latch n BLOK
Latch v BLOK JOIN
Late j TIME
Late j DEAD PAST
Late j NEW
Lately d NEW
Latency n REST
Lateness n TIME
Latent j REST
Later d TIME
Lateral j PLAC
Lateral n GO PLAY
Latest j NEW

Latest j TIME
Latex n MTRL
Lathe n MECH
Lather n CLEN FLOW
Lather n FLOW
Lather v DAMG
Latin n TALK
Latin n GRUP
Latitude n OPEN
Latitude n MSMT
Latrine n CLEN HOME
Latter j BACK
Latter j NEW
Lattice n FORM
Laud v AGRE GOOD
Laugh n GLAD
Launch n BGIN GO
Launch n FLOW VEHC
Launder v CLEN FLOW
Laundress n CLEN LADY
Laundries n CLEN MART
Laundromat n CLEN MART
Laundry n CLEN MART
Laureate j POWR
Laurel n VEGT
Laurel n POWR VEGT
Lava n ERTH FLOW
Lavaliere n GARB GOOD
Lavatory n CLEN HOME
Lavender n COLR
Lavender n VEGT
Lavish j MUCH GOOD
Law n LAW
Lawabiding j GOOD LAW
Lawbreaker n CRIM LAW
Lawmaker n LEAD LAW
Lawn n VEGT
Laws n LAW
Lawsuit n LAW MOTV
Lawyer n LAW
Lax j EASY WEAK
Laxative j EASY SOMA
Laxative n MEDC SOMA
Laxity n EASY WEAK
Lay v REST
Lay v BGIN
Lay j GRUP
Lay j GRUP HOLY
Lay n JOIN SEX
Lay v NSCR
Layer n FORM
Layer n ANML BGIN
Layette n GARB YNG
Layman n GRUP
Layout n FORM
Lazy j REST
Lead v LEAD FORW
Lead v FORW
Lead n ERTH MTRL
Lead n DAMG MTRL
Leaded v ERTH MTRL
Leader n LEAD FORW
Leaf n BODY VEGT
Leaf n WRIT
Leaf n FORM

Leaflet n WRIT
League n AGRE GRUP
League n MSMT
League n GRUP PLAY
Leak v OUT FLOW
Lean v VARY
Lean j LITL
Lean v AID
Lean v AGRE MOTV
Lean n ANML FOOD
Leaned v VARY
Leaned v AID
Leaned v AGRE MOTV
Leaning v VARY
Leaning v AID
Leaning v AGRE MOTV
Leans v VARY
Leans v AID
Leans v AGRE MOTV
Leanto n HOME
Leap n QUIK GO
Learn v EDUC
Lease n WRIT HAVE
Lease v MART MONY
Leash n BLOK FABR
Least j LITL
Leather n ANML FABR
Leave v GO SEP
Leave v EVER SEP
Leaven v EASY VEGT
Leaven v VARY EASY
Leaves n BODY VEGT
Leaves v GO SEP
Leaves v EVER SEP
Leaves n WRIT
Leaves n FORM
Lecher n BAD SEX
Lectern n FURN WRIT
Lecture n TALK EDUC
Led v LEAD FORW
Ledge n ERTH BULG
Ledge n BULG
Ledger n WRIT
Lee n WEA AID
Leech n BUG JOIN
Leek n FOOD VEGT
Leer n AGGR VIEW
Leerier j BLUR PANG
Leering v AGGR VIEW
Leery j BLUR PANG
Left j BODY PLAC
Left v GO SEP
Left v EVER SEP
Left n GRUP
Lefthanded j BODY PLAC
Leg n BODY
Leg n SOME
Legacy n AID LAW
Legal j LAW
Legation n LEAD GRUP
Legation n LEAD HOME
Legend n WRIT
Legend n TALK MYTH
Legerdemain n FALS MYTH
Legged j BODY

Legging n GARB BODY
Legible j WRIT SHRP
Legion n DAMG GRUP
Legion n MUCH GRUP
Legionnaire n DAMG GRUP
Legislate v LEAD LAW
Legitimacy n LAW TRUE
Legume n FOOD VEGT
Lei n FORM VEGT
Leis n FORM VEGT
Leisure j GLAD REST
Lemming n ANML
Lemon n FOOD VEGT
Lemon n WEAK VEGT
Lemon n COLR
Lemonade n SIP VEGT
Lemur n ANML
Lend v AID
Length n MSMT
Leniency n EASY AID
Lens n VIEW
Lent v AID
Lent n HOLY TIME
Lentil n FOOD VEGT
Leo n ANML MALE
Leo n ASTR MYTH
Leonine j ANML
Leopard n ANML
Leopardess n ANML LADY
Leotard n GARB
Leper n SICK
Leprechaun n MYTH
Leprosy n SICK
Lesbian j SIML SEX
Lesion n DAMG
Less n LITL
Lesson n EDUC
Lest c NSCR
Let v AGRE
Let v MART MONY
Letdown n DOWN PANG
Lethal j DAMG DEAD
Lethargy n REST
Letter n WRIT
Letterhead n FORW WRIT
Letting v AGRE
Letting v MART MONY
Lettuce n FOOD VEGT
Levee n ERTH BULG
Level v SIML FORM
Level v TRUE
Lever n WORK
Levied v MONY HAVE
Levied v DAMG
Levied v GRUP JOIN
Levity n GLAD
Levy v MONY HAVE
Levy v DAMG
Levy v GRUP JOIN
Lewd j BAD SEX
Lexicon n FORW WRIT
Liability n MOTV
Liaison n JOIN
Liar n FALS TALK
Lib n OPEN

Libation n HOLY FLOW
Libel v AGGR FALS
Liberal j OPEN
Liberal j AID OPEN
Liberate v OPEN
Libertarian n OPEN
Liberties n OPEN
Libertine j BAD OPEN
Liberty n OPEN
Libido n SEX MOTV
Libra n ASTR MYTH
Librarian n WRIT
Libraries n HOME WRIT
Library n HOME WRIT
Libretto n WRIT MUSC
Lice n BUG DIRT
License n AGRE WRIT
License n OPEN
Licentious j BAD OPEN
Lichen n VEGT
Lick n FOOD SOMA
Lick v POWR WEAK
Lick v DAMG
Lick n LITL SOME
Lick n ERTH FOOD
Licked v FOOD SOMA
Licked v POWR WEAK
Licked v DAMG
Licking v FOOD SOMA
Licking v POWR WEAK
Licking v DAMG
Licorice n FOOD VEGT
Lid n COVR
Lid n BODY COVR
Lie v REST
Lie v FALS TALK
Lie v NSCR
Lied v FALS TALK
Lien n LAW MOTV
Lies v REST
Lies v FALS TALK
Lies v NSCR
Lieu n OPPO
Lieutenant n LEAD
Life n LIVE
Life n QUIK LIVE
Lifeblood n SOMA LIVE
Lifeboat n FLOW VEHC
Lifebuoy n AID FLOW
Lifegiving j AID LIVE
Lifeless j DEAD TRIV
Lifeless j DEAD LACK
Lifelike j SIML LIVE
Lifeline n AID LIVE
Lifelong j EVER LIVE
Lifer n BLOK CRIM
Lifesaver n AID LIVE
Lifesaver n FOOD
Lifesize j SIML LIVE
Lifetime n LIVE TIME
Lift n GO UP
Lift n AID UP
Lift n GO AID
Lift v CRIM
Ligament n SOMA JOIN

Ligature n BLOK
Light j VIEW
Light j EASY
Light j COLR
Light j GLAD TRIV
Light n HEAT VIEW
Light v DOWN GO
Lighted v VIEW
Lighted v HEAT VIEW
Lighted v DOWN GO
Lighten v EASY
Lighten v VIEW
Lighten v COLR
Lighthearted j GLAD SOMA
Lighthouse n HOME VIEW
Lighting v VIEW
Lighting v HEAT VIEW
Lighting v DOWN GO
Lightly d EASY
Lightly d GLAD TRIV
Lightning n WEA VIEW
Lights v VIEW
Lights v HEAT VIEW
Lights v DOWN GO
Lightweight j EASY MSMT
Like b SIML
Like v FOND
Likelihood n MUCH
Likely j MUCH
Liken v SIML
Likewise d SIML
Lilac n VEGT
Lilac n COLR
Lilies n VEGT
Lilt n MUSC
Lilt n VARY EASY
Lily n VEGT
Limb n BODY
Limb n BODY VEGT
Limbed j BODY
Limbed j BODY VEGT
Limber j VARY EASY
Limbo n DEAD MYTH
Limbo n BLOK LACK
Lime n ERTH MTRL
Lime n FOOD VEGT
Lime n COLR
Limelight n POWR VIEW
Limerick n GLAD TALK
Limit n END
Limousine n VEHC
Limp j EASY WEAK
Limp n GO WEAK
Limped v GO WEAK
Limpid j SHRP
Limping v GO WEAK
Linden n VEGT
Line n FORM
Line n WRIT
Line n FORW
Line n WORK
Line n MART VEHC
Line n FORW PLAY
Line n PAST KIN
Line n TALK

Line n FABR
Line v COVR
Lineage n PAST KIN
Linear j FORM
Linen n VEGT FABR
Linen n FURN FABR
Liner n COVR
Liner n FLOW VEHC
Linger v EVER REST
Lingerie n GARB LADY
Lingering v EVER REST
Lingo n TALK
Linguistics n TALK IDEA
Liniment n MEDC
Lining n COVR
Lining v FORW
Lining n FABR
Link v JOIN
Linoleum n MTRL
Linseed n MTRL VEGT
Lint n DIRT FABR
Lion n ANML
Lion n ANML POWR
Lioness n ANML LADY
Lionize v ANML POWR
Lip n BODY
Lips n BODY
Lipstick n COLR BODY
Liqueur n SIP VEGT
Liquid j FLOW
Liquid j EASY
Liquidate v END
Liquidate v DAMG END
Liquor n SIP VEGT
Lira n MONY
Lisp n TALK WEAK
Lissome j POWR EASY
List n FORW WRIT
List n VARY
Listed v FORW WRIT
Listed v VARY
Listen v HEAR
Listless j TRIV PANG
Lit v HEAT VIEW
Litany n TALK HOLY
Liter n MSMT
Literacy n WRIT EDUC
Literal j SIML WRIT
Literary j WRIT
Literate j WRIT EDUC
Literature n WRIT
Lithe j VARY EASY
Lithium n ERTH MTRL
Lithograph n WRIT VIEW
Lithograph n WRIT MECH
Litigation n OPPO LAW
Litmus n MTRL
Litter n ANML YNG
Litter n DIRT
Litter n MTRL VEGT
Litter n FURN REST
Littered v DIRT
Littering v DIRT
Little j LITL
Liturgy n HOLY FORM

Live v LIVE
Livelihood n AID LIVE
Liveliness n QUIK LIVE
Lively j QUIK LIVE
Liven v QUIK LIVE
Liver n SOMA
Liver n ANML FOOD
Liverwurst n ANML FOOD
Lives v LIVE
Livestock n ANML GRUP
Livid j COLR
Living n LIVE
Living n AID LIVE
Lizard n ANML
Lizard n ANML FABR
Llama n ANML
Lo i EMPH
Load v BULG
Load v FALS BULG
Loaf n FOOD
Loaf v REST
Loafed v REST
Loafer n REST
Loafer n GARB
Loafing v REST
Loam n ERTH
Loan n AID
Loan n AID MONY
Loathe v AGGR PANG
Lob v GO
Lobbed v GO
Lobbies n HOME
Lobbies n GRUP LAW
Lobbing v GO
Lobby n HOME
Lobby n GRUP LAW
Lobe n BODY
Lobo n ANML
Lobster n ANML FLOW
Lobster n FOOD FLOW
Local j NEAR PLAC
Local n REST VEHC
Locale n PLAC
Locality n NEAR PLAC
Locate v PLAC
Locate v OPEN
Lock n BLOK MECH
Lock n BODY SOME
Locked v BLOK MECH
Locker n BLOK HOLW
Locket n GARB HOLW
Loco j FOOL SICK
Locomotion n GO
Locomotive n MECH VEHC
Locus n PLAC
Locus n JOIN FORM
Locust n BUG UP
Locust n VEGT
Locution n TALK
Lodge n HOME
Lodge n GRUP HOME
Lodge v NSCR
Lodger n HOME LIVE
Loft n HOME UP
Loft v GO UP

Lofted v GO UP
Loftier j UP
Loftier j GOOD UP
Lofting v GO UP
Lofty j UP
Lofty j GOOD UP
Log n MTRL VEGT
Log n WRIT
Loganberry n FOOD VEGT
Loge n PLAY REST
Logged v WRIT
Logged v MTRL VEGT
Logging v WRIT
Logging v MTRL VEGT
Logic n IDEA FORM
Logier j REST
Logistic j AID
Logy j REST
Loin n BODY
Loiter v REST
Lollipop n FOOD
Lone j SOLE SEP
Lonely j SOLE PANG
Lonesome j SOLE PANG
Long j EVER
Long j MSMT
Long j AFAR
Long v MOTV
Longed v MOTV
Longer j EVER
Longer j AFAR
Longest j EVER
Longest j AFAR
Longevity n EVER LIVE
Longing v MOTV
Longitude n MSMT
Longterm j EVER TIME
Look n VIEW
Lookout n VIEW
Loom n MECH FABR
Loom v BLUR VIEW
Loomed v BLUR VIEW
Looming v BLUR VIEW
Loon n ANML UP
Loonier j FOOL SICK
Loony j FOOL SICK
Loop n HOLW FORM
Loophole n OPEN
Loose j OPEN
Loose j BAD OPEN
Loosed v OPEN
Loosen v OPEN
Loosing v OPEN
Loot v CRIM
Lop v SHRP
Lop j DOWN
Lope v EASY GO
Loping v EASY GO
Lopped v SHRP
Loquacious j MUCH TALK
Lord n LEAD MALE
Lord n LEAD HOLY
Lore n GRUP MYTH
Lorgnette n AID VIEW
Lorry n VEHC

Lose v LACK
Lose v WEAK LACK
Lot n MUCH
Lot n ERTH
Lot n MOTV
Lot n END
Lotion n AID FLOW
Lottery n MOTV
Lotus n VEGT
Loud j HEAR
Loudspeaker n HEAR TALK
Lounge n HOME REST
Lounge n FURN REST
Lounge v REST
Lounged v REST
Lounging v REST
Louse n BUG DIRT
Lousier j BUG DIRT
Lousier j BAD DIRT
Lousy j BUG DIRT
Lousy j BAD DIRT
Lout n FOOL
Louver n BLOK OPEN
Love n FOND
Love n FOND SEX
Love n NUMR PLAY
Lovely j FOND GOOD
Low j DOWN
Low j DOWN LITL
Low j DOWN SUB
Low j DOWN PANG
Low j BAD DOWN
Low v ANML TALK
Lower v DOWN
Lower v AGGR
Lowest j DOWN
Loyal j AGRE
Lozenge n FOOD LITL

Lozenge n FORM
LSD n MEDC MYTH
Lubricate v EASY MTRL
Lucid j VIEW
Lucid j IDEA SHRP
Luck n AID
Lucrative j MUCH MONY
Ludicrous j FOOL
Lug v GO
Lug n BULG
Lug n FOOL
Luggage n HOLW
Lugged v GO
Lugging v GO
Lugubrious j FOOL PANG
Lukewarm j HEAT
Lukewarm j TRIV MOTV
Lull n GLAD REST
Lullaby n REST MUSC
Lumber n MTRL VEGT
Lumber n FURN TRIV
Lumber n GO
Lumbered v GO
Lumbering v GO
Lumberyard n MART MTRL
Luminary n ASTR
Luminary n POWR VIEW
Luminous j VIEW
Lump n BULG
Lump v BULG JOIN
Lump n AGGR BULG
Lunacy n FOOL SICK
Lunar j ASTR
Lunatic j FOOL SICK
Lunch n FOOD
Luncheon n FOOD
Luncheonette n FOOD
Luncheonette n MART FOOD

Lung n SOMA
Lunge n QUIK GO
Lunging v QUIK GO
Lunkhead n FOOL
Lurch n VARY
Lurch n AGGR
Lure v MOTV
Lure n BLOK SHRP
Lurid j PANG
Lurid j VIEW
Lurid j COLR
Luring v MOTV
Lurk v COVR
Luscious j GOOD
Lush j MUCH GOOD
Lush n SIP PANG
Lust n MOTV
Lust n SEX MOTV
Lusted v MOTV
Lusted v SEX MOTV
Luster n VIEW
Luster n GOOD VIEW
Lustier j POWR
Lusting v MOTV
Lusting v SEX MOTV
Lustrous j VIEW
Lusty j POWR
Lute n MUSC
Luxury n MUCH GOOD
Lyceum n HOME EDUC
Lye n MTRL
Lying v REST
Lying v FALS TALK
Lying v NSCR
Lynch v DAMG DEAD
Lynx n ANML
Lyonnaise j FOOD
Lyre n MUSC

M

M n WRIT
Ma n LADY KIN
Ma n LADY AID
Maam n LADY
Macabre j DEAD PANG
Macaroni n FOOD
Macaroon n FOOD
Macaw n ANML UP
Machete n SHRP
Machine n MECH
Mackerel n ANML FLOW
Mackerel n FOOD FLOW
Mackintosh n GARB
Macroscopic j LARG VIEW
Mad j AGGR
Mad j FOOL
Mad j FOND MOTV
Mad j FOOL SICK
Madam n LADY
Madcap j FOOL
Made v FORM
Made v GO
Made v POWR
Made v MONY HAVE

Made v NSCR
Madras n PLAC FABR
Madrigal n TALK MUSC
Maestro n LEAD MUSC
Mafia n CRIM GRUP
Magazine n WRIT
Magazine n HOLW
Magenta n COLR
Maggot n BUG DIRT
Magic j MYTH
Magistrate n LEAD LAW
Magnanimity n GOOD AID
Magnate n LEAD
Magnesium n MTRL
Magnet n JOIN ION
Magnetism n JOIN ION
Magnetism n FOND JOIN
Magnificence n POWR GOOD
Magnified v LARG
Magnify v LARG
Magniloquence n LARG TALK
Magnitude n MSMT
Magnolia n VEGT
Magpie n ANML UP

Magpie n MUCH TALK
Maharaja n LEAD MALE
Maharani n LEAD LADY
Mahatma n POWR IDEA
Mahogany n MTRL VEGT
Mahogany n COLR
Maid n LADY
Maid n LADY AID
Maiden n LADY YNG
Mail n GO WRIT
Mail n DAMG AID
Mailing v GO WRIT
Mails v GO WRIT
Maim v DAMG
Main j CRUX
Main n HOLW PATH
Main n FLOW
Mains n HOLW PATH
Mainstay n CRUX AID
Maintain v EVER HAVE
Maintain v IDEA
Maintain v EVER AID
Maintenance n EVER HAVE
Maintenance n EVER AID

Maize n FOOD VEGT
Majestic j LEAD GOOD
Majesties n LEAD
Majesty n LEAD
Major j POWR CRUX
Major n LEAD
Major n POWR EDUC
Majordomo n LEAD AID
Majored v POWR EDUC
Majorette n LADY PLAY
Majoring v POWR EDUC
Majority n MUCH
Majors n LEAD
Majors n POWR EDUC
Make v FORM
Make v GO
Make v POWR
Make v MONY HAVE
Make v NSCR
Makebelieve j FALS MYTH
Maker n FORM
Maker n LEAD HOLY
Makes v FORM
Makes v GO
Makes v POWR
Makes v MONY HAVE
Makes v NSCR
Makeshift j VARY
Makeup n BODY FORM
Makeup n CRUX FORM
Makeup n SIML
Maladaptation n BAD OPPO
Maladies n SICK
Maladjustment n BAD OPPO
Maladminister v BAD LEAD
Maladroit j WEAK
Malady n SICK
Malaise n PANG
Malapropos j OPPO
Malaria n SICK
Malcontent j AGGR PANG
Male n MALE
Malediction n BAD TALK
Malefaction n BAD CRIM
Malevolence n BAD AGGR
Malfeasance n CRIM
Malformation n FALS FORM
Malice n BAD AGGR
Malign v BAD AGGR
Malignancy n BAD AGGR
Malignancy n BAD SICK
Malinger v FALS SICK
Mall n PATH
Mallard n ANML UP
Malleable j VARY
Mallet n PLAY
Mallet n WORK
Malnutrition n SICK LACK
Malodorous j VAPR DIRT
Malpractice n FALS WORK
Malt n SIP VEGT
Maltreat v DAMG

Mamma n LADY KIN
Mamma n LADY AID
Mammal n ANML
Mammary j BODY LADY
Mammoth j LARG
Mammoth n ANML
Mammy n LADY KIN
Mammy n LADY AID
Man n MALE
Man n WHOL GRUP
Man v AID
Manacle v BLOK MECH
Manage v LEAD
Mandarin n LEAD
Mandarin n FOOD VEGT
Mandate n LEAD
Mandatory j LEAD
Mandolin n MUSC
Mane n ANML BODY
Maneuver v POWR GO
Maneuver n POWR EVNT
Manganese n ERTH MTRL
Mange n SICK
Manger n FOOD HOLW
Mangle v DAMG
Mangle v EASY MECH
Mango n FOOD VEGT
Mangrove n VEGT
Mangy j DIRT
Manhood n MALE
Mania n SICK PANG
Mania n PANG MOTV
Maniac n SICK PANG
Manic j SICK PANG
Manicure n CLEN BODY
Manifest j OPEN
Manifest n MART WRIT
Manifested v OPEN
Manifesting v OPEN
Manifold j MUCH
Manifold n HOLW FORM
Manikin n SIML FORM
Manipulate v LEAD
Mankind n WHOL GRUP
Manna n FOOD HOLY
Manned v AID
Mannequin n SIML FORM
Manner n EVNT
Mannerly j GOOD
Manofwar n DAMG FLOW
Manor n HOME
Mans v AID
Manse n HOME HOLY
Manservant n MALE SUB
Mansion n HOME
Manslaughter n DAMG DEAD
Mantel n FURN
Mantelpiece n FURN
Mantis n BUG UP
Mantle n GARB
Mantle n COVR
Mantle n FURN

Mantle v LARG
Manual j BODY
Manual n WRIT
Manufacture v MART WORK
Manure n DIRT SOMA
Manuscript n WRIT
Many j MUCH
Map n IDEA FORM
Maple n VEGT
Maple n MTRL VEGT
Mar v DIRT
Maraca n MUSC
Maraschino n VEGT
Marathon n EVER GO
Marble n ERTH MTRL
Marble n MTRL PLAY
Marble n COLR
Marbled v COLR
Marbling v COLR
Marcel v BODY AID
March n GO
March n GO MUSC
March n TIME
Marched v GO
Marching v GO
Mare n ANML LADY
Margarine n FOOD VEGT
Margin n END
Margin n SOME
Marigold n VEGT
Marijuana n MEDC VEGT
Marimba n MUSC
Marinate v FOOD FLOW
Marine j FLOW
Marine n DAMG FLOW
Mariner n FLOW
Marines n DAMG FLOW
Marionette n PLAY SUB
Marital j SEX KIN
Maritime j FLOW
Marjoram n FOOD VEGT
Mark v WRIT
Mark v VIEW
Mark n SHRP
Mark n MONY
Marked j EMPH
Marked v WRIT
Marked v VIEW
Market n MART MONY
Market n MART FOOD
Marketplace n MART PLAC
Marking v WRIT
Marking v VIEW
Marksman n DAMG SHRP
Marlin n ANML FLOW
Marmalade n FOOD VEGT
Marmoset n ANML
Marmot n ANML
Maroon j COLR
Maroon v SEP
Marooned v SEP
Marooning v SEP

Parts of speech: a article; b preposition; c conjunction; d adverb; f prefix; i interjection;
j adjective; n noun; p pronoun; r phrase; v verb.

Marquee n PLAY VIEW
Marred v DIRT
Marriage n SEX KIN
Married v SEX KIN
Marring v DIRT
Marrow n CRUX SOMA
Marry v SEX KIN
Mars n ASTR
Mars n DAMG MYTH
Mars v DIRT
Marsh n ERTH FLOW
Marshal n LEAD
Marshmallow n FOOD VEGT
Marsupial j ANML
Mart n MART
Marten n ANML
Marten n ANML FABR
Martial j DAMG
Martian n ASTR
Martin n ANML UP
Martini n SIP VEGT
Martyr n DEAD HOLY
Marvelous j POWR GOOD
Mascara n COLR
Mascot n AID
Masculine j MALE
Mash n SIP VEGT
Mash v EASY
Mask n ANML BODY
Mask n COVR
Mask n GARB COVR
Masochism n DAMG SOLE
Mason n FORM WORK
Masque n FALS PLAY
Masquerade v FALS PLAY
Mass j MUCH GRUP
Mass n MUCH
Mass n TALK HOLY
Mass n MSMT
Massacre v DAMG DEAD
Massage v BODY AID
Massed v MUCH GRUP
Masseur n AID MALE
Masseuse n LADY AID
Massing v MUCH GRUP
Massive j LARG
Mast n FORM
Mastectomy n MEDC BODY
Master n POWR LEAD
Master n LEAD EDUC
Master n MALE YNG
Mastered v POWR LEAD
Mastering v POWR LEAD
Masterpiece n POWR LEAD
Masthead n FORW FORM
Masticate v FOOD SOMA
Mastiff n ANML
Masturbate v SOLE SEX
Mat n DOWN FURN
Mat n JOIN FORM
Mat n COLR
Matador n ANML DAMG
Match n HEAT
Match n SIML
Match n PLAY

Matched v SIML
Matches n HEAT
Matches n SIML
Matches n PLAY
Matching v SIML
Matchless j POWR
Mate n SEX KIN
Mate n SIML
Mate v JOIN SEX
Mate n LEAD FLOW
Mate v POWR PLAY
Mated v JOIN SEX
Mated v POWR PLAY
Mater n LADY KIN
Mater n LADY AID
Material n MTRL
Material n FABR
Material j TRUE
Material j CRUX
Materialize v TRUE
Maternal j LADY KIN
Maternal j LADY AID
Math n NUMR
Mathematics n NUMR
Matinee n PLAY TIME
Mating v JOIN SEX
Mating v POWR PLAY
Matriarch n LEAD LADY
Matriarch n LADY KIN
Matriculate v JOIN EDUC
Matrimony n SEX KIN
Matron n LADY AID
Matted v JOIN FORM
Matter n CRUX
Matter n MTRL
Matter n CRUX PANG
Mattered v CRUX
Mattering v CRUX
Matteroffact j TRUE
Matters v CRUX
Mattress n FURN REST
Mature v POWR
Mature v END
Maudlin j FOOL PANG
Mausoleum n DEAD HOLW
Mauve n COLR
Maverick n ANML OPPO
Mawkish j PANG
Maxim n TALK IDEA
Maximal j LARG
Maximize v LARG
Maximum j LARG
May v NSCR
May n TIME
Maybe d SOME
Mayhem n DAMG
Mayonnaise n FOOD
Mayor n LEAD LAW
Maze n BLUR PATH
Me p SOLE WE
Meadow n ERTH VEGT
Meager j LITL
Meal n FOOD
Meal n FOOD VEGT
Mealtime n FOOD TIME

Mealy j FOOD VEGT
Mealymouth j FALS BODY
Mean v IDEA
Mean v MOTV
Mean j BAD AGGR
Mean j NUMR
Mean j WEAK
Mean n EASY
Meander v VARY GO
Meaning n IDEA
Meaning v MOTV
Meaningless j FOOL
Means v IDEA
Means v MOTV
Means n AID
Means n NUMR
Meant v IDEA
Meant v MOTV
Meantime n TIME
Meanwhile d TIME
Measles n SICK
Measly j BAD LITL
Measure n MSMT
Measure n SOME
Measure n LAW
Measure n AID
Measure n MSMT MUSC
Measured v MSMT
Measuring v MSMT
Meat n ANML FOOD
Meat n FOOD
Meat n CRUX
Mechanic n MECH WORK
Mechanism n MECH
Mechanize v MECH
Medal n POWR
Meddle v AGGR
Media n AID
Media n TALK WRIT
Median j NUMR
Median j PLAC
Mediate v AID
Medical j MEDC
Medicine n MEDC
Medieval j PAST
Mediocre j WEAK
Meditate v IDEA
Medium j EASY
Medium n AID
Medium n MYTH
Medley n JOIN
Meek j WEAK
Meet v JOIN
Meet v GRUP JOIN
Meet v SIML
Megaphone n HEAR
Melancholia n PANG
Meld v JOIN
Meld v JOIN PLAY
Melee n DAMG
Mellifluous j EASY
Mellow j EASY
Melodies n MUSC
Melodrama n PLAY PANG
Melody n MUSC

Melon n FOOD VEGT
Melt v VARY EASY
Member n GRUP JOIN
Member n BODY
Membrane n SOMA
Membrane n MTRL
Memento n IDEA PAST
Memo n WRIT
Memoir n WRIT PAST
Memorable j GOOD IDEA
Memorandum n WRIT
Memorial j IDEA PAST
Memory n IDEA PAST
Men n MALE
Menace n DAMG
Menagerie n ANML HOME
Mend v AID
Mendacity n FALS
Mendicant n MOTV LACK
Menial j SUB TRIV
Menopause n LADY SOMA
Menstrual j LADY SOMA
Mental j IDEA
Mention v TALK
Mentor n LEAD EDUC
Menu n FOOD WRIT
Meow v ANML TALK
Mercenary j DAMG MONY
Merchandise n MART
Merchant n MART
Merciful j GOOD AID
Merciless j AGGR
Mercurial j VARY
Mercury n MTRL
Mercury n TALK MYTH
Mercury n ASTR
Mercy n GOOD AID
Mere j TRIV
Merge v JOIN
Meridian n ASTR TIME
Meridian n POWR UP
Meridian n ERTH MSMT
Meringue n FOOD
Merit n GOOD
Merit v MOTV
Mermaid n LADY MYTH
Merry j GLAD
Merrygoround n GO PLAY
Merrymaking n GLAD PLAY
Mesa n ERTH BULG
Mesh n FABR
Mesh v JOIN
Meshed v JOIN
Meshing v JOIN
Mesmerize v REST
Mesomorph n BODY
Meson n ION
Mesozoic j PAST
Mesquite n VEGT
Mess n BLUR DIRT
Mess n FOOD
Message n TALK
Messenger n TALK
Messy j BLUR DIRT
Mestizo n GRUP

Met v JOIN
Met v GRUP JOIN
Met v SIML
Metal n MTRL
Metallurgy n MTRL IDEA
Metaphor n SIML TALK
Metaphysical j IDEA EVNT
Meteor n ASTR
Meteorology n ASTR IDEA
Meter n MSMT
Meter n MECH MSMT
Meter n MSMT MUSC
Method n FORM
Meticulous j SHRP
Metric j MSMT
Metronome n MSMT TIME
Metropolitan j PLAC
Mettle n POWR
Mew n ANML TALK
Mezzanine n HOME UP
Mica n ERTH MTRL
Mice n ANML
Mice n ANML WEAK
Microanalysis n LITL IDEA
Microbe n BUG SICK
Microcosm n WHOL LITL
Microorganism n LITL LIVE
Microphone n HEAR
Microscope n MECH VIEW
Mid j PLAC
Midden n DIRT BULG
Middle j PLAC
Middleaged j TIME
Middleclass j GRUP
Middleman n AID
Middling j EASY
Middy n GARB
Midget n LITL
Midnight n TIME
Midst n IN JOIN
Midstream n IN FLOW
Midsummer j HEAT TIME
Midway d GO SOME
Midway n PATH
Midwife n BGIN LADY
Midwinter j COLD TIME
Mien n EVNT
Miff v AGGR
Might v NSCR
Might n POWR
Mightier j POWR
Mighty j POWR
Mighty d EMPH
Migraine n SICK
Migrant n GO
Migrate v GO
Mikado n LEAD
Mike n HEAR
Mil n MSMT
Milady n LADY
Milch j ANML SIP
Mild j EASY
Milder j EASY
Mildew n DIRT
Mile n MSMT

Miles n MSMT
Milestone n CRUX MSMT
Milieu n WHOL HOLW
Militancy n AGGR
Military j DAMG
Militate v OPPO
Militia n DAMG GRUP
Milk n ANML SIP
Milk n SIP
Milkman n SIP MALE
Mill v GO GRUP
Mill n MECH WORK
Mill n MONY
Milled v GO GRUP
Milled v MECH WORK
Millennium n NUMR TIME
Millennium n FORW TIME
Millet n FOOD VEGT
Millimeter n MSMT
Millinery n GARB MART
Milling v GO GRUP
Milling v MECH WORK
Million n NUMR
Millionaire n MUCH MONY
Milord n LEAD MALE
Milt n SOMA MALE
Mime n SIML PLAY
Mimeograph v WRIT MECH
Mimic v FOOL SIML
Miming v SIML PLAY
Mimosa n VEGT
Minaret n HOME UP
Mince n FOOD LITL
Mince v LITL SEP
Mince v WEAK
Mince v GO WEAK
Mincemeat n FOOD LITL
Mind n IDEA
Mind v AID
Mind v MOTV
Mine n DAMG
Mine n ERTH WORK
Mine p SOLE WE
Mined v DAMG
Mined v ERTH WORK
Mineral n MTRL
Mines n DAMG
Mines n ERTH WORK
Mingle v JOIN
Miniature j LITL
Minimize v LITL
Minimum n LITL
Mining v DAMG
Mining v ERTH WORK
Minion n SUB
Minion n FOND
Minister n LEAD HOLY
Minister n LEAD LAW
Minister v AID
Ministered v AID
Ministering v AID
Ministry n LEAD HOLY
Ministry n LEAD LAW
Mink n ANML
Mink n ANML FABR

Minnow n ANML FLOW
Minor j SUB
Minor n EDUC SUB
Minor j TRIV
Minored v EDUC SUB
Minoring v EDUC SUB
Minority n GRUP SUB
Minority n LITL NUMR
Minstrel n TALK MUSC
Mint j NEW
Mint n FOOD VEGT
Mint n MUCH MONY
Mint v BGIN MONY
Minted v BGIN MONY
Minting v BGIN MONY
Minuet n GO MUSC
Minus b NUMR SEP
Minus b LACK
Minute j MSMT TIME
Minute j LITL
Minutes n MSMT TIME
Minutes n WRIT
Minx n POWR LADY
Miracle n GOOD MYTH
Mirage n VIEW MYTH
Mire n ERTH FLOW
Mire v BLOK ERTH
Mirror n VIEW
Mirth n GLAD
Misadventure n DAMG
Misalliance n BAD JOIN
Misanthropy n AGGR
Misapply v FALS
Misapprehend v FALS IDEA
Misbegotten j BAD BGIN
Misbehave v BAD EVNT
Miscalculate v FALS IDEA
Miscarriage n FALS WEAK
Miscarriage n BGIN FALS
Miscarry v FALS WEAK
Miscegenation n JOIN SEX
Miscellany n OPPO JOIN
Mischance n DAMG
Mischief n BAD
Misconception n FALS IDEA
Misconstrue v FALS IDEA
Miscount v FALS NUMR
Miscreant j BAD
Miscue n FALS
Misdeal v FALS PLAY
Misdeed n BAD
Misdemeanor n CRIM
Misdirect v LEAD FALS
Miser n AGGR HAVE
Miserable j PANG
Miseries n PANG
Misery n PANG
Misfire v FALS WEAK
Misfire v DAMG FALS
Misfit n FALS WEAK
Misfortune n DAMG
Misgiving n BLUR PANG
Misgovern v LEAD FALS
Misguide v FALS AID
Mishap n DAMG

Mishmash n BLUR JOIN
Misinform v FALS TALK
Misinterpret v FALS IDEA
Misjudge v FALS IDEA
Mislay v LACK
Mislead v FALS
Mismanage v LEAD FALS
Misprint n FALS WRIT
Misquote v FALS TALK
Misread v FALS WRIT
Misrepresent v FALS
Miss v VARY
Miss n LADY
Miss v LACK
Missed v VARY
Missed v LACK
Missile n DAMG
Missing v VARY
Missing v LACK
Mission n MOTV
Mission n HOLY MOTV
Missionary n HOLY MOTV
Missive n WRIT
Misspell v FALS TALK
Misstate v FALS TALK
Misstep n FALS GO
Missus n LADY KIN
Mist n WEA BLUR
Mist n VAPR FLOW
Mistake n FALS WEAK
Misted v WEA BLUR
Misted v VAPR FLOW
Mister n MALE
Mistletoe n VEGT
Mistreat v DAMG
Mistress n LEAD LADY
Mistress n LADY SEX
Mistrial n FALS LAW
Mistrust v BLUR AGGR
Misunderstand v FALS IDEA
Misuse v AGGR FALS
Mite n BUG LITL
Mite n LITL
Mitigate v EASY AID
Mitosis n SOMA SEP
Mitt n GARB PLAY
Mitten n GARB
Mix v JOIN
Mix v BLUR JOIN
Mixture n JOIN
Mnemonic j AID IDEA
Moan v TALK PANG
Moat n ERTH HOLW
Mob v AGGR GRUP
Mobile j GO
Mobile j VARY EASY
Mobile n VIEW FORM
Mobilize v GRUP
Mobilize v GO
Moccasin n GARB
Moccasin n ANML
Mocha j FOOD VEGT
Mock j SIML FALS
Mock v FOOL AGGR
Mockery n FOOL AGGR

Mocking v FOOL AGGR
Mocks v FOOL AGGR
Mode n EVNT
Mode n NEW
Mode n NUMR
Model n SIML FORM
Model j SIML GOOD
Moderate j EASY
Modern j NEW
Modes n EVNT
Modes n NUMR
Modest j GOOD
Modicum n LITL SOME
Modify v VARY
Modish j NEW
Modulate v VARY
Module n MSMT
Modus n FORM
Mohair n ANML FABR
Mohammed n LEAD HOLY
Moisture n FLOW
Molasses n FOOD VEGT
Mold n DIRT VEGT
Mold n FORM
Molded v FORM
Molding v FORM
Moldy j DIRT VEGT
Mole n ANML
Mole n BODY
Mole n BLOK FLOW
Molecule n MTRL ION
Molest v DAMG
Mollify v GLAD EASY
Mollusk n ANML FLOW
Molt v VARY BODY
Molted v VARY BODY
Molten j HEAT FLOW
Mom n LADY KIN
Mom n LADY AID
Moment n TIME
Moment n CRUX
Momentary j VARY TIME
Momentous j CRUX
Momentum n POWR GO
Monarch n LEAD
Monastery n HOME HOLY
Monastic j HOLY
Monday n TIME
Monetary j MONY
Money n MONY
Monger n MART
Mongolian n SICK YNG
Mongoose n ANML
Mongrel n ANML TRIV
Moniker n TALK
Monitor v LEAD
Monk n MALE HOLY
Monkey n ANML
Monkey v FOOL ANML
Monochromatic j SIML COLR
Monocle n AID VIEW
Monody n PANG MUSC
Monogamy n SEX KIN
Monogram n WRIT
Monolith n SOLE FORM

Monologue n SOLE TALK
Monomania n SOLE IDEA
Monoplane n VEHC UP
Monopoly n SOLE HAVE
Monorail n VEHC
Monosyllable n SOLE TALK
Monotheism n LEAD HOLY
Monotone n SIML HEAR
Monotonous j SIML EVER
Monsoon n WEA DAMG
Monster n BAD AFAR
Montage n JOIN VIEW
Month n TIME
Monument n EVER FORM
Moo v ANML TALK
Mooch v MOTV
Mood n MOTV
Moody j PANG
Moon n ASTR
Moon v PANG
Moonbeam n ASTR VIEW
Mooned v PANG
Mooning v PANG
Moonlight n ASTR VIEW
Moonlight v CRIM WORK
Moons n ASTR
Moons v PANG
Moonshine n ASTR VIEW
Moonshine n CRIM SIP
Moonstone n ERTH MTRL
Moor v BLOK
Moor n ERTH FLOW
Moor n GRUP
Moored v BLOK
Mooring v BLOK
Moose n ANML
Moot j BLUR TALK
Mop n CLEN
Mope v REST PANG
Mopped v CLEN
Moppet n YNG
Moral j GOOD IDEA
Morale n GOOD MOTV
Morass n ERTH FLOW
Morbid j PANG
Mordant j AGGR
More j MUCH
Mores n EVER GOOD
Morgue n DEAD HOLW
Moribund j DEAD
Morning n TIME
Morocco n ANML FABR
Moron n FOOL
Morose j PANG
Morpheme n TALK FORM
Morphine n MEDC REST
Morrow n FOR W TIME
Morsel n FOOD LITL
Mortal j DEAD LIVE
Mortar n JOIN MTRL
Mortar n DAMG MECH
Mortar n HOLW
Mortgage v MART MONY
Mortician n MART DEAD
Mortify v AGGR PANG

Mosaic n COLR FORM
Mosey v GO
Moslem n GRUP HOLY
Mosque n HOME HOLY
Mosquito n BUG UP
Moss n VEGT
Most j MUCH
Mote n DIRT LITL
Motel n MART HOME
Moth n BUG UP
Mother n LADY KIN
Mother n LADY AID
Mother n LADY HOLY
Motherinlaw n LADY KIN
Motherinlaw n LADY AID
Motherless j KIN LACK
Motherless j LADY LACK
Motif n IDEA
Motion n GO
Motion n IDEA MOTV
Motion v BODY EVNT
Motioned v BODY EVNT
Motioning v BODY EVNT
Motionless j REST
Motivate v MOTV
Motive n MOTV
Motive j GO
Motley j OPPO
Motor n MECH
Motor j BODY EVNT
Motor v GO VEHC
Motorboat n FLOW VEHC
Motorcade n VEHC
Motorcycle n VEHC
Motored v GO VEHC
Motoring v GO VEHC
Mottle v COLR
Motto n TALK IDEA
Mound n ERTH BULG
Mound n BULG
Mount v GO UP
Mount n ERTH BULG
Mount n ANML UP
Mountain n ERTH BULG
Mounted v GO UP
Mounting v GO UP
Mourn v PANG
Mouse n ANML
Mouse n ANML WEAK
Mouse v ANML BLOK
Moused v ANML BLOK
Mousing v ANML BLOK
Mousse n FOOD
Mouth n BODY HOLW
Move v GO
Move v MOTV
Move v EVNT
Movement n GO
Movement n MOTV
Movement n EVNT
Movement n MUSC
Movies n PLAY VIEW
Moving v GO
Moving v MOTV
Moving v EVNT

Mow v SHRP
Mr n MALE
Mrs n LADY KIN
Mrs n LADY
Ms n WRIT
Ms n LADY
Much j MUCH
Mucilage n JOIN
Mucous n SOMA
Mud n ERTH FLOW
Mud n DIRT ERTH
Muddies v DIRT ERTH
Muddies v BLUR
Muddle n BLUR WEAK
Muff n GARB
Muff v WEAK
Muffed v WEAK
Muffin n FOOD
Muffing v WEAK
Muffle v BLOK
Muffler n GARB
Muffler n BLOK
Mug n SIP HOLW
Mug n BODY
Mug v DAMG
Mugged v DAMG
Muggier j HEAT FLOW
Mugging v DAMG
Mugging v BODY
Muggy j HEAT FLOW
Mulatto j COLR
Mulberry n VEGT
Mulberry n FOOD VEGT
Mulberry n COLR
Mulch n AID VEGT
Mule n ANML
Mull v IDEA
Multifarious j MUCH OPPO
Multilateral j MUCH
Multimillionaire n MUCH MONY
Multiple j MUCH
Multiple n LARG NUMR
Multiply v LARG
Multiply v LARG NUMR
Multitude n MUCH GRUP
Multitude n MUCH
Mum j HEAR
Mumble n BLUR TALK
Mummer n PLAY
Mummies n DEAD EVER
Mummy n DEAD EVER
Mumps n SICK
Munch v FOOD SOMA
Mundane j EVER TRIV
Municipal j LAW PLAC
Munition n DAMG
Mural n COLR
Murder v CRIM DEAD
Murder v DAMG DEAD
Murky j BLUR
Murmur n HEAR TALK
Muscatel n SIP VEGT
Muscle n BODY
Muscle v POWR BODY
Muscled v POWR BODY

Muscling v POWR BODY
Muscular j BODY
Muse v IDEA
Museum n HOME
Mush n EASY FOOD
Mush n FOOL
Mush v COLD GO
Mushroom n FOOD VEGT
Mushroom v LARG QUIK
Mushroomed v LARG QUIK
Mushrooming v LARG QUIK
Music n MUSC
Musing v IDEA
Musk n ANML SOMA
Musket n DAMG MECH
Muskmelon n FOOD VEGT
Muskrat n ANML
Muskrat n ANML FABR
Muslin n FABR

Muss v BLUR
Mussed v BLUR
Mussel n FOOD FLOW
Mussel n ANML FLOW
Must v MOTV
Must n SIP VEGT
Must n DIRT
Mustache n BODY
Mustang n ANML
Mustard n FOOD VEGT
Muster v GRUP
Musty j DIRT
Mutate v VARY
Mute j TALK LACK
Mutilate v DAMG
Mutiny n DAMG
Mutt n ANML TRIV
Mutter n BLUR TALK
Mutton n ANML FOOD

Mutual j SIML
Muzzle n ANML BODY
Muzzle n BLOK BODY
Muzzle n HOLW
Muzzled v BLOK BODY
Muzzling v BLOK BODY
My p SOLE WE
Myelin n SOMA
Mynah n ANML UP
Myopia n SICK VIEW
Myriad n MUCH
Myrrh n MTRL VEGT
Myrtle n VEGT
Myself p SOLE WE
Mystery n BLUR
Mystic j BLUR HOLY
Mystify v BLUR
Myth n MYTH

N

N n WRIT
Nab v BLOK HAVE
Nag n ANML
Nag v AGGR TALK
Nagged v AGGR TALK
Nail n JOIN SHRP
Nail n BODY SHRP
Nailed v JOIN SHRP
Nailing v JOIN SHRP
Naive j WEAK
Naked j BODY OPEN
Nambypamby j WEAK
Name n TALK
Name n POWR TALK
Named v TALK
Names v TALK
Namesake n SIML TALK
Naming v TALK
Nap n REST
Nap n FABR
Napalm n DAMG MTRL
Nape n BACK BODY
Napkin n CLEN
Narcotic n MEDC REST
Narrate v TALK
Narrow j LITL
Narrows n LITL FLOW
Narrows v LITL
Nary j NO
Nasal j SOMA
Nastier j AGGR DIRT
Nasturtium n VEGT
Nasty j AGGR DIRT
Nation n GRUP
National j GRUP
Nationwide j LARG GRUP
Native n BGIN NEAR
Natty j CLEN
Natural j CRUX
Natural j WHOL

Natural j EASY
Naturalize v LAW NEAR
Naturalize v CRUX
Nature n CRUX
Nature n WHOL
Naught n NO
Naught n NUMR
Naughtier j BAD
Naughty j BAD
Nausea n SICK PANG
Nautical j FLOW
Naval j DAMG FLOW
Navel n BODY
Navies n DAMG FLOW
Navigate v GO
Navy n DAMG FLOW
Navy n COLR
Nay n NO
Nazi n GRUP
Neanderthal j PAST
Near j NEAR
Neat j CLEN
Nebula n ASTR BLUR
Nebulous j BLUR
Necessity n CRUX MOTV
Neck n BODY
Neck v BODY SEX
Necking v BODY SEX
Necklace n GARB BODY
Nectar n SIP VEGT
Nectarine n FOOD VEGT
Nee j BGIN
Need n MOTV LACK
Needle n SHRP
Needle v AGGR SHRP
Needled v AGGR SHRP
Needlepoint n SHRP FABR
Needlework n SHRP FABR
Needling v AGGR SHRP
Nefarious j BAD

Negate v OPPO NO
Negating v OPPO NO
Negative j NO
Negative n OPPO VIEW
Negative j OPPO NO
Negative j OPPO ION
Neglect v AGGR LACK
Neglect v WEAK
Negligence n AGGR LACK
Negligible j TRIV
Negotiate v AGRE
Negotiate v GO
Negro n COLR GRUP
Neigh n ANML TALK
Neighbor n NEAR
Neighborhood n NEAR PLAC
Neither j NO
Neo f NEW
Neolithic j PAST
Neologism n FOOL TALK
Neon n MTRL
Neophyte n WEAK
Nephew n MALE KIN
Nepotism n FOND KIN
Neptune n ASTR
Neptune n FLOW MYTH
Nerve n SOMA
Nerve n POWR
Nerves n SOMA
Nerves n PANG
Nervier j POWR
Nervous j SOMA
Nervous j PANG
Nervy j POWR
Nest n ANML HOME
Nestle v JOIN NEAR
Nestling v JOIN NEAR
Nestling n ANML YNG
Net n BLOK
Net n JOIN FORM

Parts of speech: a article; b preposition; c conjunction; d adverb; f prefix; i interjection;
j adjective; n noun; p pronoun; r phrase; v verb.

Net j SOME
Nether j DOWN
Nettle n SHRP VEGT
Nettle v AGGR PANG
Nettled v AGGR PANG
Nettling v AGGR PANG
Neurology n MEDC SOMA
Neurosis n SICK PANG
Neurotic j SICK PANG
Neuter j SEX LACK
Neutral j EASY
Neutron n ION
Never d EVER NO
Nevertheless d OPPO
New j NEW
Newcomer n GO NEW
Newfangled j NEW
Newfound j OPEN NEW
News n TALK NEW
Newsboy n WRIT YNG
Newspaper n WRIT NEW
Newsreel n VIEW NEW
Next d NEAR
Next d FORW
Niacin n MTRL
Nib n SHRP
Nibble v FOOD LITL
Nice j GOOD
Niche n HOLW
Nick v DAMG SHRP
Nicked v DAMG SHRP
Nickel n MONY
Nickel n MTRL
Nickelodeon n MECH MUSC
Nickname n TALK
Nicotine n MTRL
Niece n LADY KIN
Nifty j GOOD
Niggard n AGGR HAVE
Niggling j TRIV
Nigh d NEAR
Night n TIME
Nightcap n SIP TIME
Nightcap n GARB REST
Nightcap n END TIME
Nightfall n TIME
Nightgown n GARB REST
Nightingale n ANML UP
Nightmare n MYTH PANG
Nightstick n DAMG LAW
Nighttime n TIME
Nihilism n NO IDEA
Nil n NO
Nimble j POWR QUIK
Nimbus n VAPR VIEW
Nimbus n BLUR WEA
Nincompoop n FOOL
Nine n NUMR
Nineteen n NUMR
Ninety n NUMR
Ninny n FOOL
Ninth n NUMR
Nip v SHRP
Nip v BLOK
Nip v SIP SOMA

Nipandtuck r NEAR
Nipped v SHRP
Nipped v BLOK
Nipped v SIP SOMA
Nipple n SIP BULG
Nirvana n GLAD OPEN
Nit n BUG DIRT
Nitrate n MTRL
Nitrogen n VAPR
Nitroglycerin n MTRL
Nitwit n FOOL
Nix n NO
No d NO
Nobility n LEAD GOOD
Noble j LEAD GOOD
Nobody n SOLE NO
Nobody n SOLE WEAK
Nock n HOLW
Nocturnal j TIME
Nod v AGRE
Nod v VARY REST
Noel n HOLY MUSC
Nog n SIP
Noise n HEAR
Noiseless j HEAR
Nomad n GO GRUP
Nomenclature n TALK
Nominal j TRIV
Nominate v MOTV
Nominative j MOTV
Nominative j TALK FORM
Nominee n MOTV
Non f NO
Nonchalance n GLAD REST
Noncom n LEAD
Noncommittal j BLUR
Nonconductor n BLOK
Nonconformist n OPPO
Noncooperation n OPPO
Nondescript j TRIV
None p NO
Nonentity n TRIV
Nonpartisan j OPEN MOTV
Nonplus v BLUR
Nonsense n FOOL
Noodle n FOOD
Noodle n BODY IDEA
Nook n HOLW
Noon n TIME
Noose n BLOK
Nor c NO
Norm n EVER
Normal j EVER
North n PLAC PATH
Nose n BODY
Nostalgia n PANG MOTV
Nostril n BODY
Nostrum n MEDC
Nosy j AGGR MOTV
Not d NO
Notable j POWR
Notary n WRIT LAW
Notation n WRIT
Notch n HOLW
Note n SOME

Note n WRIT
Note n IDEA
Note n WRIT MONY
Note n POWR
Note n MUSC
Notebook n WRIT
Noted j POWR
Noted v WRIT
Noted v IDEA
Nothing n NO
Notice v VIEW
Notice n IDEA
Notify v IDEA
Noting v IDEA
Noting v WRIT
Notion n IDEA
Notion n MART TRIV
Notoriety n BAD OPEN
Notwithstanding b OPPO
Noun n TALK FORM
Nourish v FOOD AID
Nova n ASTR
Novel j NEW
Novel n WRIT
Novels n WRIT
Novelty n NEW
Novelty n MART NEW
November n TIME
Novena n FOND HOLY
Novice n WEAK
Novitiate n HOLY SUB
Now d NEW
Noxious j BAD DAMG
Nozzle n OUT FLOW
Nth j NUMR
Nuance n VARY COLR
Nub n CRUX
Nub n BULG
Nubile j SEX KIN
Nuclear j CRUX ION
Nucleus n CRUX
Nucleus n CRUX ION
Nude j BODY OPEN
Nudge v JOIN
Nugget n ERTH MTRL
Nuisance n AGGR PANG
Null j NO
Numb v REST
Numbed v REST
Number n NUMR
Numbs v REST
Numbskull n FOOL BODY
Numeral n NUMR
Numerator n NUMR
Numerical j NUMR
Numerous j MUCH
Nun n LADY HOLY
Nunnery n HOME HOLY
Nuptial j SEX KIN
Nurse n LADY AID
Nurse n MEDC AID
Nurse v SIP YNG
Nursery n HOME YNG
Nursery n AID VEGT
Nurture v AID

Nut n FOOD VEGT
Nut n BLOK MECH
Nut n FOOL
Nutcracker n FOOD SEP
Nutcracker n ANML UP
Nutmeg n FOOD VEGT

Nutria n ANML MTRL
Nutrient j FOOD AID
Nutriment n FOOD AID
Nutrition n FOOD AID
Nutshell n LITL
Nutshell n HOLW VEGT

Nuzzle v BODY JOIN
Nylon n FABR
Nylon n GARB LADY
Nymph n LADY MYTH

O

O n WRIT
O i EMPH
O n WRIT FORM
O n NUMR
Oaf n FOOL
Oak n VEGT
Oak n MTRL VEGT
Oar n AID FLOW
Oasis n ERTH AID
Oat n FOOD VEGT
Oath n BAD TALK
Oath n TALK HOLY
Obduracy n AGGR EVER
Obedience n AGRE SUB
Obeisance n SUB
Obelisk n FORM
Obese j LARG BODY
Obey v AGRE SUB
Obfuscate v BLUR
Obituary n DEAD WRIT
Object n NSCR
Object n END MOTV
Object n TALK FORM
Object v OPPO
Objected v OPPO
Objecting v OPPO
Objective j TRUE
Objective j TALK FORM
Objective n END MOTV
Objectivity n TRUE
Objector n OPPO
Obligate v MOTV
Oblige v AGRE MOTV
Oblique j FORM
Oblique j VARY
Obliterate v DAMG
Obliterate v BLUR
Oblivion n BLUR
Oblong j FORM
Obloquy n AGGR TALK
Obnoxious j AGGR
Oboe n MUSC
Obscene j BAD SEX
Obscure j BLUR
Obsequious j FOND SUB
Observable j VIEW
Observatory n ASTR VIEW
Observation n VIEW
Observation n AGRE
Observation n TALK
Observe v VIEW
Observe v AGRE
Observe v TALK
Observing v VIEW
Observing v AGRE
Observing v TALK

Obsess v EVER PANG
Obsidian n ERTH MTRL
Obsolete j PAST TRIV
Obstacle n BLOK
Obstetric j BGIN MEDC
Obstinacy n AGGR EVER
Obstreperous j AGGR HEAR
Obstruct v BLOK
Obtain v HAVE
Obtuse j FORM
Obtuse j FOOL
Obtuse j BLUR
Obviate v BLOK
Obvious j OPEN
Ocarina n MUSC
Occasion n EVNT
Occasional j SOME
Occident n PLAC
Occult j MYTH COVR
Occupancy n IN HAVE
Occupation n IN HAVE
Occupation n WORK
Occupation n MOTV
Occupied v IN HAVE
Occupied v WORK
Occupied v MOTV
Occupy v IN HAVE
Occupy v WORK
Occupy v MOTV
Occur v EVNT
Ocean n FLOW
Oceanography n IDEA FLOW
Ocelot n ANML
Ochre n COLR
Ochre n ERTH MTRL
Oclock n TIME
Octagon n FORM
Octane n MTRL
Octave n NUMR MUSC
October n TIME
Octopus n ANML FLOW
Oculist n MEDC VIEW
Odd j OPPO
Odd j AFAR
Oddball n FOOL AFAR
Ode n TALK MUSC
Odious j AGGR
Odor n VAPR SOMA
Of b NSCR
Off j SEP
Off j NSCR
Offal n DIRT
Offend v AGGR
Offense n DAMG
Offense n AGGR
Offer n AID

Offhand j EASY TRIV
Office n MART HOME
Office n LEAD
Office n AID
Office n HOLY
Officer n LEAD
Officer n LEAD LAW
Official n LEAD
Officiate v LEAD
Officious j AGGR
Offing n FORW TIME
Offing n FLOW
Offset n WRIT MECH
Offset n OPPO
Offset n VARY
Offsets v OPPO
Offsets v VARY
Offshoot n SEP
Offspring n KIN YNG
Often d MUCH
Ogle v VIEW
Ogre n DAMG MYTH
Oh i EMPH
Ohm n ION MSMT
Oil v EASY MTRL
Oil n ERTH MTRL
Oil n FOOD VEGT
Oil n COLR
Oiled v EASY MTRL
Oiling v EASY MTRL
Oils v EASY MTRL
Oils n ERTH MTRL
Oils n FOOD VEGT
Oils n COLR
Oilskin n GARB
Ointment n EASY MTRL
OK j AGRE
Okay j AGRE
Okra n FOOD VEGT
Old j PAST
Oldfashioned j PAST
Oldfashioned n SIP PAST
Oldtime j PAST
Oleander n VEGT
Oleomargarine n FOOD VEGT
Olfactory j VAPR SOMA
Oligarchy n LEAD GRUP
Olive n FOOD VEGT
Olive n COLR
Olympic j PLAY
Omelet n FOOD
Omen n FORW MYTH
Ominous j BAD
Omission n LACK
Omit v LACK
Omnibus n VEHC

Omnibus n MUCH WRIT
Omnipotence n WHOL POWR
Omnipresence n WHOL NEAR
Omniscient j WHOL IDEA
Omnivorous j WHOL FOOD
On d NSCR
On d FORW
Onanism n SOLE SEX
Once d PAST
Once n QUIK
Once d NUMR
One n NUMR
One n SOLE
Onerous j PANG
Onesided j FALS MOTV
Ongoing j FORW
Onion n FOOD VEGT
Onlooker n VIEW
Only j SOLE
Only d TRIV
Only c NSCR
Onset n BGIN
Onset n DAMG
Onslaught n DAMG
Ontogeny n SOLE PAST
Onus n PANG
Oocyte n BGIN SOMA
Oodles n MUCH
Oosperm n BGIN SOMA
Ooze v FLOW
Ooze n ERTH FLOW
Opacity n BLUR VIEW
Opal n ERTH MTRL
Opalescent j VIEW
Opaque j BLUR VIEW
Open v OPEN
Open v BGIN OPEN
Opera n TALK MUSC
Operate v WORK
Operate v MEDC SHRP
Operatic j TALK MUSC
Operating v WORK
Operating v MEDC SHRP
Operetta n TALK MUSC
Ophthalmology n MEDC VIEW
Opiate n MEDC REST
Opinion n IDEA
Opinionated j AGGR IDEA
Opium n MEDC VEGT
Opossum n ANML
Opponent n OPPO
Opportunity n AID
Oppose v OPPO
Oppress v DAMG
Opprobrium n AGGR
Optic j SOMA VIEW
Optician n MEDC VIEW
Optics n SOMA VIEW
Optimism n GLAD MOTV
Optimum n GOOD
Option n MOTV
Opulence n MUCH GOOD
Opus n WORK
Or c NSCR
Oracle n LEAD HOLY

Oral j TALK
Oral j BODY HOLW
Orange n FOOD VEGT
Orange n COLR
Orangutan n ANML
Oration n TALK
Orator n TALK
Oratorical j TALK
Oratorio n TALK MUSC
Oratory n TALK
Orbit n GO HOLW
Orbit n HOLW FORM
Orchard n ERTH VEGT
Orchestra n GRUP MUSC
Orchestra n PLAY REST
Orchestral j GRUP MUSC
Orchestrate v GRUP MUSC
Orchid n VEGT
Orchid n COLR
Ordain v LEAD LAW
Ordain v LEAD HOLY
Ordain v LEAD END
Ordeal n PANG
Order n LEAD MOTV
Order n GRUP
Order n FORW FORM
Order n GOOD
Orderly j GOOD
Orderly n AID
Ordinal j FORW NUMR
Ordinance n LAW
Ordinary j EVER
Ordinary j TRIV
Ore n ERTH MTRL
Organ n MUSC
Organ n BODY
Organdy n FABR
Organic j SOMA LIVE
Organism n LIVE
Organism n BUG LIVE
Organist n MUSC
Organization n FORM
Organization n GRUP FORM
Organize v FORM
Orgasm n SOMA SEX
Orgiastic j GLAD PLAY
Orgiastic j PLAY SEX
Orgy n GLAD PLAY
Orgy n PLAY SEX
Orient n PLAC
Orient v NEAR IDEA
Orient v FORW
Oriental n PLAC
Orientate v NEAR IDEA
Oriented v NEAR IDEA
Oriented v FORW
Orienting v NEAR IDEA
Orienting v FORW
Orients v NEAR IDEA
Orients v FORW
Orifice n HOLW OPEN
Origin n BGIN
Original j BGIN
Oriole n ANML UP
Ornament n GOOD

Ornate j GOOD
Ornery j BAD
Ornithology n ANML UP
Orphan n KIN LACK
Orthodox j EVER HOLY
Orthodox j EVER
Orthopedic j MEDC BODY
Oscillate v VARY
Oscilloscope n MECH VIEW
Osmosis n SOMA IN
Osprey n ANML UP
Ostensible j OPEN
Ostentation n OPEN VIEW
Osteopath n MEDC
Ostracism n BLOK SEP
Ostrich n ANML
Other j OPPO
Other p SOLE
Others p SOLE
Otherwise j OPPO
Otter n ANML
Ouch i DAMG EMPH
Ought v MOTV
Ounce n MSMT
Our p WE
Ours p WE
Oust v OUT SEP
Out d OUT
Out d OUT SEP
Out d END OUT
Out d OPPO
Out n OUT PLAY
Outburst n AGGR OUT
Outcast n OUT SEP
Outcome n END
Outcry n HEAR PANG
Outdo v POWR
Outdoor j OUT
Outer j OUT
Outfield n ERTH PLAY
Outfit n GARB
Outfit n GRUP
Outfit v AID
Outgrowth n END
Outing n OUT PLAY
Outlandish j FOOL AFAR
Outlast v EVER
Outlaw n CRIM
Outlay n MONY OUT
Outlet n OUT
Outline n SIML FORM
Outlook n IDEA VIEW
Outlying j AFAR OUT
Outmoded j PAST TRIV
Outpatient j SICK OUT
Outplay v POWR PLAY
Outpost n AID OUT
Output n END
Outrage n BAD DAMG
Outright j EMPH
Outset n BGIN
Outshine v POWR VIEW
Outside j OUT
Outsider n OUT SEP
Outskirts n END OUT

Outsmart v POWR IDEA
Outspoken j TALK OPEN
Outstanding j POWR
Outstanding j OUT
Outstrip v POWR
Outward d OUT
Outwit v POWR IDEA
Oval j FORM
Ovary n LADY SOMA
Ovation n FOND HEAR
Oven n HOLW HEAT
Over b UP
Over b NSCR
Over j END
Overabundant j MUCH LARG
Overactive j QUIK
Overall j WHOL
Overalls n GARB
Overanxious j PANG
Overawe v WEAK PANG
Overbearing j AGGR POWR
Overboard d FLOW SEP
Overburden v BULG
Overburden v PANG
Overcame v POWR WEAK
Overcapacity n LARG BULG
Overcareful j AID MOTV
Overcast j WEA BLUR
Overcautious j AID MOTV
Overclothes n GARB
Overcoat n GARB
Overcome v POWR WEAK
Overcompensate v LARG MONY
Overcompensate v SIML LARG
Overconfident j POWR MOTV
Overcook v FOOD HEAT
Overcook v LARG HEAT
Overcrowd v LARG GRUP
Overdependent j AID SUB
Overdevelop v LARG VARY
Overdevelop v VARY
Overdid v LARG
Overdo v LARG
Overdone v LARG

Overdose n LARG SOME
Overdrive n MECH VEHC
Overdue j PAST
Overeager j MOTV
Overeat v FOOD BULG
Overeat v FOOD SOMA
Overemotional j PANG
Overemphasis n EMPH
Overenthusiastic j MOTV
Overestimate v LARG IDEA
Overexcite v PANG
Overextend v LARG
Overfeed v FOOD SOMA
Overflew v GO UP
Overflight n GO UP
Overflow v BULG FLOW
Overfly v GO UP
Overground j ERTH UP
Overhang n DOWN UP
Overhaul v AID
Overhaul v GO NEAR
Overhead j UP
Overhead n MART MONY
Overhear v HEAR
Overheat v LARG HEAT
Overindulge v LARG AID
Overjoyed j GLAD
Overlaid n UP
Overland j ERTH UP
Overlap v SIML JOIN
Overlay n UP
Overleap v GO UP
Overlearn v EDUC
Overlie v UP
Overload v BULG
Overlook v VIEW UP
Overlook v FALS VIEW
Overlord n LEAD
Overly d EMPH
Overlying n UP
Overmaster v POWR LEAD
Overnight d TIME
Overoptimist n GLAD MOTV
Overpass n UP PATH

Overpay v LARG MONY
Overpopulate v LARG GRUP
Overpower v POWR WEAK
Overprice v LARG MONY
Overran v DAMG GO
Override v OPPO
Overrule v OPPO
Overrun v DAMG GO
Oversaw v LEAD VIEW
Oversea j AFAR FLOW
Oversee v LEAD VIEW
Overseer n LEAD
Overshirt n GARB
Overshoe n GARB
Overshoot v GO
Overshot v GO
Oversight n FALS
Oversimplify v EASY
Oversize j LARG
Overt j OPEN
Overtake v GO NEAR
Overthrow v POWR WEAK
Overtone n BLUR IDEA
Overtone n MUSC
Overtone n VIEW
Overtook v GO NEAR
Overture n MUSC
Overture n IDEA MOTV
Overturn v VARY
Overview n WHOL VIEW
Overweening j AGGR POWR
Overweight j LARG MSMT
Overwhelm v POWR WEAK
Overwrought j PANG
Ovulate v LADY SOMA
Owe v MOTV
Owl n ANML UP
Own v HAVE
Ox n ANML
Oxide n MTRL
Oxygen n VAPR
Oyster n FOOD FLOW
Oyster n ANML FLOW
Ozone n VAPR

P

P n WRIT
Pa n MALE KIN
Pa n LEAD MALE
Pace v GO
Pacemaker n POWR GO
Pachyderm n ANML
Pacific n PLAC FLOW
Pacific j GLAD
Pacifies v GLAD
Pacifist n GLAD
Pacify v GLAD
Pack n BLOK BULG
Pack n ANML GRUP
Pack v FALS GRUP
Package n BULG HOLW
Packed v BLOK BULG
Packed v FALS GRUP
Packet n BULG HOLW

Packet n FLOW VEHC
Packing v BLOK BULG
Packing v FALS GRUP
Packrat n ANML
Pact n AGRE
Pad n EASY BULG
Pad n WRIT
Pad v GO
Pad n HOME
Padded v EASY BULG
Padded v GO
Paddle v GO FLOW
Paddle v DAMG
Paddock n BLOK HOME
Paddywagon n BLOK VEHC
Padlock n BLOK
Padre n LEAD HOLY
Padrone n LEAD

Pagan j OPPO HOLY
Page n WRIT
Page n AID YNG
Page v TALK
Pageant n PLAY
Paged v TALK
Pagination n FORW WRIT
Paging v TALK
Pagoda n HOME HOLY
Paid v MONY
Paid v AID
Paid v GO
Pail n HOLW
Pailful n BULG HOLW
Pain n DAMG PANG
Painless j GLAD
Pains n DAMG PANG
Painstaking j AID MOTV

Paint v COLR
Pair n SIML JOIN
Pair n NUMR
Paisley j FABR
Pajamas n GARB
Pal n FOND
Palace n LEAD HOME
Paladin n POWR
Palatable j FOND FOOD
Palatal j SOMA
Palate n SOMA
Palatial j LEAD HOME
Palaver v TALK
Pale j COLR
Pale j COLR WEAK
Pale n BLOK
Paleolithic j PAST
Paleontology n IDEA PAST
Paleozoic j PAST
Palette n COLR HOLW
Paling v COLR
Paling n BLOK
Palisade n ERTH BULG
Pall n PANG COVR
Pall v TRIV PANG
Pallbearer n DEAD GO
Palled v TRIV PANG
Palled v FOND
Pallet n HOLW FORM
Pallet n FURN REST
Pallet n MECH TIME
Pallet n WORK
Palliate v GLAD EASY
Pallid j COLR WEAK
Palling v TRIV PANG
Palling v FOND
Pallor n COLR WEAK
Palm n BODY
Palm n VEGT
Palm n POWR VEGT
Palm v FALS
Palmed v BODY
Palmed v FALS
Palmer n GO HOLY
Palmetto n VEGT
Palming v BODY
Palming v FALS
Palmist n BODY MYTH
Palomino n ANML COLR
Palpable j OPEN
Palpate v MEDC JOIN
Palpitate v VARY SOMA
Pals n FOND
Palsy n SICK REST
Palter v FALS
Paltry j TRIV
Pampas n ERTH
Pamper v AID
Pamphlet n WRIT
Pan n HOLW
Pan v VIEW
Pan f WHOL

Pan v END
Pan v AGGR
Panatela n FOOD HEAT
Pancake n FOOD
Pancake n FORM
Pancaked v FORM
Pancaking v FORM
Pancreas n SOMA
Panda n ANML
Pandemic j WHOL
Pandemonium n DAMG HEAR
Pander v BAD SEX
Pander v BAD AID
Pane n MTRL VIEW
Panel n GRUP
Panel n SOME
Panel v MTRL FORM
Paneled v MTRL FORM
Paneling v MTRL FORM
Panelled v MTRL FORM
Panetella n FOOD HEAT
Pang n PANG
Panhandle n ERTH BULG
Panhandle v MOTV
Panic n PANG
Panned v END
Panned v AGGR
Panned v VIEW
Pannier n GARB LADY
Pannier n HOLW
Panning v END
Panning v AGGR
Panning v VIEW
Panorama n WHOL VIEW
Pansy n VEGT
Pansy n SIML SEX
Pant v VAPR SOMA
Pantaloon n GARB
Pantheism n WHOL HOLY
Pantheon n HOME HOLY
Pantheon n LEAD HOLY
Panther n ANML
Panties n GARB LADY
Pantomime n SIML PLAY
Pantry n FOOD HOME
Pants n GARB MALE
Panty n GARB LADY
Pantywaist n WEAK YNG
Pap n EASY FOOD
Papa n MALE KIN
Papa n LEAD MALE
Papacy n LEAD HOLY
Papal j LEAD HOLY
Papaya n FOOD VEGT
Paper n MTRL
Paper n WRIT MTRL
Paperback n WRIT
Papered v MTRL
Papering v MTRL
Papiermache n MTRL
Papoose n YNG
Paprika n FOOD VEGT

Papyrus n WRIT MTRL
Par n SIML
Parable n TALK MYTH
Parabola n FORM
Parachute v DOWN GO
Parade n GO GRUP
Paradigm n SIML
Parading v GO GRUP
Paradise n GLAD GOOD
Paradox n BLUR OPPO
Paraffin n MTRL
Paragon n SIML GOOD
Paragraph n WRIT SOME
Parakeet n ANML UP
Parallax n ASTR OPPO
Parallel n SIML
Parallelogram n SIML FORM
Paralysis n SICK REST
Paramecium n BUG
Parameter n NUMR
Paramount j LEAD
Paramour n FOND SEX
Paranoia n AGGR SICK
Parapet n FORM COVR
Paraphernalia n AID
Paraphrase v TALK
Paraplegia n SICK REST
Parasite n BUG SUB
Parasite n AID SUB
Parasol n GARB LADY
Paratroop n DAMG DOWN
Parcel n BULG HOLW
Parcel n SOME
Parcel v SEP SOME
Parch v HEAT LACK
Parchment n WRIT MTRL
Pardon v AGRE
Pardon v AGRE OPEN
Pare v SEP SHRP
Parent n LEAD KIN
Parent n BGIN LEAD
Parenthesis n WRIT SEP
Parfait n FOOD
Pariah n SEP WEAK
Parimutuel j GRUP HAVE
Paring v SEP SHRP
Parish n GRUP HOLY
Parishioner n GRUP HOLY
Parity n SIML
Park n ERTH VEGT
Park v REST VEHC
Parka n GARB
Parked v REST VEHC
Parking v REST VEHC
Parkway n PATH
Parlance n TALK
Parlay n MONY MOTV
Parley n JOIN TALK
Parliament n GRUP LAW
Parlor n HOME
Parlor n MART HOME
Parmesan n ANML FOOD

Parts of speech: a article; b preposition; c conjunction; d adverb; f prefix; i interjection;
j adjective; n noun; p pronoun; r phrase; v verb.

Parochial j GRUP HOLY
Parochial j BLOK GRUP
Parody n FOOL SIML
Parole n AGRE TALK
Parole n OPEN
Paroled v OPEN
Paroling v OPEN
Paroxysm n VARY PANG
Parquet n FORM
Parquet n PLAY REST
Parricide n DAMG LEAD
Parried v VARY BLOK
Parrot n ANML UP
Parrot v SIML TALK
Parroted v SIML TALK
Parroting v SIML TALK
Parry n VARY BLOK
Parse v TALK FORM
Parsimony n LITL HAVE
Parsing v TALK FORM
Parsley n FOOD VEGT
Parsnip n FOOD VEGT
Parson n LEAD HOLY
Part n SOME
Part v GO SEP
Part n SEP
Part n SIML
Partake v HAVE
Parted v GO SEP
Parted v SEP
Partial j SOME
Partial j MOTV
Partiality n MOTV
Partially d SOME
Participate v JOIN
Participial j TALK FORM
Participle n TALK FORM
Particle n LITL SOME
Particolor j MUCH COLR
Particular j SHRP
Particularly d SHRP
Parties n GRUP
Parties n GRUP PLAY
Parties n SOLE
Parting v GO SEP
Parting v SEP
Partisan j AGRE MOTV
Partisan j DAMG MOTV
Partition n SEP
Partner n JOIN
Partner n KIN
Partook v HAVE
Partridge n ANML UP
Parttime j SOME TIME
Parturition n BGIN YNG
Party n GRUP
Party n GRUP PLAY
Party n SOLE
Pasha n LEAD
Pass v GO
Pass n PATH
Pass n GO WRIT
Pass v POWR
Pass n SEX
Pass v IDEA

Pass v DEAD GO
Pass v EVNT
Pass v AGRE
Passable j GO
Passable j AGRE
Passage n GO
Passage n WRIT SOME
Passage n AGRE
Passageway n PATH
Passe j PAST
Passed v GO
Passed v POWR
Passed v IDEA
Passed v DEAD GO
Passed v EVNT
Passed v AGRE
Passenger n GO
Passes v GO
Passes n PATH
Passes n GO WRIT
Passes n POWR
Passes n SEX
Passes v IDEA
Passes v DEAD GO
Passes v EVNT
Passes v AGRE
Passing v GO
Passing v POWR
Passing v IDEA
Passing v DEAD GO
Passing v EVNT
Passing v AGRE
Passion n MOTV
Passion n HOLY PANG
Passive j REST WEAK
Passover n HOLY TIME
Passport n GO WRIT
Past b AFAR
Past j PAST
Paste n JOIN
Paste n FOOD
Paste j FALS
Paste v DAMG
Pasteboard n JOIN MTRL
Pasted v JOIN
Pasted v DAMG
Pastel n COLR WRIT
Pastern n ANML BODY
Pasteurize v CLEN HEAT
Pastime n PLAY TIME
Pasting v JOIN
Pasting v DAMG
Pastor n LEAD HOLY
Pastoral j ERTH VEGT
Pastoral n WRIT HOLY
Pastorale n ERTH MUSC
Pastorate n LEAD HOLY
Pastrami n ANML FOOD
Pastries n FOOD
Pastry n FOOD
Pasture n FOOD VEGT
Pasty j COLR
Pat n EASY JOIN
Pat n EASY HEAR
Pat n SOME

Pat j EVER
Patch n AID COVR
Patch n SOME
Patchwork n JOIN FABR
Pate n FOOD
Pate n BODY
Patella n SOMA
Patent j OPEN
Patent n LAW HAVE
Patent j ANML FABR
Patented v LAW HAVE
Patenting v LAW HAVE
Patents v LAW HAVE
Paterfamilias n MALE KIN
Paterfamilias n LEAD MALE
Paternity n MALE KIN
Paternity n LEAD MALE
Path n PATH
Pathetic j WEAK PANG
Pathologist n MEDC IDEA
Pathology n MEDC IDEA
Pathology n SICK IDEA
Pathos n PANG
Patience n EVER REST
Patient n SICK
Patient j EVER REST
Patients n SICK
Patina n COLR
Patio n HOME PLAC
Patriarch n MALE KIN
Patriarch n LEAD MALE
Patriarch n LEAD HOLY
Patrician j LEAD
Patricide n DEAD LEAD
Patriot n FOND GRUP
Patrol v GO AID
Patrolman n LAW MALE
Patron n LEAD AID
Patron n MART AID
Patted v EASY JOIN
Patted v EASY HEAR
Patten n GARB
Patter n HEAR
Patter n HEAR TALK
Pattern n FORM
Patties n FOOD LITL
Patting v EASY JOIN
Patting v EASY HEAR
Patty n FOOD LITL
Paucity n LITL LACK
Paunch n BODY BULG
Pauper n MONY LACK
Pause n REST
Pave v AID PATH
Pavement n AID PATH
Pavilion n HOME
Paw n ANML BODY
Pawl n BLOK MECH
Pawn n PLAY SUB
Pawn v MART MONY
Pawned v MART MONY
Pawning v MART MONY
Pay v MONY
Pay v AID
Pay v GO

Payoff n MONY
Payoff n AID
Payroll n WRIT MONY
Pea n FOOD VEGT
Peace n GLAD
Peacemaker n GLAD AID
Peach n FOOD VEGT
Peach n GOOD
Peach n COLR
Peacock n ANML UP
Peajacket n GARB FLOW
Peak n ERTH UP
Peak n POWR UP
Peaked j PANG LACK
Peaked j ERTH UP
Peal n MUSC
Peanut n FOOD VEGT
Pear n FOOD VEGT
Pearl n MTRL FLOW
Pearl n GOOD
Pearl n COLR
Peas n FOOD VEGT
Peasant n ERTH WORK
Peat n ERTH VEGT
Pebble n ERTH
Pecan n FOOD VEGT
Peck n FOOD
Peck n JOIN
Peck n FOND JOIN
Peck n MSMT
Pectoral j SOMA
Peculate v CRIM MONY
Peculiar j AFAR
Peculiar j SIML CRUX
Pecuniary j MONY
Pedagogy n EDUC
Pedal n MECH VEHC
Pedal v GO VEHC
Pedant n EDUC TRIV
Peddle v MART MONY
Peddlepusher n GARB
Pederasty n BAD SEX
Pedestal n AID FORM
Pedestrian j GO
Pedestrian j TRIV
Pediatric j MEDC YNG
Pedicure n MEDC BODY
Pediform j BODY FORM
Pedigree n BGIN PAST
Pedometer n GO MSMT
Peek v VIEW
Peekaboo n VIEW
Peel v SEP
Peep n VIEW
Peep n ANML TALK
Peer n SIML
Peer n LEAD
Peer v VIEW
Peered v VIEW
Peering v VIEW
Peerless j POWR
Peeve v AGGR PANG
Peg n BULG
Peg v GO
Peg v EVER

Peg v JOIN
Pejorative j BAD AGGR
Pekingese n ANML
Pekoe n SIP VEGT
Pelican n ANML UP
Pellagra n SICK
Pellet n DAMG
Pellet n LITL
Pellmell j BLUR QUIK
Pelt n ANML FABR
Pelt v DAMG
Pelvis n SOMA
Pen n WRIT
Pen n BLOK HOME
Pen n ANML HOME
Penal j CRIM LAW
Penalize v AGGR
Penalty n AGGR
Penance n PANG
Pence n MONY
Penchant n MOTV
Pencil n WRIT
Pendant n GARB DOWN
Pendant j DOWN
Pendant n SIML
Pending b EVER TIME
Pendulous j DOWN
Pendulum n VARY DOWN
Pendulum n VARY TIME
Penetrate v IN
Penguin n ANML FLOW
Penicillin n MEDC
Peninsula n ERTH FLOW
Penis n MALE SEX
Penitence n PANG
Penitent j PANG
Penitentiary n BLOK HOME
Penknife n SHRP
Penmanship n WRIT
Pennant n VIEW
Penned v WRIT
Penned v BLOK HOME
Pennies n MONY
Penniless j MONY LACK
Penning v WRIT
Penning v BLOK HOME
Penny n MONY
Penology n BLOK CRIM
Pens v WRIT
Pens v BLOK HOME
Pension n MONY
Pensive j IDEA
Pent j BLOK
Pentagon n FORM
Pentagon n DAMG HOME
Pentameter n TALK MSMT
Pentathlon n PLAY
Pentecost n HOLY TIME
Penthouse n HOME UP
Pentode n MECH ION
Penumbra n BLUR
Penury n MONY LACK
Peon n SUB WORK
People n GRUP
Pepper n FOOD VEGT

Pepper v AGGR
Peppermint n FOOD VEGT
Peppermint n COLR
Per b SOLE
Per b SIML
Perambulate v GO
Perambulator n VEHC YNG
Perceive v IDEA VIEW
Percent n NUMR SOME
Percept n IDEA VIEW
Perch n REST UP
Perch n ANML FLOW
Perch n FOOD FLOW
Perchance d AFAR EVNT
Percipient j IDEA
Percolate v IN FLOW
Percussion n DAMG HEAR
Percussion n MUSC
Percussion n HEAR
Perdition n BAD DAMG
Perdurable j EVER
Peregrinate v GO
Peremptory j AGGR POWR
Perennial j EVER
Perfect j POWR GOOD
Perfect j EMPH
Perfect j TALK FORM
Perfected v POWR GOOD
Perfection n POWR GOOD
Perfecto n FOOD HEAT
Perfects v POWR GOOD
Perfidy n BAD
Perforate v HOLW SHRP
Perform v EVNT
Perform v PLAY
Perfume n SOMA GOOD
Perfunctory j TRIV
Perhaps d SOME
Peril n DAMG
Perimeter n HOLW OUT
Period n TIME
Period n LADY SOMA
Period n END WRIT
Periodic j VARY EVER
Periodical n WRIT
Periphery n HOLW OUT
Periscope n MECH VIEW
Perish v DEAD
Peristalsis n VARY SOMA
Perjury n FALS
Perk v QUIK
Permanence n EVER
Permanent j EVER
Permanent n EVER BODY
Permeate v IN
Permission n AGRE
Permit v AGRE
Permit n AGRE WRIT
Permitted v AGRE
Permutation n VARY
Pernicious j DAMG
Peroration n END TALK
Peroxide n MTRL
Peroxide n COLR MTRL
Perpendicular j FORM UP

Perpetrate v BAD
Perpetuate v EVER
Perpetuity n EVER TIME
Perplex v BLUR
Persecute v DAMG
Persevere v EVER MOTV
Persimmon n FOOD VEGT
Persist v EVER
Person n SOLE
Persona n SOLE
Personable j AGRE SOLE
Personal j SOLE
Personality n SOLE
Personify v SIML SOLE
Personnel n GRUP WORK
Perspective n VIEW
Perspicacity n POWR IDEA
Perspire v SOMA FLOW
Persuade v IDEA MOTV
Pert j POWR QUIK
Pertain v JOIN
Pertinacity n EVER
Pertinence n CRUX JOIN
Perturb v PANG
Pertussis n SICK
Peruse v WRIT VIEW
Pervade v WHOL IN
Perversion n BAD
Pesky j AGGR PANG
Peso n MONY
Pessimism n PANG
Pest n AGGR PANG
Pest n BUG AGGR
Pester v AGGR PANG
Pesticide n BUG DEAD
Pestiferous j BUG SICK
Pestilence n BUG SICK
Pestle n WORK
Pet n FOND ANML
Pet n FOND
Pet n AGGR PANG
Pet v FOND JOIN
Pet v FOND SEX
Petal n BODY VEGT
Petcock n BLOK MECH
Peter v WEAK
Petite j LITL
Petition n MOTV
Petitmal n SICK
Petrel n ANML UP
Petrify v EVER
Petrify v REST PANG
Petrol n MTRL FLOW
Petroleum n MTRL FLOW
Petted v FOND JOIN
Petted v FOND SEX
Petticoat n GARB LADY
Pettier j TRIV
Petting v FOND JOIN
Petting v FOND SEX
Petty j TRIV
Petulance n AGGR PANG
Petunia n VEGT
Pew n HOLY REST
Pewter n ERTH MTRL

Phaeton n VEHC
Phalanx n DAMG GRUP
Phallic j MALE SEX
Phantasma n VIEW MYTH
Phantom n MYTH
Pharaoh n LEAD
Pharisee n FALS HOLY
Pharisee n GRUP HOLY
Pharmaceutic j MEDC
Pharmacist n MART MEDC
Pharmacology n MEDC IDEA
Pharmacopoeia n MEDC WRIT
Pharmacy n MART MEDC
Pharynx n SOMA
Phase n SOME
PhD n POWR EDUC
Pheasant n ANML UP
Pheasant n ANML FOOD
Phenomena n EVNT
Phenomenal j AFAR EVNT
Phenomenon n EVNT
Phenotype n CRUX GRUP
PhiBetaKappa n POWR EDUC
Philander v SEX TRIV
Philanthropy n GOOD AID
Philately n WRIT VIEW
Philharmonic j MUSC
Philistine n GRUP
Philistine n FOOL OPPO
Philology n WRIT IDEA
Philosophy n IDEA
Philter n SIP MYTH
Phlegm n SOMA
Phlegmatic j REST
Phobia n PANG
Phoebe n ANML UP
Phoenix n ANML MYTH
Phone v TALK MECH
Phoneme n TALK FORM
Phonetic j TALK FORM
Phonic j TALK FORM
Phoning v TALK MECH
Phonograph n MECH MUSC
Phony n FALS
Phosphate n MTRL
Phosphate n SIP
Phosphoresce v VIEW
Photo n VIEW
Photoelectric j ION VIEW
Photogenic j GOOD VIEW
Photograph n VIEW
Photogravure n MECH VIEW
Photostat n SIML VIEW
Photosynthesis n SOMA VIEW
Phrase n TALK FORM
Phrenetic j DAMG PANG
Phrenology n BODY IDEA
Phylactery n WRIT HOLY
Phylogeny n GRUP PAST
Phylum n GRUP SOME
Physic n MEDC SOMA
Physical j MTRL
Physical j BODY
Physician n MEDC
Physicist n MTRL IDEA

Physics n MTRL IDEA
Physiognomy n BODY
Physiology n SOMA IDEA
Physique n BODY
Pi n WRIT NUMR
Pi n WRIT
Pianissimo j EASY MUSC
Pianist n MUSC
Piano n MUSC
Piaster n MONY
Piazza n PLAC PATH
Piazza n HOME
Pica n WRIT MSMT
Pica n SICK MOTV
Picador n DAMG SHRP
Picalilly n FOOD VEGT
Picaresque j BAD POWR
Picyune j TRIV
Piccolo n MUSC
Pick v SHRP
Pick v HAVE
Pick v MOTV
Pick v CRIM
Pickax n SHRP WORK
Picked v SHRP
Picked v HAVE
Picked v MOTV
Picked v CRIM
Pickerel n ANML FLOW
Pickerel n FOOD FLOW
Picket n BLOK WORK
Picket n SHRP
Picket n DAMG AID
Pickle n FOOD VEGT
Pickle v CLEN FLOW
Pickle v EVER FOOD
Pickle n BLUR PANG
Pickled j EVER FOOD
Pickled j SIP PANG
Pickled j CLEN FLOW
Pickling v EVER FOOD
Pickling v CLEN FLOW
Pickup n VEHC
Picnic n FOOD PLAY
Pictograph n WRIT VIEW
Pictorial j VIEW
Picture n VIEW
Picture n SIML
Pictures n VIEW
Picturesque j GOOD VIEW
Piddle v TRIV
Pidgin n TALK
Pie n FOOD
Piece n SOME
Piece n SOLE
Piece n DAMG MECH
Pieced v SOME
Piecederesistance r POWR CRUX
Piecemeal j SOME
Piecing v SOME
Pied j COLR
Piedmont n ERTH
Pier n BLOK FLOW
Pier n AID FORM
Pierce v IN SHRP

Pies n FOOD
Piety n GOOD HOLY
Piezoelectric j MTRL ION
Pig n ANML
Pig n ANML BAD
Pig n ERTH MTRL
Pigeon n ANML UP
Pigeonhole v BLOK HOLW
Pigeonhole n ANML HOLW
Pigeonhole v GRUP HOLW
Pigheaded j AGGR
Pigiron n ERTH MTRL
Pigment n COLR
Pigskin n ANML FABR
Pigskin n PLAY FABR
Pigtail n BACK BODY
Pike n ANML FLOW
Pike n FOOD FLOW
Pike n DAMG SHRP
Pike n ERTH BULG
Pike n PATH
Piked v DAMG SHRP
Piker n TRIV
Piking v DAMG SHRP
Pile n BULG
Pile n FORM
Pile n MECH ION
Pile n SICK
Piled v BULG
Piledriver n POWR FORM
Pilfer v CRIM
Pilgrim n GO HOLY
Piling v BULG
Pill n FOOD LITL
Pillage v DAMG CRIM
Pillar n AID FORM
Pillbox n DAMG HOME
Pillbox n GARB LADY
Pillion n ANML REST
Pillory v AGGR
Pillow n EASY FURN
Pilot n LEAD VEHC
Pilot n LEAD
Piltdown j PAST
Pimento n FOOD VEGT
Pimp n BAD SEX
Pimped v BAD SEX
Pimpernel n VEGT
Pimple n DIRT BODY
Pin n BLOK SHRP
Pin n JOIN SHRP
Pin n GARB SHRP
Pin n PLAY FORM
Pincenez n AID VIEW
Pincer n BLOK SHRP
Pincer n BODY SHRP
Pinch v BLOK
Pinch n SOME
Pinch n BLOK LAW
Pinch v CRIM
Pinch n BLOK PANG
Pine n VEGT
Pine n MTRL VEGT
Pine v PANG MOTV
Pineapple n FOOD VEGT

Pined v PANG MOTV
Ping n MUSC
Pingpong n PLAY
Pining v PANG MOTV
Pinion n MECH
Pinion v BLOK
Pinion n BODY UP
Pinioned v BLOK
Pinioned j BODY UP
Pinioning v BLOK
Pink n COLR
Pink n COLR GOOD
Pink n VEGT
Pink v SHRP
Pinked v SHRP
Pinkeye n SICK VIEW
Pinkie n BODY
Pinking v SHRP
Pinnacle n ERTH UP
Pinnacle n POWR UP
Pinned v BLOK SHRP
Pinned v JOIN SHRP
Pinning v BLOK SHRP
Pinning v JOIN SHRP
Pinochle n PLAY
Pint n MSMT
Pintail n ANML UP
Pinto n ANML COLR
Pinup n VIEW
Pinwheel n PLAY
Pioneer n BGIN FORW
Pious j GOOD HOLY
Pip n BGIN VEGT
Pip n POWR
Pip n LITL
Pip v ANML TALK
Pipe n HOLW
Pipe n FOOD HEAT
Pipe n MUSC
Pipe v HEAR
Piped v HOLW
Piped v HEAR
Piper n MUSC
Pipette n HOLW FLOW
Piping n HOLW
Piping n HEAR
Piping n MUSC
Piping j HEAT
Piping n GARB FABR
Pipped v ANML TALK
Pippin n FOOD VEGT
Pipping v ANML TALK
Pips n BGIN VEGT
Pips n POWR
Pips n LITL
Pips n ANML TALK
Pipsqueak n LITL WEAK
Piquancy n AGRE SOMA
Pique v MOTV
Pique v AGGR
Piracy n CRIM FLOW
Pirouette n VARY GO
Pisces n ASTR MYTH
Pistachio n FOOD VEGT
Pistil n BODY VEGT

Pistol n DAMG MECH
Piston n MECH
Pit n HOLW
Pit n VEGT
Pit v OPPO
Pitch n VARY
Pitch n GO
Pitch n MUSC
Pitch n TALK MOTV
Pitch n COLR MTRL
Pitch v FORM
Pitchblende n ERTH MTRL
Pitched v VARY
Pitched v GO
Pitched v MUSC
Pitched v FORM
Pitcher n HOLW
Pitcher n GO PLAY
Pitchfork n SHRP WORK
Pitching v VARY
Pitching v GO
Pitching v MUSC
Pitching v FORM
Pitchpipe n MUSC
Piteous j WEAK PANG
Pitfall n DAMG HOLW
Pith n POWR CRUX
Pith n CRUX SOMA
Pithy j POWR CRUX
Pitied v PANG
Pitiful j WEAK
Pitiful j PANG
Pitiless j AGGR
Pittance n LITL MONY
Pitted v HOLW
Pitted v OPPO
Pitted v OUT VEGT
Pitterpatter n HEAR
Pitting v HOLW
Pitting v OPPO
Pitting v OUT VEGT
Pituitary j SOMA
Pity v PANG
Pivot n VARY CRUX
Pixy n GLAD MYTH
Pizza n FOOD
Pizzeria n MART FOOD
Pizzicato j MUSC
Placard n WRIT VIEW
Placate v GLAD AID
Place n PLAC
Placenta n LADY SOMA
Placid j GLAD
Placing v PLAC
Placket n GARB SEP
Plagiarism n CRIM WRIT
Plague n SICK
Plague v PANG
Plaid j FORM FABR
Plain j OPEN SHRP
Plain j EASY
Plain n ERTH
Plainclothes j GARB LAW
Plains n ERTH
Plainsman n ERTH MALE

Plaint n PANG
Plaintiff n LAW MOTV
Plaintive j PANG
Plait v VARY FORM
Plan n IDEA FORM
Plane n VEHC UP
Plane n FORM
Plane n EASY WORK
Plane n VEGT
Planed v EASY WORK
Planet n ASTR
Planetarium n ASTR HOME
Planetary j ASTR
Planing v EASY WORK
Planish v EASY
Plank n MTRL VEGT
Plank n FORM
Plankton n FLOW VEGT
Plant n ERTH VEGT
Plant n MART WORK
Plant n FALS
Plantain n VEGT
Plantation n ERTH VEGT
Planted v ERTH VEGT
Planting v ERTH VEGT
Plaque n VIEW
Plasma n SOMA
Plaster n MTRL
Plaster v SIP PANG
Plasterboard n MTRL FORM
Plastic j MTRL
Plastic j FABR
Plastic j VARY EASY
Plasticity n VARY EASY
Plat n ERTH SOME
Plat n IDEA FORM
Plate n FOOD HOLW
Plate n FORM
Plate n VIEW
Plate n ERTH MTRL
Plateau n ERTH UP
Plated v FORM
Platform n FORM
Plating v FORM
Platinum n COLR
Platinum n ERTH MTRL
Platitude n TRIV
Platonic j FOND IDEA
Platoon n GRUP
Platter n FOOD HOLW
Platypus n ANML FLOW
Plaudit n AGRE HEAR
Plausible j AGRE IDEA
Play v PLAY
Play v VARY
Play v MUSC
Playback n PLAY SIML
Playground n ERTH PLAY
Playmate n JOIN PLAY
Playpen n PLAY YNG
Plaything n PLAY
Playwright n WRIT PLAY

Plaza n PLAC PATH
Plea n MOTV
Plead v MOTV
Pleas n MOTV
Pleasant j FOND GLAD
Please v FOND GLAD
Pleasing j FOND GLAD
Pleasure n FOND GLAD
Pleat n VARY
Plebe n EDUC SUB
Plebeian j GRUP WORK
Plebiscite n LAW MOTV
Pledge n AGRE
Plenary j WHOL
Plenipotentiary n LEAD
Plenty j MUCH
Plethora n MUCH BULG
Plethora n SICK
Plexiglass n MTRL VIEW
Pliable j VARY EASY
Plied j VARY FORM
Plied v EVER GO
Plied v EVER
Plier n WORK
Plier n EVER
Plier n EVER GO
Plight n PANG
Plight v AGRE
Plod v GO REST
Plop v DOWN HEAR
Plot n IDEA COVR
Plot n IDEA FORM
Plot n ERTH SOME
Plotted v IDEA COVR
Plotted v IDEA FORM
Plover n ANML UP
Plow v ERTH WORK
Ploy n POWR EVNT
Ploy n GLAD PLAY
Pluck n POWR
Pluck v SEP
Pluck v MUSC
Plucked v SEP
Plucked v MUSC
Plucking v SEP
Plucking v MUSC
Plucky j POWR
Plug n BLOK
Plug n AGRE AID
Plug n ANML WEAK
Plug n FOOD VEGT
Plug v DAMG
Plug v EVER
Plugged v BLOK
Plugged v DAMG
Plugged v AGRE AID
Plugged v EVER
Plum n FOOD VEGT
Plum n COLR
Plumage n ANML BODY
Plumb d EMPH
Plumb v MSMT

Plumbed v MSMT
Plumber n FLOW WORK
Plumbing n MECH FLOW
Plumbing v MSMT
Plume n ANML BODY
Pluming n ANML BODY
Plummet v DOWN GO
Plump j LARG BODY
Plump n DOWN
Plumped v DOWN
Plumper j LARG BODY
Plumpest j LARG BODY
Plumping v DOWN
Plunder v CRIM
Plunge v QUIK GO
Plunk v HEAR
Pluperfect n TALK FORM
Plural j MUCH
Plus b LARG NUMR
Plus n AID
Plusfours n GARB MALE
Plush j EASY FABR
Pluto n ASTR
Pluto n DEAD MYTH
Plutocracy n LEAD GRUP
Plutonium n MTRL
Pluvial j WEA FLOW
Ply n VARY FORM
Ply v EVER GO
Ply v EVER
PM n TIME
Pneumatic j VAPR
Pneumonia n SICK
Poach v ANML CRIM
Poach v HEAT
Poach v ERTH GO
Pock v HOLW
Pocket n HOLW
Pocketbook n GARB HOLW
Pocketful n BULG HOLW
Pockmark n BODY HOLW
Pod n HOLW VEGT
Pod n ANML GRUP
Podiatry n MEDC BODY
Podium n LEAD FORM
Poem n TALK
Poet n TALK
Poetaster n TALK TRIV
Poetess n LADY TALK
Pogostick n PLAY FORM
Pogrom n DAMG DEAD
Poignant j SOMA SHRP
Poignant j PANG
Poinsettia n VEGT
Point n SHRP
Point n CRUX IDEA
Point n NUMR
Point n ERTH SHRP
Pointblank j SHRP
Pointed v SHRP
Pointing v SHRP
Pointless j TRIV

Parts of speech: a article; b preposition; c conjunction; d adverb; f prefix; i interjection;
j adjective; n noun; p pronoun; r phrase; v verb.

Poise n EVNT
Poise n POWR
Poise n REST
Poison n DAMG
Poke v BULG
Poke v BULG JOIN
Poke n DAMG
Poke v REST
Poke n HOLW
Poker n PLAY
Poker n BULG
Pokey n BLOK HOME
Poky j REST
Polar j COLD PLAC
Polar j OPPO END
Polaris n ASTR
Polarity n OPPO END
Polarize v OPPO END
Polaroid n MTRL VIEW
Pole n FORM
Pole n COLD PLAC
Pole n END
Pole v GO FORM
Poleax n DAMG SHRP
Polecat n ANML
Poled v GO FORM
Polemic n AGGR TALK
Police n LAW
Police v CLEN
Policeman n LAW MALE
Policies n IDEA FORM
Policy n IDEA FORM
Policy n MONY MOTV
Poling v GO FORM
Polio n SICK REST
Polish n CLEN EASY
Polish n EASY GOOD
Polished v CLEN EASY
Polished v EASY GOOD
Polishing v CLEN EASY
Polishing v EASY GOOD
Politburo n LEAD LAW
Polite j GOOD
Politician n LEAD LAW
Politics n LEAD LAW
Polities n GRUP LAW
Polity n GRUP LAW
Polka n GO MUSC
Polkadot j LITL FORM
Poll n GRUP MOTV
Poll n FORM
Poll n BODY
Polled v GRUP MOTV
Pollen n BGIN VEGT
Pollinate v BGIN VEGT
Polling v GRUP MOTV
Polliwog n ANML FLOW
Pollute v DIRT
Polo n PLAY
Polo j GARB
Polonium n ERTH MTRL
Poltroon n WEAK
Polyandry n SEX KIN
Polychromatic j MUCH COLR
Polygamy n SEX KIN

Polyglot j MUCH TALK
Polygon n FORM
Polygraph n WRIT MECH
Polygyny n SEX KIN
Polyhedron n FORM
Polymorphous j MUCH FORM
Polynomial n MUCH NUMR
Polyphony n MUCH MUSC
Polystyrene n MTRL
Polytechnic j MUCH EDUC
Polytheism n MUCH HOLY
Pomace n FOOD MTRL
Pomade n EASY MTRL
Pomegranate n FOOD VEGT
Pomeranian n ANML
Pommel n BULG
Pommel v DAMG
Pommeled v DAMG
Pommeling v DAMG
Pommelled v DAMG
Pomp n POWR GOOD
Pompadour n BODY AID
Pompom n DAMG MECH
Pompon n VEGT
Pompon n GARB
Pomposity n FOOL POWR
Pompous j FOOL POWR
Poncho n GARB
Pond n FLOW
Ponder v IDEA
Ponderous j LARG
Poniard n DAMG SHRP
Pontifical j LEAD HOLY
Pontoon n FLOW VEHC
Pony n ANML
Pony n LITL
Pony n CRIM WRIT
Pony v MONY
Pooch n ANML
Poodle n ANML
Pooh i TRIV
Pool n FLOW
Pool n PLAY
Pool n MONY MOTV
Pool n GRUP JOIN
Pooled v GRUP JOIN
Pooling v GRUP JOIN
Poop n FLOW VEHC
Poop v WEAK
Pooped v WEAK
Pooping v WEAK
Poor j WEAK LACK
Poor j MONY LACK
Poorhouse n HOME LACK
Pop n HEAR
Pop n MALE KIN
Pop n LEAD MALE
Pop n GRUP
Pop n SIP
Pop v GO
Popcorn n FOOD HEAR
Pope n LEAD HOLY
Poplar n VEGT
Poplin n FABR
Popped v HEAR

Popped v GO
Poppies n VEGT
Popping v HEAR
Popping v GO
Poppy n VEGT
Populace n GRUP
Popular j AGRE GRUP
Popular j GRUP
Populate v GRUP
Populous j MUCH GRUP
Porcelain n MTRL
Porch n HOME
Porcine j ANML
Porcupine n ANML
Pore n SOMA OPEN
Pore v IDEA
Pored v IDEA
Porgy n ANML FLOW
Porgy n FOOD FLOW
Poring v IDEA
Pork n ANML FOOD
Porkpie n GARB
Pornography n BAD SEX
Porosity n HOLW
Porpoise n ANML FLOW
Porridge n FOOD
Port n HOME FLOW
Port n PLAC FLOW
Port n SIP VEGT
Port n OPEN
Port n EVNT
Portable j GO
Portage n GO
Portal n BLOK OPEN
Portent n DAMG FORW
Porter n GO AID
Porter n SIP VEGT
Porterhouse n ANML FOOD
Portfolio n HOLW WRIT
Portfolio n LEAD LAW
Porthole n OPEN
Portico n HOME
Portiere n FURN COVR
Portion n SOME
Portion n MONY SOME
Portly j LARG BODY
Portray v SIML VIEW
Pose v REST FORM
Pose v FALS
Pose v BLUR
Posies n VEGT
Posing v REST FORM
Posing v FALS
Posing v BLUR
Position n PLAC
Position n IDEA
Position n WORK
Positioned v PLAC
Positioning v PLAC
Positive j SHRP
Positive j LARG
Positive j AGRE
Positive j ION
Positive j IDEA EVNT
Positively d EMPH

Positively d AGRE
Positivism n IDEA EVNT
Posse n GRUP LAW
Possess v HAVE
Possibility n SOME
Possum n ANML
Possum n ANML FALS
Post n FORM
Post n PLAC
Post n GO WRIT
Post n WORK
Post d BACK
Post v WRIT
Postage n WRIT MONY
Postal j GO WRIT
Postcard n GO WRIT
Posted v PLAC
Posted v GO WRIT
Posted v WRIT VIEW
Poster n WRIT VIEW
Posterior j BACK
Posterity n FORW YNG
Posthaste d QUIK EMPH
Posthumous j BACK DEAD
Posting v PLAC
Posting v GO WRIT
Posting v WRIT VIEW
Postmortem n BACK DEAD
Postoffice n HOME WRIT
Postpone v BLOK REST
Posts n FORM
Posts n PLAC
Posts n WORK
Posts v GO WRIT
Posts v WRIT VIEW
Postscript n BACK WRIT
Postulate v IDEA
Posture n BODY EVNT
Posture n MOTV
Posy n VEGT
Pot n HOLW
Pot n MONY MOTV
Pot n MEDC VEGT
Potable j SIP SOMA
Potash n MTRL
Potation n SIP SOMA
Potato n FOOD VEGT
Potbelly n BODY BULG
Potboiler n MONY TRIV
Potency n POWR
Potent j POWR
Potentate n LEAD
Potential n POWR
Potential n POWR ION
Potential n SOME
Potentiometer n ION MSMT
Pothole n HOLW
Pothook n BLOK HOLW
Potion n SIP
Potlatch n FOOD PLAY
Potluck n FOOD
Potpie n FOOD HOLW
Potpourri n JOIN
Pots n HOLW
Pots n MONY MOTV

Potshot n DAMG
Potted j HOLW
Potted j SIP PANG
Potter n ERTH HOLW
Pottersfield n DEAD PLAC
Pottery n ERTH HOLW
Potting v HOLW
Pouch n HOLW
Poultry n ANML FOOD
Pounce v QUIK GO
Pound n MSMT
Pound n MONY
Pound n ANML HOME
Pound v DAMG
Pound v HEAR
Poundcake n FOOD
Pounded v DAMG
Pounded v HEAR
Pounder n MSMT
Pounding v DAMG
Pounding v HEAR
Pour v FLOW
Pour v WEA FLOW
Pout n AGGR PANG
Poverty n MONY LACK
Poverty n WEAK LACK
Powder n MTRL
Powder n DAMG MTRL
Power n POWR
Power n NUMR
Powerless j WEAK LACK
Powwow n GRUP TALK
Pox n SICK
Practical j AID
Practice n EVER EVNT
Practice n EVER WORK
Practitioner n EVER WORK
Pragmatism n AID EVNT
Prairie n ERTH VEGT
Praise v AGRE
Praline n FOOD
Prance v POWR GO
Prank n FOOL GLAD
Prate v TALK TRIV
Prattle v TALK TRIV
Prawn n FOOD FLOW
Prawn n ANML FLOW
Prayer n TALK HOLY
Preach v TALK HOLY
Preamble n FORW TALK
Prearrangement n AGRE FORW
Precarious j DAMG
Precarious j BLUR
Precaution n AID MOTV
Precedence n FORW PAST
Precept n LEAD IDEA
Preceptor n LEAD EDUC
Precinct n PLAC
Precious j CRUX GOOD
Precious j GOOD TRIV
Precipice n ERTH BULG
Precipitate j QUIK
Precipitate v BGIN QUIK
Precipitate v SEP
Precipitate v WEA FLOW

Precipitate v QUIK GO
Precipitous j QUIK
Precipitous j BULG
Precis n TALK LITL
Precise j SHRP
Precisely d EMPH
Precision n SHRP
Preclude v BLOK
Precocity n POWR YNG
Preconception n FORW IDEA
Precursor n FORW PAST
Predate v FORW PAST
Predator n DAMG
Predecessor n FORW PAST
Predestination n END FORW
Predetermine v FORW IDEA
Predicament n BLUR PANG
Predicate n TALK FORM
Predicate v IDEA
Predict v FORW IDEA
Predilection n MOTV
Predispose v MOTV
Predominance n LEAD
Preeminence n POWR
Preempt v HAVE
Preen v CLEN
Preexist v LIVE PAST
Prefabricate v FORW FORM
Preface n FORW TALK
Prefect n LEAD LAW
Prefer v MOTV
Prefix n TALK FORM
Pregnability n WEAK
Pregnancy n BGIN SOMA
Preheat v FORW HEAT
Prehensile j BLOK HAVE
Prehistory n FORW PAST
Prejudge v FORW IDEA
Prejudice n FALS MOTV
Prelate n LEAD HOLY
Preliminary j FORW
Prelude n FORW
Prelude n FORW MUSC
Premature j FORW WEAK
Premedical j MEDC FORW
Premeditate v FORW IDEA
Premier j LEAD
Premier j FORW
Premier n LEAD LAW
Premiere n FORW PLAY
Premiere n LEAD LADY
Premise n FORW IDEA
Premise n ERTH HAVE
Premium n AID
Premium n AID MONY
Premonition n FORW PANG
Prenatal j BGIN FORW
Preoccupy v MOTV
Prep j AID EDUC
Prepaid j FORW MONY
Prepare v AID
Prepay v FORW MONY
Preponderance n MUCH
Preposition n TALK FORM
Prepossessing j MOTV

Preposterous j FOOL
Prepotency n POWR
Prerequisite n CRUX
Prerogative n MOTV
Presage n FORW IDEA
Presbyter n LEAD HOLY
Presbyterian n GRUP HOLY
Preschool j FORW EDUC
Prescience n FORW IDEA
Prescription n LEAD AID
Prescription n MEDC
Presence n NEAR
Presence n EVNT
Present j NEAR
Present j NEW
Present n AID
Presentable j GOOD
Presentation n AID
Presentday j NEW TIME
Presented v AID
Presentiment n FORW PANG
Presenting v AID
Presently d NEAR TIME
Presently d NEW
Presents v AID
Preserve v EVER
Preserves v EVER
Preserves n FOOD
Preshrunk j FORW LITL
Preside v LEAD
Presidency n LEAD LAW
Presiding v LEAD
Presidium n LEAD LAW
Press n WRIT MECH
Press n POWR
Press n POWR MECH
Press v CLEN GARB
Pressed v CLEN GARB
Pressed v POWR
Pressing j CRUX
Pressing v CLEN GARB
Pressing v POWR
Pressure n POWR
Prestidigitation n FALS MYTH
Prestige n POWR
Presto d QUIK
Presume v IDEA
Presumption n IDEA
Presumptuous j POWR MOTV
Presuppose v FORW IDEA
Pretend v FALS
Pretend v MOTV
Pretense n FALS
Pretense n MOTV
Pretentious j POWR FALS
Pretext n FALS IDEA
Prettier j GOOD
Pretty d EMPH
Pretty j GOOD
Pretzel n FOOD
Prevail v MUCH
Prevail v POWR
Prevalence n MUCH
Prevaricate v FALS TALK
Prevent v BLOK

Preview n FORW VIEW
Previous j PAST
Prewar j DAMG FORW
Prey n DAMG WEAK
Price n MONY
Priceless j CRUX MONY
Prick n SHRP
Prickle n SHRP
Prickly j SHRP
Pride n FOND POWR
Pried v OPEN SEP
Pried v OPEN
Pries v OPEN SEP
Pries v OPEN
Priest n LEAD HOLY
Priestess n LADY HOLY
Priesthood n LEAD HOLY
Prig n FOOL GOOD
Prim j GOOD
Primacy n LEAD FORW
Primadonna n LEAD LADY
Primafacie j OPEN TRUE
Primal j FORW PAST
Primal j CRUX FORW
Primary j CRUX FORW
Primate n LEAD HOLY
Primate n ANML
Prime j CRUX FORW
Prime j POWR
Prime n NUMR
Prime v AID
Primed v AID
Primer n WRIT
Primer n AID
Primes v AID
Primeval j FORW PAST
Priming v AID
Primitive j PAST
Primitive j BGIN
Primitive j WEAK
Primogenitor n BGIN KIN
Primordial j FORW PAST
Primp v CLEN
Primrose n VEGT
Prince n LEAD MALE
Princes n LEAD MALE
Princess n LEAD LADY
Principal j CRUX
Principal n MONY
Principal n LEAD EDUC
Principality n LEAD PLAC
Principle n GOOD IDEA
Principle n CRUX IDEA
Prink v CLEN
Print v WRIT MECH
Print n WRIT VIEW
Prior j FORW
Prior j PAST
Prior n LEAD HOLY
Prioress n LADY HOLY
Priority n CRUX FORW
Prism n FORM
Prism n VIEW FORM
Prison n BLOK HOME
Prisoner n BLOK

Prissy j TRIV MOTV
Pristine j GOOD PAST
Privacy n SEP COVR
Private j SEP COVR
Private j SOLE SEP
Private n SUB
Privateer n DAMG FLOW
Privation n LACK
Privilege n AID MOTV
Privy j AID MOTV
Privy n CLEN HOME
Prize v POWR AID
Prize v OPEN SEP
Pro n AGRE
Pro n POWR
Probability n MUCH
Probate n LAW TRUE
Probating v LAW TRUE
Probation n OPEN TRUE
Probe v IN OPEN
Probity n GOOD
Problem n BLUR
Proboscis n ANML BODY
Procedure n FORW
Proceed v FORW GO
Proceeded v FORW GO
Proceeding v FORW GO
Proceedings n EVNT
Proceeds v FORW GO
Proceeds n MONY
Process n FORW
Process n WRIT LAW
Procession n GO GRUP
Proclamation n TALK OPEN
Proclivity n MOTV
Procrastinate v BLOK REST
Procreate v BGIN
Procrustean j SIML DAMG
Proctology n MEDC SOMA
Proctor v LEAD EDUC
Procure v HAVE
Procure v BAD SEX
Prod v MOTV
Prod v DAMG SHRP
Prodigal j MUCH
Prodigious j POWR AFAR
Prodigy n POWR AFAR
Produce v VEGT
Produce v OPEN
Produce v END
Product n END
Product n NUMR
Production n END
Production n OPEN
Profane j BAD
Profess v AGRE TALK
Profession n WORK
Profession n GRUP WORK
Profession n AGRE TALK
Professional j POWR
Professor n LEAD EDUC
Proffer v AID
Proficiency n POWR
Profile n SIML FORM
Profit n AID

Profligacy n BAD
Profound j DOWN CRUX
Profound j DOWN EMPH
Profound j DOWN
Profundity n DOWN CRUX
Profundity n DOWN
Profuse j MUCH
Progenitor n BGIN KIN
Progeny n BGIN KIN
Prognathous j BODY
Prognosis n FORW IDEA
Program n IDEA FORM
Program n WRIT FORM
Progress n FORW GO
Prohibit v BLOK
Project n IDEA FORM
Project v BULG
Project v OUT MOTV
Projectile n DAMG GO
Projection v BULG
Projecting v IDEA FORM
Projecting v OUT MOTV
Projectionist n MECH VIEW
Prolapse n DOWN SOMA
Prolegomenon n FORW TALK
Proletarian n GRUP WORK
Proliferate v MUCH BGIN
Prolific j MUCH BGIN
Prologue n FORW TALK
Prolong v LARG EVER
Prom n PLAY MUSC
Promenade n GO
Promenade n PATH
Promenade n PLAY MUSC
Prominence n POWR
Prominence n BULG
Promiscuity n BAD SEX
Promiscuous j OPEN
Promiscuous j BAD SEX
Promise n AGRE
Promise n POWR
Promissory j AGRE
Promontory n ERTH BULG
Promote v FORW AID
Prompt j QUIK
Prompt v MOTV
Prompt v AID
Prompted v MOTV
Prompted v AID
Prompting v MOTV
Prompting v AID
Promptly d QUIK
Promptness n QUIK
Prompts v MOTV
Prompts v AID
Promulgate v AID OPEN
Prone j DOWN
Prone v MOTV
Prong n SHRP
Pronoun n TALK FORM
Pronounce v TALK
Pronounced v TALK
Pronounced j EMPH
Pronunciation n TALK
Proof n TRUE

Prop n AID
Prop n GO MECH
Propaganda n OPEN IDEA
Propagate v BGIN LARG
Propagate v LARG GO
Propane n VAPR MTRL
Propel v GO
Propeller n GO MECH
Propensity n MOTV
Proper j GOOD
Proper j CRUX
Property n HAVE
Prophecy n FORW IDEA
Prophylaxis n MEDC AID
Propinquity n JOIN NEAR
Propitiate v GLAD AID
Propitious j AID
Proponent n AGRE
Proportion n NUMR SOME
Proportion n SIML
Propose v IDEA
Propose v TALK KIN
Proposition n IDEA
Proposition v TALK SEX
Propound v IDEA
Propped v AID
Propping v AID
Proprietor n MART HAVE
Propriety n GOOD
Propulsion n GO
Prorate v SIML
Pros n AGRE
Pros n POWR
Prosaic j TRIV
Proscenium n FORW FORM
Proscribe v BLOK AGGR
Prose n TALK
Prosecute v AGGR LAW
Prosecute v FORW
Proselyte n AGRE
Prosody n TALK
Prospect n VIEW
Prospect n FORW MOTV
Prospect v OPEN MOTV
Prospected v OPEN MOTV
Prospecting v OPEN MOTV
Prospective j FORW MOTV
Prospector n OPEN MOTV
Prospectus n FORW WRIT
Prosper v AID
Prostate j SOMA MALE
Prosthesis n BODY AID
Prostitute n BAD SEX
Prostrate v DOWN WEAK
Protagonist n LEAD
Protagonist n AGRE
Protean j VARY FORM
Protect v AID
Protege n AID SUB
Protein n FOOD MTRL
Protest v AGGR
Protestant n GRUP HOLY
Protocol n WRIT
Protocol n IDEA FORM
Protoerozoic j PAST

Proton n ION
Protoplasm n SOMA MTRL
Prototype n SIML CRUX
Protract v LARG EVER
Protractor n MSMT
Protrusion n BULG
Proud j FOND POWR
Prove v TRUE
Proverb n TALK IDEA
Provide v AID
Provided c NSCR
Provided v AID
Providence n AID
Providing c NSCR
Providing v AID
Province n PLAC
Provincial j PLAC WEAK
Provincial j PLAC
Proving v TRUE
Provision n FOOD
Provision n AID
Provisional j VARY
Proviso n AGRE
Provocation n AGGR MOTV
Provoke v AGGR MOTV
Provost n LEAD
Prow n FORW
Prowed j FORW
Prowess n POWR
Prowl v GO COVR
Proximity n NEAR
Proxy n SIML MOTV
Prude n FOOL GOOD
Prudence n GOOD
Prune n FOOD VEGT
Prune v CLEN SHRP
Prune v CLEN
Pruned v CLEN SHRP
Pruned v CLEN
Pruning v CLEN SHRP
Pruning v CLEN
Pry v OPEN SEP
Pry v OPEN
Psalm n TALK HOLY
Pseudo j FALS
Pseudonym n FALS TALK
Pseudopod n BUG BODY
Psoriasis n DIRT SICK
Psychasthenia n SICK IDEA
Psyche n IDEA
Psychiatry n MEDC IDEA
Psychic j IDEA
Psychoanalysis n MEDC IDEA
Psychogenic j IDEA
Psychology n IDEA
Psychomotor j BODY IDEA
Psychoneurosis n SICK IDEA
Pschopathology n SICK IDEA
Psychosis n SICK IDEA
Psychosomatic j SOMA SICK
Psychotherapy n MEDC IDEA
Psychotic j SICK IDEA
Pub n MART SIP
Puberty n SEX YNG
Pubescence n SEX YNG

Pubic j BODY SEX
Public j GRUP
Public j GRUP OPEN
Publication n WRIT OPEN
Publicity n GRUP OPEN
Publicly d GRUP OPEN
Publicspirited j GRUP AID
Publish v WRIT OPEN
Puck n PLAY
Puck n GLAD MYTH
Pucker v VARY
Pudding n FOOD
Puddle n FLOW
Puddle n ERTH FLOW
Pudgy j LARG LITL
Puerile j WEAK YNG
Puff n VAPR
Puff n CLEN EASY
Puff v LARG BULG
Puff n FABR
Pug n ANML
Pug n DAMG
Pug n ERTH MTRL
Pugilism n DAMG PLAY
Pugnacious j DAMG
Pugnose n BODY
Puke v SOMA OUT
Pulchritude n GOOD
Pull v GO
Pull v SEP
Pull v EVNT
Pull n POWR
Pull v VARY
Pull v WEAK
Pull v SIP SOMA
Pull v PANG
Pulled v GO
Pulled v SEP
Pulled v EVNT
Pulled v VARY
Pulled v WEAK
Pulled v SIP SOMA
Pulled v PANG
Pullet n ANML YNG
Pulley n MECH
Pullman n REST VEHC
Pullover n GARB
Pulmonary j SOMA
Pulp n EASY MTRL
Pulpit n TALK HOLY
Pulse n VARY SOMA
Pulverize v VARY LITL
Pulverize v VARY DAMG
Pumice n EASY MTRL
Pummel v DAMG
Pump n MECH FLOW

Pump n VAPR MECH
Pump n GARB LADY
Pump v OPEN IDEA
Pumped v MECH FLOW
Pumped v VAPR MECH
Pumped v OPEN IDEA
Pumpernickel n FOOD VEGT
Pumping v MECH FLOW
Pumping v VAPR MECH
Pumping v OPEN IDEA
Pumpkin n FOOD VEGT
Pun v GLAD TALK
Punch n DAMG
Punch n HOLW
Punch n PLAY MYTH
Punch v ANML GRUP
Punch n SIP
Punched v DAMG
Punched v HOLW
Punched v ANML GRUP
Punching v DAMG
Punching v HOLW
Punching v ANML GRUP
Punctilious j SHRP
Punctual j SHRP TIME
Punctuate v WRIT
Punctuate v BLOK
Punctuation n WRIT
Puncture v HOLW SHRP
Pungent j SOMA SHRP
Punily d WEAK
Punish v DAMG
Punitive j DAMG
Punk j WEAK
Punk n VEGT
Punt n GO PLAY
Punt n FLOW VEHC
Puny j WEAK
Pup n ANML YNG
Pupil n EDUC
Pupil n SOMA VIEW
Puppet n PLAY SUB
Puppet n SUB
Puppies n ANML YNG
Puppies n FOOL YNG
Puppy n ANML YNG
Puppy n FOOL YNG
Purchase n MART MONY
Purchase n BLOK
Pure j CLEN
Pure j CLEN GOOD
Pure j EMPH
Purely d EMPH
Purgatory n DAMG HOLY
Purge v CLEN OUT
Purge v DAMG SEP

Purim n HOLY TIME
Puritan n GRUP HOLY
Puritan n GOOD
Purity n CLEN
Purity n CLEN GOOD
Purloin v CRIM
Purple n COLR
Purport n CRUX IDEA
Purpose n MOTV
Purr n ANML TALK
Purse n GARB HOLW
Purse n HOLW MONY
Purse v VARY
Pursed v VARY
Purser n LEAD FLOW
Pursing v VARY
Pursuant d SIML
Pursue v GO MOTV
Pursuing v GO MOTV
Pursuit n WORK
Pursuit n GO MOTV
Pus n DIRT SOMA
Push v GO
Push v POWR GO
Pushcart n VEHC
Pusher n CRIM MEDC
Pusher n GO
Pushover n EASY WEAK
Pushup n WORK
Puss n ANML
Pussy n ANML
Pussyfoot v EASY GO
Pussywillow n VEGT
Pustule n DIRT BODY
Put v NSCR
Put v GO
Put v GO PLAY
Putrefy v DIRT
Putrid j DIRT
Putt n GO PLAY
Putties v EASY MTRL
Putting v NSCR
Putting v GO
Putting v GO PLAY
Putty v EASY MTRL
Puzzle n BLUR
Pygmy n LITL
Pylon n FORM
Pyramid n FORM
Pyramid v LARG FORM
Pyre n BULG HEAT
Pyrex n HEAT MTRL
Pyromaniac n HEAT MOTV
Pyrotechnic j HEAT VIEW
Python n ANML

Q

Q n WRIT
Quack n MEDC FALS
Quack n ANML TALK

Quadrangle n FORM
Quadrangle n HOME PLAC
Quadrennial j NUMR TIME

Quadroon n COLR GRUP
Quadruple n NUMR
Quadruplet n SIML KIN

Parts of speech: a article; b preposition; c conjunction; d adverb; f prefix; i interjection; j adjective; n noun; p pronoun; r phrase; v verb.

Quaff v SIP SOMA
Quagmire n ERTH FLOW
Quagmire n BLUR BLOK
Quail n ANML UP
Quail v WEAK PANG
Quailed v WEAK PANG
Quailing v WEAK PANG
Quaint j AFAR
Quake n VARY ERTH
Quake v VARY PANG
Quake v VARY
Quaker n GRUP HOLY
Qualify v POWR CRUX
Qualify v VARY CRUX
Quality n CRUX
Qualm n PANG
Quandary n BLUR
Quanta n ION MSMT
Quantify v NUMR
Quantitative j NUMR
Quantity n SOME
Quantity n NUMR
Quantum n ION MSMT
Quarantine n BLOK SEP
Quarrel n AGGR
Quarried v ERTH HOLW
Quarries v ERTH HOLW
Quarries n DAMG WEAK
Quarry n ERTH HOLW
Quarry n DAMG WEAK
Quarrying v ERTH HOLW
Quart n MSMT
Quarter n MONY
Quarter n NUMR SOME
Quarter n PLAC
Quarter n PLAY SOME

Quarter v SEP SOME
Quarter n AID
Quarter n HOME
Quarter n ANML BODY
Quarterback n LEAD PLAY
Quarterdeck n FLOW FORM
Quartered v HOME
Quartered v NUMR SOME
Quartered v SEP SOME
Quartering v NUMR SOME
Quartering v HOME
Quartering v SEP SOME
Quarterly j NUMR TIME
Quarterly n WRIT TIME
Quartermaster n LEAD AID
Quartet n GRUP NUMR
Quartz n ERTH MTRL
Quash v BLOK
Quasi d SIML
Quatrain n WRIT
Quaver v VARY HEAR
Quaver n VARY MUSC
Queasy j PANG
Queen n LEAD LADY
Queen n LEAD PLAY
Queer j FOOL
Queer n MALE SEX
Queer n FALS MONY
Queered v FOOL
Queering v FOOL
Quell v BLOK DAMG
Quell v GLAD AID
Quench v END
Queries v BLUR TALK
Querulous j AGGR
Query n BLUR TALK

Quest n OPEN
Question n BLUR TALK
Quibble v TALK TRIV
Quick j QUIK
Quicksand n ERTH FLOW
Quicksilver n VARY MTRL
Quiescent j REST
Quiet j HEAR REST
Quill n ANML BODY
Quill n WRIT
Quilt n FURN REST
Quince n FOOD VEGT
Quinine n MEDC VEGT
Quinsy n SICK
Quintet n GRUP NUMR
Quintuplet n SIML KIN
Quip n GLAD TALK
Quirk n FOOL
Quirk n VARY
Quit v END
Quit v GO SEP
Quite d EMPH
Quiver n VARY
Quiver n HOLW
Quiver v VARY PANG
Quiz v BLUR TALK
Quizzed v BLUR TALK
Quizzical j FOOL
Quizzical j BLUR TALK
Quizzing v BLUR TALK
Quoits n PLAY
Quorum n GRUP LAW
Quota n NUMR SOME
Quote v TALK
Quotient n NUMR
Quoting v TALK

R

R n WRIT
Rabbet n HOLW
Rabbi n LEAD HOLY
Rabbit n ANML
Rabbit n ANML FABR
Rabble n AGGR GRUP
Rabid j AGGR
Rabid j ANML SICK
Rabies n ANML SICK
Raccoon n ANML
Raccoon n ANML FABR
Race n QUIK GO
Race n GRUP
Raced v QUIK GO
Racer n QUIK GO
Racer n ANML
Racial j GRUP
Racing v QUIK GO
Racism n AGGR GRUP
Rack n FORM
Rack n DAMG
Rack n DAMG FORM
Rack n MECH
Racked v DAMG
Racked v FORM
Racket n HEAR

Racket n PLAY
Racket n CRIM
Racketeer n CRIM
Racking v DAMG
Racking v FORM
Racks n FORM
Racks v DAMG
Radar n MECH ION
Radial j FORM
Radian n NUMR FORM
Radiance n GLAD VIEW
Radiant j GLAD VIEW
Radiant j OUT
Radiate v OUT
Radiate v VIEW
Radiator n HEAT
Radical j OPPO
Radio n HEAR TALK
Radio n ION
Radioactive j ION
Radioisotope n MTRL ION
Radiology n MEDC ION
Radish n FOOD VEGT
Radium n MTRL ION
Radius n MSMT
Raft n FLOW VEHC

Raft n MUCH GRUP
Rafter n FORM UP
Rag n TRIV FABR
Rag v AGGR TALK
Ragamuffin n DIRT YNG
Rage n AGGR
Rage n NEW MOTV
Raid n DAMG
Rail n FORM
Rail n VEHC
Rail v AGGR TALK
Railroad n VEHC
Railroad v FALS VEHC
Railroaded v FALS VEHC
Railroading v FALS VEHC
Railway n VEHC
Raiment n GARB
Rain n WEA FLOW
Rainbow n WEA COLR
Raincoat n WEA GARB
Raindrop n WEA FLOW
Rainfall n WEA FLOW
Raise v GO UP
Raisin n FOOD VEGT
Raising v GO UP
Rajah n LEAD MALE

Rake v WORK
Rake v DAMG
Rakeoff n CRIM MONY
Rally n POWR GRUP
Rally v POWR
Ram n ANML MALE
Ram v POWR
Ramble v GO
Ramble v BLUR TALK
Ramification n SEP
Rammed v POWR
Ramp n GO FORM
Rampant j OPEN
Rampart n BLOK AID
Ramrod n DAMG FORM
Rams n ANML MALE
Rams v POWR
Ramshackle j FORM WEAK
Ran v QUIK GO
Ran v GO MOTV
Ran v LEAD
Ranch n ERTH WORK
Rancid j DIRT SOMA
Rancor n AGGR PANG
Random n BLUR AFAR
Rang v MUSC
Range n FORW
Range n ERTH
Range n HEAT FURN
Range v GO
Ranged v FORW
Ranged v GO
Ranger n GO
Ranger n LAW
Ranginess n BODY
Ranging v FORW
Ranging v GO
Rangy j BODY
Rank j BAD
Rank n FORW
Ranked v FORW
Ranking v FORW
Rankle v AGGR PANG
Ranks v FORW
Ransack v DAMG OPEN
Ransom v AID MONY
Ransom v AID
Rant v AGGR TALK
Rap n HEAR
Rap n DAMG
Rap v JOIN TALK
Rapacious j DAMG MOTV
Rape n DAMG SEX
Rapid j QUIK
Rapids n QUIK FLOW
Rapine n DAMG
Raping v DAMG SEX
Rapist n DAMG SEX
Rapped v HEAR
Rapped v DAMG
Rapped v JOIN TALK
Rapprochement n AGRE
Rapt j MOTV
Rapture n GLAD
Rare j AFAR

Rare j LITL
Rarefy v LITL
Rarely d AFAR
Raring j MOTV
Rarity n AFAR
Rascal n BAD
Rash j DAMG QUIK
Rash n SICK
Rasp v HEAR
Rasp v HEAR PANG
Rasp n HEAR WORK
Raspberry n FOOD VEGT
Raspberry n AGGR HEAR
Rat n ANML
Rat n ANML BAD
Rate n MONY
Rate n FORW
Rate n NUMR
Rate v FORW IDEA
Rate v AGGR TALK
Rather d EMPH
Rather d MOTV
Rather d OPPO
Ratify v AGRE
Rating v FORW
Rating v NUMR
Rating v FORW IDEA
Rating v AGGR TALK
Ratio n NUMR
Ration v SOME
Rational j IDEA
Rationale n IDEA
Ratted v ANML BAD
Rattle n HEAR
Rattle v PANG
Rattles v HEAR
Rattles v PANG
Rattlesnake n ANML HEAR
Raucous j HEAR
Ravage v DAMG
Rave v FOND TALK
Rave v TALK PANG
Raven n ANML UP
Raven n COLR
Ravenous j FOOD MOTV
Ravine n ERTH HOLW
Raving v FOND TALK
Raving v TALK PANG
Ravish v DAMG
Ravish v GLAD MOTV
Ravish v DAMG SEX
Raw j WEAK
Raw j AGGR
Rawhide n ANML FABR
Ray n VIEW
Ray n ION
Ray n ANML FLOW
Ray n FORM
Rayon n FABR
Raze v DAMG DOWN
Razor n SHRP
Razz v AGGR TALK
Reach n LARG
Reach v GO
React v EVNT

React v OPPO EVNT
Reactance n ION
Reaction n EVNT
Reaction n OPPO EVNT
Reactionary j OPPO EVNT
Reactor n MECH ION
Read v WRIT VIEW
Readied v AID
Readied v MOTV
Readily d EASY
Reading v WRIT VIEW
Readjust v VARY
Ready j AID
Ready j MOTV
Readymade j MART
Real j TRUE
Real j EMPH TRUE
Realestate n ERTH HAVE
Reality n TRUE
Realize v IDEA TRUE
Realize v END
Really d EMPH TRUE
Realm n PLAC
Realty n ERTH HAVE
Reap v HAVE VEGT
Reappear v VIEW
Rear n BACK
Rear n BACK BODY
Rear v AID
Rear v UP
Reared v AID
Reared v UP
Rearing v AID
Rearing v UP
Rearrange v FORM
Rearward d BACK
Reason n IDEA
Reassemble v GRUP
Reassure v AID
Reawaken v QUIK
Rebate n BACK MONY
Rebel v DAMG OPPO
Rebound v BACK GO
Rebuff n AGGR
Rebuild v FORM WORK
Rebuke n AGGR
Recalcitrant j AGGR
Recall v IDEA PAST
Recall v BACK TALK
Recant v OPPO TALK
Recapitulate v SIML TALK
Recapture v BLOK HAVE
Recede v BACK GO
Receipt n WRIT HAVE
Receipt n HAVE
Receive v HAVE
Receive v AGRE
Receive v HEAR TALK
Receiver n HAVE
Receiver n HOLW HAVE
Receiver n LAW HAVE
Receiver n HEAR TALK
Recent j NEAR PAST
Receptacle n HOLW
Reception n HAVE

Reception n HEAR TALK
Reception n AGRE JOIN
Receptive j AGRE
Recess n SEP TIME
Recess n HOLW
Recessing v SEP TIME
Recessing v HOLW
Recession n BACK GO
Recipe n MSMT FORM
Recipient n HAVE
Reciprocity n SIML
Recital n MUSC
Recital n TALK
Recite v TALK
Reciting v TALK
Reck v IDEA
Reckless j DAMG
Reckon v IDEA
Reckon v NUMR IDEA
Reclaim v HAVE
Reclaim v AID
Recline v VARY REST
Recluse j SOLE SEP
Recognition n AGRE NEAR
Recoil v BACK GO
Recollect v IDEA PAST
Recollect v GRUP JOIN
Recommence v BGIN
Recommend v AGRE
Recompense v MONY
Reconcile v AGRE
Recondite j BLUR COVR
Reconnaissance n OPEN IDEA
Reconnoitre v OPEN IDEA
Reconsider v IDEA
Reconstruct v FORM WORK
Record n WRIT
Record n TALK MUSC
Record n POWR
Recorder n TALK MECH
Recorder n WRIT
Recorder n MUSC
Recount v TALK
Recount v NUMR
Recourse n AID
Recover v HAVE
Recover v MEDC
Recreant n OPPO
Recreant n WEAK
Recreation n PLAY
Recreation n SIML BGIN
Recruit n JOIN
Recruit v AID
Rectal j DIRT SOMA
Rectangle n FORM
Rectify v TRUE
Rectilinear j FORM
Rectum n DIRT SOMA
Recumbent j REST
Recuperate v MEDC
Recur v SIML
Red n COLR
Red n COLR GRUP
Red n COLR LACK
Redden v COLR

Redeem v AID HAVE
Redeem v AID
Redhead n COLR BODY
Redouble v LARG
Redouble v BACK GO
Redound v LARG AID
Redress n AID
Redskin n COLR GRUP
Reduce v LITL
Redundant j BULG TRIV
Redwood n COLR VEGT
Redwood n MTRL VEGT
Reed n VEGT
Reed n MUSC
Reef n ERTH FLOW
Reek v VAPR DIRT
Reel v VARY
Reel v VARY WEAK
Reel n GO MUSC
Refer v TALK
Referee n LEAD IDEA
Reference n TALK
Referendum n GRUP LAW
Refine v GOOD
Reflect v SIML VIEW
Reflect v IDEA
Reflex j SOMA EVNT
Reflexive j TALK FORM
Reform n VARY GOOD
Reform v SIML FORM
Reformatory n BLOK HOME
Refraction n VARY VIEW
Refractory j AGGR
Refractory j HEAT MTRL
Refrain v BLOK LACK
Refrain n TALK MUSC
Refresh v AID
Refreshment n FOOD AID
Refrigerate v COLD
Refrigerator n COLD HOLW
Refuge n AID
Refugee n GO SEP
Refund v BACK MONY
Refurbish v CLEN NEW
Refuse n DIRT
Refuse v OPPO
Refused v OPPO
Refusing v OPPO
Refute v OPPO
Regain v HAVE
Regal j LEAD
Regale v GLAD
Regaling v GLAD
Regard n VIEW
Regard n FOND
Regard n NSCR
Regarded v VIEW
Regarding b NSCR
Regarding v VIEW
Regardless j OPPO
Regards n FOND
Regards v VIEW
Regards v NSCR
Regatta n FLOW VEHC
Regenerate v SIML BGIN

Regime n LEAD GRUP
Regime n IDEA FORM
Regimen n IDEA FORM
Regiment n DAMG GRUP
Regiment v LEAD GRUP
Region n PLAC
Register n WRIT
Register n FORW
Register n FORW MUSC
Register n MART MECH
Register v VIEW
Registered v WRIT
Registered v VIEW
Registering v WRIT
Registering v VIEW
Registrar n WRIT
Registration n WRIT
Regress v BACK GO
Regret v PANG
Regular j EVER
Regulate v LEAD
Regurgitate v SOMA OUT
Rehabilitate v AID
Rehash v TALK
Rehearse v TALK
Reich n LEAD GRUP
Reify v MTRL
Reign n LEAD
Reimburse v MONY
Rein n BLOK LEAD
Reincarnation n DEAD LIVE
Reindeer n ANML
Reinforce v POWR AID
Reiterate v TALK
Reject v AGGR SEP
Rejoice v GLAD
Rejoin v JOIN
Rejoin v TALK
Rejoinder n TALK
Rejuvenate v AID NEW
Relapse n WEAK
Relate v TALK
Relate v SIML JOIN
Related j SIML JOIN
Related j KIN
Related v TALK
Relating v TALK
Relating v SIML JOIN
Relative j SIML JOIN
Relative n KIN
Relax v GLAD REST
Relax v EASY
Relay n GO
Relay n JOIN MECH
Release v OPEN
Relegate v SEP
Relent v EASY
Relentless j AGGR EVER
Relevant j SIML JOIN
Reliable j AID
Reliance n AID
Relic n PAST
Relied v AID
Relief n AID
Relief n VIEW FORM

Relies v AID
Relieve v AID
Religion n HOLY
Relinquish v SEP LACK
Relish n FOOD
Relish n FOND SOMA
Relish n FOND
Reluctance n OPPO
Rely v AID
Remain v EVER
Remainder n SOME
Remains v EVER
Remains n SOME
Remains n DEAD
Remark n TALK
Remarkable j GOOD
Remarkable j AFAR
Remedy n MEDC AID
Remembrance n IDEA PAST
Remind v IDEA
Reminiscence n IDEA PAST
Remiss j WEAK
Remission n END
Remission n AGRE
Remission n GO
Remit v GO
Remit v AGRE
Remit v END
Remnant n SOME
Remnant n SOME FABR
Remodel v VARY FORM
Remonstrate v AGGR TALK
Remorse n PANG
Remote j AFAR
Remove v SEP
Remunerate v MONY
Renaissance j PAST
Renaissance n BGIN POWR
Rend v DAMG SEP
Rended v DAMG SEP
Render v AID
Render v VARY
Render v EVNT
Render v TALK
Rendezvous n JOIN
Rending v DAMG SEP
Rendition n EVNT
Renegade n AGGR
Renege v OPPO NO
Renew v BGIN NEW
Renounce v AGGR LACK
Renovate v AID NEW
Renown n POWR
Rent n MART MONY
Rent n DAMG SEP
Rented v MART MONY
Renter n MART MONY
Renting v MART MONY
Rents v MART MONY
Renunciation n AGGR LACK
Reorganize v FORM
Repair v AID
Repair v GO
Repairman n AID WORK
Repartee n GLAD TALK

Repeal v OPPO END
Repeat v SIML TALK
Repeat v SIML
Repel v AGGR SEP
Repent v PANG
Repercussion n OPPO
Repertoire n GRUP
Repitition n SIML
Rephrase v TALK
Replace v SIML VARY
Replenish v BULG
Replete j BULG
Replica n SIML
Replies v TALK
Reply n TALK
Report n TALK
Report n HEAR
Reporter n WRIT
Reporter n TALK
Repose n REST
Reprehend v AGGR TALK
Represent v SIML
Represent v SIML LAW
Repress v BLOK
Reprieve n AID
Reprimand n AGGR TALK
Reprisal n AGGR
Reproach n AGGR TALK
Reprobate n BAD
Reproduce v SIML
Reproduce v SIML BGIN
Reproof n AGGR TALK
Reprove v AGGR TALK
Reptile n ANML
Republic n GRUP LAW
Republican n GRUP
Repudiate v OPPO
Repugnance n AGGR PANG
Repulse v AGGR SEP
Reputable j GOOD
Reputation n CRUX
Reputation n POWR CRUX
Repute n CRUX
Repute n POWR CRUX
Repute v IDEA
Reputed v IDEA
Reputes v IDEA
Reputing v IDEA
Request n MOTV
Requiem n DEAD HOLY
Require v MOTV
Requisite j MOTV
Requisition n MOTV
Rescind v OPPO END
Rescue v AID
Research n OPEN IDEA
Resemble v SIML
Resent v AGGR PANG
Reservation n HAVE
Reservation n OPPO
Reservation n ERTH
Reserve v HAVE
Reserve n OPPO
Reserve n ERTH
Reserve n DAMG GRUP

Reserved v HAVE
Reserved j OPPO
Reserving v HAVE
Rservist n DAMG GRUP
Reservoir n HOLW FLOW
Reside v HOME LIVE
Residence n HOME LIVE
Residue n SOME
Resign v SEP
Resign v WEAK
Resilient j VARY EASY
Resist v BLOK
Resist v BLOK DAMG
Resolute j MOTV
Resolution n MOTV
Resolution n AGRE END
Resolve v MOTV
Resolve v AGRE END
Resonant j MUSC
Resort n AID
Resort n PLAY
Resound v HEAR
Resource n AID
Respect n FOND AGRE
Respect n SOME
Respect n NSCR
Respectable j GOOD
Respected v FOND AGRE
Respectful j FOND AGRE
Respecting b NSCR
Respecting v FOND AGRE
Respective j SIML
Respiration n VAPR SOMA
Respirator n VAPR MECH
Respite n REST
Resplendent j GOOD
Response n TALK
Response n EVNT
Responsibility n MOTV
Rest n REST
Rest n END REST
Rest n SOME
Restaurant n MART FOOD
Restless j PANG
Restore v AID
Restrain v BLOK
Restrict v BLOK
Result n END
Resume v BGIN
Resume n LITL IDEA
Resumed v BGIN
Resuming v BGIN
Resurrect v DEAD LIVE
Resuscitate v DEAD LIVE
Retail n MART MONY
Retain v EVER HAVE
Retaliate v AGGR
Retard v BLOK REST
Retention n EVER HAVE
Reticent j WEAK
Retina n SOMA VIEW
Retinue n GRUP SUB
Retire v GO SEP
Retire v GO REST
Retort n AGGR TALK

Retort n HOLW	Rib v GLAD	Ring n HOLW FORM
Retorted v AGGR TALK	Ribald j BAD GLAD	Ring n MUSC
Retorting v AGGR TALK	Ribbed j FORM	Ring n GRUP HOLW
Retrace v BACK GO	Ribbed v GLAD	Ring n HOME PLAY
Retrace v SIML WRIT	Ribbon n FABR	Ringed v HOLW FORM
Retract v BACK HAVE	Ribbon n POWR FABR	Ringing n MUSC
Retreat n BACK GO	Ribbon n LITL	Ringing v HOLW FORM
Retreat n HOLY COVR	Rice n FOOD VEGT	Ringleader n LEAD GRUP
Retreat n HOME COVR	Rich j MUCH MONY	Rink n HOME PLAY
Retreated v BACK GO	Rich j MUCH GOOD	Rinse v CLEN FLOW
Retreating v BACK GO	Rickety j WEAK	Riot n DAMG
Retrieve v HAVE	Rickety j SICK	Rip n SEP
Retroactive j PAST	Ricochet v VARY GO	Rip v AGGR SEP
Retrospect n BACK VIEW	Rid v SEP	Rip n VARY FLOW
Return n BACK GO	Ridding v SEP	Ripe j NEW
Reveal v OPEN	Riddle n BLUR	Ripe j POWR
Revel n GLAD PLAY	Riddle v HOLW	Ripped v SEP
Revelation n OPEN	Riddle v SEP	Ripped v AGGR SEP
Revenge n DAMG	Ride v GO	Ripple n VARY
Revenue n MART MONY	Ride v AGGR	Rise v GO UP
Reverberation n HEAR	Rider n GO	Rise n BULG UP
Revere v FOND	Rider n JOIN LAW	Risen v GO UP
Reverie n IDEA MYTH	Ridge n ERTH BULG	Risk v DAMG MOTV
Revering v FOND	Ridicule n FOOL AGGR	Rite n HOLY FORM
Reverse n BACK VARY	Riding v GO	Ritual j HOLY FORM
Reverse n VARY OPPO	Riding v AGGR	Rival n OPPO
Review n IDEA VIEW	Rifle n DAMG MECH	River n FLOW
Review n WRIT IDEA	Rifle v CRIM	Rivers n FLOW
Revile v AGGR TALK	Rifled v CRIM	Riverside n NEAR FLOW
Revise v VARY	Rifling v CRIM	Rivet v JOIN
Revive v DEAD LIVE	Rift n SEP	Roach n BUG
Revolt n DAMG	Rig n AID	Road n PATH
Revolt n PANG	Rig n VEHC	Roadway n PATH
Revolution n VARY GO	Rig n GARB	Roam v GO
Revolution n VARY DAMG	Rig v FALS	Roar n HEAR
Revolve v VARY GO	Right d BODY PLAC	Roar n ANML TALK
Revolver n DAMG MECH	Right d SHRP EMPH	Roast v HEAT
Revulsion n PANG	Right d GOOD TRUE	Roast n FOOD HEAT
Reward n AID	Right j FORM	Rob v CRIM
Rh n SOMA	Right n TRUE MOTV	Robe n GARB
Rhapsody n MUSC	Right n GRUP	Robin n ANML UP
Rheostat n VARY ION	Right v FORM UP	Robot n MECH
Rhesus n ANML	Righted v GOOD TRUE	Robust j POWR
Rhesus n MYTH	Righted v FORM UP	Rock n ERTH
Rhesus n SOMA	Righteous j GOOD TRUE	Rock v VARY
Rhetoric n TALK	Righthanded j BODY PLAC	Rocked v VARY
Rheumatism n SICK	Righting v GOOD TRUE	Rocker n VARY
Rhinal j BODY	Righting v FORM UP	Rocker n FURN REST
Rhine n PLAC FLOW	Rightly d GOOD TRUE	Rocket n VEHC UP
Rhinencephalon n SOMA	Rights n TRUE MOTV	Rocket v GO UP
Rhinestone n MTRL VIEW	Rights n BODY PLAC	Rocking v VARY
Rhinitis n SICK	Rights v GOOD TRUE	Rococo j VARY FORM
Rhinoceros n ANML	Rights v FORM UP	Rod n FORM
Rhododendron n VEGT	Rigid j EVER	Rod n DAMG FORM
Rhombus n FORM	Rigmarole n FOOL	Rod n DAMG MECH
Rhubarb n FOOD VEGT	Rigor n AGGR	Rod n MSMT
Rhubarb n DAMG	Rigor n EVER	Rod n SOMA VIEW
Rhumba n GO MUSC	Rigorous j AGGR	Rode v GO
Rhyme v SIML TALK	Rile v DIRT	Rode v AGGR
Rhythm n VARY MUSC	Rile v AGGR PANG	Rodent n ANML
Rib n SOMA	Rim n END	Rodeo n ANML PLAY
Rib n FORM	Rind n BODY VEGT	Roentgen n ION MSMT

Parts of speech; a article; b preposition; c conjunction; d adverb; f prefix; i interjection;
j adjective; n noun; p pronoun; r phrase; v verb.

Roger n AGRE
Rogue n BAD
Roil v DIRT
Roil v AGGR
Roister v GLAD PLAY
Role n SIML
Roll n FORM
Roll n FORW WRIT
Roll n FOOD VEGT
Roll v GO
Roll n MUSC
Roll n MONY
Roll v CRIM
Rolled v FORM
Rolled v GO
Rolled v MUSC
Rolled v CRIM
Romance n FOND SEX
Romantic j FOND SEX
Romp v GLAD GO
Rondeau n TALK MUSC
Rondeau n TALK
Roof n UP COVR
Rook n PLAY
Rook n ANML UP
Rook v FALS
Rooked v FALS
Rookie n WEAK
Rooking v FALS
Room n HOME
Roommate n HOME JOIN
Roost n ANML HOME
Rooster n ANML UP
Root n BGIN VEGT
Root n BGIN CRUX
Root n CRUX NUMR
Root v AGRE TALK
Root v SOMA OUT
Root v IN
Rope n FABR
Rope n DEAD FABR
Rope n JOIN
Rope v BLOK FABR
Roped v BLOK FABR
Roping v BLOK FABR
Rorschach n BLUR TRUE
Rosary n GARB HOLY
Rose n VEGT
Rose n COLR
Rose v GO UP
Rosecolored j COLR GOOD
Rosicrucian n GRUP HOLY
Rosily d COLR GOOD
Rosily d COLR
Rosiness n COLR GOOD
Rosiness n COLR
Roster n FORW WRIT
Rostrum n TALK FORM
Rosy j COLR GOOD
Rosy j COLR
Rosy j VEGT
Rot v DIRT
Rotary n VARY PATH
Rotate v VARY GO
Rote n EVER TRIV

Rotund j BULG FORM
Rotunda n HOME FORM
Rouge n COLR
Rouge n EASY MTRL
Rough j VARY
Rough j BLUR
Rough j DAMG
Rough n VARY ERTH
Roughed v VARY
Roughed v DAMG
Roughing v VARY
Roughing v DAMG
Roulette n PLAY MOTV
Round j FORM
Round v VARY GO
Round n SOME
Round n DAMG
Round n TALK MUSC
Round v BLOK HOLW
Round v END
Roundabout j VARY
Rounded v FORM
Rounded v VARY GO
Rounded v BLOK HOLW
Rounded v END
Rounder j FORM
Roundest j FORM
Rounding v FORM
Rounding v VARY GO
Rounding v BLOK HOLW
Rounding v END
Roundly d EMPH
Roundness n FORM
Rounds v FORM
Rounds n VARY GO
Rounds n SOME
Rounds n DAMG
Rounds n TALK MUSC
Rounds v BLOK HOLW
Rounds v END
Roundup n BLOK HOLW
Rouse v QUIK
Rout n GO WEAK
Rout v HOLW SHRP
Rout n AGGR GRUP
Route n PATH
Routed v PATH
Routed v GO WEAK
Routed v HOLW SHRP
Router n HOLW MECH
Routine n EVER
Routing v PATH
Routing v GO WEAK
Routing v HOLW SHRP
Rove v GO
Row n FORW
Row n DAMG
Row n PATH
Row v GO FLOW
Rowboat n FLOW VEHC
Rowdy j DAMG
Rowed v GO FLOW
Rowing v GO FLOW
Royal j LEAD
Royalty n LEAD

Royalty n MONY
Rub v VARY JOIN
Rub v CLEN
Rub v AGGR
Rub v DAMG DEAD
Rubbed v VARY JOIN
Rubbed v CLEN
Rubbed v AGGR
Rubbed v DAMG DEAD
Rubber n MTRL
Rubber n FABR
Rubber n PLAY SOME
Rubber n CLEN
Rubbers n GARB
Rubbing v VARY JOIN
Rubbing v CLEN
Rubbing v AGGR
Rubbing v DAMG DEAD
Rubbish n DIRT
Rubble n DIRT
Rubies n ERTH MTRL
Ruble n MONY
Ruby n ERTH MTRL
Ruby n COLR
Rudder n LEAD FORM
Ruddiness n COLR
Ruddy j COLR
Rude j AGGR
Rudiment n BGIN
Rue v PANG
Ruffian n DAMG
Ruffle v VARY
Ruffle n VARY GARB
Ruffle v PANG
Rug n DOWN FURN
Rugged j POWR
Ruin v DAMG DIRT
Ruing v PANG
Rule n LEAD
Rule n MSMT FORM
Rule n IDEA FORM
Rule n EVER
Ruled v LEAD
Ruled v MSMT FORM
Ruler n MSMT FORM
Ruler n LEAD
Ruling v LEAD
Ruling v MSMT FORM
Rum n SIP VEGT
Rumba n GO MUSC
Rumble n HEAR
Rumble n DAMG HEAR
Ruminate v IDEA
Ruminate v FOOD SOMA
Rummage n TRIV
Rummage v OPEN
Rummaged v OPEN
Rummaging v OPEN
Rumor n TALK
Rump n BACK BODY
Rump n ANML FOOD
Rumple v VARY
Rumpus n PLAY
Rumpus n DAMG
Run v QUIK GO

Run v GO MOTV
Run v LEAD
Runabout n VEHC
Runaway j GO OPEN
Rung v MUSC
Rung n DOWN UP
Rung n FORM
Runt n LITL
Rupture n DAMG SEP
Rupture n SICK SEP
Rural j ERTH PLAC
Ruse n FALS
Rush n QUIK GO

Rush n VEGT
Rushed v QUIK GO
Rushes v QUIK GO
Rushes n VEGT
Rushing v QUIK GO
Russet j COLR
Rust n DIRT
Rust n COLR
Rust n SICK VEGT
Rustic j ERTH
Rustic n ERTH WEAK
Rustier j DIRT
Rustier j WEAK

Rusting v DIRT
Rustle v VARY HEAR
Rustle v ANML CRIM
Rustler n ANML CRIM
Rusty j DIRT
Rusty j WEAK
Rusty j COLR
Rut n EVER HOLW
Rut n HOLW
Rut n ANML SEX
Ruthless j AGGR
Rye n FOOD VEGT
Rye n SIP VEGT

S

S n WRIT
S n WRIT FORM
Sabbath n HOLY TIME
Sable n COLR
Sable n ANML
Sable n ANML FABR
Sabotage v DAMG
Sabre n DAMG SHRP
Sac n SOMA HOLW
Saccharin n FOOD
Sacerdotal j HOLY
Sachem n LEAD
Sack n HOLW
Sack n FABR
Sack n SIP VEGT
Sack v DAMG CRIM
Sack n HOLW REST
Sack v SEP
Sackcloth n GARB PANG
Sacked v HOLW
Sacked v DAMG CRIM
Sacked v HOLW REST
Sacked v SEP
Sacking n FABR
Sacking v HOLW
Sacking v DAMG CRIM
Sacking v HOLW REST
Sacking v SEP
Sacrament n HOLY
Sacred j HOLY
Sacrifice n DAMG LACK
Sacrifice n HOLY LACK
Sacrifice n LACK
Sacrificial j HOLY LACK
Sad j PANG
Sad j WEAK
Sadden v PANG
Saddle n ANML REST
Saddle n ANML BODY
Saddle n ANML FABR
Saddle n FORM
Saddlebag n HOLW REST
Sadism n DAMG
Safari n GO GRUP
Safe j AID
Safe n AID HOLW
Safeguard n AID
Safety n AID
Safety n AID MECH

Safety n PLAY
Saffron n COLR
Saffron n VEGT
Sag v DOWN
Saga n TALK MYTH
Sagacity n POWR IDEA
Sagamore n LEAD
Sage n GOOD IDEA
Sage n FOOD VEGT
Sagebrush n VEGT
Sagittal j PLAC BODY
Sagittal j SHRP
Sagittarius n ASTR MYTH
Sahara n HEAT PLAC
Sahib n LEAD MALE
Said v TALK
Sail n FLOW FABR
Sail v GO FLOW
Sail v GO UP
Sailboat n FLOW VEHC
Sailed v GO FLOW
Sailed v GO UP
Sailing v GO FLOW
Sailing v GO UP
Sailor n FLOW
Saint n GOOD HOLY
Sake n AID
Sake n SIP VEGT
Sal n MTRL
Salad n FOOD
Salamander n ANML FLOW
Salamander n ANML MYTH
Salamander n HEAT
Salami n ANML FOOD
Salary n MONY WORK
Sale n MART MONY
Salient j BULG
Salient j QUIK GO
Saline j MTRL
Saliva n SOMA FLOW
Sallied v GO
Sallied v DAMG GO
Sallow j COLR
Sallow n VEGT
Sally n GO
Sally n DAMG GO
Salmon n ANML FLOW
Salmon n FOOD FLOW
Salmon n COLR

Salon n HOME
Salon n GRUP HOME
Saloon n HOME
Saloon n MART SIP
Salt n FOOD
Salt n MTRL
Salt n FLOW
Salt n AGGR
Salt v EVER
Salt v FALS
Salted v FOOD
Salted v EVER
Salted v FALS
Salting v FOOD
Salting v EVER
Salting v FALS
Saltpeter n MTRL
Saltwater j MTRL FLOW
Salubrious j MEDC AID
Salutary j MEDC AID
Salute v AGRE
Salvage v AID
Salvation n AID
Salve n AID
Salve n AID MTRL
Salvo n DAMG GRUP
Salvo n GRUP HEAR
Samaritan n GOOD AID
Samba n GO MUSC
Same j SIML
Samovar n SIP HOLW
Sampan n FLOW VEHC
Sample v SOME
Sanatorium n MEDC HOME
Sanctify v GOOD HOLY
Sanctimonious j FALS HOLY
Sanction n DAMG
Sanction v AGRE
Sanctity n GOOD HOLY
Sanctuary n AID HOLY
Sanctum n HOME HOLY
Sand n ERTH
Sand v ERTH EASY
Sandal n GARB
Sandalwood n MTRL VEGT
Sandalwood n VEGT
Sandbag n ERTH HOLW
Sandbag v DAMG
Sandbox n ERTH HOLW

Sandglass n MSMT TIME
Sandhog n HOLW WORK
Sandier j ERTH
Sandier j COLR
Sandlot j ERTH
Sandman n MALE REST
Sandpaper v ERTH EASY
Sandpiper n ANML UP
Sandstone n ERTH MTRL
Sandwich n FOOD
Sandwich n COVR
Sandwiched v COVR
Sandwiching v COVR
Sandy j ERTH
Sandy j COLR
Sane j MEDC IDEA
Sang v TALK MUSC
Sangfroid n GLAD POWR
Sanguine j COLR SOMA
Sanguine j SOMA MOTV
Sanguine j DAMG SOMA
Sanhedrin n LEAD GRUP
Sanitarium n MEDC HOME
Sanitary j CLEN MEDC
Sanitation n CLEN MEDC
Sanity n MEDC IDEA
Sank v DOWN GO
Sanka n SIP VEGT
Sans b LACK
Sanskrit n TALK
SantaClaus n PLAY HOLY
Sap n SOMA VEGT
Sap n CRUX SOMA
Sap n FOOL WEAK
Sap v DAMG WEAK
Sap v WEAK LACK
Sapling n VEGT YNG
Sapped v DAMG WEAK
Sapped v WEAK LACK
Sapper n DAMG
Sapphire n ERTH MTRL
Sapphire n COLR
Saran n MTRL
Sarcasm n AGGR
Sarcoma n SICK
Sarcophagus n DEAD HOLW
Sardine n FOOD FLOW
Sardine n ANML FLOW
Sardonic j AGGR
Sari n GARB LADY
Sarong n GARB
Sarsaparilla n VEGT
Sarsaparilla n SIP VEGT
Sartorial j GARB
Sash n GARB
Sash n FORM VIEW
Sashay v GO
Sass v AGGR TALK
Sassafras n VEGT
Sat v REST
Satan n BAD LEAD
Satchel n HOLW
Sated j AID BULG
Sateen n FABR
Satellite n ASTR SUB

Satiate v AID BULG
Satiety n AID BULG
Satin n FABR
Satire n FOOL AGGR
Satisfaction n AGRE AID
Satisfactory j GOOD
Satisfied v AGRE AID
Satisfy v AGRE AID
Saturate v BULG FLOW
Saturate v BULG
Saturday n TIME
Saturn n ASTR
Saturn n LEAD MYTH
Saturnine j PANG
Satyr n MALE MYTH
Satyr n MALE SEX
Satyriasis n MALE SEX
Sauce n FOOD
Sauce n AGGR
Saucer n FOOD HOLW
Saucy j AGGR
Sauerkraut n FOOD VEGT
Saunter v GO REST
Saurian n ANML
Sausage n ANML FOOD
Saute j FOOD HEAT
Sauterne n SIP VEGT
Savage j DAMG
Savant n POWR EDUC
Save v AID
Save v EVER HAVE
Save v EVER
Save b OPPO
Saving v AID
Saving v EVER HAVE
Saving v EVER
Savings n MONY HAVE
Savior n LEAD HOLY
Savoirfaire n POWR
Savor n SOMA GOOD
Saw v VIEW
Saw n SHRP WORK
Saw n TALK IDEA
Sawdust n DIRT MTRL
Sax n MUSC
Saxon n GRUP
Saxon n TALK
Saxophone n MUSC
Say v TALK
Saying v TALK
Saying n TALK IDEA
Scab n AGGR WORK
Scab n DIRT BODY
Scabbard n HOLW SHRP
Scabbed v AGGR WORK
Scabbed v DIRT BODY
Scabbing v AGGR WORK
Scabbing v DIRT BODY
Scabby j BAD
Scabby j DIRT BODY
Scabrous j BAD
Scabrous j DIRT BODY
Scads n MUCH
Scaffold n FORM
Scaffold n DEAD FORM

Scalar n NUMR
Scald v HEAT
Scald v DAMG HEAT
Scale n MECH MSMT
Scale n MSMT
Scale n ANML BODY
Scale n FOR W
Scale n FOR W MUSC
Scale n FORM COVR
Scale v GO
Scale v GO UP
Scallion n FOOD VEGT
Scallop n FOOD FLOW
Scallop n ANML FLOW
Scallop n FORM
Scallop v FOOD HEAT
Scalloped j FORM
Scalloped v FOOD HEAT
Scalp n BODY
Scalp v DAMG BODY
Scalp v CRIM MONY
Scalped v DAMG BODY
Scalped v CRIM MONY
Scalpel n SHRP
Scalping v DAMG BODY
Scalping v CRIM MONY
Scamp n BAD
Scamper v QUIK GO
Scan v VIEW
Scandal n BAD PANG
Scant j LITL
Scapegoat n ANML WEAK
Scar n DAMG BODY
Scarab n BUG
Scarce j AFAR
Scarce j LITL
Scarcely d LITL
Scarcely d TRIV
Scare v PANG
Scarecrow n ANML PANG
Scarf n GARB
Scarlet j COLR
Scat v GO SEP
Scathing j AGGR
Scatology n BAD SEX
Scatter v SEP
Scatterbrain n FOOL
Scavenge v DIRT FOOD
Scavenge v CLEN
Scene n VIEW
Scene n PLAY
Scene n PANG
Scenery n VIEW
Scenic j VIEW
Scent n VAPR SOMA
Scepter n LEAD FORM
Sceptic n BLUR OPPO
Schedule v FOR W WRIT
Schematize v IDEA FORM
Scheme n IDEA FORM
Scheme v FALS IDEA
Schemed v FALS IDEA
Schemer n FALS IDEA
Scheming v FALS IDEA
Scherzo n MUSC

Schism n SEP
Schizoid j SICK IDEA
Schizophrenia n SICK IDEA
Schmo n FOOL
Schmooze v TALK
Schnapps n SIP VEGT
Schnauzer n ANML
Schnitzel n ANML FOOD
Schnook n FOOL
Schnorrer n MOTV LACK
Scholar n POWR EDUC
Scholastic j EDUC
School n HOME EDUC
School n GRUP EDUC
School n GRUP
School v EDUC
Schoolboy n EDUC YNG
Schooled v EDUC
Schoolgirl n EDUC YNG
Schoolhouse n HOME EDUC
Schooling v EDUC
Schoolmaster n LEAD EDUC
Schoolmate n JOIN EDUC
Schoolroom n HOME EDUC
Schoolteacher n LEAD EDUC
Schooner n FLOW VEHC
Science n IDEA TRUE
Scimitar n DAMG SHRP
Scintillate v VIEW
Scintillate v POWR VIEW
Scissor n SHRP
Scoff v AGGR
Scold v AGGR TALK
Scoop v HOLW
Scoop v POWR WRIT
Scoot v QUIK GO
Scooted v QUIK GO
Scooter n VEHC
Scope n LARG
Scorch v DAMG HEAT
Score n NUMR
Score n SHRP
Score v AGGR
Score n IDEA
Score n MOTV
Score v POWR NUMR
Score n WRIT MUSC
Scorn n AGGR
Scorpio n ASTR MYTH
Scorpion n BUG
Scotch n SIP VEGT
Scotch v BLOK
Scoundrel n BAD
Scour v GO OPEN
Scour v CLEN
Scourge n DAMG
Scout n GRUP OPEN
Scout n GO OPEN
Scout v AGGR
Scouted v GO OPEN
Scouted v AGGR
Scoutmaster n LEAD GRUP
Scow n FLOW VEHC
Scowl n AGGR
Scram v GO SEP

Scramble v AGGR GO
Scramble v VARY JOIN
Scrap n SOME
Scrap n TRIV
Scrap n DAMG
Scrapbook n WRIT
Scrape v HEAR
Scrape v CLEN SEP
Scrape v HAVE
Scrape n DAMG
Scraping v HEAR
Scraping v CLEN SEP
Scraping v HAVE
Scrapped v DAMG
Scrapple n FOOD
Scratch n DAMG SHRP
Scratch n WRIT SHRP
Scratch n BGIN
Scratch v SHRP
Scratch v SEP
Scrawl n WRIT
Scrawny j BODY LITL
Scream v HEAR TALK
Screech v HEAR TALK
Screen v COVR
Screen v VIEW
Screen v SEP
Screw n JOIN
Screw n GO MECH
Screw v AGGR
Screw v JOIN SEX
Screwball n FOOL
Screwball n VARY PLAY
Screwdriver n JOIN WORK
Screwy j FOOL
Scribble v WRIT
Scribe n WRIT
Scribe n SHRP
Scrimmage v PLAY
Scrimshaw n VIEW SHRP
Script n WRIT
Scripture n WRIT HOLY
Scroll n WRIT
Scroll n WRIT FORM
Scrounge v MOTV
Scrub v CLEN
Scrub n VEGT
Scrub n PLAY SUB
Scrubbed v CLEN
Scrubbed v PLAY SUB
Scrupulous j GOOD
Scrutiny n IDEA VIEW
Scuba j VAPR MECH
Scuffle v DAMG
Sculpture n VIEW FORM
Scum n DIRT
Scurried v QUIK GO
Scurrilous j BAD
Scurry v QUIK GO
Scurvy j BAD AGGR
Scurvy n SICK
Scythe n SHRP WORK
Sea n FLOW
Sea n BLUR FLOW
Seaboard n ERTH FLOW

Seafaring j GO FLOW
Seal v BLOK COVR
Seal n ANML FLOW
Seal n VIEW
Seal n ANML FABR
Seal v AGRE
Sealed v BLOK COVR
Sealed v AGRE
Sealing v BLOK COVR
Sealing v AGRE
Sealing v ANML FLOW
Seam n GARB JOIN
Seam n JOIN
Seam n SOME
Seaman n MALE FLOW
Seamed v GARB JOIN
Seamed v JOIN
Seamen n MALE FLOW
Seaming v GARB JOIN
Seaming v JOIN
Seams n GARB JOIN
Seams n JOIN
Seams n SOME
Seamstress n GARB LADY
Seamy j BAD
Seance n GRUP MYTH
Seance n GRUP JOIN
Sear v DAMG HEAT
Search n OPEN MOTV
Seas n FLOW
Seashore n ERTH FLOW
Seasick j SICK FLOW
Season n TIME
Season v FOOD
Season v POWR TIME
Seasoned v FOOD
Seasoned v POWR TIME
Seasoning n FOOD
Seasoning v POWR TIME
Seat n FURN REST
Seat n PLAC REST
Seat n BODY REST
Seaward d FORW FLOW
Seaweed n FLOW VEGT
Secant n NUMR FORM
Secede v SEP
Secession n SEP
Seclusion n SEP COVR
Second j NUMR
Second j MSMT TIME
Second j SUB
Second n AGRE NUMR
Second n AID NUMR
Second n NUMR MUSC
Secondary j SUB
Secondary j EDUC
Secondclass j GRUP SUB
Seconded v AGRE NUMR
Seconded v AID NUMR
Secondhand j TRIV
Seconding v AGRE NUMR
Seconding v AID NUMR
Secondrate j SUB TRIV
Secrecy n COVR
Secret j COVR

Secretary n WRIT
Secretary n LEAD WRIT
Secretary n FURN WRIT
Secrete v COVR
Secrete v OUT
Secreting v COVR
Secreting v OUT
Sect n GRUP
Section n SOME
Section v SHRP SOME
Secular j GRUP HOLY
Secure v HAVE
Secure j AID
Secure v BLOK
Security n AID
Security n MART MONY
Sedate j REST
Sedate v MEDC REST
Sedated v MEDC REST
Sedating v MEDC REST
Sedge n VEGT
Sedition n AGGR
Seduction n BAD SEX
Seduction n BAD MOTV
See v VIEW
See n LEAD HOLY
Seed n BGIN
Seed n BGIN VEGT
Seek v OPEN MOTV
Seem v IDEA VIEW
Seen v VIEW
Seep v FLOW
Sees v VIEW
Seesaw n VARY
Segment n SOME
Segment v SEP SOME
Segregate v BLOK SEP
Seize v BLOK HAVE
Seizure n BLOK SICK
Seizure n BLOK HAVE
Seldom d AFAR
Select j GOOD
Select v MOTV
Self n SOLE
Selfassured j POWR SOLE
Selfconfidence n POWR SOLE
Selfconscious j SOLE IDEA
Selfconscious j SOLE PANG
Selfdefense n AID SOLE
Selfish j SOLE MOTV
Selfless j GOOD AID
Selfmade j POWR SOLE
Selfpity n SOLE WEAK
Selfpreservation n AID SOLE
Selfrighteous j FALS GOOD
Selfsame j SIML SOLE
Sell v MART MONY
Semen n SOMA MALE
Semester n EDUC TIME
Semi f SOME
Semicolon n WRIT
Seminar n GRUP EDUC

Seminary n EDUC HOLY
Semitic j GRUP
Semitic j TALK
Senate n LEAD LAW
Send v GO
Senile j SICK PAST
Senior j LEAD
Senior j LEAD PAST
Senior n LEAD EDUC
Sensation n SOMA IDEA
Sensation n MOTV
Sensational j POWR
Sensational j MOTV
Sense n SOMA IDEA
Senseless j FOOL
Sensible j IDEA
Sensing v SOMA IDEA
Sensitive j MOTV
Sensory j SOMA IDEA
Sensuous j MOTV
Sent v GO
Sentence n TALK FORM
Sentence n TALK LAW
Sentiment n MOTV
Sentimental j MOTV
Sentinel n DAMG AID
Sentry n DAMG AID
Separate j SEP
September n TIME
Sepulchre n DEAD HOLW
Sequence n FORW
Serenade n TALK MUSC
Serene j GLAD
Serenity n GLAD
Sergeant n LEAD
Serial n FORW
Series n FORW
Serigraph n COLR
Serious j CRUX
Sermon n TALK HOLY
Serum n SOMA
Servant n AID SUB
Serve v AID
Serve v GO PLAY
Service n AID
Service n DAMG AID
Service n TALK HOLY
Service n GO PLAY
Service n FOOD FURN
Serviced v AID
Servicing v AID
Servile j SUB
Serving v AID
Serving v GO PLAY
Session n GRUP TIME
Set n GRUP
Set v BGIN
Set v GO
Set v REST
Set v AID
Set v EVER
Set v NSCR

Setback n BACK WEAK
Settee n FURN REST
Setter n ANML
Setting n EVNT
Setting v BGIN
Setting v GO
Setting v REST
Setting v AID
Setting v EVER
Setting v NSCR
Settle v EVER LIVE
Settle v AGRE
Settle v DOWN
Settle v GLAD
Settlement n EVER LIVE
Settlement n AGRE
Seven n NUMR
Seventeen n NUMR
Seventy n NUMR
Sever v SEP SHRP
Several j SOME
Severe j AGGR
Sew v GARB JOIN
Sewage n DIRT
Sex n SEX
Sextant n MECH MSMT
Sextet n GRUP NUMR
Sexton n AID HOLY
Shabby j DIRT
Shack n HOME
Shackle v BLOK JOIN
Shad n ANML FLOW
Shad n FOOD FLOW
Shade n COLR
Shade n BLUR COVR
Shade n LITL
Shade n MYTH
Shadow n BLUR
Shadow n MYTH
Shaft n FORM
Shaft n HOLW
Shag n FABR
Shag n FOOD VEGT
Shag n BULG FABR
Shag n GO MUSC
Shagbark n VEGT
Shaggy j BULG
Shake n VARY
Shake v VARY PANG
Shake v VARY JOIN
Shake n SIP
Shake n MTRL FORM
Shake n MUSC
Shakedown n CRIM MONY
Shakedown n TRUE
Shaking v VARY
Shaking v VARY PANG
Shaking v VARY JOIN
Shaky j VARY WEAK
Shallow j LITL
Shallow j TRIV
Sham j FALS

Parts of speech: a article; b preposition; c conjunction; d adverb; f prefix; i interjection;
j adjective; n noun; p pronoun; r phrase; v verb.

Shame n BAD PANG
Shamefaced j BODY PANG
Shameless j BAD
Shaming v BAD PANG
Shampoo v CLEN
Shape n FORM
Shapeless j BLUR
Shapely j GOOD FORM
Shard n SOME
Share v HAVE SOME
Sharecropper n VEGT WORK
Shareholder n MART HAVE
Shark n ANML FLOW
Shark n ANML FALS
Sharp j SHRP
Sharp j AGGR SHRP
Sharp j SHRP MUSC
Sharp j POWR SHRP
Sharpen v SHRP
Sharpshooter n DAMG SHRP
Shatter v DAMG SEP
Shave n CLEN SHRP
Shawl n GARB LADY
She p HSCR
Sheaf n GRUP
Shear v SEP SHRP
Sheath n HOLW
Shed n HOME
Shed v SEP
Shed v AID
Shed v DAMG OUT
Sheen n VIEW
Sheep n ANML
Sheep n ANML WEAK
Sheep n ANML FABR
Sheepskin n ANML FABR
Sheepskin n POWR WRIT
Sheer j EMPH
Sheer j BULG
Sheer j OPEN VIEW
Sheer v VARY
Sheered v VARY
Sheering v VARY
Sheet n FORM
Sheet n FORM FABR
Shekel n MONY
Shelf n FORM
Shell n HOLW
Shell n DAMG HOLW
Shell n BODY VEGT
Shell n ANML BODY
Shell n FLOW VEHC
Shellack n MTRL
Shellack v POWR WEAK
Shellfish n ANML FLOW
Shellfish n FOOD FLOW
Shelter n AID HOME
Shelve v FORM
Shepherd n ANML AID
Sherbert n FOOD
Sheriff n LEAD LAW
Sherry n SIP VEGT
Shied v VARY WEAK
Shield n AID
Shield n VIEW

Shield n GARB AID
Shift n VARY
Shift n GARB LADY
Shimmer v VARY VIEW
Shin n BODY
Shin v BODY GO
Shine n VIEW
Shine v CLEN VIEW
Shine v POWR VIEW
Shine n FOND
Shiner n VIEW
Shiner n ANML FLOW
Shiner n COLR BODY
Shingle n FORM
Shingle n VIEW FORM
Ship n FLOW VEHC
Ship n VEHC
Ship v GO VEHC
Shipboard n FLOW VEHC
Shipmate n JOIN FLOW
Shipwreck n DAMG FLOW
Shirk v VARY FALS
Shirt n GARB MALE
Shirtsleeve n GARB
Shit v DIRT SOMA
Shiver v VARY
Shock n DAMG
Shock n BULG
Shock n PANG
Shock n GRUP
Shoddy j WEAK
Shoe n GARB
Shoe n MECH
Shoemaker n GARB MART
Shoestring n GARB JOIN
Shoestring n LITL
Shone v VIEW
Shone v POWR VIEW
Shoo v GO SEP
Shook v VARY
Shook v VARY PANG
Shook v VARY JOIN
Shoot v DAMG
Shoot n BGIN VEGT
Shoot v QUIK GO
Shoot v MOTV
Shoot v VIEW
Shoot v MSMT
Shop n MART HOME
Shop n MART WORK
Shopkeeper n MART HAVE
Shore n ERTH FLOW
Shore v AID
Shoreline n ERTH FLOW
Shorn v SEP SHRP
Short j LITL
Short j LITL LACK
Shortage n LITL LACK
Shortcake n FOOD
Shortcircuit n LITL PATH
Shortcoming n WEAK
Shortcut n LITL PATH
Shorten v LITL
Shorthand n WRIT LITL
Shortlived j LITL TIME

Shortly d LITL TIME
Shorts n GARB LITL
Shortsighted j LITL VIEW
Shot n DAMG
Shot v QUIK GO
Shot n MOTV
Shot n SOME
Shot n VIEW
Shot n SIP
Shot n PLAY
Shot j TRIV
Shotgun n DAMG MECH
Should v NSCR
Shoulder n BODY
Shout v HEAR TALK
Shove v AGGR GO
Shovel n HOLW WORK
Show n VIEW
Show n PLAY
Showed v VIEW
Shower n CLEN FLOW
Shower n WEA FLOW
Shower n AID PLAY
Showing v VIEW
Shown v VIEW
Shrank v LITL
Shrank v PANG
Shred n SEP SOME
Shrewd j POWR IDEA
Shriek v HEAR TALK
Shrill j HEAR
Shrimp n FOOD FLOW
Shrimp n ANML FLOW
Shrimp n LITL
Shrine n HOME HOLY
Shrink v LITL
Shrink v PANG
Shrivel v VARY LITL
Shrivel v WEAK
Shroud v COVR
Shroud v GARB DEAD
Shrub n VEGT
Shrug v VARY BODY
Shudder v VARY PANG
Shuffle v VARY JOIN
Shuffle v GO REST
Shun v VARY
Shunt v VARY GO
Shut v BLOK COVR
Shutter n BLOK COVR
Shy j WEAK
Shy j LACK
Shy v VARY PANG
Shyster n FALS
Sibilant j HEAR
Sibling n KIN
Sick j SICK
Side n FORM
Side n PLAC
Side n BODY
Side n AGRE
Sideboard n FOOD FURN
Sidekick n JOIN SUB
Sidelong j VARY
Sidestep v VARY GO

Sidetrack v VARY GO
Sidewalk n PATH
Sideway j FORM
Siding n FORM
Siding v AGRE
Siding n PATH
Siege n DAMG EVER
Sieve n SEP
Sift v SEP
Sigh n HEAR
Sight n VIEW
Sight n BODY VIEW
Sights n VIEW
Sightseeing n PLAY VIEW
Sign v WRIT
Sign n VIEW
Sign n SIML IDEA
Signal j POWR
Signal n VIEW
Signal n HEAR
Signal n IDEA
Signature n WRIT
Signed v WRIT
Signet n VIEW
Significance n IDEA
Significance n CRUX
Signified v IDEA
Signify v IDEA
Silence n HEAR
Silhouette n SIML FORM
Silicon n ERTH MTRL
Silk j BUG FABR
Silks n BUG FABR
Silkscreen n COLR FABR
Sill n FORM
Silly j FOOL
Silver n COLR
Silver n ERTH MTRL
Silver n FOOD FURN
Silver n MONY
Silverware n FOOD FURN
Similar j SIML
Simile n SIML TALK
Simmer v HEAT
Simple j EASY
Simple j FOOL
Simpleton n FOOL
Simplicity n EASY
Simplify v EASY
Simply d EASY
Simply d TRIV
Simply d EMPH
Simulate v SIML FALS
Simultaneous j SIML TIME
Sin n BAD
Since d TIME
Since c NSCR
Sincere j GOOD TRUE
Sing v TALK MUSC
Singe v DAMG HEAT
Singe v HEAT
Single j SOLE NUMR
Single n NUMR PLAY
Singlehanded d BODY SOLE
Singular j SOLE

Singular j AFAR SOLE
Sink v DOWN GO
Sink n HOLW FLOW
Sink n BAD HOLW
Sinker n DOWN GO
Sinker n FOOD
Sinuous j VARY
Sip v SIP SOMA
Sir n MALE
Sire n BGIN MALE
Siren n DAMG LADY
Siren n MUSC
Siring v BGIN MALE
Sirloin n ANML FOOD
Sissy n WEAK
Sister n LADY KIN
Sister n LADY HOLY
Sisterhood n LADY KIN
Sisterinlaw n LADY KIN
Sit v REST
Site n PLAC
Situate v PLAC
Situation n EVNT
Situation n PLAC
Situation n WORK
Six n NUMR
Sixteen n NUMR
Sixth n NUMR
Sixth n NUMR MUSC
Sixty n NUMR
Size n MSMT
Size v AID MTRL
Sizzle v HEAR HEAT
Skate v GO PLAY
Skate n ANML FLOW
Skated v GO PLAY
Skating v GO PLAY
Skee v GO PLAY
Skeleton n SOMA FORM
Skeptic n BLUR OPPO
Sketch n SIML VIEW
Ski v GO PLAY
Skid n EASY GO
Skied v GO PLAY
Skier n GO PLAY
Skies v GO PLAY
Skies n ASTR UP
Skiff n FLOW VEHC
Skiing v GO PLAY
Skill n POWR
Skim v SEP
Skim v QUIK GO
Skimp v LITL
Skin n BODY
Skin v BODY SEP
Skinned j BODY
Skinned v BODY SEP
Skinning v BODY SEP
Skinny j BODY LITL
Skip v VARY
Skip v VARY GO
Skirmish n DAMG
Skirt n GARB LADY
Skirt v VARY GO
Skirting v VARY GO

Skis v GO PLAY
Skit n PLAY
Skull n SOMA
Skull n SOMA IDEA
Skunk n ANML
Skunk n ANML FABR
Skunk n ANML BAD
Sky n ASTR UP
Skylight n VIEW UP
Skyscraper n FORM UP
Slab n SOME FORM
Slack j REST
Slack j EASY
Slacks n GARB
Slacks v REST
Slacks v EASY
Slain v DAMG DEAD
Slake v AID FLOW
Slake v FLOW
Slam n HEAR
Slam n DAMG
Slam n POWR PLAY
Slander n AGGR FALS
Slang n TALK
Slant n VARY
Slap n DAMG
Slapdash j QUIK TRIV
Slapstick j FOOL GLAD
Slash v DAMG SHRP
Slate n ERTH MTRL
Slate n WRIT
Slate n COLR
Slate v FORW MOTV
Slated v FORW MOTV
Slating v FORW MOTV
Slaughter n DAMG DEAD
Slave n SUB
Slavic j GRUP
Slavic j TALK
Slay v DAMG DEAD
Sled n COLD VEHC
Sledge n WORK
Sledge n COLD VEHC
Sleek j CLEN EASY
Sleep v REST
Sleeper n REST
Sleeper n REST VEHC
Sleeper n POWR REST
Sleet n WEA COLD
Sleeve n GARB HOLW
Sleigh n COLD VEHC
Sleight n FALS
Slender j LITL
Slept v REST
Sleuth n LAW
Slew v DAMG DEAD
Slew n MUCH
Slew v VARY
Slice v SHRP
Slick j EASY
Slicker n GARB
Slicker n FALS
Slid v EASY GO
Slide n EASY GO
Slide n VIEW

Slight j LITL
Slight n AGGR LITL
Slighted v AGGR LITL
Slighting v AGGR LITL
Slightly d LITL
Slim j LITL
Slime n DIRT
Sling n DOWN
Sling n AID
Sling n DAMG MECH
Sling v GO
Slink v GO COVR
Slip n EASY WEAK
Slip v EASY GO
Slip n SOME
Slip n GARB LADY
Slip n HOLW FABR
Slip n ERTH FLOW
Slip n BLOK FLOW
Slipped v EASY GO
Slipper n GARB
Slippery j EASY GO
Slippery j EASY FALS
Slipping v EASY GO
Slipshod j DIRT WEAK
Slit n HOLW SHRP
Slither v EASY GO
Sliver n LITL SEP
Slogan n TALK
Sloop n FLOW VEHC
Slope n VARY
Sloppy j DIRT
Slosh v GO FLOW
Slot n HOLW
Sloth n REST
Sloth n ANML REST
Slouch n REST WEAK
Slouch n DOWN
Slow j REST
Slow v GO REST
Slue v VARY
Slug n BUG REST
Slug n DAMG
Slug n MTRL
Slug n SIP
Sluggard n REST
Slugged v DAMG
Slugging v DAMG
Sluggish j REST
Sluice n BLOK FLOW
Slum n DIRT PLAC
Slumber n REST
Slump n DOWN WEAK
Slung v DOWN
Slung v GO
Slunk v GO COVR
Slur n AGGR TALK
Slur n BLUR
Slur n MUSC
Slush n DIRT FLOW
Slut n DIRT LADY
Sly j FALS COVR
Smack n HEAR
Smack n DAMG HEAR
Smack n FLOW VEHC

Small j LITL
Smallpox n SICK
Smart j POWR IDEA
Smart j POWR QUIK
Smart j POWR GOOD
Smart v PANG
Smarted v PANG
Smarting v PANG
Smash v DAMG
Smattering n LITL
Smear v BLUR
Smear v DIRT
Smear v AGGR DIRT
Smell n VAPR SOMA
Smile n GLAD
Smirk n GLAD FALS
Smith n WORK
Smock n GARB
Smog n WEA BLUR
Smog n VAPR BLUR
Smoke n VAPR HEAT
Smoke v FOOD HEAT
Smolder v HEAT
Smolder v AGGR HEAT
Smooth j EASY
Smother v BLOK DEAD
Smother v BLOK
Smudge v DIRT
Smuggle v CRIM COVR
Smut n DIRT
Snack n FOOD
Snag n BLOK
Snail n ANML REST
Snail n ANML FOOD
Snake n ANML
Snake n ANML BAD
Snake n ANML WORK
Snake v ANML GO
Snaked v ANML GO
Snaking v ANML GO
Snap n HEAR
Snap n EASY
Snap n QUIK VIEW
Snap n FOOD
Snap n HEAR JOIN
Snap n QUIK TIME
Snap n QUIK
Snap v DAMG SEP
Snap v QUIK HAVE
Snap v QUIK GO
Snapped v HEAR
Snapped v DAMG SEP
Snapped v QUIK HAVE
Snapped v QUIK GO
Snapped v QUIK VIEW
Snapped v HEAR JOIN
Snaps v HEAR
Snaps v DAMG SEP
Snaps v QUIK HAVE
Snaps v QUIK GO
Snaps v QUIK VIEW
Snaps v HEAR JOIN
Snapshot n VIEW
Snare n BLOK MECH
Snare n MUSC

Snarl v AGGR TALK
Snarl v BLOK
Snatch v HAVE
Snatch n LITL
Sneak v GO COVR
Sneaked v GO COVR
Sneaker n GARB
Sneer n AGGR
Sneeze n SOMA OUT
Snide j AGGR
Sniff n VAPR SOMA
Snip v SHRP
Snip n SHRP SOME
Snipe n ANML UP
Snipe v DAMG COVR
Sniped v DAMG COVR
Sniper n DAMG COVR
Sniping v DAMG COVR
Snivel v TALK PANG
Snob n POWR FALS
Snoop v OPEN VIEW
Snooze n REST
Snore n SOMA HEAR
Snorkel n VAPR MECH
Snort n HEAR
Snort n SIP
Snout n ANML BODY
Snow n WEA COLD
Snowball n WEA COLD
Snowball n VEGT
Snowball v LARG
Snowflake n WEA COLD
Snowplow n COLD VEHC
Snows n WEA COLD
Snowshoe n GARB COLD
Snowstorm n WEA DAMG
Snowsuit n GARB COLD
Snowwhite j WEA COLR
Snub v AGGR
Snub j BODY
Snubbed v AGGR
Snuck v GO COVR
Snug j GLAD
Snug j BLOK
Snuggle v GLAD JOIN
So c NSCR
So d SIML
So d EMPH
Soak v FLOW
Soak v SIP PANG
Soak v DAMG
Soak v MONY
Soap n CLEN
Soar v GO UP
Sob v TALK PANG
Sober j PANG
Sober j CRUX
Sobriety n CRUX
Socalled j TALK
Soccer n PLAY
Sociable j AGRE GRUP
Social j GRUP
Socialist n GRUP
Socialize v AGRE GRUP
Society n GRUP

Sociology n GRUP IDEA
Sock n GARB
Sock n DAMG
Socked v DAMG
Socket n HOLW
Socking v DAMG
Sod n ERTH VEGT
Soda n SIP
Soda n MTRL
Sodded v ERTH VEGT
Sodden j FLOW
Sodding v ERTH VEGT
Sofa n FURN REST
Soft j EASY
Soggy j FLOW
Soil n ERTH
Soil v DIRT
Soiled v DIRT
Soiling v DIRT
Sojourn v GO
Solace v GLAD AID
Solar j ASTR HEAT
Solder v HEAT JOIN
Soldier n DAMG
Soldier v FALS WORK
Sole j SOLE
Sole n DOWN
Sole n FOOD FLOW
Sole n ANML FLOW
Sole v GARB DOWN
Soled v GARB DOWN
Solely d SOLE
Solemn j CRUX
Solicit v MOTV
Solicit v SEX MOTV
Solicitor n LAW
Solicitor n MOTV
Solid j FORM
Solid j EVER
Solid j WHOL
Solid j POWR
Solidarity n WHOL GRUP
Soliloquy n SOLE TALK
Soling v GARB DOWN
Solitaire n SOLE PLAY
Solitaire n ERTH MTRL
Solitary j SOLE SEP
Solitude n SOLE SEP
Solo j SOLE
Soluble j VARY FLOW
Soluble j IDEA
Solution n IDEA
Solution n FLOW
Solve v IDEA
Somatic j SOMA
Somber j PANG
Some j SOME
Some j EMPH
Some j NSCR
Somebody p SOLE
Someday d TIME
Somehow d BLUR
Someone p SOLE
Somersault n VARY GO
Something n NSCR

Sometime d TIME
Sometime j PAST
Sometimes d SOME TIME
Somewhat d SOME
Somewhere d PLAC
Somnambulism n GO REST
Somnolent j REST
Son n MALE KIN
Song n TALK MUSC
Soninlaw n MALE KIN
Sonnet n TALK
Sonorous j MUSC
Soon d NEAR TIME
Soot n DIRT
Soothe v GLAD AID
Sop n FOOD FLOW
Sop n AID TRIV
Sop v FLOW
Sophism n FALS IDEA
Sophistication n POWR IDEA
Sophistry n FALS IDEA
Sophomore n EDUC SUB
Soporific j REST
Soprano n MUSC
Sorcery n MYTH
Sordid j BAD DIRT
Sore j PANG
Sore j AGGR
Sore n DAMG BODY
Sores n DAMG BODY
Sorrow n PANG
Sorry j PANG
Sorry j WEAK
Sort n SIML GRUP
Sort v SEP
Sorted v SEP
Sortie n DAMG GO
Sorting v SEP
Sorts n SIML GRUP
Sorts n PANG
SOS n DAMG WRIT
Sot n SIP PANG
Souffle n FOOD
Soul n CRUX MYTH
Soul n CRUX SOLE
Sound n HEAR
Sound n FLOW
Sound v DOWN FLOW
Sound j POWR
Sounded v HEAR
Sounded v DOWN FLOW
Sounding v HEAR
Sounding v DOWN FLOW
Soundless j HEAR
Soundproof v BLOK HEAR
Soup n SIP FOOD
Soup v POWR
Souped v POWR
Souping v POWR
Soupspoon n FOOD FURN
Sour j FOOD SOMA
Sour j DIRT SOMA
Sour j AGGR PANG
Source n BGIN
Soured v DIRT SOMA

Soured v AGGR PANG
Souring v DIRT SOMA
Souring v AGGR PANG
South n PLAC PATH
Souvenir n IDEA PAST
Sovereign n LEAD
Sovereign n MONY
Soviet n LEAD GRUP
Sow v BGIN VEGT
Sow n ANML LADY
Sowed v BGIN VEGT
Sowing v BGIN VEGT
Space v SEP
Space n HOLW
Space n VAPR ASTR
Space n SOME
Space n TIME
Spacecraft n ASTR VEHC
Spaced v SEP
Spaces v SEP
Spaces n HOLW
Spaces n SOME
Spacing v SEP
Spacious j LARG
Spade n WORK
Spade n PLAY
Spaghetti n FOOD
Span n TIME
Span n LARG
Span v JOIN
Spangle n MTRL VIEW
Spangle v VIEW
Spaniel n ANML
Spank v DAMG
Spar n FORM
Spar v DAMG PLAY
Spare v AID
Spare j MUCH
Spare j LITL
Spare n POWR PLAY
Spared v AID
Sparing v AID
Spark v HEAT VIEW
Spark v BGIN MOTV
Sparkle v VIEW
Sparrow n ANML UP
Sparse j LITL
Spasm n VARY QUIK
Spasmodic j VARY QUIK
Spastic j VARY
Spat v SOMA OUT
Spat n AGGR
Spate n MUCH QUIK
Spats n GARB
Spats n AGGR
Spatter v DIRT FLOW
Spatula n FOOD FURN
Spawn v BGIN YNG
Spay v MEDC SOMA
Speak v TALK
Speakeasy n CRIM SIP
Spear n DAMG SHRP
Spear n SHRP
Special j CRUX
Specialist n POWR CRUX

Specialty n POWR CRUX
Species n GRUP
Specific j SHRP
Specify v SHRP
Specimen n SOLE
Specimen n SOME
Specious j FALS
Speck n LITL
Speck n DIRT LITL
Speckling n COLR
Spectacle n VIEW
Spectacles n AID VIEW
Spectacles n VIEW
Spectacular j POWR VIEW
Spectator n VIEW
Specter n MYTH
Spectral j MYTH
Spectroscope n COLR VIEW
Spectrum n COLR FORW
Speculate v IDEA
Speculate v MONY MOTV
Speech n TALK
Speed v QUIK GO
Speedometer n QUIK MSMT
Spell v TALK
Spell n TIME
Spell n PANG
Spell n MYTH
Spellbound j MOTV
Spelled v TALK
Spelled v TIME
Spelling v TALK
Spelling v TIME
Spend v MONY LACK
Spend v LACK
Sperm n SOMA MALE
Spew v OUT
Sphere n HOLW
Sphere n FORM
Spherical j FORM
Sphincter n BLOK SOMA
Sphinx n BLUR MYTH
Spice n FOOD VEGT
Spice n FOOD SOMA
Spice n MOTV
Spicy j FOOD SOMA
Spicy j SEX
Spider n BUG
Spied v VIEW COVR
Spiel n TALK
Spies v VIEW COVR
Spiffy j GOOD
Spigot n BLOK MECH
Spike n JOIN SHRP
Spill v FLOW
Spill v DAMG FLOW
Spill v DOWN GO
Spill v OPEN
Spin v VARY GO
Spin v WORK FABR
Spinach n FOOD VEGT
Spindle n FORM

Spindle n MECH
Spine n SOMA
Spineless j SOMA WEAK
Spinster n LADY SOLE
Spiral j VARY FORM
Spire n FORM UP
Spirit n CRUX MOTV
Spirit n CRUX MYTH
Spirit n SIP
Spirit v GO COVR
Spirited j CRUX MOTV
Spirited v GO COVR
Spiriting v GO COVR
Spiritual j HOLY MYTH
Spiritual n HOLY MUSC
Spit v SOMA OUT
Spit n SHRP
Spite n AGGR
Splash v HEAR FLOW
Splash v DIRT FLOW
Spleen n SOMA
Spleen n AGGR SOMA
Splendor n POWR GOOD
Splenetic j AGGR PANG
Splice v JOIN
Splinter n SEP
Splinter n LITL SEP
Split j SEP
Splutter v BLUR TALK
Spoil v DAMG DIRT
Spoil v BAD AID
Spoils v DAMG DIRT
Spoils v BAD AID
Spoils n DAMG HAVE
Spoke v TALK
Spoke n FORM
Spoken v TALK
Spokes n FORM
Spokesman n TALK
Sponge n CLEN FLOW
Sponge n MOTV
Sponge n MTRL FLOW
Spontaneity n EASY OPEN
Spoof v FALS
Spook n MYTH
Spool n FORM
Spoon n FOOD FURN
Sporadic j VARY
Sport n PLAY
Sport n GLAD
Sport n VARY
Spot n DIRT
Spot n PLAC
Spot n COLR
Spot v SOME
Spot v VIEW
Spotless j CLEN
Spotlight n VIEW SHRP
Spotted v VIEW
Spotted v DIRT
Spotted v PLAC
Spotted j COLR

Spouse n SEX KIN
Spout v OUT FLOW
Spout v TALK OUT
Sprain n DAMG
Sprang v QUIK GO
Sprang v BGIN
Sprawl v REST
Spray n FLOW
Spray n GRUP VEGT
Sprayed v FLOW
Spraying v FLOW
Spread n LARG
Spread n LARG FOOD
Spread n FURN COVR
Spreading v LARG
Spree n GLAD
Sprightly j QUIK
Spring n BGIN
Spring n QUIK GO
Spring n FLOW
Spring n TIME
Spring n VARY MECH
Springing v BGIN
Springing v QUIK GO
Springtime n TIME
Sprinkle n FLOW
Sprint v QUIK GO
Sprout v BGIN VEGT
Spruce n VEGT
Spruce n MTRL VEGT
Spruce v CLEN GOOD
Spruced v CLEN GOOD
Sprucing v CLEN GOOD
Spry j POWR
Spun v VARY GO
Spun v WORK FABR
Spur n BULG
Spur n SHRP MOTV
Spur n VARY PATH
Spurious j FALS
Spurn v AGGR
Spurred v SHRP MOTV
Spurring v SHRP MOTV
Spurt n QUIK
Spurt n FLOW
Sputnik n ASTR VEHC
Sputter n HEAR
Spy n VIEW COVR
Spyglass n MECH VIEW
Squabble v AGGR
Squad n GRUP
Squalid j DIRT
Squall n WEA DAMG
Squall v AGGR TALK
Squalor j DIRT
Squander v LACK
Square n FORM
Square n NUMR
Square n PLAC PATH
Square v SIML
Square j GOOD TRUE
Squared v FORM

Parts of speech: a article; b preposition; c conjunction; d adverb; f prefix; i interjection;
j adjective; n noun; p pronoun; r phrase; v verb.

Squared v NUMR
Squared v SIML
Squarely d EMPH
Squarely d SHRP
Squarely d GOOD TRUE
Squaring v FORM
Squaring v NUMR
Squaring v SIML
Squash n FOOD VEGT
Squash v BLOK
Squash n PLAY
Squashed v BLOK
Squashing v BLOK
Squat j LARG LITL
Squat v REST
Squat v EVER REST
Squats v REST
Squats v EVER REST
Squatted v REST
Squatted v EVER REST
Squawk v ANML TALK
Squawk v AGGR TALK
Squeak v HEAR
Squeal v HEAR
Squeal v TALK OPEN
Squeamish j PANG
Squeeze v BLOK
Squint v VARY VIEW
Squirrel n ANML
Squirrel n ANML FABR
Squirt n TRIV YNG
Squirt v FLOW
Stab v DAMG SHRP
Stability n EVER
Stable j EVER
Stable n ANML HOME
Stabled v ANML HOME
Stables n ANML HOME
Stabling v ANML HOME
Staccato j MUSC
Stack n BULG
Stack n HOLW
Stadium n HOME PLAY
Staff n FORM
Staff n WRIT MUSC
Staff n GRUP AID
Stag n ANML MALE
Stage n PLAY FORM
Stage n SOME
Stage n VEHC
Stagecoach n VEHC
Stagger v VARY
Stagger v VARY GO
Stagnate v DIRT REST
Staid j REST
Stain n COLR
Stain n DIRT
Stainless j CLEN
Stair n DOWN UP
Stake n SHRP
Stake n MOTV
Stale j DIRT
Stale j DIRT WEAK
Stalemate n BLOK END
Stalk n BODY VEGT

Stalk v GO
Stalked v GO
Stalking v GO
Stall n ANML HOME
Stall n MART HOME
Stall n BLOK
Stalled v BLOK
Stalling v BLOK
Stallion n ANML MALE
Stalwart j POWR
Stamina n POWR
Stammer v TALK WEAK
Stamp n WRIT
Stamp n FORM
Stamp n WRIT VIEW
Stamp v DAMG
Stamp v AGGR HEAR
Stamped v WRIT
Stamped v FORM
Stamped v WRIT VIEW
Stamped v DAMG
Stamped v AGGR HEAR
Stampede v DAMG GO
Stance n BODY EVNT
Stance n MOTV
Stand v REST
Stand v UP
Stand v EVER
Stand v AGRE
Stand v SIML
Stand n FORM
Stand v EVNT
Stand v MOTV
Stand n MART HOME
Stand n GRUP VEGT
Standard j EVER
Standard n MSMT
Standard n VIEW
Standard n FORM
Standardbearer n LEAD
Standby j NEAR REST
Standing v REST
Standing v UP
Standing v EVER
Standing v AGRE
Standing v SIML
Standing v EVNT
Standing v MOTV
Standpoint n IDEA
Stank v VAPR DIRT
Stanza n WRIT SOME
Staple n CRUX
Staple v JOIN
Stapled v JOIN
Stapling v JOIN
Star n ASTR
Star n POWR
Star n FORM
Starboard n PLAC FLOW
Starch n MTRL VEGT
Stare n VIEW
Starfish n ANML FLOW
Staring v VIEW
Stark j EMPH
Stark j AGGR

Starlight n ASTR VIEW
Starling n ANML UP
Starry j ASTR
Stars n ASTR
Stars n POWR
Stars n FORM
Starspangled j VIEW FORM
Start v BGIN
Start v PANG
Started v BGIN
Starting v BGIN
Startle v PANG
Starve v FOOD LACK
Stash v COVR
State n EVNT
State n PLAC
State v TALK
Stated v TALK
Statement n TALK
Stateroom n HOME VEHC
States n EVNT
States n PLAC
States v TALK
Statesman n LEAD LAW
Stating v TALK
Station n PLAC
Stationary j EVER REST
Stationer n MART WRIT
Stationery n WRIT
Statistic n NUMR
Statue n FORM
Stature n UP
Stature n POWR
Status n POWR
Statusquo n EVER NEW
Statute n WRIT LAW
Staunch j POWR
Staunch v BLOK
Staunched v BLOK
Staunching v BLOK
Staunchly d POWR
Stay v REST
Stay v EVER
Stay n BLOK
Stay n AID
Stead n OPPO
Stead n AID
Steadied v EVER
Steady j EVER
Steak n ANML FOOD
Steal v CRIM
Steal v GO COVR
Steam n VAPR HEAT
Steam v VAPR GO
Steamboat n FLOW VEHC
Steamed v VAPR HEAT
Steamed v VAPR GO
Steamer n FLOW VEHC
Steamer n HOLW HEAT
Steams v VAPR HEAT
Steams v VAPR GO
Steamship n FLOW VEHC
Steel n ERTH MTRL
Steel n POWR
Steeled v POWR

Steeling v POWR
Steep j BULG
Steep v BULG FLOW
Steeped v BULG FLOW
Steeping v BULG FLOW
Steeple n FORM UP
Steer v LEAD
Steer n ANML MALE
Steered v LEAD
Steering v LEAD
Steers v LEAD
Stein n SIP HOLW
Stellar j ASTR
Stellar j LEAD
Stem n BODY VEGT
Stem n FORM
Stem v BGIN
Stem v BLOK
Stem n FORW FLOW
Stemmed j BODY VEGT
Stemmed j FORM
Stemmed v BGIN
Stemmed v BLOK
Stemming v BGIN
Stemming v BLOK
Stench n VAPR DIRT
Stencil v WRIT
Stenography n WRIT
Step v GO
Step n DOWN UP
Stepbrother n MALE KIN
Stepchild n KIN YNG
Stepdaughter n LADY KIN
Stepfather n MALE KIN
Stepfather n LEAD MALE
Stepladder n DOWN UP
Stepmother n LADY KIN
Stepmother n LADY AID
Steps n GO
Steps n DOWN UP
Stepsister n LADY KIN
Stepson n MALE KIN
Stereophonic j MUSC
Stereoscopy n MECH VIEW
Stereotype n SIML TRIV
Stereotype n WRIT MECH
Sterile j BGIN LACK
Sterile j CLEN
Stern j AGGR
Stern n BACK FLOW
Stew n FOOD HEAT
Stew n HEAT PANG
Stew v HEAT
Steward n LEAD AID
Stewardess n LADY AID
Stick n FORM
Stick v SHRP
Stick v JOIN
Stick v BULG
Stick v BLOK
Sticker n JOIN WRIT
Stickler n AGGR TRIV
Stickler n BLUR BLOK
Stickup n CRIM
Sticky j JOIN

Sties n DIRT HOME
Sties n SICK VIEW
Stiff j EVER
Stiff n DEAD BODY
Stiffen v EVER
Stifle v BLOK
Stifle v BLOK DEAD
Stigma n BAD VIEW
Still d EVER TIME
Still d REST
Still d HEAR
Still d EMPH
Still n SIP HOLW
Still n VIEW REST
Stilled v REST
Stilled v HEAR
Stilling v REST
Stilling v HEAR
Stills v REST
Stills v HEAR
Stills n SIP HOLW
Stills n VIEW REST
Stilt n FORM UP
Stilted j FOOL
Stimulate v BGIN MOTV
Sting v DAMG SHRP
Stingy j AGGR HAVE
Stink v VAPR DIRT
Stint v BLOK
Stint n MOTV
Stipend n MONY
Stipple v COLR LITL
Stipulate v AGRE
Stir v VARY
Stir v MOTV
Stir n BLOK HOME
Stirred v VARY
Stirred v MOTV
Stitch n JOIN SHRP
Stock n HAVE
Stock n MART MONY
Stock n ANML
Stock n FORM
Stock n BGIN
Stock n CRUX
Stock n PLAY
Stock n BLOK
Stock n ANML FOOD
Stocked v HAVE
Stockholder n MART HAVE
Stocking n GARB
Stocking v HAVE
Stockmarket n MART MONY
Stocks n HAVE
Stocks n MART MONY
Stocks n FORM
Stocks n BLOK
Stockstill j EVER REST
Stocky j LARG BODY
Stoke v HEAT
Stole v CRIM
Stole v GO COVR
Stole n GARB
Stolen j CRIM
Stolen v GO COVR

Stoles n GARB
Stomach n BODY SOMA
Stomp n GO MUSC
Stomp v AGGR HEAR
Stone n ERTH
Stone v DAMG ERTH
Stoned v DAMG ERTH
Stoneware j ERTH
Stoning v DAMG ERTH
Stood v REST
Stood v UP
Stood v EVER
Stood v AGRE
Stood v SIML
Stood v EVNT
Stood v MOTV
Stooge n SUB
Stool n FURN REST
Stool n DIRT SOMA
Stool n FALS OPEN
Stoop v VARY DOWN
Stoop n HOME
Stop v BLOK END
Store n MART HOME
Store v EVER HAVE
Stored v EVER HAVE
Storehouse n HOME HAVE
Storekeeper n MART HAVE
Storeroom n HOME HAVE
Storey n FORM
Storied j FORM
Storied j TALK
Stories n TALK
Stories n FORM
Storing v EVER HAVE
Storm n WEA DAMG
Storm v DAMG GO
Story n TALK
Story n FORM
Stout j LARG BODY
Stout j POWR
Stout n SIP VEGT
Stove n HEAT FURN
Stow v COVR
Straggle v GO SEP
Straight j SIML FORM
Straight j SHRP
Straight n FORW PLAY
Straighten v SIML FORM
Straightforward j FORW SHRP
Strain n SOME
Strain v SEP
Strain n POWR
Strain n PANG
Strained v SEP
Strained v POWR
Strained v PANG
Straining v SEP
Straining v POWR
Straining v PANG
Strait n BLOK
Strait n BLOK PANG
Strand n SOME
Strand v BLOK SEP
Stranded v BLOK SEP

Stranding v BLOK SEP
Strange j AFAR
Strangle v BLOK DEAD
Strap v BLOK
Strap v DAMG
Stratagem n FALS IDEA
Strategic j IDEA FORM
Strategic j POWR CRUX
Strategies n IDEA FORM
Strategy n IDEA FORM
Stratosphere n VAPR ASTR
Stratum n SOME
Straw n MTRL VEGT
Strawberry n FOOD VEGT
Strawberry n COLR
Stray v GO SEP
Streak n SOME
Streak v COLR SOME
Streak v QUIK GO
Streaked v COLR SOME
Streaked v QUIK GO
Streaking v COLR SOME
Streaking v QUIK GO
Stream n GO FLOW
Streamline v EASY FORM
Street n PATH
Strength n POWR
Strenuous j WORK
Stress n EMPH
Stress n PANG
Stress n POWR
Stretch v LARG
Strew v GO SEP
Stricken j DAMG WEAK
Strict j BLOK AGGR
Strict j SHRP
Stricture n BLOK
Stride n GO
Strident j HEAR
Strike v DAMG
Strike v JOIN
Strike v BLOK WORK
Strike v PLAY
Strike v IDEA
Strike v SEP
Strike v HEAR
Strike v GO
Strike v NSCR
Striking j EMPH
Striking v DAMG
Striking v JOIN
Striking v BLOK WORK
Striking v PLAY
Striking v IDEA
Striking v SEP
Striking v HEAR
Striking v GO
Striking v NSCR
String n FABR
String n GRUP JOIN
String n MUSC
String v FORW GO
String v FALS
Stringing v FORW GO
Stringing v FALS

Stringing v GRUP JOIN
Strip n SOME
Strip v SEP
Strip v GARB SEP
Stripe n COLR FORM
Stripe n DAMG
Striping n COLR FORM
Stripling n MALE YNG
Stripped v SEP
Stripped v GARB SEP
Strive v MOTV
Stroke n VARY JOIN
Stroke n GO FLOW
Stroke n HEAR
Stroke n SICK REST
Stroke n DAMG
Stroked v VARY JOIN
Stroked v GO FLOW
Stroked v HEAR
Stroking v VARY JOIN
Stroking v GO FLOW
Stroking v HEAR
Stroll n GO
Strong j POWR
Strong j EMPH
Stronghold n POWR HOME
Strove v MOTV
Struck v DAMG
Struck v JOIN
Struck v BLOK WORK
Struck v PLAY
Struck v IDEA
Struck v SEP
Struck v HEAR
Struck v GO
Struck v NSCR
Structure n FORM
Struggle n DAMG
Strum v MUSC
Strung v FORW GO
Strung v FALS
Strung v GRUP JOIN
Strut n POWR GO
Strut n AID JOIN
Stub n LITL
Stub n WRIT LITL
Stub v BLOK
Stubbed v BLOK
Stubbed j LITL
Stubble n VEGT
Stubble n BODY
Stubborn j AGGR EVER
Stubby j LARG LITL
Stucco n MTRL
Stuck v SHRP
Stuck v JOIN
Stuck v BULG
Stuck v BLOK
Student n EDUC
Studied v IDEA
Studies v IDEA
Studies n HOME IDEA
Studio n HOME WORK
Studious j IDEA
Study n IDEA

Study n HOME IDEA
Stuff n MTRL
Stuff n FABR
Stuff v BULG
Stuffed v BULG
Stuffing n BULG
Stuffs v BULG
Stuffy j BLOK
Stumble v VARY WEAK
Stump n FORM
Stump v GO HEAR
Stump v BLOK
Stump v GO TALK
Stumped v GO HEAR
Stumped v BLOK
Stumped v GO TALK
Stumping v GO HEAR
Stumping v BLOK
Stumping v GO TALK
Stun v DAMG REST
Stung v DAMG SHRP
Stunk v VAPR DIRT
Stunned v DAMG REST
Stunning j POWR GOOD
Stunning v DAMG REST
Stunt n PLAY
Stunt v BLOK
Stunted v BLOK
Stunting v BLOK
Stupendous j POWR GOOD
Stupid j FOOL
Stupor n BLUR REST
Sturdy j POWR
Stutter v TALK WEAK
Sty n DIRT HOME
Sty n SICK VIEW
Style n GARB
Style n EVNT
Style n NEW
Styled v GARB
Styled v EVNT
Styling v GARB
Styling v EVNT
Stylish j NEW
Stylus n SHRP
Styx n DEAD FLOW
Suave j EASY
Sub f DOWN
Sub j SUB
Sub n SIML VARY
Sub n FLOW VEHC
Sub n FOOD
Subaltern n SUB
Subbed v SIML VARY
Subcommittee n GRUP SUB
Subconscious j IDEA COVR
Subcontract v AGRE MART
Subcutaneous j BODY SOMA
Subdivide v SEP
Subdue v POWR WEAK
Subject n IDEA
Subject n SUB
Subject v EVNT
Subject n SOLE
Subject n TALK FORM

Subjected v SUB
Subjected v EVNT
Subjecting v SUB
Subjecting v EVNT
Subjective j SOLE
Subjective j TALK FORM
Subjoin v JOIN
Subjugate v LEAD SUB
Subjunctive n TALK FORM
Sublease v MART MONY
Sublet v MART MONY
Sublimation n GOOD MOTV
Sublime j POWR GOOD
Submachine j MECH
Submarine j DOWN FLOW
Submarine n FLOW VEHC
Submarine n DAMG FLOW
Submarine n FOOD
Submerge v DOWN FLOW
Submission n WEAK SUB
Submission n AID
Submissive j WEAK SUB
Submit v AID
Submit v WEAK SUB
Subordinate j SUB
Suborn v CRIM FALS
Subplot n IDEA FORM
Subpoena n LAW MOTV
Subregion n PLAC
Subs v SIML VARY
Subs n FLOW VEHC
Subs n FOOD
Subscribe v AGRE
Subscribe v AGRE MONY
Subscript n DOWN WRIT
Subscription n AGRE MONY
Subsequent j BACK
Subservient j SUB
Subside v END
Subside v DOWN
Subsidiary j SUB
Subsidies n AID
Subsidies n AID MONY
Subsiding v END
Subsiding v DOWN
Subsidize v AID MONY
Subsidy n AID
Subsidy n AID MONY
Subsist v LIVE
Subsoil n DOWN ERTH
Subspecies n GRUP
Substance n CRUX
Substance n MTRL
Substandard j WEAK
Substantial j MUCH
Substantial j POWR
Substantial j MTRL
Substantiate v TRUE
Substantive j CRUX
Substitute v SIML VARY
Substratum n DOWN FORM
Substructure n DOWN FORM
Subsume v GRUP
Subterfuge n FALS
Subterranean j DOWN ERTH

Subtle j BLUR
Subtle j LITL
Subtract v NUMR SEP
Subtropical j HEAT PLAC
Suburb n NEAR PLAC
Subvene v AID
Subvert v DAMG WEAK
Subway n DOWN VEHC
Succeed v FORW
Succeed v POWR
Success n POWR
Successive j FORW
Successor n FORW
Succinct j LITL
Succumb v WEAK
Succumb v DEAD WEAK
Such j EMPH
Such j SIML
Suck v VAPR IN
Suck v SIP SOMA
Sucked v VAPR IN
Sucked v SIP SOMA
Sucker n FALS WEAK
Sucker n SIP SOMA
Sucker n VAPR IN
Sucker n VEGT
Suckling n SIP YNG
Suction n VAPR IN
Sudden j QUIK
Sue v LAW MOTV
Sue v MOTV
Sued v LAW MOTV
Sued v MOTV
Suede n ANML FABR
Suffer v PANG
Suffer v AGRE
Suffice v MUCH
Sufficient j MUCH
Suffix n TALK FORM
Suffocate v BLOK DEAD
Sugar n FOOD VEGT
Suggest v IDEA
Suggestion n IDEA
Suggestion n SOME
Suicide n DAMG DEAD
Suing v LAW MOTV
Suing v MOTV
Suit n GARB
Suit v SIML
Suit n MOTV
Suit n SEX MOTV
Suitcase n GARB HOLW
Suite n GRUP MUSC
Suite n GRUP HOME
Suite n GRUP SUB
Suited v SIML
Suited j GARB
Suiting v SIML
Suitor n MOTV
Suitor n SEX MOTV
Sulk v AGGR PANG
Sulkies n VEHC
Sulking v AGGR PANG
Sulky d AGGR PANG
Sulky n VEHC

Sullen j AGGR PANG
Sullied v DIRT
Sully v DIRT
Sulphur n ERTH MTRL
Sum n WHOL NUMR
Sum n WHOL
Summary j LITL
Summed v WHOL NUMR
Summed v WHOL
Summer n HEAT TIME
Summing v WHOL NUMR
Summing v WHOL
Summit n UP
Summon v MOTV
Summons n LAW MOTV
Sumptuous j MUCH GOOD
Sun n ASTR HEAT
Sunbeam n ASTR VIEW
Sunburn n ASTR HEAT
Sundae n FOOD
Sunday n TIME
Sundial n MSMT TIME
Sundown n ASTR DOWN
Sunflower n ASTR VEGT
Sunlight n ASTR VIEW
Sunned v ASTR HEAT
Sunny j ASTR HEAT
Sunrise n ASTR UP
Suns n ASTR HEAT
Sunset n ASTR DOWN
Sunshine n ASTR HEAT
Sunstroke n ASTR SICK
Sup v FOOD
Super j POWR
Superb j POWR GOOD
Supercilious j AGGR POWR
Superficial j TRIV
Superfluous j TRIV
Superhuman j POWR AFAR
Superior j LEAD
Superior j POWR GOOD
Superior j UP
Superior j GOOD
Superiority n POWR GOOD
Superiority n GOOD
Superiors n LEAD
Superlative j POWR GOOD
Superman n POWR MALE
Supermarket n LARG MART
Supernatural j AFAR MYTH
Supersede v SIML VARY
Supersonic j QUIK HEAR
Superstition n MYTH
Supervise v LEAD
Supped v FOOD
Supper n FOOD
Supping v FOOD
Supplant v SIML VARY
Supple j VARY EASY
Supplement n LARG
Supplicate v MOTV
Supplied v AID SOME
Supplied v SOME
Supply n AID SOME
Supply v AID

Support v AID
Support v AGRE
Supported v AID
Supported v AGRE
Supporter n AID
Supporter n AGRE
Supporter n GARB AID
Suppose v IDEA
Suppress v BLOK
Supremacy n LEAD
Sure j SHRP
Sure j EMPH
Surefooted j BODY SHRP
Surf n VARY FLOW
Surface n FORM UP
Surge v GO BULG
Surgeon n MEDC SHRP
Surgery n MEDC SHRP
Surgical j MEDC SHRP
Surly j AGGR
Surmise v IDEA
Surmount v POWR
Surname n TALK
Surpass v POWR
Surplus n MUCH BULG
Surprise n AFAR PANG
Surrealism n FORM MYTH
Surrender n WEAK
Surreptitious j COVR
Surround v BLOK HOLW
Survey n VIEW
Survey n IDEA VIEW
Survey n MSMT
Surveyor n MSMT
Survive v LIVE
Susceptible j WEAK MOTV
Suspect v BLUR IDEA
Suspect v BLUR AGGR
Suspend v DOWN
Suspend v BLOK END
Suspended v DOWN
Suspended v BLOK END
Suspender n GARB DOWN
Suspense n BLUR PANG
Suspense n BLOK
Suspension n DOWN
Suspension n BLOK
Suspicion n BLUR AGGR
Sustain v AID

Sustain v HAVE
Sustenance n AID
Swab v CLEN
Swagger v POWR
Swallow n FOOD SOMA
Swallow n ANML UP
Swallowed v FOOD SOMA
Swallowing v FOOD SOMA
Swam v GO FLOW
Swam v BLUR
Swamp n ERTH FLOW
Swamp v BULG FLOW
Swamped v BULG FLOW
Swamping v BULG FLOW
Swan n ANML UP
Swarm n GO GRUP
Swastika n FORM
Sway v VARY
Sway n POWR
Swear v TALK HOLY
Swear v BAD TALK
Sweat v SOMA FLOW
Sweated v SOMA FLOW
Sweater n GARB
Sweep v CLEN
Sweep v GO
Sweeps v CLEN
Sweeps v GO
Sweepstake n MONY MOTV
Sweet j FOND GOOD
Sweet j SOMA GOOD
Sweetheart n FOND SEX
Swell v LARG BULG
Swell n LARG FLOW
Swept v CLEN
Swept v GO
Swerve v VARY GO
Swift j QUIK
Swig v SIP SOMA
Swill n DIRT FOOD
Swill v SIP SOMA
Swill v CLEN
Swim v GO FLOW
Swim v BLUR
Swindle v CRIM FALS
Swine n ANML
Swine n ANML BAD
Swing v VARY GO
Swish n HEAR

Switch n VARY
Switch n DAMG
Switchboard n JOIN TALK
Swivel v VARY
Swollen j LARG BULG
Swoon v BLUR REST
Swoop v QUIK GO
Sword n DAMG SHRP
Swordfish n ANML FLOW
Swordfish n FOOD FLOW
Swore v TALK HOLY
Swore v BAD TALK
Swum v GO FLOW
Swum v BLUR
Swung v VARY GO
Sycamore n VEGT
Sycophant n FOND SUB
Syllable n TALK FORM
Syllabus n WRIT
Symbol n SIML IDEA
Symmetry n SIML
Sympathetic j FOND
Sympathetic j SOMA
Sympathy n FOND
Symphony n MUSC
Symposium n GRUP IDEA
Symptom n SIML SICK
Synagogue n HOME HOLY
Synchrony n SIML
Syncopate v VARY MUSC
Syncopate v JOIN
Syncope n BLUR REST
Syndicate n MART GRUP
Syndrome n SICK
Synod n LEAD GRUP
Synonym n SIML TALK
Synopsis n TALK LITL
Syntax n TALK FORM
Synthesis n JOIN
Synthetic j FALS
Synthetic j JOIN
Syphilis n SICK SEX
Syringe n HOLW FLOW
Syrup n FOOD
System n FORM
Syzygy n ASTR
Syzygy n JOIN

T

T n WRIT
T n WRIT FORM
Tab n BULG
Tab n WRIT MONY
Tab n IDEA
Tabbed v BULG
Tabbed v IDEA
Tabbies n ANML
Tabbies n LADY TALK
Tabbing v BULG

Tabbing v IDEA
Tabby n FABR
Tabby n ANML
Tabernacle n HOME HOLY
Tabes n SICK
Tabetic j SICK
Table n FURN
Table n FORM
Table n WRIT FORM
Table v BLOK

Tableau n VIEW
Tablecloth n FURN FABR
Tabled v BLOK
Tables n FURN
Tables n FORM
Tables n WRIT FORM
Tables v BLOK
Tablespoon n FOOD FURN
Tablet n FORM
Tablet n WRIT

Parts of speech: a article; b preposition; c conjunction; d adverb; f prefix; i interjection;
          j adjective; n noun; p pronoun; r phrase; v verb.

Tabling v BLOK
Taboo v BLOK
Tabor n MUSC
Tabular j FORM
Tabular j WRIT FORM
Tabulate v WRIT FORM
Tacit j IDEA COVR
Taciturn j TALK LITL
Tack n JOIN SHRP
Tack n VARY GO
Tack n FOOD
Tackle n MECH
Tackle n BLOK
Tackle v MOTV
Tackled v BLOK
Tackled v MOTV
Tackling v BLOK
Tackling v MOTV
Tact n POWR
Tactic n POWR EVNT
Tactile j BODY JOIN
Tactless j FOOL
Tadpole n ANML FLOW
Taffeta n FABR
Tag v JOIN WRIT
Tag v JOIN
Tag v GO JOIN
Tail n BACK BODY
Tail v BACK GO
Tailing v BACK GO
Tailor n GARB MART
Tailor v VARY FORM
Tails n BACK BODY
Tails n GARB MALE
Tails v BACK GO
Taint v DIRT
Take v HAVE
Take v GO
Take v FOND
Take v POWR
Take v DAMG DEAD
Take v FALS
Take v NSCR
Talc n MTRL
Talcum n MTRL
Tale n TALK MYTH
Talent n POWR
Talisman n POWR MYTH
Talk n TALK
Tall j LARG
Tall j FOOL LARG
Tallied v NUMR
Tallied v SIML
Tallow n ANML MTRL
Tally v NUMR
Tally v SIML
Talon n ANML BODY
Tambourine n MUSC
Tame j GLAD SUB
Taming v GLAD SUB
Tamoshanter n GARB
Tamper v BAD VARY
Tan n COLR
Tan v COLR DAMG
Tang n SOMA

Tang n BULG
Tangent n VARY JOIN
Tangent n NUMR FORM
Tangible j TRUE
Tangle v BLOK JOIN
Tank n HOLW FLOW
Tank n DAMG VEHC
Tankard n SIP HOLW
Tantalize v PANG
Tantrum n AGGR PANG
Tap n HEAR
Tap n JOIN OPEN
Tap n JOIN
Tap n MECH
Tap n NEAR
Tap n MART SIP
Tap n BLOK MECH
Tape v MTRL COVR
Tape v HEAR MTRL
Tape v MSMT
Taper n VIEW
Taper n LITL
Tapered v LITL
Tapering v LITL
Tapes v MTRL COVR
Tapes v HEAR MTRL
Tapes v MSMT
Tapestry n COLR FABR
Taping v MTRL COVR
Taping v HEAR MTRL
Taping v MSMT
Tapioca n FOOD VEGT
Taproot n BGIN VEGT
Tar n MTRL
Tar n FLOW
Tarantula n BUG
Tardy j REST
Target n SHRP
Tariff n MART MONY
Tarn n FLOW
Tarnish v DIRT
Tarpaulin n FABR COVR
Tarred v MTRL
Tarried v EVER REST
Tarring v MTRL
Tarry v EVER REST
Tart j FOOD SOMA
Tart j AGGR
Tart n FOOD
Tart n BAD LADY
Tartan n FABR
Tartan n FLOW VEHC
Tartar n VEGT
Tartar n GRUP
Tartar n AGGR
Tartar n DIRT BODY
Task n WORK
Taskmaster n LEAD WORK
Taste n FOOD SOMA
Taste n GOOD MOTV
Taste n MOTV
Tasteless j TRIV
Tasty j FOOD GOOD
Tatter v TRIV FABR
Tattle v TALK OPEN

Tattoo n VIEW
Tattoo n HEAR
Taught v EDUC
Taunt v AGGR TALK
Taurus n ASTR MYTH
Taut j BLOK
Taut j BLOK PANG
Tavern n MART SIP
Tawny j COLR
Tax n MONY
Tax v AGGR
Taxi n VEHC
Taxi v GO VEHC
Taxicab n VEHC
Taxing v MONY
Taxing v AGGR
Taxpayer n MONY
Tea n SIP VEGT
Teach v EDUC
Teacher n LEAD EDUC
Teaching v EDUC
Teakettle n SIP HOLW
Team n AGRE GRUP
Teamwork n AGRE GRUP
Teapot n SIP HOLW
Tear n SEP
Tear n SOMA FLOW
Tear v QUIK GO
Tearful j SOMA PANG
Tease v AGGR
Teaspoon n FOOD FURN
Teat n BODY LADY
Technique n FORM
Tedious j TRIV PANG
Teem v MUCH
Teen j NUMR TIME
Teeth n FOOD BODY
Teeth n BULG
Telegram n WRIT
Telemeter n ION MSMT
Telepathy n TALK MYTH
Telephone v TALK MECH
Telescope n MECH VIEW
Telescope v LITL
Television n TALK VIEW
Tell v TALK
Tell v TALK IDEA
Tell v POWR
Teller n MART MONY
Teller n TALK
Teller n TALK NUMR
Telltale j TALK OPEN
Temerity n POWR
Temper n AGGR
Temper n MOTV
Temper n EVER FORM
Temper v GLAD AID
Tempera n COLR
Temperament n MOTV
Temperance n EASY MOTV
Temperate j EASY MOTV
Temperate j WEA EASY
Temperature n HEAT MSMT
Tempering v GLAD AID
Tempering v EVER FORM

Tempest n WEA DAMG
Temple n HOME HOLY
Temple n BODY
Tempo n QUIK
Temporary j VARY
Tempt v MOTV
Ten n NUMR
Tenable j POWR
Tenacity n POWR EVER
Tenant n LIVE
Tend v AID
Tend v MOTV
Tend v GO
Tended v AID
Tended v MOTV
Tended v GO
Tendency n MOTV
Tender j EASY
Tender j EASY PANG
Tender j FOND EASY
Tender n FLOW VEHC
Tender v AID
Tendered v AID
Tendering v AID
Tendon n SOMA
Tenement n HOME
Tennis n PLAY
Tenor n MUSC
Tenor n IDEA
Tens n NUMR
Tense j PANG
Tense j BLOK
Tense n TALK FORM
Tension n PANG
Tension n BLOK
Tensor n SOMA
Tensor n NUMR
Tent n HOME
Tentacle n ANML BODY
Tentative j VARY
Tenth n NUMR
Tenure n HAVE TIME
Tepid j HEAT
Term n EVER TIME
Term n EDUC TIME
Term n TALK
Term n AGRE
Terminal n END
Terming v TALK
Termite n BUG
Terrace n ERTH BULG
Terracotta j ERTH MTRL
Terracotta j COLR ERTH
Terrain n ERTH
Terrestrial j ERTH
Terrible j EMPH
Terrible j BAD DAMG
Terrible j BAD PANG
Terrier n ANML
Terrific j BAD DAMG
Terrific j GOOD
Terrified v PANG
Terrify v PANG
Territory n ERTH PLAC
Terror n BAD DAMG

Terror n PANG
Terry n FABR
Terse j LITL SHRP
Tertiary j NUMR
Test n TRUE
Testament n WRIT HOLY
Testament n WRIT MOTV
Testament n AGRE TALK
Tested v TRUE
Testes n MALE SEX
Testicle n MALE SEX
Testify v TALK TRUE
Testimony n TALK TRUE
Testing v TRUE
Testis n MALE SEX
Testy j AGGR PANG
Tetanus n SICK
Teutonic j GRUP
Teutonic j TALK
Text n WRIT
Textbook n WRIT EDUC
Textile n FABR
Textual j WRIT
Texture n FORM
Than c NSCR
Thanatopsis n DEAD
Thank v FOND AID
Thankless j AGGR
Thanks n FOND AID
Thanksgiving n AID TIME
That c NSCR
Thaw n VARY FLOW
The a NSCR
Theater n HOME PLAY
Theater n PLAC
Theatrical j PLAY
Theft n CRIM
Their p HSCR
Them p HSCR
Theme n IDEA
Then d NSCR
Then n PAST
Thence p NSCR
Thenceforth d FORW TIME
Theology n IDEA HOLY
Theory n IDEA FORM
Therapy n MEDC AID
There d NSCR
There d PLAC
Thereafter d FORW TIME
Therefore d NSCR
Thermal j HEAT
Thermodynamic j POWR HEAT
Thermometer n HEAT MSMT
Thermonuclear j HEAT ION
Thermostat n HEAT MECH
Thesaurus n FORW WRIT
These j NSCR
Theses n WRIT IDEA
Thesis n IDEA
Thesis n WRIT IDEA
Thespian n PLAY
They p HSCR
Thick j FABR
Thick j LARG
Thick j MSMT

Thick j FOOL
Thief n CRIM
Thigh n BODY
Thimble n GARB HOLW
Thin j LITL
Thing n NSCR
Think v IDEA
Third n NUMR
Third n NUMR MUSC
Thirst n SIP MOTV
Thirteen n NUMR
Thirty n NUMR
This j NSCR
Thistle n SHRP VEGT
Thither d NSCR
Thorazine n MEDC
Thorn n SHRP VEGT
Thorn n AGGR SHRP
Thorough j WHOL
Thoroughbred j ANML POWR
Thoroughbred j BGIN POWR
Thoroughfare n PATH
Thoroughgoing j WHOL
Those j NSCR
Though c OPPO
Though c NSCR
Thought n IDEA
Thoughtless j FOOL
Thousand n NUMR
Thrash v VARY AGGR
Thrash v DAMG
Thread n FABR
Thread v GO FABR
Threadbare j TRIV FABR
Threaded v GO FABR
Threading v GO FABR
Threat n DAMG
Three n NUMR
Threshold n IN FORM
Threshold n BGIN
Threw v GO
Threw v POWR WEAK
Threw v EVNT
Threw v FALS
Threw v FORM
Thrift n HAVE
Thrill v FOND
Thrive v POWR
Throat n BODY SOMA
Throb n VARY
Throe n DAMG PANG
Throne n LEAD FURN
Throng n GRUP
Throttle n BLOK MECH
Throttle v BLOK DEAD
Through b IN
Through b END
Through b AID
Throughout b WHOL
Throw v GO
Throw v POWR WEAK
Throw v EVNT
Throw v FALS
Throw v FORM
Thrust v POWR GO

Thud n HEAR
Thug n BAD CRIM
Thumb n BODY
Thumbnail j BODY LITL
Thump n HEAR
Thunder n WEA HEAR
Thunderbolt n WEA DAMG
Thunders v WEA HEAR
Thunderstorm n WEA DAMG
Thursday n TIME
Thus d SIML
Thwart v BLOK
Tic n BODY SICK
Tick n HEAR
Tick v WRIT
Tick n BUG
Tick n FABR
Ticked v HEAR
Ticked v WRIT
Ticket n WRIT
Ticking n HEAR
Ticking v WRIT
Ticking n FABR
Tickle v GLAD BODY
Tide n FLOW
Tide v AID
Tided v AID
Tidily d CLEN
Tidiness n CLEN
Tiding v AID
Tidings n TALK NEW
Tidy j CLEN
Tie v BLOK JOIN
Tie n GARB
Tie n SIML
Tied v BLOK JOIN
Tied v SIML
Tieing v BLOK JOIN
Tieing v SIML
Tiger n ANML
Tight j BLOK
Tight j SIP PANG
Tighten v BLOK
Tights n GARB
Tile n MTRL
Till c TIME
Till n HOLW MONY
Till v ERTH WORK
Tilled v ERTH WORK
Tilling v ERTH WORK
Tills n HOLW MONY
Tills v ERTH WORK
Tilt n VARY
Tilt n DAMG SHRP
Tilt n QUIK GO
Timber n MTRL VEGT
Time n TIME
Timepiece n MECH TIME
Times n TIME
Times n NUMR
Times n WRIT TIME
Timid j WEAK
Timing v TIME
Tin n ERTH MTRL
Tin n HOLW MTRL

Tincture n COLR
Tinder n HEAT MTRL
Tinge n SOME
Tinge n COLR SOME
Tingle v SOMA
Tinier j LITL
Tinker n MTRL WORK
Tinker v TRIV WORK
Tinkle n MUSC
Tinsel n MTRL VIEW
Tint n COLR
Tiny j LITL
Tip n END
Tip n MONY
Tip n AID
Tip n VARY
Tips n END
Tips v MONY
Tips v AID
Tips v VARY
Tipsy j SIP PANG
Tirade n AGGR TALK
Tire n VEHC
Tire v WEAK
Tired v WEAK
Tireless j POWR
Tiring v WEAK
Tissue n FORM
Tissue n MTRL
Tissue n SOMA
Title n TALK
Title n HAVE
Tizzy n PANG
To b NSCR
Toad n ANML
Toads n ANML
Toadstool n VEGT
Toast n FOOD HEAT
Toast n FOND SIP
Tobacco n FOOD VEGT
Today n NEW TIME
Toe n BODY
Toe v VARY
Toenail n BODY SHRP
Together d JOIN
Toggle n JOIN MECH
Togs n GARB
Toil v WORK
Toiled v WORK
Toilet n CLEN HOME
Toilet n CLEN GARB
Token j TRIV
Token n SIML
Token n MONY
Tokened v SIML
Tokening v SIML
Told v TALK
Told v POWR
Tolerance n AGRE
Toll n MONY
Toll n MUSC
Toll n LACK
Tolled v MUSC
Tolling v MUSC
Tom j ANML MALE

Tomato n FOOD VEGT
Tomato n LADY VEGT
Tomb n DEAD HOLW
Tomboy n LADY MALE
Tombs n DEAD HOLW
Tombstone n DEAD ERTH
Tome n WRIT
Tomorrow d FORW TIME
Tomtom n MUSC
Ton n MSMT
Tone n MUSC
Tone n POWR
Tone n COLR
Tong n BLOK MECH
Tongue n BODY
Tongue n ANML FOOD
Tongue n BODY TALK
Tongue n BULG
Tonic n MEDC
Tonic j AID
Tonic j MUSC
Tonic j COLR
Tonight n TIME
Tons n MSMT
Tonsil n SOMA
Tonsilectomy n MEDC SOMA
Too d EMPH
Too d SIML
Took v HAVE
Took v GO
Took v FOND
Took v POWR
Took v DAMG DEAD
Took v FALS
Took v NSCR
Tool n WORK
Toot v MUSC
Tooth n FOOD BODY
Tooth n BULG
Toothache n BODY PANG
Toothpaste n CLEN BODY
Toothpick n BODY SHRP
Top n UP
Top n UP COVR
Top n PLAY
Top v SHRP UP
Top v POWR UP
Top v END
Topaz n ERTH MTRL
Topaz n COLR
Topaz n ANML UP
Topic n IDEA
Topless j UP LACK
Topless j GARB LACK
Topmost j EMPH UP
Topped v UP
Topped v UP COVR
Topped v SHRP UP
Topped v POWR UP
Topped v END
Topple v DOWN
Tops n UP
Tops n UP COVR
Tops n PLAY
Tops v SHRP UP

Tops v POWR UP	Track n GO PLAY	Transmission n MECH
Tops v END	Track v DIRT GO	Transmit v GO
Topsyturvy j BLUR OPPO	Track v BACK GO	Transparent j OPEN VIEW
Torch n VIEW	Tracked v GO	Transpire v EVNT
Torch n HEAT VIEW	Tracked v DIRT GO	Transplant v VARY VEGT
Tore v SEP	Tracked v BACK GO	Transplant v VARY GO
Tore v QUIK GO	Tracking v GO	Transport n GO VEHC
Toreador n ANML DAMG	Tracking v DIRT GO	Transport n GLAD
Tories n GRUP	Tracking v BACK GO	Transportation n GO VEHC
Torment n DAMG PANG	Tract n ERTH	Transpose v VARY
Torn j SEP	Tract n WRIT	Trap n BLOK
Tornado n WEA DAMG	Tract n SOMA	Trap n MUSC
Torpedo n DAMG	Tractable j SUB	Trap n MECH PLAY
Torpor n REST	Tractor n VEHC	Trapdoor n BLOK OPEN
Torque n VARY POWR	Trade n MART	Trapeze n PLAY UP
Torrent n DAMG FLOW	Trade n MART WORK	Trapped v BLOK
Torrid j HEAT	Trademark n MART VIEW	Trapping n BLOK
Torso n BODY	Trading v MART	Trappings n GARB TRIV
Tort n BAD LAW	Tradition n EVER PAST	Trash n DIRT
Tortoise n ANML	Traffic n GO VEHC	Trauma n DAMG PANG
Tortuous j VARY	Traffic n MART	Travail n PANG WORK
Torture v DAMG PANG	Tragedy n DAMG	Travel n GO
Tory n GRUP	Trail n PATH	Travesty n FOOL
Toss v GO	Trail v BACK GO	Tray n HOLW
Toss v VARY	Trailed v·BACK GO	Treacherous j DAMG FALS
Total j WHOL	Trailer n VEHC	Tread v GO
Total n WHOL NUMR	Train n VEHC	Treason n AGGR FALS
Totaling v WHOL	Train n EDUC	Treasure n CRUX
Totaling v WHOL NUMR	Train n FORW	Treasure v FOND CRUX
Totalitarian j LEAD GRUP	Train n BACK GARB	Treasured v FOND CRUX
Totter v VARY WEAK	Train n GRUP SUB	Treasurer n LEAD MONY
Touch n JOIN	Train v AID	Treasuries n MONY
Touch n BODY JOIN	Train v SHRP	Treasuring v FOND CRUX
Touch n SOME	Trained v EDUC	Treasury n MONY
Touch v PANG MOTV	Trained v AID	Treat v AID
Touchback n POWR PLAY	Trained v SHRP	Treat v MEDC AID
Touchball n JOIN PLAY	Trainer n LEAD EDUC	Treat v EVNT
Touchdown n POWR PLAY	Trait n CRUX	Treaties n AGRE
Tough j AGGR	Traitor n AGGR FALS	Treating v AID
Tough j POWR	Tramp v GO	Treating v MEDC AID
Tough j BLUR BLOK	Tramp n GO OPEN	Treating v EVNT
Toupee n GARB BODY	Trample v DAMG GO	Treatise n WRIT
Tour n GO	Trance n REST	Treatment n AID
Tour n EVER TIME	Tranquil j GLAD	Treatment n MEDC AID
Tourist n GO	Transact v EVNT	Treatment n EVNT
Tournament n PLAY	Transatlantic j AFAR FLOW	Treaty n AGRE
Tow v GO AID	Transcend v POWR	Treble j MUSC
Toward b FORW	Transcribe v SIML WRIT	Treble j LARG NUMR
Towed v GO AID	Transfer v GO	Tree n VEGT
Towel n CLEN	Transfix v DAMG SHRP	Tree n FORM VEGT
Tower n HOME UP	Transform v VARY	Treetop n UP VEGT
Tower v UP	Transfusion n MEDC IN	Trek n GO
Towered v UP	Transgress v BAD	Trellis n FORM
Towering v UP	Transgress v CRIM	Tremble n VARY PANG
Towhead n BODY	Transient j VARY SEP	Tremendous j LARG
Town n PLAC	Transistor n MECH ION	Tremor n VARY
Toxic j DAMG	Transit n GO	Tremulous j VARY PANG
Toy n PLAY	Transit n MECH VIEW	Trench n ERTH HOLW
Trace n SOME	Transition n VARY	Trench v AGGR GO
Trace v BACK GO	Transitive j TALK FORM	Trenchant j SHRP
Trace v SIML WRIT	Transitory j VARY SEP	Trend n PATH
Traced v BACK GO	Translate v VARY	Trepidation n PANG
Traced v SIML WRIT	Translate v VARY TALK	Trespass v CRIM GO
Track n PATH	Translucent j VIEW	Triad n GRUP NUMR
Track v GO	Transmission n GO	Trial n LAW TRUE

Trial n TRUE	Trounce v DAMG	Tuna n FOOD FLOW
Trial n PANG	Troupe n GRUP PLAY	Tuna n ANML FLOW
Triangle n FORM	Trouser j GARB MALE	Tune n MUSC
Triangle n FORM MUSC	Trout n ANML FLOW	Tuning v MUSC
Triangular j FORM	Trout n FOOD FLOW	Tunnel n HOLW PATH
Tribe n GRUP	Trowel n WORK	Turban n GARB
Tribulation n PANG	Truce n DAMG END	Turbid j BLUR
Tribunal n LEAD LAW	Truce n REST	Turbine n MECH
Tribute n FOND	Truck n VEHC	Turbulent j AGGR
Trick n FALS	Truck n MART	Turf n ERTH VEGT
Trick n POWR	Truck v GO VEHC	Turgid j BULG
Trick n PLAY	Trucked v GO VEHC	Turkey n ANML UP
Trickle v FLOW	Trucking v GO VEHC	Turkey n ANML FOOD
Tricycle n VEHC	Truckle v SUB	Turmoil n BLUR PANG
Tried v MOTV	Trucks n VEHC	Turn n VARY GO
Tried j TRUE	Trucks v GO VEHC	Turn n VARY AID
Tried v LAW TRUE	Trudge v GO	Turn n VARY PANG
Tried v PANG	True j TRUE	Turnabout n VARY PATH
Trifle n TRIV	Truism n TRIV TRUE	Turnbuckle n JOIN MECH
Trigger n BGIN	Trump v POWR PLAY	Turncoat n VARY AGGR
Trigger n BGIN MECH	Trump v FALS	Turnkey n BLOK OPEN
Trigonometry n NUMR FORM	Trumped v POWR PLAY	Turnout n GO GRUP
Trill n MUSC	Trumped v FALS	Turnover n VARY
Trim v SHRP	Trumpet n MUSC	Turnover n FOOD
Trim j GOOD	Trunk n BODY	Turnpike n PATH
Trim n FORM	Trunk n BODY VEGT	Turpentine n MTRL VEGT
Trim v POWR WEAK	Trunk n HOLW	Turpitude n BAD
Trimmed v SHRP	Trunk n JOIN PATH	Turquoise n COLR
Trimmed v POWR WEAK	Trunks n HOLW	Turquoise n ERTH MTRL
Trinity n HOLY KIN	Trunks n BODY VEGT	Turret n HOME UP
Trinity n GRUP NUMR	Trunks n GARB MALE	Turtle n ANML
Trinket n TRIV	Trust n FOND AID	Turtle n ANML FOOD
Trio n GRUP NUMR	Trust n AID MONY	Tusk n ANML BODY
Trio n NUMR MUSC	Trust n MART JOIN	Tussle v DAMG
Triode n MECH ION	Truth n TRUE	Tutor n LEAD EDUC
Trip n GO	Try v MOTV	Tutor v EDUC
Trip v VARY WEAK	Try v TRUE	Tutored v EDUC
Trip v BGIN	Try v LAW TRUE	Tutoring v EDUC
Tripe n ANML FOOD	Try v PANG	Tuxedo n GARB MALE
Tripe n TRIV	Tub n HOLW	TV n TALK VIEW
Triple j NUMR	Tube n HOLW	Twang n MUSC
Triple n NUMR PLAY	Tube n HOLW VEHC	Tweed n FABR
Triplet n NUMR	Tuber n VEGT	Tweet n ANML TALK
Triplet n NUMR MUSC	Tuberculosis n SICK	Tweezer n BLOK MECH
Triplet n SIML KIN	Tubing n HOLW	Twelve n NUMR
Tripod n FORM	Tubular j HOLW	Twenty n NUMR
Trite j TRIV	Tuck v COVR	Twice d NUMR
Triumph n POWR	Tuck n VARY GARB	Twig n BODY VEGT
Trivial j TRIV	Tucked v COVR	Twilight n BLUR TIME
Troika n ANML VEHC	Tucker v WEAK	Twin n SIML KIN
Trombone n MUSC	Tucking v COVR	Twine n JOIN FABR
Troop n GRUP	Tuesday n TIME	Twine v VARY JOIN
Troop v GO GRUP	Tuft n SOME	Twinge n PANG
Trooped v GO GRUP	Tug n GO	Twining v VARY JOIN
Trooper n LAW	Tug n FLOW VEHC	Twinkle n VARY VIEW
Trooping v GO GRUP	Tuition n MONY EDUC	Twirl v VARY GO
Trophy n POWR	Tulip n VEGT	Twist n VARY
Tropic j HEAT PLAC	Tumble v VARY GO	Twist n VARY FOOD
Trot v GO	Tumbled v VARY GO	Twist n VARY SOME
Trouble n PANG	Tumbledown j VARY WEAK	Twisted v VARY
Trough n HOLW	Tumor n SICK	Twister n WEA DAMG
Trounce v POWR WEAK	Tumult n HEAR PANG	Twisting v VARY

Parts of speech: a article; b preposition; c conjunction; d adverb; f prefix; i interjection;
j adjective; n noun; p pronoun; r phrase; v verb.

Twit v FOOL TALK
Twitch n VARY
Twitted v FOOL TALK
Twitter n ANML TALK
Twitter n PANG
Two n NUMR
Twofaced j FALS BODY

Tycoon n LEAD
Tying v BLOK JOIN
Tying v SIML
Type n SIML GRUP
Type n WRIT
Type v WRIT MECH
Typewrite v WRIT MECH

Typical j SIML
Typify v SIML
Typing v WRIT MECH
Typing v SIML GRUP
Typist n WRIT MECH
Tyranny n AGGR LEAD
Tyro n WEAK

U

U n WRIT
U n WRIT FORM
Udder n BODY LADY
Ugh i PANG
Ugly j BAD
Ulcer n SICK
Ulterior j AFAR
Ulterior j COVR
Ultimate j END
Ultimatum n END MOTV
Ultra j AFAR
Umbilical j BODY JOIN
Umbrella n WEA GARB
Umbrella n AID COVR
Umpire n LEAD PLAY
Unabashed j POWR
Unabated j EVER
Unable j WEAK
Unabridged j WHOL
Unacceptable j OPPO
Unaccompanied j SOLE SEP
Unaccountable j BLUR
Unaccustomed j AFAR
Unadulterated j CLEN
Unaffected j EVER
Unaffected j EASY TRUE
Unafraid j POWR
Unalike j OPPO
Unalloyed j CLEN
Unalterable j EVER
UnAmerican j OPPO GRUP
Unanimous j AGRE WHOL
Unanticipated j AFAR
Unappetizing j FOOD PANG
Unassuming j WEAK
Unattached j OPEN
Unattainable j BLOK
Unattended j OPEN
Unattractive j BAD
Unauthorized j OPPO
Unavailable j LACK
Unavoidable j EVER
Unaware j BLUR
Unbearable j PANG
Unbeatable j POWR
Unbecoming j BAD
Unbelievable j FALS
Unbeliever n OPPO IDEA
Unbiased j TRUE
Unborn j BGIN
Unbreakable j EVER
Unbroken j EVER
Unburden v OPEN
Unburied j OPEN COVR
Unburned j HEAT

Unbutton v GARB OPEN
Uncalled j OPPO
Uncanny j AFAR MYTH
Uncared j AGGR
Unceasing j EVER
Uncensored j OPEN
Unceremonious j AGGR
Uncertain j BLUR
Unchanged j EVER
Uncivil j BAD AGGR
Unclad j GARB SEP
Unclaimed j LACK
Uncle n MALE KIN
Unclean j DIRT
Unclothe v GARB SEP
Uncoil v VARY FORM
Uncomfortable j PANG
Uncommitted j OPEN
Uncommon j AFAR
Uncommunicative j OPPO TALK
Uncomplimentary j AGGR
Uncompromising j AGGR
Unconcealed j OPEN
Unconcern n TRIV
Unconditional j WHOL
Unconfirmed j BLUR
Unconscious j IDEA COVR
Unconscious j BLUR REST
Unconstitutional j OPPO LAW
Uncontrollable j POWR OPEN
Unconventional j OPPO
Uncooperative j OPPO
Uncork v BLOK OPEN
Uncouple v SEP
Uncouth j AGGR
Uncover v OPEN
Uncritical j AGRE
Uncrowded j GRUP LITL
Unction n MTRL HOLY
Unction n AID
Unction n EASY MTRL
Unctuous j EASY FALS
Uncultured j FOOL
Uncut j WHOL
Undamaged j AID
Undated j TIME
Undaunted j POWR
Undecided j BLUR
Undeclared j TALK COVR
Undefeated j POWR
Undemocratic j OPPO GRUP
Undeniable j TRUE
Under b DOWN
Under b DOWN SUB
Underbrush n VEGT

Undercarriage n DOWN FORM
Underclothes n GARB DOWN
Undercurrent n DOWN FLOW
Undercurrent n BLUR MOTV
Underdeveloped j WEAK
Underdog n ANML WEAK
Undergo v EVNT
Undergraduate n EDUC SUB
Underground n DOWN ERTH
Underground n DAMG COVR
Underground n DOWN VEHC
Underhand j FALS COVR
Underhand j DOWN BODY
Underlying j DOWN CRUX
Undermine v DAMG WEAK
Underneath b DOWN
Underneath b DOWN SUB
Undernourished j FOOD LACK
Underpass n DOWN PATH
Underprivileged j WEAK LACK
Underrate v FALS
Undersea j DOWN FLOW
Undershirt n GARB DOWN
Understand v IDEA
Understood v IDEA
Understudy n EDUC SUB
Undertake v BGIN MOTV
Undertaker n MART DEAD
Undertone n BLUR TALK
Underwear n GARB DOWN
Underwent v EVNT
Underworld n WHOL DOWN
Underworld n CRIM
Underwrite v AID WRIT
Undeserved j OPPO
Undesirable j BAD
Undetected j COVR
Undeveloped j WEAK
Undid v VARY
Undid v OPEN
Undid v WEAK
Undies n GARB LADY
Undignified j BAD
Undivided j WHOL
Undo v VARY
Undo v OPEN
Undo v WEAK
Undoubted j TRUE
Undress v GARB SEP
Undue j OPPO
Undulate v VARY
Unduly j OPPO
Undying j DEAD EVER
Unearned j OPPO HAVE
Unearth v ERTH OPEN

Unearthly j AFAR MYTH
Uneasy j PANG
Uneaten j FOOD
Uneducated j EDUC LACK
Unemotional j MOTV LACK
Unemployment n LACK WORK
Unending j EVER
Unenlightened j FOOL
Unenviable j PANG
Unequal j OPPO
Unequal j VARY
Unequal j OPPO WEAK
Unequalled j POWR
Unequivocal j SHRP
Unessential j TRIV
Uneven j VARY
Uneventful j TRIV
Unexcelled j POWR
Unexpected j AFAR
Unfailing j EVER
Unfair j BAD
Unfaithful j AGGR
Unfamiliar j AFAR
Unfasten v OPEN
Unfavorable j AGGR
Unfeeling j AGGR
Unfeigned j TRUE
Unfilled j LACK
Unfinished j SOME
Unfinished j LACK
Unfit j WEAK
Unflinching j POWR
Unfold v VARY OPEN
Unforeseen j AFAR
Unforgettable j EVER IDEA
Unfortunate j WEAK
Unfounded j FALS
Unfriendly j AGGR
Unfurl v VARY OPEN
Ungainly j WEAK
Ungrateful j AGGR
Unguarded j OPEN WEAK
Unhappy j PANG
Unharmed j AID
Unheard j AFAR HEAR
Unhurried j REST
Unicellular j SOMA SOLE
Unicorn n ANML MYTH
Unidentified j BLUR
Unified v JOIN
Uniform j SIML WHOL
Uniform n GARB
Unify v JOIN
Unimpeachable j GOOD TRUE
Unimportant j TRIV
Unimproved j WEAK
Uninformed j FOOL
Uninhabited j LIVE LACK
Uninhibited j OPEN
Uninspired j WEAK TRIV
Unintelligent j FOOL
Unintelligible j BLUR
Unintentional j OPPO MOTV
Uninteresting j TRIV
Uninterrupted j EVER

Union n JOIN
Union n GRUP JOIN
Unique j AFAR SOLE
Unison n SIML
Unit n GRUP SOLE
Unit n SOLE MSMT
Unit n SOLE
Unite v JOIN
UnitedStates n PLAC
Uniting v JOIN
Unity n JOIN
Universal j WHOL
Universe n WHOL
University n HOME EDUC
Unjust j BAD
Unkempt j DIRT
Unkind j AGGR
Unknown j BLUR COVR
Unlawful j CRIM LAW
Unlawful j OPPO LAW
Unlearn v OPPO EDUC
Unleavened j VEGT LACK
Unless c OPPO
Unlighted j BLUR
Unlike b OPPO
Unlikely j AFAR
Unlimber v AID
Unlimited j OPEN
Unlisted j WRIT
Unload v SEP
Unlock v OPEN
Unloved j AGGR
Unlucky j WEAK
Unman v MALE LACK
Unmanageable j OPPO
Unmanned v MALE LACK
Unmannerly d BAD AGGR
Unmarked j BLUR WRIT
Unmarried j SEP SEX
Unmask v OPEN
Unmerciful j AGGR
Unmistakable j SHRP
Unmitigated j EVER
Unmotivated j MOTV LACK
Unnatural j OPPO AFAR
Unnecessary j TRIV
Unnerve v PANG
Unnoticed j VIEW COVR
Unobtrusive j WEAK
Unoccupied j OPEN
Unofficial j OPPO
Unopened j COVR
Unorganized j BLUR
Unoriginal j EVER TRIV
Unorthodox j OPPO
Unpack v OPEN SEP
Unpaid j MONY LACK
Unpardonable j BAD
Unpatriotic j OPPO GRUP
Unperceived j VIEW COVR
Unperturbed j GLAD EASY
Unplanned j BLUR
Unpleasant j PANG
Unpolished j WEAK
Unpolished j DIRT

Unpopular j AGGR GRUP
Unprecedented j AFAR
Unpredictable j BLUR
Unprejudiced j TRUE
Unpremeditated j EASY
Unprepared j WEAK
Unproductive j WEAK TRIV
Unprofitable j TRIV
Unprotected j WEAK
Unproved j BLUR
Unpublished j WRIT COVR
Unqualified j WEAK
Unqualified j EMPH
Unquestionable j TRUE
Unravel v OPEN SEP
Unreal j AFAR MYTH
Unreasonable j FOOL
Unrelated j OPPO
Unrelenting j EVER
Unreliable j WEAK
Unresponsive j OPPO MOTV
Unrest n PANG
Unrestrained j OPEN
Unrestricted j OPEN
Unripe j WEAK
Unrivaled j POWR
Unroll v VARY FORM
Unruffled j GLAD EASY
Unruly j AGGR
Unsafe j DAMG WEAK
Unsanitary j DIRT
Unsatiated j LACK
Unsatisfactory j BAD
Unsatisfactory j WEAK
Unsatisfied j LACK
Unsavory j BAD AGGR
Unsavory j AGGR SOMA
Unscathed j AID
Unscientific j FALS IDEA
Unscrew v SEP
Unscrupulous j BAD
Unseasonable j OPPO TIME
Unseen j VIEW COVR
Unselfish j GOOD AID
Unsettled j VARY
Unsettled j VARY PANG
Unsettled j LIVE LACK
Unsettled j VARY OPPO
Unsightly j BAD VIEW
Unsinkable j EVER FLOW
Unskilled j WEAK
Unsold j MONY LACK
Unsolicited j OPPO MOTV
Unsolved j BLUR
Unsophisticated j WEAK
Unsound j WEAK
Unspeakably d TALK EMPH
Unspoiled j CLEN
Unspoken j TALK COVR
Unstable j VARY WEAK
Unsteady j VARY WEAK
Unsuccessful j WEAK
Unsure j BLUR WEAK
Unsweetened j FOOD SOMA
Unsympathetic j AGGR

Unsystematic j BLUR
Untactful j WEAK
Untamed j DAMG
Untangle v OPEN SEP
Untenable j FALS
Untenable j WEAK
Untended j OPEN
Untested j BLUR
Untie v OPEN SEP
Until b TIME
Untimely j OPPO TIME
Untold j MUCH TALK
Untold j TALK COVR
Untouched j OPEN
Untoward j PANG
Untrained j EDUC WEAK
Untreated j EVER
Untreated j AID LACK
Untried j BLUR
Untrue j FALS
Untrustworthy j AGGR WEAK
Untying v OPEN SEP
Unused j NEW
Unused j AFAR
Unusual j AFAR
Unveil v OPEN
Unwanted j AGGR
Unwary j WEAK
Unwed j SEP SEX
Unwelcome j AGGR
Unwieldy j WEAK
Unwilling j OPPO

Unwind v VARY
Unwitting j BLUR OPPO
Unwonted j AFAR
Unworthy j WEAK
Unwrap v OPEN
Unwritten j WRIT
Unyielding j EVER
Up b UP
Up j END UP
Upbraid v AGGR TALK
Upbringing n AID UP
Upend v VARY WEAK
Upheaval n VARY DAMG
Upheld v AID
Uphill d BULG UP
Uphold v AID
Upholster v FURN FABR
Upkeep n AID
Upon b NSCR
Upper j UP
Upright j UP
Upright j GOOD UP
Uproar n HEAR PANG
Uproot v DAMG SEP
Upset v PANG
Upset v VARY WEAK
Upset v POWR WEAK
Upside n UP
Upstairs d UP
Upstanding j GOOD UP
Upstate j PLAC UP
Upstream d FLOW UP

Uptodate r NEW
Uptown d PLAC UP
Upward d UP
Uranus n ASTR
Uranus n LEAD MYTH
Urban j PLAC
Urge n MOTV
Urgent j CRUX
Urine n DIRT SOMA
Urn n HOLW
Us p WE
Usage n EVER
Usage n EVNT
Use v AID
Used j EVER
Used j TRIV
Used v AID
Useful j AID
Useless j TRIV
Usher v AID
Using v AID
Usual j EVER
Usurp v DAMG HAVE
Utensil n FOOD FURN
Utility n AID
Utilize v AID
Utmost j EMPH
Utmost j AFAR
Utopia n PLAC MYTH
Utter v TALK
Utter j EMPH
Utterly d EMPH

V

V n WRIT
V n WRIT FORM
Vacancy n SEP LACK
Vacating v SEP LACK
Vacation n PLAY
Vaccinate v MEDC
Vacillate v BLUR VARY
Vacuous j TRIV
Vacuum n VAPR LACK
Vacuum n CLEN MECH
Vagabond n GO OPEN
Vagina n LADY SEX
Vagrant j GO OPEN
Vague j BLUR
Vain j WEAK TRIV
Vain j FOOL
Vale n ERTH HOLW
Valedictorian n POWR TALK
Valence n JOIN ION
Valentine n FOND PLAY
Valet n AID MALE
Valiant j POWR
Valid j TRUE
Valise n HOLW
Valley n ERTH HOLW
Valor n POWR
Value v CRUX
Valueless j TRIV
Valve n BLOK MECH
Vamoose v GO SEP

Van n FORW GRUP
Van n VEHC
Vandal n DAMG CRIM
Vane n WEA FORM
Vane n FORM
Vanguard n FORW GRUP
Vanilla j FOOD VEGT
Vanish v VIEW SEP
Vanity n FOOL
Vanity n FURN
Vanity n HOLW FURN
Vanquish v POWR WEAK
Vapid j TRIV
Vapor n VAPR BLUR
Variable j VARY
Varicose j SICK
Varied v VARY
Varied v VARY OPPO
Various j VARY
Varnish n MTRL VIEW
Vary v VARY
Vary v VARY OPPO
Vase n HOLW
Vasectomy n MEDC SOMA
Vassal n SUB
Vast j LARG
Vat n HOLW
Vatican n PLAC HOLY
Vault n HOME FORM
Vault n DEAD HOLW

Vault v GO UP
Vaulted j HOME FORM
Vaulted v GO UP
Vaulting v GO UP
Vaunt v POWR TALK
Vector n NUMR
Veer v VARY
Vegetable n FOOD VEGT
Vegetation n VEGT
Vehement j AGGR
Vehicle n VEHC
Veil n COVR
Veil n GARB COVR
Veil n GARB HOLY
Vein n HOLW
Vein n SOME
Vein n SOMA
Velocity n QUIK
Velvet j FABR
Vendor n MART MONY
Veneer n MTRL COVR
Venerable j FOND PAST
Venerate v FOND
Vengeance n DAMG
Venom n DAMG
Vent n OPEN OUT
Venture n DAMG MOTV
Venus n ASTR
Venus n LADY MYTH
Veracity n TRUE

Veranda n HOME
Verb n TALK FORM
Verbal j TALK
Verbatim d SIML TALK
Verbiage n TALK TRIV
Verbose j MUCH TALK
Verdict n LAW IDEA
Verdict n IDEA
Verge n NEAR
Verge v VARY NEAR
Verge n FORM
Verge n MECH TIME
Verge n END
Verify v TRUE
Verily d EMPH
Vermilion n COLR
Vermin n BUG BAD
Vermouth n SIP VEGT
Vernacular n TALK
Versatile j POWR
Verse n TALK
Versed j POWR
Version n IDEA
Versus b OPPO
Vertebra n SOMA
Vertebrate j ANML SOMA
Vertex n UP
Vertical n FORM
Vertigo n BLUR PANG
Very d EMPH
Very j SIML EMPH
Vessel n FLOW VEHC
Vessel n HOLW
Vessel n VEHC
Vest n GARB
Vest v AID
Vested v AID
Vestibule n HOME
Vestige n SOME
Vesting v AID
Veteran n DAMG PAST
Veteran n POWR PAST
Veto v BLOK
Vex v AGGR PANG
Via b PATH
Viable j POWR LIVE
Viaduct n PATH
Vial n HOLW
Viand n FOOD
Vibrate v VARY
Vice n BAD
Vice f SIML
Viceversa r VARY OPPO
Vicinity n NEAR PLAC
Vicious j DAMG
Victim n DAMG WEAK
Victor n POWR

Victorian j PAST
Victories n POWR
Victorious j POWR
Victory n POWR
Victual n FOOD
Vie v OPPO
View n VIEW
View n IDEA
Vigilance n QUIK AID
Vignette n VIEW
Vigor n POWR
Vile j BAD
Vilify v BAD AGGR
Villa n HOME
Village n PLAC
Villain n DAMG
Vim n POWR
Vin n SIP VEGT
Vindicate v OPEN TRUE
Vindictive j DAMG
Vine n VEGT
Vinegar n FOOD VEGT
Vineyard n ERTH VEGT
Vintage j TIME VEGT
Vinyl n FABR
Vinyl n MTRL
Violate v DAMG
Violence n DAMG
Violet n VEGT
Violet n COLR
Violin n MUSC
Viper n ANML DAMG
Viral j SICK
Virgin j BGIN NEW
Virgin n LADY HOLY
Virgin n LADY SEX
Virgo n ASTR MYTH
Virile j POWR MALE
Virtual j NEAR
Virtue n POWR
Virtue n GOOD
Virtuoso n POWR
Virtuous j GOOD
Virulent j DAMG
Virus n SICK
Visa n AID WRIT
Visage n BODY
Viscosity n FLOW REST
Vise n BLOK MECH
Visibility n VIEW
Vision n VIEW
Vision n FORW VIEW
Vision n VIEW MYTH
Visionary j FORW VIEW
Visit v GO JOIN
Vista n VIEW
Visual j VIEW

Vital j CRUX
Vital j CRUX LIVE
Vital j DEAD CRUX
Vitality n POWR
Vitamin n FOOD AID
Vitiate v BAD WEAK
Vituperate v AGGR TALK
Vivacious j QUIK
Vivendi n LIVE
Vivid j VIEW EMPH
Vivify v QUIK LIVE
Vocabulary n TALK
Vocal j TALK
Vocation n WORK
Vociferous j HEAR TALK
Vodka n SIP VEGT
Vogue n NEW MOTV
Voice n TALK
Void j END TRIV
Void j LACK
Volatile j VARY
Volcano n DAMG ERTH
Volition n MOTV
Volley n DAMG GRUP
Volley n GRUP
Volley n GO PLAY
Volleyed v GO PLAY
Volleying v GO PLAY
Volt n ION MSMT
Voltmeter n ION MSMT
Voluble j MUCH TALK
Volume n WRIT
Volume n MSMT
Voluminous j LARG
Voluntary j MOTV
Volunteer n AID MOTV
Voluptuous j GLAD MOTV
Vomit v SOMA OUT
Voracious j FOOD MOTV
Votary n FOND
Vote n MOTV
Voting v MOTV
Vouch v TRUE
Vouched v TRUE
Voucher n WRIT TRUE
Vouchsafe v AGRE AID
Vow v AGRE TALK
Vowed v AGRE TALK
Vowel n TALK FORM
Voyage n GO
Voyeur n VIEW SEX
Vulgar j BAD AGGR
Vulnerable j WEAK
Vulture n ANML UP
Vulture n ANML AGGR
Vulva n LADY SEX
Vying v OPPO

W

W n WRIT
Wacky j FOOL
Wad n BULG
Wad n BULG MONY

Wadded v BULG
Waddle n VARY GO
Wade v GO
Wading v GO

Wafer n FORM
Wafer n FOOD
Waffle n FOOD
Waft v VAPR GO

Wag n VARY
Wag n GLAD TALK
Wage n MONY WORK
Wage v DAMG
Wager v MONY MOTV
Waging v DAMG
Wagon n VEHC
Waif n SOLE YNG
Wail n TALK PANG
Waist n BODY
Waist n GARB BODY
Waistcoat n GARB
Waistline n BODY
Wait v REST
Wait v AID
Waited v REST
Waited v AID
Waiter n AID MALE
Waitress n LADY AID
Waive v SEP LACK
Waive v REST
Waiver n SEP LACK
Wake v QUIK
Wake n DEAD REST
Wake n BACK FLOW
Waked v QUIK
Waken v QUIK
Waking v QUIK
Walk n GO
Walk n PATH
Walk v GO PLAY
Wall n BLOK FORM
Walled v BLOK FORM
Wallet n GARB HOLW
Wallop v DAMG
Wallow v BAD VARY
Walnut n MTRL VEGT
Walnut n FOOD VEGT
Walnut n COLR
Walrus n ANML FLOW
Waltz n GO MUSC
Wan j COLR WEAK
Wand n FORM
Wand n FORM MYTH
Wander v GO
Wane v LITL WEAK
Wane v LITL
Waning v LITL WEAK
Waning v LITL
Want v MOTV
Want v LACK
Wanton j BAD MOTV
Wanton j BAD SEX
War n DAMG
Warble n ANML TALK
Ward n MEDC HOME
Ward n AID
Ward n PLAC
Ward v BLOK
Warded v BLOK
Warden n LEAD LAW
Warding v BLOK

Wardrobe n GARB HOLW
Wardrobe n GARB
Ware n MART
Warehouse n MART HOME
Warily d AID MOTV
Warm j HEAT
Warm j FOND HEAT
Warn v AGGR
Warp n VARY FALS
Warp n FORM FABR
Warp v VARY FLOW
Warped v VARY FALS
Warped v VARY FLOW
Warping v VARY FALS
Warping v VARY FLOW
Warrant n WRIT LAW
Warrant n AID TRUE
Warrant n TRUE
Warranted v AID TRUE
Warranted v TRUE
Warranting v AID TRUE
Warranting v TRUE
Warranty n AID TRUE
Warred v DAMG
Warren n ANML HOME
Warring v DAMG
Warrior n DAMG
Warship n DAMG FLOW
Wart n DIRT BODY
Wartime n DAMG TIME
Wary j AID MOTV
Was v NSCR
Was v EVNT
Wash v CLEN FLOW
Wash n GO FLOW
Wash n COLR FLOW
Washed v CLEN FLOW
Washed v GO FLOW
Washer n CLEN FLOW
Washer n BLOK
Wasp n BUG UP
Waste n TRIV LACK
Waste n DIRT TRIV
Waste n ERTH TRIV
Watch v VIEW
Watch v AID VIEW
Watch n MECH TIME
Watchdog n ANML AID
Watchman n AID VIEW
Watchtower n VIEW UP
Water n FLOW
Water n SIP FLOW
Water n DIRT SOMA
Water n MSMT
Watercloset n CLEN HOME
Watercolor n COLR FLOW
Watercool v COLD FLOW
Watercourse n FLOW PATH
Watercress n FOOD VEGT
Watered v FLOW
Watered v SIP FLOW
Waterfall n DOWN FLOW

Waterfowl n ANML FLOW
Waterfront n FORW FLOW
Waterhole n HOLW FLOW
Watering v FLOW
Watering v SIP FLOW
Waterless j FLOW LACK
Waterline n FLOW FORM
Waterlog v BULG FLOW
Waterloo n PLAC WEAK
Watermelon n FOOD VEGT
Waterproof j BLOK FLOW
Watershed n FLOW SEP
Watertight j BLOK FLOW
Waterworks n MECH FLOW
Watt n ION MSMT
Wave n VARY
Wave n VARY BULG
Wave n VARY FLOW
Waver v VARY
Waver v VARY WEAK
Wax n CLEN MTRL
Wax n MTRL
Wax v LARG
Way n PATH
Way n EVNT
Waylay v DAMG COVR
Wayside j NEAR PATH
Wayward j BAD GO
Wayward j VARY GO
We p WE
Weak j WEAK
Wealth n MUCH MONY
Wean v SEP
Weapon n DAMG
Wear v GARB
Wear v TRIV
Wear v EVER
Wear v HAVE
Wear v WEAK PANG
Wearily d WEAK PANG
Weariness n WEAK PANG
Wearing v GARB
Wearing v TRIV
Wearing v EVER
Wearing v HAVE
Wearing v WEAK PANG
Weary j WEAK PANG
Weasel n ANML
Weasel v ANML FALS
Weaseled v ANML FALS
Weaseling v ANML FALS
Weather n WEA
Weather v WEA POWR
Weathervane n WEA FORM
Weave v VARY GO
Weave v JOIN
Web n BUG HOME
Web n FORM
Web n BLOK
Webbed j FORM
Wed v SEX KIN
Wedge n SOME FORM

Parts of speech: a article; b preposition; c conjunction; d adverb; f prefix; i interjection;
j adjective; n noun; p pronoun; r phrase; v verb.

Wedge n SEP
Wedge v BLOK
Wednesday n TIME
Wee j LITL
Weed n VEGT
Weed v CLEN VEGT
Week n TIME
Weekend n END TIME
Weep v SOMA PANG
Weigh v MSMT
Weigh v IDEA
Weigh v PANG
Weigh v FLOW UP
Weight n MSMT
Weight n CRUX
Weight n PANG
Weird j AFAR MYTH
Welcome n FOND
Weld v JOIN
Welfare n AID
Well d GOOD
Well d EMPH
Well i NSCR
Well j MEDC GOOD
Well n HOLW
Well n HOLW FLOW
Well v FLOW
Wellbeing n MEDC GOOD
Wellbred j BGIN GOOD
Welled v FLOW
Welling v FLOW
Wells n HOLW FLOW
Wells v FLOW
Welltodo j MUCH MONY
Wellwisher n GOOD MOTV
Welt n DAMG BULG
Weltanschauung n WHOL IDEA
Welter n BLUR
Welter v BAD VARY
Welterweight n MSMT
Wench n LADY
Wend v GO
Wept v SOMA PANG
Were v NSCR
Were v EVNT
West n PLAC PATH
Wet j FLOW
Wet j FOOL FLOW
Wetland n ERTH FLOW
Wets v FLOW
Wetted v FLOW
Whack n DAMG
Whack n HEAR
Whack n EVNT
Whale n ANML FLOW
Whale n ANML LARG
Whalebone n ANML MTRL
Wharf n BLOK FLOW
What p NSCR
Whatever j NSCR
Whatnot n TRIV
Whatsoever j NSCR
Wheat n FOOD VEGT
Wheedle v FALS
Wheel n MECH

Wheel n FORM
Wheel n POWR
Wheel n VEHC
Wheel v VARY QUIK
Wheel v GO VEHC
Wheelbarrow n VEHC WORK
Wheelchair n GO REST
Wheeled v VARY QUIK
Wheeled v GO VEHC
Wheeling v VARY QUIK
Wheeling v GO VEHC
Wheeze n SOMA HEAR
When d NSCR
When d TIME
Whence d PLAC
Where c NSCR
Where d PLAC
Whereabout d PLAC
Whereas c NSCR
Whereby d NSCR
Wherefore d NSCR
Wherein d NSCR
Whereof d NSCR
Whereupon d NSCR
Wherever d PLAC
Wherewithal n AID
Whet v SHRP
Whet v SHRP MOTV
Whether c NSCR
Whets v SHRP
Whets v SHRP MOTV
Whetstone n ERTH SHRP
Which j NSCR
Whichever j NSCR
Whiff n VAPR
Whiff n VAPR SOMA
Whig n GRUP
While c TIME
While c OPPO
Whim n VARY MOTV
Whimper v TALK PANG
Whine v TALK PANG
Whinny n ANML TALK
Whip n DAMG
Whip v POWR WEAK
Whip v VARY
Whip v QUIK
Whippersnapper n TRIV
Whir n VARY HEAR
Whirl n VARY QUIK
Whirl v VARY GO
Whirlpool n VARY FLOW
Whirlwind n WEA VARY
Whisker n BODY
Whiskey n SIP VEGT
Whisper n HEAR TALK
Whistle n MUSC
Whit n LITL TRIV
White j COLR
White j COLR GOOD
Whitecollar j GARB MART
Whitefish n FOOD FLOW
Whitefish n ANML FLOW
Whitewash v CLEN COLR
Whither d PLAC

Whiting n ANML FLOW
Whiting n FOOD FLOW
Whiting n COLR MTRL
Whittle v SHRP
Whittle v LITL SHRP
Whiz v QUIK GO
Whiz n POWR
Who p NSCR
Whoever p SOLE
Whole j WHOL
Wholehearted j WHOL TRUE
Wholesale j MART MONY
Wholesome j GOOD
Wholewheat j WHOL VEGT
Wholly d WHOL EMPH
Whom p NSCR
Whoop v ANML TALK
Whoopee n GLAD HEAR
Whopper n LARG
Whopper n FALS
Whore n BAD SEX
Whose p NSCR
Why d IDEA
Wick n HEAT MTRL
Wicked j BAD
Wicker n MTRL VEGT
Wicker n HOLW VEGT
Wide j LARG
Wide j MSMT
Wideawake j QUIK
Wideeyed j BODY VIEW
Widespread j LARG
Widow n DEAD KIN
Widow n DEAD LADY
Widow n BUG LADY
Widowed v DEAD KIN
Widowed v DEAD LADY
Widower n DEAD KIN
Widower n DEAD MALE
Width n MSMT
Wield v POWR
Wife n LADY KIN
Wife n LADY SEX
Wig n GARB BODY
Wigged v GARB BODY
Wiggle v VARY
Wild j DAMG
Wild j VARY
Wild j FOOL
Wild j FOND
Wild n ERTH VEGT
Wildcat j OPPO
Wildcat n ANML DAMG
Wilderness n ERTH VEGT
Wile n FALS
Will v NSCR
Will n MOTV
Will v LAW MOTV
Willed v MOTV
Willed v LAW MOTV
Willing j AGRE MOTV
Willing v MOTV
Willing v LAW MOTV
Willow n MTRL VEGT
Willow n MTRL VEGT

Willow n MECH VEGT
Willow v CLEN VEGT
Willynilly d NO MOTV
Wilt v WEAK
Wily j FALS
Win v POWR
Win v POWR HAVE
Wince v PANG
Winch n MECH
Wind n VAPR WEA
Wind v VARY
Wind v VARY GO
Wind v VARY END
Wind n VAPR IDEA
Windbreaker n WEA GARB
Windfall n WEA AID
Windfall n WEA DOWN
Windjammer n FLOW VEHC
Windmill n WEA WORK
Window n VIEW
Windows n VIEW
Windowsill n VIEW FORM
Winds n VAPR WEA
Winds v VARY
Winds v VARY GO
Winds v VARY END
Windshield n AID VIEW
Windy j VAPR WEA
Wine n SIP VEGT
Wing n BODY UP
Wing n FORM UP
Wing n FORM
Wing n GRUP
Wing n PLAY FORM
Wing v GO UP
Wing v DAMG
Winged j BODY UP
Winged j FORM UP
Winged v GO UP
Winged v DAMG
Winging v GO UP
Winging v DAMG
Wining v SIP VEGT
Wink n VARY VIEW
Wink n VARY QUIK
Winning v POWR
Winning v POWR HAVE
Winnow n MECH SEP
Winnow v SEP
Winnow v GO UP
Winter n COLD TIME
Wipe v CLEN
Wipe v DAMG
Wire n MTRL
Wire n WRIT
Wisdom n GOOD IDEA
Wise j GOOD IDEA
Wise j FOOL IDEA
Wiseacre n FOOL IDEA
Wisecrack n GLAD TALK
Wish v MOTV
Wishywashy j WEAK
Wisp n LITL SOME
Wisteria n VEGT
Wistful j MOTV

Wit n GLAD IDEA
Wit n IDEA
Witch n BAD LADY
Witchcraft n BAD MYTH
With b NSCR
With b JOIN
Withdraw v GO SEP
Withdraw v SEP
Wither v WEAK
Withhold v BLOK HAVE
Within b IN
Within b NSCR
Without b LACK
Without d OUT
Withstand v OPPO POWR
Witness n VIEW
Witticism n GLAD IDEA
Witting j AGRE MOTV
Wives n LADY KIN
Wives n LADY SEX
Wizard n POWR MYTH
Wizen v WEAK
Wobble v VARY WEAK
Woe n PANG
Woke v QUIK
Wolf n ANML
Wolf v ANML FOOD
Wolfed v ANML FOOD
Wolfing v ANML FOOD
Wolfs v ANML FOOD
Wolves n ANML
Woman n LADY
Womb n LADY SOMA
Womb n BGIN HOLW
Women n LADY
Won v POWR
Won v POWR HAVE
Wonder v BLUR IDEA
Wonder n GOOD
Wonderful j GOOD
Wont n EVER
Woo v FOND SEX
Wood n MTRL VEGT
Wood n VEGT
Woodchuck n ANML
Woodcraft n POWR MTRL
Woodcut n VIEW SHRP
Wooded j VEGT
Woodpile n BULG MTRL
Woods n MTRL VEGT
Woods n VEGT
Woodwork n MTRL FORM
Woof n FORM FABR
Woof n ANML TALK
Woofer n MUSC
Wool n ANML FABR
Woolen j ANML FABR
Woolens n GARB FABR
Woozy j BLUR PANG
Word n TALK
Word n AGRE TALK
Wordy j MUCH TALK
Wore v GARB
Wore v TRIV
Wore v EVER

Wore v HAVE
Wore v WEAK PANG
Work n WORK
Work n FORM WORK
Work v PANG WORK
Worked v WORK
Worked v PANG WORK
Working v WORK
Working v PANG WORK
Workman n MALE WORK
Works v WORK
Works n FORM WORK
Works v PANG WORK
Workshop n HOME WORK
World n WHOL
Worldwide j WHOL LARG
Worm n BUG
Worm n BUG BAD
Worm n MECH
Worm v BUG MEDC
Worm v FALS
Worm n BUG SICK
Wormed v BUG MEDC
Wormed v FALS
Worming v BUG MEDC
Worming v FALS
Wormwood n BUG VEGT
Worn v GARB
Worn v TRIV
Worn v EVER
Worn v HAVE
Worn v WEAK PANG
Wornout j TRIV
Wornout j WEAK PANG
Worry v PANG
Worse j BAD
Worship v FOND HOLY
Worst j BAD
Worth n CRUX GOOD
Worthless j TRIV
Worthwhile j CRUX GOOD
Would v NSCR
Wound v VARY
Wound v DAMG
Wound v VARY GO
Wound v VARY END
Wounded v DAMG
Wounding v DAMG
Wounds v DAMG
Wove v VARY GO
Wove v JOIN
Wow i EMPH
Wow n POWR GOOD
Wrangle v AGGR TALK
Wrangle v ANML BLOK
Wrap n COVR
Wrap n GARB
Wrapped v COVR
Wrath n AGGR
Wreath n FORM VEGT
Wreath n HOLW FORM
Wreathe v VARY FORM
Wreathing v VARY FORM
Wreck v DAMG
Wren n ANML UP

Wrench n WORK
Wrench n DAMG
Wrenched v DAMG
Wrenches n WORK
Wrenches v DAMG
Wrenching v DAMG
Wrest v DAMG SEP
Wrestle v DAMG JOIN
Wretch n BAD PANG
Wriggle v VARY
Wring v BLOK DAMG

Wring v BLOK FLOW
Wringer n BLOK MECH
Wrinkle v VARY
Wrist n BODY
Wristband n BODY HOLW
Wristwatch n MECH TIME
Writ n WRIT LAW
Write v WRIT
Writhe v VARY PANG
Writing v WRIT
Written v WRIT

Wrong j FALS
Wrong j BAD
Wrongdoing n BAD CRIM
Wrought j FORM
Wrought j PANG
Wrung v BLOK DAMG
Wrung v BLOK FLOW
Wry j VARY
Wry j FOOL

X

X n WRIT
X n WRIT FORM
Xenon n VAPR

Xenophobe n AGGR AFAR
Xerox v SIML WRIT
Xmas n HOLY TIME

Xray n MEDC ION
Xray n ION VIEW
Xylophone n MUSC

Y

Y n WRIT
Y n WRIT FORM
Yacht n FLOW VEHC
Yak n ANML
Yak v TALK
Yakked v TALK
Yam n FOOD VEGT
Yammer v TALK
Yank n QUIK
Yank n GRUP
Yanked v QUIK
Yankee n GRUP
Yanking v QUIK
Yap n ANML TALK
Yard n MSMT
Yard n PLAC
Yard n FORM
Yards n MSMT
Yards n PLAC
Yards n FORM
Yardstick n MSMT FORM
Yarn n FABR
Yarn n TALK MYTH
Yaw v VARY
Yawl n FLOW VEHC

Yawn v LARG OPEN
Yawn n BODY OPEN
Yea d AGRE
Yeah d AGRE
Year n TIME
Yearbook n WRIT TIME
Yearling n ANML YNG
Yearlong j EVER TIME
Yearly d TIME
Yearn v MOTV
Yeast n FOOD VEGT
Yegg n CRIM
Yell v HEAR TALK
Yellow j COLR
Yellow j COLR WEAK
Yelp n ANML TALK
Yen n MOTV
Yen n MONY
Yeoman n MALE
Yes d AGRE
Yeshiva n EDUC HOLY
Yesterday d PAST
Yet d NSCR
Yet d EVER
Yew n VEGT

Yiddish n TALK
Yield v AID
Yield v WEAK
Yip v ANML TALK
Yodel n TALK MUSC
Yoga n IDEA HOLY
Yoghurt n ANML FOOD
Yogi n IDEA HOLY
Yoke n JOIN FORM
Yokel n WEAK
Yolk n ANML FOOD
YomKippur n HOLY TIME
Yon d AFAR
Yonder d AFAR
Yore n PAST
You p HSCR
Young j YNG
Youngster n YNG
Your p HSCR
Youth n YNG
Yowl n ANML TALK
Yoyo n PLAY
Yule n PLAY HOLY
Yummy j GOOD

Z

Z n WRIT
Zany j FOOL
Zeal n MOTV
Zealot n MOTV
Zebra n ANML
Zen n HOLY
Zenith n UP
Zephyr n VAPR WEA
Zephyr n GARB
Zeppelin n VEHC UP
Zero n NUMR
Zero v SHRP
Zest n MOTV

Zeus n LEAD MYTH
Zigzag j VARY
Zigzag v VARY GO
Zinc n ERTH MTRL
Zinnia n VEGT
Zion n PLAC HOLY
Zip n POWR
Zip v QUIK GO
Zip v GARB JOIN
Zipped v QUIK GO
Zipped v GARB JOIN
Zipper n GARB JOIN
Zither n MUSC

Zodiac n ASTR MYTH
Zombie n DEAD MYTH
Zombie n SIP VEGT
Zone n PLAC
Zoo n ANML HOME
Zoological j ANML IDEA
Zoom v QUIK GO
Zoysia n VEGT
Zucchini n FOOD VEGT
Zwieback n FOOD
Zygote n BGIN SOMA

Parts of speech: a article; b preposition; c conjunction; f prefix; i interjection;
j adjective; n noun; p pronoun; r phrase; v verb.

4

category listing
of words

Categories are listed in alphabetic sequence in this section, and within each category, words are alphabetized. For each word there is a letter symbol for part of speech (explained by footnotes repeated at intervals throughout the text), and possibly one additional category. It is to be understood that a word receives the category under whose heading it appears, as well as the additional category, if any, shown.

Abnormal j OPPO
Abnormity n BAD
Abroad d
Accident n EVNT
Accidental j EVNT
Across b
Afar d
Aloof j SEP
Beyond b
Beyond n DEAD
Chance n EVNT
Curio n
Curios n
Curious j
Distance n
Distant j
Eccentric j
Eerie j PANG
Erratic j VARY
Esoteric j COVR
Exceptional j
Exotic j
Extraordinary j GOOD
Extraordinary j
Extrasensory j SOMA
Extreme j OPPO

Extreme j
Extremity n END
Fabulous j MYTH
Far d
Faraway j
Farfetched j FOOL
Farreaching j LARG
Farsighted j VIEW
Farther d
Fluke n AID
Foreign j
Fortuitous j EVNT
Freak n
Further d
Hap n EVNT
Hazard n EVNT
Hinterland n ERTH
Horizon n ASTR
Idiosyncrasy n SOLE
Improbable j
Incredible j
Infrequency n
Long j
Longer j
Longest j
Monster n BAD

Odd j
Oddball n FOOL
Outlandish j FOOL
Outlying j OUT
Oversea j FLOW
Past b
Peculiar j
Perchance d EVNT
Phenomenal j EVNT
Prodigious j POWR
Prodigy n POWR
Quaint j
Random n BLUR
Rare j
Rarely d
Rarity n
Remarkable j
Remote j
Scarce j
Seldom d
Singular j SOLE
Strange j
Superhuman j POWR
Supernatural j MYTH
Surprise n PANG
Transatlantic j FLOW

Ulterior j
Ultra j
Unaccustomed j
Unanticipated j
Uncanny j MYTH
Uncommon j
Unearthly j MYTH
Unexpected j
Unfamiliar j
Unforeseen j
Unheard j HEAR
Unique j SOLE
Unlikely j
Unnatural j OPPO
Unprecedented j
Unreal j MYTH
Unused j
Unusual j
Unwonted j
Utmost j
Weird j MYTH
Xenophobe n AGGR
Yon d
Yonder d

AGGR

Abhor v
Abjure v LACK
Abominable j
Abrasive n MTRL
Abrupt j QUIK
Abuse n
Accursed j BAD
Accuse v
Acid j
Acrid j
Acrid j SOMA
Acrimony n
Admonish v TALK
Affront v
Aggravate v PANG
Aggression n
Anathema n
Anger n
Anglophobe n PLAC
Angry j
Animadversion n TALK
Animosity n
Annoy v PANG
Antagonize v
Antipathy n
Argue v TALK
Arraign v LAW
Arrogant j POWR
Askance d VARY
Asperity n
Aspersion n TALK
Astringent j
Audacity n POWR

Austere j
Averse j
Aversion n
Bait v
Baleful j
Balk v
Beef v TALK
Beefed v TALK
Beefing v TALK
Beefs v TALK
Begrudge v
Belittle v LITL
Berate v TALK
Betray v FALS
Bicker v TALK
Bile n SOMA
Bird n TALK
Bitch v TALK
Bitched v TALK
Bitches v TALK
Bitching v TALK
Bitter j PANG
Bitterly d PANG
Black j COLR
Blackball v COLR
Blame v MOTV
Blunt j OPEN
Bluster v WEA
Bluster v TALK
Boil v HEAT
Boiled v HEAT
Boisterous j HEAR
Boo v TALK

Boos n TALK
Bother v PANG
Brat n YNG
Bridle v
Bristle v
Browbeat v
Brusque j
Bug v PANG
Bugged v PANG
Bugging v PANG
Bullheaded j BODY
Bumptious j
Burn v HEAT
Burning j HEAT
Busybody n MOTV
Buzzard n ANML
Callous j
Calumny n FALS
Cantankerous j
Captious j
Carp v TALK
Carped v TALK
Carping v TALK
Carps v TALK
Castigate v
Cattier j ANML
Catty j ANML
Caustic j
Cavalier j POWR
Caveat n
Cavil n TRIV
Censorious j
Censure v

Chafe v JOIN
Champ v FOOD
Champed v FOOD
Champing v FOOD
Charge n
Cheek n BODY
Chide v TALK
Choleric j PANG
Churl n
Coarse j
Codger n WEAK
Coerce v POWR
Cold j COLD
Comeback n TALK
Complain v PANG
Complaint n PANG
Condemn v
Conflict n
Contemn v
Contempt n
Contentious j
Contumacy n
Cool j COLD
Crab n PANG
Crabbed v PANG
Crabbier j PANG
Crabbing v PANG
Crabby j PANG
Crank n PANG
Crankiness n PANG
Cranks n PANG
Cranky j PANG
Critic n IDEA

Parts of speech: a article; b preposition; c conjunction; d adverb; f prefix; i interjection;
j adjective; n noun; p pronoun; r phrase; v verb.

Critical j IDEA
Criticism n IDEA
Cross j PANG
Crude j BAD
Crust n
Culpable j MOTV
Cur n ANML
Curs n ANML
Curse n BAD
Curt j LITL
Cynic n
Damn v BAD
Dander n
Deaf j HEAR
Decried v TALK
Decry v TALK
Defame v FALS
Defied v OPPO
Defile v DIRT
Defy v OPPO
Degrade v SUB
Dehumanize v BAD
Denounce v TALK
Denunciation n TALK
Deprecate v
Depreciate v
Deride v FOOL
Derision n FOOL
Derogate v
Despicable j BAD
Despise v
Despite n
Despot n LEAD
Detest v
Detract v
Detriment n
Devil v BAD
Diatribe n TALK
Dig n
Disagreeable j
Discord n
Discountenance v PANG
Discourage v PANG
Discourteous j
Discredit v BAD
Discriminate v
Disdain n
Disfavor n
Disgruntle v PANG
Disharmony n
Dishonor n BAD
Disinherit v SEP
Dislike v
Disloyal j FALS
Disobedient j
Disown v SEP
Disparage v
Displease v
Dispute n
Disrespect n
Disrupt v BLOK
Dissatisfy v
Disservice n
Distasteful j
Distemper n PANG

Distrust v
Dog v ANML
Dogged v ANML
Dogging v ANML
Dress v TALK
Dressed v TALK
Dresses v TALK
Dressing v TALK
Effrontery n
Embitter v PANG
Embroil v PANG
Emeries n MTRL
Emery n MTRL
Encroach v GO
Enemy n
Enmity n
Enrage v
Entrench v GO
Envious j MOTV
Envy v MOTV
Exacerbate v
Exasperate v PANG
Execrable j
Exploit v AID
Exploitation n AID
Exploited v AID
Exploiting v AID
Expostulate v IDEA
Faithless j
Faultfinding n FALS
Fine n MONY
Fined v MONY
Fines v MONY
Fining v MONY
Fishwife n LADY
Fix v
Flare v
Flout v
Foe n
Foment v BGIN
Forbidding j
Forewarn v FORW
Forswear v LACK
Fractious j
Fresh j
Fret v PANG
Frosty j COLD
Frown n
Frustrate v BLOK
Fume v PANG
Fuming v PANG
Furious j
Fury n
Gad v SHRP
Gadfly n BUG
Gaff n
Gaffed v
Gall n POWR
Gall v PANG
Galled v PANG
Galling v PANG
Galls v PANG
Gibe n TALK
Gibing v TALK
Glare n VIEW

Glower v VIEW
Gnash v
Grate v PANG
Grating v PANG
Grim j PANG
Grouch n PANG
Grouse v TALK
Growl n TALK
Grudge n
Gruff j
Grumble v TALK
Grumpy j PANG
Haggle v TALK
Harass v PANG
Hard j
Hardbitten j
Hardboiled j
Hardhearted j SOMA
Harsh j
Hate n
Hating v
Hatred n
Haughty j POWR
Hauteur n POWR
Haze v PANG
Hazed v PANG
Hazing v PANG
Heartless j
Heckle v TALK
Heel n BAD
Henpeck v SUB
Hex n MYTH
Hiss n TALK
Hoot n HEAR
Hostility n
Hound v
Hoyden n LADY
Huff n
Humiliate v WEAK
Hypercritical j
Icy j COLD
Impeach v LAW
Impeach v
Impertinence n TRIV
Impinge v JOIN
Implacable j EVER
Impolite j
Impose v POWR
Impudence n
Impugn v
Incense v PANG
Incivility n
Inclement j
Inconsiderate j
Indelicate j
Indict v LAW
Indignation n
Indignity n
Indurate j EVER
Inflame v HEAT
Inflammatory j HEAT
Infringe v
Infuriate v
Ingrate n
Ingratitude n

Inhospitable j
Inimical j
Insensate j REST
Insensitive j REST
Insolence n
Instigate v BGIN
Insubordinate j
Insult n
Intemperance n
Intemperance n MOTV
Intolerance n
Intractable j
Intransigent j
Intrusion n IN
Inure v EVER
Invective n TALK
Inveigh v TALK
Invidious j
Irascible j PANG
Irate j
Ire n
Irk v PANG
Ironic j FOOL
Ironies n FOOL
Irony n FOOL
Irreverence n BAD
Irritate v PANG
Jar v VARY
Jar v PANG
Jarred v VARY
Jarred v PANG
Jaundice v
Jaw v TALK
Jawed v TALK
Jawing v TALK
Jealous j
Jeer v TALK
Jilt v SEP
Kibitz v TALK
Knock v
Lampoon v FOOL
Leer n VIEW
Leering v VIEW
Libel v FALS
Loathe v PANG
Lower v
Lump n BULG
Lurch n
Mad j
Malcontent j PANG
Malevolence n BAD
Malice n BAD
Malign v BAD
Malignancy n BAD
Mean j BAD
Meddle v
Merciless j
Miff v
Militancy n
Misanthropy n
Miser n HAVE
Mistrust v BLUR
Misuse v FALS
Mob v GRUP
Mock v FOOL

Mockery n FOOL
Mocking v FOOL
Mocks v FOOL
Mordant j
Mortify v PANG
Nag v TALK
Nagged v TALK
Nastier j DIRT
Nasty j DIRT
Needle v SHRP
Needled v SHRP
Needling v SHRP
Neglect v LACK
Negligence n LACK
Nettle v PANG
Nettled v PANG
Nettling v PANG
Niggard n HAVE
Nosy j MOTV
Nuisance n PANG
Obduracy n EVER
Obloquy n TALK
Obnoxious j
Obstinacy n EVER
Obstreperous j HEAR
Odious j
Offend v
Offense n
Officious j
Opinionated j IDEA
Opprobrium n
Outburst n OUT
Overbearing j POWR
Overweening j POWR
Pan v
Panned v
Panning v
Paranoia n SICK
Peeve v PANG
Pejorative j BAD
Penalize v
Penalty n
Pepper v
Peremptory j POWR
Pesky j PANG
Pest n PANG
Pest n BUG
Pester v PANG
Pet n PANG
Petulance n PANG
Pigheaded j
Pillory v
Pique v
Pitiless j
Polemic n TALK
Pout n PANG
Proscribe v BLOK
Prosecute v LAW
Protest v
Provocation n MOTV

Provoke v MOTV
Quarrel n
Querulous j
Rabble n GRUP
Rabid j
Racism n GRUP
Rag v TALK
Rage n
Rail v TALK
Rancor n PANG
Rankle v PANG
Rant v TALK
Raspberry n HEAR
Rate v TALK
Rating v TALK
Raw j
Razz v TALK
Rebuff n
Rebuke n
Recalcitrant j
Refractory j
Reject v SEP
Relentless j EVER
Remonstrate v TALK
Renegade n
Renounce v LACK
Renunciation n LACK
Repel v SEP
Reprehend v TALK
Reprimand n TALK
Reprisal n
Reproach n TALK
Reproof n TALK
Reprove v TALK
Repugnance n PANG
Repulse v SEP
Resent v PANG
Retaliate v
Retort n TALK
Retorted v TALK
Retorting v TALK
Revile v TALK
Ride v
Ridicule n FOOL
Riding v
Rigor n
Rigorous j
Rile v PANG
Rip v SEP
Ripped v SEP
Rode v
Roil v
Rout n GRUP
Rub v
Rubbed v
Rubbing v
Rude j
Ruthless j
Salt n
Sarcasm n

Sardonic j
Sass v TALK
Satire n FOOL
Sauce n
Saucy j
Scab n WORK
Scabbed v WORK
Scabbing v WORK
Scathing j
Scoff v
Scold v TALK
Score v
Scorn n
Scout v
Scouted v
Scowl n
Scramble v GO
Screw v
Scurvy j BAD
Sedition n
Severe j
Sharp j SHRP
Shove v GO
Slander n FALS
Slight n LITL
Slighted v LITL
Slighting v LITL
Slur n TALK
Smear v DIRT
Smolder v HEAT
Snarl v TALK
Sneer n
Snide j
Snub v
Snubbed v
Sore j
Sour j PANG
Soured v PANG
Souring v PANG
Spat n
Spats n
Spite n
Spleen n SOMA
Splenetic j PANG
Spurn v
Squabble v
Squall v TALK
Squawk v TALK
Stamp v HEAR
Stamped v HEAR
Stark j
Stern j
Stickler n TRIV
Stingy j HAVE
Stomp v HEAR
Strict j BLOK
Stubborn j EVER
Sulk v PANG
Sulking v PANG
Sulky d PANG

Sullen j PANG
Supercilious j POWR
Surly j
Suspect v BLUR
Suspicion n BLUR
Tantrum n PANG
Tart j
Tartar n
Taunt v TALK
Tax v
Taxing v
Tease v
Temper n
Testy j PANG
Thankless j
Thorn n SHRP
Thrash v VARY
Tirade n TALK
Tough j
Traitor n FALS
Treason n FALS
Trench v GO
Turbulent j
Turncoat n VARY
Tyranny n LEAD
Uncared j
Unceremonious j
Uncivil j BAD
Uncomplimentary j
Uncompromising j
Uncouth j
Unfaithful j
Unfavorable j
Unfeeling j
Unfriendly j
Ungrateful j
Unkind j
Unloved j
Unmannerly d BAD
Unmerciful j
Unpopular j GRUP
Unruly j
Unsavory j BAD
Unsavory j SOMA
Unsympathetic j
Untrustworthy j WEAK
Unwanted j
Unwelcome j
Upbraid v TALK
Vehement j
Vex v PANG
Vilify v BAD
Vituperate v TALK
Vulgar j BAD
Vulture n ANML
Warn v
Wrangle v TALK
Wrath n
Xenophobe n AFAR

Abide v EVER
Absolution n OPEN
Absolution n HOLY
Absolve v OPEN
Accede v
Accept v
Accession n
Acclaim v POWR
Accolade n POWR
Accord v AID
According v AID
Accredit v
Acknowledge v
Acquiesce v
Adhere v JOIN
Adhesion n JOIN
Admissible j
Admission n
Admit v
Adopt v HAVE
Adopt v
Advocate n
Affirmative j
Agree v
Agreeable j
Allegiance n JOIN
Alliance n JOIN
Allied j JOIN
Allies n JOIN
Allow v
Allowance n
Allright d
Ally n JOIN
Alright d
Amen i HOLY
Amenable j
Amnesty n OPEN
Apology n IDEA
Applause n HEAR
Approbation n
Approve v
Arrange v
Assent v
Atone v
Atonement n HOLY
Atonement n
Authorize v LEAD
Avow v TALK
Axis n JOIN
Aye d
Bargain n MART
Bear v
Bearing v
Belief n IDEA
Believe v IDEA
Bipartisan j MOTV
Bore v
Borne v
Brook v
Brooked v
Brooking v
Cede v AID
Ceding v AID
Cheer n TALK
Cheering v TALK

Clap n HEAR
Clapped v HEAR
Claque n GRUP
Clear v OPEN
Collaborate v JOIN
Commend v
Commit v MOTV
Committed v MOTV
Compact n
Compliance n
Complied v
Compliment n
Comply v
Compound v
Compromise v
Concede v
Concede v WEAK
Concede v AID
Concert n
Concerted j
Concession n
Concession n WEAK
Concession n AID
Conciliate v
Concord n
Concur v
Condescend v LEAD
Condition n CRUX
Conditional j CRUX
Condone v
Confess v
Confess v HOLY
Confessing v
Confessing v HOLY
Confirm v TRUE
Congenial j
Connive v BAD
Consensus n
Consent v
Consign v AID
Conspire v JOIN
Contract n
Contract n WRIT
Contracting v
Contractor n WORK
Contractor n
Contractual j
Convention n GRUP
Conventional j GRUP
Conviction n IDEA
Convince v IDEA
Coop n AID
Cooperate v AID
Countenance v BODY
Covenant n
Credence n IDEA
Credit n
Credo n IDEA
Credulous j IDEA
Creed n IDEA
Deal n
Deals n
Dedicate v
Defer v SUB
Deference n SUB

Deign v LEAD
Disarm v
Eclat n
Endorse v WRIT
Entente n GRUP
Entitle v MOTV
Espouse v JOIN
Eulogy n TALK
Euphony n HEAR
Exculpate v OPEN
Excuse v IDEA
Excuse v OPEN
Exonerate v OPEN
Expiate v
Exponent n
Extol v
Faith n
Faith n HOLY
Fall v
Falling v
Felicitous j GLAD
Fell v
Fidelity n
Follow v SUB
For b MOTV
Forgive v
Grateful j AID
Gratify v AID
Gratitude n AID
Guaranty n AID
Hail v TALK
Hails v TALK
Hand n BODY
Heed v
Hi i
Hobnob v NEAR
Homage n
Hosanna i HOLY
Imprimatur n WRIT
Indulge v AID
Laud v GOOD
League n GRUP
Lean v MOTV
Leaned v MOTV
Leaning v MOTV
Leans v MOTV
Let v
Letting v
License n WRIT
Loyal j
Negotiate v
Nod v
Obedience n SUB
Obey v SUB
Oblige v MOTV
Observation n
Observe v
Observing v
OK j
Okay j
Pact n
Pardon v
Pardon v OPEN
Parole n TALK
Partisan j MOTV

Pass v
Passable j
Passage n
Passed v
Passes v
Passing v
Permission n
Permit v
Permit n WRIT
Permitted v
Personable j SOLE
Piquancy n SOMA
Plaudit n HEAR
Plausible j IDEA
Pledge n
Plight v
Plug n AID
Plugged v AID
Popular j GRUP
Positive j
Positively d
Praise v
Prearrangement n FORW
Pro n
Profess v TALK
Profession n TALK
Promise n
Promissory j
Proponent n
Pros n
Proselyte n
Protagonist n
Proviso n
Rapprochement n
Ratify v
Receive v
Reception n JOIN
Receptive j
Recognition n NEAR
Recommend v
Reconcile v
Remission n
Remit v
Resolution n END
Resolve v END
Respect n FOND
Respected v FOND
Respectful j FOND
Respecting v FOND
Roger n
Root v TALK
Salute v
Sanction v
Satisfaction n AID
Satisfied v AID
Satisfy v AID
Seal v
Sealed v
Sealing v
Second n NUMR
Seconded v NUMR
Seconding v NUMR
Settle v
Settlement n
Side n

Siding v
Sociable j GRUP
Socialize v GRUP
Stand v
Standing v
Stipulate v
Stood v
Subcontract v MART
Subscribe v

Subscribe v MONY
Subscription n MONY
Suffer v
Support v
Supported v
Supporter n
Team n GRUP
Teamwork n GRUP
Term n

Testament n TALK
Tolerance n
Treaties n
Treaty n
Unanimous j WHOL
Uncritical j
Vouchsafe v AID
Vow v TALK
Vowed v TALK

Willing j MOTV
Witting j MOTV
Word n TALK
Yea d
Yeah d
Yes d

AID

Abet v
Abutment n FORM
Accessory n SUB
Accomodate v SIML
Accomplice n CRIM
Accord v AGRE
According v AGRE
Accouterment n GARB
Acolyte n HOLY
Ad n PLAY
Adjutant n
Administer v
Advance v FORW
Advantage n
Advice n IDEA
Advise v IDEA
Aegis n
Afford v
Agency n
Agent n
Aid v
Aid n
Aliment n FOOD
Alimentary j FOOD
Alleviate v
Allocate v SOME
Allot v SOME
Alms n
Altruism n GOOD
Ameliorate v
Amend n
Amulet n MYTH
Anaclitic j
Ancillary j SUB
Anodyne n GLAD
Appeal n MOTV
Appease v GLAD
Apportion v SOME
Armature n DAMG
Armor n DAMG
Asset n CRUX
Assist v
Assuage v GLAD
Assure v
Asylum n
Attend v JOIN
Attendant n
Attendant n JOIN
Auspice n LEAD
Auspicious j

Auxiliary j SUB
Auxiliary n GRUP
Avail v
Award n POWR
Award n
Babied v YNG
Babies v YNG
Baby v YNG
Babying v YNG
Back v BACK
Bandage v COVR
Bank v
Bartender n SIP
Behalf n
Behind b BACK
Benediction n HOLY
Beneficial j
Beneficiary n HAVE
Benefit n
Benevolent j GOOD
Benign j GOOD
Bequeath v
Bestow v
Better v
Betterment n
Bifocal j VIEW
Big j LARG
Black n COLR
Bless v HOLY
Bodyguard n DAMG
Bolster v
Bolstered v
Bolstering v
Bonus n MONY
Boost v
Bounty n MUCH
Brace n
Break n
Bridesmaid n LADY
Brownie n MYTH
Buffer n
Bulwark n FORM
Bumper n DAMG
Busboy n MALE
Butler n MALE
Buttress n FORM
Caddy n PLAY
Caddy n FURN
Cane n FORM
Capitalize v

Care n
Cared v
Careful j MOTV
Cares v
Caretaker n WORK
Carhop n VEHC
Caring v
Carried v
Carry v
Cater v
Cater v FOOD
Caution n MOTV
Cede v AGRE
Ceding v AGRE
Chambermaid n LADY
Champion n POWR
Chaperone v JOIN
Charity n GOOD
Chauffeur n VEHC
Chip v
Chipped v
Chipping v
Circumspect j MOTV
Clemency n GOOD
Clew n OPEN
Clue n OPEN
Coddle v FOND
Collateral n MART
Comfort v GLAD
Comforted v GLAD
Commodious j LARG
Commodity n
Commonweal n WHOL
Compost n MTRL
Concede v AGRE
Concession n MART
Concession n AGRE
Concierge n OPEN
Condition v
Conditioned v
Conditioning v
Conduce v
Confer v
Conference n
Conservation n EVER
Conservator n EVER
Conserve v EVER
Considerate j GOOD
Consideration n GOOD
Consign v AGRE

Console v GLAD
Consoled v GLAD
Consoling v GLAD
Constructive j
Consult v IDEA
Contribute v
Contribute v MONY
Convenience n
Coop n AGRE
Cooperate v AGRE
Counsel n IDEA
Counsel n LAW
Count v CRUX
Counted v CRUX
Counting v CRUX
Cover v
Coverage n
Covert n COVR
Cradle n FORM
Creche n YNG
Crutch n FORM
Cue n IDEA
Culture n
Curable j MEDC
Curative j MEDC
Curator n LEAD
Cure n MEDC
Curing v MEDC
Custodian n WORK
Custodian n HAVE
Custody n HAVE
Defend v
Defense n
Deliver v OPEN
Deliverance n OPEN
Depend v
Depend v SUB
Dependability n
Develop v VARY
Dispensation n
Dispensation n OPEN
Dispense v
Dispensing v
Distribute v
Distributor n
Dole v
Doling v
Domestic n HOME
Donate v
Donor n

Parts of speech: a article; b preposition; c conjunction; d adverb; f prefix; i interjection;
j adjective; n noun; p pronoun; r phrase; v verb.

Doorkeeper n OPEN	Footing n BODY	Guy n	Intervene v SEP
Doorman n MALE	Footman n MALE	Guyed v	Invocation n MOTV
Dot n MONY	Foots v BODY	Guying v	Invoke v MOTV
Dowry n MONY	Fortify v POWR	Habilitate v	Janitor n WORK
Dress v	Fortunate j	Hairdo n BODY	Keep v EVER
Dressed v	Fortune n	Hairdresser n BODY	Keeps v EVER
Dresser n	Fortune n END	Hand n BODY	Kept v EVER
Dresses v	Forward v FORW	Handbook n WRIT	Kind j GOOD
Dressing v	Forwarded v FORW	Handed v BODY	Kinder j GOOD
Dumbwaiter n MECH	Forwarding v FORW	Handing v BODY	Kindest j GOOD
Edit v WRIT	Forwards v FORW	Handle n BULG	Kindhearted j GOOD
Editing v WRIT	Foster v	Handmaid n LADY	Kindliness n GOOD
Editor n WRIT	Fructify v BGIN	Hands v BODY	Kindly d GOOD
Eke v	Fruitful j VEGT	Handyman n WORK	Kit n
Embattle v DAMG	Fruition n END	Harbor n FLOW	Lean v
Emissary n	Fulcrum n	Harbor v HOME	Leaned v
Employ v	Fulfill v	Harmless j TRIV	Leaning v
Employed v	Furnish v	Harness n	Leans v
Encourage v	Further v	Haven n HOME	Lee n WEA
Endow v HAVE	Furthered v	Heal v MEDC	Legacy n LAW
Enlist v	Furthering v	Health n MEDC	Lend v
Enrich v GOOD	Furthers v	Hearten v POWR	Leniency n EASY
Ensure v SHRP	Gamekeeper n ANML	Helmet n GARB	Lent v
Entrust v FOND	Gave v	Help n	Liberal j OPEN
Equip v	Gear n	Help n WORK	Lifebuoy n FLOW
Equipment n	Generosity n GOOD	Hitch v GO	Lifegiving j LIVE
Equipment n HAVE	Generous j GOOD	Hitched v GO	Lifeline n LIVE
Errand n GO	Gift n	Hitchhike v GO	Lifesaver n LIVE
Escort v JOIN	Gift n POWR	Hospitable j GOOD	Lift n UP
Exercise v	Gifted j POWR	Hospitality n GOOD	Lift n GO
Exorcise v BAD	Gird v	Host n	Livelihood n LIVE
Expediency n	Girded v	Hosted v	Living n LIVE
Expedite v QUIK	Give v	Hostess n LADY	Loan n
Expediting v QUIK	Glass n VIEW	Hosting v	Loan n MONY
Expedition n QUIK	Glasses n VIEW	Housekeeper n HOME	Logistic j
Exploit v AGGR	Goatherd n ANML	Humane j GOOD	Lorgnette n VIEW
Exploit v	Godmother n LADY	Humanism n GOOD	Lotion n FLOW
Exploitation n AGGR	Goggles n VIEW	Humanitarian n GOOD	Luck n
Exploited v AGGR	Grace n GOOD	Humanity n GOOD	Ma n LADY
Exploited v	Graced v GOOD	Humanize v GOOD	Magnanimity n GOOD
Exploiting v AGGR	Graceful j GOOD	Husband v	Maid n LADY
Exploiting v	Gracing v GOOD	Husbanded v	Mail n DAMG
Extend v	Gracious j GOOD	Husbanding v	Mainstay n CRUX
Extension n	Grandma n LADY	Husbandry n	Maintain v EVER
Extra n PLAY	Grandmother n LADY	Immune j MEDC	Maintenance n EVER
Facilitate v	Grant n	Immune j OPEN	Majordomo n LEAD
Facility n	Grateful j AGRE	Impart v	Mamma n LADY
Factor n MART	Gratify v AGRE	Imparting v	Mammy n LADY
Favor n FOND	Gratis d	Implement v	Man v
Favoring v FOND	Gratitude n AGRE	Improve v GOOD	Manned v
Feasibility n	Gratuities n MONY	Improving v GOOD	Mans v
Fed v	Gratuitous j OPEN	Indemnify v MONY	Marcel v BODY
Feed v	Gratuity n MONY	Indemnity v	Mascot n
Feedback n BACK	Gravy n	Indemnity n MONY	Massage v BODY
Fend v BLOK	Groom v	Indulge v AGRE	Masseur n MALE
Fender n BLOK	Groomed v	Innocuous j TRIV	Masseuse n LADY
Fertilize v BGIN	Grooming v	Inoffensive j TRIV	Mater n LADY
Fiduciary n	Guaranty n AGRE	Instrument n	Maternal j LADY
Fireproof j HEAT	Guard n BLOK	Instrument n MECH	Matron n LADY
Fix v	Guardian n	Insure v MART	Means n
Flameproof j HEAT	Guarding v BLOK	Insure v	Measure n
Fledge v POWR	Guest n JOIN	Intact j WHOL	Media n
Fluke n AFAR	Guidance n LEAD	Intercede v	Mediate v
Foot v BODY	Guide n LEAD	Interdependence n JOIN	Medium n
Foothold n BODY	Guidebook n WRIT	Intermediary n JOIN	Mend v

Merciful j GOOD
Mercy n GOOD
Middleman n
Mind v
Minister v
Ministered v
Ministering v
Misguide v FALS
Mitigate v EASY
Mnemonic j IDEA
Mom n LADY
Monocle n VIEW
Mother n LADY
Motherinlaw n LADY
Mulch n VEGT
Nourish v FOOD
Nurse n LADY
Nurse n MEDC
Nursery n VEGT
Nurture v
Nutrient j FOOD
Nutriment n FOOD
Nutrition n FOOD
Oar n FLOW
Oasis n ERTH
Offer n
Office n
Opportunity n
Orderly n
Outfit v
Outpost n OUT
Overcareful j MOTV
Overcautious j MOTV
Overdependent j SUB
Overhaul v
Overindulge v LARG
Page n YNG
Paid v
Painstaking j MOTV
Pamper v
Pander v BAD
Paraphernalia n
Parasite n SUB
Patch n COVR
Patrol v GO
Patron n LEAD
Patron n MART
Pave v PATH
Pavement n PATH
Pay v
Payoff n
Peacemaker n GLAD
Pedestal n FORM
Philanthropy n GOOD
Picket n DAMG
Pier n FORM
Pillar n FORM
Pincenez n VIEW
Placate v GLAD
Plug n AGRE
Plugged v AGRE
Plus n
Pompadour n BODY
Porter n GO
Practical j

Pragmatism n EVNT
Precaution n MOTV
Premium n
Premium n MONY
Prep j EDUC
Prepare v
Prescription n LEAD
Present n
Presentation n
Presented v
Presenting v
Presents v
Prime v
Primed v
Primer n
Primes v
Priming v
Privilege n MOTV
Privy j MOTV
Prize v POWR
Proffer v
Profit n
Promote v FORW
Prompt v
Prompted v
Prompting v
Prompts v
Promulgate v OPEN
Prop n
Prophylaxis n MEDC
Propitiate v GLAD
Propitious j
Propped v
Propping v
Prosper v
Prosthesis n BODY
Protect v
Protege n SUB
Provide v
Provided v
Providence n
Providing v
Provision n
Publicspirited j GRUP
Quarter n
Quartermaster n LEAD
Quell v GLAD
Rampart n BLOK
Ransom v MONY
Ransom v
Readied v
Ready j
Rear v
Reared v
Rearing v
Reassure v
Reclaim v
Recourse n
Recruit v
Redeem v HAVE
Redeem v
Redound v LARG
Redress n
Refresh v
Refreshment n FOOD

Refuge n
Rehabilitate v
Reinforce v POWR
Rejuvenate v NEW
Reliable j
Reliance n
Relied v
Relief n
Relies v
Relieve v
Rely v
Remedy n MEDC
Render v
Renovate v NEW
Repair v
Repairman n WORK
Reprieve n
Rescue v
Resort n
Resource n
Restore v
Reward n
Rig n
Safe j
Safe n HOLW
Safeguard n
Safety n
Safety n MECH
Sake n
Salubrious j MEDC
Salutary j MEDC
Salvage v
Salvation n
Salve n
Salve n MTRL
Samaritan n GOOD
Sanctuary n HOLY
Sated j BULG
Satiate v BULG
Satiety n BULG
Satisfaction n AGRE
Satisfied v AGRE
Satisfy v AGRE
Save v
Saving v
Second n NUMR
Seconded v NUMR
Seconding v NUMR
Secure j
Security n
Selfdefense n SOLE
Selfless j GOOD
Selfpreservation n SOLE
Sentinel n DAMG
Sentry n DAMG
Servant n SUB
Serve v
Service n
Service n DAMG
Serviced v
Servicing v
Serving v
Set v
Setting v
Sexton n HOLY

Shed v
Shelter n HOME
Shepherd n ANML
Shield n
Shield n GARB
Shore v
Shower n PLAY
Size v MTRL
Slake v FLOW
Sling n
Solace v GLAD
Soothe v GLAD
Sop n TRIV
Spare v
Spared v
Sparing v
Spectacles n VIEW
Spoil v BAD
Spoils v BAD
Staff n GRUP
Stay n
Stead n
Stepmother n LADY
Steward n LEAD
Stewardess n LADY
Strut n JOIN
Submission n
Submit v
Subsidies n
Subsidies n MONY
Subsidize v MONY
Subsidy n
Subsidy n MONY
Subvene v
Supplied v SOME
Supply n SOME
Supply v
Support v
Supported v
Supporter n
Supporter n GARB
Sustain v
Sustenance n
Temper v GLAD
Tempering v GLAD
Tend v
Tended v
Tender v
Tendered v
Tendering v
Thank v FOND
Thanks n FOND
Thanksgiving n TIME
Therapy n MEDC
Through b
Tide v
Tided v
Tiding v
Tip n
Tips v
Tonic j
Tow v GO
Towed v GO
Train v
Trained v

Treat v	Unscathed j	Vest v	Warranted v TRUE
Treat v MEDC	Unselfish j GOOD	Vested v	Warranting v TRUE
Treating v	Untreated j LACK	Vesting v	Warranty n TRUE
Treating v MEDC	Upbringing n UP	Vigilance n QUIK	Wary j MOTV
Treatment n	Upheld v	Visa n WRIT	Watch v VIEW
Treatment n MEDC	Uphold v	Vitamin n FOOD	Watchdog n ANML
Trust n FOND	Upkeep n	Volunteer n MOTV	Watchman n VIEW
Trust n MONY	Use v	Vouchsafe v AGRE	Welfare n
Turn n VARY	Used v	Wait v	Wherewithal n
Umbrella n COVR	Useful j	Waited v	Windfall n WEA
Unction n	Usher v	Waiter n MALE	Windshield n VIEW
Undamaged j	Using v	Waitress n LADY	Yield v
Underwrite v WRIT	Utility n	Ward n	
Unharmed j	Utilize v	Warily d MOTV	
Unlimber v	Valet n MALE	Warrant n TRUE	

ANML

Adder n	Beaked j BODY	Bulling v POWR	Charger n
Aerie n HOME	Bear n	Bulls n MALE	Chat n UP
Airedale n	Beast n	Bulls v POWR	Cheddar n FOOD
Albatross n UP	Beast n BAD	Bunny n	Cheep n TALK
Alligator n FLOW	Beaver n	Burro n	Cheese n FOOD
Alligator n FABR	Beaver n FABR	Bush n BODY	Cheeseburger n FOOD
Alpaca n	Beef n FOOD	Butter n FOOD	Cheetah n
Alpaca n FABR	Beefier j FOOD	Buttermilk n SIP	Chick n YNG
Ambergris n MTRL	Beefsteak n FOOD	Buzzard n UP	Chicken n UP
Anaconda n	Beefy j FOOD	Buzzard n AGGR	Chicken n FOOD
Anchovy n FLOW	Beige n FABR	Cabob n FOOD	Chicken n WEAK
Angora n FABR	Bestial j BAD	Cackle n TALK	Chickened v WEAK
Animal n	Bill n BODY	Calf n YNG	Chickening v WEAK
Anteater n	Billygoat n MALE	Calf n FABR	Chihuahua n
Antelope n	Bird n UP	Calve v BGIN	Chimpanzee n
Antenna n BODY	Birds n UP	Calved v BGIN	Chinchilla n
Anthropoid n	Bitch n LADY	Calves n YNG	Chinchilla n FABR
Antler n BODY	Bitches n LADY	Calves v BGIN	Chipmunk n
Ape n	Blackbird n UP	Calving v BGIN	Chirp v TALK
Ape v FOOL	Bleat v TALK	Camel n	Chop n FOOD
Apish j	Bloodhound n SOMA	Canary n UP	Chops n FOOD
Apish j FOOL	Blubber n SOMA	Canine n	Chow n
Aquiline j UP	Bluebird n UP	Capon n FOOD	Chuck n FOOD
Armadillo n	Bluefish n FLOW	Cardinal n UP	Cinch n GARB
Asinine j FOOL	Bluejay n UP	Cardinals n UP	Clam n FLOW
Asp n DAMG	Boar n	Caribou n	Clam v BLOK
Ass n	Bobcat n	Carnassial j BODY	Clammed v FLOW
Ass n FOOL	Bobolink n UP	Carnivorous j FOOD	Clammed v BLOK
Asses n	Bobwhite n UP	Carp n FLOW	Clamming v FLOW
Asses n FOOL	Bossy n LADY	Cashmere n FABR	Clamming v BLOK
Auk n UP	Bovine j	Castor n GARB	Clod n FOOD
Aviary n HOME	Bowwow n TALK	Castor n MTRL	Cluck v TALK
Baa n TALK	Boxer n	Cat n	Clutch n BGIN
Bacon n FOOD	Bray n TALK	Catbird n UP	Coat n BODY
Baloney n FOOD	Bristle n MTRL	Catcall n TALK	Cobra n
Bark n TALK	Broiler n FOOD	Catfish n FLOW	Cock n MALE
Barn n HOME	Bronco n	Catgut n MTRL	Cockandbull j FOOL
Barns n HOME	Brush n BODY	Cattier j AGGR	Cockle n FLOW
Barnyard n HOME	Buck n MALE	Cattle n	Cockpit n DAMG
Bass n FLOW	Buff n FABR	Catty j AGGR	Cocks n MALE
Bat n UP	Buffalo n	Cavalier n DAMG	Cocktail n
Bay v TALK	Buffalo v FALS	Cavalry n DAMG	Cod n FLOW
Bayed v TALK	Bull n MALE	Caw n TALK	Collie n
Baying v TALK	Bull v POWR	Centaur n MYTH	Colt n YNG
Bays v TALK	Bulldog n	Cervine j	Comb n BODY
Beagle n	Bulled v POWR	Chanticleer n MALE	Condor n UP
Beak n BODY	Bullfight n DAMG	Chap n BODY	Conger n FLOW

Constrictor n BLOK	Dickey n	Flicker n UP	Hamburger n FOOD
Coo v TALK	Dinosaur n	Flipper n BODY	Hammerhead n FLOW
Coon n	Dobbin n	Flock n GRUP	Hamster n
Coop n HOME	Doe n LADY	Flounder n FLOW	Hangbird n UP
Copperhead n	Does n LADY	Fluke n FLOW	Hardhead n FLOW
Coral n FLOW	Dog n	Foal n YNG	Hare n
Cornu n BODY	Dog n BAD	Fold n GRUP	Harrier n
Coronet n BODY	Dog v AGGR	Fold n HOME	Harrier n UP
Corral n HOME	Dogged v AGGR	Fowl n UP	Hatchery n BGIN
Cossack n DAMG	Dogging v AGGR	Fox n	Hawk n UP
Cote n HOME	Doghouse n HOME	Fox n FABR	Hedgehog n
Cottontail n	Dogleg n VARY	Fox v FALS	Heehaw n TALK
Cougar n	Dolphin n FLOW	Foxed v FALS	Heifer n YNG
Courser n QUIK	Donkey n	Foxhound n	Hen n LADY
Courser n UP	Donkey n FOOL	Foxing v FALS	Hennery n HOME
Covey n GRUP	Dories n FLOW	Frankfurter n FOOD	Herd n GRUP
Cow n LADY	Dory n FLOW	Fricassee n FOOD	Heron n UP
Cowbird n UP	Dove n UP	Frog n	Herring n FLOW
Cowboy n MALE	Drafthorse n WORK	Frog n HEAR	Hide n FABR
Cowcatcher n BLOK	Dragon n MYTH	Fryer n FOOD	Hind n LADY
Cowgirl n LADY	Drake n UP	Fur n FABR	Hind n FLOW
Cowhide n FABR	Dromedary n	Furry j BODY	Hippopotamus n
Cowpuncher n MALE	Drumstick n FOOD	Gabble v TALK	Hiss n TALK
Coyote n	Duck n UP	Game n FOOD	Hog n
Crab n FLOW	Duckbill n FLOW	Gamekeeper n AID	Hog n FOOD
Crab n ASTR	Duckling n YNG	Gander n UP	Hognose n
Crabbed v FLOW	Eagle n UP	Gazelle n	Hogwash n DIRT
Crabbing v FLOW	Eagle n MONY	Geese n UP	Homer n UP
Crackling n FOOD	Eel n FLOW	Gibbon n	Honk v TALK
Crane n UP	Egg n FOOD	Giblet n FOOD	Hoof n BODY
Crawfish n FLOW	Eggnog n SIP	Giraffe n	Hoot n TALK
Crayfish n FLOW	Egret n UP	Girth n GARB	Hooves n BODY
Cream n SIP	Elephant n	Gizzard n SOMA	Horn n BODY
Creamery n FOOD	Elephantine j LARG	Glutton n	Horn n MTRL
Creature n	Elk n	Gnu n	Horned j BODY
Creeper n UP	Elks n	Goat n	Horse n
Crest n BODY	Elks n GRUP	Goat n WEAK	Horse n FORM
Croak v TALK	Ermine n	Goatherd n AID	Horse n FOOL
Croaked v TALK	Ermine n FABR	Gobble v TALK	Horseback n BODY
Croaker n TALK	Ewe n LADY	Goldfish n FLOW	Horses n
Crocodile n FLOW	Falcon n UP	Goose n UP	Horses n FORM
Crop n FABR	Fang n BODY	Goose n FOOD	Horses v FOOL
Crop n BODY	Fauna n	Goose n FOOL	Horseshoe n GARB
Crow n UP	Fawn n YNG	Gopher n	Horsing v FOOL
Crow v TALK	Feather n BODY	Gorilla n	Hotdog n FOOD
Crustacean n FLOW	Feline j	Gorilla n DAMG	Hound n
Cub n YNG	Ferret n	Gosling n YNG	Howl n TALK
Cubbed v YNG	Ferret v OPEN	Grackle n UP	Hummingbird n UP
Cuckoo n UP	Fetlock n BODY	Grenadier n FLOW	Hunt v DAMG
Cuckoo n TALK	Filet n FOOD	Griffin n MYTH	Huskies n
Cur n AGGR	Fillet n FOOD	Grizzly n COLR	Husky n
Curr v TALK	Fillies n	Grouse n UP	Hyena n
Curs n AGGR	Filly n YNG	Guano n MTRL	Ibex n
Cutlet n FOOD	Fin n BODY	Gull n UP	Ibis n UP
Dace n FLOW	Finch n UP	Guppy n FLOW	Ivory n MTRL
Dachshund n	Fish n FLOW	Hack n WEAK	Jackal n
Dairy j FOOD	Fished v FLOW	Hackle n BODY	Jackal n SUB
Dalmatian n PLAC	Fishier j FALS	Hackney n	Jackass n
Dam n LADY	Fishy j FLOW	Haddock n FLOW	Jackass n FOOL
Dams n LADY	Fishy j FALS	Hagfish n FLOW	Jackrabbit n
Dane n PLAC	Flamingo n UP	Haggard n UP	Jade n WEAK
Dapple n COLR	Flank n BODY	Hake n FLOW	Jaguar n
Darter n FLOW	Flatfish n FLOW	Halcyon n UP	Jay n UP
Daw n UP	Fleece n FABR	Halibut n FLOW	Jellyfish n FLOW
Deer n	Fleece v SHRP	Ham n FOOD	Jellyfish n WEAK

Jersey n PLAC	Martin n UP	Pachyderm n	Possum n
Jockey n PLAY	Mask n BODY	Pack n GRUP	Possum n FALS
Kabob n FOOD	Mastiff n	Packrat n	Poultry n FOOD
Kangaroo n	Matador n DAMG	Palomino n COLR	Pound n HOME
Kennel n HOME	Maverick n OPPO	Panda n	Prawn n FLOW
Kennel n GRUP	Meat n FOOD	Panther n	Primate n
Kid n YNG	Menagerie n HOME	Parakeet n UP	Proboscis n BODY
Kid n FABR	Meow v TALK	Parmesan n FOOD	Pug n
Kidney n FOOD	Mew n TALK	Parrot n UP	Pullet n YNG
Kipper n FLOW	Mice n	Partridge n UP	Punch v GRUP
Kite n UP	Mice n WEAK	Pastern n BODY	Punched v GRUP
Kitten n YNG	Milch j SIP	Pastrami n FOOD	Punching v GRUP
Kitties n YNG	Milk n SIP	Patent j FABR	Pup n YNG
Kitty n YNG	Mink n	Paw n BODY	Puppies n YNG
Koala n	Mink n FABR	Peacock n UP	Puppy n YNG
Lair n HOME	Minnow n FLOW	Peep n TALK	Purr n TALK
Lamb n YNG	Moccasin n	Pekingese n	Puss n
Lamb n FOOD	Mohair n FABR	Pelican n UP	Pussy n
Lamb n FABR	Mole n	Pelt n FABR	Python n
Lanolin n MTRL	Mollusk n FLOW	Pen n HOME	Quack n TALK
Lard n MTRL	Mongoose n	Penguin n FLOW	Quail n UP
Larded v MTRL	Mongrel n TRIV	Perch n FLOW	Quarter n BODY
Lark n UP	Monkey n	Pet n FOND	Quill n BODY
Layer n BGIN	Monkey v FOOL	Petrel n UP	Rabbit n
Lean n FOOD	Moo v TALK	Pheasant n UP	Rabbit n FABR
Leather n FABR	Moose n	Pheasant n FOOD	Rabid j SICK
Lemming n	Morocco n FABR	Phoebe n UP	Rabies n SICK
Lemur n	Mount n UP	Phoenix n MYTH	Raccoon n
Leo n MALE	Mouse n	Pickerel n FLOW	Raccoon n FABR
Leonine j	Mouse n WEAK	Pig n	Racer n
Leopard n	Mouse v BLOK	Pig n BAD	Ram n MALE
Leopardess n LADY	Moused v BLOK	Pigeon n UP	Rams n MALE
Lion n	Mousing v BLOK	Pigeonhole n HOLW	Rat n
Lion n POWR	Mule n	Pigskin n FABR	Rat n BAD
Lioness n LADY	Musk n SOMA	Pike n FLOW	Ratted v BAD
Lionize v POWR	Muskrat n	Pillion n REST	Rattlesnake n HEAR
Litter n YNG	Muskrat n FABR	Pintail n UP	Raven n UP
Liver n FOOD	Mussel n FLOW	Pinto n COLR	Rawhide n FABR
Liverwurst n FOOD	Mustang n	Pip v TALK	Ray n FLOW
Livestock n GRUP	Mutt n TRIV	Pipped v TALK	Reindeer n
Lizard n	Mutton n FOOD	Pipping v TALK	Reptile n
Lizard n FABR	Muzzle n BODY	Pips n TALK	Rhesus n
Llama n	Mynah n UP	Platypus n FLOW	Rhinoceros n
Lobo n	Nag n	Plover n UP	Roar n TALK
Lobster n FLOW	Neigh n TALK	Plug n WEAK	Robin n UP
Loon n UP	Nest n HOME	Plumage n BODY	Rodent n
Low v TALK	Nestling n YNG	Plume n BODY	Rodeo n PLAY
Lynx n	Nightingale n UP	Pluming n BODY	Rook n UP
Macaw n UP	Nutcracker n UP	Poach v CRIM	Roost n HOME
Mackerel n FLOW	Nutria n MTRL	Pod n GRUP	Rooster n UP
Magpie n UP	Ocelot n	Polecat n	Rump n FOOD
Mallard n UP	Octopus n FLOW	Polliwog n FLOW	Rustle v CRIM
Mammal n	Opossum n	Pomeranian n	Rustler n CRIM
Mammoth n	Orangutan n	Pony n	Rut n SEX
Mane n BODY	Oriole n UP	Pooch n	Sable n
Mare n LADY	Ornithology n UP	Poodle n	Sable n FABR
Marlin n FLOW	Osprey n UP	Porcine j	Saddle n REST
Marmoset n	Ostrich n	Porcupine n	Saddle n BODY
Marmot n	Otter n	Porgy n FLOW	Saddle n FABR
Marsupial j	Owl n UP	Pork n FOOD	Salamander n FLOW
Marten n	Ox n	Porpoise n FLOW	Salamander n MYTH
Marten n FABR	Oyster n FLOW	Porterhouse n FOOD	Salami n FOOD

Parts of speech: a article; b preposition; c conjunction; d adverb; f prefix; i interjection;
j adjective; n noun; p pronoun; r phrase; v verb.

Salmon n FLOW
Sandpiper n UP
Sardine n FLOW
Saurian n
Sausage n FOOD
Scale n BODY
Scallop n FLOW
Scapegoat n WEAK
Scarecrow n PANG
Schnauzer n
Schnitzel n FOOD
Seal n FLOW
Seal n FABR
Sealing v FLOW
Setter n
Shad n FLOW
Shark n FLOW
Shark n FALS
Sheep n
Sheep n WEAK
Sheep n FABR
Sheepskin n FABR
Shell n BODY
Shellfish n FLOW
Shepherd n AID
Shiner n FLOW
Shrimp n FLOW
Sirloin n FOOD
Skate n FLOW
Skunk n
Skunk n FABR
Skunk n BAD
Sloth n REST
Snail n REST
Snail n FOOD
Snake n

Snake n BAD
Snake n WORK
Snake v GO
Snaked v GO
Snaking v GO
Snipe n UP
Snout n BODY
Sole n FLOW
Sow n LADY
Spaniel n
Sparrow n UP
Squawk v TALK
Squirrel n
Squirrel n FABR
Stable n HOME
Stabled v HOME
Stables n HOME
Stabling v HOME
Stag n MALE
Stall n HOME
Stallion n MALE
Starfish n FLOW
Starling n UP
Steak n FOOD
Steer n MALE
Stock n
Stock n FOOD
Suede n FABR
Swallow n UP
Swan n UP
Swine n
Swine n BAD
Swordfish n FLOW
Tabbies n
Tabby n
Tadpole n FLOW

Tallow n MTRL
Talon n BODY
Tentacle n BODY
Terrier n
Thoroughbred j POWR
Tiger n
Toad n
Toads n
Tom j MALE
Tongue n FOOD
Topaz n UP
Toreador n DAMG
Tortoise n
Tripe n FOOD
Troika n VEHC
Trout n FLOW
Tuna n FLOW
Turkey n UP
Turkey n FOOD
Turtle n
Turtle n FOOD
Tusk n BODY
Tweet n TALK
Twitter n TALK
Underdog n WEAK
Unicorn n MYTH
Vertebrate j SOMA
Viper n DAMG
Vulture n UP
Vulture n AGGR
Walrus n FLOW
Warble n TALK
Warren n HOME
Watchdog n AID
Waterfowl n FLOW
Weasel n

Weasel v FALS
Weaseled v FALS
Weaseling v FALS
Whale n FLOW
Whale n LARG
Whalebone n MTRL
Whinny n TALK
Whitefish n FLOW
Whiting n FLOW
Whoop v TALK
Wildcat n DAMG
Wolf n
Wolf v FOOD
Wolfed v FOOD
Wolfing v FOOD
Wolfs v FOOD
Wolves n
Woodchuck n
Woof n TALK
Wool n FABR
Woolen j FABR
Wrangle v BLOK
Wren n UP
Yak n
Yap n TALK
Yearling n YNG
Yelp n TALK
Yip v TALK
Yoghurt n FOOD
Yolk n FOOD
Yowl n TALK
Zebra n
Zoo n HOME
Zoological j IDEA

ASTR

Alpha n VIEW
Aquarius n MYTH
Aries n MYTH
Astrology n MYTH
Astronaut n VEHC
Astronomical j IDEA
Astronomical j LARG
Astronomy n IDEA
Astrophysics n IDEA
Atmosphere n VAPR
Atmospheric j VAPR
Aurora n VIEW
Beta n VIEW
Cancer n MYTH
Capricorn n MYTH
Celestial j UP
Comet n
Constellation n GRUP
Copernican j
Corona n VIEW
Cosmonaut n VEHC
Crab n ANML
Crescent n FORM
Dipper n HOLW
Earth n ERTH
Ether n VAPR

Firmament n UP
Galactic j GRUP
Galaxy n GRUP
Gemini n MYTH
Heaven n UP
Heavenward d UP
Heliocentric j HEAT
Heliotrope n VEGT
Heliotropism n HEAT
Hercules n POWR
Horizon n AFAR
Horoscope n MYTH
Interstellar j
Jupiter n
Leo n MYTH
Libra n MYTH
Luminary n
Lunar j
Mars n
Martian n
Mercury n
Meridian n TIME
Meteor n
Meteorology n IDEA
Moon n
Moonbeam n VIEW

Moonlight n VIEW
Moons n
Moonshine n VIEW
Nebula n BLUR
Neptune n
Nova n
Observatory n VIEW
Parallax n OPPO
Pisces n MYTH
Planet n
Planetarium n HOME
Planetary j
Pluto n
Polaris n
Sagittarius n MYTH
Satellite n SUB
Saturn n
Scorpio n MYTH
Skies n UP
Sky n UP
Solar j HEAT
Space n VAPR
Spacecraft n VEHC
Sputnik n VEHC
Star n
Starlight n VIEW

Starry j
Stars n
Stellar j
Stratosphere n VAPR
Sun n HEAT
Sunbeam n VIEW
Sunburn n HEAT
Sundown n DOWN
Sunflower n VEGT
Sunlight n VIEW
Sunned v HEAT
Sunny j HEAT
Sunrise n UP
Suns n HEAT
Sunset n DOWN
Sunshine n HEAT
Sunstroke n SICK
Syzygy n
Taurus n MYTH
Uranus n
Venus n
Virgo n MYTH
Zodiac n MYTH

Aback d	Behind n BODY	Kickback n MONY	Retreat n GO
Aback d PANG	Behinds n BODY	Last j END	Retreated v GO
Abaft d FLOW	Breech n BODY	Latter j	Retreating v GO
Aft j FLOW	Butt n	Nape n BODY	Retrospect n VIEW
After b	Buttock n BODY	Pigtail n BODY	Return n GO
Afterward d	Can n BODY	Post d	Reverse n VARY
Ass n BODY	Cans n BODY	Posterior j	Rump n BODY
Assed j BODY	Chase n GO	Posthumous j DEAD	Setback n WEAK
Asses n BODY	Chased v GO	Postmortem n DEAD	Stern n FLOW
Astern d FLOW	Chaser n GO	Postscript n WRIT	Subsequent j
Back n	Countermarch n GO	Rear n	Tail n BODY
Back n BODY	Croup n BODY	Rear n BODY	Tail v GO
Back n PLAY	Derriere n BODY	Rearward d	Tailing v GO
Back v GO	Dorsal j	Rebate n MONY	Tails n BODY
Back v AID	Ebb v FLOW	Rebound v GO	Tails v GO
Backbone n BODY	Ensue v	Recall v TALK	Trace v GO
Backfield n PLAY	Feedback n AID	Recede v GO	Traced v GO
Background n	Follow v GO	Recession n GO	Track v GO
Background n CRUX	Halfback n PLAY	Recoil v GO	Tracked v GO
Backward d	Heel n	Redouble v GO	Tracking v GO
Backward j WEAK	Heeled j	Refund v MONY	Trail v GO
Backwood j VEGT	Heeling v	Regress v GO	Trailed v GO
Behind b	Hind j	Retrace v GO	Train n GARB
Behind b AID	Hindermost j	Retract v HAVE	Wake n FLOW

BAD

Abandon n	Bum n WEAK	Derelict j WEAK	Heel n AGGR
Abase v WEAK	Cad n	Despicable j AGGR	Heinous j DAMG
Abnormity n AFAR	Callgirl n SEX	Deuce n	Hell n PANG
Accursed j AGGR	Coarse j	Devil n LEAD	Hideous j
Adulterer n SEX	Collude v JOIN	Devil n	Hussy n LADY
Adulterous j SEX	Collusion n JOIN	Devil v AGGR	Ignoble j WEAK
Adultery n SEX	Confound v	Diabolic j	Ignominy n
Amoral j	Connive v AGRE	Dirt n DIRT	Ill j
Arrant j	Conscienceless j IDEA	Discredit v AGGR	Illicit j CRIM
Atrocious j	Conspire v JOIN	Disgrace v	Immoderate j
Atrocious j DAMG	Corrupt j DIRT	Dishonest j FALS	Immodest j
Atrocity n DAMG	Crude j AGGR	Dishonor n AGGR	Immoral j
Atrocity n	Cruel j DAMG	Disorderly j SEX	Imp n YNG
Awful j	Culprit n CRIM	Disreputable j	Impish j YNG
Awfully d	Curse n TALK	Dissolute j	Improper j
Bad j	Curse n AGGR	Dog n ANML	Impropriety n
Bad j DAMG	Cursing v TALK	Eclat n OPEN	Imprudent j
Bad j DIRT	Cuss n TALK	Enormity n LARG	Incorrigible j
Bad j FALS	Cyprian n SEX	Epithet n TALK	Indecency n
Bad j PANG	Daemon n MYTH	Error n FALS	Indecorous j
Base j	Damn v AGGR	Evil n	Indefensible j
Basely d	Dark j BLUR	Exorcise v AID	Indiscretion n
Baseness n	Dastard n WEAK	Fall n DOWN	Inexcusable j
Baser j	Debase v	Fault n FALS	Inexpiable j
Basest j	Debauch v MOTV	Fie i	Infamy n
Bastard n	Decadence n	Fiend n DAMG	Infernal j
Bastard n KIN	Deform v VARY	Flagrant j OPEN	Inferno n DAMG
Bawdy j SEX	Degeneracy n	Forebode v FORW	Inglorious j WEAK
Beast n ANML	Degenerate j	Fornicate v SEX	Iniquity n
Bedevil v PANG	Degrade v	Foul j	Injudicious j
Bestial j ANML	Dehumanize v AGGR	Ghoul n MYTH	Injustice n
Bewitch v MYTH	Demean v	Goblin n MYTH	Insincere j FALS
Bitch n LADY	Demerit n	Gorgon n LADY	Irreverence n AGGR
Bitches n LADY	Demerit n FALS	Grisly j PANG	Jezebel n LADY
Black j COLR	Demon n MYTH	Gross j	Knave n
Blasphemy n TALK	Demoniac j MYTH	Gutter n HOLW	Lascivious j SEX
Blasted j	Denigrate v	Hag n LADY	Lecher n SEX
Bloody j SOMA	Deprave v	Harlot n SEX	Lewd j SEX

Libertine j OPEN
Licentious j OPEN
Loose j OPEN
Lousier j DIRT
Lousy j DIRT
Low j DOWN
Maladaptation n OPPO
Maladjustment n OPPO
Maladminister v LEAD
Malediction n TALK
Malefaction n CRIM
Malevolence n AGGR
Malice n AGGR
Malign v AGGR
Malignancy n AGGR
Malignancy n SICK
Mean j AGGR
Measly j LITL
Misalliance n JOIN
Misbegotten j BGIN
Misbehave v EVNT
Mischief n
Miscreant j
Misdeed n
Monster n AFAR
Naughtier j
Naughty j
Nefarious j
Notoriety n OPEN
Noxious j DAMG
Oath n TALK
Obscene j SEX
Ominous j

Ornery j
Outrage n DAMG
Pander v SEX
Pander v AID
Pederasty n SEX
Pejorative j AGGR
Perdition n DAMG
Perfidy n
Perpetrate v
Perversion n
Picaresque j POWR
Pig n ANML
Pimp n SEX
Pimped v SEX
Pornography n SEX
Procure v SEX
Profane j
Profligacy n
Promiscuity n SEX
Promiscuous j SEX
Prostitute n SEX
Rank j
Rascal n
Rat n ANML
Ratted v ANML
Reprobate n
Ribald j GLAD
Rogue n
Satan n LEAD
Scabby j
Scabrous j
Scamp n
Scandal n PANG

Scatology n SEX
Scoundrel n
Scurrilous j
Scurvy j AGGR
Seamy j
Seduction n SEX
Seduction n MOTV
Shame n PANG
Shameless j
Shaming v PANG
Sin n
Sink n HOLW
Skunk n ANML
Snake n ANML
Sordid j DIRT
Spoil v AID
Spoils v AID
Stigma n VIEW
Swear v TALK
Swine n ANML
Swore v TALK
Tamper v VARY
Tart n LADY
Terrible j DAMG
Terrible j PANG
Terrific j DAMG
Terror n DAMG
Thug n CRIM
Tort n LAW
Transgress v
Turpitude n
Ugly j
Unattractive j

Unbecoming j
Uncivil j AGGR
Undesirable j
Undignified j
Unfair j
Unjust j
Unmannerly d AGGR
Unpardonable j
Unsatisfactory j
Unsavory j AGGR
Unscrupulous j
Unsightly j VIEW
Vermin n BUG
Vice n
Vile j
Vilify v AGGR
Vitiate v WEAK
Vulgar j AGGR
Wallow v VARY
Wanton j MOTV
Wanton j SEX
Wayward j GO
Welter v VARY
Whore n SEX
Wicked j
Witch n LADY
Witchcraft n MYTH
Worm n BUG
Worse j
Worst j
Wretch n PANG
Wrong j
Wrongdoing n CRIM

BGIN

Aborigine n NEAR
Abortion n BLOK
Accouchement n REST
Activate v
Actuate v
Aetiology n IDEA
Alpha n
Arise v UP
Arose v UP
Autochthonous j NEAR
Bear v
Bearer n
Bearing v
Began v
Begin v
Begun v
Birth n
Birthday n TIME
Birthmark n VIEW
Blaze v VIEW
Bore v
Born v
Borne v
Bred v
Breed n GRUP
Breed v
Breeding n
Breeding n GOOD
Brew v SIP

Brood j YNG
Bud v VEGT
Budded v VEGT
Budding v VEGT
Bulb n VEGT
Burgeon v
Caesarian j SHRP
Calve v ANML
Calved v ANML
Calves v ANML
Calving v ANML
Cause n
Childbirth n YNG
Clutch n ANML
Coin v
Commence v
Commencement n EDUC
Commencement n
Compose v FORM
Composing v FORM
Composition n FORM
Conceive v YNG
Conception n YNG
Congenital j SOMA
Constitute v FORM
Constituting v FORM
Constitution n FORM
Contraceptive j BLOK
Create v

Creator n
Creator n HOLY
Dawn v TIME
Daybreak n TIME
Debut n
Debutante n LADY
Deliver v
Deliveries n
Delivery n
Derive v
Descendant n KIN
Descendent n KIN
Egg n SOMA
Embark v GO
Embryo n SOMA
Endogenous j IN
Engender v
Establish v EVER
Establishment n EVER
Etiology n IDEA
Etymology n TALK
Eugenic j GOOD
Evoke v OUT
Exogenous j OUT
Extraction n OUT
Fecund j MUCH
Fertilize v AID
Fetal j SOMA
Fetus n SOMA

Firstborn j FORW
Firstborn n KIN
Firsthand d FORW
Foetus n SOMA
Foment v AGGR
Found v
Founded v
Founder n
Founds v
Fountainhead n FLOW
Fructify v AID
Gamete n SOMA
Gene n SOMA
Generate v
Generating v
Generation n GRUP
Generation n
Generator n
Genes n SOMA
Genesis n
Genetic j
Germ n
Germ n VEGT
Germ n SOMA
Germinate v LARG
Gestate v
Hatch v
Hatched v
Hatchery n ANML

Heredity n HAVE
Heritage n HAVE
Heterozygous j OPPO
Homozygous j SIML
Hybrid j JOIN
Ignition n HEAT
Impetus n POWR
Impregnate v
Improvise v EASY
Inaugurate v
Inchoate j BLUR
Incipient j
Incite v MOTV
Incubate v
Indigenous j NEAR
Induce v
Induct v JOIN
Induction n JOIN
Induction n
Infertile j LACK
Initial j
Initiate v
Innate j IN
Innovate v
Install v
Instigate v AGGR
Institute v
Instituted v
Instituting v
Institution n
Interbreed v KIN
Introduce v NEAR
Introduce v

Invent v
Invent v FALS
Invest v LEAD
Investing v LEAD
Issue n KIN
Kernel n VEGT
Knock v SEX
Laid v
Launch n GO
Lay v
Layer n ANML
Midwife n LADY
Mint v MONY
Minted v MONY
Minting v MONY
Misbegotten j BAD
Miscarriage n FALS
Native n NEAR
Nee j
Obstetric j MEDC
Onset n
Oocyte n SOMA
Oosperm n SOMA
Open v OPEN
Origin n
Original j
Outset n
Parent n LEAD
Parturition n YNG
Pedigree n PAST
Pioneer n FORW
Pip n VEGT
Pips n VEGT

Pollen n VEGT
Pollinate v VEGT
Precipitate v QUIK
Pregnancy n SOMA
Prenatal j FORW
Primitive j
Primogenitor n KIN
Procreate v
Progenitor n KIN
Progeny n KIN
Proliferate v MUCH
Prolific j MUCH
Propagate v LARG
Recommence v
Recreation n SIML
Regenerate v SIML
Renaissance n POWR
Renew v NEW
Reproduce v SIML
Resume v
Resumed v
Resuming v
Root n VEGT
Root n CRUX
Rudiment n
Scratch n
Seed n
Seed n VEGT
Set v
Setting v
Shoot n VEGT
Sire n MALE
Siring v MALE

Source n
Sow v VEGT
Sowed v VEGT
Sowing v VEGT
Spark v MOTV
Spawn v YNG
Sprang v
Spring n
Springing v
Sprout v VEGT
Start v
Started v
Starting v
Stem v
Stemmed v
Stemming v
Sterile j LACK
Stimulate v MOTV
Stock n
Taproot n VEGT
Thoroughbred j POWR
Threshold n
Trigger n
Trigger n MECH
Trip v
Unborn j
Undertake v MOTV
Virgin j NEW
Wellbred j GOOD
Womb n HOLW
Zygote n SOMA

BLOK

Abeyance n REST
Abortion n BGIN
Abstain v LACK
Abstemious j LACK
Abstention n LACK
Abstinence n LACK
Afoul d
Aground d ERTH
Anchor v
Anchorage n
Apprehension n
Arrest v LAW
Arrest v
Astringent j
Attach v LAW
Attached v LAW
Attaches v LAW
Avert v VARY
Baffle n
Bag v HOLW
Bagged v HOLW
Bagging v HOLW
Balk v
Ban n
Banish v SEP
Bank v BULG
Banned v
Bans n
Bar n

Barred v
Barricade n
Barrier n
Barring v
Bay n
Bind v
Bit n
Bite n
Block n
Blockade n DAMG
Blot v FLOW
Blotted v FLOW
Blotter n FLOW
Bluelaw n LAW
Bog v
Bogged v
Bolt n MECH
Bond n JOIN
Bondage n SUB
Bottleneck n
Bound j
Bounds n
Box v
Boxed v
Boxing v
Boycott v SEP
Brake n MECH
Breakwater n FLOW
Bridle v

Brig n HOME
Bulkhead n FORM
Bunker n ERTH
Bushing n MECH
Buttonhole v GARB
Cage n HOME
Caging v HOME
Calaboose n HOME
Calk v MTRL
Captive j
Captor n
Capture v
Catch v
Catches v
Caught v
Caulk v MTRL
Cell n HOME
Censor v IDEA
Censoring v IDEA
Chain n JOIN
Check n
Checked v
Checkmate v PLAY
Chock n FORM
Choke v DAMG
Choke v
Choker n
Chuck n MECH
Cinch n HAVE

Cinched v HAVE
Cinching v HAVE
Circumscribe v HOLW
Clam v ANML
Clammed v ANML
Clamming v ANML
Clamp v
Clamp v JOIN
Clasp n JOIN
Clasp v HAVE
Claustrophobia n PANG
Cleat n FORM
Clench v JOIN
Clench v HAVE
Clinch v JOIN
Clink n HOME
Clog n
Clot n SOMA
Clothespin n GARB
Clutch n HAVE
Clutch n MECH
Clutch n CRUX
Cock n MECH
Cocks n MECH
Collar n GARB
Commit v
Committed v
Compass v HOLW
Compassed v HOLW

Compassing v HOLW	Disrupt v AGGR	Guardhouse n HOME	Insolvable j EVER
Compress v LITL	Dock n FLOW	Guarding v AID	Insulate v SEP
Compressor n MECH	Docked v FLOW	Gum v JOIN	Insuperable j EVER
Con n CRIM	Door n OPEN	Gummed v JOIN	Insurmountable j EVER
Concentration n	Dragnet n	Hairpin n BODY	Intercept v
Confine v	Dungeon n HOME	Halt n END	Interdict v
Confiscate v HAVE	Earthbound j ERTH	Halted v END	Interfere v
Congest v BULG	Embargo n LAW	Halter n	Interlock v JOIN
Constipate v SOMA	Embrace n JOIN	Halter n DEAD	Intern v
Constrain v	Encircle v HOLW	Hamper v	Interned v
Constrict v	Enclosure n HOLW	Hamstring v SOMA	Internee n
Constrictor n ANML	Encompass v	Handcuff n BODY	Interrupt v END
Constrictor n	Encumber v	Handicap n WEAK	Iron n MTRL
Contain v IN	Enjoin v	Hangup n	Jail n HOME
Continence n LACK	Enmesh v JOIN	Harness n GARB	Jam n
Continent j LACK	Enslave v SUB	Harness v	Jammed v
Continently d LACK	Ensnare v	Hasp n	Jaw n
Contraceptive j BGIN	Exclude v SEP	Hatch n OPEN	Jetties n FLOW
Convict v CRIM	Exclusive j SEP	Hatched v OPEN	Jetty n FLOW
Convicting v CRIM	Exile v SEP	Headlock n BODY	Jug n HOME
Conviction n CRIM	Fast d	Hedge n VEGT	Kill v DEAD
Cooler n COLD	Fasten v	Hedge n	Knot n JOIN
Coop v HOME	Faucet n MECH	Hedgehog n DAMG	Land v HAVE
Cooped v HOME	Fence n	Held v	Landed v HAVE
Cooping v HOME	Fend v AID	Held v CRIM	Landing v HAVE
Cordon n	Fender n AID	Hem v	Lanyard n FABR
Cork n MTRL	Fetter v	Hermetic j	Lariat n FABR
Corner v	Filibuster v TALK	Hidebound j BODY	Lash v
Corners v	Firebreak n HEAT	Hidebound j FOOL	Lashing v
Corral v HOME	Firetrap n HEAT	Hinder v	Lasso n FABR
Cowcatcher n ANML	Floodgate n FLOW	Hindrance n	Latch n
Cramp n SOMA	Fluke n SHRP	Hitch n	Latch v JOIN
Cramp n	Foil v WEAK	Hitched v	Leash n FABR
Creeper n GO	Foiled v WEAK	Hobble v	Lifer n CRIM
Crimp v	Foiling v WEAK	Hobbled v	Ligature n
Curb n	Forbade v	Hold n	Limbo n LACK
Curfew n TIME	Forbear v LACK	Hold v CRIM	Lock n MECH
Curtail v LITL	Forbid v	Holdfast n HAVE	Locked v MECH
Custodian n HAVE	Forbidding v	Holdfast n	Locker n HOLW
Custody n HAVE	Foreclose v	Hook n SHRP	Louver n OPEN
Cut v SHRP	Forestall v FORW	Hoosegow n HOME	Lure n SHRP
Cutoff n SHRP	Frustrate v AGGR	Hostage n	Manacle v MECH
Cutout n SHRP	Gaff n SHRP	Hung j	Mire v ERTH
Cutting v SHRP	Gaffed v SHRP	Hurdle n	Mole n FLOW
Dam n FLOW	Gag n TALK	Illiberal j	Moor v
Damp v	Gagged v TALK	Immure v IN	Moored v
Dams n FLOW	Gagging v TALK	Impassable j	Mooring v
Deadlock n	Garnish v LAW	Impasse n END	Mouse v ANML
Debar v	Gasket n MECH	Impede v	Moused v ANML
Defer v REST	Gate n OPEN	Impenetrable j	Mousing v ANML
Delay n REST	Ghetto n GRUP	Impermeable j	Muffle v
Delimit v	Gird v HOLW	Impervious j	Muffler n
Demarcate v SEP	Girded v HOLW	Impossible j BLUR	Muzzle n BODY
Detain v	Glassy j PANG	Impound v HAVE	Muzzled v BODY
Detention n	Gorge n BULG	Imprison v HOME	Muzzling v BODY
Deter v	Grapnel n	Inaccessible j	Nab v HAVE
Diaphragm n SOMA	Grapple v JOIN	Incarcerate v HOME	Net n
Diaphragm n	Gremlin n MYTH	Incommunicado j TALK	Nip v
Difficult j BLUR	Grip n	Inextricable j	Nipped v
Dike n FLOW	Gripped v	Infeasible j	Nonconductor n
Dilatory j REST	Guard n AID	Inhibit v	Noose n
Disbar v SEP	Guard n PLAY	Injunction n LAW	Nut n MECH

Obstacle n
Obstruct v
Obviate v
Ostracism n SEP
Pack n BULG
Packed v BULG
Packing v BULG
Paddock n HOME
Paddywagon n VEHC
Padlock n
Pale n
Paling n
Parochial j GRUP
Parried v VARY
Parry n VARY
Pawl n MECH
Pen n HOME
Penitentiary n HOME
Penned v HOME
Penning v HOME
Penology n CRIM
Pens v HOME
Pent j
Petcock n MECH
Picket n WORK
Pier n FLOW
Pigeonhole v HOLW
Pin n SHRP
Pincer n SHRP
Pinch v
Pinch n LAW
Pinch n PANG
Pinion v
Pinioned v
Pinioning v
Pinned v SHRP
Pinning v SHRP
Plug n
Plugged v
Pokey n HOME
Portal n OPEN
Postpone v REST
Pothook n HOLW
Preclude v
Prehensile j HAVE
Prevent v
Prison n HOME
Prisoner n
Procrastinate v REST
Prohibit v
Proscribe v AGGR
Punctuate v

Purchase n
Quagmire n BLUR
Quarantine n SEP
Quash v
Quell v DAMG
Rampart n AID
Recapture v HAVE
Reformatory n HOME
Refrain v LACK
Rein n LEAD
Repress v
Resist v
Resist v DAMG
Restrain v
Restrict v
Retard v REST
Rope v FABR
Roped v FABR
Roping v FABR
Round v HOLW
Rounded v HOLW
Rounding v HOLW
Rounds v HOLW
Roundup n HOLW
Scotch v
Seal v COVR
Sealed v COVR
Sealing v COVR
Secure v
Segregate v SEP
Seize v HAVE
Seizure n SICK
Seizure n HAVE
Shackle v JOIN
Shut v COVR
Shutter n COVR
Slip n FLOW
Sluice n FLOW
Smother v DEAD
Smother v
Snag n
Snare n MECH
Snarl v
Snug j
Soundproof v HEAR
Sphincter n SOMA
Spigot n MECH
Squash v
Squashed v
Squashing v
Squeeze v
Stalemate n END

BLUR

Stall n
Stalled v
Stalling v
Staunch v
Staunched v
Staunching v
Stay n
Stem v
Stemmed v
Stemming v
Stick v
Stickler n BLUR
Stifle v
Stifle v DEAD
Stint v
Stir n HOME
Stock n
Stocks n
Stop v END
Strait n
Strait n PANG
Strand v SEP
Stranded v SEP
Stranding v SEP
Strangle v DEAD
Strap v
Strict j AGGR
Stricture n
Strike v WORK
Striking v WORK
Struck v WORK
Stub v
Stubbed v
Stuck v
Stuffy j
Stump v
Stumped v
Stumping v
Stunt v
Stunted v
Stunting v
Suffocate v DEAD
Suppress v
Surround v HOLW
Suspend v END
Suspended v END
Suspense n
Suspension n
Table v
Tabled v
Tables v
Tabling v

Taboo v
Tackle n
Tackled v
Tackling v
Tangle v JOIN
Tap n MECH
Taut j
Taut j PANG
Tense j
Tension n
Throttle n MECH
Throttle v DEAD
Thwart v
Tie v JOIN
Tied v JOIN
Tieing v JOIN
Tight j
Tighten v
Tong n MECH
Tough j BLUR
Trap n
Trapdoor n OPEN
Trapped v
Trapping n
Turnkey n OPEN
Tweezer n MECH
Tying v JOIN
Unattainable j
Uncork v OPEN
Valve n MECH
Veto v
Vise n MECH
Wall n FORM
Walled v FORM
Ward v
Warded v
Warding v
Washer n
Waterproof j FLOW
Watertight j FLOW
Web n
Wedge v
Wharf n FLOW
Withhold v HAVE
Wrangle v ANML
Wring v DAMG
Wring v FLOW
Wringer n MECH
Wrung v DAMG
Wrung v FLOW

Abstruse j COVR
Addle v
Adumbrate v FORW
Aimless j
Ambiguous j
Ambivalent j MOTV
Amnesia n SICK
Amorphous j
Anarchy n LAW
Baffle v

Ball v
Balled v
Bamboozle v FALS
Bedlam n HEAR
Befuddle v
Bewilder v
Blackout n COLR
Blackout n REST
Bleary j
Blob n

Blunt j
Blur v
Chaos n
Chaotic j
Charade n PLAY
Cloud n WEA
Cloud v
Cloud n VAPR
Clutter n DIRT
Clutter n HEAR

Coma n REST
Complex j
Complicate v
Confound v
Confuse v
Conjecture n IDEA
Crossexamine v TALK
Cryptic j COVR
Dark j COLR
Dark j BAD

Dateless j TIME
Daub v
Daze v PANG
Dazzle v VIEW
Difficult j BLOK
Diffuse j
Dilemma n PANG
Dim v
Dishevel v
Disjointed j SEP
Disorder n
Disorderly j
Disorganize v
Dissolve v
Dizzy j PANG
Doubt v
Dubious j
Dull j
Dulled v
Dulling v
Dulls v
Dumbfound v PANG
Dusk n TIME
Eclipse v COVR
Enigma n
Enquire v TALK
Equivocal j
Fade v COLR
Fade v
Fading v COLR
Fading v
Faint v REST
Faint j
Fainted v REST
Fainting v REST
Film n
Fog n WEA
Fog n VAPR
Foreshadow v FORW
Forget v IDEA
Formless j FORM
Fuzzier j
Fuzzy j
Garble v FALS
Giddy j PANG
Gloom n
Gloom n PANG
Goo n FLOW
Greek n TALK
Grill v TALK
Grilled v TALK
Grope v
Guess v IDEA
Haphazard j
Harangue v TALK
Harumscarum j DAMG
Hash n JOIN
Hashed v JOIN

Hashing v JOIN
Haywire d
Haze n WEA
Haze n VAPR
Hazier j WEA
Hazier j VAPR
Hazy j WEA
Hazy j VAPR
Helterskelter j QUIK
Hesitate v REST
Hieroglyphic n WRIT
Higgledypiggledy d
Hodgepodge n JOIN
If n
Illegible j WRIT
Imbroglio n OPPO
Impossible j BLOK
Inarticulate j TALK
Incalculable j LARG
Inchoate j BGIN
Incoherence n FOOL
Incomprehensible j IDEA
Inconceivable j IDEA
Inconclusive j
Inconspicuous j VIEW
Indecipherable j
Indecision n
Indefinable j
Indefinite j
Indescribable j
Indeterminate j
Indiscernible j
Indiscriminate j
Indistinct j
Indistinguishable j
Ineffable j
Inexact j FALS   .
Inexplainable j IDEA
Inexplicable j IDEA
Inexpressible j TALK
Inexpressive j
Inquire v TALK
Inquisitive j TALK
Inscrutable j COVR
Interrogate v TALK
Intricacy n
Involved j
Jumble n JOIN
Labyrinth n PATH
Leerier j PANG
Leery j PANG
Loom v VIEW
Loomed v VIEW
Looming v VIEW
Maze n PATH
Mess n DIRT
Messy j DIRT
Misgiving n PANG

Mishmash n JOIN
Mist n WEA
Misted v WEA
Mistrust v AGGR
Mix v JOIN
Moot j TALK
Muddies v
Muddle n WEAK
Mumble n TALK
Murky j
Muss v
Mussed v
Mutter n TALK
Mystery n
Mystic j HOLY
Mystify v
Nebula n ASTR
Nebulous j
Nimbus n WEA
Noncommital j
Nonplus v
Obfuscate v
Obliterate v
Oblivion n
Obscure j
Obtuse j
Opacity n VIEW
Opaque j VIEW
Overcast j WEA
Overtone n IDEA
Paradox n OPPO
Pellmell j QUIK
Penumbra n
Perplex v
Pickle n PANG
Pose v
Posing v
Precarious j
Predicament n PANG
Problem n
Puzzle n
Quagmire n BLOK
Quandary n
Queries v TALK
Query n TALK
Question n TALK
Quiz v TALK
Quizzed v TALK
Quizzical j TALK
Quizzing v TALK
Ramble v TALK
Random n AFAR
Recondite j COVR
Riddle n
Rorschach n TRUE
Rough j
Sceptic n OPPO
Sea n FLOW

Shade n COVR
Shadow n
Shapeless j
Skeptic n OPPO
Slur n
Smear v
Smog n WEA
Smog n VAPR
Somehow d
Sphinx n MYTH
Splutter v TALK
Stickler n BLOK
Stupor n REST
Subtle j
Suspect v IDEA
Suspect v AGGR
Suspense n PANG
Suspicion n AGGR
Swam v
Swim v
Swoon v REST
Swum v
Syncope n REST
Topsyturvy j OPPO
Tough j BLOK
Turbid j
Turmoil n PANG
Twilight n TIME
Unaccountable j
Unaware j
Uncertain j
Unconfirmed j
Unconscious j REST
Undecided j
Undercurrent n MOTV
Undertone n TALK
Unidentified j
Unintelligible j
Unknown j COVR
Unlighted j
Unmarked j WRIT
Unorganized j
Unplanned j
Unpredictable j
Unproved j
Unsolved j
Unsure j WEAK
Unsystematic j
Untested j
Untried j
Unwitting j OPPO
Vacillate v VARY
Vague j
Vapor n VAPR
Vertigo n PANG
Welter n
Wonder v IDEA
Woozy j PANG

BODY

Abdomen n HOLW
Ablebodied j POWR
Acne n DIRT
Akimbo j VARY

Ambidextrous j POWR
Amputate v SEP
Ankle n
Antenna n ANML

Antler n ANML
Arch n
Arches n
Arm n

Armed j
Armful n BULG
Armpit n HOLW
Arms n

Articular j JOIN
Ass n BACK
Assed j BACK
Asses n BACK
Astride j SEP
Attitude n EVNT
Back n BACK
Backbone n POWR
Backbone n BACK
Bald j LACK
Bang n
Bare j OPEN
Barefoot j OPEN
Bareheaded j OPEN
Bark n VEGT
Beak n ANML
Beaked j ANML
Bean n
Bean v DAMG
Beard n
Beautician n GOOD
Beefy j LARG
Behead v DEAD
Behind n BACK
Behinds n BACK
Bellied v BULG
Bellies n SOMA
Bellies v BULG
Belly n SOMA
Belly v BULG
Bellying v BULG
Bicep n
Bill n ANML
Bill v SEX
Billed v SEX
Billing v SEX
Binocular j VIEW
Blade n VEGT
Blade n
Blonde n COLR
Bloom v VEGT
Bloomed v VEGT
Blossom v VEGT
Blush v COLR
Bob v SHRP
Bobbed v SHRP
Bobbing v SHRP
Bobbypin n JOIN
Bobs v SHRP
Bodies n
Bodies n DEAD
Bodily j
Body n
Body n DEAD
Body n SOLE
Boil n DIRT
Bonehead n FOOL
Bosom n LADY
Bosom j FOND
Bottom n DOWN
Bough n VEGT
Branch n VEGT
Breast n
Breast n LADY
Breech n BACK

Bridge n
Brow n
Bruise v DAMG
Brunette n COLR
Brush n ANML
Build n FORM
Bullheaded j AGGR
Bullseye n SHRP
Bun n
Bush n ANML
Bust n FORM
Bust n LADY
Buttock n BACK
Buxom j LADY
Cadaver n DEAD
Calf n
Callous j
Callus n
Calves n
Calyx n VEGT
Can n BACK
Canine n FOOD
Cans n BACK
Carbuncle n DIRT
Carcass n DEAD
Carnal j
Carnal j SEX
Carnassial j ANML
Chap n DAMG
Chap n ANML
Chapped v DAMG
Cheek n
Cheek n AGGR
Cheekbone n
Chest n
Chin n
Chiropractor n MEDC
Chop n
Chops n
Chubby j LARG
Cilia n
Claw n SHRP
Clubfoot n SICK
Coat n ANML
Cob n VEGT
Cockeyed j FOOL
Cockeyed j VARY
Coiffure n GARB
Collarbone n SOMA
Comb n ANML
Complected j COLR
Complexion n COLR
Cone n VEGT
Coniferous j VEGT
Contortionist n VARY
Contuse v DAMG
Corn n
Cornu n ANML
Corny j
Coronet n ANML
Corpora n DEAD
Corporal j
Corporally d
Corporation n BULG

Corporeal j
Corpse n DEAD
Corpulence n LARG
Cortex n VEGT
Cortices n VEGT
Cosmetic j GOOD
Countenance n
Countenance v AGRE
Crawl v PANG
Creep v PANG
Crest n ANML
Crop n SHRP
Crop n ANML
Cropped v SHRP
Crotch n SEP
Croup n BACK
Crown n UP
Crown v DAMG
Curl n VARY
Cuspid n FOOD
Cutaneous j
Cuticle n
Daddylonglegs n BUG
Daglock n DIRT
Dandruff n DIRT
Decapitate v SEP
Deciduous j VARY
Decollate v SEP
Dental j FOOD
Dentate j FOOD
Dentifrice n CLEN
Dentist n MEDC
Dentition n FOOD
Denture n FOOD
Dermal j
Dermatitis n SICK
Dermatologist n MEDC
Derriere n BACK
Digit n
Dimple n HOLW
Disfigure v DIRT
Dismember v SEP
Down n
Ear n HEAR
Ear n VEGT
Earache n PANG
Eardrum n HEAR
Earring n GARB
Earshot n HEAR
Ectomorph n LITL
Eczema n DIRT
Egghead n IDEA
Elbow n
Elbow v GO
Embody v IN
Endomorph n LARG
Epidermis n
Erupt v OUT
Extremity n END
Eye n VIEW
Eye n VEGT
Eyeball n VIEW
Eyebrow n VIEW
Eyeglass n VIEW
Eyelash n VIEW

Eyelid n COVR
Face n
Face v FORW
Facial j
Facing v FORW
Fairhaired j COLR
Fang n ANML
Fat j LARG
Fathead n FOOL
Feather n ANML
Feathercut n SHRP
Featherless j LACK
Feature n
Feel v JOIN
Feet n
Felt v JOIN
Fetlock n ANML
Figurehead n FLOW
Fillip v QUIK
Fin n ANML
Finger n
Finger n MSMT
Finger v JOIN
Fingernail n SHRP
Fingerprint n WRIT
Fist n DAMG
Flank n ANML
Flatfoot n FORM
Flatfoot n LAW
Flatfooted j FORM
Flesh n
Flesh n COLR
Flipper n ANML
Flush n COLR
Flushed v COLR
Flushing v COLR
Foliage n VEGT
Follicle n HOLW
Foot n
Foot n DOWN
Foot v AID
Foot v GO
Football n PLAY
Foothold n AID
Footing n AID
Footing v GO
Footpath n PATH
Footprint n WRIT
Foots v AID
Foots v GO
Footsore j PANG
Footstep n GO
Footstool n REST
Forearm n
Forefinger n
Forehead n
Freckle n COLR
Frond n VEGT
Furry j ANML
Gape v OPEN
Gaping v OPEN
Genital j SEX
Genuflect v VARY
Gesticulate v EVNT
Gesture n EVNT

Gill n
Goatee n
Goose v GLAD
Goosed v GLAD
Goosing v GLAD
Gourd n VEGT
Graft n JOIN
Greasepaint n COLR
Grinder n FOOD
Groin n
Growth n LARG
Hackle n ANML
Hair n
Hairbrush n CLEN
Haircloth n FABR
Haircut n SHRP
Hairdo n AID
Hairdresser n AID
Hairless j LACK
Hairpin n BLOK
Ham n
Hand n
Hand n AID
Hand n WRIT
Hand n AGRE
Hand n WORK
Hand n NEAR
Hand n PLAY
Hand n MSMT
Hand n GRUP
Handbag n GARB
Handcuff n BLOK
Handed j
Handed v AID
Handful n SOME
Handicraft n WORK
Handier j POWR
Handily d POWR
Handing v AID
Handiwork n WORK
Handle v JOIN
Handle v LEAD
Handmade j FORM
Hands n
Hands v AID
Hands n WORK
Hands n PLAY
Hands n MSMT
Hands n GRUP
Handshake n JOIN
Handwriting n WRIT
Handy j POWR
Harelip n SICK
Haunch n
Head n
Head n IDEA
Headache n PANG
Headed j
Header n
Headier j PANG
Headless j LACK
Headlock n BLOK
Headlong j QUIK
Headlong j FORW
Headpiece n GARB

Heads n
Heads n IDEA
Headstrong j POWR
Heady j PANG
Heel n
Hide n
Hide v DAMG
Hidebound j BLOK
Hip n
Hipshot j SICK
Hirsute j
Hoof n ANML
Hoof v GO
Hooves n ANML
Horn n ANML
Horned j ANML
Horseback n ANML
Hulk n LARG
Hull n VEGT
Hump n BULG
Hunchback n VARY
Husk n VEGT
Incarnate j SIML
Incisor n SHRP
Index n
Instep n
Iris n VIEW
Jaw n
Jawed j
Joint n JOIN
Kick n GO
Kick n DAMG
Knee n
Kneecap n
Kneel v DOWN
Knockkneed j VARY
Knot n VEGT
Knuckle n
Laceration n DAMG
Lap n
Lapful n BULG
Lash n
Leaf n VEGT
Leaves n VEGT
Left j PLAC
Lefthanded j PLAC
Leg n
Legged j
Legging n GARB
Lid n COVR
Limb n
Limb n VEGT
Limbed j
Limbed j VEGT
Lip n
Lips n
Lipstick n COLR
Lobe n
Lock n SOME
Loin n
Makeup n FORM
Mammary j LADY
Mane n ANML
Manicure n CLEN
Manual j

Marcel v AID
Mask n ANML
Massage v AID
Mastectomy n MEDC
Mealymouth j FALS
Member n
Mesomorph n
Mole n
Molt v VARY
Molted v VARY
Motion v EVNT
Motioned v EVNT
Motioning v EVNT
Motor j EVNT
Mouth n HOLW
Mug n
Mugging v
Muscle n
Muscle v POWR
Muscled v POWR
Muscling v POWR
Muscular j
Mustache n
Muzzle n ANML
Muzzle n BLOK
Muzzled v BLOK
Muzzling v BLOK
Nail n SHRP
Naked j OPEN
Nape n BACK
Navel n
Neck n
Neck v SEX
Necking v SEX
Necklace n GARB
Noodle n IDEA
Nose n
Nostril n
Nude j OPEN
Numbskull n FOOL
Nuzzle v JOIN
Obese j LARG
Oral j HOLW
Organ n
Orthopedic j MEDC
Palm n
Palmed v
Palming v
Palmist n MYTH
Pastern n ANML
Pate n
Paunch n BULG
Paw n ANML
Pedicure n MEDC
Pediform j FORM
Permanent n EVER
Petal n VEGT
Phrenology n IDEA
Physical j
Physiognomy n
Physique n
Pigtail n BACK
Pimple n DIRT
Pincer n SHRP
Pinion n UP

Pinioned j UP
Pinkie n
Pistil n VEGT
Plumage n ANML
Plume n ANML
Pluming n ANML
Plump j LARG
Plumper j LARG
Plumpest j LARG
Pockmark n HOLW
Podiatry n MEDC
Poll n
Pompadour n AID
Portly j LARG
Posture n EVNT
Potbelly n BULG
Proboscis n ANML
Prognathous j
Prosthesis n AID
Pseudopod n BUG
Psychomotor j IDEA
Pubic j SEX
Pugnose n
Pustule n DIRT
Quarter n ANML
Quill n ANML
Ranginess n
Rangy j
Rear n BACK
Redhead n COLR
Rhinal j
Right d PLAC
Righthanded j PLAC
Rights n PLAC
Rind n VEGT
Rump n BACK
Saddle n ANML
Sagittal j PLAC
Scab n DIRT
Scabbed v DIRT
Scabbing v DIRT
Scabby j DIRT
Scabrous j DIRT
Scale n ANML
Scalp n
Scalp v DAMG
Scalped v DAMG
Scalping v DAMG
Scar n DAMG
Scrawny j LITL
Seat n REST
Shamefaced j PANG
Shell n VEGT
Shell n ANML
Shin n
Shin v GO
Shiner n COLR
Shoulder n
Shrug v VARY
Side n
Sight n VIEW
Singlehanded d SOLE
Skin n
Skin v SEP
Skinned j

Skinned v SEP
Skinning v SEP
Skinny j LITL
Snout n ANML
Snub j
Sore n DAMG
Sores n DAMG
Stalk n VEGT
Stance n EVNT
Stem n VEGT
Stemmed j VEGT
Stiff n DEAD
Stocky j LARG
Stomach n SOMA
Stout j LARG
Stubble n
Subcutaneous j SOMA

Surefooted j SHRP
Tactile j JOIN
Tail n BACK
Tails n BACK
Talon n ANML
Tartar n DIRT
Teat n LADY
Teeth n FOOD
Temple n
Tentacle n ANML
Thigh n
Throat n SOMA
Thumb n
Thumbnail j LITL
Tic n SICK
Tickle v GLAD
Toe n

Toenail n SHRP
Tongue n
Tongue n TALK
Tooth n FOOD
Toothache n PANG
Toothpaste n CLEN
Toothpick n SHRP
Torso n
Touch n JOIN
Toupee n GARB
Towhead n
Trunk n
Trunk n VEGT
Trunks n VEGT
Tusk n ANML
Twig n VEGT
Twofaced j FALS

Udder n LADY
Umbilical j JOIN
Underhand j DOWN
Visage n
Waist n
Waist n GARB
Waistline n
Wart n DIRT
Whisker n
Wideeyed j VIEW
Wig n GARB
Wigged v GARB
Wing n UP
Winged j UP
Wrist n
Wristband n HOLW
Yawn n OPEN

BUG

Amebic j
Amoeba n
Ant n
Aphid n DIRT
Apiary n HOME
Arachnid n
Bacteria n
Bee n UP
Beehive n HOME
Beetle n UP
Blackwidow n LADY
Bug n
Bug n SICK
Bug n FALS
Bumblebee n UP
Butterflies n UP
Butterflies n PANG
Butterfly n UP
Butterfly n FORM
Caterpillar n
Centipede n
Cicada n UP
Cobweb n HOME
Cockroach n
Cocoon n HOME

Cricket n
Cutworm n
Daddylonglegs n BODY
Darningneedle n UP
Delouse v CLEN
Dragonfly n UP
Drone n UP
Drosophila n UP
Earthworm n ERTH
Firefly n UP
Flea n
Fleabitten j DIRT
Fleabitten j COLR
Flies n UP
Fly n UP
Gadfly n AGGR
Germ n SICK
Gnat n UP
Grasshopper n
Grub n YNG
Grubbier j DIRT
Grubby j DIRT
Hive n HOME
Hives n HOME
Honey n FOOD

Hornet n UP
Insect n
Insecticide n DEAD
Katydid n
Larva n YNG
Leech n JOIN
Lice n DIRT
Locust n UP
Louse n DIRT
Lousier j DIRT
Lousy j DIRT
Maggot n DIRT
Mantis n UP
Microbe n SICK
Mite n LITL
Mosquito n UP
Moth n UP
Nit n DIRT
Organism n LIVE
Paramecium n
Parasite n SUB
Pest n AGGR
Pesticide n DEAD
Pestiferous j SICK
Pestilence n SICK

Pseudopod n BODY
Roach n
Scarab n
Scorpion n
Silk j FABR
Silks n FABR
Slug n REST
Spider n
Tarantula n
Termite n
Tick n
Vermin n BAD
Wasp n UP
Web n HOME
Widow n LADY
Worm n
Worm n BAD
Worm v MEDC
Worm n SICK
Wormed v MEDC
Worming v MEDC
Wormwood n VEGT

BULG

Accumulate v LARG
Aerial n UP
Alpine j PLAC
Alps n PLAC
Andes n PLAC
Antenna n UP
Appalachian j PLAC
Armful n BODY
Avalanche n DOWN
Balloon v
Bank n ERTH
Bank v BLOK
Bank v
Bay n

Bays n
Bellied v BODY
Bellies v BODY
Belly v BODY
Bellying v BODY
Berg n
Big j LARG
Bilge n
Billow n FLOW
Billow n
Blister n DIRT
Blister n HOLW
Bloat v
Bluff n ERTH

Brim v
Bulge v
Bump n
Bumpier j
Bumpy j
Bundle n
Bunion n SICK
Bushy j
Butte n ERTH
Button n
Carload n VEHC
Cliff n ERTH
Cloy v
Clump n

Cog v JOIN
Collect v LARG
Congest v BLOK
Corporation n BODY
Crag n ERTH
Cram v
Cram v IDEA
Cumulate v LARG
Cumuli n LARG
Cumulus n LARG
Cupful n HOLW
Cusp n SHRP
Deluge n FLOW
Deluge n

Parts of speech: a article; b preposition; c conjunction; d adverb; f prefix; i interjection;
        j adjective; n noun; p pronoun; r phrase; v verb.

Diluvial j FLOW
Downhill d DOWN
Dune n ERTH
Dunghill n DIRT
Earthwork n ERTH
Emboss v GOOD
Eminence n UP
Engorge v FOOD
Fill n
Filled v
Filling v
Flood n FLOW
Flush j HAVE
Foothill n DOWN
Fraught j
Full j
Full j WHOL
Glut v FOOD
Glut v
Glutted v FOOD
Glutted v
Glutton n FOOD
Gorge n BLOK
Gorge v FOOD
Gorged v FOOD
Gorging v FOOD
Haft n
Handle n AID
Haycock n VEGT
Haystack n VEGT
Head n ERTH
Heap n
Heap n MUCH
Hernia n SICK
Hill n ERTH
Hill n
Hillbilly n WEAK
Hillock n ERTH
Hillside n ERTH
Hilt n
Hob n HEAT
Hob n PLAY

Horn n
Houseful n HOME
Hummock n
Hump n BODY
Hump n
Hunch n VARY
Hunched v VARY
Hunching v VARY
Inflate v VAPR
Inflating v VAPR
Inflation n VAPR
Inundate v FLOW
Jut v
Knob n
Knot n JOIN
Laden j
Lading n
Lapful n BODY
Ledge n ERTH
Ledge n
Levee n ERTH
Load v
Load v FALS
Lug n
Lump n
Lump v JOIN
Lump n AGGR
Mesa n ERTH
Midden n DIRT
Mound n ERTH
Mound n
Mount n ERTH
Mountain n ERTH
Nipple n SIP
Nub n
Overburden v
Overcapacity n LARG
Overeat v FOOD
Overflow v FLOW
Overload v
Pack n BLOK
Package n HOLW

Packed v BLOK
Packet n HOLW
Packing v BLOK
Pad n EASY
Padded v EASY
Pailful n HOLW
Palisade n ERTH
Panhandle n ERTH
Parcel n HOLW
Paunch n BODY
Peg n
Pike n ERTH
Pile n
Piled v
Piling v
Plethora n MUCH
Pocketful n HOLW
Poke v
Poke v JOIN
Poker n
Pommel n
Potbelly n BODY
Precipice n ERTH
Precipitous j
Project v
Projecting v
Prominence n
Promontory n ERTH
Protrusion n
Puff v LARG
Pyre n HEAT
Redundant j TRIV
Replenish v
Replete j
Ridge n ERTH
Rise n UP
Rotund j FORM
Salient j
Sated j AID
Satiate v AID
Satiety n AID
Saturate v FLOW

Saturate v
Shag n FABR
Shaggy j
Sheer j
Shock n
Spur n
Stack n
Steep j
Steep v FLOW
Steeped v FLOW
Steeping v FLOW
Stick v
Stuck v
Stuff v
Stuffed v
Stuffing n
Stuffs v
Surge v GO
Surplus n MUCH
Swamp v FLOW
Swamped v FLOW
Swamping v FLOW
Swell v LARG
Swollen j LARG
Tab n
Tabbed v
Tabbing v
Tang n
Teeth n
Terrace n ERTH
Tongue n
Tooth n
Turgid j
Uphill d UP
Wad n
Wad n MONY
Wadded v
Waterlog v FLOW
Wave n VARY
Welt n DAMG
Woodpile n MTRL

CLEN

Ablution n FLOW
Aerate v VAPR
Antimacassar n FURN
Aseptic j MEDC
Autoclave n HEAT
Bath n FLOW
Bath n HOME
Bathe v FLOW
Bathrobe n GARB
Bathroom n HOME
Bathtub n HOLW
Brainwash v IDEA
Broom n
Broomstick n FORM
Brush n
Buff v
Buffed v
Burnish v VIEW
Can n HOME
Card v SEP

Carded v SEP
Carding v SEP
Catharsis n OUT
Chimneysweep n WORK
Chlorinate v VAPR
Clarify v SHRP
Clean j
Clean j WHOL
Cleanliness n
Cleanse v
Clear j
Closet n HOME
Comb n
Combed v
Combing v
Commode n HOLW
Curried v
Curry v
Currycomb v
Decontaminate v

Delouse v BUG
Dentifrice n BODY
Deodorant n SOMA
Deodorize v SOMA
Detergent n
Dishcloth n
Dishwasher n FURN
Disinfect v MEDC
Dust v ERTH
Dusted v ERTH
Duster n ERTH
Dusting v ERTH
Expurgate v OUT
Flatiron n EASY
Fumigate v
Gargle v FLOW
Groom v
Groomed v
Grooming v
Hairbrush n BODY

Head n HOME
Hygiene n MEDC
Immaculate j
Iron n EASY
Ironed v EASY
Ironing v EASY
Kleenex n
Lather n FLOW
Latrine n HOME
Launder v FLOW
Laundress n LADY
Laundries n MART
Laundromat n MART
Laundry n MART
Lavatory n HOME
Manicure n BODY
Mop n
Mopped v
Napkin n
Natty j

Neat j
Pasteurize v HEAT
Pickle v FLOW
Pickled j FLOW
Pickling v FLOW
Police v
Polish n EASY
Polished v EASY
Polishing v EASY
Preen v
Press v GARB
Pressed v GARB
Pressing v GARB
Primp v
Prink v
Privy n HOME
Prune v SHRP
Prune v
Pruned v SHRP
Pruned v

Pruning v SHRP
Pruning v
Puff n EASY
Pure j
Pure j GOOD
Purge v OUT
Purity n
Purity n GOOD
Refurbish v NEW
Rinse v FLOW
Rub v
Rubbed v
Rubber n
Rubbing v
Sanitary j MEDC
Sanitation n MEDC
Scavenge v
Scour v
Scrape v SEP
Scraping v SEP

Scrub v
Scrubbed v
Shampoo v
Shave n SHRP
Shine v VIEW
Shower n FLOW
Sleek j EASY
Soap n
Sponge n FLOW
Spotless j
Spruce v GOOD
Spruced v GOOD
Sprucing v GOOD
Stainless j
Sterile j
Swab v
Sweep v
Sweeps v
Swept v
Swill v

Tidily d
Tidiness n
Tidy j
Toilet n HOME
Toilet n GARB
Toothpaste n BODY
Towel n
Unadulterated j
Unalloyed j
Unspoiled j
Vacuum n MECH
Wash n FLOW
Washed v FLOW
Washer n FLOW
Watercloset n HOME
Wax n MTRL
Weed v VEGT
Whitewash v COLR
Willow v VEGT
Wipe v

COLD

Antarctic n PLAC
Arctic n PLAC
Bobsled n VEHC
Chill n
Cold j
Cold j AGGR
Coldcuts n FOOD
Cool j
Cool j GLAD
Cool j GOOD
Cool j AGGR
Coolant n
Cooler j
Cooler j GLAD
Cooler n HOLW
Cooler n BLOK
Cooling v

Cooling v GLAD
Defrost v VARY
Fan v VARY
Fanned v VARY
Floe n FLOW
Freeze v
Freeze v PANG
Freezer n HOLW
Frigid j
Frigid j SEX
Frost n FLOW
Frost n FOOD
Frosty j FLOW
Frosty j AGGR
Froze v
Froze v PANG
Glacier n FLOW

Glaze n FLOW
Glazing v FLOW
Hibernal j TIME
Ice n FLOW
Ice n FOOD
Iceberg n FLOW
Icebox n HOLW
Icecream n FOOD
Icicle n FLOW
Iciness n FLOW
Icing n FLOW
Icing n FOOD
Icy j FLOW
Icy j AGGR
JackFrost n WEA
Midwinter j TIME
Mush v GO

Polar j PLAC
Pole n PLAC
Refrigerate v
Refrigerator n HOLW
Sled n VEHC
Sledge n VEHC
Sleet n WEA
Sleigh n VEHC
Snow n WEA
Snowball n WEA
Snowflake n WEA
Snowplow n VEHC
Snows n WEA
Snowshoe n GARB
Snowsuit n GARB
Watercool v FLOW
Winter n TIME

COLR

Acrylic n
Albino n LACK
Amber n
Amethyst n
Apricot n
Aquamarine n
Aquatint n
Ash n
Ashen j
Auburn j
Azure j
Batik n FABR
Bay n
Beige j
Biscuit n
Black j
Black j BAD
Black j AGGR
Black j CRIM
Black j DIRT
Black n AID
Black n GRUP

Blackball v AGGR
Blackboard n FORM
Blacken v
Blacken v DIRT
Blackjack n DAMG
Blackjack n PLAY
Blackjack n VIEW
Blackjack n VEGT
Blackout n BLUR
Blanch v
Bleach v
Bleached v
Bled v OUT
Bleed v OUT
Blonde j
Blonde n BODY
Blue j
Blue j PANG
Blues n PANG
Blues n
Bluest j
Bluest j PANG

Blush v BODY
Brass n
Brassy j
Bronze j
Brown n
Brown v HEAT
Brownie n FOOD
Browning v
Browning v HEAT
Brownstone j ERTH
Brunette j
Brunette n BODY
Buff n
Burgundy n
Canary n
Carbuncle n
Cardinal j
Carmine n
Carnation n
Cast n
Charcoal n MTRL
Chartreuse n

Cherry n
Chestnut n
Chiaroscuro n
Chlorophyll n VEGT
Chocolate n
Chromatic j
Chrome n
Claret n
Cloisonne n FORM
Cocoa n
Coffee n
Color n
Colorless j LACK
Colorless j TRIV
Complected j BODY
Complexion n BODY
Copper n
Coral n
Crayon n WRIT
Cream n
Crimson j
Daffodil n

Damask n
Dapple n ANML
Dapple v
Dark j
Dark j BLUR
Decolor v
Dichromatic j
Discolor v DIRT
Distemper n
Drab j TRIV
Drab n FABR
Dull j
Dun j
Dusk j
Dye n
Dyestuff n MTRL
Ebony n
Eggshell n FOOD
Emblazon v VIEW
Emerald n
Enamel n MTRL
Fade v BLUR
Fading v BLUR
Fair j
Fairhaired j BODY
Fawn n
Flame n HEAT
Flat j
Fleabitten j BUG
Flesh n BODY
Florid j
Flush n BODY
Flushed v BODY
Flushing v BODY
Freckle n BODY
Fresco n
Fuchsia n
Garnet n
Gild v MTRL
Gilt j MTRL
Glaze n MTRL
Glazing v MTRL
Gold n
Golden j
Golden j GOOD
Gouache n
Grape n
Gray j
Greasepaint n BODY
Green j
Green j WEAK
Green n VEGT
Greenback n MONY
Greenery n VEGT
Grey j

Grizzly n ANML
Grizzly j
Hazel n
Heliotrope n
Heterochromatic j MUCH
Hoar j PAST
Homochromatic j SIML
Hue n
Hyacinth n
Indigo n
Indigo n VEGT
Infrared j
Ink n WRIT
Iridescence n VIEW
Isochromatic j SIML
Ivory j
Jade n
Jasper n
Jaundice n SICK
Jet n
Khaki n
Khaki n GARB
Khakis n GARB
Lacquer v MTRL
Lavender n
Lemon n
Light j
Lighten v
Lilac n
Lime n
Lipstick n BODY
Livid j
Lurid j
Magenta n
Mahogany n
Marble n
Marbled v
Marbling v
Maroon j
Mascara n
Mat n
Mauve n
Monochromatic j SIML
Mosaic n FORM
Mottle v
Mulatto j
Mulberry n
Mural n
Navy n
Negro n GRUP
Nuance n VARY
Ochre n
Oil n
Oils n
Olive n

Orange n
Orchid n
Paint v
Pale j
Pale j WEAK
Palette n HOLW
Paling v
Pallid j WEAK
Pallor n WEAK
Palomino n ANML
Particolor j MUCH
Pastel n WRIT
Pasty j
Patina n
Peach n
Pearl n
Peppermint n
Peroxide n MTRL
Pied j
Pigment n
Pink n
Pink n GOOD
Pinto n ANML
Pitch n MTRL
Platinum n
Plum n
Polychromatic j MUCH
Purple n
Quadroon n GRUP
Rainbow n WEA
Raven n
Red n
Red n GRUP
Red n LACK
Redden v
Redhead n BODY
Redskin n GRUP
Redwood n VEGT
Rose n
Rosecolored j GOOD
Rosily d GOOD
Rosily d
Rosiness n GOOD
Rosiness n
Rosy j GOOD
Rosy j
Rouge n
Ruby n
Ruddiness n
Ruddy j
Russet j
Rust n
Rusty j
Sable n
Saffron n

Sallow j
Salmon n
Sandier j
Sandy j
Sanguine j SOMA
Sapphire n
Scarlet j
Serigraph n
Shade n
Shiner n BODY
Silkscreen n FABR
Silver n
Slate n
Snowwhite j WEA
Speckling n
Spectroscope n VIEW
Spectrum n FORW
Spot n
Spotted j
Stain n
Stipple v LITL
Strawberry n
Streak v SOME
Streaked v SOME
Streaking v SOME
Stripe n FORM
Striping n FORM
Tan n
Tan v DAMG
Tapestry n FABR
Tawny j
Tempera n
Terracotta j ERTH
Tincture n
Tinge n SOME
Tint n
Tone n
Tonic j
Topaz n
Turquoise n
Vermilion n
Violet n
Walnut n
Wan j WEAK
Wash n FLOW
Watercolor n FLOW
White j
White j GOOD
Whitewash v CLEN
Whiting n MTRL
Yellow j
Yellow j WEAK

COVR

Abstruse j BLUR
Ambush n DAMG
Anonymous j TALK
Apron n
Arcane j
Awning n UP
Bandage v AID

Bedspread n FURN
Blanket n
Blind j VIEW
Blindfold n VIEW
Blot v VIEW
Blotted v VIEW
Board v MTRL

Boarded v MTRL
Boarding v MTRL
Boards v MTRL
Bonnet n MECH
Bug v HEAR
Bugged v HEAR
Bugging v HEAR

Buried v
Buried v DEAD
Burrow v
Bury v
Bury v DEAD
Cabal n GRUP
Cabala n HOLY

Cache n HOLW
Camera n HOME
Camouflage v FALS
Canopy n UP
Cant n TALK
Cap n
Caps v
Ceiling n UP
Cipher n WRIT
Clandestine j
Classify v GRUP
Cloak n
Close v
Closed v
Closing v
Coat n
Code n IDEA
Coding v IDEA
Conceal v
Conclave n HOME
Conclave n JOIN
Confidant n FOND
Confide v FOND
Confidence n FOND
Confident j FOND
Confidential j FOND
Confidential j
Cope v FORM
Coping n FORM
Cot n
Counterpane n FURN
Cover n
Coverage n
Coverlet n FURN
Covert j
Covert n AID
Crust n FOOD
Crust n
Cryptic j BLUR
Cryptogram n WRIT
Curtain n FURN
Curtain n
Curtain n PLAY
Cypher n WRIT
Disguise n FALS

Dome n UP
Domino n GARB
Drape v FABR
Drapery n FURN
Eavesdrop v HEAR
Eclipse v BLUR
Enclose v IN
Enclosure n IN
Encrust v DIRT
Ensconce v
Envelop v HOLW
Enveloped v HOLW
Esoteric j AFAR
Espionage n VIEW
Eyelid n BODY
Ferrule n HOLW
Fifthcolumn n DAMG
Film n
Furtive j
Grapevine n TALK
Hidden v
Hide v
Hideout n HOME
Hoard n HAVE
Hood n
Imperceptible j VIEW
Inclose v IN
Incognito d FALS
Incrustation n DIRT
Inhume v DEAD
Inscrutable j BLUR
Inter v DEAD
Interment n DEAD
Interred v DEAD
Intrigue n FALS
Invisible j VIEW
Jacket n
Lid n
Lid n BODY
Line v
Liner n
Lining n
Lurk v
Mantle n
Mask n

Mask n GARB
Occult j MYTH
Pall n PANG
Parapet n FORM
Patch n AID
Plot n IDEA
Plotted v IDEA
Portiere n FURN
Privacy n SEP
Private j SEP
Prowl v GO
Recondite j BLUR
Retreat n HOLY
Retreat n HOME
Roof n UP
Sandwich n
Sandwiched v
Sandwiching v
Scale n FORM
Screen v
Seal v BLOK
Sealed v BLOK
Sealing v BLOK
Seclusion n SEP
Secrecy n
Secret j
Secrete v
Secreting v
Shade n BLUR
Shroud v
Shut v BLOK
Shutter n BLOK
Slink v GO
Slunk v GO
Sly j FALS
Smuggle v CRIM
Sneak v GO
Sneaked v GO
Snipe v DAMG
Sniped v DAMG
Sniper n DAMG
Sniping v DAMG
Snuck v GO
Spied v VIEW
Spies v VIEW

Spirit v GO
Spirited v GO
Spiriting v GO
Spread n FURN
Spy n VIEW
Stash v
Steal v GO
Stole v GO
Stolen v GO
Stow v
Subconscious j IDEA
Surreptitious j
Tacit j IDEA
Tape v MTRL
Tapes v MTRL
Taping v MTRL
Tarpaulin n FABR
Top n UP
Topped v UP
Tops n UP
Tuck v
Tucked v
Tucking v
Ulterior j
Umbrella n AID
Unburied j OPEN
Unconscious j IDEA
Undeclared j TALK
Underground n DAMG
Underhand j FALS
Undetected j
Unknown j BLUR
Unnoticed j VIEW
Unopened j
Unperceived j VIEW
Unpublished j WRIT
Unseen j VIEW
Unspoken j TALK
Untold j TALK
Veil n
Veil n GARB
Veneer n MTRL
Waylay v DAMG
Wrap n
Wrapped v

CRIM

Abduct v SEP
Abscond v GO
Accomplice n AID
Apache n GRUP
Argot n TALK
Arson n HEAT
Bandit n
Black j COLR
Blackmail v MONY
Bootleg j
Break n DAMG
Bribe n MONY
Buccaneer n FLOW
Bunco n FALS
Bunko n FALS
Burglar n
Caper n

Case v IDEA
Cased v IDEA
Casing v IDEA
Cheat v FALS
Chisel v FALS
Con j FALS
Con n BLOK
Confederate n JOIN
Conned v FALS
Conning v FALS
Cons v FALS
Contraband j MART
Convict v BLOK
Convicting v BLOK
Conviction n BLOK
Corsair n FLOW
Crib n WRIT

Cribbed v WRIT
Cribbing v WRIT
Crime n
Criminal j
Criminology n LAW
Crook n
Culprit n BAD
Cutpurse n
Cutthroat n DAMG
Defalcate v MONY
Defraud v FALS
Delinquency n
Depredate v DAMG
Desperado n
Despoil v DAMG
Embezzle v
Extort v

Felony n
Fence n
Filch v
Firebug n HEAT
Fleece v
Flimflam v FALS
Frameup n FALS
Fraud n FALS
Gangster n
Gouge v MONY
Graft n
Guilt n PANG
Held v BLOK
Highwayman n MALE
Hijack v
Hocus v FALS
Hold v BLOK

Homicide n DEAD
Hood n
Hoodlum n
Hot j HEAT
Illegal j
Illegitimate j
Illicit j BAD
Incest n SEX
Incriminate v
Kidnap v SEP
Larceny n
Lawbreaker n LAW
Lifer n BLOK
Lift v
Loot v
Mafia n GRUP
Malefaction n BAD
Malfeasance n
Misdemeanor n

Moonlight v WORK
Moonshine n SIP
Murder v DEAD
Outlaw n
Peculate v MONY
Penal j LAW
Penology n BLOK
Pick v
Picked v
Pilfer v
Pillage v DAMG
Pinch v
Piracy n FLOW
Plagiarism n WRIT
Plunder v
Poach v ANML
Pony n WRIT
Purloin v
Pusher n MEDC

Racket n
Racketeer n
Rakeoff n MONY
Rifle v
Rifled v
Rifling v
Rob v
Roll v
Rolled v
Rustle v ANML
Rustler n ANML
Sack v DAMG
Sacked v DAMG
Sacking v DAMG
Scalp v MONY
Scalped v MONY
Scalping v MONY
Shakedown n MONY
Smuggle v COVR

Speakeasy n SIP
Steal v
Stickup n
Stole v
Stolen j
Suborn v FALS
Swindle v FALS
Theft n
Thief n
Thug n BAD
Transgress v
Trespass v GO
Underworld n
Unlawful j LAW
Vandal n DAMG
Wrongdoing n BAD
Yegg n

CRUX

ABC n WRIT
Appraise v IDEA
Archetype n SIML
Assess v IDEA
Asset n AID
Attribute n HAVE
Background n BACK
Base n HOME
Base n
Based v
Based v HOME
Bases n HOME
Bases n
Basic j
Basing v
Basis n
Body n
Capital j
Cardinal j
Cardinal j NUMR
Central j SHRP
Character n
Characteristic j
Characterize v
Climacteric n TIME
Climactic j UP
Climax n UP
Clutch n BLOK
Condition n AGRE
Conditional j AGRE
Consequence n
Core n SHRP
Core n VEGT
Coring v VEGT
Cornerstone n ERTH
Count v AID
Counted v AID
Counting v AID
Crisis n DAMG
Critical j

Crucial j
Crux n
Deep j DOWN
Denature v VARY
Denominator n NUMR
Depreciable j LITL
Depreciate v LITL
Earnest j MOTV
Element n SOME
Elementary j SOME
Elements n SOME
Equities n SIML
Equity n SIML
Essence n
Essential j
Evaluate v IDEA
Feature n VIEW
Featuring v VIEW
Figure v
Figured v
Figuring v
Foundation n FORM
Founded j
Founds v FORM
Fundamental n
Germane j SIML
Gist n
Grave j PANG
Gravity n PANG
Grist n SOME
Ground n IDEA
Heart n
Home n
Hub n SHRP
Idiosyncrasy n SOLE
Imperative j MOTV
Imperious j MOTV
Import n IDEA
Importance n
Indispensable j

Ingrained j IN
Inherent j EVER
Integral j WHOL
Intrinsic j IN
Invaluable j
Kernel n
Key n
Keyed v
Keying v
Keynote n
Keys n
Keystone n FORM
Main j
Mainstay n AID
Major j POWR
Makeup n FORM
Marrow n SOMA
Material j
Matter n
Matter n PANG
Mattered v
Mattering v
Matters v
Meat n
Milestone n MSMT
Moment n
Momentous j
Natural j
Naturalize v
Nature n
Necessity n MOTV
Nub n
Nuclear j ION
Nucleus n
Nucleus n ION
Peculiar j SIML
Pertinence n JOIN
Phenotype n GRUP
Piecederesistance r POWR
Pith n POWR

Pith n SOMA
Pithy j POWR
Pivot n VARY
Point n IDEA
Precious j GOOD
Prerequisite n
Pressing j
Priceless j MONY
Primal j FORW
Primary j FORW
Prime j FORW
Principal j
Principle n IDEA
Priority n FORW
Profound j DOWN
Profundity n DOWN
Proper j
Prototype n SIML
Purport n IDEA
Qualify v POWR
Qualify v VARY
Quality n
Reputation n
Reputation n POWR
Repute n
Repute n POWR
Root n BGIN
Root n NUMR
Sap n SOMA
Serious j
Significance n
Sober j
Sobriety n
Solemn j
Soul n MYTH
Soul n SOLE
Special j
Specialist n POWR
Specialty n POWR
Spirit n MOTV

Parts of speech: a article; b preposition; c conjunction; d adverb; f prefix; i interjection;
          j adjective; n noun; p pronoun; r phrase; v verb.

Spirit n MYTH
Spirited j MOTV
Staple n
Stock n
Strategic j POWR
Substance n

Substantive j
Trait n
Treasure n
Treasure v FOND
Treasured v FOND
Treasuring v FOND

Underlying j DOWN
Urgent j
Value v
Vital j
Vital j LIVE
Vital j DEAD

Weight n
Worth n GOOD
Worthwhile j GOOD

DAMG

Abrade v
Abrasion n
Abrasive j
Abuse n
Accident n
Ace n POWR
Action n
Adventure n
Afflict v
Affray n
Aftermath n END
Aggression n
Altercation n
Ambush n COVR
Ammunition n
Amuck j PANG
Annihilate v END
Antebellum j PAST
Apocalypse n FORW
Archer n SHRP
Arm n MECH
Armada n VEHC
Armageddon n PLAC
Armament n MECH
Armature n AID
Armed v MECH
Armies n GRUP
Arming v MECH
Armistice n END
Armor n AID
Armories n HOME
Armory n HOME
Arms n MECH
Army n GRUP
Arrow n SHRP
Arsenal n HOLW
Arsenic n MTRL
Artillery n MECH
Asp n ANML
Asphyxiate v DEAD
Assail v
Assassinate v DEAD
Assault n
Ate v FOOD
Atrocious j BAD
Atrocity n BAD
Attack v
Attempt n
Automatic n MECH
Avenge v
Bad j BAD
Ball n FORM
Bang v
Barbarian n
Barbaric j
Barrage n GRUP

Bash v
Bat v
Battalion n GRUP
Batted v
Batter v
Batteries n GRUP
Battering v
Batters v
Battery n
Batting v
Battle n
Battlefield n ERTH
Battleship n FLOW
Bayonet n SHRP
Bean v BODY
Beat v
Beaten j
Belch v OUT
Belligerent j
Belt v
Beset v
Besiege v
Beware v MOTV
Billies n FORM
Billy n FORM
Bit v
Bite n
Biting v
Bitten v
Blackjack n COLR
Blank n LACK
Blast n HEAR
Blast n WEA
Blasted v HEAR
Blastoff n SEP
Blew v
Blight n SICK
Blizzard n WEA
Blockade n BLOK
Bloodied v SOMA
Bloodshed n SOMA
Bloodthirsty j SOMA
Bloody j SOMA
Bloodying v SOMA
Blow n
Bluebeard n MYTH
Blunderbuss n MECH
Bodyguard n AID
Bolt n
Bomb n
Bombard v
Bombardier n
Bomber n
Bomber n VEHC
Bounce v GO
Bouncer n GO

Bow n
Bowl v
Bowled v
Bowling v
Box v
Box v PLAY
Boxed v
Boxed v PLAY
Boxer n PLAY
Boxing v
Boxing v PLAY
Brain v SOMA
Brandish v
Brawl n
Breach n SEP
Break n SEP
Break n CRIM
Breaker n FLOW
Broadside n
Broke v SEP
Broken j SEP
Bruise v BODY
Bruise v
Brunt n
Brush n JOIN
Brute n
Bulldoze v
Bullet n
Bullfight n ANML
Bullies n
Bully n
Bump v JOIN
Bump v DEAD
Bumped v JOIN
Bumped v DEAD
Bumper n AID
Bumping v JOIN
Bumping v DEAD
Bunker n HOME
Burn v HEAT
Burning j HEAT
Burst n HEAR
Burst n SEP
Bushwhacker n VEGT
Bust n
Busted v
Buster n
Busting v
Butcher n DEAD
Butt n
Butted v
Butting v
Caisson n HOLW
Caisson n VEHC
Calamity n
Campaign n

Cane v FORM
Caned v FORM
Caning v FORM
Cannibal n FOOD
Cannibalize v SEP
Cannon n MECH
Cap n PLAY
Caps n PLAY
Capsize v VARY
Carbine n MECH
Carnage n DEAD
Cartridge n
Casualty n
Cataclysm n
Catapult n MECH
Catastrophe n
Caustic n MTRL
Cavalier n ANML
Cavalry n ANML
Cave v WEAK
Caving v WEAK
Chafe v
Chair n DEAD
Chap n BODY
Chapped v BODY
Char v HEAT
Charge n
Chase n GO
Chasten v
Chastise v
Chevies n GO
Chevy n GO
Choke v BLOK
Chop n SHRP
Chopped v SHRP
Chops n SHRP
Claw v SHRP
Clip n
Clipped v
Clout n
Club v
Clubbed v
Clubbing v
Cockpit n ANML
Collide v JOIN
Collision n JOIN
Combat n
Commando n
Concussion n
Conflagration n HEAT
Conflict n
Conquistador n POWR
Consume v
Consumption n
Contuse v BODY
Corpsman n MEDC

Cossack n ANML
Coup n POWR
Crack n
Cracked v
Crash n HEAR
Cripple v WEAK
Crisis n CRUX
Crown v BODY
Crucified v
Crucifixion n HOLY
Crucify v
Cruel j BAD
Crusade v HOLY
Crush n
Cudgel n
Cuff n
Curried v
Curry v
Cut v SHRP
Cutlass n SHRP
Cutthroat n CRIM
Cutting v SHRP
Cyclone n WEA
Damage n
Danger n
Dash v GO
Dashing v GO
Debacle n WEAK
Decimate v
Deface v DIRT
Deflower v SEX
Deleterious j
Demilitarize v END
Demobilize v END
Demolish v
Demolition n
Depopulate v GRUP
Depredate v CRIM
Derringer n MECH
Desecrate v HOLY
Desolate v
Despoil v CRIM
Destroy v
Destroyer n
Destroyer n FLOW
Destruction n
Detonate v HEAR
Devastate v
Devour v
Dire j
Dirk n SHRP
Disarm v WEAK
Disaster n
Discharge v OUT
Discipline v LEAD
Disintegrate v SEP
Disorder n
Disorderly j
Division n GRUP
Dogfight n UP
Dragoon n
Dreadnaught n FLOW
Drub v
Duel n
Dump n HOLW

Dynamite v MTRL
Earthquake n ERTH
Eat v FOOD
Electrocute v DEAD
Embattle v AID
Emergency n
Encounter n JOIN
Endanger v
Engage v JOIN
Erupt v OUT
Execute v DEAD
Executing v DEAD
Explode v HEAR
Explosion n HEAR
Explosive n HEAR
Exterminate v DEAD
Extirpate v OUT
Fall v DOWN
Falling v DOWN
Fatal j DEAD
Fell v DOWN
Ferocity n
Feud n
Fiend n BAD
Fierce j
Fifthcolumn n COVR
Fight n
Fire v HEAT
Firearm n MECH
Firebrand n
Fired v HEAT
Firepower n POWR
Fires v HEAT
Firing v HEAT
Fist n BODY
Flagellate v
Flail v
Flak n
Flog v
Floor v DOWN
Foray v
Forearm v FORW
Forearmed v FORW
Forearming v FORW
Fought v
Fracas n
Fracture v SEP
Fray n
Front n FORW
Fusillade n
Gale n WEA
Gantlet n
Garrison n HOME
Garrison n GRUP
Gas n VAPR
Gash n SHRP
Gat n MECH
Gauntlet n GARB
Get v
Gladiator n
Goon n FOOL
Gore n SOMA
Gore v SHRP
Gorier j SOMA
Gorilla n ANML

Gory j SOMA
Got v
Grapple v JOIN
Grenade n
Grenadier n
Grind v
Grinds v
Ground v VARY
Gruel v
Grueling j
Guerrilla j
Gun n MECH
Gunboat n FLOW
Gunman n MALE
Gunned v MECH
Gunpowder n MTRL
Gunshot n HEAR
Gut v
Gutted v
Hack v
Hammer n MECH
Harm n
Harpoon n SHRP
Harried v PANG
Harrier n PANG
Harrow v PANG
Harry v PANG
Harumscarum j BLUR
Havoc n
Haymaker n REST
Hazard n MOTV
Headsman n
Hector v
Hedgehog n BLOK
Heinous j BAD
Hide v BODY
Hit v
Holocaust n HEAT
Hook n VARY
Hooligan n
Howitzer n MECH
Hunt v ANML
Hurl v GO
Hurricane n WEA
Hurt v
Illfated j END
Illtreat v
Impact n JOIN
Impair v WEAK
Imperil v
Impetuous j QUIK
Implode v IN
Implosion n IN
Incautious j
Incendiary n HEAT
Infantry n
Inferno n BAD
Infest v MUCH
Inflict v
Inhuman j
Inhumane j
Injure v
Injury n
Inroad n
Insidious j

Insurgence n
Internecine j DEAD
Invade v IN
Invasion n IN
Jab n
Jabbed v
Javelin n SHRP
Jeopardy n
Jolt n
Jolt n VARY
Jump v
Jumped v
Jumping v
Keel v VARY
Kick n BODY
Kill v DEAD
Knife v SHRP
Knight n
Knock v
Knockout n REST
Lace v
Laceration n BODY
Lam v
Lance n SHRP
Lash n
Lashing v
Lather v
Lead n MTRL
Legion n GRUP
Legionnaire n GRUP
Lesion n
Lethal j DEAD
Levied v
Levy v
Lick v
Licked v
Licking v
Liquidate v END
Lynch v DEAD
Mail n AID
Maim v
Maltreat v
Mangle v
Manofwar n FLOW
Manslaughter n DEAD
Marine n FLOW
Marines n FLOW
Marksman n SHRP
Mars n MYTH
Martial j
Masochism n SOLE
Massacre v DEAD
Matador n ANML
Mayhem n
Melee n
Menace n
Mercenary j MONY
Military j
Militia n GRUP
Mine n
Mined v
Mines n
Mining v
Misadventure n
Mischance n

Misfire v FALS	Plugged v	Rended v SEP	Sharpshooter n SHRP
Misfortune n	Pogrom n DEAD	Rending v SEP	Shatter v SEP
Mishap n	Poison n	Rent n SEP	Shed v OUT
Missile n	Poke n	Reserve n GRUP	Shell n HOLW
Mistreat v	Poleax n SHRP	Reservist n GRUP	Shipwreck n FLOW
Molest v	Pommel v	Resist v BLOK	Shock n
Monsoon n WEA	Pommeled v	Revenge n	Shoot v
Mortar n MECH	Pommeling v	Revolt n	Shot n
Mug v	Pommelled v	Revolution n VARY	Shotgun n MECH
Mugged v	Pompom n MECH	Revolver n MECH	Siege n EVER
Mugging v	Poniard n SHRP	Rhubarb n	Singe v HEAT
Munition n	Portent n FORW	Rifle n MECH	Siren n LADY
Murder v DEAD	Potshot n	Riot n	Skirmish n
Musket n MECH	Pound v	Risk v MOTV	Slain v DEAD
Mutilate v	Pounded v	Rod n FORM	Slam n
Mutiny n	Pounding v	Rod n MECH	Slap n
Napalm n MTRL	Powder n MTRL	Rough j	Slash v SHRP
Naval j FLOW	Precarious j	Roughed v	Slaughter n DEAD
Navies n FLOW	Predator n	Roughing v	Slay v DEAD
Navy n FLOW	Prewar j FORW	Round n	Slew v DEAD
Nick v SHRP	Prey n WEAK	Rounds n	Sling n MECH
Nicked v SHRP	Privateer n FLOW	Row n	Slug n
Nightstick n LAW	Procrustean j SIML	Rowdy j	Slugged v
Noxious j BAD	Prod v SHRP	Rub v DEAD	Slugging v
Obliterate v	Projectile n GO	Rubbed v DEAD	Smack n HEAR
Offense n	Pug n	Rubbing v DEAD	Smash v
Ogre n MYTH	Pugilism n PLAY	Ruffian n	Snap v SEP
Onset n	Pugnacious j	Ruin v DIRT	Snapped v SEP
Onslaught n	Pulverize v VARY	Rumble n HEAR	Snaps v SEP
Oppress v	Pummel v	Rumpus n	Snipe v COVR
Ouch i EMPH	Punch n	Rupture n SEP	Sniped v COVR
Outrage n BAD	Punched v	Sabotage v	Sniper n COVR
Overran v GO	Punching v	Sabre n SHRP	Sniping v COVR
Overrun v GO	Punish v	Sack v CRIM	Snowstorm n WEA
Paddle v	Punitive j	Sacked v CRIM	Soak v
Pain n PANG	Purgatory n HOLY	Sacking v CRIM	Sock n
Pains n PANG	Purge v SEP	Sacrifice n LACK	Socked v
Pandemonium n HEAR	Quarries n WEAK	Sadism n	Socking v
Paratroop n DOWN	Quarry n WEAK	Sallied v GO	Soldier n
Parricide n LEAD	Quell v BLOK	Sally n GO	Sore n BODY
Partisan j MOTV	Rack n	Salvo n GRUP	Sores n BODY
Paste v	Rack n FORM	Sanction n	Sortie n GO
Pasted v	Racked v	Sandbag v	SOS n WRIT
Pasting v	Racking v	Sanguine j SOMA	Spank v
Pellet n	Racks v	Sap v WEAK	Spar v PLAY
Pelt v	Raid n	Sapped v WEAK	Spear n SHRP
Pentagon n HOME	Rake v	Sapper n	Spill v FLOW
Percussion n HEAR	Ramrod n FORM	Savage j	Spoil v DIRT
Perdition n BAD	Ransack v OPEN	Scald v HEAT	Spoils v DIRT
Peril n	Rap n	Scalp v BODY	Spoils n HAVE
Pernicious j	Rapacious j MOTV	Scalped v BODY	Sprain n
Persecute v	Rape n SEX	Scalping v BODY	Squall n WEA
Phalanx n GRUP	Rapine n	Scar n BODY	Stab v SHRP
Phrenetic j PANG	Raping v SEX	Scimitar n SHRP	Stamp v
Picador n SHRP	Rapist n SEX	Scorch v HEAT	Stamped v
Picket n AID	Rapped v	Scourge n	Stampede v GO
Piece n MECH	Rash j QUIK	Scrap n	Sting v SHRP
Pike n SHRP	Ravage v	Scrape n	Stone v ERTH
Piked v SHRP	Ravish v	Scrapped v	Stoned v ERTH
Piking v SHRP	Ravish v SEX	Scratch n SHRP	Stoning v ERTH
Pillage v CRIM	Raze v DOWN	Scuffle v	Storm n WEA
Pillbox n HOME	Rebel v OPPO	Sear v HEAT	Storm v GO
Pistol n MECH	Reckless j	Sentinel n AID	Strap v
Pitfall n HOLW	Regiment n GRUP	Sentry n AID	Stricken j WEAK
Plug v	Rend v SEP	Service n AID	Strike v

Striking v
Stripe n
Stroke n
Struck v
Struggle n
Stun v REST
Stung v SHRP
Stunned v REST
Stunning v REST
Submarine n FLOW
Subvert v WEAK
Suicide n DEAD
Switch n
Sword n SHRP
Take v DEAD
Tan v COLR
Tank n VEHC
Tempest n WEA
Terrible j BAD
Terrific j BAD
Terror n BAD
Thrash v
Threat n
Throe n PANG
Thunderbolt n WEA

Thunderstorm n WEA
Tilt n SHRP
Took v DEAD
Toreador n ANML
Torment n PANG
Tornado n WEA
Torpedo n
Torrent n FLOW
Torture v PANG
Toxic j
Tragedy n
Trample v GO
Transfix v SHRP
Trauma n PANG
Treacherous j FALS
Trounce v
Truce n END
Tussle v
Twister n WEA
Underground n COVR
Undermine v WEAK
Unsafe j WEAK
Untamed j
Upheaval n VARY
Uproot v SEP

Usurp v HAVE
Vandal n CRIM
Vengeance n
Venom n
Venture n MOTV
Veteran n PAST
Vicious j
Victim n WEAK
Villain n
Vindictive j
Violate v
Violence n
Viper n ANML
Virulent j
Volcano n ERTH
Volley n GRUP
Wage v
Waging v
Wallop v
War n
Warred v
Warring v
Warrior n
Warship n FLOW
Wartime n TIME

Waylay v COVR
Weapon n
Welt n BULG
Whack n
Whip n
Wild j
Wildcat n ANML
Wing v
Winged v
Winging v
Wipe v
Wound v
Wounded v
Wounding v
Wounds v
Wreck v
Wrench n
Wrenched v
Wrenches v
Wrenching v
Wrest v SEP
Wrestle v JOIN
Wring v BLOK
Wrung v BLOK

DEAD

Antemortem j FORW
Asphyxiate v DAMG
Assassinate v DAMG
Autopsy n IDEA
Behead v BODY
Bereave v LACK
Beyond n AFAR
Bier n HOLW
Block n FORM
Bodies n BODY
Body n BODY
Bump v DAMG
Bumped v DAMG
Bumping v DAMG
Buried v COVR
Bury v COVR
Butcher n DAMG
Cadaver n BODY
Capital j
Carcass n BODY
Carnage n DAMG
Casket n HOLW
Catacomb n HOLW
Cemetery n HOLW
Cenotaph n FORM
Cerecloth n FABR
Cerement n GARB
Chair n DAMG
Charnel j HOLW
Coffin n HOLW
Coroner n LEAD
Corpora n BODY
Corpse n BODY
Cremate v HEAT
Croak v
Croaked v
Crypt n HOLW

Dead j
Dead j TRIV
Deadbeat n WEAK
Deaden v REST
Deaden v TRIV
Deadwood n TRIV
Death n
Deathbed n REST
Deathless j EVER
Decease v
Decedent n
Defunct j END
Deicide n HOLY
Demise n
Departed j SEP
Die v
Diehard n OPPO
Dispatch v
Dispatched v
Dispatching v
Doom n END
Drown v FLOW
Dying v
Dying v MOTV
Electrocute v DAMG
Embalm v EVER
End n END
Epitaph n WRIT
Execute v DAMG
Executing v DAMG
Expire v
Exterminate v DAMG
Extinct j END
Fatal j DAMG
Fratricide n KIN
Funeral n
Funereal j PANG

Gallow n FORM
Genocide n GRUP
Grave n HOLW
Gravestone n ERTH
Graveyard n HOLW
Guillotine n SHRP
Hades n MYTH
Halter n BLOK
Hang v DOWN
Hanged v DOWN
Hangman n MALE
Harakiri n SHRP
Headstone n ERTH
Hearse n VEHC
Hearse n FORM
Heaven n MYTH
Hell n MYTH
Homicide n CRIM
Hung v DOWN
Inanimate j
Infanticide n YNG
Inhume v COVR
Insecticide n BUG
Inter v COVR
Interment n COVR
Internecine j DAMG
Interred v COVR
Kick v
Kill v DAMG
Kill v BLOK
Knell n MUSC
Late j PAST
Lethal j DAMG
Lifeless j TRIV
Lifeless j LACK
Limbo n MYTH
Lynch v DAMG

Macabre j PANG
Manslaughter n DAMG
Martyr n HOLY
Massacre v DAMG
Mausoleum n HOLW
Morgue n HOLW
Moribund j
Mortal j LIVE
Mortician n MART
Mummies n EVER
Mummy n EVER
Murder v CRIM
Murder v DAMG
Obituary n WRIT
Pallbearer n GO
Pass v GO
Passed v GO
Passes v GO
Passing v GO
Patricide n LEAD
Perish v
Pesticide n BUG
Pluto n MYTH
Pogrom n DAMG
Posthumous j BACK
Postmortem n BACK
Pottersfield n PLAC
Reincarnation n LIVE
Remains n
Requiem n HOLY
Resurrect v LIVE
Resuscitate v LIVE
Revive v LIVE
Rope n FABR
Rub v DAMG
Rubbed v DAMG
Rubbing v DAMG

Sarcophagus n HOLW	Stiff n BODY	Throttle v BLOK	Wake n REST
Scaffold n FORM	Stifle v BLOK	Tomb n HOLW	Widow n KIN
Sepulchre n HOLW	Strangle v BLOK	Tombs n HOLW	Widow n LADY
Shroud v GARB	Styx n FLOW	Tombstone n ERTH	Widowed v KIN
Slain v DAMG	Succumb v WEAK	Took v DAMG	Widowed v LADY
Slaughter n DAMG	Suffocate v BLOK	Undertaker n MART	Widower n KIN
Slay v DAMG	Suicide n DAMG	Undying j EVER	Widower n MALE
Slew v DAMG	Take v DAMG	Vault n HOLW	Zombie n MYTH
Smother v BLOK	Thanatopsis n	Vital j CRUX	

DIRT

Abscess n SICK	Dirt n ERTH	Lousier j BUG	Sawdust n MTRL
Acne n BODY	Disarray n	Lousier j BAD	Scab n BODY
Addle v	Discolor v COLR	Lousy j BUG	Scabbed v BODY
Adulterate v	Disfigure v BODY	Lousy j BAD	Scabbing v BODY
Anal j SOMA	Disrepair n	Maggot n BUG	Scabby j BODY
Anus n SOMA	Dowdy j GARB	Malodorous j VAPR	Scabrous j BODY
Aphid n BUG	Dreg n	Mangy j	Scavenge v FOOD
Bad j BAD	Dross n	Manure n SOMA	Scum n
Besmirch v	Dump n HOLW	Mar v	Sewage n
Bilge n FLOW	Dung n SOMA	Marred v	Shabby j
Black j COLR	Dunghill n BULG	Marring v	Shit v SOMA
Blacken v COLR	Dust n ERTH	Mars v	Slime n
Blemish n	Eczema n BODY	Mess n BLUR	Slipshod j WEAK
Blister n BULG	Encrust v COVR	Messy j BLUR	Sloppy j
Blot n	Excrement n OUT	Midden n BULG	Slum n PLAC
Blotch n	Excrete v OUT	Mildew n	Slush n FLOW
Blotted v	Faeces n SOMA	Mold n VEGT	Slut n LADY
Boil n BODY	Feces n SOMA	Moldy j VEGT	Smear v
Bowel n SOMA	Fester v SICK	Mote n LITL	Smear v AGGR
Carbuncle n BODY	Fetid j SOMA	Mud n ERTH	Smudge v
Cesspool n HOLW	Filth n	Muddies v ERTH	Smut n
Cloaca n SOMA	Fleabitten j BUG	Must n	Soil v
Clutter n BLUR	Fleck n SOME	Musty j	Soiled v
Colon n SOMA	Foul j	Nastier j AGGR	Soiling v
Contaminate v	Frowzy j	Nasty j AGGR	Soot n
Corrode v WEAK	Fume n VAPR	Nit n BUG	Sordid j BAD
Corrosion n WEAK	Garbage n	Offal n	Sour j SOMA
Corrupt j BAD	Greasier j MTRL	Pimple n BODY	Soured v SOMA
Crap n SOMA	Greasy j MTRL	Pollute v	Souring v SOMA
Craps v SOMA	Grime n	Psoriasis n SICK	Spatter v FLOW
Daggle v	Griminess n	Pus n SOMA	Speck n LITL
Daglock n BODY	Grimy j	Pustule n BODY	Splash v FLOW
Dandruff n BODY	Grubbier j BUG	Putrefy v	Spoil v DAMG
Debris n	Grubbier j	Putrid j	Spoils v DAMG
Decay n WEAK	Grubby j BUG	Ragamuffin n YNG	Spot n
Decompose v SEP	Grubby j	Rancid j SOMA	Spotted v
Decrepit j WEAK	Halitosis n SOMA	Rectal j SOMA	Squalid j
Decrepitude n WEAK	Hogwash n ANML	Rectum n SOMA	Squalor j
Deface v DAMG	Impetigo n SICK	Reek v VAPR	Stagnate v REST
Defecate v SOMA	Impure j	Refuse n	Stain n
Defile v AGGR	Incrustation n COVR	Rile v	Stale j
Deform v VARY	Infect v SICK	Roil v	Stale j WEAK
Degenerate v	Insanitary j	Rot v	Stank v VAPR
Deteriorate v WEAK	Junk n TRIV	Rubbish n	Stench n VAPR
Diarrhea n SICK	Lice n BUG	Rubble n	Sties n HOME
Dilapidate v	Lint n FABR	Ruin v DAMG	Stink v VAPR
Dingier j	Litter n	Rust n	Stool n SOMA
Dingy j	Littered v	Rustier j	Stunk v VAPR
Dirt n	Littering v	Rusting v	Sty n HOME
Dirt n BAD	Louse n BUG	Rusty j	Sullied v

Parts of speech: a article; b preposition; c conjunction; d adverb; f prefix; i interjection;
        j adjective; n noun; p pronoun; r phrase; v verb.

Sully v
Swill n FOOD
Taint v
Tarnish v
Tartar n BODY

Track v GO
Tracked v GO
Tracking v GO
Trash n
Unclean j

Unkempt j
Unpolished j
Unsanitary j
Urine n SOMA
Wart n BODY

Waste n TRIV
Water n SOMA

DOWN

Abyss n HOLW
Alight v GO
Artesian j ERTH
Avalanche n BULG
Base n FORM
Basement n HOME
Bases n FORM
Basing v FORM
Below b
Below b SUB
Beneath b
Beneath b SUB
Bottom n
Bottom n BODY
Bottomless j
Bow n VARY
Bow v SUB
Bowed v VARY
Bowed v SUB
Bowing v VARY
Bowing v SUB
Carpet n FURN
Cascade n FLOW
Cataract n FLOW
Cellar n HOME
Chute n GO
Couch v
Countersank v HOLW
Countersink v HOLW
Countersunk v HOLW
Cropper n WEAK
Crouch v VARY
Dangle v
DavyJones n FLOW
Declension n GO
Decline v GO
Declivity n
Deep j
Deep j CRUX
Deep j EMPH
Deep n FLOW
Deepsea j FLOW
Depress v
Depression n HOLW
Depression n
Depth n
Descend v GO
Descended v GO
Descent n GO
Dip n
Dipped v
Dismount v SEP
Ditch v FLOW
Dive n GO

Dive n FLOW
Diver n GO
Diver n FLOW
Divers n GO
Divers n FLOW
Diving v GO
Diving v FLOW
Dove v GO
Dove v FLOW
Down d
Down d PANG
Down n PLAY
Downcast j PANG
Downed v
Downfall n WEAK
Downgrade v SUB
Downgrade n PATH
Downhill d BULG
Downing v
Downstairs d UP
Downstream d FLOW
Downtown d PLAC
Downtrodden j SUB
Downward d
Droop v WEAK
Drop n GO
Dropped v GO
Dropping v GO
Duck v FLOW
Ducked v FLOW
Ducking v FLOW
Dump n PANG
Dump v GO
Dumped v GO
Dumping v GO
Elevator n UP
Fall n GO
Fall n BAD
Fall n FLOW
Fall v DAMG
Falling v GO
Falling v DAMG
Fell v GO
Fell v DAMG
Floor n FORM
Floor n TALK
Floor v DAMG
Flop v
Foot n BODY
Foothill n BULG
Footlight n VIEW
Footnote n WRIT
Gainer n VARY
Hang v

Hang v DEAD
Hanged v DEAD
Hanger n
Hung v
Hung v DEAD
Inferior j SUB
Inferior j
Kneel v BODY
Kowtow v SUB
Ladder n UP
Letdown n PANG
Light v GO
Lighted v GO
Lighting v GO
Lights v GO
Lop j
Low j
Low j LITL
Low j SUB
Low j PANG
Low j BAD
Lower v
Lowest j
Mat n FURN
Nether j
Overhang n UP
Parachute v GO
Paratroop n DAMG
Pendant n GARB
Pendant j
Pendulous j
Pendulum n VARY
Plop v HEAR
Plummet v GO
Plump n
Plumped v
Plumping v
Profound j CRUX
Profound j EMPH
Profound j
Profundity n CRUX
Profundity n
Prolapse n SOMA
Prone j
Prostrate v WEAK
Raze v DAMG
Rug n FURN
Rung n UP
Sag v
Sank v GO
Settle v
Sink v GO
Sinker n GO
Sling n

Slouch n
Slump n WEAK
Slung v
Sole n
Sole v GARB
Soled v GARB
Soling v GARB
Sound v FLOW
Sounded v FLOW
Sounding v FLOW
Spill v GO
Stair n UP
Step n UP
Stepladder n UP
Steps n UP
Stoop v VARY
Sub f
Submarine j FLOW
Submerge v FLOW
Subscript n WRIT
Subside v
Subsiding v
Subsoil n ERTH
Substratum n FORM
Substructure n FORM
Subterranean j ERTH
Subway n VEHC
Sundown n ASTR
Sunset n ASTR
Suspend v
Suspended v
Suspender n GARB
Suspension n
Topple v
Under b
Under b SUB
Undercarriage n FORM
Underclothes n GARB
Undercurrent n FLOW
Underground n ERTH
Underground n VEHC
Underhand j BODY
Underlying j CRUX
Underneath b
Underneath b SUB
Underpass n PATH
Undersea j FLOW
Undershirt n GARB
Underwear n GARB
Underworld n WHOL
Waterfall n FLOW
Windfall n WEA

Adlib v TALK
Airy j VAPR
Artless j
Average j
Bearing n MECH
Bearings n MECH
Bland j
Bolster n FURN
Breeze n VAPR
Brush n JOIN
Calender v MECH
Calm j GLAD
Caress v JOIN
Casual j
Casual j GARB
Cinch n
Coast v GO
Coasted v GO
Coasting v GO
Cream n
Creamed v
Cursive j WRIT
Cushier j
Cushion n
Cushy j
Dishabille n GARB
Ductile j VARY
Ease n GLAD
Easier j GLAD
Easy j GLAD
Easygoing j GLAD
Effortless j
Elastic j VARY
Extemporize v
Facile j
Facility n
Featherweight n MSMT
Finish n END
Flabbier j WEAK
Flabby j WEAK
Flaccid j WEAK
Flatiron n CLEN
Flexible j VARY
Flow v
Flowed v
Fluent j
Fluent j TALK
Fluff n MTRL
Fluffy j MTRL
Fluid j
Fondle v JOIN

Fuzz n MTRL
Fuzzier j MTRL
Fuzzy j MTRL
Gentle j
Glassy j
Glib j
Glide v GO
Glider n FURN
Glissade n GO
Glissando n MUSC
Gloss n VIEW
Glossy j VIEW
Gossamer j FABR
Graze v JOIN
Grease v MTRL
Guileless j GOOD
Impromptu j QUIK
Improvise v BGIN
Informal j
Informality n
Ingenuous j OPEN
Innocence n GOOD
Iron n CLEN
Ironed v CLEN
Ironing v CLEN
Jauntily d GLAD
Jaunty j GLAD
Lambent j VIEW
Lank j
Lax j WEAK
Laxative j SOMA
Laxity n WEAK
Leaven v VEGT
Leaven v VARY
Leniency n AID
Light j
Lighten v
Lightly d
Lightweight j MSMT
Lilt n VARY
Limber j VARY
Limp j WEAK
Liquid j
Lissome j POWR
Lithe j VARY
Lope v GO
Loping v GO
Lubricate v MTRL
Mangle v MECH
Mash v
Mean n

Medium j
Mellifluous j
Mellow j
Melt v VARY
Middling j
Mild j
Milder j
Mitigate v AID
Mobile j VARY
Moderate j
Mollify v GLAD
Mush n FOOD
Natural j
Neutral j
Offhand j TRIV
Oil v MTRL
Oiled v MTRL
Oiling v MTRL
Oils v MTRL
Ointment n MTRL
Oversimplify v
Pad n BULG
Padded v BULG
Palliate v GLAD
Pap n FOOD
Pat n JOIN
Pat n HEAR
Patted v JOIN
Patted v HEAR
Patting v JOIN
Patting v HEAR
Pianissimo j MUSC
Pillow n FURN
Plain j
Plane n WORK
Planed v WORK
Planing v WORK
Planish v
Plastic j VARY
Plasticity n VARY
Pliable j VARY
Plush j FABR
Polish n CLEN
Polish n GOOD
Polished v CLEN
Polished v GOOD
Polishing v CLEN
Polishing v GOOD
Pomade n MTRL
Puff n CLEN
Pulp n MTRL

Pumice n MTRL
Pushover n WEAK
Pussyfoot v GO
Putties v MTRL
Putty v MTRL
Readily d
Relax v
Relent v
Resilient j VARY
Rouge n MTRL
Sand v ERTH
Sandpaper v ERTH
Simple j
Simplicity n
Simplify v
Simply d
Skid n GO
Slack j
Slacks v
Sleek j CLEN
Slick j
Slid v GO
Slide n GO
Slip n WEAK
Slip v GO
Slipped v GO
Slippery j GO
Slippery j FALS
Slipping v GO
Slither v GO
Smooth j
Snap n
Soft j
Spontaneity n OPEN
Streamline v FORM
Suave j
Supple j VARY
Temperance n MOTV
Temperate j MOTV
Temperate j WEA
Tender j
Tender j PANG
Tender j FOND
Unaffected j TRUE
Unction n MTRL
Unctuous j FALS
Unperturbed j GLAD
Unpremeditated j
Unruffled j GLAD

EDUC

A n WRIT
Academic j
Academies n GRUP
Academies n HOME
Academy n GRUP
Academy n HOME
Almamater n HOME
Alumna n LADY
Alumni n MALE
Alumnus n MALE
Arts n POWR

B n WRIT
Bachelor n POWR
C n WRIT
Cadet n
Campus n HOME
Class n GRUP
Classmate n JOIN
Classroom n HOME
Coed n LADY
Coeducation n JOIN
College n HOME

Commencement n BGIN
Convocation n GRUP
Course n
Credit n
Curriculum n
D n WRIT
Dean n LEAD
Degree n
Didactic j
Discipline n
Doctor n POWR

Doctorate n POWR
Drill v
E n WRIT
Educate v
Educator n LEAD
Elective n MOTV
Erudite j
Exercise n
F n WRIT
Faculty n LEAD
Form n GRUP

Freshman n SUB	Majors n POWR	Scholar n POWR	Teach v
Frosh n SUB	Master n LEAD	Scholastic j	Teacher n LEAD
Grade n FORW	Matriculate v JOIN	School n HOME	Teaching v
Graduate v POWR	Mentor n LEAD	School n GRUP	Term n TIME
Gymnasium n HOME	Minor n SUB	School v	Textbook n WRIT
Highschool n HOME	Minored v SUB	Schoolboy n YNG	Train v
Humanities n GOOD	Minoring v SUB	Schooled v	Trained v
Inculcate v	Overlearn v	Schoolgirl n YNG	Trainer n LEAD
Instruct v	Pedagogy n	Schoolhouse n HOME	Tuition n MONY
Instructive j	Pedant n TRIV	Schooling v	Tutor n LEAD
Instructor n LEAD	PhD n POWR	Schoolmaster n LEAD	Tutor v
Junior j SUB	PhiBetaKappa n POWR	Schoolmate n JOIN	Tutored v
Kindergarten n YNG	Plebe n SUB	Schoolroom n HOME	Tutoring v
Learn v	Polytechnic j MUCH	Schoolteacher n LEAD	Undergraduate n SUB
Lecture n TALK	Preceptor n LEAD	Secondary j	Understudy n SUB
Lesson n	Prep j AID	Semester n TIME	Uneducated j LACK
Literacy n WRIT	Preschool j FORW	Seminar n GRUP	University n HOME
Literate j WRIT	Principal n LEAD	Seminary n HOLY	Unlearn v OPPO
Lyceum n HOME	Proctor v LEAD	Senior n LEAD	Untrained j WEAK
Major n POWR	Professor n LEAD	Sophomore n SUB	Yeshiva n HOLY
Majored v POWR	Pupil n	Student n	
Majoring v POWR	Savant n POWR	Taught v	

EMPH

Absolute j WHOL	Exclamation n TALK	Interjection n TALK	Sheer j
Accent n	Expletive n TALK	Italicize v WRIT	Simply d
Accent n TALK	Exquisite j	Just d	So d
Accentuate v	Extra d MUCH	Lo i	Some j
Acute j	Extreme j LARG	Marked j	Squarely d
Amazingly d PANG	Fairly d	Mighty d	Stark j
Asterisk n WRIT	Fiddlesticks i FOOL	O i	Still d
Awfully d	Flat j	Oh i	Stress n
Certainly d	Flatfooted j	Ouch i DAMG	Striking j
Circumflex n WRIT	Flatly d	Outright j	Strong j
Completely d WHOL	Foremost j FORW	Overemphasis n	Such j
Darn i	Forte j MUSC	Overly d	Sure j
Darned j	Fortissimo j MUSC	Perfect j	Terrible j
Dead d	Hallelujah i GLAD	Plumb d	Too d
Decided j	Headmost j FORW	Positively d	Topmost j UP
Decidedly d	Heck i	Posthaste d QUIK	Unqualified j
Deep j DOWN	Hey i	Precisely d	Unspeakably d TALK
Definitely d	High j	Pretty d	Utmost j
Diacritic n WRIT	Hist i HEAR	Profound j DOWN	Utter j
Dogtired j WEAK	Ho i	Pronounced j	Utterly d
Downright d	Hurrah i GLAD	Pure j	Verily d
Drastic j	Huzza i GLAD	Purely d	Very d
Emphasis n	Implicit j	Quite d	Very j SIML
Especially d	Indeed d	Rather d	Vivid j VIEW
Even d	Infinitely d	Real j TRUE	Well d
Exactly d	Inmost j IN	Really d TRUE	Wholly d WHOL
Exceedingly d	Innermost j IN	Right d SHRP	Wow i
Exclaim v TALK	Intensity n	Roundly d	

END

Abolish v	Bound n NEAR	Can v	Close n
Abrogate v	Boundary n	Cancel v	Closed v
Adjourn v	Bounded v NEAR	Canned v	Closing v
Aftermath n DAMG	Bounding v NEAR	Canning v	Closure n
Annihilate v DAMG	Bounds v NEAR	Cans v	Cloture n LAW
Annul v NO	Brim n	Cap v	Compass n
Armistice n DAMG	Brink n	Caps v	Complete v WHOL
Border v	Brow n UP	Cease v	Conclude v IDEA
Border v NEAR	Byproduct n NEAR	Cessation n	Conclusion n IDEA

Consequence n
Consume v LACK
Consummate v
Consumption n LACK
Coterminous j SIML
Culdesac n PATH
Culminate v
Deadline n TIME
Defunct j DEAD
Demilitarize v DAMG
Demobilize v DAMG
Denouement n OPEN
Desist v
Destine v
Disband v SEP
Discontinue v
Dissolution n SEP
Dissolve v SEP
Disuse n
Done v
Doom n DEAD
Douse v FLOW
Douse v
Edge n SHRP
Effect n
Effected v
Effecting v
Electrode n ION
End n
End n MOTV
End n PLAY
End n DEAD
Ended v
Ending v
Epilogue n TALK

Eventual j
Exhaust v LACK
Exhausting v LACK
Exhaustive j WHOL
Expire v
Extinct j DEAD
Extinguish v
Extremity n AFAR
Extremity n BODY
Extremity n PANG
Fate n
Final j
Finish n
Finish n POWR
Finish n EASY
Finite j
Fortune n AID
Fringe n
Frontier n FORW
Fruit n VEGT
Fruition n AID
Goal n
Goal n PLAY
Goalie n PLAY
Halt n BLOK
Halted v BLOK
Hem n GARB
Illfated j DAMG
Impasse n BLOK
Interrupt v BLOK
Kaput j WEAK
Knock v
Lapse v
Last j BACK
Last n

Limit n
Liquidate v
Liquidate v DAMG
Lot n
Margin n
Mature v
Nightcap n TIME
Object n MOTV
Objective n MOTV
Ordain v LEAD
Out d OUT
Outcome n
Outgrowth n
Output n
Outskirts n OUT
Over j
Pan v
Panned v
Panning v
Period n WRIT
Peroration n TALK
Polar j OPPO
Polarity n OPPO
Polarize v OPPO
Pole n
Predestination n FORW
Produce v
Product n
Production n
Quench v
Quit v
Realize v
Remission n
Remit v
Repeal v OPPO

Rescind v OPPO
Resolution n AGRE
Resolve v AGRE
Rest n REST
Result n
Rim n
Round v
Rounded v
Rounding v
Rounds v
Stalemate n BLOK
Stop v BLOK
Subside v
Subsiding v
Suspend v BLOK
Suspended v BLOK
Terminal n
Through b
Tip n
Tips n
Top v
Topped v
Tops v
Truce n DAMG
Ultimate j
Ultimatum n MOTV
Up j UP
Verge n
Void j TRIV
Weekend n TIME
Wind v VARY
Winds v VARY
Wound v VARY

ERTH

Acre n MSMT
Adamant n MTRL
Adobe j MTRL
Agate n MTRL
Agrarian j VEGT
Agriculture n VEGT
Agronomy n VEGT
Aground d BLOK
Alabaster n MTRL
Alluvial j FLOW
Amber n MTRL
Amethyst n MTRL
Amphibious j FLOW
Aquamarine n MTRL
Arable j VEGT
Archaeology n PAST
Archeology n PAST
Archipelago n FLOW
Arroyo n HOLW
Artesian j DOWN
Asbestos n MTRL
Ashore d FLOW
Asphalt n MTRL
Atoll n FLOW
Bank n FLOW
Bank n BULG
Battlefield n DAMG

Beach n FLOW
Bed n
Beds n
Biscuit n MTRL
Bluff n BULG
Bog n FLOW
Boulder n
Brass n MTRL
Brassy j MTRL
Brazen j MTRL
Bronze n MTRL
Brownstone j COLR
Bucolic j
Bunker n BLOK
Burrow n HOME
Burrow v IN
Bush n VEGT
Bushes n VEGT
Butte n BULG
Canyon n HOLW
Cape n FLOW
Carbuncle n MTRL
Castiron j MTRL
Cave n HOME
Cavern n HOME
Ceramic j MTRL
Chasm n HOLW

Clay n MTRL
Cliff n BULG
Clod n
Clodhopper n FOOL
Clodhopper n GARB
Coast n FLOW
Coastal j FLOW
Coastward d FLOW
Coastwise d FLOW
Cobble v FORM
Cobbled v FORM
Cobbles v FORM
Cobblestone n FORM
Col n PATH
Collier n WORK
Concrete j MTRL
Continent n PLAC
Continental j PLAC
Copper n MTRL
Cornerstone n CRUX
Country n PLAC
Countryside n PLAC
Course n PATH
Cove n HOLW
Crag n BULG
Crosscountry j GO
Cultivate v WORK

Dale n HOLW
Damask n MTRL
Dell n HOLW
Delta n FLOW
Desert n HEAT
Diamond n MTRL
Dirt n DIRT
Disinter v OUT
Ditch n HOLW
Divot n LITL
Down n
Dozer n VEHC
Dugout n HOME
Dune n BULG
Dust n DIRT
Dust n
Dust v CLEN
Dusted v CLEN
Duster n CLEN
Dusting v CLEN
Earth n
Earth n ASTR
Earthbound j BLOK
Earthenware j
Earthling n LIVE
Earthquake n DAMG
Earthward d FORW

Earthwork n BULG	Homestead n HOME	Oasis n AID	Quicksand n FLOW
Earthworm n BUG	Humus n MTRL	Obsidian n MTRL	Ranch n WORK
Earthy j	Hyacinth n MTRL	Ochre n MTRL	Range n
Embankment n FORM	Idyl n TALK	Oil n MTRL	Ravine n HOLW
Emerald n MTRL	Idyl n GOOD	Oils n MTRL	Realestate n HAVE
Endomorph n FORM	Inland j IN	Ooze n FLOW	Realty n HAVE
Entrench v HOLW	Insular j FLOW	Opal n MTRL	Reef n FLOW
Estate n HAVE	Iron n MTRL	Orchard n VEGT	Reservation n
Exhume v OUT	Ironmonger n MART	Ore n MTRL	Reserve n
Fallow j REST	Island n FLOW	Outfield n PLAY	Ridge n BULG
Farm n WORK	Isle n FLOW	Overground j UP	Rock n
Farmhouse n HOME	Isthmus n JOIN	Overland j UP	Rough n VARY
Fault n SEP	Jade n MTRL	Palisade n BULG	Rubies n MTRL
Ferro f MTRL	Jasper n MTRL	Pampas n	Ruby n MTRL
Field n	Jet n MTRL	Panhandle n BULG	Rural j PLAC
Field n PLAY	Kerosene n MTRL	Park n VEGT	Rustic j
Fielder n PLAY	Key n FLOW	Pastoral j VEGT	Rustic n WEAK
Fielding v PLAY	Keys n FLOW	Pastorale n MUSC	Sand n
Flag n FORM	Kolkohz n WORK	Peak n UP	Sand v EASY
Flags n FORM	Land n	Peaked j UP	Sandbag n HOLW
Flagstone n FORM	Land n PLAC	Peasant n WORK	Sandbox n HOLW
Flat n	Land v GO	Peat n VEGT	Sandier j
Flats n	Landed j	Pebble n	Sandlot j
Flint n MTRL	Landed v GO	Peninsula n FLOW	Sandpaper v EASY
Foreground n FORW	Landing v GO	Pewter n MTRL	Sandstone n MTRL
Foxhole n HOME	Landmark n VIEW	Piedmont n	Sandy j
Garden n VEGT	Landowner n HAVE	Pig n MTRL	Sapphire n MTRL
Garnet n MTRL	Landscape v VEGT	Pigiron n MTRL	Seaboard n FLOW
Geocentric j SHRP	Landward d	Pike n BULG	Seashore n FLOW
Geochemist n IDEA	Lava n FLOW	Pinnacle n UP	Shore n FLOW
Geography n IDEA	Lead n MTRL	Pitchblende n MTRL	Shoreline n FLOW
Geology n IDEA	Leaded v MTRL	Plain n	Silicon n MTRL
Geophysics n IDEA	Ledge n BULG	Plains n	Silver n MTRL
Glen n HOLW	Levee n BULG	Plainsman n MALE	Slate n MTRL
Globe n WHOL	Lick n FOOD	Plant n VEGT	Slip n FLOW
Gold n MTRL	Lime n MTRL	Plantation n VEGT	Sod n VEGT
Gorge n HOLW	Lithium n MTRL	Planted v VEGT	Sodded v VEGT
Grange n HOME	Loam n	Planting v VEGT	Sodding v VEGT
Grange n GRUP	Lot n	Plat n SOME	Soil n
Granite n	Manganese n MTRL	Plate n MTRL	Solitaire n MTRL
Graphite n MTRL	Marble n MTRL	Plateau n UP	Steel n MTRL
Gravel n	Marsh n FLOW	Platinum n MTRL	Stone n
Gravestone n DEAD	Meadow n VEGT	Playground n PLAY	Stone v DAMG
Grit n	Meridian n MSMT	Plot n SOME	Stoned v DAMG
Grotto n HOME	Mesa n BULG	Plow v WORK	Stoneware j
Ground n	Mica n MTRL	Poach v GO	Stoning v DAMG
Gulch n HOLW	Mine n WORK	Point n SHRP	Subsoil n DOWN
Gulf n HOLW	Mined v WORK	Polonium n MTRL	Subterranean j DOWN
Gullies n HOLW	Mines n WORK	Potter n HOLW	Sulphur n MTRL
Gully n HOLW	Mining v WORK	Pottery n HOLW	Swamp n FLOW
Gumbo n	Mire n FLOW	Prairie n VEGT	Terrace n BULG
Hammock n VEGT	Mire v BLOK	Precipice n BULG	Terracotta j MTRL
Hardpan n	Moat n HOLW	Premise n HAVE	Terracotta j COLR
Harrow v MECH	Moonstone n MTRL	Promontory n BULG	Terrain n
Head n BULG	Moor n FLOW	Puddle n FLOW	Terrestrial j
Headstone n DEAD	Morass n FLOW	Pug n MTRL	Territory n PLAC
Heath n VEGT	Mound n BULG	Quagmire n FLOW	Till v WORK
Heliotrope n MTRL	Mount n BULG	Quake n VARY	Tilled v WORK
Highland n UP	Mountain n BULG	Quarried v HOLW	Tilling v WORK
Hill n BULG	Mud n FLOW	Quarries v HOLW	Tills v WORK
Hillock n BULG	Mud n DIRT	Quarry n HOLW	Tin n MTRL
Hillside n BULG	Muddies v DIRT	Quarrying v HOLW	Tombstone n DEAD
Hinterland n AFAR	Nugget n MTRL	Quartz n MTRL	Topaz n MTRL

Tract n
Trench n HOLW
Turf n VEGT
Turquoise n MTRL

Underground n DOWN
Unearth v OPEN
Vale n HOLW
Valley n HOLW

Vineyard n VEGT
Volcano n DAMG
Waste n TRIV
Wetland n FLOW

Whetstone n SHRP
Wild n VEGT
Wilderness n VEGT
Zinc n MTRL

EVER

Abide v AGRE
Abide v LIVE
Abiding j
Acclimate v SIML
Accustom v SIML
Across b
Adamant j
Adinfinitum d
Aeon n TIME
Ageless j TIME
Always d
Arbitrary j MOTV
Assiduous j MOTV
Beaten j
Ceaseless j
Ceremony n FORM
Changeless j
Chronic j
Classic j POWR
Classic j PAST
Cling v JOIN
Clung v JOIN
Common j
Conservation n AID
Conservatism n
Conservative j
Conservator n AID
Conserve v AID
Conserve v
Consistency n SIML
Consistent j SIML
Constant j
Continual j
Continuation n
Continuation n GO
Continue v
Continue v GO
Continuing v
Continuing v GO
Continuity n
Continuous j
Continuum n
Convention n
Conventional j
Conventional j TRIV
Corn v FOOD
Corned j FOOD
Course n
Curable j
Cure n
Curing v
Custom n
Customary j
Daily j TIME
Deathless j DEAD
Determine v MOTV
Diligence n MOTV
Diligent j MOTV

Dogged j
Durable j
Duration n TIME
During b TIME
Dwell v REST
Embalm v DEAD
Endless j
Endure v
Endure v PANG
Establish v BGIN
Establishment n BGIN
Establishment n GRUP
Eternal j
Ever d
Everlasting j
Evermore d
Everyday j
Firm j
Fix v
Fixative n
Fixture n
Forever d
Formal j FORM
Frequent v
Frequented v
Frequenting v
Habit n
Habitual j
Habitude n
Hang v HAVE
Hangover n
Hard j
Harp v TALK
Harped v TALK
Harping v TALK
Haunt v MYTH
Heirloom n HAVE
Held v
Hitherto d NEW
Hold v
Holdover n
Homeostasis n SOMA
Hung v HAVE
Immanent j IN
Immemorial j PAST
Immortal j LIVE
Immovable j REST
Immutable j
Imperishable j LIVE
Implacable j AGGR
Inalienable j
Incessant j
Incurable j SICK
Indelible j
Indestructible j POWR
Indissoluble j
Indurate j AGGR
Indurate j

Industrious j WORK
Industry n WORK
Ineffaceable j
Inelastic j
Ineluctable j POWR
Ineradicable j
Inerasable j
Inescapable j POWR
Inevitable j POWR
Inexhaustible j POWR
Inexorable j
Inextinguishable j
Inextirpable j
Infallible j POWR
Infallible j
Infinite j LARG
Infinities n LARG
Infinity n LARG
Inflexible j
Inherent j CRUX
Inseparable j JOIN
Insoluble j
Insolvable j BLOK
Institution n FORM
Insuperable j BLOK
Insurmountable j BLOK
Interminable j
Inure v AGGR
Invariable j
Inveterate j
Irredeemable j
Irremediable j
Irremovable j
Irreparable j
Irreversible j
Irrevocable j
Keep v
Keep v AID
Keep v HAVE
Keeps v
Keeps v AID
Keeps v HAVE
Kept v
Kept v AID
Kept v HAVE
Last v
Lasting j
Leave v SEP
Leaves v SEP
Left v SEP
Lifelong j LIVE
Linger v REST
Lingering v REST
Long j
Longer j
Longest j
Longevity n LIVE
Longterm j TIME

Maintain v HAVE
Maintain v AID
Maintenance n HAVE
Maintenance n AID
Marathon n GO
Monotonous j SIML
Monument n FORM
Mores n GOOD
Mummies n DEAD
Mummy n DEAD
Mundane j TRIV
Never d NO
Norm n
Normal j
Obduracy n AGGR
Obsess v PANG
Obstinacy n AGGR
Ordinary j
Orthodox j HOLY
Orthodox j
Outlast v
Pat j
Patience n REST
Patient j REST
Peg v
Pending b TIME
Perdurable j
Perennial j
Periodic j VARY
Permanence n
Permanent j
Permanent n BODY
Perpetuate v
Perpetuity n TIME
Persevere v MOTV
Persist v
Pertinacity n
Petrify v
Pickle v FOOD
Pickled j FOOD
Pickling v FOOD
Plied v GO
Plied v
Plier n
Plier n GO
Plug v
Plugged v
Ply v GO
Ply v
Practice n EVNT
Practice n WORK
Practitioner n WORK
Preserve v
Preserves v
Prolong v LARG
Protract v LARG
Regular j
Relentless j AGGR

Remain v
Remains v
Retain v HAVE
Retention n HAVE
Rigid j
Rigor n
Rote n TRIV
Routine n
Rule n
Rut n HOLW
Salt v
Salted v
Salting v
Save v HAVE
Save v
Saving v HAVE
Saving v
Set v
Setting v
Settle v LIVE
Settlement n LIVE

Siege n DAMG
Solid j
Squat v REST
Squats v REST
Squatted v REST
Stability n
Stable j
Stand v
Standard j
Standing v
Stationary j REST
Statusquo n NEW
Stay v
Steadied v
Steady j
Stiff j
Stiffen v
Still d TIME
Stockstill j REST
Stood v
Store v HAVE

Stored v HAVE
Storing v HAVE
Stubborn j AGGR
Tarried v REST
Tarry v REST
Temper n FORM
Tempering v FORM
Tenacity n POWR
Term n TIME
Tour n TIME
Tradition n PAST
Unabated j
Unaffected j
Unalterable j
Unavoidable j
Unbreakable j
Unbroken j
Unceasing j
Unchanged j
Undying j DEAD
Unending j

Unfailing j
Unforgettable j IDEA
Uninterrupted j
Unmitigated j
Unoriginal j TRIV
Unrelenting j
Unsinkable j FLOW
Untreated j
Unyielding j
Usage n
Used j
Usual j
Wear v
Wearing v
Wont n
Wore v
Worn v
Yearlong j TIME
Yet d

EVNT

Accident n AFAR
Accidental j AFAR
Acquit v
Act n
Acting j SIML
Acting v
Action n
Action n QUIK
Active j
Active j QUIK
Activity n
Activity n QUIK
Affair n
Am v
Are v
Attitude n BODY
Be v
Bear v
Bearing n
Became v
Become v
Been v
Behave v
Behavior n
Being v
Bore v
Borne v
Business n
Carriage n
Carried v
Carry v
Case n SOLE
Chance n AFAR
Circumstance n
Circumstantial j
Coincide v SIML
Commission n
Commit v
Committed v
Comport v
Condition n

Conduct v
Conducting v
Contingency n
Contingent n
Deal v
Dealing v
Deals v
Dealt v
Deed n
Demean v
Demeanor n
Deport v
Did v
Do v
Does v
Doing v
Done v
Empirical j
Episode n
Estate n
Event n
Execute v
Executing v
Exist v
Existence n
Experience n
Fashion n
Fortuitous j AFAR
Function n
Functioned v
Functioning v
Gesticulate v BODY
Gesture n BODY
Go v
Gone v
Grew v
Grow v
Grown v
Hap n AFAR
Happen v
Hazard n AFAR

Held v
Hold v
Incident n
Instance n SOLE
Is v
Maneuver n POWR
Manner n
Metaphysical j IDEA
Mien n
Misbehave v BAD
Mode n
Modes n
Motion v BODY
Motioned v BODY
Motioning v BODY
Motor j BODY
Move v
Movement n
Moving v
Occasion n
Occur v
Pass v
Passed v
Passes v
Passing v
Perchance d AFAR
Perform v
Phenomena n
Phenomenal j AFAR
Phenomenon n
Ploy n POWR
Poise n
Port n
Positive j IDEA
Positivism n IDEA
Posture n BODY
Practice n EVER
Pragmatism n AID
Presence n
Proceedings n
Pull v

Pulled v
React v
React v OPPO
Reaction n
Reaction n OPPO
Reactionary j OPPO
Reflex j SOMA
Render v
Rendition n
Response n
Setting n
Situation n
Stance n BODY
Stand v
Standing v
State n
States n
Stood v
Style n
Styled v
Styling v
Subject v
Subjected v
Subjecting v
Tactic n POWR
Threw v
Throw v
Transact v
Transpire v
Treat v
Treating v
Treatment n
Undergo v
Underwent v
Usage n
Was v
Way n
Were v
Whack n

Alligator n ANML
Alpaca n ANML
Angora n ANML
Batik n COLR
Beaver n ANML
Beige n ANML
Birdseye j FORM
Bolt n
Broadcloth n
Brocade n
Buff n ANML
Burlap n VEGT
Calf n ANML
Calico j VEGT
Canvas n
Canvas n FLOW
Cashmere n ANML
Cerecloth n DEAD
Cheesecloth n VEGT
Chiffon n
Chinchilla n ANML
Chintz n VEGT
Cloth n
Cop n FORM
Cord n
Cording n
Cordon n GARB
Cordovan j PLAC
Corduroy j VEGT
Corduroys n GARB
Cotton n VEGT
Covert n
Cowhide n ANML
Crash n VEGT
Crepe n
Crop n ANML
Dacron n
Damask n PLAC
Denier n MSMT
Denim n VEGT
Dimity n VEGT
Doily n FURN
Drab n COLR
Drape v COVR
Duck n VEGT
Duffle n

Dufflebag n HOLW
Dungaree n
Elastic n VARY
Ermine n ANML
Fabric n
Felt n
Fiber n
Fibrous j
Filet n FORM
Fillet n FORM
Flannel n
Fleece n ANML
Floss n
Fox n ANML
Fur n ANML
Gabardine n
Gauze n
Gingham n VEGT
Goods n MART
Gossamer j EASY
Gunny n
Haircloth n BODY
Hemp n VEGT
Hessian n VEGT
Hide n ANML
Holland n PLAC
Homespun j HOME
Interline v IN
Jersey n
Jute n VEGT
Khaki n VEGT
Kid n ANML
Lace n FORM
Lamb n ANML
Lanyard n BLOK
Lariat n BLOK
Lasso n BLOK
Lasting n
Leash n BLOK
Leather n ANML
Line n
Linen n VEGT
Linen n FURN
Lining n
Lint n DIRT
Lizard n ANML

Loom n MECH
Madras n PLAC
Marten n ANML
Material n
Mesh n
Mink n ANML
Mohair n ANML
Morocco n ANML
Muskrat n ANML
Muslin n
Nap n
Needlepoint n SHRP
Needlework n SHRP
Nylon n
Organdy n
Paisley j
Patchwork n JOIN
Patent j ANML
Pelt n ANML
Pigskin n ANML
Pigskin n PLAY
Piping n GARB
Plaid j FORM
Plastic j
Plush j EASY
Poplin n
Puff n
Rabbit n ANML
Raccoon n ANML
Rag n TRIV
Rawhide n ANML
Rayon n
Remnant n SOME
Ribbon n
Ribbon n POWR
Rope n
Rope n DEAD
Rope v BLOK
Roped v BLOK
Roping v BLOK
Rubber n
Sable n ANML
Sack n
Sacking n
Saddle n ANML
Sail n FLOW

Sateen n
Satin n
Seal n ANML
Shag n
Shag n BULG
Sheep n ANML
Sheepskin n ANML
Sheet n FORM
Silk j BUG
Silks n BUG
Silkscreen n COLR
Skunk n ANML
Slip n HOLW
Spin v WORK
Spun v WORK
Squirrel n ANML
String n
Stuff n
Suede n ANML
Tabby n
Tablecloth n FURN
Taffeta n
Tapestry n COLR
Tarpaulin n COVR
Tartan n
Tatter v TRIV
Terry n
Textile n
Thread n
Thread v GO
Threadbare j TRIV
Threaded v GO
Threading v GO
Tick n
Ticking n
Tweed n
Twine n JOIN
Upholster v FURN
Velvet j
Vinyl n
Warp n FORM
Woof n FORM
Wool n ANML
Woolen j ANML
Woolens n GARB
Yarn n

FALS

Affect v
Affectation n
Airs n VAPR
Alias n TALK
Amiss j
Anachronism n PAST
Apocryphal j
Artifice n
Artificial j
Assume v HAVE
Astray d GO
Awry j VARY
Bad j BAD
Balk v PLAY
Bamboozle v BLUR
Baseless j

Beguile v
Belie v
Betray v AGGR
Betray v OPEN
Bias n MOTV
Bigot n MOTV
Bilk v
Blandish v
Blarney n TALK
Bluff n
Bluffed v
Bluffing v
Blunder n WEAK
Bogus j
Boner n FOOL
Buffalo v ANML

Bug n BUG
Bunco n CRIM
Bunk n FOOL
Bunko n CRIM
Butter v FOOD
Cajole v FOND
Calumny n AGGR
Camouflage v COVR
Cant n TALK
Canted v TALK
Casuistry n IDEA
Charlatan n
Cheat v CRIM
Chicanery n
Chisel v CRIM
Circumvent v VARY

Claptrap n FOOL
Cog n
Con j CRIM
Confabulate v TALK
Conned v CRIM
Conning v CRIM
Cons v CRIM
Counterfeit j
Craft n POWR
Craftier j POWR
Crafty j POWR
Cunning j POWR
Deacon v
Deceit n
Deceive v
Deception n

Decoy n
Defame v AGGR
Defraud v CRIM
Delude v
Delusion n
Demagogue n LEAD
Demerit n BAD
Device n
Discount v
Discounted v
Discredit v
Disguise n COVR
Dishonest j BAD
Disloyal j AGGR
Disprove v
Distort v VARY
Doctor v
Double j
Doublecross v NUMR
Dummy n
Dupe n
Duplicity n
Embroider v GOOD
Errant j VARY
Error n BAD
Error n WEAK
Exaggerate v LARG
Fabricate v
Factitious j
Fake n
Faking v
Fallacy n
False j
Falsetto n MUSC
Fault n
Fault n BAD
Faultfinding n AGGR
Fauxpas n
Feign v
Fib n
Fiction n MYTH
Fictitious j MYTH
Figurehead n LEAD
Finagle v
Fishier j ANML
Fishy j ANML
Fix v
Flatter v FOND
Flaw n WEAK
Flimflam v CRIM
Foist v
Fool v
Forge v WRIT
Forgery n WRIT
Forgery n
Foul n PLAY
Fox v ANML
Foxed v ANML
Foxing v ANML
Frame v
Frameup n CRIM
Fraud n CRIM
Front n FORW
Fudge v
Fudged v

Fudging v
Fulsome j PANG
Gag n GLAD
Garble v BLUR
Gerrymander v LAW
Gimmick n
Gloss n VIEW
Grandiose j POWR
Guff n TALK
Guile n
Guise n GARB
Gull v
Gulled v
Gulling v
Gyp v
Hankypanky n
Hightoned j POWR
Hoax n
Hocus v CRIM
Hocuspocus n FOOL
Humbug n FOOL
Hypocrisy n
Illegitimate j
Illogical j IDEA
Imitate v SIML
Impersonate v SIML
Implausible j
Impostor n
Improper j
Inaccuracy n
Inadvertent j
Incognito d COVR
Incorrect j
Indefensible j
Inexact j BLUR
Insincere j BAD
Intrigue n COVR
Invalid j
Inveigle v MOTV
Invent v BGIN
Jockey v
Joker n
Juggle v VARY
Kangaroo n LAW
Legerdemain n MYTH
Liar n TALK
Libel v AGGR
Lie v TALK
Lied v TALK
Lies v TALK
Load v BULG
Lying v TALK
Makebelieve j MYTH
Malformation n FORM
Malinger v SICK
Malpractice n WORK
Masque n PLAY
Masquerade v PLAY
Mealymouth j BODY
Mendacity n
Misapply v
Misapprehend v IDEA
Miscalculate v IDEA
Miscarriage n WEAK
Miscarriage n BGIN

Miscarry v WEAK
Misconception n IDEA
Misconstrue v IDEA
Miscount v NUMR
Miscue n
Misdeal v PLAY
Misdirect v LEAD
Misfire v WEAK
Misfire v DAMG
Misfit n WEAK
Misgovern v LEAD
Misguide v AID
Misinform v TALK
Misinterpret v IDEA
Misjudge v IDEA
Mislead v
Mismanage v LEAD
Misprint n WRIT
Misquote v TALK
Misread v WRIT
Misrepresent v
Misspell v TALK
Misstate v TALK
Misstep n GO
Mistake n WEAK
Mistrial n LAW
Misunderstand v IDEA
Misuse v AGGR
Mock j SIML
Onesided j MOTV
Overlook v VIEW
Oversight n
Pack v GRUP
Packed v GRUP
Packing v GRUP
Palm v
Palmed v
Palming v
Palter v
Paste j
Perjury n
Pharisee n HOLY
Phony n
Plant n
Pose v
Posing v
Possum n ANML
Prejudice n MOTV
Prestidigitation n MYTH
Pretend v
Pretense n
Pretentious j POWR
Pretext n IDEA
Prevaricate v TALK
Pseudo j
Pseudonym n TALK
Quack n MEDC
Queer n MONY
Railroad v VEHC
Railroaded v VEHC
Railroading v VEHC
Rig v
Rook v
Rooked v
Rooking v

Ruse n
Salt v
Salted v
Salting v
Sanctimonious j HOLY
Scheme v IDEA
Schemed v IDEA
Schemer n IDEA
Scheming v IDEA
Selfrighteous j GOOD
Sham j
Shark n ANML
Shirk v VARY
Shyster n
Simulate v SIML
Slander n AGGR
Sleight n
Slicker n
Slippery j EASY
Sly j COVR
Smirk n GLAD
Snob n POWR
Soldier v WORK
Sophism n IDEA
Sophistry n IDEA
Specious j
Spoof v
Spurious j
Stool n OPEN
Stratagem n IDEA
String v
Stringing v
Strung v
Suborn v CRIM
Subterfuge n
Sucker n WEAK
Swindle v CRIM
Synthetic j
Take v
Threw v
Throw v
Took v
Traitor n AGGR
Treacherous j DAMG
Treason n AGGR
Trick n
Trump v
Trumped v
Twofaced j BODY
Unbelievable j
Unctuous j EASY
Underhand j COVR
Underrate v
Unfounded j
Unscientific j IDEA
Untenable j
Untrue j
Warp n VARY
Warped v VARY
Warping v VARY
Weasel v ANML
Weaseled v ANML
Weaseling v ANML
Wheedle v
Whopper n

Wile n	Worm v	Worming v	
Wily j	Wormed v	Wrong j	

FLOW

Abaft d BACK	Bluefish n ANML	Commodore n LEAD	Ditch v DOWN
Ablution n CLEN	Bluefish n FOOD	Conch n HOLW	Dive n DOWN
Admiral n LEAD	Boat n VEHC	Condense v VARY	Diver n DOWN
Adrift d GO	Bog n ERTH	Conger n ANML	Divers n DOWN
Afloat j GO	Breaker n DAMG	Conger n FOOD	Diving v DOWN
Aft j BACK	Breakwater n BLOK	Conning n VEHC	Dock n BLOK
Ahoy i TALK	Bridge n VEHC	Coral n MTRL	Docked v BLOK
Algae n VEGT	Brig n VEHC	Coral n ANML	Doldrums n REST
Alligator n ANML	Brook n	Corsair n CRIM	Dolphin n ANML
Alluvial j ERTH	Bubble n HOLW	Cove n HOLW	Dories n VEHC
Amazon n PLAC	Bubble n HEAR	Crab n ANML	Dories n ANML
Amphibious j ERTH	Buccaneer n CRIM	Crab n FOOD	Dory n VEHC
Anchovy n FOOD	Buoy n VIEW	Crabbed v ANML	Dory n ANML
Anchovy n ANML	Buoy v UP	Crabbing v ANML	Douse v END
Angle v SHRP	Buoyant j UP	Crawfish n ANML	Douse v
Angler n SHRP	Cabana n HOME	Crawl n GO	Dove v DOWN
Angling v SHRP	Caisson n HOLW	Crawl n HOLW	Downpour n WEA
Anoint v MTRL	Canal n PATH	Crayfish n ANML	Downstream d DOWN
Anoint v HOLY	Canoe n VEHC	Creek n	Draft n
Antediluvian j PAST	Canvas n FABR	Crocodile n ANML	Drain v OUT
Aqua n	Cape n ERTH	Cruise v GO	Draughts n
Aquacade n PLAY	Capstan n MECH	Crustacean n ANML	Draw v
Aquarium n HOME	Caribbean j PLAC	Current n	Dreadnaught n DAMG
Aquatic j	Carp n ANML	Cutter n VEHC	Drench v
Aqueduct n PATH	Carp n FOOD	Dabble v	Dribble v
Archipelago n ERTH	Carrier n VEHC	Dace n ANML	Driftwood n VEGT
Argosy n VEHC	Cascade n DOWN	Dam n BLOK	Drip n
Arid j LACK	Castaway j SEP	Damp v	Drizzle n WEA
Ark n VEHC	Catamaran n VEHC	Dams n BLOK	Drool v SOMA
Ashore d ERTH	Cataract n DOWN	Dank j	Drop n LITL
Astern d BACK	Catfish n ANML	Danube n PLAC	Drought n LACK
Atlantic n PLAC	Catfish n FOOD	Darter n ANML	Drown v DEAD
Atoll n ERTH	Caviar n FOOD	DavyJones n DOWN	Dry j LACK
Bail v HOLW	Channel n PATH	Deadeye n MECH	Duck v DOWN
Bank n ERTH	Chum n FOOD	Debark v SEP	Duckbill n ANML
Baptize v HOLY	Cistern n HOLW	Decoct v HEAT	Ducked v DOWN
Barge n VEHC	Clam n ANML	Deep n DOWN	Ducking v DOWN
Barges n VEHC	Clam n FOOD	Deepsea j DOWN	Dugout n VEHC
Bark n VEHC	Clammed v ANML	Dehumidify v OUT	Dunk v IN
Bass n ANML	Clammier j	Dehydrate v LACK	Ebb v BACK
Bass n FOOD	Clamming v ANML	Deliquesce v VARY	Eddy n VARY
Bath n CLEN	Clammy j	Delta n ERTH	Eel n ANML
Bathe v CLEN	Clipper n VEHC	Deluge n BULG	Eel n FOOD
Battleship n DAMG	Cloudburst n WEA	Desiccate v LACK	Effervesce v HEAR
Bay n HOLW	Coast n ERTH	Destroyer n DAMG	Emulsion n
Bays n HOLW	Coastal j ERTH	Dew n	Ensign n LEAD
Beach n ERTH	Coaster n VEHC	Dhow n VEHC	Estuary n
Beachcomber n REST	Coastward d ERTH	Dike n BLOK	Evaporate v VAPR
Becalm v REST	Coastwise d ERTH	Diluvial j BULG	Fall n DOWN
Berth n REST	Cockle n ANML	Dinghy n VEHC	Fathom n MSMT
Beverage n SIP	Cod n ANML	Dip n IN	Ferries n VEHC
Bilge n DIRT	Cod n FOOD	Dipped v IN	Ferry n VEHC
Bilge n HOLW	Collier n VEHC	Dipper n HOLW	Figurehead n BODY
Billow n BULG	Comb v VARY	Dissolve v VARY	Fiord n
Blot v BLOK	Combed v VARY	Distill v	Fireboat n HEAT
Blotted v BLOK	Comber n VARY	Distillate n	Fireplug n HEAT
Blotter n BLOK	Combing v VARY	Distilled v	Fish n ANML

Parts of speech: a article; b preposition; c conjunction; d adverb; f prefix; i interjection;
j adjective; n noun; p pronoun; r phrase; v verb.

Fish n FOOD
Fished v ANML
Fisherman n MALE
Fishy j ANML
Fjord n
Flagship n LEAD
Flatboat n VEHC
Flatfish n ANML
Flatfish n FOOD
Float v GO
Floated v GO
Floating v GO
Floe n COLD
Flood n BULG
Floodgate n BLOK
Flotilla n GRUP
Flotsam n TRIV
Flounder n ANML
Flounder n FOOD
Flow v
Flowed v
Fluid n
Fluke n ANML
Fluke n FOOD
Flush v GO
Flushed v GO
Flushing v GO
Flux n
Foam n
Font n HOLW
Ford v GO
Forecastle n HOME
Fountain n HOLW
Fountain n
Fountainhead n BGIN
Freighter n VEHC
Frigate n VEHC
Frost n COLD
Frosty j COLD
Froth v
Froth v SOMA
Fry n YNG
Fuse v HEAT
Fused v HEAT
Fusible j HEAT
Fusing v HEAT
Galleon n VEHC
Galley n VEHC
Gangplank n PATH
Gargle v CLEN
Gas n MTRL
Gasoline n MTRL
Geyser n HEAT
Gill n SOMA
Glacier n COLD
Glaze n COLD
Glazing v COLD
Gob n
Goldfish n ANML
Gondola n VEHC
Goo n BLUR
Grenadier n ANML
Gulf n
Gunboat n DAMG
Gunwale n FORM

Guppy n ANML
Gurgle v HEAR
Gush v
Haddock n ANML
Haddock n FOOD
Hagfish n ANML
Hail v WEA
Hails v WEA
Hailstone n WEA
Hake n ANML
Hake n FOOD
Halibut n ANML
Halibut n FOOD
Hammerhead n ANML
Harbor n AID
Hardhead n ANML
Herring n ANML
Herring n FOOD
Hind n ANML
Hose n HOLW
Hosing v HOLW
Hulk n VEHC
Hull n FORM
Humid j
Humidify v
Humor n SOMA
Hydrant n HOLW
Hydraulic j MECH
Hydrodynamic j POWR
Hydroelectric j ION
Ice n COLD
Iceberg n COLD
Icicle n COLD
Iciness n COLD
Icing n COLD
Icy j COLD
Inlet n IN
Insular j ERTH
Inundate v BULG
Irrigate v
Island n ERTH
Isle n ERTH
Jellyfish n ANML
Jet n QUIK
Jetted v QUIK
Jetties n BLOK
Jetting v QUIK
Jetty n BLOK
Juice n
Junk n VEHC
Kayak n VEHC
Keel n FORM
Kelp n VEGT
Ketch n VEHC
Key n ERTH
Keys n ERTH
Kipper n ANML
Kipper n FOOD
Lagoon n
Lake n
Lap v
Lapped v
Larboard n PLAC
Lather n CLEN
Lather n

Launch n VEHC
Launder v CLEN
Lava n ERTH
Leak v OUT
Libation n HOLY
Lifeboat n VEHC
Lifebuoy n AID
Liner n VEHC
Liquid j
Lobster n ANML
Lobster n FOOD
Lotion n AID
Mackerel n ANML
Mackerel n FOOD
Main n
Manofwar n DAMG
Marinate v FOOD
Marine j
Marine n DAMG
Mariner n
Marines n DAMG
Maritime j
Marlin n ANML
Marsh n ERTH
Mate n LEAD
Midstream n IN
Minnow n ANML
Mire n ERTH
Mist n VAPR
Misted v VAPR
Moisture n
Mole n BLOK
Mollusk n ANML
Molten j HEAT
Moor n ERTH
Morass n ERTH
Motorboat n VEHC
Mud n ERTH
Muggier j HEAT
Muggy j HEAT
Mussel n FOOD
Mussel n ANML
Narrows n LITL
Nautical j
Naval j DAMG
Navies n DAMG
Navy n DAMG
Neptune n MYTH
Nozzle n OUT
Oar n AID
Ocean n
Oceanography n IDEA
Octopus n ANML
Offing n
Ooze v
Ooze n ERTH
Overboard d SEP
Overflow v BULG
Oversea j AFAR
Oyster n FOOD
Oyster n ANML
Pacific n PLAC
Packet n VEHC
Paddle v GO
Peajacket n GARB

Pearl n MTRL
Penguin n ANML
Peninsula n ERTH
Perch n ANML
Perch n FOOD
Percolate v IN
Perspire v SOMA
Petrol n MTRL
Petroleum n MTRL
Pickerel n ANML
Pickerel n FOOD
Pickle v CLEN
Pickled j CLEN
Pickling v CLEN
Pier n BLOK
Pike n ANML
Pike n FOOD
Pipette n HOLW
Piracy n CRIM
Plankton n VEGT
Platypus n ANML
Plumber n WORK
Plumbing n MECH
Pluvial j WEA
Polliwog n ANML
Pond n
Pontoon n VEHC
Pool n
Poop n VEHC
Porgy n ANML
Porgy n FOOD
Porpoise n ANML
Port n HOME
Port n PLAC
Pour v
Pour v WEA
Prawn n FOOD
Prawn n ANML
Precipitate v WEA
Privateer n DAMG
Puddle n
Puddle n ERTH
Pump n MECH
Pumped v MECH
Pumping v MECH
Punt n VEHC
Purser n LEAD
Quagmire n ERTH
Quarterdeck n FORM
Quicksand n ERTH
Raft n VEHC
Rain n WEA
Raindrop n WEA
Rainfall n WEA
Rapids n QUIK
Ray n ANML
Reef n ERTH
Regatta n VEHC
Reservoir n HOLW
Rhine n PLAC
Rinse v CLEN
Rip n VARY
River n
Rivers n
Riverside n NEAR

Row v GO
Rowboat n VEHC
Rowed v GO
Rowing v GO
Sail n FABR
Sail v GO
Sailboat n VEHC
Sailed v GO
Sailing v GO
Sailor n
Salamander n ANML
Saliva n SOMA
Salmon n ANML
Salmon n FOOD
Salt n
Saltwater j MTRL
Sampan n VEHC
Sardine n FOOD
Sardine n ANML
Saturate v BULG
Scallop n FOOD
Scallop n ANML
Schooner n VEHC
Scow n VEHC
Sea n
Sea n BLUR
Seaboard n ERTH
Seafaring j GO
Seal n ANML
Sealing v ANML
Seaman n MALE
Seamen n MALE
Seas n
Seashore n ERTH
Seasick j SICK
Seaward d FORW
Seaweed n VEGT
Seep v
Shad n ANML
Shad n FOOD
Shark n ANML
Shell n VEHC
Shellfish n ANML
Shellfish n FOOD
Shiner n ANML
Ship n VEHC
Shipboard n VEHC
Shipmate n JOIN
Shipwreck n DAMG
Shore n ERTH
Shoreline n ERTH
Shower n CLEN
Shower n WEA

Shrimp n FOOD
Shrimp n ANML
Sink n HOLW
Skate n ANML
Skiff n VEHC
Slake v AID
Slake v
Slip n ERTH
Slip n BLOK
Sloop n VEHC
Slosh v GO
Sluice n BLOK
Slush n DIRT
Smack n VEHC
Soak v
Sodden j
Soggy j
Sole n FOOD
Sole n ANML
Soluble j VARY
Solution n
Sop n FOOD
Sop v
Sound n
Sound v DOWN
Sounded v DOWN
Sounding v DOWN
Spatter v DIRT
Spill v
Spill v DAMG
Splash v HEAR
Splash v DIRT
Sponge n CLEN
Sponge n MTRL
Spout v OUT
Spray n
Sprayed v
Spraying v
Spring n
Sprinkle n
Spurt n
Squirt v
Starboard n PLAC
Starfish n ANML
Steamboat n VEHC
Steamer n VEHC
Steamship n VEHC
Steep v BULG
Steeped v BULG
Steeping v BULG
Stem n FORW
Stern n BACK
Stream n GO

Stroke n GO
Stroked v GO
Stroking v GO
Styx n DEAD
Sub n VEHC
Submarine j DOWN
Submarine n VEHC
Submarine n DAMG
Submerge v DOWN
Subs n VEHC
Surf n VARY
Swam v GO
Swamp n ERTH
Swamp v BULG
Swamped v BULG
Swamping v BULG
Sweat v SOMA
Sweated v SOMA
Swell n LARG
Swim v GO
Swordfish n ANML
Swordfish n FOOD
Swum v GO
Syringe n HOLW
Tadpole n ANML
Tank n HOLW
Tar n
Tarn n
Tartan n VEHC
Tear n SOMA
Tender n VEHC
Thaw n VARY
Tide n
Torrent n DAMG
Transatlantic j AFAR
Trickle v
Trout n ANML
Trout n FOOD
Tug n VEHC
Tuna n FOOD
Tuna n ANML
Undercurrent n DOWN
Undersea j DOWN
Unsinkable j EVER
Upstream d UP
Vessel n VEHC
Viscosity n REST
Wake n BACK
Walrus n ANML
Warp v VARY
Warped v VARY
Warping v VARY
Warship n DAMG

Wash n CLEN
Wash v GO
Wash n COLR
Washed v CLEN
Washed v GO
Washer n CLEN
Water n
Water n SIP
Watercolor n COLR
Watercool v COLD
Watercourse n PATH
Watered v
Watered v SIP
Waterfall n DOWN
Waterfowl n ANML
Waterfront n FORW
Waterhole n HOLW
Watering v
Watering v SIP
Waterless j LACK
Waterline n FORM
Waterlog v BULG
Waterproof j BLOK
Watershed n SEP
Watertight j BLOK
Waterworks n MECH
Wave n VARY
Weigh v UP
Well n HOLW
Well v
Welled v
Welling v
Wells n HOLW
Wells v
Wet j
Wet j FOOL
Wetland n ERTH
Wets v
Wetted v
Whale n ANML
Wharf n BLOK
Whirlpool n VARY
Whitefish n FOOD
Whitefish n ANML
Whiting n ANML
Whiting n FOOD
Windjammer n VEHC
Wring v BLOK
Wrung v BLOK
Yacht n VEHC
Yawl n VEHC

FOND

Admire v
Adore v
Adulate v SUB
Affable j
Affection n
Affinity n JOIN
Agape n HOLY
Allure n
Amatory j SEX

Amiable j
Amicable j
Amity n
Amorous j SEX
Amour n SEX
Anglophile n PLAC
Appeal n
Appreciate v IDEA
Appreciate v

Ardent j
Attach v JOIN
Attached v JOIN
Attaches v JOIN
Attractive j MOTV
Beau n MALE
Befriend v
Bewitch v MYTH
Bosom j BODY

Boyfriend n MALE
Buddies n
Buddy n
Buff n MOTV
Buss n SEX
Bussed v SEX
Busses v SEX
Bussing v SEX
Cajole v FALS

Camaraderie n JOIN
Caress v JOIN
Charm n GOOD
Chauvinism n GRUP
Cherish v
Chuck n JOIN
Chucked v JOIN
Chucking v JOIN
Chucks v JOIN
Chum n
Chummy j
Close j NEAR
Coax v MOTV
Coddle v AID
Comity n GOOD
Commiserate v PANG
Companion n JOIN
Company n JOIN
Compassion n
Complaisance n
Comrade n JOIN
Condole v PANG
Confessional n HOLY
Confidant n COVR
Confide v COVR
Confidence n COVR
Confident j COVR
Confidential j COVR
Congratulate v
Coo v TALK
Cordial j
Cotton v
Court v SEX
Courted v SEX
Courting v SEX
Courts v SEX
Courtship n SEX
Crazier j
Crazy j
Crony n
Crush n SEX
Cuddle v JOIN
Cult n HOLY
Cupid n MYTH

Curtsy n
Dandle v JOIN
Darling j
Dazzle v MOTV
Dear j
Delight v GLAD
Devote v
Devotion n
Devotion n HOLY
Dig v IDEA
Dote v
Effusive j
Embrace n JOIN
Empathy n
Enamor v SEX
Enchant v
Enchantress n LADY
Enthrall v
Entrance v
Entranced v
Entrancing v
Entrust v AID
Esteem n IDEA
Fan n MOTV
Fancied v
Fancier n
Fancies v
Fancy n
Fascinate v
Favor n AID
Favoring v AID
Favorite j
Fawn v SUB
Fawned v SUB
Fawning v SUB
Felicitate v GLAD
Fellowship n
Fetching j
Fetish n MYTH
Flatter v FALS
Fond j
Fondle v JOIN
Fraternize v JOIN
Friend n

Girlfriend n LADY
Greet v
Gush v
Honey n GOOD
Honeymoon n SEX
Hug v JOIN
Idol n HOLY
Infatuate v
Ingratiate v
Intimacy n JOIN
Intimate j JOIN
Keepsake n HAVE
Kiss v SEX
Like v
Love n
Love n SEX
Lovely j GOOD
Mad j MOTV
Magnetism n JOIN
Minion n
Nepotism n KIN
Novena n HOLY
Obsequious j SUB
Ovation n HEAR
Pal n
Palatable j FOOD
Palled v
Palling v
Pals n
Paramour n SEX
Patriot n GRUP
Peck n JOIN
Pet n ANML
Pet n
Pet v JOIN
Pet v SEX
Petted v JOIN
Petted v SEX
Petting v JOIN
Petting v SEX
Platonic j IDEA
Pleasant j GLAD
Please v GLAD
Pleasing j GLAD

Pleasure n GLAD
Pride n POWR
Proud j POWR
Rave v TALK
Raving v TALK
Regard n
Regards n
Relish n SOMA
Relish n
Respect n AGRE
Respected v AGRE
Respectful j AGRE
Respecting v AGRE
Revere v
Revering v
Romance n SEX
Romantic j SEX
Shine n
Sweet j GOOD
Sweetheart n SEX
Sycophant n SUB
Sympathetic j
Sympathy n
Take v
Tender j EASY
Thank v AID
Thanks n AID
Thrill v
Toast n SIP
Took v
Treasure v CRUX
Treasured v CRUX
Treasuring v CRUX
Tribute n
Trust n AID
Valentine n PLAY
Venerable j PAST
Venerate v
Votary n
Warm j HEAT
Welcome n
Wild j
Woo v SEX
Worship v HOLY

FOOD

Acid j SOMA
Acorn n VEGT
Alacarte j WRIT
Alamode j
Aliment n AID
Alimentary j SOMA
Alimentary j AID
Almond n VEGT
Anchovy n FLOW
Angel n
Anise n VEGT
Antipasto n
Appetite n MOTV
Apple n VEGT
Applesauce n VEGT
Applesauce n FOOL
Apricot n VEGT

Artichoke n VEGT
Asparagus n VEGT
Ate v SOMA
Ate v PANG
Ate v DAMG
Automat n MART
Avocado n VEGT
Bacon n ANML
Bake v HEAT
Bakery n MART
Baloney n ANML
Baloney n FOOL
Banana n VEGT
Banquet n
Barbecue n HEAT
Bass n FLOW
Baste v

Batter n
Bean n VEGT
Beef n ANML
Beefier j ANML
Beefsteak n ANML
Beefy j ANML
Berry n VEGT
Biscuit n
Bistro n HOME
Bit v SOMA
Bite n SOMA
Biting v SOMA
Bitten v SOMA
Bitter j SOMA
Blueberry n VEGT
Bluefish n FLOW
Board n LIVE

Boarded v LIVE
Boarder n LIVE
Boarding v LIVE
Boardinghouse n HOME
Boards v LIVE
Bolt v QUIK
Bonbon n
Borsch n SIP
Bouillon n SIP
Bread n VEGT
Breadbasket n SOMA
Breakfast n
Broccoli n VEGT
Broiler n ANML
Broth n SIP
Brownie n COLR
Browse v VEGT

Buffet n
Bun n
Butcher n MART
Butt n HEAT
Butter n ANML
Butter v FALS
Cabbage n VEGT
Cabob n ANML
Cafe n MART
Cafeteria n MART
Caffeine n MTRL
Cake n
Calory n MSMT
Canape n
Candies n
Candy n
Cane n VEGT
Canine n BODY
Cannibal n DAMG
Cantaloupe n VEGT
Canteen n MART
Caper n VEGT
Capon n ANML
Caramel n VEGT
Carbohydrate n MTRL
Carnivorous j ANML
Carp n FLOW
Carrot n VEGT
Cashew n VEGT
Casserole n HOLW
Cater v AID
Catfish n FLOW
Cauliflower n VEGT
Caviar n FLOW
Celery n VEGT
Cereal n VEGT
Champ v AGGR
Champed v AGGR
Champing v AGGR
Cheddar n ANML
Cheer n GLAD
Cheese n ANML
Cheeseburger n ANML
Cheesecake n
Chef n LEAD
Cheroot n HEAT
Cherry n VEGT
Chestnut n VEGT
Chew v SOMA
Chicken n ANML
Chicle n VEGT
Chicory n VEGT
Chili n VEGT
China n FURN
Chip n LITL
Chive n VEGT
Chocolate n VEGT
Chop n ANML
Chops n ANML
Chopstick n
Chopsuey n
Chow n
Chowder n SIP
Chowmein n
Chuck n ANML

Chum n FLOW
Chump v SOMA
Cigar n HEAT
Cigarette n HEAT
Cinnamon n VEGT
Citric j VEGT
Citron n VEGT
Citrus j VEGT
Clam n FLOW
Clod n ANML
Clove n VEGT
Cobbler n VEGT
Cockle n VEGT
Cocktail n
Cocoanut n VEGT
Coconut n VEGT
Cod n FLOW
Coddle v HEAT
Coldcuts n COLD
Coleslaw n VEGT
Collard n VEGT
Comestible n
Comfit n VEGT
Communion n HOLY
Condiment n
Cone n FORM
Confection n
Confiture n
Conger n FLOW
Conserve n
Consomme n SIP
Consume v SOMA
Consumption n SOMA
Cook v HEAT
Cookbook n WRIT
Cookie n
Cooking v HEAT
Copra n VEGT
Corn n VEGT
Corn v EVER
Corned j EVER
Cornstarch n VEGT
Corny j VEGT
Corona n HEAT
Cosey n HOLW
Costermonger n MART
Cosy n HOLW
Course n
Cozy n HOLW
Crab n FLOW
Crabapple n VEGT
Cracker n
Crackerjack n
Crackling n ANML
Cranberry n VEGT
Cream n
Cream v SEP
Creamed v
Creamed v SEP
Creamer n SEP
Creamery n ANML
Cress n VEGT
Cruller n
Crumb n LITL
Crumpet n

Crust n COVR
Cucumber n VEGT
Cud n
Cuisine n
Culinary j
Cupboard n HOLW
Cupcake n
Currant n VEGT
Curried v VEGT
Curry n VEGT
Cuspid n BODY
Custard n
Cutlery n FURN
Cutlet n ANML
Dairy j ANML
Danish n PLAC
Date n VEGT
Delicacy n GOOD
Delicatessen n MART
Dental j BODY
Dentate j BODY
Dentition n BODY
Denture n BODY
Dessert n
Devil v
Devour v SOMA
Dextrose n MTRL
Diet n
Digest v SOMA
Digestion n SOMA
Dill j VEGT
Dine v SOMA
Diner n SOMA
Diner n MART
Dinette n HOME
Dinner n
Dinnerware n FURN
Dip n IN
Dish n HOLW
Dished v HOLW
Donut n
Dough n VEGT
Doughnut n
Dress v
Dressed v
Dresses v
Dressing v
Drumstick n ANML
Dumpling n
Eat v SOMA
Eat v PANG
Eat v DAMG
Eclair n
Edible j
Eel n FLOW
Egg n ANML
Eggplant n VEGT
Eggshell n HOLW
Eggshell n COLR
Endive n VEGT
Engorge v BULG
Entree n
Epicure n MOTV
Escarole n VEGT
Eucharist n HOLY

Fag n HEAT
Famine n LACK
Famish v LACK
Fare n
Farina n VEGT
Fast n LACK
Fasted v LACK
Fasting v LACK
Feast n
Fed v
Fed v SOMA
Feed n
Feed v SOMA
Fig n VEGT
Filbert n VEGT
Filet n ANML
Fillet n ANML
Fish n FLOW
Fishmonger n MART
Flatfish n FLOW
Flavor n SOMA
Flounder n FLOW
Flour n VEGT
Fluke n FLOW
Fodder n
Food n
Forage v OPEN
Fork n FURN
Frankfurter n ANML
Fricassee n ANML
Fried v HEAT
Fries v HEAT
Fritter n VEGT
Frost n COLD
Fruit n VEGT
Fruited j VEGT
Fruiter n VEGT
Fruitful j VEGT
Fry v HEAT
Fryer n ANML
Frying v HEAT
Fudge n
Galley n HOME
Game n ANML
Garlic n VEGT
Garnish v GOOD
Gastronomy n SOMA
Gelatine n
Gherkin n VEGT
Giblet n ANML
Ginger n VEGT
Glaze n
Glazing v
Glucose n
Glut v BULG
Glutted v BULG
Glutton n BULG
Gnaw v SOMA
Gnaw v PANG
Gobble v SOMA
Goose n ANML
Gorge v BULG
Gorged v BULG
Gorging v BULG
Goulash n

Gourmet n MOTV	Kitchen n HOME	Molasses n VEGT	Pecan n VEGT
Grape n VEGT	Kohlrabi n VEGT	Morsel n LITL	Peck n
Grapefruit n VEGT	Kosher j HOLY	Mousse n	Pepper n VEGT
Grapevine n VEGT	Kumquat n VEGT	Muffin n	Peppermint n VEGT
Gravy n	Lamb n ANML	Mulberry n VEGT	Perch n FLOW
Graze v VEGT	Larder n HOLW	Munch v SOMA	Perfecto n HEAT
Griddle n HEAT	Lean n ANML	Mush n EASY	Persimmon n VEGT
Grill n HEAT	Leek n VEGT	Mushroom n VEGT	Pheasant n ANML
Grill n MART	Legume n VEGT	Muskmelon n VEGT	Picalilly n VEGT
Grilled v HEAT	Lemon n VEGT	Mussel n FLOW	Pickerel n FLOW
Grinder n	Lentil n VEGT	Mustard n VEGT	Pickle n VEGT
Grinder n BODY	Lettuce n VEGT	Mutton n ANML	Pickle v EVER
Grits n VEGT	Lick n SOMA	Nectarine n VEGT	Pickled j EVER
Groats n VEGT	Lick n ERTH	Nibble v LITL	Pickling v EVER
Grocer n MART	Licked v SOMA	Noodle n	Picnic n PLAY
Grub n	Licking v SOMA	Nourish v AID	Pie n
Gruel n	Licorice n VEGT	Nut n VEGT	Pies n
Guava n VEGT	Lifesaver n	Nutcracker n SEP	Pike n FLOW
Gulp n SOMA	Lime n VEGT	Nutmeg n VEGT	Pill n LITL
Gum n VEGT	Liver n ANML	Nutrient j AID	Pimento n VEGT
Gumbo n SIP	Liverwurst n ANML	Nutriment n AID	Pineapple n VEGT
Gumdrop n	Loaf n	Nutrition n AID	Pipe n HEAT
Gustation n SOMA	Lobster n FLOW	Oat n VEGT	Pippin n VEGT
Haddock n FLOW	Loganberry n VEGT	Oil n VEGT	Pistachio n VEGT
Hake n FLOW	Lollipop n	Oils n VEGT	Pizza n
Halibut n FLOW	Lozenge n LITL	Okra n VEGT	Pizzeria n MART
Ham n ANML	Lunch n	Oleomargarine n VEGT	Plate n HOLW
Hamburger n ANML	Luncheon n	Olive n VEGT	Platter n HOLW
Hardtack n	Luncheonette n	Omelet n	Plug n VEGT
Hash n	Luncheonette n MART	Omnivorous j WHOL	Plum n VEGT
Havana n PLAC	Lyonnaise j	Onion n VEGT	Pomace n MTRL
Herb n VEGT	Macaroni n	Orange n VEGT	Pomegranate n VEGT
Herbivore n VEGT	Macaroon n	Overcook v HEAT	Popcorn n HEAR
Hermit n	Mackerel n FLOW	Overeat v BULG	Porgy n FLOW
Herring n FLOW	Maize n VEGT	Overeat v SOMA	Pork n ANML
Hibachi n HEAT	Mandarin n VEGT	Overfeed v SOMA	Porridge n
Hog n ANML	Manger n HOLW	Oyster n FLOW	Porterhouse n ANML
Hollandaise n	Mango n VEGT	Palatable j FOND	Potato n VEGT
Honey n BUG	Manna n HOLY	Panatela n HEAT	Potlatch n PLAY
Hookah n HOLW	Margarine n VEGT	Pancake n	Potluck n
Horseradish n VEGT	Marinate v FLOW	Panetella n HEAT	Potpie n HOLW
Host n HOLY	Marjoram n VEGT	Pantry n HOME	Poultry n ANML
Hotdog n ANML	Market n MART	Pap n EASY	Poundcake n
Huckleberry n VEGT	Marmalade n VEGT	Papaya n VEGT	Praline n
Hunger n MOTV	Marshmallow n VEGT	Paprika n VEGT	Prawn n FLOW
Hungry j MOTV	Masticate v SOMA	Parfait n	Preserves n
Ice n COLD	Mayonnaise n	Parmesan n ANML	Pretzel n
Icecream n COLD	Meal n	Parsley n VEGT	Protein n MTRL
Icing n COLD	Meal n VEGT	Parsnip n VEGT	Provision n
Indigestion n SICK	Mealtime n TIME	Paste n	Prune n VEGT
Inedible j OPPO	Mealy j VEGT	Pastrami n ANML	Pudding n
Ingest v SOMA	Meat n ANML	Pastries n	Pumpernickel n VEGT
Jam n VEGT	Meat n	Pastry n	Pumpkin n VEGT
Jellies n	Melon n VEGT	Pasture n VEGT	Quince n VEGT
Jello n	Menu n WRIT	Pate n	Radish n VEGT
Jelly n	Meringue n	Patties n LITL	Raisin n VEGT
Junket n VEGT	Mess n	Patty n LITL	Raspberry n VEGT
Kabob n ANML	Millet n VEGT	Pea n VEGT	Ravenous j MOTV
Kale n VEGT	Mince n LITL	Peach n VEGT	Refreshment n AID
Ketchup n VEGT	Mincemeat n LITL	Peanut n VEGT	Relish n
Kidney n ANML	Mint n VEGT	Pear n VEGT	Restaurant n MART
Kipper n FLOW	Mocha j VEGT	Peas n VEGT	Rhubarb n VEGT

Parts of speech: a article; b preposition; c conjunction; d adverb; f prefix; i interjection; j adjective; n noun; p pronoun; r phrase; v verb.

Rice n VEGT
Roast n HEAT
Roll n VEGT
Ruminate v SOMA
Rump n ANML
Rye n VEGT
Saccharin n
Sage n VEGT
Salad n
Salami n ANML
Salmon n FLOW
Salt n
Salted v
Salting v
Sandwich n
Sardine n FLOW
Sauce n
Saucer n HOLW
Sauerkraut n VEGT
Sausage n ANML
Saute j HEAT
Scallion n VEGT
Scallop n FLOW
Scallop v HEAT
Scalloped v HEAT
Scavenge v DIRT
Schnitzel n ANML
Scrapple n
Season v
Seasoned v
Seasoning n
Service n FURN
Shad n FLOW
Shag n VEGT

Shellfish n FLOW
Sherbert n
Shortcake n
Shrimp n FLOW
Sideboard n FURN
Silver n FURN
Silverware n FURN
Sinker n
Sirloin n ANML
Smoke v HEAT
Snack n
Snail n ANML
Snap n
Sole n FLOW
Sop n FLOW
Souffle n
Soup n SIP
Soupspoon n FURN
Sour j SOMA
Spaghetti n
Spatula n FURN
Spice n VEGT
Spice n SOMA
Spicy j SOMA
Spinach n VEGT
Spoon n FURN
Spread n LARG
Squash n VEGT
Starve v LACK
Steak n ANML
Stew n HEAT
Stock n ANML
Strawberry n VEGT
Sub n

Submarine n
Subs n
Sugar n VEGT
Sundae n
Sup v
Supped v
Supper n
Supping v
Swallow n SOMA
Swallowed v SOMA
Swallowing v SOMA
Swill n DIRT
Swordfish n FLOW
Syrup n
Tablespoon n FURN
Tack n
Tapioca n VEGT
Tart j SOMA
Tart n
Taste n SOMA
Tasty j GOOD
Teaspoon n FURN
Teeth n BODY
Toast n HEAT
Tobacco n VEGT
Tomato n VEGT
Tongue n ANML
Tooth n BODY
Tripe n ANML
Trout n FLOW
Tuna n FLOW
Turkey n ANML
Turnover n
Turtle n ANML

Twist n VARY
Unappetizing j PANG
Undernourished j LACK
Uneaten j
Unsweetened j SOMA
Utensil n FURN
Vanilla j VEGT
Vegetable n VEGT
Viand n
Victual n
Vinegar n VEGT
Vitamin n AID
Voracious j MOTV
Wafer n
Waffle n
Walnut n VEGT
Watercress n VEGT
Watermelon n VEGT
Wheat n VEGT
Whitefish n FLOW
Whiting n FLOW
Wolf v ANML
Wolfed v ANML
Wolfing v ANML
Wolfs v ANML
Yam n VEGT
Yeast n VEGT
Yoghurt n ANML
Yolk n ANML
Zucchini n VEGT
Zwieback n

FOOL

Abracadabra n TALK
Absentminded j IDEA
Absurd j
Antic n
Ape v ANML
Apish j ANML
Applesauce n FOOD
Asinine j ANML
Ass n ANML
Asses n ANML
Baloney n FOOD
Banter v TALK
Battier j SICK
Batty j SICK
Benighted j
Blather n TALK
Blithering j TALK
Blockhead n
Bombast n TALK
Bonehead n BODY
Boner n FALS
Brainless j
Brash j POWR
Brass n POWR
Brassy j POWR
Brazen j POWR
Buffoon n GLAD
Bull n TALK

Bunk n FALS
Burlesque n
Burlesque n PLAY
Caricature n SIML
Cartoon n VIEW
Childish j YNG
Chump n
Claptrap n FALS
Clod n
Clodhopper n ERTH
Clown n GLAD
Cockandbull j ANML
Cockeyed j BODY
Conceit n POWR
Conceit n IDEA
Conceited j POWR
Corn n TRIV
Cornier j TRIV
Corny j TRIV
Crackpot n
Crass j
Crazier j
Crazily d
Craziness n
Crazy j
Cretin n SICK
Cuckoo n
Cuss n

Daffier j
Daffy j
Daft j
Dandies n GARB
Dandy n GARB
Dense j
Density n
Deride v AGGR
Derision n AGGR
Dolt n
Donkey n ANML
Dope n
Dotage n PAST
Drip n
Drivel n TALK
Dude n GARB
Dullard n
Dumb j
Dumbbell n
Dummy n
Dunce n
Falderol n
Fanatic n MOTV
Farce n
Farfetched j AFAR
Fathead n BODY
Fatuous j
Featherbrain n

Fiddlesticks i EMPH
Flightier j VARY
Flighty j VARY
Folly n
Fool n
Foolhardy j POWR
Fop n GARB
Fudge n
Funnier j GLAD
Funniest j GLAD
Funny j GLAD
Gargoyle n FORM
Gawk n WEAK
Gawk v VIEW
Gawkier j WEAK
Gawky j WEAK
Geezer n PAST
Gibberish n TALK
Gink n
Goof v WEAK
Goofy j
Goon n DAMG
Goon n
Goose n ANML
Grotesque j
Halfbaked j
Halfwit n
Ham v WEAK

Hammed v WEAK
Harebrain j
Hidebound j BLOK
Highfalutin j UP
Hocuspocus n FALS
Hooey n
Horse v ANML
Horses v ANML
Horsing v ANML
Humbug n FALS
Idiocy n
Idiot n
Ignorance n
Illiteracy n WRIT
Imbecile n
Inane j TRIV
Incoherence n BLUR
Insane j
Insensate j
Ironic j AGGR
Ironies n AGGR
Irony n AGGR
Irrational j
Jabber v TALK
Jackass n ANML
Jargon n TALK
Jerk n
Jest n GLAD
Jinks n GLAD
Joke n GLAD

Joked v GLAD
Kid v GLAD
Kidded v GLAD
Lampoon v AGGR
Loco j SICK
Loonier j SICK
Loony j SICK
Lout n
Ludicrous j
Lug n
Lugubrious j PANG
Lunacy n SICK
Lunatic j SICK
Lunkhead n
Mad j
Mad j SICK
Madcap j
Maudlin j PANG
Meaningless j
Mimic v SIML
Mock v AGGR
Mockery n AGGR
Mocking v AGGR
Mocks v AGGR
Monkey v ANML
Moron n
Mush n
Neologism n TALK
Nincompoop n
Ninny n

Nitwit n
Nonsense n
Numbskull n BODY
Nut n
Oaf n
Obtuse j
Oddball n AFAR
Outlandish j AFAR
Parody n SIML
Philistine n OPPO
Pomposity n POWR
Pompous j POWR
Prank n GLAD
Preposterous j
Prig n GOOD
Prude n GOOD
Puppies n YNG
Puppy n YNG
Queer j
Queered v
Queering v
Quirk n
Quizzical j
Ridicule n AGGR
Rigmarole n
Sap n WEAK
Satire n AGGR
Scatterbrain n
Schmo n
Schnook n

Screwball n
Screwy j
Senseless j
Silly j
Simple j
Simpleton n
Slapstick j GLAD
Stilted j
Stupid j
Tactless j
Tall j LARG
Thick j
Thoughtless j
Travesty n
Twit v TALK
Twitted v TALK
Uncultured j
Unenlightened j
Uninformed j
Unintelligent j
Unreasonable j
Vain j
Vanity n
Wacky j
Wet j FLOW
Wild j
Wise j IDEA
Wiseacre n IDEA
Wry j
Zany j

FORM

Abscissa n
Abutment n AID
Adjective n TALK
Adverb n TALK
Altar n HOLY
Angle n
Angular j
Anneal v HEAT
Anvil n WORK
Arabesque n VARY
Arc n
Arch n
Arched v
Arches n
Arching v
Architect n IDEA
Armature n
Arrange v
Article n TALK
Asymmetry n VARY
Atlas n IDEA
Axes n
Axis n
Ball n
Ball n PLAY
Ball n DAMG
Balled v
Band n
Banded v
Banding v
Bands n

Bar n
Bar n SIP
Barbell n WORK
Baroque j VARY
Baroque j PAST
Barred v
Barring v
Base n DOWN
Baseboard n MTRL
Bases n DOWN
Basing v DOWN
Basketry n HOLW
Bat n
Bat n PLAY
Baton n LEAD
Batted v PLAY
Batter n PLAY
Batters n PLAY
Batting v PLAY
Bead n GARB
Bead n LITL
Bead n HOLY
Beam n
Bed n
Beds n
Belt n
Bench n
Billboard n WRIT
Billies n DAMG
Billy n DAMG
Birdseye j FABR

Blackboard n COLR
Block n
Block n PLAY
Block n DEAD
Blueprint n IDEA
Board n
Boards n
Bob n
Bobbin n
Boom n
Bow n
Box n HOLW
Boxed v HOLW
Boxing v HOLW
Bracket n
Braid n
Brick n MTRL
Bricklayer n WORK
Bridge n
Broadside n LARG
Broomstick n CLEN
Build v WORK
Build n BODY
Building n HOME
Building v WORK
Bulkhead n BLOK
Bulwark n AID
Bust n BODY
Butterfly n BUG
Buttress n AID
Cadre n GRUP

Cake n
Cameo n GARB
Candelabrum n VIEW
Cane n AID
Cane v DAMG
Caned v DAMG
Caning v DAMG
Canon n IDEA
Canonical j IDEA
Capital n UP
Carpenter n WORK
Cartographer n IDEA
Carve v SHRP
Case n TALK
Casement n VIEW
Cast n
Casting n
Cenotaph n DEAD
Ceremony n HOLY
Ceremony n EVER
Chart n IDEA
Chassis n MECH
Checkerboard n PLAY
Chock n BLOK
Chord n
Chorography n IDEA
Circle n HOLW
Circular j
Clause n TALK
Cleat n BLOK
Clew n

Cloisonne n COLR
Clot v VARY
Cloverleaf j VEGT
Club n
Clubbed j
Clue n
Coagulate v VARY
Cobble v ERTH
Cobbled v ERTH
Cobbles v ERTH
Cobblestone n ERTH
Code n IDEA
Codify v IDEA
Coding v IDEA
Coil v VARY
Collage n JOIN
Collinear j SIML
Collocate v JOIN
Colonnade n
Colossus n LARG
Column n
Column n FORW
Complect v JOIN
Complected v JOIN
Complex n
Compose v BGIN
Compose v
Composing v BGIN
Composing v
Composition n WRIT
Composition n
Composition n BGIN
Concave j HOLW
Concoct v
Cone n
Cone n FOOD
Confect v
Confecting v
Configuration n
Congeal v VARY
Conic j
Conjugate v TALK
Conjunction n TALK
Consistency n SIML
Consistent j SIML
Consonant n TALK
Constitute v BGIN
Constitute v
Constituting v BGIN
Constituting v
Constitution n BGIN
Constitution n
Construct v WORK
Construct n IDEA
Constructing v WORK
Contour n
Contrive v IDEA
Convex j
Cop n FABR
Cope v COVR
Coping n COVR
Copulative n TALK
Corner n
Corners n
Corrugate v VARY

Cosecant n NUMR
Cosine n NUMR
Cosines n NUMR
Cosmic j WHOL
Cosmos n WHOL
Cotangent n NUMR
Counter n MART
Counters n MART
Course n
Cove n HOLW
Cradle n AID
Crankshaft n MECH
Crescent j
Crescent n ASTR
Crop n
Cross n
Cross n HOLY
Crosshatch n WRIT
Crossways d
Crosswise d
Crotch n SEP
Crotched j SEP
Crowbar n WORK
Crucifix n HOLY
Crutch n AID
Crux n
Crystal n MTRL
Crystallize v MTRL
Crystallize v SHRP
Cube n
Cubic j
Cubism n
Cylinder n HOLW
Cylindrical j HOLW
Dada n OPPO
Dado n
Dais n POWR
Dash n WRIT
Dative j TALK
Decagonal j
Deck n
Decked v
Decking v
Declension n TALK
Decline v TALK
Deform v VARY
Delineate v SHRP
Design n IDEA
Devise v IDEA
Diagonal j
Diagram n IDEA
Dial n VIEW
Dialed v VIEW
Dialing v VIEW
Diamond n
Dihedral n
Dimension n
Dimorphic j OPPO
Diphthong n TALK
Disc n
Discus n PLAY
Dish n HOLW
Dished v HOLW
Disk n
Dispose v

Doctrine n IDEA
Dogma n IDEA
Dovetail v JOIN
Draft n WRIT
Drafted v WRIT
Draughtsman n WRIT
Easel n
Eave n UP
Eaves n UP
Eccentric j VARY
Echelon n FORW
Edifice n
Ellipse n
Elliptic j
Embankment n ERTH
Endomorph n ERTH
Engineer n MECH
Erect v UP
Erection n UP
Fashion v WORK
Fashioning v WORK
Festoon v PLAY
Figure n
Figurine n
Filament n LITL
Filet n FABR
Filigree n
Fillet n FABR
Fin n
Flag n ERTH
Flags n ERTH
Flagstaff n VIEW
Flagstone n ERTH
Flap n VARY
Flapped v VARY
Flat j
Flatcar n VEHC
Flatfoot n BODY
Flatfooted j BODY
Flatten v
Floor n DOWN
Flounce n GARB
Flute n HOLW
Fold n VARY
Folder n VARY
Form n
Form n WRIT
Formal j EVER
Format n
Formation n
Formative j
Formed v
Forming v
Formless j BLUR
Formulate v IDEA
Foundation n CRUX
Founds v CRUX
Frame n VIEW
Frame n
Framework n
Fret n
Frieze n
Frill n TRIV
Furring n MTRL
Fuselage n VEHC

Gable n UP
Gallow n DEAD
Gantry n
Gargoyle n FOOL
Garland n VEGT
Gatepost n OPEN
Genitive j TALK
Geometry n NUMR
Gerund n TALK
Girder n
Globe n
Globule n LITL
Grained v
Graining v
Grammar n TALK
Granule n LITL
Graph n IDEA
Graphing v IDEA
Grate n
Grating n
Grid n
Gridded v
Gridiron n HEAT
Gridiron n PLAY
Gridiron n
Grille n
Gunwhale n FLOW
Handmade j BODY
Hatch n WRIT
Hatched v WRIT
Hearse n DEAD
Helical j VARY
Helicoid j VARY
Helm n LEAD
Hemicycle n SOME
Hemisphere n SOME
Heptagon n
Herringbone j
Hexagon n
Hip n
Hipped j
Homemade j HOME
Hoop n HOLW
Horizontal j
Horse n ANML
Horses n ANML
Hull n FLOW
Hyperbola n
Hyperbolic j
Hypotenuse n
I n WRIT
Icon n
Icon n HOLY
Ideology n IDEA
Imperfect j TALK
Indoctrinate v IDEA
Infinitve n TALK
Inflect v TALK
Ingot n
Inlaid j IN
Inlay n IN
Install v
Institution n EVER
Intransitive j TALK
Ism n IDEA

Isomorphic j SIML	Orbit n HOLW	Polkadot j LITL	Ringing v HOLW
Isosceles j SIML	Order n FORW	Poll n	Rite n HOLY
Jamb n	Organization n	Polygon n	Ritual j HOLY
Jell v VARY	Organization n GRUP	Polyhedron n	Rococo j VARY
Jig n	Organize v	Polymorphous j MUCH	Rod n
Keel n FLOW	Outline n SIML	Pose v REST	Rod n DAMG
Keyboard n FORW	Oval j	Posing v REST	Roll n
Keystone n CRUX	Pallet n HOLW	Post n	Rolled v
L n WRIT	Pancake n	Posts n	Rostrum n TALK
Lace n FABR	Pancaked v	Predicate n TALK	Rotund j BULG
Lace v	Pancaking v	Prefabricate v FORW	Rotunda n HOME
Last n	Panel v MTRL	Prefix n TALK	Round j
Lattice n	Paneled v MTRL	Preposition n TALK	Rounded v
Layer n	Paneling v MTRL	Prism n	Rounder j
Layout n	Panelled v MTRL	Prism n VIEW	Roundest j
Leaf n	Parabola n	Profile n SIML	Rounding v
Leaves n	Parallelogram n SIML	Program n IDEA	Roundness n
Lei n VEGT	Parapet n COVR	Program n WRIT	Rounds v
Leis n VEGT	Parquet n	Project n IDEA	Rudder n LEAD
Level v SIML	Parse v TALK	Projecting v IDEA	Rule n MSMT
Line n	Parsing v TALK	Pronoun n TALK	Rule n IDEA
Linear j	Participial j TALK	Proscenium n FORW	Ruled v MSMT
Liturgy n HOLY	Participle n TALK	Protean j VARY	Ruler n MSMT
Locus n JOIN	Pattern n	Protocol n IDEA	Ruling v MSMT
Logic n IDEA	Pedestal n AID	Pylon n	Rung n
Loop n HOLW	Pediform j BODY	Pyramid n	S n WRIT
Lozenge n	Pentagon n	Pyramid v LARG	Saddle n
Made v	Perfect j TALK	Quadrangle n	Sash n VIEW
Make v	Perpendicular j UP	Quarterdeck n FLOW	Scaffold n
Maker n	Phoneme n TALK	Rack n	Scaffold n DEAD
Makes v	Phonetic j TALK	Rack n DAMG	Scale n COVR
Makeup n BODY	Phonic j TALK	Racked v	Scallop n
Makeup n CRUX	Phrase n TALK	Racking v	Scalloped j
Malformation n FALS	Pier n AID	Racks n	Scepter n LEAD
Manifold n HOLW	Pile n	Radial j	Schematize v IDEA
Manikin n SIML	Piledriver n POWR	Radian n NUMR	Scheme n IDEA
Mannequin n SIML	Pillar n AID	Rafter n UP	Scroll n WRIT
Map n IDEA	Pin n PLAY	Rail n	Sculpture n VIEW
Mason n WORK	Pitch v	Ramp n GO	Secant n NUMR
Mast n	Pitched v	Ramrod n DAMG	Sentence n TALK
Masthead n FORW	Pitching v	Ramshackle j WEAK	Shaft n
Mat n JOIN	Plaid j FABR	Ray n	Shake n MTRL
Matted v JOIN	Plait v VARY	Rearrange v	Shape n
Method n	Plan n IDEA	Rebuild v WORK	Shapely j GOOD
Mobile n VIEW	Plane n	Recipe n MSMT	Sheet n
Model n SIML	Plank n	Reconstruct v WORK	Sheet n FABR
Modus n	Plasterboard n MTRL	Rectangle n	Shelf n
Mold n	Plat n IDEA	Rectilinear j	Shelve v
Molded v	Plate n	Reflexive j TALK	Shingle n
Molding v	Plated v	Reform v SIML	Shingle n VIEW
Monolith n SOLE	Platform n	Regime n IDEA	Side n
Monument n EVER	Plating v	Regimen n IDEA	Sideway j
Morpheme n TALK	Plied j VARY	Relief n VIEW	Siding n
Mosaic n COLR	Plot n IDEA	Remodel v VARY	Silhouette n SIML
Net n JOIN	Plotted v IDEA	Reorganize v	Sill n
Nominative j TALK	Pluperfect n TALK	Rhombus n	Skeleton n SOMA
Noun n TALK	Ply n VARY	Rib n	Skyscraper n UP
O n WRIT	Podium n LEAD	Ribbed j	Slab n SOME
Obelisk n	Pogostick n PLAY	Right j	Solid j
Object n TALK	Pole n	Right v UP	Spar n
Objective j TALK	Pole v GO	Righted v UP	Sphere n
Oblique j	Poled v GO	Righting v UP	Spherical j
Oblong j	Policies n IDEA	Rights v UP	Spindle n
Obtuse j	Policy n IDEA	Ring n HOLW	Spiral j VARY
Octagon n	Poling v GO	Ringed v HOLW	Spire n UP

Spoke n	Streamline v EASY	Tense n TALK	Wand n
Spokes n	Stripe n COLR	Texture n	Wand n MYTH
Spool n	Striping n COLR	Theory n IDEA	Warp n FABR
Square n	Structure n	Threshold n IN	Waterline n FLOW
Squared v	Stump n	Threw v	Weathervane n WEA
Squaring v	Subject n TALK	Throw v	Web n
Staff n	Subjective j TALK	Tissue n	Webbed j
Stage n PLAY	Subjunctive n TALK	Transitive j TALK	Wedge n SOME
Stamp n	Subplot n IDEA	Tree n VEGT	Wheel n
Stamped v	Substratum n DOWN	Trellis n	Windowsill n VIEW
Stand n	Substructure n DOWN	Triangle n	Wing n UP
Standard n	Suffix n TALK	Triangle n MUSC	Wing n
Star n	Surface n UP	Triangular j	Wing n PLAY
Stars n	Surrealism n MYTH	Trigonometry n NUMR	Winged j UP
Starspangled j VIEW	Swastika n	Trim n	Woodwork n MTRL
Statue n	Syllable n TALK	Tripod n	Woof n FABR
Steeple n UP	Syntax n TALK	U n WRIT	Work n WORK
Stem n	System n	Uncoil v VARY	Works n WORK
Stemmed j	T n WRIT	Undercarriage n DOWN	Wreath n VEGT
Stick n	Table n	Unroll v VARY	Wreath n HOLW
Stilt n UP	Table n WRIT	V n WRIT	Wreathe v VARY
Stock n	Tables n	Vane n WEA	Wreathing v VARY
Stocks n	Tables n WRIT	Vane n	Wrought j
Storey n	Tablet n	Vault n HOME	X n WRIT
Storied j	Tabular j	Vaulted j HOME	Y n WRIT
Stories n	Tabular j WRIT	Verb n TALK	Yard n
Story n	Tabulate v WRIT	Verge n	Yards n
Straight j SIML	Tailor v VARY	Vertical n	Yardstick n MSMT
Straighten v SIML	Tangent n NUMR	Vowel n TALK	Yoke n JOIN
Strategic j IDEA	Technique n	Wafer n	
Strategies n IDEA	Temper n EVER	Wall n BLOK	
Strategy n IDEA	Tempering v EVER	Walled v BLOK	

FORW

Adumbrate v BLUR	Boding v	Face n	Forerunner n GO
Advance n GO	Bow n	Face v BODY	Foresee v VIEW
Advance n	By n PLAY	Facing v	Foreshadow v BLUR
Advance n SEX	Bye n PLAY	Facing v BODY	Foresight n VIEW
Advance v AID	Catalogue n WRIT	File v GO	Forestall v BLOK
Aforementioned j TALK	Chain n JOIN	File v WRIT	Foretaste n SOMA
Aforesaid j TALK	Chronology n TIME	Filing v GO	Foretell v TALK
Aforethought n IDEA	Clockwise j TIME	Filing v WRIT	Forethought n IDEA
Ahead d	Column n FORM	First j NUMR	Foretold v TALK
Along d	Concatenate v JOIN	Firstborn j BGIN	Forewarn v AGGR
Alphabet n WRIT	Concordance n WRIT	Firstclass j POWR	Foreword n TALK
Ante f	Confront v JOIN	Firsthand d BGIN	Former j
Antecede v PAST	Consecutive j	Firstrate j POWR	Forth d
Antechamber n HOME	Cycle n VARY	Fore n	Forthcoming j TIME
Antedate v PAST	Cyclic j VARY	Forearm v DAMG	Forthright j SHRP
Antemortem j DEAD	Defile v GO	Forearmed v DAMG	Forward d
Anterior j	Dictionary n WRIT	Forearming v DAMG	Forward v GO
Anteroom n HOME	Directory n WRIT	Forebode v BAD	Forward j POWR
Anticipate v MOTV	Earlier j TIME	Forecast n TALK	Forward n PLAY
Apocalypse n DAMG	Early j TIME	Forefront n	Forward v AID
Apron n	Earthward d ERTH	Forego v GO	Forwarded v GO
Array n	Echelon n FORM	Foregone j SHRP	Forwarded v AID
Augur v MYTH	Encyclopedia n WRIT	Foreground n ERTH	Forwarding v GO
Avantgarde n NEW	Eve n TIME	Foreknowledge n IDEA	Forwarding v AID
Bank n	Evolve v VARY	Foremost j POWR	Forwards v GO
Before c	Exordium n TALK	Foremost j EMPH	Forwards n PLAY
Bode v	Facade n	Forename n TALK	Forwards v AID

Parts of speech: a article; b preposition; c conjunction; d adverb; f prefix; i interjection;
j adjective; n noun; p pronoun; r phrase; v verb.

Front j
Front n FALS
Front n DAMG
Frontier n END
Frontiersman n MALE
Fronting v
Frontispiece n VIEW
Future n TIME
Gamut n
Glossary n WRIT
Gradation n
Grade n MSMT
Grade n EDUC
Graduate v MSMT
Harbinger n TIME
Head v GO
Head n
Headed v GO
Headed v
Header n
Heading n WRIT
Heading v GO
Heading v
Headlight n VIEW
Headline n WRIT
Headlong j BODY
Headmost j EMPH
Heads v GO
Heads v
Headway n GO
Hedgerow n VEGT
Hence d TIME
Henceforth d TIME
Herald n TALK
Hereafter d TIME
Hierarchy n LEAD
Homeward j HOME
Keyboard n MUSC
Keyboard n FORM
Lead v LEAD
Lead v
Leader n LEAD
Led v LEAD
Letterhead n WRIT
Lexicon n WRIT

Line n
Line n PLAY
Lining v
List n WRIT
Listed v WRIT
Masthead n FORM
Millennium n TIME
Morrow n TIME
Next d
Offing n TIME
Omen n MYTH
On d
Ongoing j
Order n FORM
Ordinal j NUMR
Orient v
Oriented v
Orienting v
Orients v
Pagination n WRIT
Pioneer n BGIN
Portent n DAMG
Posterity n YNG
Preamble n TALK
Prearrangement n AGRE
Precedence n PAST
Preconception n IDEA
Precursor n PAST
Predate v PAST
Predecessor n PAST
Predestination n END
Predetermine v IDEA
Predict v IDEA
Prefabricate v FORM
Preface n TALK
Preheat v HEAT
Prehistory n PAST
Prejudge v IDEA
Preliminary j
Prelude n
Prelude n MUSC
Premature j WEAK
Premedical j MEDC
Premeditate v IDEA
Premier j

Premiere n PLAY
Premise n IDEA
Premonition n PANG
Prenatal j BGIN
Prepaid j MONY
Prepay v MONY
Presage n IDEA
Preschool j EDUC
Prescience n IDEA
Presentiment n PANG
Preshrunk j LITL
Presuppose v IDEA
Preview n VIEW
Prewar j DAMG
Primacy n LEAD
Primal j PAST
Primal j CRUX
Primary j CRUX
Prime j CRUX
Primeval j PAST
Primordial j PAST
Prior j
Priority n CRUX
Procedure n
Proceed v GO
Proceeded v GO
Proceeding v GO
Proceeds v GO
Process n
Prognosis n IDEA
Progress n GO
Prolegomenon n TALK
Prologue n TALK
Promote v AID
Prophecy n IDEA
Proscenium n FORM
Prosecute v
Prospect n MOTV
Prospective j MOTV
Prospectus n WRIT
Prow n
Prowed j
Range n
Ranged v
Ranging v

Rank n
Ranked v
Ranking v
Ranks v
Rate n
Rate v IDEA
Rating v
Rating v IDEA
Register n
Register n MUSC
Roll n WRIT
Roster n WRIT
Row n
Scale n
Scale n MUSC
Schedule v WRIT
Seaward d FLOW
Sequence n
Serial n
Series n
Slate v MOTV
Slated v MOTV
Slating v MOTV
Spectrum n COLR
Stem n FLOW
Straight n PLAY
Straightforward j SHRP
String v GO
Stringing v GO
Strung v GO
Succeed v
Successive j
Successor n
Thenceforth d TIME
Thereafter d TIME
Thesaurus n WRIT
Tomorrow d TIME
Toward b
Train n
Van n GRUP
Vanguard n GRUP
Vision n VIEW
Visionary j VIEW
Waterfront n FLOW

FURN

Andiron n HEAT
Antimacassar n CLEN
Appliance n MECH
Appointed v
Appointment n
Armchair n REST
Bed n REST
Beds n REST
Bedspread n COVR
Bedstead n REST
Bench n REST
Blanket n REST
Bolster n EASY
Bricabrac n TRIV
Buffet n HOLW
Bunk n REST
Bunked v REST

Bunking v REST
Bureau n HOLW
Cabinet n HOLW
Caddy n AID
Carpet n DOWN
Caster n HOLW
Castor n HOLW
Centerpiece n GOOD
Chair n REST
Chaise n REST
Chandelier n VIEW
Chest n HOLW
Chesterfield n REST
China n FOOD
Chippendale j
Coaster n HOLW
Comforter n REST

Commode n HOLW
Console n HOLW
Cot n REST
Couch n REST
Couches n REST
Counterpane n COVR
Coverlet n COVR
Credence n HOLW
Credenza n HOLW
Curtain n COVR
Cutlery n FOOD
Davenport n REST
Desk n WRIT
Dinnerware n FOOD
Dishwasher n CLEN
Divan n REST
Doily n FABR

Drapery n COVR
Drawer n HOLW
Drawers n HOLW
Dresser n HOLW
Fixture n
Fork n FOOD
Furnish v
Furniture n
Glider n EASY
Hammock n REST
Hassock n REST
Highboy n HOLW
Household j HOME
Knickknack n TRIV
Lectern n WRIT
Linen n FABR
Litter n REST

Lounge n REST
Lumber n TRIV
Mantel n
Mantelpiece n
Mantle n
Mat n DOWN
Mattress n REST
Pallet n REST
Pillow n EASY
Portiere n COVR

Quilt n REST
Range n HEAT
Rocker n REST
Rug n DOWN
Seat n REST
Secretary n WRIT
Service n FOOD
Settee n REST
Sideboard n FOOD
Silver n FOOD

Silverware n FOOD
Sofa n REST
Soupspoon n FOOD
Spatula n FOOD
Spoon n FOOD
Spread n COVR
Stool n REST
Stove n HEAT
Table n
Tablecloth n FABR

Tables n
Tablespoon n FOOD
Teaspoon n FOOD
Throne n LEAD
Upholster v FABR
Utsensil n FOOD
Vanity n
Vanity n HOLW

GARB

Accouterment n AID
Afghan n
Alb n HOLY
Anklet n
Apparel n
Apron n
Arctics n
Array n
Ascot n
Attire n
Bag n HOLW
Band n
Bandana n
Bands n HOLW
Baste v JOIN
Bathrobe n CLEN
Bead n FORM
Belt n
Beret n
Bermudas n PLAC
Bib n YNG
Bib n
Bikini n LADY
Blazer n
Bloomers n LADY
Blouse n LADY
Bobbysox n YNG
Bodice n LADY
Bolero n
Bonnet n
Boot n
Boot n GO
Boot n SEP
Boot v WEAK
Booted v
Booted v GO
Booted v WEAK
Bootee n YNG
Bootery n MART
Boutonniere n VEGT
Bow n
Bowler n
Bra n LADY
Bracelet n HOLW
Bras n LADY
Brassiere n LADY
Breeches n MALE
Briefs n LITL
Brogue n
Brooch n
Buckle n JOIN
Bustle n LADY

Button n JOIN
Buttonhole n HOLW
Buttonhole v BLOK
Cameo n FORM
Cap n
Cape n
Capote n
Caps n
Cardigan n
Cardinal n LADY
Cardinals n LADY
Cassock n HOLY
Castor n ANML
Casual j EASY
Cerement n DEAD
Chapeau n
Chemise n LADY
Chesterfield n
Chiffon n LADY
Choker n
Cinch n ANML
Circlet n HOLW
Clad v
Clip n
Cloak n
Clodhopper n ERTH
Clog n
Clothe v
Clothes n
Clothespin n BLOK
Clothier n MART
Clothing n
Clout n
Coat n
Cobble v
Cobbled v
Cobbler n
Cobbles v
Coiffure n BODY
Collar n
Collar n BLOK
Comforter n
Commode n LADY
Compact n LADY
Cordon n FABR
Corduroys n FABR
Coronary j LEAD
Coronation n LEAD
Coronet n LEAD
Coronet n
Corsage n VEGT
Corsage n LADY

Corselet n LADY
Corset n LADY
Costume n
Coverall n
Crape n PANG
Cravat n
Crochet v JOIN
Crown n LEAD
Cuff n
Culottes n LADY
Cutaway n
Dalmatic n
Dandies n FOOL
Dandy n FOOL
Dapper j GOOD
Darn v JOIN
Darned v JOIN
Darning v JOIN
Dart n JOIN
Deck v GOOD
Decked v GOOD
Decking v GOOD
Decolletage n LADY
Derby n MALE
Diadem n LEAD
Diaper n YNG
Dickey n
Dishabille n EASY
Disrobe v SEP
Doll v GOOD
Dolled v GOOD
Dolling v GOOD
Domino n COVR
Don v
Donned v
Dowdy j DIRT
Drawers n
Dress n LADY
Dress v
Dressed v
Dresser n
Dresses v
Dresses n LADY
Dressier j GOOD
Dressing v
Dressmaker n MART
Dressy j GOOD
Dude n FOOL
Duds n
Dungarees n
Duster n
Earring n BODY

Embroider v GOOD
Ensemble n GRUP
Fashion n
Fatigues n WORK
Fedora n
Fell v JOIN
Fez n
Finery n GOOD
Flies n
Flounce n FORM
Fly n
Fob n JOIN
Fob n HOLW
Fop n FOOL
Frock n HOLY
Frock n
Frog n
Furrier n MART
Gaberdine n
Gallow n
Galosh n
Garb n
Garment n
Garter n
Gauntlet n DAMG
Gird v
Girded v
Girdle n LADY
Girth n ANML
Glove n
Glove n PLAY
Gown n
Guise n FALS
Haberdasher n MART
Habiliment n
Habilitate v
Habit n
Halter n LADY
Handbag n BODY
Handkerchief n
Harness n BLOK
Hat n
Haversack n HOLW
Headpiece n BODY
Heel n
Heeled j
Heeling v
Heelless j LACK
Helmet n AID
Hem n END
Hood n
Horseshoe n ANML

Hose n
Hosier n MART
Housecoat n LADY
Jacket n
Jeans n
Jerkin n
Jersey n
Jewel n GOOD
Jumper n
Kerchief n
Khaki n COLR
Khakis n COLR
Kilt n MALE
Kimono n
Knapsack n HOLW
Knit v JOIN
Lapel n
Lavaliere n GOOD
Layette n YNG
Legging n BODY
Leotard n
Lingerie n LADY
Loafer n
Locket n HOLW
Mackintosh n
Mantle n
Mask n COVR
Middy n
Millinery n MART
Mitt n PLAY
Mitten n
Moccasin n
Muff n
Muffler n
Necklace n BODY
Nightcap n REST
Nightgown n REST
Nylon n LADY
Oilskin n
Outfit n
Overalls n
Overclothes n
Overcoat n
Overshirt n
Overshoe n
Pajamas n

Pannier n LADY
Pantaloon n
Panties n LADY
Panty n LADY
Pants n MALE
Parasol n LADY
Parka n
Patten n
Peajacket n FLOW
Peddlepusher n
Pendant n DOWN
Petticoat n LADY
Pillbox n LADY
Pin n SHRP
Piping n FABR
Placket n SEP
Plainclothes j LAW
Plusfours n MALE
Pocketbook n HOLW
Polo j
Pompon n
Poncho n
Porkpie n
Press v CLEN
Pressed v CLEN
Pressing v CLEN
Pullover n
Pump n LADY
Purse n HOLW
Raiment n
Raincoat n WEA
Rig n
Robe n
Rosary n HOLY
Rubbers n
Ruffle n VARY
Sackcloth n PANG
Sandal n
Sari n LADY
Sarong n
Sartorial j
Sash n
Scarf n
Seam n JOIN
Seamed v JOIN
Seaming v JOIN

Seams n JOIN
Seamstress n LADY
Sew v JOIN
Shawl n LADY
Shield n AID
Shift n LADY
Shirt n MALE
Shirtsleeve n
Shoe n
Shoemaker n MART
Shoestring n JOIN
Shorts n LITL
Shroud v DEAD
Skirt n LADY
Slacks n
Sleeve n HOLW
Slicker n
Slip n LADY
Slipper n
Smock n
Sneaker n
Snowshoe n COLD
Snowsuit n COLD
Sock n
Sole v DOWN
Soled v DOWN
Soling v DOWN
Spats n
Stocking n
Stole n
Stoles n
Strip v SEP
Stripped v SEP
Style n
Styled v
Styling v
Suit n
Suitcase n HOLW
Suited j
Supporter n AID
Suspender n DOWN
Sweater n
Tailor n MART
Tails n MALE
Tamoshanter n
Thimble n HOLW

Tie n
Tights n
Togs n
Toilet n CLEN
Topless j LACK
Toupee n BODY
Train n BACK
Trappings n TRIV
Trouser j MALE
Trunks n MALE
Tuck n VARY
Turban n
Tuxedo n MALE
Umbrella n WEA
Unbutton v OPEN
Unclad j SEP
Unclothe v SEP
Underclothes n DOWN
Undershirt n DOWN
Underwear n DOWN
Undies n LADY
Undress v SEP
Uniform n
Veil n COVR
Veil n HOLY
Vest n
Waist n BODY
Waistcoat n
Wallet n HOLW
Wardrobe n HOLW
Wardrobe n
Wear v
Wearing v
Whitecollar j MART
Wig n BODY
Wigged v BODY
Windbreaker n WEA
Woolens n FABR
Wore v
Worn v
Wrap n
Zephyr n
Zip v JOIN
Zipped v JOIN
Zipper n JOIN

GLAD

Allay v
Amuse v
Analgesic n MEDC
Anodyne n AID
Appease v AID
Assuage v AID
Bask v REST
Basked v REST
Beam v
Beguile v
Bender n SIP
Binge n SIP
Bliss n
Blithe j
Buffoon n FOOL
Buoy v

Buoyant j
Bust n
Calm j EASY
Caper n GO
Card n
Carefree j
Celebrant n PLAY
Celebrate v PLAY
Celebrated v PLAY
Chaff n TALK
Cheer n
Cheer n FOOD
Cheerful j
Cheering v
Chipper j
Chuckle v

Clemency n
Clement j
Clown n FOOL
Collect v
Comedian n PLAY
Comedy n PLAY
Comfort v AID
Comfortable j
Comforted v AID
Comic j
Comics n WRIT
Complacence n
Compose v
Composing v
Composure n
Console v AID

Consoled v AID
Consoling v AID
Content j
Convivial j
Cool j COLD
Cooler j COLD
Cooling v COLD
Cosey j
Cosie j
Cosily d
Cosiness n
Cosy j
Cozy j
Crack n TALK
Cracked v TALK
Debonair j

Delight v FOND
Desensitize v
Dispassionate j
Docile j SUB
Droll j
Ease n EASY
Easier j EASY
Easy j EASY
Easygoing j EASY
Ecstasy n
Effervesce v
Enjoy v
Enjoy v HAVE
Enjoyable j
Enrapture v
Ensconce v REST
Epicure n MOTV
Equanimity n
Euphoria n
Exhilarate v
Exuberant j
Exult v
Facetious j
Felicitate v FOND
Felicitous j AGRE
Festival n PLAY
Festive j PLAY
Flip j TRIV
Flippancy n TRIV
Frisk v
Friskier j
Frisky j
Frivolous j TRIV
Frolic v PLAY
Fun n
Funnier j FOOL
Funnier j
Funnies n VIEW
Funniest j FOOL
Funniest j
Funny j FOOL
Funny j
Gag n FALS
Gaiety n

Gala j PLAY
Gambol v GO
Gay j
Genial j
Giggle v
Glad j
Glee n
Gloat v
Goose v BODY
Goosed v BODY
Goosing v BODY
Grin n
Guffaw n HEAR
Halcyon j
Hallelujah i EMPH
Happier j
Happily d
Happy j
Harlequin n PLAY
Heaven n GOOD
Hedonism n
High j UP
Hilarity n
Humor n
Humoresque n MUSC
Hurrah i EMPH
Huzza i EMPH
Imperturbable j
Insouciance n
Jauntily d EASY
Jaunty j EASY
Jest n
Jest n FOOL
Jinks n FOOL
Joke n FOOL
Joked v FOOL
Jolly j
Josh v TALK
Jovial j
Joy n
Jubilation n
Jubilee n TIME
Kick n
Kid v FOOL

Kidded v FOOL
Lark n
Laugh n
Leisure j REST
Levity n
Light j TRIV
Lighthearted j SOMA
Lightly d TRIV
Limerick n TALK
Lull n REST
Merry j
Merrymaking n PLAY
Mirth n
Mollify v EASY
Nirvana n OPEN
Nonchalance n REST
Optimism n MOTV
Orgiastic j PLAY
Orgy n PLAY
Overjoyed j
Overoptimist n MOTV
Pacific j
Pacifies v
Pacifist n
Pacify v
Painless j
Palliate v EASY
Paradise n GOOD
Peace n
Peacemaker n AID
Pixy n MYTH
Placate v AID
Placid j
Pleasant j FOND
Please v FOND
Pleasing j FOND
Pleasure n FOND
Ploy n PLAY
Prank n FOOL
Propitiate v AID
Puck n MYTH
Pun v TALK
Quell v AID
Quip n TALK

Radiance n VIEW
Radiant j VIEW
Rapture n
Ravish v MOTV
Regale v
Regaling v
Rejoice v
Relax v REST
Repartee n TALK
Revel n PLAY
Rib v
Ribald j BAD
Ribbed v
Roister v PLAY
Romp v GO
Sangfroid n POWR
Serene j
Serenity n
Settle v
Slapstick j FOOL
Smile n
Smirk n FALS
Snug j
Snuggle v JOIN
Solace v AID
Soothe v AID
Sport n
Spree n
Tame j SUB
Taming v SUB
Temper v AID
Tempering v AID
Tickle v BODY
Tranquil j
Transport n
Unperturbed j EASY
Unruffled j EASY
Voluptuous j MOTV
Wag n TALK
Whoopee n HEAR
Wisecrack n TALK
Wit n IDEA
Witticism n IDEA

GO

Abscond v CRIM
Accelerate v QUIK
Access n
Accessible j
Accession n POWR
Admission n IN
Admit v IN
Adrift d FLOW
Advance n FORW
Advent n
Afloat j FLOW
Alight v DOWN
Alsoran n WEAK
Amble v
Ambulant j
Ambulatory j
Approach v NEAR
Arise v UP

Arose v UP
Arrive v
Arrive v POWR
Ascend v UP
Ascension n UP
Astray d FALS
Attain v POWR
Attend v JOIN
Attendance n JOIN
Attract v JOIN
Auto v VEHC
Autoed v VEHC
Back v BACK
Bail v
Ballet n MUSC
Bank v VARY
Barge v POWR
Barged v POWR

Barges v POWR
Barging v POWR
Barnstorm v TALK
Barnstorm v UP
Barrel v QUIK
Bear v
Bearing v
Beat v QUIK
Bicycle v VEHC
Bike v VEHC
Biked v VEHC
Biking v VEHC
Blew v VAPR
Blow v VAPR
Bolero n MUSC
Bolt v QUIK
Bonvoyage i SEP
Boomerang v VARY

Boot n GARB
Booted v GARB
Bore v
Borne v
Bounce v VARY
Bounce v DAMG
Bouncer n DAMG
Bound j
Bound n QUIK
Bounded v QUIK
Bounding v QUIK
Bounds v QUIK
Bring v
Brought v
Budge v
Burst v QUIK
Bus v VEHC
Busing v VEHC

Bussed v VEHC	Climb v UP	Dart n QUIK	Emerge v OUT
Busses v VEHC	Clip n QUIK	Darted v QUIK	Emigrant j SEP
Bussing v VEHC	Close v NEAR	Darting v QUIK	Emigrate v SEP
Bustle n QUIK	Closed v NEAR	Dash n QUIK	Encroach v AGGR
Bypass v SEP	Closing v NEAR	Dash v DAMG	Enter v IN
Call n JOIN	Clump n HEAR	Dashing v QUIK	Entrance n IN
Calling v JOIN	Coast v EASY	Dashing v DAMG	Entree n IN
Came v	Coasted v EASY	Debouch v OUT	Entrench v AGGR
Cancan n MUSC	Coasting v EASY	Decamp v SEP	Entries n IN
Canter v	Come v	Decelerate v REST	Entry n IN
Caper n GLAD	Comeback n POWR	Declension n DOWN	Errand n AID
Career v QUIK	Comedown n WEAK	Decline v DOWN	Errant j VARY
Carom n VARY	Comer n	Defile v FORW	Escalate v UP
Carried v HAVE	Comer n POWR	Deflect v VARY	Escapade n OPEN
Carrier n HAVE	Comes v	Deliver v	Escape n OPEN
Carry v HAVE	Coming v	Deliveries n	Excursion n
Cart v VEHC	Commute v VEHC	Delivery n	Exit n OUT
Cartage n VEHC	Commuter n VEHC	Depart v SEP	Exodus n OUT
Carted v VEHC	Commuting v VEHC	Departed v SEP	Expedition n
Carter n VEHC	Compass v VARY	Deploy v LARG	Expedition n GRUP
Carting v VEHC	Compassed v VARY	Deport v SEP	Explore v OPEN
Cartwheel n VARY	Compassing v VARY	Derail v VARY	Explorer n OPEN
Cast n	Conduct v	Derby n QUIK	Extend v LARG
Castaway j SEP	Conducting v	Descend v DOWN	Extension n LARG
Caster n MECH	Conduction v	Descended v DOWN	Extradite v LAW
Casting v	Conga n MUSC	Descent n DOWN	Fall n DOWN
Castor n MECH	Continuation n EVER	Describe v SIML	Falling v DOWN
Catapult n MECH	Continue v EVER	Detour n VARY	Fare v
Catch v JOIN	Continuing v EVER	Devolve v	Fared v
Catches v JOIN	Convection n HEAT	Diffuse v LARG	Fares v
Caught v JOIN	Converge v JOIN	Dispatch v	Farewell n SEP
Cavalcade n GRUP	Convey v	Dispatched v	Faring v
Centrifugal j SEP	Conveyance n	Dispatching v	Fell v DOWN
Centripetal j IN	Convoy v JOIN	Disperse v SEP	Ferried v VEHC
Charge n QUIK	Cotillion n MUSC	Dive n DOWN	Ferries v VEHC
Chase n BACK	Countermarch n BACK	Diver n DOWN	Ferry v VEHC
Chase n DAMG	Courier n WRIT	Divers n DOWN	Fetch v
Chased v BACK	Course v QUIK	Diving v DOWN	Fetching v
Chaser n BACK	Coursed v QUIK	Dodge v VARY	File v FORW
Chevies n DAMG	Cover v	Double v VARY	Filing v FORW
Chevy n DAMG	Coverage n	Dove v DOWN	Flamenco n MUSC
Chip v PLAY	Crawl n REST	Drag v	Flank v VARY
Chipped v PLAY	Crawl n FLOW	Draw v	Flanked v VARY
Chipping v PLAY	Creep v REST	Drawn v	Flanking v VARY
Choreography n MUSC	Creeper n VEGT	Drew v	Fled v QUIK
Chuck v	Creeper n REST	Dribble v PLAY	Flee v QUIK
Chucked v	Creeper n BLOK	Drift v REST	Flew v UP
Chucking v	Crept v REST	Drive v VEHC	Flew v QUIK
Chucks v	Crisscross v VARY	Drop n DOWN	Flier n UP
Chug v HEAR	Cross v	Dropped v DOWN	Flies v UP
Chute n DOWN	Crosscountry j ERTH	Dropping v DOWN	Flies v QUIK
Circle v VARY	Cruise v FLOW	Drove v VEHC	Flight n SEP
Circuit n VARY	Cruise v VEHC	Dump v DOWN	Fling n MUSC
Circulate v VARY	Cut v VARY	Dumped v DOWN	Fling n QUIK
Circulating v VARY	Cutting v VARY	Dumping v DOWN	Flit v QUIK
Circulation n SOMA	Cycle n VARY	Edge v	Float v FLOW
Circulation n VARY	Cycle v VEHC	Efferent j SEP	Float v UP
Circulatory j SOMA	Cycled v VARY	Elbow v BODY	Floated v FLOW
Circumnavigate v VARY	Cycled v VEHC	Elevate v UP	Floated v UP
Clamber v	Cycling v VARY	Elevation n UP	Floating v FLOW
Clatter v HEAR	Cycling v VEHC	Elope v SEP	Floating v UP
Clear v OPEN	Dance n MUSC	Embark v BGIN	Flock v GRUP

Parts of speech: a article; b preposition; c conjunction; d adverb; f prefix; i interjection; j adjective; n noun; p pronoun; r phrase; v verb.

Flocked v GRUP
Flocking v GRUP
Flounce v VARY
Flown v UP
Flown v QUIK
Flung v QUIK
Flush v FLOW
Flushed v FLOW
Flushing v FLOW
Fly v UP
Fly v QUIK
Flyer n UP
Follow v BACK
Foot v BODY
Footing v BODY
Footloose j OPEN
Foots v BODY
Footstep n BODY
Ford v FLOW
Forego v FORW
Forerunner n FORW
Forge v
Forward v FORW
Forwarded v FORW
Forwarding v FORW
Forwards v FORW
Foxtrot n MUSC
Frank n OPEN
Fugitive n SEP
Gad v
Gadabout n
Gait n
Gallivant v
Gallop n QUIK
Gambol v GLAD
Gavotte n MUSC
Get v
Girdle v VARY
Glance v VARY
Glide v EASY
Glissade n EASY
Go v
Gone v
Got v
Gravitate v JOIN
Gravity n JOIN
Gypsy n GRUP
Gyrate v VARY
Hail v
Hails v
Hale v
Haled v
Hales v
Halfway j SOME
Haling v
Harrier n QUIK
Hasten v QUIK
Haul v
Head v FORW
Headed v FORW
Heading v FORW
Heads v FORW
Headway n FORW
Heave v
Heft v UP

Hie v QUIK
Hied v QUIK
Hies v QUIK
Highball v QUIK
Highballed v QUIK
Highballing v QUIK
Hike v
Hike v UP
Hit v
Hitch n VARY
Hitch v AID
Hitched v VARY
Hitched v AID
Hitchhike v AID
Hobble v VARY
Hobble v WEAK
Hobbled v VARY
Hobbled v WEAK
Hobo n OPEN
Hoist n UP
Homing v HOME
Hoof v BODY
Hop n QUIK
Hop n MUSC
Hopped v QUIK
Hover v UP
Hula n MUSC
Hurl v
Hurl v DAMG
Hurried v QUIK
Hurry v QUIK
Hurtle v QUIK
Hustle v QUIK
Immigrate v IN
Impel v
Inch v REST
Incoming j IN
Infiltrate v IN
Influx n IN
Ingress n IN
Input n IN
Intake n IN
Itinerant j
Jaunt n
Jaywalk v OPPO
Jig n MUSC
Jigged v MUSC
Jigging v MUSC
Jitterbug n MUSC
Jog v REST
Jounce v VARY
Journey n
Jump n QUIK
Jumped v QUIK
Jumper n QUIK
Jumping v QUIK
Junket n PLAY
Kick n BODY
Kinematic j MECH
Kinetic j
Lam v
Land v ERTH
Landed v ERTH
Landing v ERTH
Lateral n PLAY

Launch n BGIN
Leap n QUIK
Leave v SEP
Leaves v SEP
Left v SEP
Lift n UP
Lift n AID
Light v DOWN
Lighted v DOWN
Lighting v DOWN
Lights v DOWN
Limp n WEAK
Limped v WEAK
Limping v WEAK
Lob v
Lobbed v
Lobbing v
Locomotion n
Loft v UP
Lofted v UP
Lofting v UP
Lope v EASY
Loping v EASY
Lug v
Lugged v
Lugging v
Lumber v
Lumbered v
Lumbering v
Lunge n QUIK
Lunging v QUIK
Made v
Mail n WRIT
Mailing v WRIT
Mails v WRIT
Make v
Makes v
Maneuver v POWR
Marathon n EVER
March n
March n MUSC
Marched v
Marching v
Meander v VARY
Merrygoround n PLAY
Midway d SOME
Migrant n
Migrate v
Mill v GRUP
Milled v GRUP
Milling v GRUP
Mince v WEAK
Minuet n MUSC
Misstep n FALS
Mobile j
Mobilize v
Momentum n POWR
Mosey v
Motion n
Motive j
Motor v VEHC
Motored v VEHC
Motoring v VEHC
Mount v UP
Mounted v UP

Mounting v UP
Move v
Movement n
Moving v
Mush v COLD
Navigate v
Negotiate v
Newcomer n NEW
Nomad n GRUP
Orbit n HOLW
Overflew v UP
Overflight n UP
Overfly v UP
Overhaul v NEAR
Overleap v UP
Overran v DAMG
Overrun v DAMG
Overshoot v
Overshot v
Overtake v NEAR
Overtook v NEAR
Pace v
Pacemaker n POWR
Pad v
Padded v
Paddle v FLOW
Paid v
Pallbearer n DEAD
Palmer n HOLY
Parachute v DOWN
Parade n GRUP
Parading v GRUP
Part v SEP
Parted v SEP
Parting v SEP
Pass v
Pass n WRIT
Pass v DEAD
Passable j
Passage n
Passed v
Passed v DEAD
Passenger n
Passes v
Passes n WRIT
Passes v DEAD
Passing v
Passing v DEAD
Passport n WRIT
Patrol v AID
Pay v
Pedal v VEHC
Pedestrian j
Pedometer n MSMT
Peg v
Perambulate v
Peregrinate v
Pilgrim n HOLY
Pirouette n VARY
Pitch n
Pitched v
Pitcher n PLAY
Pitching v
Plied v EVER
Plier n EVER

Plod v REST
Plummet v DOWN
Plunge v QUIK
Ply v EVER
Poach v ERTH
Pole v FORM
Poled v FORM
Poling v FORM
Polka n MUSC
Pop v
Popped v
Popping v
Portable j
Portage n
Porter n AID
Post n WRIT
Postal j WRIT
Postcard n WRIT
Posted v WRIT
Posting v WRIT
Posts v WRIT
Pounce v QUIK
Prance v POWR
Precipitate v QUIK
Proceed v FORW
Proceeded v FORW
Proceeding v FORW
Proceeds v FORW
Procession n GRUP
Progress n FORW
Projectile n DAMG
Promenade n
Prop n MECH
Propagate v LARG
Propel v
Propeller n MECH
Propulsion n
Prowl v COVR
Pull v
Pulled v
Punt n PLAY
Pursue v MOTV
Pursuing v MOTV
Pursuit n MOTV
Push v
Push v POWR
Pusher n
Pussyfoot v EASY
Put v
Put v PLAY
Putt n PLAY
Putting v
Putting v PLAY
Quit v SEP
Race n QUIK
Raced v QUIK
Racer n QUIK
Racing v QUIK
Raise v UP
Raising v UP
Ramble v
Ramp n FORM
Ran v QUIK
Ran v MOTV
Range v

Ranged v
Ranger n
Ranging v
Reach v
Rebound v BACK
Recede v BACK
Recession n BACK
Recoil v BACK
Redouble v BACK
Reel n MUSC
Refugee n SEP
Regress v BACK
Relay n
Remission n
Remit v
Repair v
Retire v SEP
Retire v REST
Retrace v BACK
Retreat n BACK
Retreated v BACK
Retreating v BACK
Return n BACK
Revolution n VARY
Revolve v VARY
Rhumba n MUSC
Ricochet v VARY
Ride v
Rider n
Riding v
Rise v UP
Risen v UP
Roam v
Rocket v UP
Rode v
Roll v
Rolled v
Romp v GLAD
Rose v UP
Rotate v VARY
Round v VARY
Rounded v VARY
Rounding v VARY
Rounds n VARY
Rout n WEAK
Routed v WEAK
Routing v WEAK
Rove v
Row v FLOW
Rowed v FLOW
Rowing v FLOW
Rumba n MUSC
Run v QUIK
Run v MOTV
Runaway j OPEN
Rush n QUIK
Rushed v QUIK
Rushes v QUIK
Rushing v QUIK
Safari n GRUP
Sail v FLOW
Sail v UP
Sailed v FLOW
Sailed v UP
Sailing v FLOW

Sailing v UP
Salient j QUIK
Sallied v
Sallied v DAMG
Sally n
Sally n DAMG
Samba n MUSC
Sank v DOWN
Sashay v
Saunter v REST
Scale v
Scale v UP
Scamper v QUIK
Scat v SEP
Scoot v QUIK
Scooted v QUIK
Scour v OPEN
Scout n OPEN
Scouted v OPEN
Scram v SEP
Scramble v AGGR
Screw n MECH
Scurried v QUIK
Scurry v QUIK
Seafaring j FLOW
Send v
Sent v
Serve v PLAY
Service n PLAY
Serving v PLAY
Set v
Setting v
Shag n MUSC
Shin v BODY
Ship v VEHC
Shoo v SEP
Shoot v QUIK
Shot v QUIK
Shove v AGGR
Shuffle v REST
Shunt v VARY
Sidestep v VARY
Sidetrack v VARY
Sink v DOWN
Sinker n DOWN
Skate v PLAY
Skated v PLAY
Skating v PLAY
Skee v PLAY
Ski v PLAY
Skid n EASY
Skied v PLAY
Skier n PLAY
Skies v PLAY
Skiing v PLAY
Skim v QUIK
Skip v VARY
Skirt v VARY
Skirting v VARY
Skis v PLAY
Slid v EASY
Slide n EASY
Sling v
Slink v COVR
Slip v EASY

Slipped v EASY
Slippery j EASY
Slipping v EASY
Slither v EASY
Slosh v FLOW
Slow v REST
Slung v
Slunk v COVR
Snake v ANML
Snaked v ANML
Snaking v ANML
Snap v QUIK
Snapped v QUIK
Snaps v QUIK
Sneak v COVR
Sneaked v COVR
Snuck v COVR
Soar v UP
Sojourn v
Somersault n VARY
Somnambulism n REST
Sortie n DAMG
Speed v QUIK
Spill v DOWN
Spin v VARY
Spirit v COVR
Spirited v COVR
Spiriting v COVR
Sprang v QUIK
Spring n QUIK
Springing v QUIK
Sprint v QUIK
Spun v VARY
Stagger v VARY
Stalk v
Stalked v
Stalking v
Stampede v DAMG
Steal v COVR
Steam v VAPR
Steamed v VAPR
Steams v VAPR
Step v
Steps n
Stole v COVR
Stolen v COVR
Stomp n MUSC
Storm v DAMG
Straggle v SEP
Stray v SEP
Streak v QUIK
Streaked v QUIK
Streaking v QUIK
Stream n FLOW
Strew v SEP
Stride n
Strike v
Striking v
String v FORW
Stringing v FORW
Stroke n FLOW
Stroked v FLOW
Stroking v FLOW
Stroll n
Struck v

Strung v FORW
Strut n POWR
Stump v HEAR
Stump v TALK
Stumped v HEAR
Stumped v TALK
Stumping v HEAR
Stumping v TALK
Surge v BULG
Swam v FLOW
Swarm n GRUP
Sweep v
Sweeps v
Swept v
Swerve v VARY
Swim v FLOW
Swing v VARY
Swoop v QUIK
Swum v FLOW
Swung v VARY
Tack n VARY
Tag v JOIN
Tail v BACK
Tailing v BACK
Tails v BACK
Take v
Taxi v VEHC
Tear v QUIK
Tend v
Tended v
Thread v FABR
Threaded v FABR
Threading v FABR
Threw v

Throw v
Thrust v POWR
Tilt n QUIK
Took v
Tore v QUIK
Toss v
Tour n
Tourist n
Tow v AID
Towed v AID
Trace v BACK
Traced v BACK
Track v
Track n PLAY
Track v DIRT
Track v BACK
Tracked v
Tracked v DIRT
Tracked v BACK
Tracking v
Tracking v DIRT
Tracking v BACK
Traffic n VEHC
Trail v BACK
Trailed v BACK
Tramp v
Tramp n OPEN
Trample v DAMG
Transfer v
Transit n
Transmission n
Transmit v
Transplant v VARY
Transport n VEHC

Transportation n VEHC
Travel n
Tread v
Trek n
Trench v AGGR
Trespass v CRIM
Trip n
Troop v GRUP
Trooped v GRUP
Trooping v GRUP
Trot v
Truck v VEHC
Trucked v VEHC
Trucking v VEHC
Trucks v VEHC
Trudge v
Tug n
Tumble v VARY
Tumbled v VARY
Turn n VARY
Turnout n GRUP
Twirl v VARY
Vagabond n OPEN
Vagrant j OPEN
Vamoose v SEP
Vault v UP
Vaulted v UP
Vaulting v UP
Visit v JOIN
Volley n PLAY
Volleyed v PLAY
Volleying v PLAY
Voyage n
Waddle n VARY

Wade v
Wading v
Waft v VAPR
Walk n
Walk v PLAY
Waltz n MUSC
Wander v
Wash v FLOW
Washed v FLOW
Wayward j BAD
Wayward j VARY
Weave v VARY
Wend v
Wheel v VEHC
Wheelchair n REST
Wheeled v VEHC
Wheeling v VEHC
Whirl v VARY
Whiz v QUIK
Wind v VARY
Winds v VARY
Wing v UP
Winged v UP
Winging v UP
Winnow v UP
Withdraw v SEP
Wound v VARY
Wove v VARY
Zigzag v VARY
Zip v QUIK
Zipped v QUIK
Zoom v QUIK

GOOD

Admirable j
Adonis n MALE
Adorn v
Aesthetic j
Altruism n AID
Ambrosia n SOMA
Amenity n
Angel n HOLY
Apollo n MALE
Attractive j
Beautician n BODY
Beauties n
Beautiful j
Beauty n
Bedeck v
Behave v
Belle n LADY
Benevolent j AID
Benign j AID
Best j
Better j
Blameless j
Breeding n BGIN
Brick n
Bully j
Capital j
Centerpiece n FURN
Character n

Charity n AID
Charm n FOND
Chaste j
Chastity n
Chic j
Chivalry n
Choice j
Civil j
Civility n
Civilize v
Clemency n AID
Cologne n SOMA
Comely j
Comity n FOND
Conscience n IDEA
Conscientious j IDEA
Considerate j AID
Consideration n AID
Cool j COLD
Cosmetic j BODY
Courteous j
Courtesies n
Courtesy n
Courtly j
Cream n POWR
Cricket n PLAY
Crown v
Cultivate v IDEA

Culture n IDEA
Cunning j
Cute j
Dainty j
Dandy j
Dapper j GARB
Decency n
Decent j
Deck v
Deck v GARB
Decked v
Decked v GARB
Decking v
Decking v GARB
Decor n
Decorate v
Decorate v POWR
Decorous j
Decorum n
Delectable j
Delicacy n FOOD
Delicate j
Delicious j
Desirable j MOTV
Dignify v POWR
Dignity n POWR
Discreet j
Discretion n IDEA

Divine j
Doll n LADY
Doll v GARB
Dolled v GARB
Dolling v GARB
Dream n MYTH
Dress v
Dressed v
Dresser n
Dresses v
Dressier j GARB
Dressing v
Dressy j GARB
Edified v
Edify v
Elaborate j
Elegance n
Elite j POWR
Embellish v
Emboss v BULG
Embroider v GARB
Embroider v FALS
Enhance v LARG
Ennoble v LEAD
Enrich v AID
Equitable j SIML
Equities n SIML
Equity n SIML

Esthetic j
Ethic n
Etiquette n
Eugenic j BGIN
Euphemism n TALK
Exalt v POWR
Excellence n POWR
Exemplary j
Exquisite j
Extraordinary j AFAR
Extravagance n MUCH
Extravagant j MUCH
Fabulous j
Fair j
Fairly d
Fancier j
Fanciest j
Fancy j
Fantastic j
Faultless j POWR
Fine j
Finer j
Finery n GARB
Finest j
Flawless j POWR
Florid j TRIV
Flourish n
Flowery j TRIV
Garnish v FOOD
Garnish v
Gem n MTRL
Generosity n AID
Generous j AID
Genteel j
Gentility n
Gentle j
Gentleman n MALE
Glamor n POWR
Glory n POWR
Golden j COLR
Good j
Good j POWR
Goodhearted j SOMA
Goodly j POWR
Goodness n
Gorgeous j
Grace n AID
Graced v AID
Graceful j AID
Gracing v AID
Gracious j AID
Grand j POWR
Great j POWR
Guileless j EASY
Guiltless j
Hallmark n WRIT
Halo n VIEW
Handsome j
Heartfelt j MOTV
Heaven n GLAD
High j UP
Honest j TRUE

Honey n FOND
Honor n POWR
Hospitable j AID
Hospitality n AID
Humane j AID
Humanism n AID
Humanitarian n AID
Humanities n EDUC
Humanity n AID
Humanize v AID
Ideal n IDEA
Idyl n ERTH
Impeccable j
Improve v AID
Improving v AID
Incorrupt j
Innocence n
Innocence n EASY
Integrity n
Irreproachable j
Jewel n GARB
Jeweler n MART
Judicious j IDEA
Just j TRUE
Justice n TRUE
Justify v IDEA
Justly d TRUE
Justness n TRUE
Kind j AID
Kinder j AID
Kindest j AID
Kindhearted j AID
Kindliness n AID
Kindly d AID
Knockout n
Kosher j
Laud v AGRE
Lavaliere n GARB
Lavish j MUCH
Lawabiding j LAW
Loftier j UP
Lofty j UP
Lovely j FOND
Luscious j
Lush j MUCH
Luster n VIEW
Luxury n MUCH
Magnanimity n AID
Magnificence n POWR
Majestic j LEAD
Mannerly j
Marvelous j POWR
Memorable j IDEA
Merciful j AID
Mercy n AID
Merit n
Miracle n MYTH
Model j SIML
Modest j
Moral j IDEA
Morale n MOTV
Mores n EVER

Nice j
Nifty j
Nobility n LEAD
Noble j LEAD
Optimum n
Opulence n MUCH
Order n
Orderly j
Ornament n
Ornate j
Paradise n GLAD
Paragon n SIML
Peach n
Pearl n
Perfect j POWR
Perfected v POWR
Perfection n POWR
Perfects v POWR
Perfume n SOMA
Philanthropy n AID
Photogenic j VIEW
Picturesque j VIEW
Piety n HOLY
Pink n COLR
Pious j HOLY
Polish n EASY
Polished v EASY
Polishing v EASY
Polite j
Pomp n POWR
Precious j CRUX
Precious j TRIV
Presentable j
Prettier j
Pretty j
Prig n FOOL
Prim j
Principle n IDEA
Pristine j PAST
Probity n
Proper j
Propriety n
Prude n FOOL
Prudence n
Pulchritude n
Pure j CLEN
Puritan n
Purity n CLEN
Refine v
Reform n VARY
Remarkable j
Reputable j
Respectable j
Resplendent j
Rich j MUCH
Right d TRUE
Righted v TRUE
Righteous j TRUE
Righting v TRUE
Rightly d TRUE
Rights v TRUE
Rosecolored j COLR

Rosily d COLR
Rosiness n COLR
Rosy j COLR
Sage n IDEA
Saint n HOLY
Samaritan n AID
Sanctify v HOLY
Sanctity n HOLY
Satisfactory j
Savor n SOMA
Scrupulous j
Select j
Selfless j AID
Selfrighteous j FALS
Shapely j FORM
Sincere j TRUE
Smart j POWR
Spiffy j
Splendor n POWR
Spruce v CLEN
Spruced v CLEN
Sprucing v CLEN
Square j TRUE
Squarely d TRUE
Stunning j POWR
Stupendous j POWR
Sublimation n MOTV
Sublime j POWR
Sumptuous j MUCH
Superb j POWR
Superior j POWR
Superior j
Superiority n POWR
Superiority n
Superlative j POWR
Sweet j FOND
Sweet j SOMA
Taste n MOTV
Tasty j FOOD
Terrific j
Trim j
Unimpeachable j TRUE
Unselfish j AID
Upright j UP
Upstanding j UP
Virtue n
Virtuous j
Well d
Well j MEDC
Wellbeing n MEDC
Wellbred j BGIN
Wellwisher n MOTV
White j COLR
Wholesome j
Wisdom n IDEA
Wise j IDEA
Wonder n
Wonderful j
Worth n CRUX
Worthwhile j CRUX
Wow n POWR
Yummy j

Academies n EDUC
Academy n EDUC
Acculturation n IDEA
Aggregate j WHOL
American n
Anglican j HOLY
Anglosaxon j
Anthology n WRIT
Anthropology n IDEA
Apache n
Apache n CRIM
Apartheid n SEP
Aristocracy n LEAD
Aristocrat n LEAD
Armies n DAMG
Armies n MUCH
Army n DAMG
Army n MUCH
Aryan j
Asocial j SEP
Assemble v JOIN
Assembly n JOIN
Associate v JOIN
Assort v SEP
Assortment n SEP
Attendance n JOIN
Audience n HEAR
Auxiliary n AID
Aztec j
Bale n
Baling v
Band n JOIN
Banded v JOIN
Banding v JOIN
Bands n JOIN
Bar n LAW
Barrage n DAMG
Battalion n DAMG
Batteries n
Batteries n DAMG
Battery n
Beatnik n OPPO
Black n COLR
Bloc n
Block n
Board n LEAD
Boards n LEAD
Bodies n
Body n
Bohemian j OPPO
Bouquet n VEGT
Bourgeois n
Brace n
Breed n BGIN
Brigade n
Brood n YNG
Buddhism n HOLY
Bunch n
Bundle n
Bureau n
Cabal n COVR
Cabinet n LEAD

Cadre n FORM
Calvinism n HOLY
Camp n HOME
Camporee n HOME
Caravan n VEHC
Cast n PLAY
Caste n
Casting n PLAY
Categorical j
Category n
Catholic j HOLY
Caucasian j
Caucus n LAW
Cavalcade n GO
Cell n
Census n NUMR
Chamber n LAW
Chapter n SOME
Chauvinism n FOND
Cherokee n
Cheyenne n
Choir n MUSC
Choral j MUSC
Chorus n MUSC
Chorus n PLAY
Christian j HOLY
Church n HOLY
Circle n
Citizenry n
Civic j
Civics n LAW
Civil j LAW
Civil j
Clan n KIN
Claque n AGRE
Class n
Class n EDUC
Classify v
Classify v COVR
Classing v
Clergy n HOLY
Clique n
Club n
Club n HOME
Clubhouse n HOME
Clump n
Cluster n
Cohort n
Collect v HAVE
Collect v JOIN
Collector n HAVE
College n
Colonial j
Colonialism j SUB
Colonize v
Colonize v SUB
Colony n
Colony n SUB
Comanche n
Commissariat n LEAD
Commission n
Commit v LAW

Committed v LAW
Committee n
Commoner n WEAK
Commons n LAW
Commons n HOME
Commonwealth n
Communal j WHOL
Commune n JOIN
Communicant n HOLY
Communion n JOIN
Communion n HOLY
Communism n
Community n WHOL
Communize v
Companies n
Companies n MART
Company n
Company n MART
Compatriot n SIML
Concern n MART
Condominium n HAVE
Condominium n LEAD
Confederacy n JOIN
Confederate n JOIN
Conference n JOIN
Conglomerate n JOIN
Congregate v JOIN
Congregating v JOIN
Congregation n HOLY
Congregation n JOIN
Congregational j HOLY
Congress n JOIN
Constellation n ASTR
Constituency n LAW
Constituent n LAW
Contingent n
Convene v JOIN
Convening v JOIN
Convention n JOIN
Convention n AGRE
Conventional j AGRE
Convocation n JOIN
Convocation n EDUC
Convoke v JOIN
Coopt v MOTV
Corporate j JOIN
Corporation n MART
Corporation n LEAD
Corporative j JOIN
Corps n
Cortege n JOIN
Coterie n
Council n LEAD
Council n IDEA
Councilor n LEAD
Court n
Covey n ANML
Craft n WORK
Creole n
Crew n
Crowd n
Cult n HOLY

Deck n PLAY
Delegation n MOTV
Democracy n LAW
Democrat n LAW
Democrat n
Demography n IDEA
Denomination n
Department n SOME
Depopulate v DAMG
Deputation n
Dervish n HOLY
Detachment n SOME
Detail n SOME
Division n SOME
Division n DAMG
Dominican j HOLY
Drove n
Druid n HOLY
Dutch n
Electorate n MOTV
Elks n ANML
English n
Ensemble n
Ensemble n MUSC
Ensemble n GARB
Entente n AGRE
Entourage n JOIN
Espritdecorps n POWR
Establishment n EVER
Ethnic j
Ethno f
Ethnography n IDEA
Ethnology n IDEA
Expedition n GO
Faction n OPPO
Family n KIN
Fascism n LEAD
Federal j LAW
Federation n JOIN
Fellow n JOIN
Fellowship n
Field n
Fleet n VEHC
Flock n
Flock n ANML
Flock v GO
Flocked v GO
Flocking v GO
Flotilla n FLOW
Fold n ANML
Fold n
Folk j
Folklore n MYTH
Folks n KIN
Folks n
Force n POWR
Form n EDUC
Foundation n
Foursome n NUMR
Function n PLAY
Galactic j ASTR
Galaxy n ASTR

Parts of speech: a article; b preposition; c conjunction; d adverb; f prefix; i interjection;
        j adjective; n noun; p pronoun; r phrase; v verb.

Gang n
Garrison n DAMG
Gather v JOIN
Generation n BGIN
Genocide n DEAD
Genre n
Gentile n HOLY
Gentry n LEAD
Genus n
Ghetto n BLOK
Glee n MUSC
Grange n ERTH
Gregarious j
Gringo n
Group n
Guild n
Gypsy n GO
Hand n BODY
Hands n BODY
Hebrew n
Herd n ANML
Hippie n OPPO
Hohenzollern n LEAD
Homo n MALE
Horde n
Host n MUCH
House n LAW
House n HOME
Huddle n JOIN
Human j WHOL
Humanity n WHOL
Ilk n
Institute n
Institution n
International j JOIN
Jamboree n PLAY
Jew n HOLY
Junta n LAW
Juries n LAW
Juries v IDEA
Juror n LAW
Juror n IDEA
Jury n LAW
Jury n IDEA
Kennel n ANML
Kind n SIML
Kingdom n PLAC
Klan n
Knot n JOIN
Laity n
Latin n
Lay j
Lay j HOLY
Layman n
League n AGRE
League n PLAY
Left n
Legation n LEAD
Legion n DAMG
Legion n MUCH
Legionnaire n DAMG
Levied v JOIN
Levy v JOIN
Livestock n ANML
Lobbies n LAW

Lobby n LAW
Lodge n HOME
Lore n MYTH
Mafia n CRIM
Man n WHOL
Mankind n WHOL
Mass j MUCH
Massed v MUCH
Massing v MUCH
Meet v JOIN
Member n JOIN
Mestizo n
Met v JOIN
Middleclass j
Militia n DAMG
Mill v GO
Milled v GO
Milling v GO
Minority n SUB
Mob v AGGR
Mobilize v
Moor n
Moslem n HOLY
Multitude n MUCH
Muster v
Nation n
National j
Nationwide j LARG
Nazi n
Negro n COLR
Nomad n GO
Oligarchy n LEAD
Orchestra n MUSC
Orchestral j MUSC
Orchestrate v MUSC
Order n
Organization n FORM
Outfit n
Overcrowd v LARG
Overpopulate v LARG
Pack n ANML
Pack v FALS
Packed v FALS
Packing v FALS
Panel n
Parade n GO
Parading v GO
Parimutuel j HAVE
Parish n HOLY
Parishioner n HOLY
Parliament n LAW
Parochial j HOLY
Parochial j BLOK
Parties n
Parties n PLAY
Party n
Party n PLAY
Patriot n FOND
People n
Personnel n WORK
Phalanx n DAMG
Pharisee n HOLY
Phenotype n CRUX
Philistine n
Phylogeny n PAST

Phylum n SOME
Pigeonhole v HOLW
Platoon n
Plebeian j WORK
Plutocracy n LEAD
Pod n ANML
Polities n LAW
Polity n LAW
Poll n MOTV
Polled v MOTV
Polling v MOTV
Pool n JOIN
Pooled v JOIN
Pooling v JOIN
Pop n
Populace n
Popular j AGRE
Popular j
Populate v
Populous j MUCH
Posse n LAW
Powwow n TALK
Presbyterian n HOLY
Procession n GO
Profession n WORK
Proletarian n WORK
Protestant n HOLY
Public j
Public j OPEN
Publicity n OPEN
Publicly d OPEN
Publicspirited j AID
Punch v ANML
Punched v ANML
Punching v ANML
Puritan n HOLY
Quadroon n COLR
Quaker n HOLY
Quartet n NUMR
Quintet n NUMR
Quorum n LAW
Rabble n AGGR
Race n
Racial j
Racism n AGGR
Raft n MUCH
Rally n POWR
Reassemble v
Recollect v JOIN
Red n COLR
Redskin n COLR
Referendum n LAW
Regime n LEAD
Regiment n DAMG
Regiment v LEAD
Reich n LEAD
Repertoire n
Republic n LAW
Republican n
Reserve n DAMG
Reservist n DAMG
Retinue n SUB
Right n
Ring n HOLW
Ringleader n LEAD

Rosicrucian n HOLY
Rout n AGGR
Safari n GO
Salon n HOME
Salvo n DAMG
Salvo n HEAR
Sanhedrin n LEAD
Saxon n
School n EDUC
School n
Scout n OPEN
Scoutmaster n LEAD
Seance n MYTH
Seance n JOIN
Secondclass j SUB
Sect n
Secular j HOLY
Seminar n EDUC
Semitic j
Session n TIME
Set n
Sextet n NUMR
Sheaf n
Shock n
Slavic j
Sociable j AGRE
Social j
Socialist n
Socialize v AGRE
Society n
Sociology n IDEA
Solidarity n WHOL
Sort n SIML
Sorts n SIML
Soviet n LEAD
Species n
Spray n VEGT
Squad n
Staff n AID
Stand n VEGT
String n JOIN
Stringing v JOIN
Strung v JOIN
Subcommittee n SUB
Subspecies n
Subsume v
Suite n MUSC
Suite n HOME
Suite n SUB
Swarm n GO
Symposium n IDEA
Syndicate n MART
Synod n LEAD
Tartar n
Team n AGRE
Teamwork n AGRE
Teutonic j
Throng n
Tories n
Tory n
Totalitarian j LEAD
Train n SUB
Triad n NUMR
Tribe n
Trinity n NUMR

Trio n NUMR	Turnout n GO	Union n JOIN	Volley n DAMG
Troop n	Type n SIML	Unit n SOLE	Volley n
Troop v GO	Typing v SIML	Unpatriotic j OPPO	Whig n
Trooped v GO	UnAmerican j OPPO	Unpopular j AGGR	Wing n
Trooping v GO	Uncrowded j LITL	Van n FORW	Yank n
Troupe n PLAY	Undemocratic j OPPO	Vanguard n FORW	Yankee n

HAVE

Accept v	Condominium n GRUP	Heirloom n EVER	Realty n ERTH
Accumulate v LARG	Confiscate v BLOK	Held v	Reap v VEGT
Acquire v	Contract v	Heredity n BGIN	Recapture v BLOK
Acquisition n	Contracting v	Heritage n BGIN	Receipt n WRIT
Adopt v AGRE	Cop v	Hoard n COVR	Receipt n
Amass v LARG	Copped v	Hold v	Receive v
Annex v JOIN	Copping v	Holdfast n BLOK	Receiver n
Appropriate v MONY	Copyright v LAW	Hung v EVER	Receiver n HOLW
Appropriate v	Cumulate v LARG	Imbue v IN	Receiver n LAW
Appropriated v MONY	Custodian n AID	Impound v BLOK	Reception n
Appropriated v	Custodian n BLOK	Inherit v	Recipient n
Appropriates v MONY	Custody n AID	Inventory n MART	Reclaim v
Appropriates v	Custody n BLOK	Keep v EVER	Recover v
Appropriation n MONY	Derive v	Keeps v EVER	Redeem v AID
Appropriation n	Domain n LEAD	Keepsake n FOND	Regain v
Arrogate v	Dominion n LEAD	Kept v EVER	Reservation n
Asset n	Economical j MONY	Land v BLOK	Reserve v
Assume v	Economize v MONY	Landed v BLOK	Reserved v
Assume v FALS	Economy n MONY	Landing v BLOK	Reserving v
Assumption n	Effect n	Landowner n ERTH	Retain v EVER
Attribute n CRUX	Endow v AID	Lease n WRIT	Retention n EVER
Avail v	Enjoy v GLAD	Levied v MONY	Retract v BACK
Baggage n HOLW	Equipment n AID	Levy v MONY	Retrieve v
Bear v	Estate n ERTH	Made v MONY	Save v EVER
Bearer n	Estate n	Maintain v EVER	Saving v EVER
Bearing v	Fall v	Maintenance n EVER	Savings n MONY
Belong v	Falling v	Make v MONY	Scrape v
Beneficiary n AID	Fell v	Makes v MONY	Scraping v
Booty n	Flush j BULG	Miser n AGGR	Secure v
Bore v	Frugal j LITL	Monopoly n SOLE	Seize v BLOK
Borne v	Fund n	Nab v BLOK	Seizure n BLOK
Borrow v	Gain v LARG	Niggard n AGGR	Share v SOME
Bought v MONY	Gain v	Obtain v	Shareholder n MART
Burden n PANG	Gained v LARG	Occupancy n IN	Shopkeeper n MART
Carried v GO	Gained v	Occupation n IN	Snap v QUIK
Carried v	Gainer n LARG	Occupied v IN	Snapped v QUIK
Carrier n GO	Gainful j	Occupy v IN	Snaps v QUIK
Carry v GO	Gains v LARG	Own v	Snatch v
Carry v	Gains v	Parimutuel j GRUP	Spoils n DAMG
Catch v	Garner v	Parsimony n LITL	Stingy j AGGR
Catcher n PLAY	Gather v	Partake v	Stock n
Catches v	Get v	Partook v	Stocked v
Caught v	Glean v	Patent n LAW	Stockholder n MART
Chattel n	Got v	Patented v LAW	Stocking v
Cinch n BLOK	Grab v	Patenting v LAW	Stocks n
Cinched v BLOK	Grasp n	Patents v LAW	Store v EVER
Cinching v BLOK	Had v	Pick v	Stored v EVER
Claim v	Hang v EVER	Picked v	Storehouse n HOME
Clasp n BLOK	Harvest n VEGT	Possess v	Storekeeper n MART
Clear v OPEN	Has v	Preempt v	Storeroom n HOME
Clench v BLOK	Haul n	Prehensile j BLOK	Storing v EVER
Clutch n BLOK	Have v	Premise n ERTH	Sustain v
Collect v GRUP	Haves n	Procure v	Take v
Collect v MONY	Having v	Property n	Tenure n TIME
Collector n GRUP	Heir n	Proprietor n MART	Thrift n
Commandeer v LEAD	Heiress n LADY	Realestate n ERTH	Title n

Took v	Wear v	Winning v POWR	Wore v
Unearned j OPPO	Wearing v	Withhold v BLOK	Worn v
Usurp v DAMG	Win v POWR	Won v POWR	

HEAR

Abuzz j	Clump n GO	Hack n SOMA	Pound v
Acoustic j	Clutter n BLUR	Hark v	Pounded v
Alarm n PANG	Cough n SOMA	Hawk v SOMA	Pounding v
Aloud d	Crack n	Hawked v SOMA	Quaver v VARY
Applause n AGRE	Cracked v	Hawking v SOMA	Quiet j REST
Aspirate v TALK	Crackle v	Hear v	Racket n
Aspirating v TALK	Crackling n	Hearken v	Radio n TALK
Aspiration n TALK	Crash n DAMG	Hearsay n TALK	Rap n
Assonance n SIML	Creak v	Hem v TALK	Rapped v
Audible j	Cried v TALK	Hiccup v SOMA	Rasp v
Audience n GRUP	Crier n TALK	Hiss n	Rasp v PANG
Audience n JOIN	Crunch v	Hist i EMPH	Rasp n WORK
Audio j	Cry n TALK	Hoarse j	Raspberry n AGGR
Audit v	Deaf j SICK	Holler n TALK	Rattle n
Auditor n	Deaf j AGGR	Honk v	Rattles v
Auditorium n HOME	Deafen v SICK	Hoot n AGGR	Rattlesnake n ANML
Auditory j	Decibel n MSMT	Hubbub n PANG	Raucous j
Aural j	Decrepitate v	Hullabaloo n PANG	Receive v TALK
Auscultation n MEDC	Detonate v DAMG	Hush n REST	Receiver n TALK
Babble v TALK	Din n	Huskier j	Reception n TALK
Bang n	Dinned v	Huskiest j	Report n
Barker n TALK	Dinning v	Huskily d	Resound v
Bedlam n BLUR	Dissonance n OPPO	Husky j	Reverberation n
Belch v SOMA	Drone v	Inaudible j	Roar n
Bellow v TALK	Drum n SOMA	Knock v	Rumble n
Blare v	Ear n BODY	Listen v	Rumble n DAMG
Blast n DAMG	Eardrum n BODY	Loud j	Rustle v VARY
Blast n	Earshot n BODY	Loudspeaker n TALK	Salvo n GRUP
Blasted v DAMG	Eavesdrop v COVR	Megaphone n	Scrape v
Blasted v	Echo v SIML	Microphone n	Scraping v
Boisterous j AGGR	Effervesce v FLOW	Mike n	Scream v TALK
Boom n	Euphony n AGRE	Monotone n SIML	Screech v TALK
Boomed v	Explode v DAMG	Mum j	Shout v TALK
Bubble n FLOW	Explosion n DAMG	Murmur n TALK	Shriek v TALK
Bug v COVR	Explosive n DAMG	Noise n	Shrill j
Bugged v COVR	Firecracker n HEAT	Noiseless j	Sibilant j
Bugging v COVR	Fizz n SIP	Obstreperous j AGGR	Sigh n
Burble v TALK	Fizz n	Outcry n PANG	Signal n
Burp v SOMA	Fizzle n	Ovation n FOND	Silence n
Burst n DAMG	Flap n VARY	Overhear v	Sizzle v HEAT
Buzz v	Flapped v VARY	Pandemonium n DAMG	Slam n
Cacophony n OPPO	Flapper n VARY	Pat n EASY	Smack n
Call n TALK	Flop v VARY	Patted v EASY	Smack n DAMG
Calling v TALK	Flutter n VARY	Patter n	Snap n
Channel n VIEW	Frizz v HEAT	Patter n TALK	Snap n JOIN
Chatter v VARY	Frizzle v HEAT	Patting v EASY	Snapped v
Chug n	Frog n ANML	Percussion n DAMG	Snapped v JOIN
Chug v GO	Gasp v SOMA	Percussion n	Snaps v
Clack v	Gavel n LEAD	Pipe v	Snaps v JOIN
Clamor v PANG	Grate v	Piped v	Snore n SOMA
Clank n	Grating v	Piping n	Snort n
Clap n	Grit v	Pitterpatter n	Sound n
Clap n AGRE	Grits v	Plaudit n AGRE	Sounded v
Clapped v	Growl n	Plop v DOWN	Sounding v
Clapped v AGRE	Grunt n TALK	Plunk v	Soundless j
Clash v	Guffaw n GLAD	Pop n	Soundproof v BLOK
Clatter v	Gunshot n DAMG	Popcorn n FOOD	Splash v FLOW
Clatter v GO	Gurgle v FLOW	Popped v	Sputter n
Click v	Guttural j	Popping v	Squeak v

Squeal v
Stamp v AGGR
Stamped v AGGR
Still d
Stilled v
Stilling v
Stills v
Stomp v AGGR
Strident j
Strike v
Striking v

Stroke n
Stroked v
Stroking v
Struck v
Stump v GO
Stumped v GO
Stumping v GO
Supersonic j QUIK
Swish n
Tap n
Tape v MTRL

Tapes v MTRL
Taping v MTRL
Tattoo n
Thud n
Thump n
Thunder n WEA
Thunders v WEA
Tick n
Ticked v
Ticking n
Tumult n PANG

Unheard j AFAR
Uproar n PANG
Vociferous j TALK
Whack n
Wheeze n SOMA
Whir n VARY
Whisper n TALK
Whoopee n GLAD
Yell v TALK

HEAT

Ablaze j VIEW
Acetylene n MTRL
Afire j VIEW
Aflame j VIEW
Andiron n FURN
Anneal v FORM
Anthracite n MTRL
Arson n CRIM
Ash n MTRL
Ashes n MTRL
Autoclave n CLEN
Bake v FOOD
Bake v
Barbecue n FOOD
Blacksmith n WORK
Blaze n VIEW
Boil v
Boil v AGGR
Boiled v
Boiled v AGGR
Boiler n MECH
Bonfire n
Braise v
Brand n
Brand n VIEW
Branding v
Branding v VIEW
Braze v JOIN
Broil v
Broiler n
Brown v COLR
Browning v COLR
Burn v
Burn v AGGR
Burn v DAMG
Burning j
Burning j AGGR
Burning j DAMG
Butt n FOOD
Caldron n HOLW
Calory n MSMT
Candle n VIEW
Candlelight n VIEW
Cauldron n HOLW
Cauterize v
Centigrade j MSMT
Chafe v
Char v DAMG
Charcoal n MTRL
Cheroot n FOOD
Chimney n HOLW

Cigar n FOOD
Cigarette n FOOD
Cinder n MTRL
Cinerator n HOLW
Coal n MTRL
Coddle v FOOD
Coke n MTRL
Combustion n
Conflagration n DAMG
Convection n GO
Cook v FOOD
Cook v
Cooking v FOOD
Cooking v
Corona n FOOD
Cremate v DEAD
Crucible n HOLW
Decoct v FLOW
Desert n ERTH
Diathermy n MEDC
Ember n
Equator n PLAC
Fag n FOOD
Fahrenheit j MSMT
Febrile j SICK
Fever n SICK
Fierier j
Fiery j
Fire n VIEW
Fire v DAMG
Fire v MOTV
Fireball n VIEW
Fireboat n FLOW
Firebox n HOLW
Firebrand n MTRL
Firebreak n BLOK
Firebrick n MTRL
Firebug n CRIM
Firecracker n HEAR
Fired v DAMG
Fired v MOTV
Fired v VIEW
Firelight n VIEW
Fireman n MALE
Fireplace n HOLW
Fireplug n FLOW
Fireproof j AID
Fires n VIEW
Fires v DAMG
Fires v MOTV
Fireside j NEAR

Firetrap n BLOK
Firewood n VEGT
Fireworks n VIEW
Firing v DAMG
Firing v MOTV
Firing v VIEW
Flame n VIEW
Flame n SEX
Flame n COLR
Flamed v VIEW
Flameproof j AID
Flaming v VIEW
Flare v VIEW
Forge v WORK
Foundry n WORK
Fried v FOOD
Fried v
Fries n FOOD
Fries v
Frizz v HEAR
Frizzle v HEAR
Fry v FOOD
Fry v
Frying v FOOD
Frying v
Fuel n MTRL
Furnace n HOLW
Fuse n
Fuse v FLOW
Fused v FLOW
Fusible j FLOW
Fusing v FLOW
Geyser n FLOW
Glow n VIEW
Glowed v VIEW
Griddle n FOOD
Gridiron n FORM
Grill n FOOD
Grilled v FOOD
Hearth n HOLW
Heat n
Heat n SEX
Heated v
Heating v
Heats v
Heliocentric j ASTR
Heliotropism n ASTR
Hibachi n FOOD
Hob n BULG
Holocaust n DAMG
Hot j

Hot j MOTV
Hot j POWR
Hot j PANG
Hot j SEX
Hot j CRIM
Igneous j
Ignition n BGIN
Incandescence n VIEW
Incendiary n DAMG
Incense n SOMA
Incinerate v
Inflame v
Inflame v MOTV
Inflame v AGGR
Inflammable j
Inflammation n
Inflammatory j AGGR
Isotherm n SIML
Kiln n HOLW
Kindle v
Kindling n MTRL
Light n VIEW
Lighted v VIEW
Lighting v VIEW
Lights n VIEW
Lit v VIEW
Lukewarm j
Match n
Matches n
Midsummer j TIME
Molten j FLOW
Muggier j FLOW
Muggy j FLOW
Oven n HOLW
Overcook v FOOD
Overcook v LARG
Overheat v LARG
Panatela n FOOD
Panetela n FOOD
Parch v LACK
Pasteurize v CLEN
Perfecto n FOOD
Pipe n FOOD
Piping j
Poach v
Preheat v FORW
Pyre n BULG
Pyrex n MTRL
Pyromaniac n MOTV
Pyrotechnic j VIEW
Radiator n

Range n FURN
Refractory j MTRL
Roast v
Roast n FOOD
Sahara n PLAC
Salamander n
Saute j FOOD
Scald v
Scald v DAMG
Scallop v FOOD
Scalloped v FOOD
Scorch v DAMG
Sear v DAMG
Simmer v
Singe v DAMG

Singe v
Sizzle v HEAR
Smoke n VAPR
Smoke v FOOD
Smolder v
Smolder v AGGR
Solar j ASTR
Solder v JOIN
Spark v VIEW
Steam n VAPR
Steamed v VAPR
Steamer n HOLW
Steams v VAPR
Stew n FOOD
Stew n PANG

Stew v
Stoke v
Stove n FURN
Subtropical j PLAC
Summer n TIME
Sun n ASTR
Sunburn n ASTR
Sunned v ASTR
Sunny j ASTR
Suns n ASTR
Sunshine n ASTR
Temperature n MSMT
Tepid j
Thermal j
Thermodynamic j POWR

Thermometer n MSMT
Thermonuclear j ION
Thermostat n MECH
Tinder n MTRL
Toast n FOOD
Torch n VIEW
Torrid j
Tropic j PLAC
Unburned j
Warm j
Warm j FOND
Wick n MTRL

HOLW

Abdomen n BODY
Abyss n DOWN
Agape j OPEN
Aperture n OPEN
Area n
Ark n HOLY
Armpit n BODY
Around b
Arroyo n ERTH
Arsenal n DAMG
Atmosphere n VAPR
Atmospheric j VAPR
Aura n VAPR
Aura n
Aureole n VIEW
Bag n
Bag n GARB
Bag n LADY
Bag v BLOK
Baggage n HAVE
Bagged v
Bagged v BLOK
Bagging v
Bagging v BLOK
Baggy j
Bail n
Bail v FLOW
Bands n GARB
Barrel n
Basin n
Basket n
Basketball n PLAY
Basketry n FORM
Bathtub n CLEN
Bay n FLOW
Bays n FLOW
Beaker n
Bier n DEAD
Bilge n FLOW
Billfold n MONY
Bin n
Blister n BULG
Boat n
Bookcase n WRIT

Bore v IN
Bore n
Bored v IN
Boring v IN
Bottle n
Bottle n SIP
Bowl n
Box n FORM
Boxcar n VEHC
Boxed v FORM
Boxing v FORM
Bracelet n GARB
Bracket n
Bubble n FLOW
Bucket n
Buffet n FURN
Bulb n
Bunker n
Bureau n FURN
Bushel n MSMT
Butt n
Buttonhole n GARB
Cabinet n FURN
Cache n COVR
Caisson n DAMG
Caisson n FLOW
Caldron n HEAT
Can n
Canister n
Canned v
Cannery n HOME
Canning v
Cans n
Canteen n SIP
Canyon n ERTH
Capillary j LITL
Capillary n SOMA
Capsule n LITL
Carton n
Case n
Cased v
Casement n
Casing v
Cask n

Casket n DEAD
Casket n
Casserole n FOOD
Caster n FURN
Castor n FURN
Catacomb n DEAD
Cauldron n HEAT
Cavity n
Cell n
Cellular j SOMA
Cemetery n DEAD
Cesspool n DIRT
Chalice n SIP
Chamber n
Channel n
Charnel j DEAD
Chasm n ERTH
Chest n FURN
Chimney n HEAT
Chink n SEP
Churn n VARY
Cinerator n HEAT
Circle n FORM
Circlet n GARB
Circumference n OUT
Circumscribe v BLOK
Circumscribe v WRIT
Cistern n FLOW
Clip n
Closet n
Coaster n FURN
Coffer n
Coffin n DEAD
Colander n SEP
Commode n FURN
Commode n CLEN
Compartment n
Compass v BLOK
Compassed v BLOK
Compassing v BLOK
Concave j FORM
Conch n FLOW
Conduit n PATH
Console n FURN

Contain v IN
Content n IN
Context n WRIT
Cooler n COLD
Cooper n WORK
Cornucopia n MUCH
Corner n
Cornice n HEAT
Cosey n FOOD
Cosy n FOOD
Countersank v DOWN
Countersink v DOWN
Countersunk v DOWN
Cove n FORM
Cove n FLOW
Cove n ERTH
Cover n WRIT
Cozy n FOOD
Crankcase n MECH
Cranny n
Crate n
Crater n
Crawl n FLOW
Creamer n SIP
Crease n PLAY
Credence n FURN
Credenza n FURN
Crevasse n SEP
Crevice n SEP
Crib n
Cribbed v
Cribbing v
Crucible n HEAT
Cruet n
Crypt n DEAD
Culvert n
Cup n SIP
Cup n
Cup n POWR
Cupboard n FOOD
Cupful n BULG
Cupped v
Cupping v
Cuspidor n SOMA
Cylinder n FORM

Parts of speech: a article; b preposition; c conjunction; d adverb; f prefix; i interjection;
j adjective; n noun; p pronoun; r phrase; v verb.

Cylindrical j FORM
Cyst n SOMA
Dale n ERTH
Decanter n
Dell n ERTH
Demijohn n
Demitasse n SIP
Dent v
Depository n
Depression n DOWN
Dimple n BODY
Dipper n FLOW
Dipper n ASTR
Dish n FOOD
Dish n FORM
Dished v FOOD
Dished v FORM
Ditch n ERTH
Drawer n FURN
Drawers n FURN
Dresser n FURN
Drum n
Duct n PATH
Ductless j PATH
Dufflebag n FABR
Dump n DIRT
Dump n DAMG
Eggshell n FOOD
Encircle v BLOK
Enclosure n BLOK
Entrench v ERTH
Envelop v COVR
Envelope n
Enveloped v COVR
Environment n WHOL
Excavate v OUT
Eye n OPEN
Fenestra n SOMA
Fenestrate j OPEN
Ferrule n COVR
Firebox n HEAT
Fireplace n HEAT
Fissure n SEP
Flagon n
Flask n
Flowerpot n VEGT
Flue n
Flute n FORM
Fob n GARB
Folder n WRIT
Folder n
Follicle n BODY
Font n FLOW
Fountain n FLOW
Freezer n COLD
Funnel n
Furnace n HEAT
Furrow v
Gape v OPEN
Gaping v OPEN
Gastric j SOMA
Gird v BLOK
Girded v BLOK
Girth n MSMT
Glass n MTRL

Glasses n MTRL
Glassware n MTRL
Glen n ERTH
Goblet n SIP
Gorge n ERTH
Gorge n SOMA
Gouge n
Gourd n SIP
Grail n HOLY
Granary n VEGT
Grave n DEAD
Graveyard n DEAD
Grip n
Groove n
Gulch n ERTH
Gulf n
Gulf n ERTH
Gullet n SOMA
Gullies n ERTH
Gully n ERTH
Gut n SOMA
Gutter n
Gutter n BAD
Hamper n
Haversack n GARB
Haymow n VEGT
Hearth n HEAT
Highboy n FURN
Hod n
Hogshead n MSMT
Hold n
Hole n OPEN
Holing v
Hollow n
Hollow j TRIV
Holster n
Hookah n FOOD
Hoop n FORM
Hopper n
Horn n
Hose n FLOW
Hosing v FLOW
Housing n
Humidor n
Hydrant n FLOW
Icebox n COLD
Indent v
Intestine n SOMA
Jackpot n WHOL
Jar n
Jug n
Keg n
Kettle n
Keyhole n OPEN
Kiln n HEAT
Knapsack n GARB
Knothole n VEGT
Ladle n
Larder n FOOD
Locker n BLOK
Locket n GARB
Loop n FORM
Luggage n
Magazine n
Main n PATH

Mains n PATH
Manger n FOOD
Manifold n FORM
Mausoleum n DEAD
Milieu n WHOL
Moat n ERTH
Morgue n DEAD
Mortar n
Mouth n BODY
Mug n SIP
Muzzle n
Niche n
Nock n
Nook n
Notch n
Nutshell n VEGT
Oral j BODY
Orbit n GO
Orbit n FORM
Orifice n OPEN
Oven n HEAT
Package n BULG
Packet n BULG
Pail n
Pailful n BULG
Palette n COLR
Pallet n FORM
Pan n
Pannier n
Parcel n BULG
Perforate v SHRP
Perimeter n OUT
Periphery n OUT
Pigeonhole v BLOK
Pigeonhole n ANML
Pigeonhole v GRUP
Pipe n
Piped v
Pipette n FLOW
Piping n
Pit n
Pitcher n
Pitfall n DAMG
Pitted v
Pitting v
Plate n FOOD
Platter n FOOD
Pock v
Pocket n
Pocketbook n GARB
Pocketful n BULG
Pockmark n BODY
Pod n VEGT
Poke n
Porosity n
Portfolio n WRIT
Pot n
Pothole n
Pothook n BLOK
Potpie n FOOD
Pots n
Potted j
Potter n ERTH
Pottery n ERTH
Potting v

Pouch n
Punch n
Punched v
Punching v
Puncture v SHRP
Purse n GARB
Purse n MONY
Quarried v ERTH
Quarries v ERTH
Quarry n ERTH
Quarrying v ERTH
Quiver n
Rabbet n
Ravine n ERTH
Receiver n HAVE
Receptacle n
Recess n
Recessing v
Refrigerator n COLD
Reservoir n FLOW
Retort n
Riddle v
Ring n FORM
Ring n GRUP
Ringed v FORM
Ringing v FORM
Round v BLOK
Rounded v BLOK
Rounding v BLOK
Rounds v BLOK
Roundup n BLOK
Rout v SHRP
Routed v SHRP
Router n MECH
Routing v SHRP
Rut n EVER
Rut n
Sac n SOMA
Sack n
Sack n REST
Sacked v
Sacked v REST
Sacking v
Sacking v REST
Saddlebag n REST
Safe n AID
Samovar n SIP
Sandbag n ERTH
Sandbox n ERTH
Sandhog n WORK
Sarcophagus n DEAD
Satchel n
Saucer n FOOD
Scabbard n SHRP
Scoop v
Sepulchre n DEAD
Shaft n
Sheath n
Shell n
Shell n DAMG
Shovel n WORK
Sink n FLOW
Sink n BAD
Sleeve n GARB
Slip n FABR

Slit n SHRP	Tank n FLOW	Trunks n	Vault n DEAD
Slot n	Tankard n SIP	Tub n	Vein n
Socket n	Teakettle n SIP	Tube n	Vessel n
Space n	Teapot n SIP	Tube n VEHC	Vial n
Spaces n	Thimble n GARB	Tubing n	Wallet n GARB
Sphere n	Till n MONY	Tubular j	Wardrobe n GARB
Stack n	Tills n MONY	Tunnel n PATH	Waterhole n FLOW
Steamer n HEAT	Tin n MTRL	Urn n	Well n
Stein n SIP	Tomb n DEAD	Vale n ERTH	Well n FLOW
Still n SIP	Tombs n DEAD	Valise n	Wells n FLOW
Stills n SIP	Tray n	Valley n ERTH	Wicker n VEGT
Suitcase n GARB	Trench n ERTH	Vanity n FURN	Womb n BGIN
Surround v BLOK	Trough n	Vase n	Wreath n FORM
Syringe n FLOW	Trunk n	Vat n	Wristband n BODY

HOLY

Abbe n LEAD	Canonical j WRIT	Cure n LEAD	Hallow v
Abbess n LADY	Canonical j LEAD	DalaiLama n LEAD	Hallowed j
Abbey n HOME	Canonize v LEAD	Deacon n	Hanukkah n TIME
Abbot n LEAD	Cantor n TALK	Deacon v TALK	Haphtarah n WRIT
Absolution n AGRE	Cardinal n LEAD	Deaconess n LADY	Hazzan n MUSC
Acolyte n AID	Cardinals n LEAD	Decretal n WRIT	Heathen j OPPO
Advent n	Cassock n GARB	Deicide n DEAD	Heresy n OPPO
Adventist n	Catechism n WRIT	Deify v LEAD	Heretic n OPPO
Agape n FOND	Cathedral n HOME	Deism n LEAD	Hieratic j
Agnostic j OPPO	Catholic j GRUP	Deity n LEAD	Holier j
Alb n GARB	Celestial j LEAD	Demigod n LEAD	Holy j
Almighty n LEAD	Ceremony n FORM	Dervish n GRUP	Homily n TALK
Altar n FORM	Chapel n HOME	Desecrate v DAMG	Hosanna i AGRE
Amen i AGRE	Chaplain n LEAD	Deuteronomy n WRIT	Host n FOOD
Angel n GOOD	Christ n LEAD	Devotion n FOND	Hymn n MUSC
Anglican j GRUP	Christen v	Devout j MOTV	Hymnal n WRIT
Anoint v FLOW	Christian j GRUP	Diocese n LEAD	Icon n FORM
Aphrodite n LADY	Christmas n TIME	Disciple n SUB	Iconoclast n OPPO
Apocalypse n WRIT	Church n HOME	Divine j LEAD	Idol n FOND
Apocrypha n WRIT	Church n GRUP	Divinity n LEAD	Impiety n OPPO
Apostle n LEAD	Churchyard n PLAC	Dominican j GRUP	Impious j OPPO
Apostolic j LEAD	Clergy n GRUP	Druid n GRUP	Infidel n OPPO
Apse n HOME	Clergyman n	Easter n TIME	Irreligious j OPPO
Archangel n LEAD	Cleric n	Ecclesiastes n WRIT	Jehovah n LEAD
Archbishop n LEAD	Clerical j	Ecclesiastic j	Jesus n LEAD
Ark n HOLW	Clerk n	Ecumenical j WHOL	Jew n GRUP
AshWednesday n TIME	Cloister n HOME	Enshrine v IN	Kerygma n WRIT
Assumption n POWR	Commandment n LEAD	Episcopal j	Koran n WRIT
Atheism n OPPO	Communicant n GRUP	Epistle n WRIT	Kosher j FOOD
Atonement n AGRE	Communion n GRUP	Eucharist n FOOD	Krishna n LEAD
Baptize v FLOW	Communion n FOOD	Evangel n	Lay j GRUP
Bead n FORM	Confess v AGRE	Excommunicate v SEP	Lent n TIME
Benediction n AID	Confessing v AGRE	Faith n AGRE	Libation n FLOW
Bible n WRIT	Confessional n HOME	Fakir n MYTH	Litany n TALK
Biblical j PAST	Confessional n FOND	Father n LEAD	Liturgy n FORM
Biblical j WRIT	Confirm v	Friar n MALE	Lord n LEAD
Bishop n LEAD	Congregation n GRUP	Frock n GARB	Maker n LEAD
Bishop n PLAY	Congregational j GRUP	Gentile n GRUP	Manna n FOOD
Bless v AID	Consecrate v MOTV	Gnostic j	Manse n HOME
Brother n MALE	Convent n HOME	God n LEAD	Martyr n DEAD
Buddhism n GRUP	Creator n BGIN	Goddess n LADY	Mass n TALK
Bull n WRIT	Creche n HOME	Gospel n WRIT	Minister n LEAD
Bulls n WRIT	Cross n FORM	Grace n TALK	Ministry n LEAD
Cabala n COVR	Crucifix n FORM	Grail n HOLW	Mission n MOTV
Caliph n LEAD	Crucifixion n DAMG	Guru n LEAD	Missionary n MOTV
Calvinism n GRUP	Crusade v DAMG	Haggada n WRIT	Mohammed n LEAD
Canon n WRIT	Cult n FOND	Hagiology n WRIT	Monastery n HOME
Canon n LEAD	Cult n GRUP	Halakah n LAW	Monastic j

Monk n MALE
Monotheism n LEAD
Moslem n GRUP
Mosque n HOME
Mother n LADY
Mystic j BLUR
Noel n MUSC
Novena n FOND
Novitiate n SUB
Nun n LADY
Nunnery n HOME
Oath n TALK
Office n
Oracle n LEAD
Ordain v LEAD
Orthodox j EVER
Padre n LEAD
Pagan j OPPO
Pagoda n HOME
Palmer n GO
Pantheism n WHOL
Pantheon n HOME
Pantheon n LEAD
Papacy n LEAD
Papal j LEAD
Parish n GRUP
Parishioner n GRUP
Parochial j GRUP
Parson n LEAD
Passion n PANG

Passover n TIME
Pastor n LEAD
Pastoral n WRIT
Pastorate n LEAD
Patriarch n LEAD
Pentecost n TIME
Pew n REST
Pharisee n FALS
Pharisee n GRUP
Phylactery n WRIT
Piety n GOOD
Pilgrim n GO
Pious j GOOD
Polytheism n MUCH
Pontifical j LEAD
Pope n LEAD
Prayer n TALK
Preach v TALK
Prelate n LEAD
Presbyter n LEAD
Presbyterian n GRUP
Priest n LEAD
Priestess n LADY
Priesthood n LEAD
Primate n LEAD
Prior n LEAD
Prioress n LADY
Protestant n GRUP
Psalm n TALK
Pulpit n TALK

Purgatory n DAMG
Purim n TIME
Puritan n GRUP
Quaker n GRUP
Rabbi n LEAD
Religion n
Requiem n DEAD
Retreat n COVR
Rite n FORM
Ritual j FORM
Rosary n GARB
Rosicrucian n GRUP
Sabbath n TIME
Sacerdotal j
Sacrament n
Sacred j
Sacrifice n LACK
Sacrificial j LACK
Saint n GOOD
Sanctify v GOOD
Sanctimonious j FALS
Sanctity n GOOD
Sanctuary n AID
Sanctum n HOME
SantaClaus n PLAY
Savior n LEAD
Scripture n WRIT
Secular j GRUP
See n LEAD
Seminary n EDUC

Sermon n TALK
Service n TALK
Sexton n AID
Shrine n HOME
Sister n LADY
Spiritual j MYTH
Spiritual n MUSC
Swear v TALK
Swore v TALK
Synagogue n HOME
Tabernacle n HOME
Temple n HOME
Testament n WRIT
Theology n IDEA
Trinity n KIN
Unction n MTRL
Vatican n PLAC
Veil n GARB
Virgin n LADY
Worship v FOND
Xmas n TIME
Yeshiva n EDUC
Yoga n IDEA
Yogi n IDEA
YomKippur n TIME
Yule n PLAY
Zen n
Zion n PLAC

HOME

Abbey n HOLY
Abode n LIVE
Academies n EDUC
Academy n EDUC
Aerie n ANML
Airport n UP
Alcove n
Almamater n EDUC
Amphitheater n PLAY
Antechamber n FORW
Anteroom n FORW
Apartment n
Apiary n BUG
Apse n HOLY
Aquarium n FLOW
Arbor v VEGT
Arcade n
Archives n WRIT
Arena n PLAY
Armories n DAMG
Armory n DAMG
Asylum n MEDC
Attic n UP
Auditorium n HEAR
Aviary n ANML
Balcony n UP
Ballroom n PLAY
Barn n ANML
Barns n ANML
Barnyard n ANML
Barracks n
Base n CRUX

Based v CRUX
Basement n DOWN
Bases n CRUX
Bath n CLEN
Bathroom n CLEN
Bedroom n REST
Beehive n BUG
Bigtop n PLAY
Billet v
Bistro n FOOD
Bivouac n
Boardinghouse n FOOD
Booth n
Boudoir n LADY
Bower n VEGT
Bowl n PLAY
Brig n BLOK
Building n FORM
Bungalow n
Bunker n DAMG
Burrow n ERTH
Cabana n FLOW
Cabin n
Cabinet n
Caboose n VEHC
Cage n BLOK
Caging v BLOK
Calaboose n BLOK
Camera n COVR
Camp n GRUP
Camp n
Camporee n GRUP

Campus n EDUC
Can n CLEN
Cannery n HOLW
Capitol n LEAD
Carport n VEHC
Castle n
Castle n PLAY
Castling v PLAY
Cathedral n HOLY
Cave n ERTH
Cavern n ERTH
Cell n BLOK
Cellar n DOWN
Chalet n
Chamber n
Chancellery n LEAD
Chancery n LEAD
Chapel n HOLY
Chateau n
Church n HOLY
Cinema n PLAY
Circus n PLAY
Citadel n POWR
Classroom n EDUC
Clinic n MEDC
Clink n BLOK
Cloister n HOLY
Cloister n
Cloister v SEP
Closet n CLEN
Club n GRUP
Clubhouse n GRUP

Cobweb n BUG
Cockpit n VEHC
Cocoon n BUG
Coliseum n PLAY
College n EDUC
Colosseum n PLAY
Commissaries n MART
Commissary n MART
Commons n GRUP
Compartment n
Compound n
Conclave n COVR
Confessional n HOLY
Conservatories n IDEA
Conservatories n VEGT
Conservatory n IDEA
Conservatory n VEGT
Convent n HOLY
Coop n ANML
Coop v BLOK
Cooped v BLOK
Cooping v BLOK
Corral v BLOK
Corral n ANML
Cot n
Cote n ANML
Cottage n
Court n LAW
Court n PLAY
Court n PLAC
Courthouse n LAW
Courtroom n LAW

Courts n LAW
Courts n PLAY
Courts n PLAC
Courtyard n PLAC
Creche n HOLY
Crib n
Cubbyhole n
Cubicle n
Den n
Dens n
Depot n
Dinette n FOOD
Doghouse n ANML
Domestic n AID
Domicile n LIVE
Dorm n
Dugout n ERTH
Dungeon n BLOK
Duplex n NUMR
Dwell v LIVE
Emporium n MART
Factory n WORK
Farmhouse n ERTH
Farmyard n PLAC
Flat n
Flats n
Flophouse n MART
Fold n ANML
Forecastle n FLOW
Fort n POWR
Fortress n POWR
Foxhole n ERTH
Foyer n
Gallery n
Galley n FOOD
Garage n VEHC
Garret n UP
Garrison n DAMG
Grange n ERTH
Greenhouse n VEGT
Grotto n ERTH
Guardhouse n BLOK
Gym n PLAY
Gymnasium n PLAY
Gymnasium n EDUC
Hacienda n
Hall n
Hallway n PATH
Hangar n VEHC
Harbor v AID
Haven n AID
Head n CLEN
Headquarters n LEAD
Hennery n ANML
Hideout n COVR
Highschool n EDUC
Hippodrome n PLAY
Hive n BUG
Hives n BUG
Home n

Home n PLAY
Homeless j LACK
Homelike j SIML
Homemade j FORM
Homer n PLAY
Homered v PLAY
Homering v PLAY
Homesick j PANG
Homespun j FABR
Homestead n ERTH
Homeward j FORW
Homing v GO
Hoosegow n BLOK
Hospital n MEDC
Hospitalize v MEDC
Hostel n MART
Hotel n MART
Hothouse n VEGT
House n
House n GRUP
Houseful n BULG
Household j FURN
Housekeeper n AID
Housewife n LADY
Housework n WORK
Housing n
Hovel n
Hut n
Hutch n
Igloo n
Imprison v BLOK
Incarcerate v BLOK
Infirmary n MEDC
Inn n MART
Innkeeper n MART
Institute n
Institution n
Jail n BLOK
Joint n
Jug n BLOK
Kennel n ANML
Kitchen n FOOD
Laboratory n WORK
Lair n ANML
Landing n
Landlord n MART
Latrine n CLEN
Lavatory n CLEN
Leanto n
Legation n LEAD
Libraries n WRIT
Library n WRIT
Lighthouse n VIEW
Lobbies n
Lobby n
Lodge n
Lodge n GRUP
Lodger n LIVE
Loft n UP
Lounge n REST

Lyceum n EDUC
Manor n
Manse n HOLY
Mansion n
Menagerie n ANML
Mezzanine n UP
Minaret n UP
Monastery n HOLY
Mosque n HOLY
Motel n MART
Museum n
Nest n ANML
Nunnery n HOLY
Nursery n YNG
Office n MART
Pad n
Paddock n BLOK
Pagoda n HOLY
Palace n LEAD
Palatial j LEAD
Pantheon n HOLY
Pantry n FOOD
Parlor n
Parlor n MART
Patio n PLAC
Pavilion n
Pen n BLOK
Pen n ANML
Penitentiary n BLOK
Penned v BLOK
Penning v BLOK
Pens v BLOK
Pentagon n DAMG
Penthouse n UP
Piazza n
Pillbox n DAMG
Planetarium n ASTR
Pokey n BLOK
Poorhouse n LACK
Porch n
Port n FLOW
Portico n
Postoffice n WRIT
Pound n ANML
Prison n BLOK
Privy n CLEN
Quadrangle n PLAC
Quarter n
Quartered v
Quartering v
Reformatory n BLOK
Reside v LIVE
Residence n LIVE
Retreat n COVR
Ring n PLAY
Rink n PLAY
Room n
Roommate n JOIN
Roost n ANML
Rotunda n FORM

Salon n
Salon n GRUP
Saloon n
Sanatorium n MEDC
Sanctum n HOLY
Sanitarium n MEDC
School n EDUC
Schoolhouse n EDUC
Schoolroom n EDUC
Shack n
Shed n
Shelter n AID
Shop n MART
Shrine n HOLY
Stable n ANML
Stabled v ANML
Stables n ANML
Stabling v ANML
Stadium n PLAY
Stall n ANML
Stall n MART
Stand n MART
Stateroom n VEHC
Sties n DIRT
Stir n BLOK
Stoop n
Store n MART
Storehouse n HAVE
Storeroom n HAVE
Stronghold n POWR
Studies n IDEA
Studio n WORK
Study n IDEA
Sty n DIRT
Suite n GRUP
Synagogue n HOLY
Tabernacle n HOLY
Temple n HOLY
Tenement n
Tent n
Theater n PLAY
Toilet n CLEN
Tower n UP
Turret n UP
University n EDUC
Vault n FORM
Vaulted j FORM
Veranda n
Vestibule n
Villa n
Ward n MEDC
Warehouse n MART
Warren n ANML
Watercloset n CLEN
Web n BUG
Workshop n WORK
Zoo n ANML

He p
Her p
Hers p
Herself p

Him p
Himself p
His p
It p

Its p
She p
Their p
Them p

They p
You p
Your p

IDEA

Absentminded j FOOL
Abstract j
Abstract n LITL
Account n
Acculturation n GRUP
Acquaint v NEAR
Acumen n POWR
Adage n TALK
Adduce v
Adjudge v
Adjudge v LAW
Adjudicate v LAW
Advice n AID
Advise v AID
Aetiology n BGIN
Aforethought n FORW
Alibi n
Analyze v
Anatomy n SOMA
Animism n MYTH
Answer n TALK
Anthropology n GRUP
Antithesis n OPPO
Aphorism n TALK
Apology n AGRE
Apostasy n OPPO
Appear v VIEW
Appraise v CRUX
Appreciate v FOND
Apprehension n
Apprise v
Apriori j
Arbiter n LEAD
Arbitrate v LEAD
Architect n FORM
Ascertain v SHRP
Ascribe v MOTV
Assay v
Assess v CRUX
Associate v JOIN
Assume v
Assumption n
Astronomical j ASTR
Astronomy n ASTR
Astrophysics n ASTR
Astute j POWR
Atlas n FORM
Attribute v MOTV
Audit v NUMR
Auditor n NUMR
Autopsy n DEAD
Aware j
Axiom n TRUE
Because c
Belief n AGRE

Believe v AGRE
Biochemist n SOMA
Biology n SOMA
Blueprint n FORM
Bone v
Boning v
Botany n VEGT
Brain n SOMA
Brainwash v CLEN
Brief v TALK
Briefed v TALK
Briefing v TALK
Briefs v TALK
Bright j POWR
Brilliant j POWR
Burden n
Cagey j POWR
Cagier j POWR
Caginess n POWR
Calculate v
Calculate v NUMR
Cannier j POWR
Cannily d POWR
Canny j POWR
Canon n FORM
Canonical j FORM
Canvass n MOTV
Cartographer n FORM
Case n
Case v CRIM
Cased v CRIM
Casing v CRIM
Casuistry n FALS
Censor v BLOK
Censoring v BLOK
Cerebral j SOMA
Cerebrate v
Chart n FORM
Chemist n MTRL
Chorography n FORM
Clever j POWR
Code n FORM
Code n COVR
Codify v FORM
Coding v FORM
Coding v COVR
Cogent j TRUE
Cogitate v
Cognition n
Cognizance n
Cohere v JOIN
Commemorate v PAST
Comprehend v
Compute v NUMR
Computed v NUMR

Computer n NUMR
Con v
Conceit n FOOL
Conceive v
Concentrate v SHRP
Concentration n SHRP
Concept n
Conclude v END
Conclusion n END
Conjecture n BLUR
Connoisseur n POWR
Connote v
Cons v
Conscience n GOOD
Conscienceless j BAD
Conscientious j GOOD
Conscious j
Conservatories n HOME
Conservatory n HOME
Consider v
Consideration n
Construct n FORM
Construe v
Consult v AID
Contemplate v
Contend v
Content n IN
Contention n
Contrive v FORM
Conversant j NEAR
Conviction n AGRE
Convince v AGRE
Corollary j JOIN
Cosmology n WHOL
Council n GRUP
Counsel n AID
Cram v BULG
Credence n AGRE
Credo n AGRE
Credulous j AGRE
Creed n AGRE
Critic n AGGR
Critical j AGGR
Criticism n AGGR
Critique n
Cue n AID
Cultivate v GOOD
Culture n GOOD
Cytology n SOMA
Decide v
Decided v
Decision n
Decisive j POWR
Deduce v
Deductive j

Deem v
Define v
Defining v
Definition n
Definitive j SHRP
Deliberate v MOTV
Dementia n SICK
Demography n GRUP
Demonstrate v TRUE
Denote v
Design n FORM
Determine v
Devise v FORM
Diagnosis n
Diagram n FORM
Dialectic n
Dictum n TALK
Dig v FOND
Disbelief n OPPO
Discern v
Discretion n GOOD
Discriminate v OPPO
Dissertation n WRIT
Dissuade v VARY
Distract v VARY
Diversion n VARY
Divert v VARY
Divine v
Divining v
Doctrine n FORM
Dogma n FORM
Dope n
Doped v
Doping v
Draw v
Drawn v
Dream n MYTH
Drew v
Eclectic n MOTV
Egghead n BODY
Elaborate v
Elucidate v SHRP
Enlighten v
Entertain v
Enumerate v NUMR
Epigram n TALK
ESP n MYTH
Establish v TRUE
Establishment n TRUE
Esteem n FOND
Esteem n
Estimate v
Ethnography n GRUP
Ethnology n GRUP
Etiology n BGIN

Parts of speech: a article; b preposition; c conjunction; d adverb; f prefix; i interjection;
        j adjective; n noun; p pronoun; r phrase; v verb.

Psychosis n SICK
Psychotherapy n MEDC
Psychotic j SICK
Pump v OPEN
Pumped v OPEN
Pumping v OPEN
Purport n CRUX
Rate v FORW
Rating v FORW
Rational j
Rationale n
Realize v TRUE
Reason n
Recall v PAST
Reck v
Reckon v
Reckon v NUMR
Recollect v PAST
Reconnaissance n OPEN
Reconnoitre v OPEN
Reconsider v
Referee n LEAD
Reflect v
Regime n FORM
Regimen n FORM
Remembrance n PAST
Remind v
Reminiscence n PAST
Repute v
Reputed v
Reputes v
Reputing v
Research n OPEN
Resume n LITL
Reverie n MYTH
Review n VIEW
Review n WRIT

Rule n FORM
Ruminate v
Sagacity n POWR
Sage n GOOD
Sane j MEDC
Sanity n MEDC
Saw n TALK
Saying n TALK
Schematize v FORM
Scheme n FORM
Scheme v FALS
Schemed v FALS
Schemer n FALS
Scheming v FALS
Schizoid j SICK
Schizophrenia n SICK
Science n TRUE
Score n
Scrutiny n VIEW
Seem v VIEW
Selfconscious j SOLE
Sensation n SOMA
Sense n SOMA
Sensible j
Sensing v SOMA
Sensory j SOMA
Shrewd j POWR
Sign n SIML
Signal n
Significance n
Signified v
Signify v
Skull n SOMA
Smart j POWR
Sociology n GRUP
Soluble j
Solution n

Solve v
Sophism n FALS
Sophistication n POWR
Sophistry n FALS
Souvenir n PAST
Speculate v
Standpoint n
Stratagem n FALS
Strategic j FORM
Strategies n FORM
Strategy n FORM
Strike v
Striking v
Struck v
Studied v
Studies v
Studies n HOME
Studious j
Study n
Study n HOME
Subconscious j COVR
Subject n
Subplot n FORM
Suggest v
Suggestion n
Suppose v
Surmise v
Survey n VIEW
Suspect v BLUR
Symbol n SIML
Symposium n GRUP
Tab n
Tabbed v
Tabbing v
Tacit j COVR
Tell v TALK
Tenor n

Theme n
Theology n HOLY
Theory n FORM
Theses n WRIT
Thesis n
Thesis n WRIT
Think v
Thought n
Topic n
Unbeliever n OPPO
Unconscious j COVR
Understand v
Understood v
Unforgettable j EVER
Unscientific j FALS
Verdict n LAW
Verdict n
Version n
View n
Weigh v
Weltanschauung n WHOL
Why d
Wind n VAPR
Wisdom n GOOD
Wise j GOOD
Wise j FOOL
Wiseacre n FOOL
Wit n GLAD
Wit n
Witticism n GLAD
Wonder v BLUR
Yoga n HOLY
Yogi n HOLY
Zoological j ANML

IN

Aboard b VEHC
Absorb v
Admission n GO
Admit v GO
Amid b JOIN
Board v VEHC
Boarded v VEHC
Boarder n VEHC
Boarding v VEHC
Boards v VEHC
Bore v HOLW
Bored v HOLW
Boring v HOLW
Burrow v ERTH
Centripetal j GO
Contain v HOLW
Contain v BLOK
Content n HOLW
Content n IDEA
Dip n FLOW
Dip n FOOD
Dipped v FLOW
Draw v SOMA
Drew v SOMA
Dunk v FLOW

Embody v BODY
Enclose v COVR
Enclosure n COVR
Endogenous j BGIN
Enshrine v HOLY
Enter v GO
Enter v WRIT
Entrance n GO
Entree n GO
Entries n GO
Entries n WRIT
Entry n GO
Entry n WRIT
Herein d NEAR
Imbue v HAVE
Immanent j EVER
Immerse v
Immigrate v GO
Immure v BLOK
Implant v
Implicit j IDEA
Implicit j
Implode v DAMG
Implosion n DAMG
Import n MART

Importation n MART
Impregnate v
In b
Inclose v COVR
Incoming j GO
Incorporate v JOIN
Indoor j
Infiltrate v GO
Influx n GO
Infuse v
Ingrained j CRUX
Ingress n GO
Inhabit v LIVE
Inject v
Inlaid j FORM
Inland j ERTH
Inlay n FORM
Inlet n FLOW
Inmate n LIVE
Inmost j EMPH
Innards n SOMA
Innards n
Innate j BGIN
Inner j
Innermost j EMPH

Inoculate v MEDC
Inpatient n SICK
Input n GO
Inseminate v SEX
Insert v
Inset n
Inside d
Instill v
Intake n GO
Interior n
Interject v SEP
Interline v FABR
Internal j
Interpolate v SEP
Interpose v SEP
Into b
Intramural j
Intramuscular j SOMA
Intravenous j SOMA
Intrinsic j CRUX
Introjection n IDEA
Introspect v IDEA
Introvert v MOTV
Introvert v VARY
Intrusion n AGGR

Invade v DAMG
Invasion n DAMG
Inward d
Midst n JOIN
Midstream n FLOW
Occupancy n HAVE
Occupation n HAVE

Occupied v HAVE
Occupy v HAVE
Osmosis n SOMA
Penetrate v
Percolate v FLOW
Permeate v
Pervade v WHOL

Pierce v SHRP
Probe v OPEN
Root v
Suck v VAPR
Sucked v VAPR
Sucker n VAPR
Suction n VAPR

Threshold n FORM
Through b
Transfusion n MEDC
Within b

ION

Alpha n MTRL
Ammeter n MSMT
Ampere n MSMT
Angstrom n MSMT
Anode n
Atom n MTRL
Atomic j MTRL
Batteries n MECH
Battery n MECH
Beta n MTRL
Capacitance n MSMT
Charge n
Charger n MECH
Circuit n PATH
Commutator n MECH
Condenser n
Conductance n PATH
Coulomb n MSMT
Covalence n JOIN
Current n
Cyclotron n MECH
Deuteron n MTRL
Dielectric n

Diode n MECH
Electric j
Electrician n WORK
Electricity n
Electrify v
Electro f
Electrode n END
Electromagnet n JOIN
Electrometer n MSMT
Electromotive j POWR
Electron n
Electroscope n MSMT
Electrostatic j REST
Element n MTRL
Elements n MTRL
Farad n MSMT
Galvanic j
Galvanometer n MSMT
Generator n MECH
Hydrocarbon n MTRL
Hydroelectric j FLOW
Inductance n POWR
Induction n POWR

Ion n MTRL
Isomeric j SIML
Isotope n SIML
Kilowatt n MSMT
Magnet n JOIN
Magnetism n JOIN
Meson n
Molecule n MTRL
Negative j OPPO
Neutron n
Nuclear j CRUX
Nucleus n CRUX
Ohm n MSMT
Pentode n MECH
Photoelectric j VIEW
Piezoelectric j MTRL
Pile n MECH
Positive j
Potential n POWR
Potentiometer n MSMT
Proton n
Quanta n MSMT
Quantum n MSMT

Radar n MECH
Radio n
Radioactive j
Radioisotope n MTRL
Radiology n MEDC
Radium n MTRL
Ray n
Reactance n
Reactor n MECH
Rheostat n VARY
Roentgen n MSMT
Telemeter n MSMT
Thermonuclear j HEAT
Transistor n MECH
Triode n MECH
Valence n JOIN
Volt n MSMT
Voltmeter n MSMT
Watt n MSMT
Xray n MEDC
Xray n VIEW

JOIN

Abut v
Abutment n
Accession n LARG
Accompany v
Accompany v MUSC
Accretion n LARG
Across b
Add v LARG
Added v LARG
Addendum n LARG
Adding v LARG
Addition n LARG
Additive n LARG
Adhere v
Adhere v AGRE
Adhesion n
Adhesion n AGRE
Adhesive j
Adjoin v
Adjunct n
Admixture n
Affair n SEX
Affaire n SEX
Affiliate n
Affinity n SIML
Affinity n FOND
Affix v
Agglutinate v
Allegiance n AGRE

Alliance n AGRE
Allied j AGRE
Allies n AGRE
Alloy n MTRL
Alloy n TRIV
Ally n AGRE
Along d
Amalgam n
Amid b IN
Among b
Annex n
Annex v HAVE
Append v
Appendage n
Appendices n WRIT
Appendices n SOMA
Appending v
Application n
Applicator n
Applied v
Apply v
Appointment n
Artery n PATH
Articular j BODY
Articulate v
Assemble v GRUP
Assemble v
Assembly n GRUP
Assembly n

Assignation n SEX
Associate v GRUP
Associate v IDEA
Assort v
Athwart b
Attach v
Attach v FOND
Attached v
Attached v FOND
Attaches v
Attaches v FOND
Attend v AID
Attend v
Attend v GO
Attendance n GO
Attendance n GRUP
Attendant j
Attendant n AID
Attract v GO
Audience n HEAR
Axis n AGRE
Band n
Band n GRUP
Banded v GRUP
Banding v GRUP
Bands n GRUP
Bands n
Baste v GARB
Belong v

Between b
Bind v
Blend v
Bobbypin n BODY
Bolt n MECH
Bond n
Bond n BLOK
Bonded v
Bonding v
Bound j
Brad n SHRP
Braze v HEAT
Bridge n PATH
Brush n EASY
Brush n DAMG
Buckle n GARB
Bump v DAMG
Bump v
Bumped v DAMG
Bumped v
Bumping v DAMG
Bumping v
Butt v
Butted v
Butting v
Button n GARB
Call n GO
Calling v GO
Camaraderie n FOND

Caress v FOND
Caress v EASY
Catch v GO
Catches v GO
Caught v GO
Cement n MTRL
Chafe v AGGR
Chain n BLOK
Chain n FORW
Chaperone n AID
Chuck n FOND
Chucked v FOND
Chucking v FOND
Chucks v FOND
Clamp v BLOK
Clasp n BLOK
Classmate n EDUC
Cleave v
Clench v BLOK
Clinch v BLOK
Cling v
Cling v EVER
Clip n
Clipped v
Clung v
Clung v EVER
Coalesce v
Coalition n
Coauthor n WRIT
Coeducation n EDUC
Coexist v LIVE
Cog v BULG
Cohabit v LIVE
Cohere v
Cohere v IDEA
Cohesion n
Coitus n SEX
Collaborate v AGRE
Collage n FORM
Collateral n SIML
Colleague n
Collect v GRUP
Collide v DAMG
Colligate v
Collision n DAMG
Collocate v FORM
Colloquy n TALK
Collude v BAD
Collusion n BAD
Combination n
Combination n NUMR
Combine v
Commerce n
Commerce n SEX
Commingle v
Commix v
Commixture n
Commune n GRUP
Commune n TALK
Communed v TALK
Communicable j
Communicate v
Communing v TALK
Communion n GRUP
Communion n TALK

Companion n FOND
Companion n SIML
Company n FOND
Compile v
Complect v FORM
Complected v FORM
Complicity n MOTV
Compost n
Compound n
Compound v LARG
Comprise v WHOL
Comrade n FOND
Concatenate v FORW
Conclave n COVR
Concomitant n
Concourse n PATH
Concur v
Confederacy n GRUP
Confederate n CRIM
Confederate n GRUP
Confer v TALK
Conference n TALK
Conference n GRUP
Confluence n PATH
Confrere n MALE
Confront v FORW
Conglomerate n GRUP
Congregate v GRUP
Congregating v GRUP
Congregation n GRUP
Congress n GRUP
Congress n SEX
Conjoin v
Conjugate v SIML
Conjunction n
Conjunctive j
Connect v
Consanguine j KIN
Conscript v MOTV
Consolidate v
Consort n SEX
Consort n
Consort v SIML
Conspire v BAD
Conspire v AGRE
Consummate v SEX
Contact v
Contact v TALK
Contagion n SICK
Contagion n
Contiguity n
Convene v GRUP
Convening v GRUP
Convention n GRUP
Converge v GO
Convocation n GRUP
Convoke v GRUP
Convoy v GO
Copartner n
Copulate v SEX
Copulating v SEX
Copulative j
Cord n
Corelative j
Corner n PATH

Corners n PATH
Corollary j IDEA
Corporate j GRUP
Corporative j GRUP
Correlate v
Cortege n GRUP
Couple n NUMR
Couple n
Couple v SEX
Coupled v
Coupled v SEX
Couplet n WRIT
Coupling v
Coupling v SEX
Covalence n ION
Cover v SEX
Crisscross v VARY
Crochet v GARB
Cross v
Crossover n PATH
Crossroad n PATH
Crossword j WRIT
Cuddle v FOND
Dab n SOME
Dabbed v SOME
Dandle v FOND
Darn v GARB
Darned v GARB
Darning v GARB
Dart n GARB
Date n TIME
Dating v TIME
Decal n VIEW
Desegregate v
Dovetail v FORM
Dowel n
Draft n MOTV
Drafted v MOTV
Draftee n MOTV
Electromagnet n ION
Embrace n FOND
Embrace n BLOK
Encounter n
Encounter n DAMG
Engage v
Engage v DAMG
Enlist v
Enmesh v BLOK
Enroll v WRIT
Entail v
Entourage n GRUP
Escort v AID
Espouse v AGRE
Federation n GRUP
Feel v BODY
Fell v GARB
Fellow n GRUP
Felt v BODY
Finger v BODY
Fix v
Fob n GARB
Fondle v FOND
Fondle v EASY
Fraternize v FOND
Friction n OPPO

Frog n
Fuse v
Fused v
Fusing v
Fusion n
Gantlet n PATH
Gather v
Gather v GRUP
Glue v MTRL
Graft n VEGT
Graft n BODY
Grapple v DAMG
Grapple v BLOK
Gravitate v GO
Gravity n GO
Graze v EASY
Guest n AID
Gum n MTRL
Gum v BLOK
Gummed v MTRL
Gummed v BLOK
Gummy j MTRL
Handle v BODY
Handshake n BODY
Hash n BLUR
Hashed v BLUR
Hashing v BLUR
Held v
Hello i
Heterosis n POWR
Hinge n
Hit v
Hitch n
Hitched v
Hobnail n SHRP
Hodgepodge n BLUR
Hold v
Huddle n GRUP
Hug v FOND
Hybrid j BGIN
Hybrid j OPPO
Impact n DAMG
Impact v
Impinge v AGGR
Implicate v IDEA
Incident j
Incorporate v MART
Incorporate v IN
Indivisible j WHOL
Induct v BGIN
Induction n BGIN
Inseparable j EVER
Integrate v WHOL
Interact v
Intercom n TALK
Interconnect v
Intercourse n
Intercourse n SEX
Interdependence n AID
Interlace v
Interlock v BLOK
Intermediary n AID
International j GRUP
Interplay n
Intersect v SEP

Interstate j PLAC
Interview n TALK
Intimacy n FOND
Intimacy n SEX
Intimate j FOND
Intimate j SEX
Involve v
Involved v
Isthmus n ERTH
Jack n MECH
Join v
Joint j
Joint n BODY
Jostle v VARY
Jumble n BLUR
Junction n PATH
Juxtapose v
Kindred j SIML
Knit v GARB
Knit v
Knot n BLOK
Knot n BULG
Knot n GRUP
Lace v
Laid v SEX
Lap v
Lapped v
Lard v
Larded v
Latch v BLOK
Lay n SEX
Leech n BUG
Levied v GRUP
Levy v GRUP
Liaison n
Ligament n SOMA
Link v
Locus n FORM
Lump v BULG
Magnet n ION
Magnetism n ION
Magnetism n FOND
Mat n FORM
Mate v SEX
Mated v SEX
Mating v SEX
Matriculate v EDUC
Matted v FORM
Medley n
Meet v
Meet v GRUP
Meld v
Meld v PLAY
Member n GRUP
Merge v
Mesh v
Meshed v
Meshing v

Met v
Met v GRUP
Midst n IN
Mingle v
Misalliance n BAD
Miscegenation n SEX
Miscellany n OPPO
Mishmash n BLUR
Mix v
Mix v BLUR
Mixture n
Montage n VIEW
Mortar n MTRL
Mucilage n
Nail n SHRP
Nailed v SHRP
Nailing v SHRP
Nestle v NEAR
Nestling v NEAR
Net n FORM
Nudge v
Nuzzle v BODY
Overlap v SIML
Pair n SIML
Palpate v MEDC
Parley n TALK
Participate v
Partner n
Paste n
Pasteboard n MTRL
Pasted v
Pasting v
Pat n EASY
Patchwork n FABR
Patted v EASY
Patting v EASY
Peck n
Peck n FOND
Peg v
Pertain v
Pertinence n CRUX
Pet v FOND
Petted v FOND
Petting v FOND
Pin n SHRP
Pinned v SHRP
Pinning v SHRP
Playmate n PLAY
Poke v BULG
Pool n GRUP
Pooled v GRUP
Pooling v GRUP
Potpourri n
Propinquity n NEAR
Rap v TALK
Rapped v TALK
Reception n AGRE
Recollect v GRUP

Recruit n
Rejoin v
Relate v SIML
Related j SIML
Relating v SIML
Relative j SIML
Relay n MECH
Relevant j SIML
Rendezvous n
Rider n LAW
Rivet v
Roommate n HOME
Rope n
Rub v VARY
Rubbed v VARY
Rubbing v VARY
Schoolmate n EDUC
Scramble v VARY
Screw n
Screw v SEX
Screwdriver n WORK
Seam n GARB
Seam n
Seamed v GARB
Seamed v
Seaming v GARB
Seaming v
Seams n GARB
Seams n
Seance n GRUP
Sew v GARB
Shackle v BLOK
Shake v VARY
Shaking v VARY
Shipmate n FLOW
Shoestring n GARB
Shook v VARY
Shuffle v VARY
Sidekick n SUB
Snap n HEAR
Snapped v HEAR
Snaps v HEAR
Snuggle v GLAD
Solder v HEAT
Span v
Spike n SHRP
Splice v
Staple v
Stapled v
Stapling v
Stick v
Sticker n WRIT
Sticky j
Stitch n SHRP
Strike v
Striking v
String n GRUP
Stringing v GRUP

Stroke n VARY
Stroked v VARY
Stroking v VARY
Struck v
Strung v GRUP
Strut n AID
Stuck v
Subjoin v
Switchboard n TALK
Syncopate v
Synthesis n
Synthetic j
Syzygy n
Tack n SHRP
Tactile j BODY
Tag v WRIT
Tag v
Tag v GO
Tangent n VARY
Tangle v BLOK
Tap n OPEN
Tap n
Tie v BLOK
Tied v BLOK
Tieing v BLOK
Together d
Toggle n MECH
Touch n
Touch n BODY
Touchball n PLAY
Trunk n PATH
Trust n MART
Turnbuckle n MECH
Twine n FABR
Twine v VARY
Twining v VARY
Tying v BLOK
Umbilical j BODY
Unified v
Unify v
Union n
Union n GRUP
Unite v
Uniting v
Unity n
Valence n ION
Visit v GO
Weave v
Weld v
With b
Wove v
Wrestle v DAMG
Yoke n FORM
Zip v GARB
Zipped v GARB
Zipper n GARB

Parts of speech: a article; b preposition; c conjunction; d adverb; f prefix; i interjection;
j adjective; n noun; p pronoun; r phrase; v verb.

Affianced j SEX
Ancestor n PAST
Aunt n LADY
Banns n SEX
Bastard n BAD
Betrothed j SEX
Bigamy n SEX
Brethren n MALE
Bride n LADY
Bridegroom n MALE
Brides n LADY
Brother n MALE
Brotherhood n MALE
Brotherinlaw n MALE
Child n YNG
Children n YNG
Clan n GRUP
Cognate j SIML
Conjugal j SEX
Conjugate v SEX
Connubial j SEX
Consanguine j JOIN
Consort n SEX
Cousin n
Dad n MALE
Dada n MALE
Daddy n MALE
Daughter n LADY
Descendant n BGIN
Descendent n BGIN
Endogamy n SEX
Engage v SEX
Family n GRUP
Father n MALE
Fatherinlaw n MALE
Fatherless j LACK

Fiance n MALE
Fiancee n LADY
Filial j YNG
Firstborn n BGIN
Folks n GRUP
Forebear n PAST
Forefather n PAST
Fraternal j MALE
Fraternity n MALE
Fratricide n DEAD
Frau n LADY
Genealogy n PAST
Godchild n YNG
Godfather n MALE
Godmother n LADY
Godparent n LEAD
Grandam n LADY
Grandchild n YNG
Granddaughter n LADY
Grandfather n MALE
Grandma n LADY
Grandmother n LADY
Grandpa n MALE
Grandparent n LEAD
Grandson n MALE
Granny n LADY
Groom n MALE
Housewife n LADY
Husband n MALE
Inlaw n
Interbreed v BGIN
Intermarry v SEX
Issue n BGIN
Kin n
Kindred j
Line n PAST

Lineage n PAST
Ma n LADY
Mamma n LADY
Mammy n LADY
Marital j SEX
Marriage n SEX
Married v SEX
Marry v SEX
Mate n SEX
Mater n LADY
Maternal j LADY
Matriarch n LADY
Matrimony n SEX
Missus n LADY
Mom n LADY
Monogamy n SEX
Mother n LADY
Motherinlaw n LADY
Motherless j LACK
Mrs n LADY
Nephew n MALE
Nepotism n FOND
Niece n LADY
Nubile j SEX
Nuptial j SEX
Offspring n YNG
Orphan n LACK
Pa n MALE
Papa n MALE
Parent n LEAD
Partner n
Paterfamilias n MALE
Paternity n MALE
Patriarch n MALE
Polyandry n SEX
Polygamy n SEX

Polygyny n SEX
Pop n MALE
Primogenitor n BGIN
Progenitor n BGIN
Progeny n BGIN
Propose v TALK
Quadruplet n SIML
Quintuplet n SIML
Related j
Relative n
Sibling n
Sister n LADY
Sisterhood n LADY
Sisterinlaw n LADY
Son n MALE
Soninlaw n MALE
Spouse n SEX
Stepbrother n MALE
Stepchild n YNG
Stepdaughter n LADY
Stepfather n MALE
Stepmother n LADY
Stepsister n LADY
Stepson n MALE
Trinity n HOLY
Triplet n SIML
Twin n SIML
Uncle n MALE
Wed v SEX
Widow n DEAD
Widowed v DEAD
Widower n DEAD
Wife n LADY
Wives n LADY

LACK

Abdicate v SEP
Abjure v AGGR
Abnegate v NO
Absence n SEP
Abstain v BLOK
Abstemious j BLOK
Abstention n BLOK
Abstinence n BLOK
Airless j VAPR
Albino n COLR
Apathy n PANG
Arid j FLOW
Arid j TRIV
Ascetic j
Asexual j SEX
Atrophy n WEAK
Bald j BODY
Bankrupt j MONY
Bare j
Barren j
Beg v MOTV
Beggar n MOTV
Begged v MOTV
Bereave v DEAD
Bereave v
Bereft v

Blank n
Blank n WRIT
Blank n DAMG
Blanked v
Blanked v WRIT
Broke j MONY
Careless j MOTV
Castrate v SEX
Celibacy n SEX
Childless j YNG
Colorless j COLR
Consume v END -
Consumption n END
Continence n BLOK
Continent j BLOK
Continently d BLOK
Cost n
Costly j
Dearth n
Deficiency n
Deficit n
Dehydrate v FLOW
Deplete v
Deprive v
Desiccate v FLOW
Destitute j

Devoid j
Dispense v
Dispensing v
Drought n FLOW
Dry j FLOW
Dumb j TALK
Ellipsis n TALK
Emaciate v LITL
Empty j
Empty v OUT
Exhaust v END
Exhausting v END
Exigency n
Expend v
Expending v
Expenditure n MONY
Expenditure n
Expense n MONY
Expense n
Expensive j
Famine n FOOD
Famine n
Famish v FOOD
Fast n FOOD
Fasted v FOOD
Fasting v FOOD

Fatherless j LEAD
Fatherless j KIN
Featherless j BODY
Forbear v BLOK
Forego v
Forfeit v
Forswear v AGGR
Gap n SEP
Gelding n SEX
Hairless j BODY
Headless j BODY
Headless j LEAD
Heedless j MOTV
Heelless j GARB
Hiatus n SEP
Hollow j
Homeless j HOME
Idle j REST
Impassive j MOTV
Impecunious j MONY
Impersonal j SOLE
Impoverish v WEAK
Improvident j
Indifference n TRIV
Indigent j
Infertile j BGIN

Insatiable j
Insolvent j MONY
Insufficient j WEAK
Intestate j LAW
Irreclaimable j
Irrecoverable j
Irredeemable j
Irreplaceable j
Lack n
Lacked v
Lacuna n
Lifeless j DEAD
Limbo n BLOK
Lose v
Lose v WEAK
Malnutrition n SICK
Mendicant n MOTV
Minus b
Mislay v
Miss v
Missed v
Missing v
Motherless j KIN
Motherless j LADY
Mute j TALK

Need n MOTV
Neglect v AGGR
Negligence n AGGR
Neuter j SEX
Omission n
Omit v
Orphan n KIN
Parch v HEAT
Paucity n LITL
Pauper n MONY
Peaked j PANG
Penniless j MONY
Penury n MONY
Poor j WEAK
Poor j MONY
Poorhouse n HOME
Poverty n MONY
Poverty n WEAK
Powerless j WEAK
Privation n
Red n COLR
Refrain v BLOK
Relinquish v SEP
Renounce v AGGR
Renunciation n AGGR

Sacrifice n DAMG
Sacrifice n HOLY
Sacrifice n
Sacrificial j HOLY
Sans b
Sap v WEAK
Sapped v WEAK
Schnorrer n MOTV
Short j LITL
Shortage n LITL
Shy j
Spend v MONY
Spend v
Squander v
Starve v FOOD
Sterile j BGIN
Toll n
Topless j UP
Topless j GARB
Unavailable j
Unclaimed j
Undernourished j FOOD
Underprivileged j WEAK
Uneducated j EDUC
Unemotional j MOTV

Unemployment n WORK
Unfilled j
Unfinished j
Uninhabited j LIVE
Unleavened j VEGT
Unman v MALE
Unmanned v MALE
Unmotivated j MOTV
Unpaid j MONY
Unsatiated j
Unsatisfied j
Unsettled j LIVE
Unsold j MONY
Untreated j AID
Vacancy n SEP
Vacating v SEP
Vacuum n VAPR
Void j
Waive v SEP
Waiver n SEP
Want v
Waste n TRIV
Waterless j FLOW
Without b

LADY

Abbess n HOLY
Actress n PLAY
Alumna n EDUC
Amazon n POWR
Androgynous j MALE
Aphrodite n HOLY
Aunt n KIN
Bag n HOLW
Ballerina n PLAY
Banshee n MYTH
Belle n GOOD
Bikini n GARB
Bitch n ANML
Bitch n BAD
Bitches n ANML
Bitches n BAD
Blackwidow n BUG
Bloomers n GARB
Blouse n GARB
Bodice n GARB
Bosom n BODY
Bossy n ANML
Boudoir n HOME
Bra n GARB
Bras n GARB
Brassiere n GARB
Breast n BODY
Bride n KIN
Bride n SEX
Brides n KIN
Brides n SEX
Bridesmaid n AID
Broad n
Broads n
Brownie n YNG
Bust n BODY
Bustle n GARB

Buxom j BODY
Cardinal n GARB
Cardinals n GARB
Chambermaid n AID
Cheesecake n VIEW
Chemise n GARB
Chick n YNG
Chiffon n GARB
Cinderella n MYTH
Clitoris n SEX
Coed n EDUC
Colleen n YNG
Commode n GARB
Compact n GARB
Concubine n SEX
Corsage n GARB
Corselet n GARB
Corset n GARB
Countess n LEAD
Courtesan n SEX
Cow n ANML
Cowgirl n ANML
Culottes n GARB
Curvaceous j VARY
Dam n ANML
Dame n LEAD
Dame n
Dams n ANML
Damsel n
Daughter n KIN
Dauphine n LEAD
Deaconess n HOLY
Debutante n BGIN
Decolletage n GARB
Distaff j
Diva n POWR
Doe n ANML

Does n ANML
Doll n GOOD
Dowager n PAST
Dress n GARB
Dresses n GARB
Duchess n LEAD
Effeminate j
Enchantress n FOND
Ewe n ANML
Female n
Feminine j
Fiancee n KIN
Fishwife n AGGR
Flapper n POWR
Frau n KIN
Geisha n PLAY
Girdle n GARB
Girl n YNG
Girlfriend n FOND
Goddess n HOLY
Godmother n KIN
Godmother n AID
Gorgon n BAD
Gorgon n MYTH
Governess n LEAD
Grace n MYTH
Grandam n KIN
Grandam n PAST
Granddaughter n KIN
Grandma n KIN
Grandma n AID
Grandmother n KIN
Grandmother n AID
Granny n KIN
Granny n PAST
Gynecology n MEDC
Hag n BAD

Hag n MYTH
Halter n GARB
Handmaid n AID
Harem n SEX
Heiress n HAVE
Hen n ANML
Hermaphrodite n MALE
Heroine n POWR
Hind n ANML
Hostess n AID
Housecoat n GARB
Housewife n HOME
Housewife n KIN
Hoyden n AGGR
Hussy n BAD
Hustle v SEX
Hymen n SEX
Ingenue n WEAK
Jade n
Jezebel n BAD
Ladies n
Ladies n LEAD
Lady n
Lady n LEAD
Lass n YNG
Laundress n CLEN
Leopardess n ANML
Lingerie n GARB
Lioness n ANML
Ma n KIN
Ma n AID
Maam n
Madam n
Maharani n LEAD
Maid n
Maid n AID
Maiden n YNG

Majorette n PLAY
Mamma n KIN
Mamma n AID
Mammary j BODY
Mammy n KIN
Mammy n AID
Mare n ANML
Masseuse n AID
Mater n KIN
Mater n AID
Maternal j KIN
Maternal j AID
Matriarch n LEAD
Matriarch n KIN
Matron n AID
Menopause n SOMA
Menstrual j SOMA
Mermaid n MYTH
Midwife n BGIN
Milady n
Minx n POWR
Miss n
Missus n KIN
Mistress n LEAD
Mistress n SEX
Mom n KIN

Mom n AID
Mother n KIN
Mother n AID
Mother n HOLY
Motherinlaw n KIN
Motherinlaw n AID
Motherless j LACK
Mrs n KIN
Mrs n
Ms n
Niece n KIN
Nun n HOLY
Nurse n AID
Nylon n GARB
Nymph n MYTH
Ovary n SOMA
Ovulate v SOMA
Pannier n GARB
Panties n GARB
Panty n GARB
Parasol n GARB
Period n SOMA
Petticoat n GARB
Pillbox n GARB
Placenta n SOMA
Poetess n TALK

Premiere n LEAD
Priestess n HOLY
Primadonna n LEAD
Princess n LEAD
Prioress n HOLY
Pump n GARB
Queen n LEAD
Sari n GARB
Seamstress n GARB
Shawl n GARB
Shift n GARB
Siren n DAMG
Sister n KIN
Sister n HOLY
Sisterhood n KIN
Sisterinlaw n KIN
Skirt n GARB
Slip n GARB
Slut n DIRT
Sow n ANML
Spinster n SOLE
Stepdaughter n KIN
Stepmother n KIN
Stepmother n AID
Stepsister n KIN
Stewardess n AID

Tabbies n TALK
Tart n BAD
Teat n BODY
Tomato n VEGT
Tomboy n MALE
Udder n BODY
Undies n GARB
Vagina n SEX
Venus n MYTH
Virgin n HOLY
Virgin n SEX
Vulva n SEX
Waitress n AID
Wench n
Widow n DEAD
Widow n BUG
Widowed v DEAD
Wife n KIN
Wife n SEX
Witch n BAD
Wives n KIN
Wives n SEX
Woman n
Womb n SOMA
Women n

LARG

Abroad d
Access n
Accession n JOIN
Accretion n JOIN
Accrue v
Accumulate v BULG
Accumulate v HAVE
Across b
Add v NUMR
Add v JOIN
Added v NUMR
Added v JOIN
Addendum n JOIN
Adder n NUMR
Adding v NUMR
Adding v JOIN
Addition n JOIN
Addition n NUMR
Additive n JOIN
Aggrandize v
Amass v HAVE
Amass v
Ample j MUCH
Amplify v
Amply d MUCH
Appreciable j
Appreciate v
Astronomical j ASTR
Augment v
Beefy j BODY
Big j
Big j POWR
Big j AID
Big j BULG
Blew v
Bloom v POWR

Bloomed v POWR
Blossom v POWR
Blow v
Bodies n
Body n
Boom n
Boomed v
Boundless j
Breadth n
Broad j
Broadcast n TALK
Broadside n FORM
Bulk n
Bulkier j
Bulky j
Bumper j
Burlier j
Burly j
Capacious j
Capacity n
Capital j WRIT
Capitalize v WRIT
Chubby j BODY
Chunk n SOME
Coarse j
Collect v BULG
Colossal j
Colossus n FORM
Commodious j AID
Compound v JOIN
Considerable j MUCH
Corpulence n BODY
Crane v
Craned v
Craning v
Crescendo n MUSC

Crescent j
Cumulate v HAVE
Cumulate v BULG
Cumuli n BULG
Cumulus n BULG
Curd n SIP
Curdle v SIP
Dense j
Deploy v GO
Develop v VARY
Diffuse j
Diffuse v GO
Dilate v
Dimension n
Disseminate v OPEN
Distend v
Dumpier j LITL
Dumpy j LITL
Elephantine j ANML
Elongate v
Endomorph n BODY
Enhance v GOOD
Enlarge v
Enlargement n
Enlargement n VIEW
Enormity n
Enormity n BAD
Enormous j
Escalate v
Exaggerate v FALS
Exceed v
Exceeding v
Excess n
Exorbitant j
Expand v
Expanse n

Extend v
Extend v GO
Extension n
Extension n GO
Extensive j MUCH
Extent n
Extreme j EMPH
Fan v
Fanned v
Farreaching j AFAR
Fat j BODY
Fat j
Flare v
Flourish v POWR
Flourished v POWR
Flourishing v POWR
Fullgrown j WHOL
Fulllength j WHOL
Gain v HAVE
Gained v HAVE
Gainer n HAVE
Gains v HAVE
Gangling j WEAK
Germinate v BGIN
Giant n
Gigantic j
Gigantism n SICK
Goliath n
Goodly j MUCH
Great j
Grew v VARY
Gross j
Grow v VARY
Grown v VARY
Grownup n POWR
Growth n VARY

Growth n BODY
Heavier j
Heavy j
Heavyweight n MSMT
Heft n
Heftier j
Hefty j
Heighten v UP
Huge j
Hulk n BODY
Hulk v
Hulked v
Hulking v
Huskier j POWR
Huskies n POWR
Huskiest j POWR
Husky j POWR
Hyperbole n TALK
Hyperventilate v SOMA
Illimitable j WHOL
Immeasurable j
Immense j
Incalculable j BLUR
Increase n
Increment n
Inestimable j IDEA
Infinite j EVER
Infinities n EVER
Infinity n EVER
Inflation n MONY
Inordinate j

Jumbo j
Lank j LITL
Large j
Large n OPEN
Macroscopic j VIEW
Magnified v
Magnify v
Magniloquence n TALK
Mammoth j
Mantle v
Massive j
Maximal j
Maximize v
Maximum j
Multiple n NUMR
Multiply v
Multiply v NUMR
Mushroom v QUIK
Mushroomed v QUIK
Mushrooming v QUIK
Nationwide j GRUP
Obese j BODY
Overabundant j MUCH
Overcapacity n BULG
Overcompensate v MONY
Overcompensate v SIML
Overcook v HEAT
Overcrowd v GRUP
Overdevelop v VARY
Overdid v
Overdo v

Overdone v
Overdose n SOME
Overestimate v IDEA
Overextend v
Overheat v HEAT
Overindulge v AID
Overpay v MONY
Overpopulate v GRUP
Overprice v MONY
Oversize j
Overweight j MSMT
Plump j BODY
Plumper j BODY
Plumpest j BODY
Plus b NUMR
Ponderous j
Portly j BODY
Positive j
Prolong v EVER
Propagate v BGIN
Propagate v GO
Protract v EVER
Pudgy j LITL
Puff v BULG
Pyramid v FORM
Reach n
Redouble v
Redound v AID
Scope n
Snowball v
Spacious j

Span n
Spread n
Spread n FOOD
Spreading v
Squat j LITL
Stocky j BODY
Stout j BODY
Stretch v
Stubby j LITL
Supermarket n MART
Supplement n
Swell v BULG
Swell n FLOW
Swollen j BULG
Tall j
Tall j FOOL
Thick j
Treble j NUMR
Tremendous j
Vast j
Voluminous j
Wax v
Whale n ANML
Whopper n
Wide j
Widespread j
Worldwide j WHOL
Yawn v OPEN

LAW

Act n
Action n
Adjudge v IDEA
Adjudicate v IDEA
Advocate n
Alderman n LEAD
Anarchy n BLUR
Appellate j
Aristocracy n LEAD
Arraign v AGGR
Arrest v BLOK
Attach v BLOK
Attache n LEAD
Attached v BLOK
Attaches v BLOK
Attorney n
Autocracy n LEAD
Bail n OPEN
Bar n GRUP
Beat n PATH
Bench n POWR
Bicameral j LEAD
Bill n WRIT
Bluelaw n BLOK
Bobbies n
Bobby n
Book v WRIT
Booked v WRIT
Booking v WRIT
Books v WRIT
Bull n

Bulls n
Bureaucracy n LEAD
Case n
Caucus n GRUP
Chamber n GRUP
Chancellery n LEAD
Chancellor n LEAD
Chancery n LEAD
Charter n WRIT
Civics n GRUP
Civil j GRUP
Cloture n END
Codefendant n SIML
Commit v GRUP
Committed v GRUP
Commons n GRUP
Congress n LEAD
Congressional j LEAD
Congressman n LEAD
Constable n LEAD
Constabulary n LEAD
Constituency n GRUP
Constituent n GRUP
Constitution n
Consul n LEAD
Cop n
Copyright v HAVE
Counsel n AID
Court n HOME
Courthouse n HOME
Courtsmartial n

Courtroom n HOME
Courts n HOME
Criminology n CRIM
Custom n
Deed n WRIT
Defendant n
Dejure j
Democracy n GRUP
Democrat n GRUP
Depose v TALK
Deposing v TALK
Deposition n TALK
Detective n
Devise v MOTV
Diet n LEAD
Diplomacy n POWR
Diplomat n LEAD
Disbar v SEP
Dock n REST
Docket n WRIT
Embargo n BLOK
Enact v
Extradite v GO
Federal j GRUP
Flatfoot n BODY
Forensic j
Franchise n MOTV
Fuzz n
Garnish v BLOK
Gendarme n
Gerrymander v FALS

Govern v LEAD
Governed v LEAD
Government n LEAD
Governor n LEAD
Gubernatorial j LEAD
Halakah n HOLY
Heteronomy n SUB
House n GRUP
Impeach v AGGR
Indict v AGGR
Injunction n BLOK
Inquest n OPEN
Inspector n OPEN
Intestate j LACK
Judge n LEAD
Judicial j
Junta n GRUP
Juries n GRUP
Jurisdiction n LEAD
Jurisprudence n IDEA
Juror n GRUP
Jury n GRUP
Justice n LEAD
Kangaroo n FALS
Law n
Lawabiding j GOOD
Lawbreaker n CRIM
Lawmaker n LEAD
Laws n
Lawsuit n MOTV
Lawyer n

Legacy n AID
Legal j
Legislate v LEAD
Legitimacy n TRUE
Lien n MOTV
Litigation n OPPO
Lobbies n GRUP
Lobby n GRUP
Magistrate n LEAD
Mayor n LEAD
Measure n
Minister n LEAD
Ministry n LEAD
Mistrial n FALS
Municipal j PLAC
Naturalize v NEAR
Nightstick n DAMG
Notary n WRIT
Officer n LEAD
Ordain v LEAD
Ordinance n

Parliament n GRUP
Patent n HAVE
Patented v HAVE
Patenting v HAVE
Patents v HAVE
Patrolman n MALE
Penal j CRIM
Pinch n BLOK
Plainclothes j GARB
Plaintiff n MOTV
Plebiscite n MOTV
Police n
Policeman n MALE
Politburo n LEAD
Politician n LEAD
Politics n LEAD
Polities n GRUP
Polity n GRUP
Portfolio n LEAD
Posse n GRUP
Prefect n LEAD

Premier n LEAD
Presidency n LEAD
Presidium n LEAD
Probate n TRUE
Probating v TRUE
Process n WRIT
Prosecute v AGGR
Quorum n GRUP
Ranger n
Receiver n HAVE
Referendum n GRUP
Represent v SIML
Republic n GRUP
Rider n JOIN
Senate n LEAD
Sentence n TALK
Sheriff n LEAD
Sleuth n
Solicitor n
Statesman n LEAD
Statute n WRIT

Subpoena n MOTV
Sue v MOTV
Sued v MOTV
Suing v MOTV
Summons n MOTV
Tort n BAD
Trial n TRUE
Tribunal n LEAD
Tried v TRUE
Trooper n
Try v TRUE
Unconstitutional j OPPO
Unlawful j CRIM
Unlawful j OPPO
Verdict n IDEA
Warden n LEAD
Warrant n WRIT
Will v MOTV
Willed v MOTV
Willing v MOTV
Writ n WRIT

LEAD

Abbe n HOLY
Abbot n HOLY
Above b UP
Absolutism n WHOL
Adjutant n
Administer v
Administration n
Admiral n FLOW
Alderman n LAW
Almighty n HOLY
Ambassador n
Apostle n HOLY
Apostolic j HOLY
Arbiter n IDEA
Arbitrate v IDEA
Archangel n HOLY
Archbishop n HOLY
Aristocracy n LAW
Aristocracy n GRUP
Aristocrat n GRUP
Ascendancy n UP
Attache n LAW
Auspice n AID
Authority n
Authorize v AGRE
Autocracy n LAW
Autocracy n SOLE
Baton n FORM
Bicameral j LAW
Bishop n HOLY
Board n GRUP
Boards n GRUP
Boss n
Bossy j
Brass n
Brigadier n
Bureaucracy n LAW
Cabinet n GRUP

Cadmus n MYTH
Caesar n
Caliph n HOLY
Canon n HOLY
Canonical j HOLY
Canonize v HOLY
Capital j PLAC
Capitol n HOME
Captain n
Cardinal n HOLY
Cardinals n HOLY
Celestial j HOLY
Centurion n
Chair n
Chairman n
Chancellery n HOME
Chancellery n LAW
Chancellor n LAW
Chancery n LAW
Chancery n HOME
Chaplain n HOLY
Charge n MOTV
Charisma n MOTV
Chef n FOOD
Chief j
Chieftain n
Christ n HOLY
Coach n PLAY
Cock n
Cocks n
Cockswain n VEHC
Colonel n
Command v
Commanded v
Commandeer v HAVE
Commandment n
Commandment n HOLY
Commissar n

Commissariat n GRUP
Commissaries n
Commissary n
Commission n
Commissioned v
Commissioner n
Commodore n FLOW
Comptroller n MONY
Condescend v AGRE
Condominium n GRUP
Conduct v
Conducting v
Congress n LAW
Congressional j LAW
Congressman n LAW
Constable n LAW
Constabulary n LAW
Consul n LAW
Control v
Controlled v
Controller n MONY
Controller n
Coordinate v
Coronary j GARB
Coronation n GARB
Coroner n DEAD
Coronet n GARB
Corporation n GRUP
Council n GRUP
Councilor n GRUP
Count n MALE
Countess n LADY
Coxswain n VEHC
Croupier n PLAY
Crown n GARB
Curator n AID
Cure n HOLY
Cybernetic j MECH

Dad n MALE
Dada n MALE
Daddy n MALE
DalaiLama n HOLY
Dame n LADY
Dauphin n MALE
Dauphine n LADY
Dean n
Dean n EDUC
Decree n TALK
Deify v HOLY
Deign v AGRE
Deism n HOLY
Deity n HOLY
Demagogue n FALS
Demigod n HOLY
Despot n AGGR
Devil n BAD
Diadem n GARB
Dictate v TALK
Dictator n
Diet n LAW
Diocese n HOLY
Diplomat n LAW
Direct v
Direction n
Directive n
Director n
Disciplinarian n
Discipline n
Discipline v DAMG
Divine j HOLY
Divinity n HOLY
Domain n HAVE
Domain n
Dominant j
Dominate v
Domineer v

Parts of speech: a article; b preposition; c conjunction; d adverb; f prefix; i interjection;
        j adjective; n noun; p pronoun; r phrase; v verb.

Dominion n HAVE
Don n
Driver n VEHC
Duchess n LADY
Duke n MALE
Dynasty n
Earl n MALE
Earldom n
Edict n TALK
Educator n EDUC
Elder n PAST
Embassy n
Emcee n PLAY
Emperor n MALE
Empire n
Employer n WORK
Empower v POWR
Engineer n VEHC
Enjoin v
Ennoble v GOOD
Ensign n FLOW
Executive n
Executor n
Faculty n EDUC
Fascism n GRUP
Father n MALE
Father n HOLY
Fatherinlaw n MALE
Fatherland n PLAC
Fatherless j LACK
Feudal j SUB
Fiat n TALK
Figurehead n FALS
Flagship n FLOW
Foreman n WORK
Gavel n HEAR
General n
Gentry n GRUP
God n HOLY
Godfather n MALE
Godparent n KIN
Govern v
Govern v LAW
Governed v
Governed v LAW
Governess n LADY
Government n LAW
Governor n LAW
Governor n MECH
Grandfather n MALE
Grandpa n MALE
Grandparent n KIN
Gubernatorial j LAW
Guidance n AID
Guide n AID
Guru n HOLY
Handle v BODY
Head n
Headed v
Heading v
Headless j LACK
Headquarters n HOME
Heads v
Helios n MYTH
Helm n FORM

Hierarchy n FORW
Highness n
Hohenzollern n GRUP
Imperative j
Imperial j
Imperious j
Impresario n PLAY
Instructor n EDUC
Invest v BGIN
Investing v BGIN
Jehovah n HOLY
Jesus n HOLY
Judge n IDEA
Judge n LAW
Jupiter n MYTH
Jurisdiction n LAW
Justice n LAW
Kaiser n MALE
King n MALE
King n PLAY
Kremlin n PLAC
Krishna n HOLY
Ladies n LADY
Lady n LADY
Lawmaker n LAW
Lead v FORW
Leader n FORW
Led v FORW
Legation n GRUP
Legation n HOME
Legislate v LAW
Lieutenant n
Lord n MALE
Lord n HOLY
Maestro n MUSC
Magistrate n LAW
Magnate n
Maharaja n MALE
Maharani n LADY
Majestic j GOOD
Majesties n
Majesty n
Major n
Majordomo n AID
Majors n
Maker n HOLY
Maladminister v BAD
Manage v
Mandarin n
Mandate n
Mandatory j
Manipulate v
Marshal n
Master n POWR
Master n EDUC
Mastered v POWR
Mastering v POWR
Masterpiece n POWR
Mate n FLOW
Matriarch n LADY
Mayor n LAW
Mentor n EDUC
Mikado n
Milord n MALE
Minister n HOLY

Minister n LAW
Ministry n HOLY
Ministry n LAW
Misdirect v FALS
Misgovern v FALS
Mismanage v FALS
Mistress n LADY
Mohammed n HOLY
Monarch n
Monitor v
Monotheism n HOLY
Nobility n GOOD
Noble j GOOD
Noncom n
Office n
Officer n
Officer n LAW
Official n
Officiate v
Oligarchy n GRUP
Oracle n HOLY
Ordain v LAW
Ordain v HOLY
Ordain v END
Order n MOTV
Overlord n
Overmaster v POWR
Oversaw v VIEW
Oversee v VIEW
Overseer n
Pa n MALE
Padre n HOLY
Padrone n
Palace n HOME
Palatial j HOME
Pantheon n HOLY
Papa n MALE
Papacy n HOLY
Papal j HOLY
Paramount j
Parent n KIN
Parent n BGIN
Parricide n DAMG
Parson n HOLY
Pasha n
Pastor n HOLY
Pastorate n HOLY
Paterfamilias n MALE
Paternity n MALE
Patriarch n MALE
Patriarch n HOLY
Patrician j
Patricide n DEAD
Patron n AID
Peer n
Pharaoh n
Pilot n VEHC
Pilot n
Plenipotentiary n
Plutocracy n GRUP
Podium n FORM
Politburo n LAW
Politician n LAW
Politics n LAW
Pontifical j HOLY

Pop n MALE
Pope n HOLY
Portfolio n LAW
Potentate n
Precept n IDEA
Preceptor n EDUC
Predominance n
Prefect n LAW
Prelate n HOLY
Premier j
Premier n LAW
Premiere n LADY
Presbyter n HOLY
Prescription n AID
Preside v
Presidency n LAW
Presiding v
Presidium n LAW
Priest n HOLY
Priesthood n HOLY
Primacy n FORW
Primadonna n LADY
Primate n HOLY
Prince n MALE
Princes n MALE
Princess n LADY
Principal n EDUC
Principality n PLAC
Prior n HOLY
Proctor v EDUC
Professor n EDUC
Protagonist n
Provost n
Purser n FLOW
Quarterback n PLAY
Quartermaster n AID
Queen n LADY
Queen n PLAY
Rabbi n HOLY
Rajah n MALE
Ran v
Referee n IDEA
Regal j
Regime n GRUP
Regiment v GRUP
Regulate v
Reich n GRUP
Reign n
Rein n BLOK
Ringleader n GRUP
Royal j
Royalty n
Rudder n FORM
Rule n
Ruled v
Ruler n
Ruling v
Run v
Sachem n
Sagamore n
Sahib n MALE
Sanhedrin n GRUP
Satan n BAD
Saturn n MYTH
Savior n HOLY

Scepter n FORM
Schoolmaster n EDUC
Schoolteacher n EDUC
Scoutmaster n GRUP
Secretary n WRIT
See n HOLY
Senate n LAW
Senior j
Senior j PAST
Senior n EDUC
Sergeant n

Sheriff n LAW
Sovereign n
Soviet n GRUP
Standardbearer n
Statesman n LAW
Steer v
Steered v
Steering v
Steers v
Stellar j
Stepfather n MALE

Steward n AID
Subjugate v SUB
Superior j
Superiors n
Supervise v
Supremacy n
Synod n GRUP
Taskmaster n WORK
Teacher n EDUC
Throne n FURN
Totalitarian j GRUP

Trainer n EDUC
Treasurer n MONY
Tribunal n LAW
Tutor n EDUC
Tycoon n
Tyranny n AGGR
Umpire n PLAY
Uranus n MYTH
Warden n LAW
Zeus n MYTH

LITL

Abate v
Abbreviate v
Abridge v
Abstract n IDEA
Attenuate v WEAK
Bead n FORM
Belittle v AGGR
Birdseye j VIEW
Bit n SOME
Bit n MONY
Brevity n
Brief j
Brief n TALK
Briefs n TALK
Briefs n GARB
Capillary j HOLW
Capsule n HOLW
Chip n SEP
Chip n FOOD
Chip n SIML
Chipped v SEP
Chipping v SEP
Collapse v VARY
Collapsible j VARY
Compact j
Compendium n WRIT
Compress v BLOK
Concise j
Condense v
Contract v
Contracting v
Contraction n
Contractive j
Contractor n
Crumb n FOOD
Crumb n SOME
Curt j AGGR
Curtail v BLOK
Cut v SHRP
Cutting v SHRP
Decrease n
Decrement n
Decrescendo n MUSC
Decrescent j WEAK
Deflate v VAPR
Depreciable j CRUX
Depreciate v CRUX
Devaluate v
Devaluate v WEAK
Dice v SHRP
Digest n TALK

Diminish v
Diminutive j
Discount v MONY
Discounted v MONY
Divot n ERTH
Dock v
Docked v
Dot n WRIT
Dot n
Drop n FLOW
Dumpier j LARG
Dumpy j LARG
Dwarf v
Dwindle v
Ectomorph n BODY
Elf n MYTH
Elves n MYTH
Emaciate v LACK
Epitome n TALK
Epitome n
Epitomize v
Extenuate v
Few j SOME
Filament n FORM
Fine j
Finer j
Finest j
Frugal j HAVE
Globule n FORM
Gnome n MYTH
Grain n
Granule n FORM
Grate v VARY
Grating v VARY
Grind v VARY
Grinder n VARY
Grinds v VARY
Ground v VARY
Infinitesmal j
Jot n
Laconic j TALK
Lank j LARG
Lean j
Least j
Less n
Lick n SOME
Little j
Low j DOWN
Lozenge n FOOD
Meager j
Measly j BAD

Microanalysis n IDEA
Microcosm n WHOL
Microorganism n LIVE
Midget n
Mince n FOOD
Mince v SEP
Mincemeat n FOOD
Miniature j
Minimize v
Minimum n
Minority n NUMR
Minute j
Mite n BUG
Mite n
Modicum n SOME
Morsel n FOOD
Mote n DIRT
Narrow j
Narrows n FLOW
Narrows v
Nibble v FOOD
Nutshell n
Parsimony n HAVE
Particle n SOME
Patties n FOOD
Patty n FOOD
Paucity n LACK
Pellet n
Petite j
Pill n FOOD
Pip n
Pips n
Pipsqueak n WEAK
Pittance n MONY
Polkadot j FORM
Pony n
Precis n TALK
Preshrunk j FORW
Pudgy j LARG
Pulverize v VARY
Pygmy n
Rare j
Rarefy v
Reduce v
Resume n IDEA
Ribbon n
Runt n
Scant j
Scarce j
Scarcely d
Scrawny j BODY

Shade n
Shallow j
Shoestring n
Short j
Short j LACK
Shortage n LACK
Shortcircuit n PATH
Shortcut n PATH
Shorten v
Shorthand n WRIT
Shortlived j TIME
Shortly d TIME
Shorts n GARB
Shortsighted j VIEW
Shrank v
Shrimp n
Shrink v
Shrivel v VARY
Skimp v
Skinny j BODY
Slender j
Slight j
Slight n AGGR
Slighted v AGGR
Slighting v AGGR
Slightly d
Slim j
Sliver n SEP
Small j
Smattering n
Snatch n
Spare j
Sparse j
Speck n
Speck n DIRT
Splinter n SEP
Squat j LARG
Stipple v COLR
Stub n
Stub n WRIT
Stubbed j
Stubby j LARG
Subtle j
Succinct j
Summary j
Synopsis n TALK
Taciturn j TALK
Taper n
Tapered v
Tapering v
Telescope v

Terse j SHRP
Thin j
Thumbnail j BODY
Tinier j

Tiny j
Uncrowded j GRUP
Wane v WEAK
Wane v

Waning v WEAK
Waning v
Wee j
Whit n TRIV

Whittle v SHRP
Wisp n SOME

LIVE

Abide v EVER
Abode n HOME
Alive j
Animate v QUIK
Being n
Board n FOOD
Boarded v FOOD
Boarder n FOOD
Boarding v FOOD
Boards v FOOD
Coexist v JOIN
Cohabit v JOIN
Cotenant n SIML
Denizen n
Domicile n HOME
Dwell v HOME
Earthling n ERTH
Ecology n WHOL
Enliven v QUIK

Exist v
Existence n
Existentialist n SOLE
Extant j
Habitable j
Habitant n
Habitat n
Immortal j EVER
Imperishable j EVER
Inhabit v IN
Inmate n IN
Life n
Life n QUIK
Lifeblood n SOMA
Lifegiving j AID
Lifelike j SIML
Lifeline n AID
Lifelong j EVER
Lifesaver n AID

Lifesize j SIML
Lifetime n TIME
Live v
Livelihood n AID
Liveliness n QUIK
Lively j QUIK
Liven v QUIK
Lives v
Living n
Living n AID
Lodger n HOME
Longevity n EVER
Microorganism n LITL
Mortal j DEAD
Organic j SOMA
Organism n
Organism n BUG
Preexist v PAST
Reincarnation n DEAD

Reside v HOME
Residence n HOME
Resurrect v DEAD
Resuscitate v DEAD
Revive v DEAD
Settle v EVER
Settlement n EVER
Subsist v
Survive v
Tenant n
Uninhabited j LACK
Unsettled j LACK
Viable j POWR
Vital j CRUX
Vivendi n
Vivify v QUIK

MALE

Actor n PLAY
Adonis n GOOD
Alumni n EDUC
Alumnus n EDUC
Androgynous j LADY
Apollo n MYTH
Apollo n GOOD
Bachelor n SOLE
Ball n SEX
Beau n FOND
Billygoat n ANML
Blade n POWR
Boy n YNG
Boyfriend n FOND
Brave n POWR
Breeches n GARB
Brethren n KIN
Bridegroom n KIN
Bridegroom n SEX
Brother n KIN
Brother n HOLY
Brotherhood n KIN
Brotherinlaw n KIN
Buck n ANML
Buck n
Bull n ANML
Bulls n ANML
Busboy n AID
Businessman n MART
Buster n
Butler n AID
Cadet n YNG
Chanticleer n ANML
Chap n
Cock n ANML
Cocks n ANML

Confrere n JOIN
Count n LEAD
Cowboy n ANML
Cowpuncher n ANML
Dad n KIN
Dad n LEAD
Dada n KIN
Dada n LEAD
Daddy n KIN
Daddy n LEAD
Dauphin n LEAD
Derby n GARB
Doorman n AID
Duke n LEAD
Earl n LEAD
Emperor n LEAD
Erection n SEX
Esquire n
Father n KIN
Father n LEAD
Fatherinlaw n KIN
Fatherinlaw n LEAD
Fellow n
Fiance n KIN
Fireman n HEAT
Fisherman n FLOW
Footman n AID
Fraternal j KIN
Fraternity n KIN
Friar n HOLY
Frontiersman n FORW
Gaffer n PAST
Gent n
Gentleman n GOOD
Gigolo n SEX
Godfather n KIN

Godfather n LEAD
Grandfather n KIN
Grandfather n LEAD
Grandpa n KIN
Grandpa n LEAD
Grandson n KIN
Groom n KIN
Groom n SEX
Gunman n DAMG
Guy n
Hangman n DEAD
Henchman n SUB
Hermaphrodite n LADY
Hero n POWR
Highwayman n CRIM
Homo n
Homo n GRUP
Husband n KIN
Husband n SEX
Jack n
Kaiser n LEAD
Kilt n GARB
King n LEAD
Lad n YNG
Leo n ANML
Lord n LEAD
Maharaja n LEAD
Male n
Man n
Manhood n
Manservant n SUB
Masculine j
Masseur n AID
Master n YNG
Men n
Milkman n SIP

Milord n LEAD
Milt n SOMA
Mister n
Monk n HOLY
Mr n
Nephew n KIN
Pa n KIN
Pa n LEAD
Pants n GARB
Papa n KIN
Papa n LEAD
Paterfamilias n KIN
Paterfamilias n LEAD
Paternity n KIN
Paternity n LEAD
Patriarch n KIN
Patriarch n LEAD
Patrolman n LAW
Penis n SEX
Phallic j SEX
Plainsman n ERTH
Plusfours n GARB
Policeman n LAW
Pop n KIN
Pop n LEAD
Prince n LEAD
Princes n LEAD
Prostate j SOMA
Queer n SEX
Rajah n LEAD
Ram n ANML
Rams n ANML
Sahib n LEAD
Sandman n REST
Satyr n MYTH
Satyr n SEX

Satyriasis n SEX
Seaman n FLOW
Seamen n FLOW
Semen n SOMA
Shirt n GARB
Sir n
Sire n BGIN
Siring v BGIN
Son n KIN
Soninlaw n KIN

Sperm n SOMA
Stag n ANML
Stallion n ANML
Steer n ANML
Stepbrother n KIN
Stepfather n KIN
Stepfather n LEAD
Stepson n KIN
Stripling n YNG
Superman n POWR

Tails n GARB
Testes n SEX
Testicle n SEX
Testis n SEX
Tom j ANML
Tomboy n LADY
Trouser j GARB
Trunks n GARB
Tuxedo n GARB
Uncle n KIN

Unman v LACK
Unmanned v LACK
Valet n AID
Virile j POWR
Waiter n AID
Widower n DEAD
Workman n WORK
Yeoman n

MART

Account n MONY
Accountant n NUMR
Actuaries n WRIT
Actuary n WRIT
Amortize v MONY
Auction n MONY
Automat n FOOD
Bakery n FOOD
Bank n MONY
Bar n SIP
Barber n SHRP
Bargain n AGRE
Bargain n TRIV
Barter v
Bazaar n
Bond n MONY
Bonded v MONY
Bonding v MONY
Bookkeeper n WRIT
Bookseller n WRIT
Bookstore n WRIT
Bootery n GARB
Boutique n
Brand n VIEW
Broker n MONY
Brothel n SEX
Business n
Businessman n MALE
Butcher n FOOD
Buy v MONY
Cabaret n PLAY
Cafe n FOOD
Cafeteria n FOOD
Canteen n FOOD
Capital j MONY
Capitalism n MONY
Capitalize v MONY
Cargo n VEHC
Carrier n VEHC
Cashier n MONY
Casino n PLAY
Charter v MONY
Clerical j WRIT
Clerk n WRIT
Client n MONY
Clothier n GARB
Collateral n AID
Commerce n
Commercial j
Commissaries n HOME
Commissary n HOME
Commodity n

Companies n GRUP
Company n GRUP
Concern n GRUP
Concession n AID
Contraband j CRIM
Corporation n GRUP
Costermonger n FOOD
Counter n FORM
Counters n FORM
Credit n MONY
Creditor n MONY
Curb n
Custom j
Customer n MONY
Deal v
Dealer n
Dealing v
Deals v
Dealt v
Debenture n MONY
Debit n MONY
Debt n MONY
Delicatessen n FOOD
Dicker v TALK
Diner n FOOD
Dive n SIP
Dividend n MONY
Dressmaker n GARB
Druggist n MEDC
Drugstore n MEDC
Duties n MONY
Duty n MONY
Economic j MONY
Economist n MONY
Economy n MONY
Emporium n HOME
Engage v MONY
Establishment n
Exchange n MONY
Excise n MONY
Export v OUT
Factor n AID
Finance v MONY
Firm n
Fiscal j MONY
Fishmonger n FOOD
Flophouse n HOME
Franchise n
Freight n VEHC
Furrier n GARB
Glazier n VIEW
Goods n FABR

Grill n FOOD
Grocer n FOOD
Haberdasher n GARB
Hawk v MONY
Hawked v MONY
Hawking v MONY
Hire v MONY
Honkytonk n SIP
Hosier n GARB
Hostel n HOME
Hotel n HOME
Huckster n MONY
Import n IN
Importation n IN
Incorporate v JOIN
Industrial j WORK
Industries n WORK
Industry n WORK
Inn n HOME
Innkeeper n HOME
Insure v AID
Interest n MONY
Inventory n HAVE
Invest v MONY
Investing v MONY
Invoice n WRIT
Ironmonger n ERTH
Jeweler n GOOD
Landlord n HOME
Laundries n CLEN
Laundromat n CLEN
Laundry n CLEN
Lease v MONY
Let v MONY
Letting v MONY
Line n VEHC
Lumberyard n MTRL
Luncheonette n FOOD
Manifest n WRIT
Manufacture v WORK
Market n MONY
Market n FOOD
Marketplace n PLAC
Mart n
Merchandise n
Merchant n
Millinery n GARB
Monger n
Mortgage v MONY
Mortician n DEAD
Motel n HOME
Notion n TRIV

Novelty n NEW
Office n HOME
Overhead n MONY
Parlor n HOME
Patron n AID
Pawn v MONY
Pawned v MONY
Pawning v MONY
Peddle v MONY
Pharmacist n MEDC
Pharmacy n MEDC
Pizzeria n FOOD
Plant n WORK
Proprietor n HAVE
Pub n SIP
Purchase n MONY
Readymade j
Register n MECH
Rent n MONY
Rented v MONY
Renter n MONY
Renting v MONY
Rents v MONY
Restaurant n FOOD
Retail n MONY
Revenue n MONY
Sale n MONY
Saloon n SIP
Security n MONY
Sell v MONY
Shareholder n HAVE
Shoemaker n GARB
Shop n HOME
Shop n WORK
Shopkeeper n HAVE
Stall n HOME
Stand n HOME
Stationer n WRIT
Stock n MONY
Stockholder n HAVE
Stockmarket n MONY
Stocks n MONY
Store n HOME
Storekeeper n HAVE
Subcontract v AGRE
Sublease v MONY
Sublet v MONY
Supermarket n LARG
Syndicate n GRUP
Tailor n GARB
Tap n SIP
Tariff n MONY

Tavern n SIP
Teller n MONY
Trade n
Trade n WORK

Trademark n VIEW
Trading v
Traffic n
Truck n

Trust n JOIN
Undertaker n DEAD
Vendor n MONY
Ware n

Warehouse n HOME
Whitecollar j GARB
Wholesale j MONY

MECH

Accelerator n QUIK
Action n
Apparatus n
Appliance n FURN
Appliance n
Arbor n
Arm n DAMG
Armament n DAMG
Armature n
Armed v DAMG
Arming v DAMG
Arms n DAMG
Artillery n DAMG
Aspirator n OUT
Atomizer n VAPR
Automate v
Automatic j
Automatic n DAMG
Automatism n
Axle n VEHC
Balance n MSMT
Batteries n ION
Battery n ION
Bearing n EASY
Bearings n EASY
Beetle n WORK
Binoculars n VIEW
Block n
Blower n VAPR
Blunderbuss n DAMG
Boiler n HEAT
Bolt n BLOK
Bolt n JOIN
Bonnet n COVR
Brake n BLOK
Breech n
Bushing n BLOK
Calculator n NUMR
Calender v EASY
Caliper n MSMT
Cam n
Camera n VIEW
Camshaft n
Cannon n DAMG
Capstan n FLOW
Carbine n DAMG
Cardiograph n SOMA
Carriage n
Caster n GO
Castor n GO
Catapult n GO
Catapult n DAMG
Centrifuge n SEP
Charger n ION

Chassis n FORM
Chuck n BLOK
Clock n TIME
Clockwork n TIME
Clutch n BLOK
Cock n BLOK
Cocks n BLOK
Cog n
Collimate v VIEW
Combine n VEGT
Commutator n ION
Compressor n BLOK
Computer n NUMR
Contraption n
Corkscrew n VARY
Crane n UP
Crank n
Crankcase n HOLW
Cranking v
Cranks n
Crankshaft n FORM
Cybernetic j LEAD
Cyclotron n ION
Dash n VIEW
Dashboard n VIEW
Davit n UP
Deadeye n FLOW
Derrick n
Derringer n DAMG
Device n
Dictaphone n TALK
Die n
Differential n
Diode n ION
Distributor n
Dog n
Doodad n TRIV
Drill n SHRP
Dumbwaiter n AID
Duplicator n WRIT
Dynamo n POWR
Eccentric n
Engine n
Engine n VEHC
Engineer n FORM
Escapement n TIME
Fan n VAPR
Faucet n BLOK
Firearm n DAMG
Flywheel n
Forceps n
Gadget n
Gasket n BLOK
Gat n DAMG
Gear n

Generator n ION
Gin n
Governor n LEAD
Gramophone n MUSC
Grindstone n SHRP
Gun n DAMG
Gun n QUIK
Gunned v DAMG
Gunned v QUIK
Gyroscope n VARY
Hammer n DAMG
Hardware n WORK
Harrow v ERTH
Header n VEGT
Howitzer n DAMG
Hurdygurdy n MUSC
Hydraulic j FLOW
Instrument n AID
Jack n JOIN
Jack n UP
Jacked v UP
Jacking v UP
Jig n VARY
Kinematic j GO
Lathe n
Lithograph n WRIT
Lock n BLOK
Locked v BLOK
Locomotive n VEHC
Loom n FABR
Machine n
Manacle v BLOK
Mangle v EASY
Mechanic n WORK
Mechanism n
Mechanize v
Meter n MSMT
Microscope n VIEW
Mill n WORK
Milled v WORK
Milling v WORK
Mimeograph v WRIT
Mortar n DAMG
Motor n
Musket n DAMG
Nickelodeon n MUSC
Nut n BLOK
Offset n WRIT
Oscilloscope n VIEW
Overdrive n VEHC
Pallet n TIME
Pawl n BLOK
Pedal n VEHC
Pentode n ION
Periscope n VIEW

Petcock n BLOK
Phone v TALK
Phoning v TALK
Phonograph n MUSC
Photogravure n VIEW
Piece n DAMG
Pile n ION
Pinion n
Pistol n DAMG
Piston n
Plumbing n FLOW
Polygraph n WRIT
Pompom n DAMG
Press n WRIT
Press n POWR
Print v WRIT
Projectionist n VIEW
Prop n GO
Propeller n GO
Pulley n
Pump n FLOW
Pump n VAPR
Pumped v FLOW
Pumped v VAPR
Pumping v FLOW
Pumping v VAPR
Rack n
Radar n ION
Reactor n ION
Recorder n TALK
Register n MART
Relay n JOIN
Respirator n VAPR
Revolver n DAMG
Rifle n DAMG
Robot n
Rod n DAMG
Router n HOLW
Safety n AID
Scale n MSMT
Screw n GO
Scuba j VAPR
Sextant n MSMT
Shoe n
Shotgun n DAMG
Sling n DAMG
Snare n BLOK
Snorkel n VAPR
Spigot n BLOK
Spindle n
Spring n VARY
Spyglass n VIEW
Stereoscopy n VIEW
Stereotype n WRIT
Submachine j

Parts of speech: a article; b preposition; c conjunction; d adverb; f prefix; i interjection;
j adjective; n noun; p pronoun; r phrase; v verb.

Tackle n	Tong n BLOK	Tweezer n BLOK	Watch n TIME
Tap n	Transistor n ION	Type v WRIT	Waterworks n FLOW
Tap n BLOK	Transit n VIEW	Typewrite v WRIT	Wheel n
Telephone v TALK	Transmission n	Typing v WRIT	Willow n VEGT
Telescope n VIEW	Trap n PLAY	Typist n WRIT	Winch n
Thermostat n HEAT	Trigger n BGIN	Vacuum n CLEN	Winnow n SEP
Throttle n BLOK	Triode n ION	Valve n BLOK	Worm n
Timepiece n TIME	Turbine n	Verge n TIME	Wringer n BLOK
Toggle n JOIN	Turnbuckle n JOIN	Vise n BLOK	Wristwatch n TIME

MEDC

Abreaction n OUT	Doping v REST	Medicine n	Quinine n VEGT
Ambulance n VEHC	Drug n	Morphine n REST	Radiology n ION
Analgesic n GLAD	Drug v REST	Narcotic n REST	Recover v
Antibiotic n	Drugged v REST	Neurology n SOMA	Recuperate v
Antibody n	Drugging v REST	Nostrum n	Remedy n AID
Antidote n	Druggist n MART	Nurse n AID	Salubrious j AID
Antiseptic j	Drugs n	Obstetric j BGIN	Salutary j AID
Antitoxin n	Drugs v REST	Oculist n VIEW	Sanatorium n HOME
Apothecary n	Drugstore n MART	Operate v SHRP	Sane j IDEA
Appendectomy n SOMA	Freudian j IDEA	Operating v SHRP	Sanitarium n HOME
Aseptic j CLEN	Fungicide n SICK	Ophthalmology n VIEW	Sanitary j CLEN
Aspirin n	Gammaglobulin n SOMA	Opiate n REST	Sanitation n CLEN
Astringent n	Geriatric j PAST	Opium n VEGT	Sanity n IDEA
Asylum n HOME	Germicide n	Optician n VIEW	Sedate v REST
Atropine n VEGT	Gynecology n LADY	Orthopedic j BODY	Sedated v REST
Auscultation n HEAR	Hale j POWR	Osteopath n	Sedating v REST
Better j	Hallucinogen n MYTH	Palpate v JOIN	Spay v SOMA
Biopsy n SOMA	Heal v AID	Pathologist n IDEA	Surgeon n SHRP
Bromide n	Health n AID	Pathology n IDEA	Surgery n SHRP
Cardiology n SOMA	Hemp n VEGT	Pediatric j YNG	Surgical j SHRP
Chiropractor n BODY	Herb n VEGT	Pedicure n BODY	Therapy n AID
Clinic n	Heroin n VEGT	Penicillin n	Thorazine n
Clinic n HOME	Hospital n HOME	Pharmaceutic j	Tonic n
Cocaine n VEGT	Hospitalize v HOME	Pharmacist n MART	Tonsilectomy n SOMA
Codeine n	Hygiene n CLEN	Pharmacology n IDEA	Transfusion n IN
Convalesce v	Hypodermic n SHRP	Pharmacopoeia n WRIT	Treat v AID
Corpsman n DAMG	Hysterectomy n SOMA	Pharmacy n MART	Treating v AID
Curable j AID	Immune j AID	Physic n SOMA	Treatment n AID
Curative j AID	Infirmary n HOME	Physician n	Vaccinate v
Cure n AID	Inoculate v IN	Podiatry n BODY	Vasectomy n SOMA
Curing v AID	Insulin n	Pot n VEGT	Ward n HOME
Dentist n BODY	Intern n	Premedical j FORW	Well j GOOD
Dermatologist n BODY	Interne n	Prescription n	Wellbeing n GOOD
Dexedrine n	Interned v	Proctology n SOMA	Worm v BUG
Diathermy n HEAT	Laxative n SOMA	Prophylaxis n AID	Wormed v BUG
Disinfect v CLEN	Liniment n	Psychiatry n IDEA	Worming v BUG
Dispensary n	LSD n MYTH	Psychoanalysis n IDEA	Xray n ION
Doctor n	Marijuana n VEGT	Psychotherapy n IDEA	
Dope n REST	Mastectomy n BODY	Pusher n CRIM	
Doped v REST	Medical j	Quack n FALS	

MONY

Account n MART	Appropriates v HAVE	Better n MOTV	Bob n
Affluence n MUCH	Appropriation n HAVE	Betting v MOTV	Bonanza n MUCH
Afford v	Arrears n MOTV	Bettor n MOTV	Bond n MART
Alimony n SEP	Assess v	Bill n	Bonded v MART
Allowance n	Auction n MART	Billed v	Bonding v MART
Amortize v MART	Bank n MART	Billfold n HOLW	Bonus n AID
Annuity n TIME	Banknote n	Billing v	Bookie n MOTV
Ante n	Bankroll n	Billionaire n MUCH	Bought v HAVE
Appropriate v HAVE	Bankrupt j LACK	Bit n LITL	Breadwinner n WORK
Appropriated v HAVE	Bet v MOTV	Blackmail v CRIM	Bribe n CRIM

Broke j LACK
Broker n MART
Buck n
Budget n
Bursary n
Buy v MART
Capital j MART
Capitalism n MART
Capitalize v MART
Cartage n VEHC
Cartwheel n
Cash v
Cashed v
Cashier n MART
Cashing v
Cent n
Centavo n
Change n
Charge n
Charter v MART
Cheap j TRIV
Cheapskate n TRIV
Check n WRIT
Chip n PLAY
Chit n WRIT
Client n MART
Coin n
Collect v HAVE
Compensate v
Comptroller n LEAD
Contribute v AID
Controller n LEAD
Copper n MTRL
Cost n
Costly j MUCH
Credit n MART
Creditor n MART
Crown n
Currency n
Customer n MART
Dear j MUCH
Debenture n MART
Debit n MART
Debt n MART
Defalcate v CRIM
Defray v
Denier n
Deposit n
Depositing v
Dime n
Disburse v
Discount v LITL
Discounted v LITL
Dividend n MART
Dollar n
Dot n AID
Dough n
Dowry n AID
Draft n WRIT
Draughts n WRIT
Dues n
Dun v MOTV
Dunned v MOTV
Duties n MART
Duty n MART

Eagle n ANML
Earn v WORK
Earned v WORK
Economic j MART
Economical j HAVE
Economist n MART
Economize v HAVE
Economy n MART
Economy n HAVE
Engage v MART
Enrich v MUCH
Exchange n MART
Excise n MART
Expenditure n LACK
Expense n LACK
Expensive j MUCH
Extravagance n MUCH
Extravagant j MUCH
Fare n VEHC
Fares n VEHC
Farthing n
Fee n
Fiduciary n
Fin n NUMR
Finance v MART
Fine n AGGR
Fined v AGGR
Fines v AGGR
Fining v AGGR
Fiscal j MART
Fiver n NUMR
Fortune n MUCH
Franc n
Freight n VEHC
Fund n
Gamble v MOTV
Gamester n MOTV
Gold n MTRL
Gouge v CRIM
Gratuities n AID
Gratuity n AID
Greenback n COLR
Guinea n
Halfpenny n
Hawk v MART
Hawked v MART
Hawking v MART
Heeled j
Hire v MART
Hireling n SUB
Huckster n MART
Impecunious j LACK
Income n
Indemnify v AID
Indemnity n AID
Inexpensive j TRIV
Inflation n LARG
Insolvent j LACK
Installment n SOME
Interest n MART
Invest v MART
Investing v MART
Kickback n BACK
Kitties n
Kitty n

Lease v MART
Let v MART
Letting v MART
Levied v HAVE
Levy v HAVE
Lira n
Loan n AID
Lucrative j MUCH
Made v HAVE
Make v HAVE
Makes v HAVE
Mark n
Market n MART
Mercenary j DAMG
Mill n
Millionaire n MUCH
Mint n MUCH
Mint v BGIN
Minted v BGIN
Minting v BGIN
Monetary j
Money n
Mortgage v MART
Multimillionaire n MUCH
Nickel n
Note n WRIT
Outlay n OUT
Overcompensate v LARG
Overhead n MART
Overpay v LARG
Overprice v LARG
Paid v
Parlay v MOTV
Pauper n LACK
Pawn v MART
Pawned v MART
Pawning v MART
Pay v
Payoff n
Payroll n WRIT
Peculate v CRIM
Pecuniary j
Peddle v MART
Pence n
Pennies n
Penniless j LACK
Penny n
Pension n
Penury n LACK
Peso n
Piaster n
Pittance n LITL
Policy n MOTV
Pony v
Pool n MOTV
Poor j LACK
Portion n SOME
Postage n WRIT
Pot n MOTV
Potboiler n TRIV
Pots n MOTV
Pound n
Poverty n LACK
Premium n AID
Prepaid j FORW

Prepay v FORW
Price n
Priceless j CRUX
Principal n
Proceeds n
Purchase n MART
Purse n HOLW
Quarter n
Queer n FALS
Rakeoff n CRIM
Ransom v AID
Rate n
Rebate n BACK
Recompense v
Refund v BACK
Reimburse v
Remunerate v
Rent n MART
Rented v MART
Renter n MART
Renting v MART
Rents v MART
Retail n MART
Revenue n MART
Rich j MUCH
Roll n
Royalty n
Ruble n
Salary n WORK
Sale n MART
Savings n HAVE
Scalp v CRIM
Scalped v CRIM
Scalping v CRIM
Security n MART
Sell v MART
Shakedown n CRIM
Shekel n
Silver n
Soak v
Sovereign n
Speculate v MOTV
Spend v LACK
Stipend n
Stock n MART
Stockmarket n MART
Stocks n MART
Sublease v MART
Sublet v MART
Subscribe v AGRE
Subscription n AGRE
Subsidies n AID
Subsidize v AID
Subsidy n AID
Sweepstake n MOTV
Tab n WRIT
Tariff n MART
Tax n
Taxing v
Taxpayer n
Teller n MART
Till n HOLW
Tills n HOLW
Tip n
Tips v

Token n
Toll n
Treasurer n LEAD
Treasuries n
Treasury n

Trust n AID
Tuition n EDUC
Unpaid j LACK
Unsold j LACK
Vendor n MART

Wad n BULG
Wage n WORK
Wager v MOTV
Wealth n MUCH
Welltodo j MUCH

Wholesale j MART
Yen n

MOTV

Absorb v
Account n
Accountable j
Ache n PANG
Addict n SICK
Address v
Affect n
After b
Agog j PANG
Aim n
Alert j QUIK
Alternative n
Ambition n POWR
Ambivalent j BLUR
Angle n
Angling v
Anticipate v FORW
Aphrodisiac n SEX
Appeal n AID
Appetite n FOOD
Appetite n
Applicant n
Application n
Application n WRIT
Applied v
Apply v
Appoint v
Appointed v
Appointee n
Appointment n
Apt j
Arbitrary j EVER
Arduous j PANG
Arouse v
Arrears n MONY
Ascribe v IDEA
Aspirant n
Aspiration n
Aspire v
Aspiring j
Assiduous j EVER
Assign v
Assignable j
Attack v
Attempt n
Attend v
Attention n
Attentive j
Attitude n
Attract v
Attractive j FOND
Attribute v IDEA
Avarice n
Avid j
Bait v
Ballot n
Beck n

Beckon v
Beg v LACK
Beggar n LACK
Begged v LACK
Beholden j
Beseech v
Besought v
Bet v MONY
Better n MONY
Betting v MONY
Bettor n MONY
Beware v DAMG
Bias n FALS
Bid v
Bigot n FALS
Bipartisan j AGRE
Blame v AGGR
Book v
Booked v
Bookie n MONY
Booking v
Books v
Bound j
Buck n
Buff n FOND
Business n
Busybody n AGGR
Cadge v
Call n
Calling n
Campaign n
Candidate n
Canvass n IDEA
Caprice n VARY
Captivate v
Care n
Cared v
Careful j AID
Careless j LACK
Cares n
Caring v
Carteblanche n
Cause n
Caution n AID
Chance n
Charge n LEAD
Charisma n LEAD
Choice n
Choose v
Chosen j
Circumspect j AID
Claim v
Coax v FOND
Commit v AGRE
Committed v AGRE
Complicity n JOIN
Compulsion n POWR

Compulsory j POWR
Concern n PANG
Concerned v PANG
Concerning v PANG
Concupiscent j SEX
Confidence n POWR
Confident j POWR
Conjure v
Conscript v JOIN
Consecrate v HOLY
Consume v
Coopt v GRUP
Court v
Courted v
Courting v
Courts v
Covet v
Crack n
Crave v
Craving v
Craze n NEW
Culpable j AGGR
Cultivate v
Cupidity n
Curiosity n
Curious j
Curried v
Curry v
Dare v POWR
Dazzle v FOND
Debauch v BAD
Debt n
Delegate n
Delegating v
Delegation n GRUP
Delegation n
Deliberate v IDEA
Delicacy n
Delicate j
Demand v
Deputies n
Deputy n
Derringdo n POWR
Desert n
Deserve v
Design n
Designate v
Desirable j GOOD
Desire n
Desire n SEX
Desiring v
Desiring v SEX
Detail v
Determine v EVER
Devise v LAW
Devour v
Devout j HOLY

Diligence n EVER
Diligent j EVER
Discretion n
Dispose v
Draft n JOIN
Drafted v JOIN
Draftee n JOIN
Dream n MYTH
Drive v POWR
Drove v POWR
Due j
Dun v MONY
Dunned v MONY
Duties n WORK
Duty n WORK
Dying v DEAD
Eager j
Earnest j CRUX
Eclectic n IDEA
Egg v
Egged v
Egging v
Egocentric j SOLE
Egotism n SOLE
Elect v
Elective j
Elective n EDUC
Electorate n GRUP
Electric j
Electrify v
Eligible j SIML
Emotion n
End n END
Endeavor v
Engage v
Engross v
Enterprise n POWR
Enthusiasm n
Entice v
Entitle v AGRE
Entreat v
Envious j AGGR
Envy v AGGR
Epicure n FOOD
Epicure n GLAD
Esprit n POWR
Essay v
Exact v POWR
Exacted v POWR
Exacting v POWR
Exacts v POWR
Excite v
Exhort v
Expect v
Expectancy n
Expression n
Expressionism n OPEN

Extrovert n OUT
Fad n NEW
Fan n FOND
Fanatic n FOOL
Fastidious j TRIV
Feel v
Felt v
Fervent j
Fervor n
Fiend n
Fillip v
Finicky j TRIV
Fire v HEAT
Fired v HEAT
Fires v HEAT
Firing v HEAT
Flesh v
Fling n
Flyer n
For b AGRE
Franchise n LAW
Galvanize v
Gambit n
Gamble v MONY
Game j POWR
Gamester n MONY
Gourmet n FOOD
Greed n
Gusto n
Hanker v
Hazard n DAMG
Heart n POWR
Heartfelt j GOOD
Heartstring n SOMA
Heedless j LACK
Hog v SOLE
Hogged v SOLE
Hogging v SOLE
Hope n
Hoping v
Hot j HEAT
Humor n
Humored v
Humoring v
Hunger n FOOD
Hungry j FOOD
Hunt v
Id n POWR
Impassioned j
Impassive j LACK
Impel v
Imperative j CRUX
Imperious j CRUX
Impetuous j QUIK
Implore v
Importune v
Impress v POWR
Impression n POWR
Impressive j POWR
Impulse n QUIK
Impute v IDEA
Incentive n
Incite v BGIN
Incline v
Incumbent n

Incur v
Indebted j
Induce v IDEA
Infect v
Inflame v HEAT
Insist v
Inspire v POWR
Instinct n
Intemperance n AGGR
Intend v
Intent n
Intentional j
Interest n
Intrigue v
Introvert v IN
Intuition n IDEA
Inveigle v FALS
Invite v
Invocation n AID
Invoke v AID
Itch v PANG
Juicier j
Juicy j
Keen j SHRP
Lawsuit n LAW
Lean v AGRE
Leaned v AGRE
Leaning v AGRE
Leans v AGRE
Liability n
Libido n SEX
Lien n LAW
Long v
Longed v
Longing v
Lot n
Lottery n
Lukewarm j TRIV
Lure v
Luring v
Lust n
Lust n SEX
Lusted v
Lusted v SEX
Lusting v
Lusting v SEX
Mad j FOND
Mania n PANG
Mean v
Meaning v
Means v
Meant v
Mendicant n LACK
Merit v
Mind v
Mission n
Mission n HOLY
Missionary n HOLY
Mooch v
Mood n
Morale n GOOD
Motion n IDEA
Motivate v
Motive n
Move v

Movement n
Moving v
Must v
Necessity n CRUX
Need n LACK
Nominate v
Nominative j
Nominee n
Nonpartisan j OPEN
Nostalgia n PANG
Nosy j AGGR
Object n END
Objective n END
Obligate v
Oblige v AGRE
Occupation n
Occupied v
Occupy v
Onesided j FALS
Optimism n GLAD
Option n
Order n LEAD
Ought v
Overcareful j AID
Overcautious j AID
Overconfident j POWR
Overeager j
Overenthusiastic j
Overoptimist n GLAD
Overture n IDEA
Owe v
Painstaking j AID
Panhandle v
Parlay v MONY
Partial j
Partiality n
Partisan j AGRE
Partisan j DAMG
Passion n
Penchant n
Persevere v EVER
Persuade v IDEA
Petition n
Pica n SICK
Pick v
Picked v
Pine v PANG
Pined v PANG
Pining v PANG
Pique v
Pitch n TALK
Plaintiff n LAW
Plea n
Plead v
Pleas n
Plebiscite n LAW
Policy n MONY
Poll n GRUP
Polled v GRUP
Polling v GRUP
Pool n MONY
Posture n
Pot n MONY
Pots n MONY
Precaution n AID

Predilection n
Predispose v
Prefer v
Prejudice n FALS
Preoccupy v
Prepossessing j
Prerogative n
Presumptuous j POWR
Pretend v
Pretense n
Prissy j TRIV
Privilege n AID
Privy j AID
Proclivity n
Prod v
Project v OUT
Projecting v OUT
Prompt v
Prompted v
Prompting v
Prompts v
Prone v
Propensity n
Prospect n FORW
Prospect v OPEN
Prospected v OPEN
Prospecting v OPEN
Prospective j FORW
Prospector n OPEN
Provocation n AGGR
Provoke v AGGR
Proxy n SIML
Purpose n
Pursue v GO
Pursuing v GO
Pursuit n GO
Pyromaniac n HEAT
Rage n NEW
Ran v GO
Rapacious j DAMG
Rapt j
Raring j
Rather d
Ravenous j FOOD
Ravish v GLAD
Readied v
Ready j
Request n
Require v
Requisite j
Requisition n
Resolute j
Resolution n
Resolve v
Responsibility n
Right n TRUE
Rights n TRUE
Risk v DAMG
Roulette n PLAY
Run v GO
Sanguine j SOMA
Schnorrer n LACK
Score n
Scrounge v
Search n OPEN

Seduction n BAD
Seek v OPEN
Select v
Selfish j SOLE
Sensation n
Sensational j
Sensitive j
Sensuous j
Sentiment n
Sentimental j
Shoot v
Shot n
Slate v FORW
Slated v FORW
Slating v FORW
Solicit v
Solicit v SEX
Solicitor n
Spark v BGIN
Speculate v MONY
Spellbound j
Spice n
Spirit n CRUX
Spirited j CRUX
Sponge n
Spur n SHRP
Spurred v SHRP
Spurring v SHRP
Stake n
Stance n

Stand v
Standing v
Stimulate v BGIN
Stint n
Stir v
Stirred v
Stood v
Strive v
Strove v
Sublimation n GOOD
Subpoena n LAW
Sue v LAW
Sue v
Sued v LAW
Sued v
Suing v LAW
Suing v
Suit n
Suit n SEX
Suitor n
Suitor n SEX
Summon v
Summons n LAW
Supplicate v
Susceptible j WEAK
Sweepstake n MONY
Tackle v
Tackled v
Tackling v
Taste n GOOD

Taste n
Temper n
Temperament n
Temperance n EASY
Temperate j EASY
Tempt v
Tend v
Tended v
Tendency n
Testament n WRIT
Thirst n SIP
Touch v PANG
Tried v
Try v
Ultimatum n END
Undercurrent n BLUR
Undertake v BGIN
Unemotional j LACK
Unintentional j OPPO
Unmotivated j LACK
Unresponsive j OPPO
Unsolicited j OPPO
Urge n
Venture n DAMG
Vogue n NEW
Volition n
Voluntary j
Volunteer n AID
Voluptuous j GLAD
Voracious j FOOD

Vote n
Voting v
Wager v MONY
Want v
Wanton j BAD
Warily d AID
Wary j AID
Wellwisher n GOOD
Whet v SHRP
Whets v SHRP
Whim n VARY
Will n
Will v LAW
Willed v
Willed v LAW
Willing j AGRE
Willing v
Willing v LAW
Willynilly d NO
Wish v
Wistful j
Witting j AGRE
Yearn v
Yen n
Zeal n
Zealot n
Zest n

MSMT

Acre n ERTH
Altimeter n UP
Altitude n UP
Ammeter n ION
Ampere n ION
Amplitude n
Anemometer n VAPR
Angstrom n ION
Area n
Assay n
Atmosphere n VAPR
Balance n MECH
Barometer n VAPR
Bushel n
Bushel n HOLW
Butt n
Cable n MTRL
Caliber n
Calibrate v
Calibre n
Caliper n MECH
Calory n HEAT
Calory n FOOD
Candle n VIEW
Capacitance n ION
Carat n
Centigrade j HEAT
Chronometer n TIME
Compass n PATH

Coordinate n
Cord n
Coulomb n ION
Craniology n SOMA
Cubit n
Curie n
Decibel n HEAR
Degree n
Denier n FABR
Density n
Diameter n
Dimension n
Distance n
Dram n
Dyne n POWR
Electrocardiogr n SOMA
Electrometer n ION
Electroscope n ION
Elevation n UP
Erg n POWR
Fahrenheit j HEAT
Farad n ION
Fathom n FLOW
Featherweight n EASY
Feet n
Finger n BODY
Foot n
Furlong n
Gallon n

Galvanometer n ION
Gauge v
Gill n
Girth n HOLW
Grade n FORW
Graduate v FORW
Grain n
Gram n
Hand n BODY
Hands n BODY
Hank n
Heavyweight n LARG
Height n UP
High j UP
Hogshead n HOLW
Horsepower n POWR
Hour n TIME
Hourglass n TIME
Inch n
Index n
Isometric j SIML
Jigger n SIP
Kilogram n
Kilometer n
Kilowatt n ION
Knot v QUIK
Lap n PATH
Large j
Latitude n

League n
Length n
Lightweight j EASY
Liter n
Long j
Longitude n
Magnitude n
Mass n
Measure n
Measure n MUSC
Measured v
Measuring v
Meridian n ERTH
Meter n
Meter n MECH
Meter n MUSC
Metric j
Metronome n TIME
Mil n
Mile n
Miles n
Milestone n CRUX
Millimeter n
Minute j TIME
Minutes n TIME
Module n
Ohm n ION
Ounce n
Overweight j LARG

Parts of speech: a article; b preposition; c conjunction; d adverb; f prefix; i interjection;
        j adjective; n noun; p pronoun; r phrase; v verb.

MSMT   Category Listing

Peck n	Radius n	Speedometer n QUIK	Volt n ION
Pedometer n GO	Recipe n FORM	Standard n	Voltmeter n ION
Pentameter n TALK	Rod n	Sundial n TIME	Volume n
Pica n WRIT	Roentgen n ION	Survey n	Water n
Pint n	Rule n FORM	Surveyor n	Watt n ION
Plumb v	Ruled v FORM	Tape v	Weigh v
Plumbed v	Ruler n FORM	Tapes v	Weight n
Plumbing v	Ruling v FORM	Taping v	Welterweight n
Potentiometer n ION	Sandglass n TIME	Telemeter n ION	Wide j
Pound n	Scale n MECH	Temperature n HEAT	Width n
Pounder n	Scale n	Thermometer n HEAT	Yard n
Protractor n	Second j TIME	Thick j	Yards n
Quanta n ION	Sextant n MECH	Ton n	Yardstick n FORM
Quantum n ION	Shoot v	Tons n	
Quart n	Size n	Unit n SOLE	

MTRL

Abrasive n AGGR	Bond n	Clapboard n VEGT	Firebrick n HEAT
Acetate n	Bone n SOMA	Clay n ERTH	Flint n ERTH
Acetylene n HEAT	Brass n ERTH	Coal n HEAT	Fluff n EASY
Acid n	Brassy j ERTH	Cobalt n	Fluffy j EASY
Acrylic n	Brazen j ERTH	Coke n HEAT	Foil n
Adamant n ERTH	Brick n FORM	Colloid n	Fuel n HEAT
Adobe j ERTH	Bristle n ANML	Compost n AID	Furring n FORM
Adrenalin n SOMA	Bronze n ERTH	Concrete j	Fuzz n EASY
Agate n ERTH	Cable n	Concrete j ERTH	Fuzzier j EASY
Alabaster n ERTH	Cable n MSMT	Confetti n PLAY	Fuzzy j EASY
Alcohol n VEGT	Cadmium n	Copper n ERTH	Galactose n
Alkali n	Caffeine n FOOD	Copper n MONY	Galvanize v
Alloy n JOIN	Calcium n	Coppersmith n WORK	Garnet n ERTH
Alpha n ION	Calk v BLOK	Coral n FLOW	Gas n FLOW
Alum n	Cane n VEGT	Cork n BLOK	Gasoline n FLOW
Aluminum n	Caned v VEGT	Cork n VEGT	Gelatine n
Amber n ERTH	Caning v VEGT	Crystal n VIEW	Gem n GOOD
Ambergris n ANML	Carbohydrate n FOOD	Crystal n FORM	Gild v COLR
Amethyst n ERTH	Carbon n	Crystallize v FORM	Gilt j COLR
Ammonia n	Carbonate n	Cyanide n	Glass n
Anoint v FLOW	Carbondioxide n	Cypress n VEGT	Glass n HOLW
Anthracite n HEAT	Carbuncle n ERTH	Cytoplasm n SOMA	Glassblower n WORK
Aquamarine n ERTH	Card n	Damask n ERTH	Glasses n HOLW
Arsenic n DAMG	Cardboard n	DDT n	Glassware n HOLW
Asbestos n ERTH	Castiron j ERTH	Deal n VEGT	Glaze n COLR
Ash n HEAT	Castor n ANML	Deuteron n ION	Glazing v COLR
Ash n VEGT	Castoroil n VEGT	Dextrose n FOOD	Glucose n
Ashes n HEAT	Catgut n ANML	Diamond n ERTH	Glue v JOIN
Asphalt n ERTH	Caulk v BLOK	Dioxide n	Glycerin n
Atom n ION	Caustic n DAMG	Dope n	Gold n ERTH
Atomic j ION	Cedar n VEGT	Dyestuff n COLR	Gold n MONY
Bakelite n	Cellophane n	Dynamite v DAMG	Graphite n ERTH
Balsa n VEGT	Celluloid n	Ebony n VEGT	Grease v EASY
Balsam n VEGT	Cement n JOIN	Element n ION	Greasier j DIRT
Base n	Ceramic j ERTH	Elements n ION	Greasy j DIRT
Baseboard n FORM	Chalk n WRIT	Emerald n ERTH	Guano n ANML
Beech n VEGT	Charcoal n HEAT	Emeries n AGGR	Gum n JOIN
Beta n ION	Charcoal n COLR	Emery n AGGR	Gummed v JOIN
Bicarbonate n	Chemical n	Enamel n	Gummy j JOIN
Birch n VEGT	Chemist n IDEA	Enamel n COLR	Gunpowder n DAMG
Biscuit n ERTH	Cherry n VEGT	Essence n	Gypsum n
Board n VEGT	Chestnut n VEGT	Eucalyptus n VEGT	Halogen n
Board v COVR	Chlorophyll n VEGT	Fat n	Heliotrope n ERTH
Boarded v COVR	Cholesterol n SOMA	Ferro f ERTH	Hickory n VEGT
Boarding v COVR	Chrome n	Filings n WORK	Horn n ANML
Boards n VEGT	Chromium n	Fir n VEGT	Humus n ERTH
Boards v COVR	Cinder n HEAT	Firebrand n HEAT	Hyacinth n ERTH

Hydrocarbon n ION
Indium n
Inorganic j
Ion n ION
Iron n ERTH
Iron n BLOK
Ironclad j POWR
Ivory n ANML
Jade n ERTH
Jasper n ERTH
Jellies n
Jelly n
Jet n ERTH
Kerosene n ERTH
Kindling n HEAT
Lacquer v COLR
Lanolin n ANML
Lard n ANML
Larded v ANML
Latex n
Lead n ERTH
Lead n DAMG
Leaded v ERTH
Lime n ERTH
Linoleum n
Linseed n VEGT
Lithiun n ERTH
Litmus n
Litter n VEGT
Log n VEGT
Logged v VEGT
Logging v VEGT
Lubricate v EASY
Lumber n VEGT
Lumberyard n MART
Lye n
Magnesium n
Mahogany n VEGT
Manganese n ERTH
Maple n VEGT
Marble n ERTH
Marble n PLAY
Material n
Matter n
Membrane n
Mercury n
Metal n
Metallurgy n IDEA
Mica n ERTH
Mineral n
Molecule n ION
Moonstone n ERTH
Mortar n JOIN
Myrrh n VEGT
Napalm n DAMG

Neon n
Niacin n
Nickel n
Nicotine n
Nitrate n
Nitroglycerin n
Nugget n ERTH
Nutria n ANML
Oak n VEGT
Obsidian n ERTH
Ochre n ERTH
Octane n
Oil v EASY
Oil n ERTH
Oiled v EASY
Oiling v EASY
Oils v EASY
Oils n ERTH
Ointment n EASY
Opal n ERTH
Ore n ERTH
Oxide n
Pane n VIEW
Panel v FORM
Paneled v FORM
Paneling v FORM
Panelled v FORM
Paper n
Paper n WRIT
Papered v
Papering v
Papiermache n
Papyrus n WRIT
Paraffin n
Parchment n WRIT
Pasteboard n JOIN
Pearl n FLOW
Peroxide n
Peroxide n COLR
Petrol n FLOW
Petroleum n FLOW
Pewter n ERTH
Phosphate n
Physical j
Physicist n IDEA
Physics n IDEA
Piezoelectric j ION
Pig n ERTH
Pigiron n ERTH
Pine n VEGT
Pitch n COLR
Pitchblende n ERTH
Plank n VEGT
Plaster n
Plasterboard n FORM

Plastic j
Plate n ERTH
Platinum n ERTH
Plexiglass n VIEW
Plutonium n
Polaroid n VIEW
Polonium n ERTH
Polystyrene n
Pomace n FOOD
Pomade n EASY
Porcelain n
Potash n
Powder n
Powder n DAMG
Propane n VAPR
Protein n FOOD
Protoplasm n SOMA
Pug n ERTH
Pulp n EASY
Pumice n EASY
Putties v EASY
Putty v EASY
Pyrex n HEAT
Quartz n ERTH
Quicksilver n VARY
Radioisotope n ION
Radium n ION
Redwood n VEGT
Refractory j HEAT
Reify v
Rhinestone n VIEW
Rouge n EASY
Rubber n
Rubies n ERTH
Ruby n ERTH
Sal n
Saline j
Salt n
Saltpeter n
Saltwater j FLOW
Salve n AID
Sandalwood n VEGT
Sandstone n ERTH
Sapphire n ERTH
Saran n
Sawdust n DIRT
Shake n FORM
Shellack n
Silicon n ERTH
Silver n ERTH
Size v AID
Slate n ERTH
Slug n
Soda n
Solitaire n ERTH

Spangle n VIEW
Sponge n FLOW
Spruce n VEGT
Starch n VEGT
Steel n ERTH
Straw n VEGT
Stucco n
Stuff n
Substance n
Substantial j
Sulphur n ERTH
Talc n
Talcum n
Tallow n ANML
Tape v COVR
Tape v HEAR
Tapes v COVR
Tapes v HEAR
Taping v COVR
Taping v HEAR
Tar n
Tarred v
Tarring v
Terracotta j ERTH
Tile n
Timber n VEGT
Tin n ERTH
Tin n HOLW
Tinder n HEAT
Tinker n WORK
Tinsel n VIEW
Tissue n
Topaz n ERTH
Turpentine n VEGT
Turquoise n ERTH
Unction n HOLY
Unction n EASY
Varnish n VIEW
Veneer n COVR
Vinyl n
Walnut n VEGT
Wax n CLEN
Wax n
Whalebone n ANML
Whiting n COLR
Wick n HEAT
Wicker n VEGT
Willow n VEGT
Wire n
Wood n VEGT
Woodcraft n POWR
Woodpile n BULG
Woods n VEGT
Woodwork n FORM
Zinc n ERTH

MUCH

Abound v
Abundant j
Adequate j
Adequate j POWR
Affluence n MONY
Ample j LARG
Amply d LARG

Armies n GRUP
Army n GRUP
Billionaire n MONY
Bonanza n MONY
Bounty n AID
Bulk n
Chatterbox n TALK

Commonplace j TRIV
Considerable j LARG
Copious j
Cornucopia n HOLW
Costly j MONY
Countless j NUMR
Dear j MONY

Enough d
Enrich v MONY
Expensive j MONY
Extensive j LARG
Extra d EMPH
Extra j
Extra n WRIT

Extravagance n MONY	Lot n	Numerous j	Proliferate v BGIN
Extravagance n GOOD	Lucrative j MONY	Often d	Prolific j BGIN
Extravagant j MONY	Lush j GOOD	Omnibus n WRIT	Raft n GRUP
Extravagant j GOOD	Luxury n GOOD	Oodles n	Rich j MONY
Fecund j BGIN	Magpie n TALK	Opulence n GOOD	Rich j GOOD
Fortune n MONY	Majority n	Overabundant j LARG	Scads n
Frequency n	Manifold j	Particolor j COLR	Slew n
Frequent j	Many j	Plenty j	Spare j
Further d	Mass j GRUP	Plethora n BULG	Spate n QUIK
Furthermore d	Mass n	Plural j	Substantial j
Galore j	Massed v GRUP	Polychromatic j COLR	Suffice v
Goodly j LARG	Massing v GRUP	Polyglot j TALK	Sufficient j
Heap n BULG	Millionaire n MONY	Polymorphous j FORM	Sumptuous j GOOD
Heavier j	Mint n MONY	Polynomial n NUMR	Surplus n BULG
Heavy j	More j	Polyphony n MUSC	Teem v
Heterochromatic j COLR	Most j	Polytechnic j EDUC	Untold j TALK
Host n GRUP	Much j	Polytheism n HOLY	Verbose j TALK
Infest v DAMG	Multifarious j OPPO	Populous j GRUP	Voluble j TALK
Innumerable j	Multilateral j	Preponderance n	Wealth n MONY
Lavish j GOOD	Multimillionaire n MONY	Prevail v	Welltodo j MONY
Legion n GRUP	Multiple j	Prevalence n	Wordy j TALK
Likelihood n	Multitude n GRUP	Probability n	
Likely j	Multitude n	Prodigal j	
Loquacious j TALK	Myriad n	Profuse j	

MUSC

A n WRIT	Bugle n	Crescendo n LARG	Fortissimo j EMPH
Accompany v JOIN	C n WRIT	Croon v TALK	Fourth n NUMR
Accordion n	Cadence n VARY	Cymbal n	Foxtrot n GO
Adagio n REST	Calypso n TALK	D n WRIT	Fret n
Air n	Cancan n GO	Dance n GO	Fugue n
Airs n	Canon n	Decrescendo n LITL	G n WRIT
Album n	Canonical j	Descant n	Gavotte n GO
Allegro j QUIK	Cantata n TALK	Diapason n	Glee n GRUP
Alto j	Carol n TALK	Ding n	Glissando n EASY
Andante j REST	Castanet n	Dirge n PANG	Glockenspiel n
Anthem n	Cellist n	Disc n TALK	Gong n
Antiphony n VARY	Cello n	Disk n TALK	Gramophone n MECH
Aria n	Chanson n TALK	Ditties n TALK	Guitar n
Arpeggio n QUIK	Chant v TALK	Ditty n TALK	Harmonic j SIML
B n WRIT	Chanting v TALK	Doorbell n OPEN	Harmonica n
Bagpipe n	Chime v	Drum n	Harmonious j SIML
Ball n PLAY	Chink n	Drummed v	Harmonize v SIML
Ballad n TALK	Choir n GRUP	Drumstick n	Harmony n SIML
Ballet n GO	Choral j GRUP	Duet n NUMR	Harp n
Band n	Chord n	Duo n NUMR	Harpsichord n
Bands n	Choreography n GO	E n WRIT	Hazzan n HOLY
Bandstand n	Chorus n GRUP	Eighth n NUMR	Hifi n SHRP
Bar n	Chromatic j	Ensemble n GRUP	Hop n GO
Bass n	Clang v	Etude n	Horn n
Beat n VARY	Clangor n	F n WRIT	Hula n GO
Belfry n UP	Clarinet n	Falsetto n FALS	Hum v
Bell n	Clarion j SHRP	Fanfare n POWR	Hummed v
Bell n TIME	Clavichord n	Fiddle v	Humming v
Blew v	Clef n WRIT	Fife n	Humoresque n GLAD
Blow v	Clink n	Fifth n NUMR	Hurdygurdy n MECH
Blues n PANG	Concert n	Flamenco n GO	Hymn n HOLY
Bolero n GO	Concerto n	Flat j	Instrument n
Bow n	Conga n GO	Flats n	Intermezzo n
Bowed v	Console n	Flatten v	Intone v TALK
Bower n	Contrabass n	Fling n GO	Jam n
Bowing v	Contralto n	Flute n	Jazz n
Brass n	Cornet n	Fork n	Jig n GO
Brassy j	Cotillion n GO	Forte j EMPH	Jigged v GO

Jigging v GO
Jingle n
Jitterbug n GO
Juke n
Kazoo n
Key n
Keyboard n FORW
Keyed v
Keying v
Keys n
Knell n
Knell n DEAD
Largo j REST
Libretto n WRIT
Lilt n
Lullaby n REST
Lute n
Lyre n
Madrigal n TALK
Maestro n LEAD
Mandolin n
Maraca n
March n GO
Marimba n
Measure n MSMT
Melodies n
Melody n
Meter n MSMT
Minstrel n TALK
Minuet n GO
Monody n PANG
Movement n
Music n
Nickelodeon n MECH
Noel n HOLY
Note n
Oboe n
Ocarina n
Octave n NUMR
Ode n TALK

Opera n TALK
Operatic j TALK
Operetta n TALK
Oratorio n TALK
Orchestra n GRUP
Orchestral j GRUP
Orchestrate v GRUP
Organ n
Organist n
Overtone n
Overture n
Pastorale n ERTH
Peal n
Percussion n
Philharmonic j
Phonograph n MECH
Pianissimo j EASY
Pianist n
Piano n
Piccolo n
Ping n
Pipe n
Piper n
Piping n
Pitch n
Pitched v
Pitching v
Pitchpipe n
Pizzicato j
Play v
Pluck v
Plucked v
Plucking v
Polka n GO
Polyphony n MUCH
Prelude n FORW
Prom n PLAY
Promenade n PLAY
Quaver n VARY
Rang v

Recital n
Record n TALK
Recorder n
Reed n
Reel n GO
Refrain n TALK
Register n FORW
Resonant j
Rhapsody n
Rhumba n GO
Rhythm n VARY
Ring n
Ringing v
Roll n
Rolled v
Rondeau n TALK
Round n TALK
Rounds n TALK
Rumba n GO
Rung v
Samba n GO
Sang v TALK
Sax n
Saxophone n
Scale n FORW
Scherzo n
Score n WRIT
Second n NUMR
Serenade n TALK
Shag n GO
Shake n
Sharp j SHRP
Sing v TALK
Siren n
Sixth n NUMR
Slur n
Snare n
Song n TALK
Sonorous j
Soprano n

Spiritual n HOLY
Staccato j
Staff n WRIT
Stereophonic j
Stomp n GO
String n
Strum v
Suite n GRUP
Symphony n
Syncopate v VARY
Tabor n
Tambourine n
Tenor n
Third n NUMR
Tinkle n
Toll n
Tolled v
Tolling v
Tomtom n
Tone n
Tonic j
Toot v
Trap n
Treble j
Triangle n FORM
Trill n
Trio n NUMR
Triplet n NUMR
Trombone n
Trumpet n
Tune n
Tuning v
Twang n
Violin n
Waltz n GO
Whistle n
Woofer n
Xylophone n
Yodel n TALK
Zither n

MYTH

Aladdin n YNG
Alchemist n
Allegory n
Amulet n AID
Animism n IDEA
Apollo n MALE
Apparition n VIEW
Aquarius n ASTR
Aries n ASTR
Astrology n ASTR
Atlas n POWR
Augur n FORW
Banshee n LADY
Bewitch v FOND
Bewitch v BAD
Bluebeard n DAMG
Brownie n AID
Bugaboo n PANG
Bugbear n PANG
Cadmus n LEAD
Camelot n PLAC
Cancer n ASTR

Capricorn n ASTR
Centaur n ANML
Charm n
Cinderella n LADY
Clairvoyant j VIEW
Conjure v
Cupid n FOND
Cyclops n
Daemon n BAD
Daydream n TIME
Demon n BAD
Demoniac j BAD
Demonology n
Dragon n ANML
Dream n IDEA
Dream n MOTV
Dream n GOOD
Dreamland n PLAC
Ectoplasm n SOMA
Elf n LITL
Elves n LITL
Eros n SEX

ESP n IDEA
Ethereal j VAPR
Fable n TALK
Fabulous j AFAR
Fairies n
Fairy n
Fairyland n PLAC
Fakir n HOLY
Fancied v IDEA
Fancies v IDEA
Fanciful j IDEA
Fancy n IDEA
Fantasied v IDEA
Fantastic j IDEA
Fantasy v IDEA
Fetish n FOND
Fiction n FALS
Fictitious j FALS
Figment n
Folklore n GRUP
Gemini n ASTR
Genie n POWR

Ghost n
Ghoul n BAD
Gnome n LITL
Goblin n BAD
Gorgon n LADY
Grace n LADY
Gremlin n BLOK
Griffin n ANML
Hades n DEAD
Hag n LADY
Hallucinate v IDEA
Hallucinogen n MEDC
Hallucinosis n SICK
Haunt v EVER
Heaven n DEAD
Helios n LEAD
Hell n DEAD
Hermetic j
Hex n AGGR
Horoscope n ASTR
Illusion n IDEA
Illusory j IDEA

Imaginary j IDEA
Imagine v IDEA
Immaterial j
Incantation n TALK
Intangible n
Jupiter n LEAD
Legend n TALK
Legerdemain n FALS
Leo n ASTR
Leprechaun n
Libra n ASTR
Limbo n DEAD
Lore n GRUP
LSD n MEDC
Magic j
Makebelieve j FALS
Mars n DAMG
Medium n
Mercury n TALK
Mermaid n LADY
Miracle n GOOD
Mirage n VIEW

Myth n
Neptune n FLOW
Nightmare n PANG
Nymph n LADY
Occult j COVR
Ogre n DAMG
Omen n FORW
Palmist n BODY
Parable n TALK
Phantasma n VIEW
Phantom n
Philter n SIP
Phoenix n ANML
Pisces n ASTR
Pixy n GLAD
Pluto n DEAD
Prestidigitation n FALS
Puck n GLAD
Punch n PLAY
Reverie n IDEA
Rhesus n
Saga n TALK

Sagittarius n ASTR
Salamander n ANML
Saturn n LEAD
Satyr n MALE
Scorpio n ASTR
Seance n GRUP
Shade n
Shadow n
Sorcery n
Soul n CRUX
Specter n
Spectral j
Spell n
Sphinx n BLUR
Spirit n CRUX
Spiritual j HOLY
Spook n
Supernatural j AFAR
Superstition n
Surrealism n FORM
Tale n TALK
Talisman n POWR

Taurus n ASTR
Telepathy n TALK
Uncanny j AFAR
Unearthly j AFAR
Unicorn n ANML
Unreal j AFAR
Uranus n LEAD
Utopia n PLAC
Venus n LADY
Virgo n ASTR
Vision n VIEW
Wand n FORM
Weird j AFAR
Witchcraft n BAD
Wizard n POWR
Yarn n TALK
Zeus n LEAD
Zodiac n ASTR
Zombie n DEAD

NEAR

Aborigine n BGIN
About b
Abreast d SIML
Acquaint v IDEA
Adjacent j
Against b
Almost d
Along b
Alongside d
Approach v GO
Approximate j
Approximate v SIML
Approximately d
Around b
Aside d SEP
At b
Autochthonous j BGIN
Barely d
Bedside j REST
Beside b
Border v END
Bound n END
Bounded v END
Bounding v END
Bounds v END

By b
By b TIME
Byproduct n END
Bystander n REST
Circa b TIME
Close d
Close j FOND
Close v GO
Closed v GO
Closeup n VIEW
Closing v GO
Conversant j IDEA
Domestic j
Element n
Endemic j WHOL
Familiar j
Fireside j HEAT
Flank v
Hand n BODY
Hence d
Here d
Hereabout d PLAC
Herein d IN
Hereon d
Herewith d

Hither d
Hitherto d
Hobnob v AGRE
Hug v
Immediate j
Imminence n TIME
Impend v TIME
Indigenous j BGIN
Introduce v BGIN
Just d
Knew v IDEA
Know v IDEA
Local j PLAC
Locality n PLAC
Native n BGIN
Naturalize v LAW
Near j
Neighbor n
Neighborhood n PLAC
Nestle v JOIN
Nestling v JOIN
Next d
Nigh d
Nipandtuck r
Omnipresence n WHOL

Orient v IDEA
Orientate v IDEA
Oriented v IDEA
Orienting v IDEA
Orients v IDEA
Overhaul v GO
Overtake v GO
Overtook v GO
Presence n
Present j
Presently d TIME
Propinquity n JOIN
Proximity n
Recent j PAST
Recognition n AGRE
Riverside n FLOW
Soon d TIME
Standby j REST
Suburb n PLAC
Tap n
Verge n
Verge v VARY
Vicinity n PLAC
Virtual j
Wayside j PATH

NEW

Afresh d
Alamode j SIML
Anew d
Avantgarde n FORW
Craze n MOTV
Crisp j
Currency n
Current j
Fad n MOTV

Fashion n
Fashionable j
Fresh j
Freshen v
Hitherto d EVER
Late j
Lately d
Latest j
Latter j

Mint j
Mode n
Modern j
Modish j
Neo f
New j
Newcomer n GO
Newfangled j
Newfound j OPEN

News n TALK
Newspaper n WRIT
Newsreel n VIEW
Novel j
Novelty n
Novelty n MART
Now d
Present j
Presentday j TIME

Parts of speech: a article; b preposition; c conjunction; d adverb; f prefix; i interjection;
j adjective; n noun; p pronoun; r phrase; v verb.

Presently d
Rage n MOTV
Refurbish v CLEN
Rejuvenate v AID

Renew v BGIN
Renovate v AID
Ripe j
Statusquo n EVER

Style n
Stylish j
Tidings n TALK
Today n TIME

Unused j
Uptodate r
Virgin j BGIN
Vogue n MOTV

NO

Abnegate v LACK
Annul v END
Cannot v
Denied v OPPO
Denier n OPPO
Deny v OPPO
Nary j

Naught n
Nay n
Negate v OPPO
Negating v OPPO
Negative j
Negative j OPPO
Neither j

Never d EVER
Nihilism n IDEA
Nil n
Nix n
No d
Nobody n SOLE
Non f

None p
Nor c
Not d
Nothing n
Null j
Renege v OPPO
Willynilly d MOTV

NSCR

A a
About b
Am v
An a
And c
Another j
Any j
Anyhow d
Anything p
Anyway d
Are v
Article n
As c
At b
Be v
Became v
Become v
Been v
Being v
Beside b
Besides d
By b
Can v
Concerning b
Could v
Deposit n
Depositing v
Did v
Do v
Does v
Doing v
Done v
Either c

For b
From b
Gave v
Gee i
Get v
Give v
Got v
Had v
Has v
Have v
Having v
Hence c
Hereby d
How d
However c
If c
In b
Is v
Item n
Laid v
Lay v
Lest c
Lie v
Lies v
Lodge v
Lying v
Made v
Make v
Makes v
May v
Might v
Object n
Of b

Off j
On d
Only c
Or c
Over b
Provided c
Providing c
Put v
Putting v
Regard n
Regarding b
Regards v
Respect n
Respecting b
Set v
Setting v
Should v
Since c
So c
Some j
Something n
Strike v
Striking v
Struck v
Take v
Than c
That c
The a
Then d
Thence p
There d
Therefore d
These j

Thing n
This j
Thither d
Those j
Though c
To b
Took v
Upon b
Was v
Well i
Were v
What p
Whatever j
Whatsoever j
When d
Where c
Whereas c
Whereby d
Wherefore d
Wherein d
Whereof d
Whereupon d
Whether c
Which j
Whichever j
Who p
Whom p
Whose p
Will v
With b
Within b
Would v
Yet d

NUMR

Abacus n
Accountant n MART
Actuarial j
Add v LARG
Added v LARG
Adder n LARG
Adding v LARG
Addition n LARG
Algebra n
Algorithm n
Arithmetic n

Audit v IDEA
Auditor n IDEA
Average j
Billion n
Bimonthly d TIME
Binary j
Birdie n PLAY
Bogey n PLAY
Both j
Calculate v IDEA
Calculator n MECH

Calculus n
Cardinal j CRUX
Census n GRUP
Cinque n
Cipher n
Coefficient n
Combination n JOIN
Compute v IDEA
Computed v IDEA
Computer n MECH
Computer n IDEA

Cosecant n FORM
Cosine n FORM
Cosines n FORM
Cotangent n FORM
Count n
Countdown n
Counted v
Counter n
Counters n
Counting v
Countless j MUCH

Couple n
Couple n JOIN
Cube n
Cubic j
Cypher n
Decimal n
Denominator n CRUX
Denominator n
Deuce n PLAY
Digit n
Divide v SEP
Dividend n SEP
Division n SEP
Divisor n SEP
Double j
Double n PLAY
Doublecross v FALS
Dozen n
Dual j SIML
Duet n MUSC
Duo n
Duo n MUSC
Duodecimal j
Duplex j
Duplex n HOME
Eagle n PLAY
Eight n
Eighteen n
Eighth n
Eighth n MUSC
Eighty n
Eleven n
Entropy n POWR
Enumerate v IDEA
Equation n SIML
Euclid n IDEA
Exponent n
Extrapolate v
Factor n
Factored v
Factoring v
Fifteen n
Fifth n
Fifth n MUSC
Fifth n SIP
Fifty n
Figure n
Figured v
Figuring v
Fin n MONY

First j FORW
Five n
Fiver n MONY
Forties n
Forty n
Four n
Fourscore j
Foursome n GRUP
Fourteen n
Fourth n
Fourth n MUSC
Fraction n SOME
Frequency n
Geometry n FORM
Gross n
Half n SOME
Harmonic j
Hemi f SOME
Hundred n
Integer n
Integer n WHOL
Integral j WHOL
Love n PLAY
Math n
Mathematics n
Mean j
Means n
Median j
Millennium n TIME
Million n
Minority n LITL
Minus b SEP
Miscount v FALS
Mode n
Modes n
Multiple n LARG
Multiply v LARG
Naught n
Nine n
Nineteen n
Ninety n
Ninth n
Nth j
Number n
Numeral n
Numerator n
Numerical j
O n
Octave n MUSC
Once d

One n
Ordinal j FORW
Pair n
Parameter n
Percent n SOME
Pi n WRIT
Plus b LARG
Point n
Polynomial n MUCH
Power n
Prime n
Product n
Proportion n SOME
Quadrennial j TIME
Quadruple n
Quantify v
Quantitative j
Quantity n
Quarter n SOME
Quartered v SOME
Quartering v SOME
Quarterly j TIME
Quartet n GRUP
Quintet n GRUP
Quota n SOME
Quotient n
Radian n FORM
Rate n
Rating v
Ratio n
Reckon v IDEA
Recount v
Root n CRUX
Scalar n
Score n
Score v POWR
Secant n FORM
Second j
Second n AGRE
Second n AID
Second n MUSC
Seconded v AGRE
Seconded v AID
Seconding v AGRE
Seconding v AID
Seven n
Seventeen n
Seventy n
Sextet n GRUP
Single j SOLE

Single n PLAY
Six n
Sixteen n
Sixth n
Sixth n MUSC
Sixty n
Square n
Squared v
Squaring v
Statistic n
Subtract v SEP
Sum n WHOL
Summed v WHOL
Summing v WHOL
Tallied v
Tally v
Tangent n FORM
Teen j TIME
Teller n TALK
Ten n
Tens n
Tensor n
Tenth n
Tertiary j
Third n
Third n MUSC
Thirteen n
Thirty n
Thousand n
Three n
Times n
Total n WHOL
Totaling v WHOL
Treble j LARG
Triad n GRUP
Trigonometry n FORM
Trinity n GRUP
Trio n GRUP
Trio n MUSC
Triple j
Triple n PLAY
Triplet n
Triplet n MUSC
Twelve n
Twenty n
Twice d
Two n
Vector n
Zero n

OPEN

Abandon n
Aboveboard j UP
Absolution n AGRE
Absolve v AGRE
Accessible j
Acquit v
Ad n
Advertise v
Agape j HOLW
Air v VAPR
Aired v VAPR
Airing v VAPR

Airs v VAPR
Ajar j
Amnesty n AGRE
Aperture n HOLW
Apparent j
Autonomy n SOLE
Bail n LAW
Bald j
Bare j BODY
Bare j
Barefoot j BODY
Bareheaded j BODY

Berth n
Betray v FALS
Bit n
Blab v TALK
Blatant j
Bluff j
Blunt j AGGR
Broach v TALK
Broach v
Candid j TRUE
Candor n TRUE
Clarify v SHRP

Clarity n SHRP
Clear j
Clear v HAVE
Clear v GO
Clear v AGRE
Clearly d
Clew n AID
Clue n AID
Comb v VIEW
Combed v VIEW
Comber n VIEW
Combing v VIEW

Concierge n AID
Conspicuous j VIEW
Decipher v WRIT
Decode v WRIT
Decontrol v
Deliver v AID
Deliverance n AID
Delve v
Denouement n END
Descried v VIEW
Descry v VIEW
Detect v
Detecting v
Dig v
Disclose v
Discover v
Disengage v SEP
Disentangle v SEP
Dislodge v SEP
Dispensation n AID
Display v VIEW
Disseminate v LARG
Divulge v
Door n BLOK
Doorbell n MUSC
Doorkeeper n AID
Doorway n PATH
Drawbridge n PATH
Dug v
Eclat n BAD
Elicit v OUT
Elude v VARY
Elusive j VARY
Emancipate v
Escapade n GO
Escape n GO
Escape n VARY
Evidence v SHRP
Evident j SHRP
Evince v VIEW
Examination n IDEA
Examination n TRUE
Exculpate v AGRE
Excuse v AGRE
Exempt v
Exhibit n VIEW
Exhibition n VIEW
Exonerate v AGRE
Explore v GO
Explore v IDEA
Explorer n GO
Expose v
Expose v VIEW
Exposing v
Exposing v VIEW
Exposition n VIEW
Exposure n VIEW
Exposure n
Expressionism n MOTV
Extricate v
Eye n HOLW
Fathom v IDEA
Fenestrate j HOLW

Ferret v ANML
Find v
Flagrant j BAD
Footloose j GO
Forage v FOOD
Forum n TALK
Found v
Frank j
Frank n GO
Free v
Freedom n
Frisk v
Gape v BODY
Gape v HOLW
Gaping v BODY
Gaping v HOLW
Gate n BLOK
Gatepost n FORM
Gateway n PATH
Gratuitous j AID
Hatch n BLOK
Hatched v BLOK
Hobo n GO
Hole n HOLW
Immune j AID
Impunity n
Independence n SOLE
Informer n TALK
Ingenuous j EASY
Inquest n LAW
Inspect v VIEW
Inspector n VIEW
Inspector n LAW
Investigate v IDEA
Irrepressible j
Key n
Keyhole n HOLW
Keys n
Laissezfaire n
Large n LARG
Latitude n
Lib n
Liberal j
Liberal j AID
Liberate v
Libertarian n
Liberties n
Libertine j BAD
Liberty n
License n
Licentious j BAD
Locate v
Loophole n
Loose j
Loose j BAD
Loosed v
Loosen v
Loosing v
Louver n BLOK
Manifest j
Manifested v
Manifesting v
Naked j BODY

Newfound j NEW
Nirvana n GLAD
Nonpartisan j MOTV
Notoriety n BAD
Nude j BODY
Obvious j
Open v
Open v BGIN
Orifice n HOLW
Ostensible j
Ostentation n VIEW
Outspoken j TALK
Overt j
Palpable j
Pardon v AGRE
Parole n
Paroled v
Paroling v
Patent j
Plain j SHRP
Pore n SOMA
Port n
Portal n BLOK
Porthole n
Pried v SEP
Pried v
Pries v SEP
Pries v
Primafacie j TRUE
Prize v SEP
Probation n TRUE
Probe v IN
Proclamation n TALK
Produce v
Production n
Promiscuous j
Promulgate v AID
Propaganda n IDEA
Prospect v MOTV
Prospected v MOTV
Prospecting v MOTV
Prospector n MOTV
Pry v SEP
Pry v
Public j GRUP
Publication n WRIT
Publicity n GRUP
Publicly d GRUP
Publish v WRIT
Pump v IDEA
Pumped v IDEA
Pumping v IDEA
Quest n
Rampant j
Ransack v DAMG
Reconnaissance n IDEA
Reconnoitre v IDEA
Release v
Research n IDEA
Reveal v
Revelation n
Rummage v
Rummaged v

Rummaging v
Runaway j GO
Scour v GO
Scout n GRUP
Scout n GO
Scouted v GO
Search n MOTV
Seek v MOTV
Sheer j VIEW
Snoop v VIEW
Spill v
Spontaneity n EASY
Squeal v TALK
Stool n FALS
Tap n JOIN
Tattle v TALK
Telltale j TALK
Tramp n GO
Transparent j VIEW
Trapdoor n BLOK
Turnkey n BLOK
Unattached j
Unattended j
Unburden v
Unburied j COVR
Unbutton v GARB
Uncensored j
Uncommitted j
Unconcealed j
Uncontrollable j POWR
Uncork v BLOK
Uncover v
Undid v
Undo v
Unearth v ERTH
Unfasten v
Unfold v VARY
Unfurl v VARY
Unguarded j WEAK
Uninhibited j
Unlimited j
Unlock v
Unmask v
Unoccupied j
Unpack v SEP
Unravel v SEP
Unrestrained j
Unrestricted j
Untangle v SEP
Untended j
Untie v SEP
Untouched j
Untying v SEP
Unveil v
Unwrap v
Vagabond n GO
Vagrant j GO
Vent n OUT
Vindicate v TRUE
Yawn v LARG
Yawn n BODY

Aberrant j VARY
Aberration n VARY
Abnormal j AFAR
Abnormal j SICK
Adversary n
Adverse j
Against b
Adverse j
Agnostic j HOLY
Alien j SEP
Alienate v SEP
Alienation n SEP
Although c
Anomaly n
Another j
Anti b
Antinomy n
Antipodes n PLAC
Antithesis n IDEA
Antitype n
Antonym n TALK
Apostasy n IDEA
Argue v TALK
Assortment n
Atheism n HOLY
Athwart b
Atypical j
Beatnik n GRUP
Bohemian j GRUP
Buck v
Bucked v
Bucking v
But c
Cacophony n HEAR
Challenge v
Clash v
Compete v
Con d
Conflict v
Confute v
Cons n
Contend v
Contention n
Contest n
Contradict v
Contraindicate v
Contrary j
Contrast v
Contravene v
Controversy n
Converse n
Counter d
Counter v
Counteract v
Counterbalance v SIML
Countered v
Countering v
Countermand v
Counterpoise v SIML
Counters v
Counterweight n
Cross j
Crosswise d
Crotchety j PANG
Dada n FORM
Debate n TALK

Declension n
Decline v
Defied v AGGR
Defy v AGGR
Demur v
Denied v NO
Denier n NO
Deny v NO
Despite b
Deviate v VARY
Diametrically d
Diehard n DEAD
Differ v
Difference n
Different j
Differential n
Dimorphic j FORM
Disagree v
Disallow v
Disapprove v
Disavow v
Disbelief n IDEA
Disclaim v
Discrepancy n
Discriminate v IDEA
Disparate j
Disproportion n
Disregard v
Dissension n
Dissent v
Dissident n
Dissimilar j
Dissonance n HEAR
Distinct j
Distinction n
Distinguish v
Diverge v VARY
Diverse j
Diversify v
Divisive j SEP
Else j
Elsewhere d PLAC
Except b
Exception n
Extreme j AFAR
Faction n GRUP
Friction n JOIN
Gainsay v TALK
Heathen j HOLY
Heresy n HOLY
Heretic n HOLY
Heterodox j IDEA
Heterogeneous j
Heteronym n TALK
Heterozygous j BGIN
Hippie n GRUP
Hybrid j JOIN
Iconoclast n HOLY
Ignore v
Imbalance n
Imbroglio n BLUR
Impiety n HOLY
Impious j HOLY
Inadmissible j
Inadvisable j

Inapplicable j
Inappropriate j
Inattentive j
Incomparable j
Incompatible j
Incongruity n
Inconsistency n
Inconsonant j
Incredulity n IDEA
Inedible j FOOD
Inequality n
Inequity n
Inexpedient j
Infelicitous j
Infidel n HOLY
Infraction n
Inharmonious j
Inopportune j
Instead d
Invert v VARY
Irreconcilable j
Irregular j
Irreligious j HOLY
Issue n
Jaywalk v GO
Lieu n
Litigation n LAW
Maladaptation n BAD
Maladjustment n BAD
Malapropos j
Maverick n ANML
Militate v
Miscellany n JOIN
Motley j
Multifarious j MUCH
Negate v NO
Negating v NO
Negative n VIEW
Negative j NO
Negative j ION
Nevertheless d
Nonconformist n
Noncooperation n
Notwithstanding b
Object v
Objected v
Objecting v
Objector n
Odd j
Offset n
Offsets v
Opponent n
Oppose v
Other j
Otherwise j
Out d
Override v
Overrule v
Pagan j HOLY
Paradox n BLUR
Parallax n ASTR
Philistine n FOOL
Pit v
Pitted v
Pitting v

Polar j END
Polarity n END
Polarize v END
Radical j
Rather d
React v EVNT
Reaction n EVNT
Reactionary j EVNT
Rebel v DAMG
Recant v TALK
Recreant n
Refuse v
Refused v
Refusing v
Refute v
Regardless j
Reluctance n
Renege v NO
Repeal v END
Repercussion n
Repudiate v
Rescind v END
Reservation n
Reserve n
Reserved j
Reverse n VARY
Rival n
Save b
Sceptic n BLUR
Skeptic n BLUR
Stead n
Though c
Topsyturvy j BLUR
Unacceptable j
Unalike j
Unamerican j GRUP
Unauthorized j
Unbeliever n IDEA
Uncalled j
Uncommunicative j TALK
Unconstitutional j LAW
Unconventional j
Uncooperative j
Undemocratic j GRUP
Undeserved j
Undue j
Unduly j
Unearned j HAVE
Unequal j
Unequal j WEAK
Unintentional j MOTV
Unlawful j LAW
Unlearn v EDUC
Unless c
Unlike b
Unmanageable j
Unnatural j AFAR
Unofficial j
Unorthodox j
Unpatriotic j GRUP
Unrelated j
Unresponsive j MOTV
Unseasonable j TIME
Unsettled j VARY
Unsolicited j MOTV

Untimely j TIME	Varied v VARY	Viceversa r VARY	While c
Unwilling j	Vary v VARY	Vie v	Wildcat j
Unwitting j BLUR	Versus b	Vying v	Withstand v POWR

OUT

Abreaction n MEDC	Eliminate v SEP	Extraction n	Outpost n AID
Abstract n	Emanate v	Extraction n BGIN	Outside j
Aspirate v VAPR	Emerge v GO	Extraneous j TRIV	Outsider n SEP
Aspirating v VAPR	Emetic n SOMA	Extrinsic j TRIV	Outskirts n END
Aspiration n VAPR	Emission n	Extrovert n MOTV	Outstanding j
Aspirator n MECH	Emit v	Extrude v	Outward d
Belch v DAMG	Empty v LACK	Exude v	Perimeter n HOLW
Bled v SOMA	Enucleate v SEP	Gut v SOMA	Periphery n HOLW
Bled v COLR	Erupt v DAMG	Gutted v SOMA	Pitted v VEGT
Bleed v SOMA	Erupt v BODY	Heave v SOMA	Pitting v VEGT
Bleed v COLR	Evacuate v SEP	Issuance n	Project v MOTV
Catharsis n CLEN	Evict v SEP	Issue n	Projecting v MOTV
Circumference n HOLW	Evoke v BGIN	Issued v	Puke v SOMA
Debouch v GO	Excavate v HOLW	Issuing v	Purge v CLEN
Dehumidify v FLOW	Excrement n DIRT	Leak v FLOW	Radiant j
Delete v SEP	Excrete v DIRT	Nozzle n FLOW	Radiate v
Discharge v SEP	Exhaust n	Oust v SEP	Regurgitate v SOMA
Discharge v DAMG	Exhausting v	Out d	Root v SOMA
Disinter v ERTH	Exhume v ERTH	Out d SEP	Secrete v
Drain v FLOW	Exit n GO	Out d END	Secreting v
Draw v	Exodus n GO	Out n PLAY	Shed v DAMG
Drawn v	Exogenous j BGIN	Outburst n AGGR	Sneeze n SOMA
Drew v	Expel v SEP	Outcast n SEP	Spat v SOMA
Educe v	Export v MART	Outdoor j	Spew v
Efface v SEP	Expurgate v CLEN	Outer j	Spit v SOMA
Effluvium n	Exterior n	Outing n PLAY	Spout v FLOW
Effusive j	External j	Outlay n MONY	Spout v TALK
Ejaculate v SOMA	Extirpate v DAMG	Outlet n	Vent n OPEN
Eject v SEP	Extract v	Outlying j AFAR	Vomit v SOMA
Elicit v OPEN	Extracting v	Outpatient j SICK	Without d

PANG

Aback d BACK	Apoplectic j SICK	Bitterly d AGGR	Bugging v AGGR
Abash v	Appall v	Bleak j	Burden n HAVE
Ache n	Apprehension n	Blubber v TALK	Butterflies n BUG
Ache n MOTV	Arduous j MOTV	Blue j COLR	Cain n
Ado n	Ashamed j	Blues n COLR	Care n
Afraid j	Astonish v	Blues n MUSC	Cares n
Aggravate v AGGR	Astound v	Bluest j COLR	Careworn j
Aggrieve v	Ate v FOOD	Bore n TRIV	Chafe v
Aghast j	Aura n SICK	Bored v TRIV	Chagrin n
Agitate v	Austere j	Boredom n TRIV	Charleyhorse n SOMA
Agog j MOTV	Awe n	Boring v TRIV	Cheerless j
Agony n	Awesome j	Bother v AGGR	Choleric j AGGR
Alack i	Awestricken j	Breakdown n SICK	Clamor v HEAR
Alarm n	Awful j	Breathless j SOMA	Claustrophobia n BLOK
Alarm n HEAR	Awing v	Breathtaking j SOMA	Colic n SICK
Alas i	Bad j BAD	Brokenhearted j SOMA	Comfortless j
Amaze v	Bawl v SOMA	Brood v	Commiserate v FOND
Amazingly d EMPH	Bedevil v BAD	Brooded v	Commotion n
Amuck j DAMG	Berserk j SICK	Brooding v	Complain v AGGR
Anguish n	Beset v	Bug v AGGR	Complaint n AGGR
Annoy v AGGR	Beside b	Bugaboo n MYTH	Complaint n SICK
Anxiety n	Bewail v TALK	Bugbear n MYTH	Complex n
Apathy n LACK	Bitter j AGGR	Bugged v AGGR	Compunction n

Parts of speech: a article; b preposition; c conjunction; d adverb; f prefix; i interjection;
          j adjective; n noun; p pronoun; r phrase; v verb.

Concern n MOTV
Concerned v MOTV
Concerning v MOTV
Condole v FOND
Conniption n
Consternation n
Contrite j
Convulse v VARY
Cow v WEAK
Cowed v WEAK
Cower v WEAK
Cowing v WEAK
Crab n AGGR
Crabbed v AGGR
Crabbier j AGGR
Crabbing v AGGR
Crabby j AGGR
Crank n AGGR
Crankiness n AGGR
Cranks n AGGR
Cranky j AGGR
Crape n GARB
Crawl v BODY
Craze v SICK
Crazed j SICK
Crazier j SICK
Craziness n SICK
Crazy j SICK
Creep v BODY
Crestfallen j
Crick n SOMA
Cried v SOMA
Cringe v WEAK
Cross j AGGR
Crotchety j OPPO
Cry n SOMA
Daze v BLUR
Deject v
Delirious j SICK
Deplore v
Depress v
Depression n
Desolate j SEP
Despair n
Desperate j
Despondent j
Dilemma n BLUR
Dirge n MUSC
Disappoint v
Discomfit v
Discomfort v
Discompose v
Disconcert v
Disconsolate j
Discontent j
Discountenance v AGGR
Discourage v AGGR
Disenchant v
Disgruntle v AGGR
Disgust v
Dishearten v
Disillusion v
Dismal j
Dismay n
Dispirit v

Disquiet v
Distemper n AGGR
Distract v
Distraught j
Distress n
Disturb v
Dizzy j BLUR
Doldrums n
Doleful j
Down d DOWN
Downcast j DOWN
Drama n PLAY
Drawn j VARY
Dread v
Dreary j
Drunk j SIP
Dumbfound v BLUR
Dump n DOWN
Duress n
Dysphoria n
Earache n BODY
Eat v FOOD
Edge n SHRP
Eek i
Eerie j AFAR
Elegy n TALK
Embarrass v
Embitter v AGGR
Embroil v AGGR
Emotion n
Endure v EVER
Ennui n TRIV
Exasperate v AGGR
Excite v
Excruciating j
Exercise v
Extremity n END
Faint j WEAK
Faze v
Fear v
Fed v
Ferment n VARY
Fidget v
Fit n
Fitful j VARY
Flabbergast v
Flinch v
Flurry n
Fluster v
Footsore j BODY
Forlorn j
Frantic j
Frazzle n
Freeze v COLD
Frenzy n
Fret v AGGR
Fretful j
Fright n
Froze v COLD
Fulsome j FALS
Fume v AGGR
Fuming v AGGR
Funereal j DEAD
Funk n
Furor n

Fuss n
Gag v SOMA
Gagged v SOMA
Gagging v SOMA
Gall v AGGR
Galled v AGGR
Galling v AGGR
Galls v AGGR
Gaunt j
Ghastly j
Giddy j BLUR
Glassy j BLOK
Gloom n BLUR
Glum j
Gnaw v FOOD
Grate v AGGR
Grating v AGGR
Grave j CRUX
Gravity n CRUX
Grief n
Grim j AGGR
Grimace v
Gripe v
Grisly j BAD
Groan n TALK
Groggy j WEAK
Grouch n AGGR
Gruesome j
Grumpy j AGGR
Guilt n CRIM
Haggard j
Hangover n
Harass v AGGR
Hard j
Hardship n
Harried v DAMG
Harrier n DAMG
Harrow v DAMG
Harry v DAMG
Haze v AGGR
Hazed v AGGR
Hazing v AGGR
Headache n BODY
Headier j BODY
Heady j BODY
Heartache n SOMA
Heartbreak n SOMA
Heartrending j SOMA
Heartsick j SOMA
Hectic j
Hell n BAD
Highstrung j
Homesick j HOME
Hopeless j
Horrendous j
Horrible j
Horrid j
Horrify v
Horror n
Hot j HEAT
Hubbub n HEAR
Hullabaloo n HEAR
Hurt v
Hypersensitive j
Hypochondria n SICK

Hysteria n SICK
Impatience n
Incense v AGGR
Inconsolable j
Inconvenience v
Indispose v
Inebriate v SIP
Insane j SICK
Insomnia n
Insufferable j
Intimidate v WEAK
Intolerable j
Intoxicate v SIP
Irascible j AGGR
Irk v AGGR
Irritate v AGGR
Itch v SOMA
Itch v MOTV
Jag n SIP
Jar v AGGR
Jarred v AGGR
Jitters n
Jittery j
Jumpier j
Jumpy j
Keen v TALK
Keened v TALK
Keening v TALK
Keens v TALK
Key v
Keyed v
Keying v
Keys v
Lacrymose j SOMA
Lament n TALK
Lassitude n REST
Leerier j BLUR
Leery j BLUR
Letdown n DOWN
Listless j TRIV
Loathe v AGGR
Lonely j SOLE
Lonesome j SOLE
Low j DOWN
Lugubrious j FOOL
Lurid j
Lush n SIP
Macabre j DEAD
Malaise n
Malcontent j AGGR
Mania n SICK
Mania n MOTV
Maniac n SICK
Manic j SICK
Matter n CRUX
Maudlin j FOOL
Mawkish j
Melancholia n
Melodrama n PLAY
Miserable j
Miseries n
Misery n
Misgiving n BLUR
Moan v TALK
Monody n MUSC

Moody j
Moon v
Mooned v
Mooning v
Moons v
Mope v REST
Morbid j
Morose j
Mortify v AGGR
Mourn v
Nausea n SICK
Nerves n
Nervous j
Nettle v AGGR
Nettled v AGGR
Nettling v AGGR
Neurosis n SICK
Neurotic j SICK
Nightmare n MYTH
Nostalgia n MOTV
Nuisance n AGGR
Obsess v EVER
Onerous j
Onus n
Ordeal n
Outcry n HEAR
Overanxious j
Overawe v WEAK
Overburden v
Overemotional j
Overexcite v
Overwrought j
Pain n DAMG
Pains n DAMG
Pall n COVR
Pall v TRIV
Palled v TRIV
Palling v TRIV
Pang n
Panic n
Paroxysm n VARY
Passion n HOLY
Pathetic j WEAK
Pathos n
Peaked j LACK
Peeve v AGGR
Penance n
Penitence n
Penitent j
Perturb v
Pesky j AGGR
Pessimism n
Pest n AGGR
Pester v AGGR
Pet n AGGR
Petrify v REST
Petulance n AGGR
Phobia n
Phrenetic j DAMG
Pickle n BLUR

Pickled j SIP
Pinch n BLOK
Pine v MOTV
Pined v MOTV
Pining v MOTV
Piteous j WEAK
Pitied v
Pitiful j
Pity v
Plague v
Plaint n
Plaintive j
Plaster v SIP
Plight n
Poignant j
Potted j SIP
Pout n AGGR
Predicament n BLUR
Premonition n FORW
Presentiment n FORW
Pull v
Pulled v
Quail v WEAK
Quailed v WEAK
Quailing v WEAK
Quake v VARY
Qualm n
Queasy j
Quiver v VARY
Rancor n AGGR
Rankle v AGGR
Rasp v HEAR
Rattle v
Rattles v
Rave v TALK
Raving v TALK
Regret v
Remorse n
Repent v
Repugnance n AGGR
Resent v AGGR
Restless j
Revolt n
Revulsion n
Rile v AGGR
Rue v
Ruffle v
Ruing v
Sackcloth n GARB
Sad j
Sadden v
Saturnine j
Scandal n BAD
Scare v
Scarecrow n ANML
Scene n
Selfconscious j SOLE
Shake v VARY
Shaking v VARY
Shame n BAD

Shamefaced j BODY
Shaming v BAD
Shock n
Shook v VARY
Shrank v
Shrink v
Shudder v VARY
Shy v VARY
Smart v
Smarted v
Smarting v
Snivel v TALK
Soak v SIP
Sob v TALK
Sober j
Somber j
Sore j
Sorrow n
Sorry j
Sorts n
Sot n SIP
Sour j AGGR
Soured v AGGR
Souring v AGGR
Spell n
Splenetic j AGGR
Squeamish j
Start v
Startle v
Stew n HEAT
Strain n
Strained v
Straining v
Strait n BLOK
Stress n
Suffer v
Sulk v AGGR
Sulking v AGGR
Sulky d AGGR
Sullen j AGGR
Surprise n AFAR
Suspense n BLUR
Tantalize v
Tantrum n AGGR
Taut j BLOK
Tearful j SOMA
Tedious j TRIV
Tender j EASY
Tense j
Tension n
Terrible j BAD
Terrified v
Terrify v
Terror n
Testy j AGGR
Throe n DAMG
Tight j SIP
Tipsy j SIP
Tizzy n
Toothache n BODY

Torment n DAMG
Torture v DAMG
Touch v MOTV
Trauma n DAMG
Travail n WORK
Tremble n VARY
Tremulous j VARY
Trepidation n
Trial n
Tribulation n
Tried v
Trouble n
Try v
Tumult n HEAR
Turmoil n BLUR
Turn n VARY
Twinge n
Twitter n
Ugh i
Unappetizing j FOOD
Unbearable j
Uncomfortable j
Uneasy j
Unenviable j
Unhappy j
Unnerve v
Unpleasant j
Unrest n
Unsettled j VARY
Untoward j
Uproar n HEAR
Upset v
Vertigo n BLUR
Vex v AGGR
Wail n TALK
Wear v WEAK
Wearily d WEAK
Weariness n WEAK
Wearing v WEAK
Weary j WEAK
Weep v SOMA
Weigh v
Weight n
Wept v SOMA
Whimper v TALK
Whine v TALK
Wince v
Woe n
Woozy j BLUR
Wore v WEAK
Work v WORK
Worked v WORK
Working v WORK
Works v WORK
Worn v WEAK
Wornout j WEAK
Worry v
Wretch n BAD
Writhe v VARY
Wrought j

Age v
Aged j
Aging j
Ago j
Already d
Anachronism n FALS
Ancestor n KIN
Ancient j
Annals n WRIT
Ante f
Antebellum j DAMG
Antecede v FORW
Antedate v FORW
Antediluvian j FLOW
Antiquity n
Archaeology n ERTH
Archaic j
Archeology n ERTH
Atavism n
Autobiography n SOLE
Baroque j FORM
Before d
Biblical j HOLY
Biography n WRIT
Bygone j
Cenozoic j
Centenarian n
Chronicle n WRIT
Classic j EVER
Commemorate v IDEA
Cromagnon j

Dotage n FOOL
Dowager n LADY
Earlier j
Early j
Elder n
Elder n LEAD
Elderly j
Emeritus j POWR
Erstwhile d
Fogies n
Fogy n
Forebear n KIN
Forefather n KIN
Former j
Formerly d
Fossil n
Gaffer n MALE
Geezer n FOOL
Genealogy n KIN
Geriatric j MEDC
Gothic j
Grandam n LADY
Granny n LADY
Heretofore d
History n IDEA
Hoar j COLR
Immemorial j EVER
Last j
Late j DEAD
Line n KIN
Lineage n KIN

Medieval j
Memento n IDEA
Memoir n WRIT
Memorial j IDEA
Memory n IDEA
Mesozoic j
Neanderthal j
Neolithic j
Obsolete j TRIV
Old j
Oldfashioned j
Oldfashioned n SIP
Oldtime j
Once d
Ontogeny n SOLE
Outmoded j TRIV
Overdue j
Paleolithic j
Paleontology n IDEA
Paleozoic j
Passe j
Past j
Pedigree n BGIN
Phylogeny n GRUP
Piltdown j
Precedence n FORW
Precursor n FORW
Predate v FORW
Predecessor n FORW
Preexist v LIVE
Prehistory n FORW

Previous j
Primal j FORW
Primeval j FORW
Primitive j
Primordial j FORW
Prior j
Pristine j GOOD
Protoerozoic j
Recall v IDEA
Recent j NEAR
Recollect v IDEA
Relic n
Remembrance n IDEA
Reminiscence n IDEA
Renaissance j
Retroactive j
Senile j SICK
Senior j LEAD
Sometime j
Souvenir n IDEA
Then n
Tradition n EVER
Venerable j FOND
Veteran n DAMG
Veteran n POWR
Victorian j
Yesterday d
Yore n

PATH

Aisle n
Alley n
Aqueduct n FLOW
Artery n JOIN
Autobahn n VEHC
Avenue n
Bearing n
Bearings n
Beat n LAW
Block n
Boulevard n
Bridge n JOIN
Canal n FLOW
Causeway n
Channel n FLOW
Circuit n ION
Col n ERTH
Compass n MSMT
Concourse n JOIN
Conductance n ION
Conductivity n
Conduit n HOLW
Confluence n JOIN
Corner n JOIN
Corners n JOIN
Corridor n
Course n

Course n ERTH
Crossover n JOIN
Crossroad n JOIN
Culdesac n END
Cutoff n VARY
Defile n
Direction n
Doorway n OPEN
Downgrade n DOWN
Drawbridge n OPEN
Driveway n
Duct n HOLW
Ductless j HOLW
East n PLAC
Easterly j PLAC
Eastern j PLAC
Enroute j
Footpath n BODY
Gangplank n FLOW
Gangway n
Gantlet n JOIN
Gateway n OPEN
Grade n VARY
Hallway n HOME
Highway n
Interchange n VARY
Itinerary n

Junction n JOIN
Labyrinth n BLUR
Lane n
Lap n MSMT
Main n HOLW
Mains n HOLW
Mall n
Maze n BLUR
Midway n
North n PLAC
Overpass n UP
Parkway n
Pass n
Passageway n
Passes n
Path n
Pave v AID
Pavement n AID
Piazza n PLAC
Pike n
Plaza n PLAC
Promenade n
Road n
Roadway n
Rotary n VARY
Route n
Routed v

Routing v
Row n
Shortcircuit n LITL
Shortcut n LITL
Sidewalk n
Siding n
South n PLAC
Spur n VARY
Square n PLAC
Street n
Thoroughfare n
Track n
Trail n
Trend n
Trunk n JOIN
Tunnel n HOLW
Turnabout n VARY
Turnpike n
Underpass n DOWN
Via b
Viaduct n
Walk n
Watercourse n FLOW
Way n
Wayside j NEAR
West n PLAC

Acropolis n POWR
Address n WRIT
Alpine j BULG
Alps n BULG
Amazon n FLOW
America n
American j
Andes n BULG
Anglican j
Anglicize v
Anglophile n FOND
Anglophobe n AGGR
Antarctic n COLD
Antipodes n OPPO
Anywhere d
Appalachian j BULG
Arctic n COLD
Area n
Armageddon n DAMG
Atlantic n FLOW
Bermudas n GARB
Bilateral j SIML
Borough n
Camelot n MYTH
Canton n
Capital j LEAD
Caribbean j FLOW
Center n SHRP
Central j SHRP
Churchyard n HOLY
Cities n
City n
Common n WHOL
Continent n ERTH
Continental j ERTH
Cordovan j FABR
Cosmopolitan j WHOL
Counties n
Country n
Country n ERTH
Countryside n ERTH
County n
Court n HOME
Courts n HOME
Courtyard n HOME

Coventry n SEP
Dalmatian n ANML
Damask n FABR
Dane n ANML
Danish n FOOD
Danube n FLOW
District n
Downtown d DOWN
Dreamland n MYTH
Dutch j
East n PATH
Easterly j PATH
Easterly n WEA
Eastern j PATH
Elsewhere d OPPO
England n
English j
Equator n HEAT
Everywhere d WHOL
Fairyland n MYTH
Farmyard n HOME
Fatherland n LEAD
Field n
Flank n
Hamlet n
Havana n FOOD
Hemisphere n
Hereabout d NEAR
Holland n
Holland n FABR
Intermediate j
Interstate j JOIN
Jersey n ANML
Kingdom n GRUP
Kremlin n LEAD
Land n ERTH
Larboard n FLOW
Lateral j
Left j BODY
Lefthanded j BODY
Local j NEAR
Locale n
Locality n NEAR
Locate v
Locus n

Madras n FABR
Marketplace n MART
Median j
Metropolitan j
Mid j
Middle j
Municipal j LAW
Neighborhood n NEAR
North n PATH
Occident n
Orient n
Oriental n
Pacific n FLOW
Patio n HOME
Piazza n PATH
Place n
Placing v
Plaza n PATH
Polar j COLD
Pole n COLD
Port n FLOW
Position n
Positioned v
Positioning v
Post n
Posted v
Posting v
Posts n
Pottersfield n DEAD
Precinct n
Principality n LEAD
Province n
Provincial j WEAK
Provincial j
Quadrangle n HOME
Quarter n
Realm n
Region n
Rhine n FLOW
Right d BODY
Righthanded j BODY
Rights n BODY
Rural j ERTH
Sagittal j BODY
Sahara n HEAT

Seat n REST
Side n
Site n
Situate v
Situation n
Slum n DIRT
Somewhere d
South n PATH
Spot n
Spotted v
Square n PATH
Starboard n FLOW
State n
States n
Station n
Subregion n
Subtropical j HEAT
Suburb n NEAR
Territory n ERTH
Theater n
There d
Town n
Tropic j HEAT
UnitedStates n
Upstate j UP
Uptown d UP
Urban j
Utopia n MYTH
Vatican n HOLY
Vicinity n NEAR
Village n
Ward n
Waterloo n WEAK
West n PATH
Whence d
Where d
Whereabout d
Wherever d
Whither d
Yard n
Yards n
Zion n HOLY
Zone n

PLAY

Ace n POWR
Acrobat n
Act n
Acting n
Actor n MALE
Actress n LADY
Ad n AID
Aerialist n UP
Amphitheater n HOME
Aquacade n FLOW
Arena n HOME
Artiste n POWR
Athlete n POWR
Avocation n
Back n BACK
Backfield n BACK
Balk v FALS

Ball n FORM
Ball n MUSC
Ballerina n LADY
Balloon n VAPR
Ballroom n HOME
Base n
Baseball n
Bases n
Basketball n HOLW
Bat n FORM
Batted v FORM
Batter n FORM
Batteries n
Batters n FORM
Battery n
Batting v FORM
Bee n

Bigtop n HOME
Billiard n
Bingo n
Birdie n NUMR
Bishop n HOLY
Blackjack n COLR
Bleachers n REST
Block n FORM
Bogey n NUMR
Bowl n HOME
Bowl v
Bowled v
Bowler n
Bowling n
Box n REST
Box v DAMG
Boxed v DAMG

Boxer n DAMG
Boxing v DAMG
Bridge n
Burlesque n FOOL
By n FORW
Bye n FORW
Cabaret n MART
Caddy n AID
Calisthenic j WORK
Canasta n
Cap n DAMG
Caps n DAMG
Card n
Carnival n
Carouse v SIP
Caroused v SIP
Carousel n

Carrousel n	Down n DOWN	Harlequin n GLAD	Out n OUT
Casino n MART	Drama n PANG	Header n	Outfield n ERTH
Cassino n	Draughts n	Heart n	Outing n OUT
Cast n GRUP	Draw v SIML	Heat n	Outplay v POWR
Casting n GRUP	Drawn v SIML	Heats n	Pageant n
Castle n HOME	Drew v SIML	Hippodrome n HOME	Pantomime n SIML
Castling v HOME	Dribble v GO	Hob n BULG	Parquet n REST
Catcher n HAVE	Duckpin n	Hobbies n	Parties n GRUP
Celebrant n GLAD	Dumbbell n WORK	Hobby n	Party n GRUP
Celebrate v GLAD	Dummy n	Hockey n	Pastime n TIME
Celebrated v GLAD	Eagle n NUMR	Holiday n TIME	Pawn n SUB
Charade n BLUR	Emcee n LEAD	Home n HOME	Pentathlon n
Checker n	Enact v	Homer n HOME	Perform v
Checkerboard n FORM	Encore n SIML	Homered v HOME	Picnic n FOOD
Checkmate v BLOK	End n END	Homering v HOME	Pigskin n FABR
Chess n	Entertain v	Impresario n LEAD	Pin n FORM
Chip n MONY	Exercise n	Inning n SOME	Pingpong n
Chip v GO	Extra n AID	Jack n	Pinochle n
Chipped v GO	Extravaganza n	Jamboree n GRUP	Pinwheel n
Chipping v GO	Fair n	Jockey n ANML	Pitcher n GO
Chorus n GRUP	Fairs n	Joker n	Play v
Cinema n HOME	Fence v SHRP	Junket n GO	Playback n SIML
Circus n HOME	Festival n GLAD	King n LEAD	Playground n ERTH
Club n	Festive j GLAD	Kite n UP	Playmate n JOIN
Coach n LEAD	Festoon v FORM	Kiting v UP	Playpen n YNG
Coliseum n HOME	Fiddle v	Knave n	Plaything n
Colosseum n HOME	Field n ERTH	Knight n	Playwright n WRIT
Comedian n GLAD	Fielder n ERTH	Lacrosse n	Ploy n GLAD
Comedy n GLAD	Fielding v ERTH	Lateral n GO	Pogostick n FORM
Confetti n MTRL	Fiesta n	League n GRUP	Poker n
Court n HOME	Film n VIEW	Line n FORW	Polo n
Courts n HOME	Flicker n VIEW	Loge n REST	Pool n
Crap n	Float n VEHC	Love n NUMR	Potlatch n FOOD
Craps n	Flush n SIML	Majorette n LADY	Premiere n FORW
Crease n HOLW	Foil n SHRP	Mallet n	Prom n MUSC
Crib n	Football n BODY	Marble n MTRL	Promenade n MUSC
Cribbage n	Forward n FORW	Marionette n SUB	Puck n
Cricket n	Forwards n FORW	Marquee n VIEW	Pugilism n DAMG
Cricket n GOOD	Foul n FALS	Masque n FALS	Punch n MYTH
Croquet n	Frame n SOME	Masquerade v FALS	Punt n GO
Croupier n LEAD	Frolic v GLAD	Match n	Puppet n SUB
Cue n	Function n GRUP	Matches n	Put v GO
Curler n	Furlough n	Mate v POWR	Putt n GO
Curling n	Gala j GLAD	Mated v POWR	Putting v GO
Curtain n COVR	Gambit n	Matinee n TIME	Quarter n SOME
Deal n SEP	Game n	Mating v POWR	Quarterback n LEAD
Dealer n SEP	Geisha n LADY	Meld v JOIN	Queen n LEAD
Dealing v SEP	Glove n GARB	Melodrama n PANG	Quoits n
Deals v SEP	Goal n END	Merrygoround n GO	Racket n
Dealt v SEP	Goalie n END	Merrymaking n GLAD	Recreation n
Decathlon n	Golf n	Mime n SIML	Resort n
Deck n GRUP	Grandstand n POWR	Miming v SIML	Revel n GLAD
Deuce n NUMR	Gridiron n FORM	Misdeal v FALS	Ring n HOME
Diamond n	Guard n BLOK	Mitt n GARB	Rink n HOME
Dice n	Gym n HOME	Movies n VIEW	Rodeo n ANML
Die n	Gymnasium n HOME	Mummer n	Roister v GLAD
Discus n FORM	Gymnast n	Olympic j	Rook n
Doll n	Half n SOME	Orchestra n REST	Roulette n MOTV
Dollies n	Halfback n BACK	Orgiastic j GLAD	Rubber n SOME
Dolly n	Halloween n TIME	Orgiastic j SEX	Rumpus j
Domino n	Hand n BODY	Orgy n GLAD	Safety n
Double n NUMR	Hands n BODY	Orgy n SEX	SantaClaus n HOLY

Parts of speech: a article; b preposition; c conjunction; d adverb; f prefix; i interjection;
j adjective; n noun; p pronoun; r phrase; v verb.

Scene n
Screwball n VARY
Scrimmage v
Scrub n SUB
Scrubbed v SUB
Serve v GO
Service n GO
Serving v GO
Shot n
Show n
Shower n AID
Sightseeing n VIEW
Single n NUMR
Skate v GO
Skated v GO
Skating v GO
Skee v GO
Ski v GO

Skied v GO
Skier n GO
Skies v GO
Skiing v GO
Skis v GO
Skit n
Slam n POWR
Soccer n
Solitaire n SOLE
Spade n
Spar v DAMG
Spare n POWR
Sport n
Squash n
Stadium n HOME
Stage n FORM
Stock n
Straight n FORW

Strike v
Striking v
Struck v
Stunt n
Tennis n
Theater n HOME
Theatrical j
Thespian n
Top n
Tops n
Touchback n POWR
Touchball n JOIN
Touchdown n POWR
Tournament n
Toy n
Track n GO
Trap n MECH
Trapeze n UP

Trick n
Triple n NUMR
Troupe n GRUP
Trump v POWR
Trumped v POWR
Umpire n LEAD
Vacation n
Valentine n FOND
Volley n GO
Volleyed v GO
Volleying v GO
Walk v GO
Wing n FORM
Yoyo n
Yule n HOLY

POWR

Ability n
Able j
Ablebodied j BODY
Ably d
Accede v
Accession n GO
Acclaim v AGRE
Accolade n AGRE
Accomplish v
Ace n PLAY
Ace n DAMG
Achieve v
Acropolis n PLAC
Acumen n IDEA
Address n
Adept j
Adequate j MUCH
Adroit j
Adult n
Adulthood n
Aerodynamics n VAPR
Agile j
Almighty j WHOL
Amazon n LADY
Ambidextrous j BODY
Ambition n MOTV
Aplomb n
Apt j
Aptitude n
Arch j
Arm n
Arrive v GO
Arrogant j AGGR
Art n
Artful j
Artisan n WORK
Artist n
Artiste n PLAY
Arts n
Arts n EDUC
Assert v
Assertive j
Assumption n HOLY
Astute j IDEA

Athlete n PLAY
Atlas n MYTH
Attain v GO
Audacity n AGGR
August j
Augustly d
Award n AID
Bachelor n EDUC
Backbone n BODY
Badge n VIEW
Banner j VIEW
Barge v GO
Barged v GO
Barges v GO
Barging v GO
Bear v
Beard v WEAK
Bearing v
Beat v WEAK
Beaten j WEAK
Bench n LAW
Best v WEAK
Bested v WEAK
Besting v WEAK
Better v WEAK
Big j LARG
Blade n MALE
Bloom v LARG
Bloomed v LARG
Blossom v LARG
Blow v TALK
Blueblood n
Boast n TALK
Bold j
Bore v
Brag v TALK
Braggart n TALK
Brash j FOOL
Brass n FOOL
Brassy j FOOL
Brave j
Brave n MALE
Bravo i
Brazen j FOOL

Bright j
Bright j IDEA
Brilliant j IDEA
Brilliant j
Buckle v
Bull v ANML
Bulled v ANML
Bulling v ANML
Bulls v ANML
Cagey j IDEA
Cagier j IDEA
Caginess n IDEA
Caliber n
Calibre n
Cannier j IDEA
Cannily d IDEA
Canny j IDEA
Cap v
Capable j
Capacities n
Capacity n
Caps v
Carried v
Carry v
Cavalier j AGGR
Celebrated j
Celebrity n
Champ n
Champion n
Champion n AID
Chefdoeuvre n
Ciceronian j TALK
Citadel n HOME
Class n
Classic j EVER
Classy j
Clever j IDEA
Click v
Clinch v
Cockier j
Cocksure j SHRP
Cocky j
Coerce v AGGR
Comeback n GO

Comer n GO
Commission n
Commissioned v
Compass v
Compassed v
Compassing v
Compel v
Competence n
Compulsion n MOTV
Compulsory j MOTV
Conceit n FOOL
Conceited j FOOL
Confidence n MOTV
Confident j MOTV
Connoisseur n IDEA
Conquer v WEAK
Conquest n WEAK
Conquistador n DAMG
Consolidate v
Cope v
Coping v
Coup n DAMG
Courage n
Crack j
Crackerjack n
Craft n WORK
Craft n FALS
Crafted v WORK
Craftier j FALS
Crafting v WORK
Crafty j FALS
Cream n GOOD
Cream v WEAK
Creamed v WEAK
Crow v TALK
Cunning j
Cunning j FALS
Cup n HOLW
Daedal j
Dais n FORM
Dare v MOTV
Dash n
Dashing j
Dauntless j

Decisive j IDEA
Decompress v VARY
Decorate v GOOD
Defeat v WEAK
Defeating v WEAK
Deft j
Derringdo n MOTV
Dexterity n
Dextrous j
Dignify v GOOD
Dignitary n
Dignity n GOOD
Dint n
Diploma n WRIT
Diplomacy n LAW
Distinction n
Distingue j
Distinguish v
Diva n LADY
Doctor n EDUC
Doctorate n EDUC
Doughty j
Down v WEAK
Downed v WEAK
Downing v WEAK
Drive v MOTV
Drop n
Drove v MOTV
Dynamic j
Dynamism n
Dynamo n MECH
Dyne n MSMT
Edge n SHRP
Effective j
Efficacy n
Efficiency n
Electromotive j ION
Elevate v UP
Elevation n UP
Elite j GOOD
Eloquence n TALK
Embolden v
Emeritus j PAST
Eminence n
Eminent j
Empower v LEAD
Enable v
Energy n
Enforce v
Enterprise n MOTV
Entropy n NUMR
Epic j
Erg n MSMT
Esprit n MOTV
Espritdecorps n GRUP
Exact v MOTV
Exacted v MOTV
Exacting v MOTV
Exacts v MOTV
Exalt v GOOD
Exceed v
Exceeding v
Excel v
Excellence n GOOD
Experience n

Expert j
Exploit n
Faculty n
Fame n
Fanfare n MUSC
Faultless j GOOD
Fearless j
Feat n
Feather n
Finesse n
Finish n END
Firepower n DAMG
Firm j
Firstclass j FORW
Firstrate j FORW
Fit j
Flair n
Flamboyant j VIEW
Flapper n LADY
Flashier j VIEW
Flashy j VIEW
Flatten v WEAK
Flaunt v VIEW
Flawless j GOOD
Fledge v AID
Flourish v LARG
Flourished v LARG
Flourishing v LARG
Flower n VEGT
Foolhardy j FOOL
Foolproof j
Force n
Force n GRUP
Forced v
Forcible j
Foremost j FORW
Formidable j
Fort n HOME
Forte n
Fortify v AID
Fortitude n
Fortress n HOME
Forward j FORW
Fullfledged j WHOL
Gall n AGGR
Gallant j
Game j MOTV
Genie n MYTH
Genius n IDEA
Gift n AID
Gifted j AID
Ginger n
Glamor n GOOD
Glory n GOOD
Goad v SHRP
Good j GOOD
Goodly j GOOD
Graduate v EDUC
Grand j GOOD
Grandeur n
Grandiloquence n TALK
Grandiose j FALS
Grandstand n PLAY
Great j GOOD
Grit n

Grownup n LARG
Gumption n
Gut n SOMA
Hale j MEDC
Handier j BODY
Handily d BODY
Handy j BODY
Hard j
Hardier j
Hardihood n
Hardily d
Hardy j
Haughty j AGGR
Hauteur n AGGR
Headstrong j BODY
Heart n MOTV
Hearten v AID
Heartier j
Hearty j
Heft n
Herculean j
Hercules n ASTR
Hero n MALE
Heroic j
Heroine n LADY
Heroism n
Heterosis n JOIN
Heyday n TIME
High j UP
Hightoned j FALS
Hit n
Honor n GOOD
Horsepower n MSMT
Hot j HEAT
Huskier j LARG
Huskies n LARG
Huskiest j LARG
Huskily d SOMA
Husky j LARG
Hydrodynamic j FLOW
Id n MOTV
Illustrious j
Impetus n BGIN
Impose v AGGR
Impregnable j
Impress v MOTV
Impression n MOTV
Impressive j MOTV
Incomparable j
Incontestable j TRUE
Incontrovertible j TRUE
Indefatigable j
Indestructible j EVER
Indisputable j TRUE
Indomitable j
Inductance n ION
Induction n ION
Ineluctable j EVER
Inescapable j EVER
Inevitable j EVER
Inexhaustible j EVER
Infallible j EVER
Influence n
Influential j
Ingenious j IDEA

Ingenuity n IDEA
Inspire v MOTV
Intrepid j
Invigorate v
Invincible j
Inviolable j
Invulnerable j
Ironclad j MTRL
Irresistible j
Journeyman n WORK
Juice n
Jump n
Knack n
Knowhow n IDEA
Kudos n
Laureate j
Laurel n VEGT
Lick v WEAK
Licked v WEAK
Licking v WEAK
Limelight n VIEW
Lion n ANML
Lionize v ANML
Lissome j EASY
Luminary n VIEW
Lustier j
Lusty j
Made v
Magnificence n GOOD
Mahatma n IDEA
Major j CRUX
Major n EDUC
Majored v EDUC
Majoring v EDUC
Majors n EDUC
Make v
Makes v
Maneuver v GO
Maneuver n EVNT
Marvelous j GOOD
Master n LEAD
Mastered v LEAD
Mastering v LEAD
Masterpiece n LEAD
Matchless j
Mate v PLAY
Mated v PLAY
Mating v PLAY
Mature v
Medal n
Meridian n UP
Mettle n
Might n
Mightier j
Mighty j
Minx n LADY
Momentum n GO
Muscle v BODY
Muscled v BODY
Muscling v BODY
Name n TALK
Nerve n
Nervier j
Nervy j
Nimble j QUIK

Notable j
Note n
Noted j
Omnipotence n WHOL
Outdo v
Outplay v PLAY
Outshine v VIEW
Outsmart v IDEA
Outstanding j
Outstrip v
Outwit v IDEA
Overbearing j AGGR
Overcame v WEAK
Overcome v WEAK
Overconfident j MOTV
Overmaster v LEAD
Overpower v WEAK
Overthrow v WEAK
Overweening j AGGR
Overwhelm v WEAK
Pacemaker n GO
Paladin n
Palm n VEGT
Pass v
Passed v
Passes v
Passing v
Peak n UP
Peerless j
Peremptory j AGGR
Perfect j GOOD
Perfected v GOOD
Perfection n GOOD
Perfects v GOOD
Perspicacity n IDEA
Pert j QUIK
PhD n EDUC
PhiBetaKappa n EDUC
Picaresque j BAD
Piecederesistance r CRUX
Piledriver n FORM
Pinnacle n UP
Pip n
Pips n
Pith n CRUX
Pithy j CRUX
Ploy n EVNT
Pluck n
Plucky j
Poise n
Pomp n GOOD
Pomposity n FOOL
Pompous j FOOL
Potency n
Potent j
Potential n
Potential n ION
Power n
Prance v GO
Precocity n YNG
Preeminence n
Prepotency n
Press n
Press n MECH

Pressed v
Pressing v
Pressure n
Prestige n
Presumptuous j MOTV
Pretentious j FALS
Prevail v
Pride n FOND
Prime j
Prize v AID
Pro n
Prodigious j AFAR
Prodigy n AFAR
Professional j
Proficiency n
Prominence n
Promise n
Pros n
Proud j FOND
Prowess n
Pull n
Push v GO
Qualify v CRUX
Rally n GRUP
Rally v
Ram v
Rammed v
Rams v
Record n
Reinforce v AID
Renaissance n BGIN
Renown n
Reputation n CRUX
Repute n CRUX
Ribbon n FABR
Ripe j
Robust j
Rugged j
Sagacity n IDEA
Sangfroid n GLAD
Savant n EDUC
Savoirfaire n
Scholar n EDUC
Scintillate v VIEW
Scoop v WRIT
Score v NUMR
Season v TIME
Seasoned v TIME
Seasoning v TIME
Selfassured j SOLE
Selfconfidence n SOLE
Selfmade j SOLE
Sensational j
Sharp j SHRP
Sheepskin n WRIT
Shellack v WEAK
Shine v VIEW
Shone v VIEW
Shrewd j IDEA
Signal j
Skill n
Slam n PLAY
Sleeper n REST
Smart j IDEA

Smart j QUIK
Smart j GOOD
Snob n FALS
Solid j
Sophistication n IDEA
Sound j
Soup v
Souped v
Souping v
Spare n PLAY
Specialist n CRUX
Specialty n CRUX
Spectacular j VIEW
Splendor n GOOD
Spry j
Stalwart j
Stamina n
Star n
Stars n
Stature n
Status n
Staunch j
Staunchly d
Steel n
Steeled v
Steeling v
Stout j
Strain n
Strained v
Straining v
Strategic j CRUX
Strength n
Stress n
Strong j
Stronghold n HOME
Strut n GO
Stunning j GOOD
Stupendous j GOOD
Sturdy j
Subdue v WEAK
Sublime j GOOD
Substantial j
Succeed v
Success n
Super j
Superb j GOOD
Supercilious j AGGR
Superhuman j AFAR
Superior j GOOD
Superiority n GOOD
Superlative j GOOD
Superman n MALE
Surmount v
Surpass v
Swagger v
Sway n
Tact n
Tactic n EVNT
Take v
Talent n
Talisman n MYTH
Tell v
Temerity n
Tenable j

Tenacity n EVER
Thermodynamic j HEAT
Thoroughbred j ANML
Thoroughbred j BGIN
Threw v WEAK
Thrive v
Throw v WEAK
Thrust v GO
Tireless j
Told v
Tone n
Took v
Top v UP
Topped v UP
Tops v UP
Torque n VARY
Touchback n PLAY
Touchdown n PLAY
Tough j
Transcend v
Trick n
Trim v WEAK
Trimmed v WEAK
Triumph n
Trophy n
Trounce v WEAK
Trump v PLAY
Trumped v PLAY
Unabashed j
Unafraid j
Unbeatable j
Uncontrollable j OPEN
Undaunted j
Undefeated j
Unequalled j
Unexcelled j
Unflinching j
Unrivaled j
Upset v WEAK
Valedictorian n TALK
Valiant j
Valor n
Vanquish v WEAK
Vaunt v TALK
Versatile j
Versed j
Veteran n PAST
Viable j LIVE
Victor n
Victories n
Victorious j
Victory n
Vigor n
Vim n
Virile j MALE
Virtue n
Virtuoso n
Vitality n
Weather v WEA
Wheel n
Whip v WEAK
Whiz n
Wield v
Win v

Win v HAVE	Withstand v OPPO	Won v HAVE	Zip n
Winning v	Wizard n MYTH	Woodcraft n MTRL	
Winning v HAVE	Won v	Wow n GOOD	

QUIK

Abrupt j	Flew v GO	Jiffy n TIME	Slapdash j TRIV
Abrupt j AGGR	Flick n VARY	Jump n GO	Smart j POWR
Accelerate v GO	Flicked v VARY	Jumped v GO	Snap n VIEW
Accelerator n MECH	Flicker n VARY	Jumper n GO	Snap n TIME
Action n EVNT	Flies v GO	Jumping v GO	Snap n
Active j EVNT	Fling n GO	Knot n MSMT	Snap v HAVE
Activity n EVNT	Flip n VARY	Leap n GO	Snap v GO
Alacrity n	Flipped v VARY	Life n LIVE	Snapped v HAVE
Alert j MOTV	Flipping v VARY	Liveliness n LIVE	Snapped v GO
Allegro j MUSC	Flips v VARY	Lively j LIVE	Snapped v VIEW
Animate v LIVE	Flit v GO	Liven v LIVE	Snaps v HAVE
Arouse v	Flown v GO	Lunge n GO	Snaps v GO
Arpeggio n MUSC	Flung v GO	Lunging v GO	Snaps v VIEW
Awake j	Flurry n	Mushroom v LARG	Spasm n VARY
Awoke v	Flutter n VARY	Mushroomed v LARG	Spasmodic j VARY
Barrel v GO	Fly v GO	Mushrooming v LARG	Spate n MUCH
Beat v GO	Flyer n VEHC	Nimble j POWR	Speed v GO
Bolt v GO	Forthwith d	Once n	Speedometer n MSMT
Bolt v FOOD	Gallop n GO	Overactive j	Sprang v GO
Bound n GO	Glance n VIEW	Pellmell j BLUR	Sprightly j
Bounded v GO	Glimpse n VIEW	Perk v	Spring n GO
Bounding v GO	Gun n MECH	Pert j POWR	Springing v GO
Bounds v GO	Gunned v MECH	Plunge v GO	Sprint v GO
Brisk j	Harrier n GO	Posthaste d EMPH	Spurt n
Burst n	Haste n	Pounce v GO	Streak v GO
Burst v GO	Hasten v GO	Precipitate j	Streaked v GO
Bustle n GO	Hasten v	Precipitate v BGIN	Streaking v GO
Career v GO	Headlong j BODY	Precipitate v GO	Sudden j
Celerity n	Helterskelter j BLUR	Precipitous j	Supersonic j HEAR
Charge n GO	Hie v GO	Presto d	Swift j
Clip n GO	Hied v GO	Prompt j	Swoop v GO
Course v GO	Hies v GO	Promptly d	Tear v GO
Coursed v GO	Highball v GO	Promptness n	Tempo n
Courser n ANML	Highballed v GO	Quick j	Tilt n GO
Cursory j TRIV	Highballing v GO	Race n GO	Tore v GO
Dart n GO	Hop n GO	Raced v GO	Velocity n
Darted v GO	Hopped v GO	Racer n GO	Vigilance n AID
Darting v GO	Hotrod n VEHC	Racing v GO	Vivacious j
Dash n GO	Hurried v	Ran v GO	Vivify v LIVE
Dashing v GO	Hurried v GO	Rapid j	Wake v
Derby n GO	Hurry v	Rapids n FLOW	Waked v
Dispatch n	Hurry v GO	Rash j DAMG	Waken v
Ejaculate v TALK	Hurtle v GO	Reawaken v	Waking v
Enliven v LIVE	Hustle v GO	Rouse v	Wheel v VARY
Expedite v AID	Hyperactive j	Run v GO	Wheeled v VARY
Expediting v AID	Immediate j	Rush n GO	Wheeling v VARY
Expedition n AID	Impetuous j MOTV	Rushed v GO	Whip v
Express j	Impetuous j DAMG	Rushes v GO	Whirl n VARY
Express n VEHC	Impromptu j EASY	Rushing v GO	Whiz v GO
Fast d	Impulse n MOTV	Salient j GO	Wideawake j
Faster j	Instant j	Scamper v GO	Wink n VARY
Fastest j	Instantaneous j	Scoot v GO	Woke v
Fillip v BODY	Jerk n VARY	Scooted v GO	Yank n
Flash v VIEW	Jerked v VARY	Scurried v GO	Yanked v
Fled v GO	Jerking v VARY	Scurry v GO	Yanking v
Flee v GO	Jet n FLOW	Shoot v GO	Zip v GO
Fleet j	Jetted v FLOW	Shot v GO	Zipped v GO
Fleeting j VARY	Jetting v FLOW	Skim v GO	Zoom v GO

Abeyance n BLOK
Accouchement n BGIN
Adagio n MUSC
Anaesthesia n
Andante j MUSC
Anesthesia n
Armchair n FURN
Asleep d
Autohypnosis n SOLE
Await v
Bask v GLAD
Basked v GLAD
Bassinet n YNG
Beachcomber n FLOW
Becalm v FLOW
Bed n FURN
Bedridden j SICK
Bedroom n HOME
Beds n FURN
Bedside j NEAR
Bedstead n FURN
Bedtime n TIME
Bench n FURN
Berth n FLOW
Berth n
Bide v
Biding v
Blackout n BLUR
Blanket n FURN
Bleachers n PLAY
Bode v
Box n PLAY
Breather n SOMA
Bunk n FURN
Bunked v FURN
Bunking v FURN
Bystander n NEAR
Chair n FURN
Chaise n FURN
Chesterfield n FURN
Chloroform n VAPR
Coma n SICK
Coma n BLUR
Comforter n FURN
Cot n FURN
Couch n FURN
Couch v
Couchant j
Couched v
Couches n FURN
Couches v
Couching v
Cradle n YNG
Crawl n GO
Creep v GO
Creeper n GO
Crept v GO
Crib n YNG
Cribbed v YNG
Cribbing v YNG
Dally v TRIV
Davenport n FURN

Dawdle v TRIV
Deactivate v
Deaden v DEAD
Deathbed n DEAD
Decelerate v GO
Defer v BLOK
Delay n BLOK
Desensitize v
Dilatory j BLOK
Dillydally v
Divan n FURN
Dock n LAW
Doldrums n FLOW
Dope n MEDC
Doped v MEDC
Doping v MEDC
Dormant j
Doze v
Dozer n
Drawl n TALK
Drift v GO
Drowsy j
Drug v MEDC
Drugged v MEDC
Drugging v MEDC
Drugs v MEDC
Dull v
Dulled v
Dulling v
Dulls v
Dwell v EVER
Electrostatic j ION
Ensconce v GLAD
Faint v BLUR
Fainted v BLUR
Fainting v BLUR
Fallow j ERTH
Feather v
Footstool n BODY
Gingerly d
Gradual j
Hammock n FURN
Hang v
Hangout n
Hassock n FURN
Hay n VEGT
Haymaker n DAMG
Hesitate v BLUR
Hibernate v TIME
Highchair n YNG
Howdah n
Hung v
Hush n HEAR
Hypnotism n
Hypoactive j
Idle j LACK
Idle v
Immobile j
Immovable j EVER
Inaction n
Inch v GO
Indolence n

Inert j
Inertia n
Insensate j
Insensate j AGGR
Insensible j
Insensitive j
Insensitive j AGGR
Insusceptible j
Jog v GO
Knockout n DAMG
Lackadaisical j
Lag n
Laggard j
Laid v
Languid j
Languish v WEAK
Languor n
Largo j MUSC
Lassitude n PANG
Latency n
Latent j
Lay v
Lazy j
Leisure j GLAD
Lethargy n
Lie v
Lies v
Linger v EVER
Lingering v EVER
Litter n FURN
Loaf v
Loafed v
Loafer n
Loafing v
Local n VEHC
Loge n PLAY
Logier j
Logy j
Loiter v
Lounge n HOME
Lounge n FURN
Lounge v
Lounged v
Lounging v
Lull n GLAD
Lullaby n MUSC
Lying v
Mattress n FURN
Mesmerize v
Mope v PANG
Morphine n MEDC
Motionless j
Nap n
Narcotic n MEDC
Nightcap n GARB
Nightgown n GARB
Nod v VARY
Nonchalance n GLAD
Numb v
Numbed v
Numbs v
Opiate n MEDC

Orchestra n PLAY
Pallet n FURN
Palsy n SICK
Paralysis n SICK
Paraplegia n SICK
Park v VEHC
Parked v VEHC
Parking v VEHC
Parquet n PLAY
Passive j WEAK
Patience n EVER
Patient j EVER
Pause n
Perch n UP
Petrify v PANG
Pew n HOLY
Phlegmatic j
Pillion n ANML
Plod v GO
Poise n
Poke v
Poky j
Polio n SICK
Pose v FORM
Posing v FORM
Postpone v BLOK
Procrastinate v BLOK
Pullman n VEHC
Quiescent j
Quiet j HEAR
Quilt n FURN
Recline v VARY
Recumbent j
Relax v GLAD
Repose n
Respite n
Rest n
Rest n END
Retard v BLOK
Retire v GO
Rocker n FURN
Sack n HOLW
Sacked v HOLW
Sacking v HOLW
Saddle n ANML
Saddlebag n HOLW
Sandman n MALE
Sat v
Saunter v GO
Seat n FURN
Seat n PLAC
Seat n BODY
Sedate j
Sedate v MEDC
Sedated v MEDC
Sedating v MEDC
Set v
Settee n FURN
Setting v
Shuffle v GO
Sit v
Slack j

Parts of speech: a article; b preposition; c conjunction; d adverb; f prefix; i interjection;
j adjective; n noun; p pronoun; r phrase; v verb.

Slacks v	Sofa n FURN	Stay v	Tardy j
Sleep v	Somnambulism n GO	Still d	Tarried v EVER
Sleeper n	Somnolent j	Still n VIEW	Tarry v EVER
Sleeper n VEHC	Soporific j	Stilled v	Torpor n
Sleeper n POWR	Sprawl v	Stilling v	Trance n
Slept v	Squat v	Stills v	Truce n
Sloth n	Squat v EVER	Stills n VIEW	Unconscious j BLUR
Sloth n ANML	Squats v	Stockstill j EVER	Unhurried j
Slouch n WEAK	Squats v EVER	Stood v	Viscosity n FLOW
Slow j	Squatted v	Stool n FURN	Wait v
Slow v GO	Squatted v EVER	Stroke n SICK	Waited v
Slug n BUG	Stagnate v DIRT	Stun v DAMG	Waive v
Sluggard n	Staid j	Stunned v DAMG	Wake n DEAD
Sluggish j	Stand v	Stunning v DAMG	Wheelchair n GO
Slumber n	Standby j NEAR	Stupor n BLUR	
Snail n ANML	Standing v	Swoon v BLUR	
Snooze n	Stationary j EVER	Syncope n BLUR	

SEP

Abandon v	Broke v DAMG	Creamed v FOOD	Detach v
Abdicate v LACK	Broke v	Creamer n FOOD	Detachment n
Abduct v CRIM	Broken j DAMG	Crevasse n HOLW	Dethrone v WEAK
Absence n	Broken j	Crevice n HOLW	Detrain v VEHC
Absence n LACK	Burst n DAMG	Cross v WRIT	Dialysis n
Absent v	By i	Crotch n FORM	Dichotomy n
Adieu n	Byby i	Crotch n BODY	Disappear v VIEW
Adios i	Bye i	Crotched j FORM	Disassociate v
Alien j OPPO	Byebye i	Crumble v WEAK	Disband v END
Alienate v OPPO	Bypass v GO	Cull v	Disbar v LAW
Alienation n OPPO	Cannibalize v DAMG	Cut v SHRP	Disbar v BLOK
Alienation n SICK	Card v CLEN	Cutaway j SHRP	Discard v
Alienist n SICK	Carded v CLEN	Cutter n SHRP	Discharge v
Alimony n MONY	Carding v CLEN	Cutting v SHRP	Discharge v OUT
Alone j SOLE	Cashier v	Deal n PLAY	Disconnect v
Aloof j AFAR	Castaway j FLOW	Dealer n PLAY	Discrete j
Amputate v BODY	Castaway j GO	Dealing v PLAY	Disembark v VEHC
Anchorite n SOLE	Castoff j WEAK	Deals v PLAY	Disembowel v SOMA
Apart d	Centrifugal j GO	Dealt v PLAY	Disengage v OPEN
Apartheid n GRUP	Centrifuge n MECH	Debark v FLOW	Disentangle v OPEN
Aside d NEAR	Cheerio i	Debride v SHRP	Disinherit v AGGR
Aside n TALK	Chink n HOLW	Decamp v GO	Disintegrate v DAMG
Asocial j GRUP	Chip n LITL	Decapitate v BODY	Disjointed j BLUR
Assort v GRUP	Chip v SHRP	Decollate v BODY	Dislodge v OPEN
Assortment n GRUP	Chipped v SHRP	Decompose v DIRT	Dismantle v
Astride j BODY	Chipped v LITL	Decompose v	Dismember v BODY
Asunder d	Chipper n SHRP	Deduct v	Dismiss v
Aufwiedersehen i	Chipping v LITL	Deducting v	Dismount v DOWN
Aurevoir i	Cleavage n	Defect v WEAK	Disown v AGGR
Away d	Cleave v SHRP	Deflower v VEGT	Dispel v
Banish v BLOK	Cleaver n SHRP	Defoliate v VEGT	Disperse v GO
Between b	Cleft n	Delete v OUT	Dispose v
Bisect v SHRP	Clip n SHRP	Demarcate v BLOK	Dispossess v
Blastoff n DAMG	Clipped v SHRP	Denude v	Disrobe v GARB
Bone v SOMA	Clipper n SHRP	Depart v GO	Dissect v SHRP
Boning v SOMA	Cloister v HOME	Departed v GO	Dissipate v
Bonvoyage i GO	Colander n HOLW	Departed j DEAD	Dissociate v
Boot n GARB	Coventry n PLAC	Deport v GO	Dissolution n END
Boycott v BLOK	Crack n	Depose v WEAK	Dissolve v END
Branch v	Cracked v	Deposing v WEAK	Distribute v
Breach n DAMG	Crackle v	Derelict n	Distributor n
Break n DAMG	Craze n	Desert v	Disunion n
Break n	Crazed j	Deserted v	Disunite v
Breakdown n	Crazing n	Deserting v	Ditch v
Breaker n	Cream v FOOD	Desolate j PANG	Divest v

Divide v	Hyphen n WRIT	Private j SOLE	Skim v
Divide v NUMR	Insular j	Prize v OPEN	Skin v BODY
Dividend n NUMR	Insulate v BLOK	Pry v OPEN	Skinned v BODY
Division n	Interim n TIME	Pull v	Skinning v BODY
Division n NUMR	Interject v IN	Pulled v	Sliver n LITL
Divisive j OPPO	Interlude n TIME	Purge v DAMG	Snap v DAMG
Divisor n NUMR	Intermission n TIME	Quarantine n BLOK	Snapped v DAMG
Divorce n	Interpolate v IN	Quarter v DAMG	Snaps v DAMG
Doff v	Interpose v IN	Quartered v SOME	Solitary j SOLE
Efface v OUT	Intersect v JOIN	Quartering v SOME	Solitude n SOLE
Efferent j GO	Intersperse v	Quit v GO	Sort v
Eject v OUT	Interval n TIME	Ramification n	Sorted v
Elapse v TIME	Interval n	Recess n TIME	Sorting v
Eliminate v OUT	Intervene v AID	Recessing v TIME	Space v
Elope v GO	Intervene v	Recluse j SOLE	Spaced v
Emigrant j GO	Island n	Refugee n GO	Spaces v
Emigrate v GO	Isolate v SOLE	Reject v AGGR	Spacing v
Enucleate v OUT	Jettison v	Relegate v	Splinter n
Ephemeral j VARY	Jilt v AGGR	Relinquish v LACK	Splinter n LITL
Eradicate v	Kidnap v CRIM	Remove v	Split j
Erase v	Leave v GO	Rend v DAMG	Straggle v GO
Erode v	Leave v EVER	Rended v DAMG	Strain v
Erosion n	Leaves v GO	Rending v DAMG	Strained v
Evacuate v OUT	Leaves v EVER	Rent n DAMG	Straining v
Evanesce v VARY	Left v GO	Repel v AGGR	Strand v BLOK
Evict v OUT	Left v EVER	Repulse v AGGR	Stranded v BLOK
Excise v SHRP	Lone j SOLE	Resign v	Stranding v BLOK
Excised v SHRP	Maroon v	Retire v GO	Stray v GO
Excising v SHRP	Marooned v	Rid v	Strew v GO
Exclude v BLOK	Marooning v	Ridding v	Strike v
Exclusive j BLOK	Mince v LITL	Riddle v	Striking v
Excommunicate v HOLY	Minus b NUMR	Rift n	Strip v
Exile v BLOK	Mitosis n SOMA	Rip n	Strip v GARB
Expatriate v	Nutcracker n FOOD	Rip v AGGR	Stripped v
Expel v OUT	Off j	Ripped v	Stripped v GARB
Expunge v	Offshoot n	Ripped v AGGR	Struck v
Farewell n GO	Ostracism n BLOK	Rupture n DAMG	Subdivide v
Fault n ERTH	Oust v OUT	Rupture n SICK	Subtract v NUMR
Filter v	Out d OUT	Sack v	Tear n
Filtrate n	Outcast n OUT	Sacked v	Tore v
Fire v	Outsider n OUT	Sacking v	Torn j
Fired v	Overboard d FLOW	Scat v GO	Transient j VARY
Fires v	Parcel v SOME	Scatter v	Transitory j VARY
Firing v	Pare v SHRP	Schism n	Unaccompanied j SOLE
Fission n	Parenthesis n WRIT	Scram v GO	Unclad j GARB
Fissure n HOLW	Pariah n WEAK	Scrape v CLEN	Unclothe v GARB
Flight n GO	Paring v SHRP	Scraping v CLEN	Uncouple v
Fork n	Part v GO	Scratch v	Undress v GARB
Forsake v	Part n	Screen v	Unload v
Foundling n YNG	Parted v GO	Secede v	Unmarried j SEX
Fracture v DAMG	Parted v	Secession n	Unpack v OPEN
Fro d	Parting v GO	Seclusion n COVR	Unravel v OPEN
From b	Parting v	Segment v SOME	Unscrew v
Fugitive n GO	Partition n	Segregate v BLOK	Untangle v OPEN
Gap n LACK	Peel v	Separate j	Untie v OPEN
Goodby n	Placket n GARB	Sever v SHRP	Untying v OPEN
Goodnight n TIME	Pluck v	Shatter v DAMG	Unwed j SEX
Halve v SOME	Plucked v	Shear v SHRP	Uproot v DAMG
Hence d	Plucking v	Shed v	Vacancy n LACK
Hermit n SOLE	Precipitate v	Shoo v GO	Vacating v LACK
Hermitage n SOLE	Pried v OPEN	Shorn v SHRP	Vamoose v GO
Hiatus n LACK	Pries v OPEN	Shred n SOME	Vanish v VIEW
Hooky n	Privacy n COVR	Sieve n	Waive v LACK
Hull v VEGT	Private j COVR	Sift v	Waiver n LACK

Watershed n FLOW   Wedge n   Winnow v   Withdraw v
Wean v   Winnow n MECH   Withdraw v GO   Wrest v DAMG

SEX

Accost v TALK
Adulterer n BAD
Adulterous j BAD
Adultery n BAD
Advance n FORW
Affair n JOIN
Affaire n JOIN
Affianced j KIN
Amatory j FOND
Amorous j FOND
Amour n FOND
Aphrodisiac n MOTV
Asexual j LACK
Assignation n JOIN
Autoerotic j SOLE
Ball n MALE
Banns n KIN
Bawdy j BAD
Betrothed j KIN
Bigamy n KIN
Bill v BODY
Billed v BODY
Billing v BODY
Bride n LADY
Bridegroom n MALE
Brides n LADY
Brothel n MART
Buss n FOND
Bussed v FOND
Busses v FOND
Bussing v FOND
Callgirl n BAD
Carnal j BODY
Castrate v LACK
Celibacy n LACK
Circumcise v SHRP
Clap n SICK
Clitoris n LADY
Coitus n JOIN
Commerce n JOIN
Concubine n LADY
Concupiscent j MOTV
Congress n JOIN
Conjugal j KIN
Conjugate v KIN
Connubial j KIN
Consort n JOIN
Consort n KIN
Consummate v JOIN
Copulate v JOIN
Copulating v JOIN
Coquetry n TRIV
Couple v JOIN

Coupled v JOIN
Coupling v JOIN
Court v FOND
Courted v FOND
Courtesan n LADY
Courting v FOND
Courts v FOND
Courtship n FOND
Cover v JOIN
Crush n FOND
Cyprian n BAD
Dally v TRIV
Deflower v DAMG
Desire n MOTV
Desiring v MOTV
Disorderly j BAD
Emasculate v WEAK
Enamor v FOND
Endogamy n KIN
Engage v KIN
Erection n MALE
Eros n MYTH
Erotic j
Exhibitionist n VIEW
Fag n SIML
Fairies n SIML
Fairy n SIML
Flame n HEAT
Flirt v TRIV
Fornicate v BAD
Frigid j COLD
Fruit n VEGT
Gay j SIML
Gelding n LACK
Gender n
Genital j BODY
Gigolo n MALE
Gonad n SOMA
Gonorrhea n SICK
Groom n MALE
Harem n LADY
Harlot n BAD
Heat n HEAT
Heterosexual j
Homosexual n SIML
Honeymoon n FOND
Hot j HEAT
Husband n MALE
Hustle v LADY
Hymen n LADY
Impotence n WEAK
Incest n CRIM
Inseminate v IN

Intercourse n JOIN
Intermarry v KIN
Intimacy n JOIN
Intimate j JOIN
Kiss v FOND
Knock v BGIN
Knowledge n IDEA
Laid v JOIN
Lascivious j BAD
Lay n JOIN
Lecher n BAD
Lesbian j SIML
Lewd j BAD
Libido n MOTV
Love n FOND
Lust n MOTV
Lusted v MOTV
Lusting v MOTV
Marital j KIN
Marriage n KIN
Married v KIN
Marry v KIN
Masturbate v SOLE
Mate n KIN
Mate v JOIN
Mated v JOIN
Mating v JOIN
Matrimony n KIN
Miscegenation n JOIN
Mistress n LADY
Monogamy n KIN
Neck v BODY
Necking v BODY
Neuter j LACK
Nubile j KIN
Nuptial j KIN
Obscene j BAD
Onanism n SOLE
Orgasm n SOMA
Orgiastic j PLAY
Orgy n PLAY
Pander v BAD
Pansy n SIML
Paramour n FOND
Pass n
Passes n
Pederasty n BAD
Penis n MALE
Pet v FOND
Petted v FOND
Petting v FOND
Phallic j MALE
Philander v TRIV

Pimp n BAD
Pimped v BAD
Polyandry n KIN
Polygamy n KIN
Polygyny n KIN
Pornography n BAD
Procure v BAD
Promiscuity n BAD
Promiscuous j BAD
Proposition v TALK
Prostitute n BAD
Puberty n YNG
Pubescence n YNG
Pubic j BODY
Queer n MALE
Rape n DAMG
Raping v DAMG
Rapist n DAMG
Ravish v DAMG
Romance n FOND
Romantic j FOND
Rut n ANML
Satyr n MALE
Satyriasis n MALE
Scatology n BAD
Screw v JOIN
Seduction n BAD
Sex n
Solicit v MOTV
Spicy j
Spouse n KIN
Suit n MOTV
Suitor n MOTV
Sweetheart n FOND
Syphilis n SICK
Testes n MALE
Testicle n MALE
Testis n MALE
Unmarried j SEP
Unwed j SEP
Vagina n LADY
Virgin n LADY
Voyeur n VIEW
Vulva n LADY
Wanton j BAD
Wed v KIN
Whore n BAD
Wife n LADY
Wives n LADY
Woo v FOND

SHRP

Accurate j TRUE   Adze n   Angler n FLOW   Arrow n
Acuity n   Aim n   Angling v FLOW   Arrow n DAMG
Acute j   Angle v FLOW   Archer n DAMG   Articulate v TALK

Ascertain v IDEA
Assure v
Auger n WORK
Awl n WORK
Ax n WORK
Axe n WORK
Axed v WORK
Axes n WORK
Axing v WORK
Barb n
Barbed j
Barber n MART
Bayonet n DAMG
Bead n
Beam v
Bisect v SEP
Bit n WORK
Blade n
Bob v BODY
Bobbed v BODY
Bobbing v BODY
Bobs v BODY
Brad n JOIN
Broach n
Bullseye n BODY
Caesarian j BGIN
Carve v FORM
Center n PLAC
Central j CRUX
Central j PLAC
Certain j
Certitude n
Chip v SEP
Chipped v SEP
Chipper n SEP
Chisel v WORK
Chop n DAMG
Chop v
Chopped v DAMG
Chopped v
Chopper n
Chops n DAMG
Chops v
Circumcise v SEX
Clarify v OPEN
Clarify v CLEN
Clarion j MUSC
Clarity n OPEN
Claw n BODY
Claw v DAMG
Clear j
Cleave v SEP
Cleaver n SEP
Clip n SEP
Clipped v SEP
Clipper n SEP
Cocksure j POWR
Concentrate v IDEA
Concentrate v
Concentration n IDEA
Concentration n
Concentric j SIML
Core n CRUX
Crisp j
Crop n BODY

Cropped v BODY
Crystallize v FORM
Cusp n BULG
Cut v SEP
Cut v LITL
Cut v DAMG
Cut v BLOK
Cutaway j SEP
Cutlass n DAMG
Cutoff n BLOK
Cutout n BLOK
Cutter n SEP
Cutting v SEP
Cutting v LITL
Cutting v DAMG
Cutting v BLOK
Dagger n
Dart n
Debride v SEP
Decenter v VARY
Decentralize v VARY
Definite j
Definition n
Definitive j IDEA
Delineate v FORM
Dice v LITL
Direct j
Dirk n DAMG
Dissect v SEP
Distinct j
Distinction n
Distinguish v
Doubtless j
Drill n MECH
Drill v WORK
Earmark v
Edge n
Edge n END
Edge n POWR
Edge n PANG
Elucidate v IDEA
Engrave v
Ensure v AID
Etch v VIEW
Evidence v OPEN
Evident j OPEN
Exact j
Exactly d
Excise v SEP
Excised v SEP
Excising v SEP
Explicit j
Express j
Eye n
Feathercut n BODY
Featheredge n
Fence v PLAY
Fidelity n SIML
Fingernail n BODY
Fix v
Fleece v ANML
Fluke n BLOK
Flush j
Focus n
Foil n PLAY

Foregone j FORW
Forthright j FORW
Gad v AGGR
Gaff n BLOK
Gaffed v BLOK
Gash n DAMG
Gash n
Geocentric j ERTH
Girdle v
Goad v POWR
Gore v DAMG
Graphic j VIEW
Graven j VIEW
Grindstone n MECH
Guillotine n DEAD
Hack v
Haircut n BODY
Hanger n
Harakiri n DEAD
Harpoon n DAMG
Hatchet n WORK
Hew v
Hifi n MUSC
Highlight v VIEW
Hobnail n JOIN
Homocentric j SIML
Hone v
Hones v
Hook n BLOK
Hub n CRUX
Hypodermic n MEDC
Identify v IDEA
Identity n SOLE
Impale v
Incise v
Incisor n BODY
Indicate v
Jackknife n
Jag v VARY
Jagged j VARY
Javelin n DAMG
Jig v VARY
Jigged v VARY
Jigging v VARY
Keen j
Keen j MOTV
Knife n
Knife v DAMG
Knives n
Lance n DAMG
Legible j WRIT
Limpid j
Lop v
Lopped v
Lucid j IDEA
Lure n BLOK
Machete n
Mark n
Marksman n DAMG
Meticulous j
Mow v
Nail n JOIN
Nail n BODY
Nailed v JOIN
Nailing v JOIN

Needle n
Needle v AGGR
Needled v AGGR
Needlepoint n FABR
Needlework n FABR
Needling v AGGR
Nettle n VEGT
Nib n
Nick v DAMG
Nicked v DAMG
Nip v
Nipped v
Operate v MEDC
Operating v MEDC
Pare v SEP
Paring v SEP
Particular j
Particularly d
Penknife n
Perforate v HOLW
Picador n DAMG
Pick v
Pickax n WORK
Picked v
Picket n
Pierce v IN
Pike n DAMG
Piked v DAMG
Piking v DAMG
Pin n BLOK
Pin n JOIN
Pin n GARB
Pincer n BLOK
Pincer n BODY
Pink v
Pinked v
Pinking v
Pinned v BLOK
Pinned v JOIN
Pinning v BLOK
Pinning v JOIN
Pitchfork n WORK
Plain j OPEN
Poignant j SOMA
Point n
Point n ERTH
Pointblank j
Pointed v
Pointing v
Poleax n DAMG
Poniard n DAMG
Positive j
Precise j
Precision n
Prick n
Prickle n
Prickly j
Prod v DAMG
Prong n
Prune v CLEN
Pruned v CLEN
Pruning v CLEN
Punctilious j
Punctual j TIME
Puncture v HOLW

Pungent j SOMA
Razor n
Right d EMPH
Rout v HOLW
Routed v HOLW
Routing v HOLW
Sabre n DAMG
Sagittal j
Saw n WORK
Scabbard n HOLW
Scalpel n
Scimitar n DAMG
Scissor n
Score n
Scratch n DAMG
Scratch n WRIT
Scratch v
Scribe n
Scrimshaw n VIEW
Scythe n WORK
Section v SOME
Sever v SEP
Sharp j
Sharp j AGGR

Sharp j MUSC
Sharp j POWR
Sharpen v
Sharpshooter n DAMG
Shave n CLEN
Shear v SEP
Shorn v SEP
Slash v DAMG
Slice v
Slit n HOLW
Snip v
Snip n SOME
Spear n DAMG
Spear n
Specific j
Specify v
Spike n JOIN
Spit n
Spotlight n VIEW
Spur n MOTV
Spurred v MOTV
Spurring v MOTV
Squarely d
Stab v DAMG

Stake n
Stick v
Sting v DAMG
Stitch n JOIN
Straight j
Straightforward j FORW
Strict j
Stuck v
Stung v DAMG
Stylus n
Sure j
Surefooted j BODY
Surgeon n MEDC
Surgery n MEDC
Surgical j MEDC
Sword n DAMG
Tack n JOIN
Target n
Terse j LITL
Thistle n VEGT
Thorn n VEGT
Thorn n AGGR
Tilt n DAMG
Toenail n BODY

Toothpick n BODY
Top v UP
Topped v UP
Tops v UP
Train v
Trained v
Transfix v DAMG
Trenchant j
Trim v
Trimmed v
Unequivocal j
Unmistakable j
Whet v
Whet v MOTV
Whets v
Whets v MOTV
Whetstone n ERTH
Whittle v
Whittle v LITL
Woodcut n VIEW
Zero v

SICK

Aberration n VARY
Abnormal j OPPO
Abscess n DIRT
Addict n MOTV
Ail v
Alcholic n SIP
Alcoholism n SIP
Alienation n SEP
Alienist n SEP
Allergy n
Amnesia n BLUR
Anaemic j
Anemic j
Aphasia n TALK
Apoplectic j PANG
Apoplexy n
Appendicitis n SOMA
Arthritis n
Asthma n
Astigmatism n VIEW
Aura n PANG
Autism n SOLE
Battier j FOOL
Batty j FOOL
Bedridden j REST
Bends n VARY
Berserk j PANG
Blight n DAMG
Blind j VIEW
Bloodshot j VIEW
Botulism n
Breakdown n PANG
Bronchitis n SOMA
Bug n BUG
Bunion n BULG
Bursitis n

Cancer n
Canker n
Case n SOLE
Catalepsy n
Cataract n VIEW
Catatonia n
Chickenpox n
Cholera n
Clap n SEX
Clubfoot n BODY
Cold n
Colic n PANG
Coma n REST
Complaint n PANG
Consumption n
Contagion n JOIN
Craze v PANG
Crazed j PANG
Crazier j PANG
Craziness n PANG
Crazy j PANG
Cretin n FOOL
Cripple v WEAK
Croup n
Deaf j HEAR
Deafen v HEAR
Delirious j PANG
Dementia n IDEA
Derange v
Dermatitis n BODY
Diabetes n
Diarrhea n DIRT
Diphtheria n
Dipsomaniac n SIP
Disease n
Disorder n

Distemper n
Dropsy n
Dysentery n
Dyspepsia n
Dystrophy n
Edema n
Encephalitis n
Epidemic n WHOL
Epilepsy n
Febrile j HEAT
Fester v DIRT
Fever n HEAT
Flu n
Fungicide n MEDC
Fungus j VEGT
Gall n
Gallstone n SOMA
Gangrene n
Germ n BUG
Gigantism n LARG
Glaucoma n VIEW
Gonorrhea n SEX
Gout n
Grip n
Grippe n
Hallucinosis n MYTH
Halt n WEAK
Harelip n BODY
Heartburn n SOMA
Hebephrenic j
Hectic j
Hemophilia n
Hemorrhage n
Hemorrhoid n
Hepatitis n

Hernia n BULG
Hipshot j BODY
Hives n
Hypertension n
Hypochondria n PANG
Hypotension n
Hysteria n PANG
Ill j
Illness n
Impetigo n DIRT
Incurable j EVER
Indigestion n FOOD
Infect v DIRT
Influenza n
Inpatient n IN
Insane j PANG
Invalid j WEAK
Jaundice n COLR
Lame j WEAK
Laming v WEAK
Laryngitis n SOMA
Leper n
Leprosy n
Loco j FOOL
Loonier j FOOL
Loony j FOOL
Lunacy n FOOL
Lunatic j FOOL
Mad j FOOL
Maladies n
Malady n
Malaria n
Malignancy n BAD
Malinger v FALS
Malnutrition n LACK
Mange n

Mania n PANG	Patients n	Psychosomatic j SOMA	Smallpox n
Maniac n PANG	Pellagra n	Psychotic j IDEA	Sties n VIEW
Manic j PANG	Pertussis n	Quinsy n	Stroke n REST
Measles n	Pestiferous j BUG	Rabid j ANML	Sty n VIEW
Microbe n BUG	Pestilence n BUG	Rabies n ANML	Sunstroke n ASTR
Migraine n	Petitmal n	Rash n	Symptom n SIML
Mongolian n YNG	Pica n MOTV	Rheumatism n	Syndrome n
Mumps n	Pile n	Rhinitis n	Syphilis n SEX
Myopia n VIEW	Pinkeye n VIEW	Rickety j	Tabes n
Nausea n PANG	Plague n	Rupture n SEP	Tabetic j
Neurosis n PANG	Plethora n	Rust n VEGT	Tetanus n
Neurotic j PANG	Pneumonia n	Sarcoma n	Tic n BODY
Outpatient j OUT	Polio n REST	Schizoid j IDEA	Tuberculosis n
Palsy n REST	Pox n	Schizophrenia n IDEA	Tumor n
Paralysis n REST	Psoriasis n DIRT	Scurvy n	Ulcer n
Paranoia n AGGR	Psychasthenia n IDEA	Seasick j FLOW	Varicose j
Paraplegia n REST	Psychoneurosis n IDEA	Seizure n BLOK	Viral j
Pathology n IDEA	Psychopathology n IDEA	Senile j PAST	Virus n
Patient n	Psychosis n IDEA	Sick j	Worm n BUG

SIML

Abreast d NEAR	Childlike j YNG	Counterbalance v OPPO	Evening v
Acclimate v EVER	Chip n LITL	Counterpart n	Evens v
Accommodate v AID	Codefendant n LAW	Counterpoise v OPPO	Example n
Accord n	Coequal j	Countersign n VIEW	Exemplify v
According c	Coeval j TIME	Covary v VARY	Facsimile n
Accustom v EVER	Cognate j KIN	Cover v	Fag n SEX
Acting j EVNT	Coincide v EVNT	Coworker n WORK	Fairies n SEX
Adapt v VARY	Collate v	Describe v TALK	Fairy n SEX
Adjust v VARY	Collateral n JOIN	Describe v GO	Fellow n
Affinity n JOIN	Collinear j FORM	Description n TALK	Fidelity n SHRP
Again d	Commensurate j	Ditto n WRIT	Figurative j
Agree v	Common j	Ditto n	Figure n
Akin j	Companion n JOIN	Double n	Fit v
Alamode j NEW	Compare v	Draw v PLAY	Flush j
Align v	Compatible j	Drawn v PLAY	Flush n PLAY
Alike j	Compatriot n GRUP	Drew v PLAY	For b
Aline v	Compeer n	Dual j NUMR	Gay j SEX
Alliterate v TALK	Compensate v	Due j	Germane j CRUX
Also d	Complement n	Duly d	Harmonic j MUSC
Analogy n	Comport v	Duplicate v	Harmonious j
Applicable j	Concentric j SHRP	Echo v HEAR	Harmonious j MUSC
Application n	Condign j	Effigy n	Harmonize v
Applied v	Conform v	Egalitarian j	Harmonize v MUSC
Apply v	Congruent j	Eligible j MOTV	Harmony n
Apposition n	Congruity n	Emulate v	Harmony n MUSC
Appropriate j	Conjugate v JOIN	Encore n PLAY	Homelike j HOME
Approximate v NEAR	Consistency n FORM	Equable j	Homocentric j SHRP
Apropos d	Consistency n EVER	Equal j	Homochromatic j COLR
Apt j	Consistent j EVER	Equalitarian j	Homogeneous j
Archetype n CRUX	Consistent j FORM	Equate v	Homogenize v
As c	Consonance n	Equation n NUMR	Homonym n TALK
Assimilate v SOMA	Consonant j	Equation n	Homosexual n SEX
Assimilate v	Consort v JOIN	Equilibrate v	Homozygous j BGIN
Assonance n HEAR	Contemporary j TIME	Equilibrium n	Identical j
Assort v	Converge v	Equitable j GOOD	Imitate v FALS
Aswellas r	Coordinate n	Equities n GOOD	Impersonate v FALS
Balance n	Copied v	Equities n CRUX	Incarnate j BODY
Became v	Copied v WRIT	Equity n GOOD	Instance n
Become v	Copy n	Equity n CRUX	Interchange n VARY
Belong v	Copy n WRIT	Equivalent j	Isochromatic j COLR
Bilateral j PLAC	Correspond v	Etcetera n	Isochronous j TIME
Carbon n WRIT	Cotenant n LIVE	Even d	Isomeric j ION
Caricature n FOOL	Coterminous j END	Evened v	Isometric j MSMT

Isomorphic j FORM
Isosceles j FORM
Isotherm n HEAT
Isotope n ION
Iterate v TALK
Jibe v
Justify v WRIT
Kind n GRUP
Kindred j JOIN
Lesbian j SEX
Level v FORM
Lifelike j LIVE
Lifesize j LIVE
Like b
Liken v
Likewise d
Literal j WRIT
Makeup n
Manikin n FORM
Mannequin n FORM
Match n
Matched v
Matches n
Matching v
Mate n
Meet v
Met v
Metaphor n TALK
Mime n PLAY
Mimic v FOOL
Miming v PLAY
Mock j FALS
Model n FORM
Model j GOOD
Monochromatic j COLR
Monotone n HEAR
Monotonous j EVER
Mutual j
Namesake n TALK
Outline n FORM
Overcompensate v LARG

Overlap v JOIN
Pair n JOIN
Pansy n SEX
Pantomime n PLAY
Par n
Paradigm n
Paragon n GOOD
Parallel n
Parallelogram n FORM
Parity n
Parody n FOOL
Parrot v TALK
Parroted v TALK
Parroting v TALK
Part n
Peculiar j CRUX
Peer n
Pendant n
Per b
Personify v SOLE
Photostat n VIEW
Picture n
Playback n PLAY
Portray v VIEW
Procrustean j DAMG
Profile n FORM
Proportion n
Prorate v
Prototype n CRUX
Proxy n MOTV
Pursuant d
Quadruplet n KIN
Quasi d
Quintuplet n KIN
Recapitulate v TALK
Reciprocity n
Recreation n BGIN
Recur v
Reflect v VIEW
Reform v FORM
Regenerate v BGIN

Relate v JOIN
Related j JOIN
Relating v JOIN
Relative j JOIN
Relevant j JOIN
Repeat v TALK
Repeat v
Repetition n
Replace v VARY
Replica n
Represent v
Represent v LAW
Reproduce v
Reproduce v BGIN
Resemble v
Respective j
Retrace v WRIT
Rhyme v TALK
Role n
Same j
Selfsame j SOLE
Sign n IDEA
Silhouette n FORM
Similar j
Simile n TALK
Simulate v FALS
Simultaneous j TIME
Sketch n VIEW
So d
Sort n GRUP
Sorts n GRUP
Square v
Squared v
Squaring v
Stand v
Standing v
Stereotype n TRIV
Stood v
Straight j FORM
Straighten v FORM
Sub n VARY

Subbed v VARY
Subs v VARY
Substitute v VARY
Such j
Suit v
Suited v
Suiting v
Supersede v VARY
Supplant v VARY
Symbol n IDEA
Symmetry n
Symptom n SICK
Synchrony n
Synonym n TALK
Tallied v
Tally v
Thus d
Tie n
Tied v
Tieing v
Token n
Tokened v
Tokening v
Too d
Trace v WRIT
Traced v WRIT
Transcribe v WRIT
Triplet n KIN
Twin n KIN
Tying v
Type n GRUP
Typical j
Typify v
Typing v GRUP
Uniform j WHOL
Unison n
Verbatim d TALK
Very j EMPH
Vice f
Xerox v WRIT

SIP

Absinthe n VEGT
Alcohol n VEGT
Alcoholic j VEGT
Alcoholic n SICK
Alcoholism n SICK
Ale n VEGT
Applejack n VEGT
Bar n FORM
Bar n MART
Bartender n AID
Beer n VEGT
Bender n GLAD
Beverage n FLOW
Binge n GLAD
Booze n VEGT
Borsch n FOOD
Bottle n HOLW
Bouillon n FOOD
Bourbon n VEGT
Brandies n VEGT
Brandy n VEGT

Brew n
Brew v BGIN
Broth n FOOD
Burgundy n VEGT
Buttermilk n ANML
Cafeaulait n
Canteen n HOLW
Carouse v PLAY
Caroused v PLAY
Chalice n HOLW
Champagne n VEGT
Chaser n
Chianti n VEGT
Chocolate n VEGT
Chowder n FOOD
Cider n VEGT
Claret n VEGT
Cobbler n VEGT
Cocktail n
Cocoa n VEGT
Coffee n VEGT

Cognac n VEGT
Coke n VEGT
Cola n VEGT
Consomme n FOOD
Cordial n VEGT
Cream n ANML
Creamer n HOLW
Cup n HOLW
Curd n LARG
Curdle v LARG
Daiquiri n
Demitasse n VEGT
Demitasse n HOLW
Dipsomaniac n SICK
Distillery n WORK
Dive n MART
Drank v SOMA
Drink v SOMA
Drunk j PANG
Drunk v SOMA
Eggnog n ANML

Fifth n NUMR
Fizz n HEAR
Flip n VEGT
Gin n VEGT
Goblet n HOLW
Gourd n HOLW
Grenadine n VEGT
Grog n
Gumbo n FOOD
Guzzle v SOMA
Hermitage n VEGT
Highball n
Honkytonk n MART
Imbibe v SOMA
Inebriate v PANG
Intoxicate v PANG
Jag n PANG
Jigger n MSMT
Juice n VEGT
Juicier j VEGT
Juicy j VEGT

Lactation n SOMA
Lap v SOMA
Lapped v SOMA
Lemonade n VEGT
Liqueur n VEGT
Liquor n VEGT
Lush n PANG
Malt n VEGT
Martini n VEGT
Mash n VEGT
Milch j ANML
Milk n ANML
Milk n
Milkman n MALE
Moonshine n CRIM
Mug n HOLW
Muscatel n VEGT
Must n VEGT
Nectar n VEGT
Nightcap n TIME
Nip v SOMA
Nipped v SOMA
Nipple n BULG
Nog n

Nurse v YNG
Oldfashioned n PAST
Pekoe n VEGT
Philter n MYTH
Phosphate n
Pickled j PANG
Plaster v PANG
Pop n
Port n VEGT
Porter n VEGT
Potable j SOMA
Potation n SOMA
Potion n
Potted j PANG
Pub n MART
Pull v SOMA
Pulled v SOMA
Punch n
Quaff v SOMA
Rum n VEGT
Rye n VEGT
Sack n VEGT
Sake n VEGT
Saloon n MART

Samovar n HOLW
Sanka n VEGT
Sarsaparilla n VEGT
Sauterne n VEGT
Schnapps n VEGT
Scotch n VEGT
Shake n
Sherry n VEGT
Shot n
Sip v SOMA
Slug n
Snort n
Soak v PANG
Soda n
Sot n PANG
Soup n FOOD
Speakeasy n CRIM
Spirit n
Stein n HOLW
Still n HOLW
Stills n HOLW
Stout n VEGT
Suck v SOMA
Sucked v SOMA

Sucker n SOMA
Suckling n YNG
Swig v SOMA
Swill v SOMA
Tankard n HOLW
Tap n MART
Tavern n MART
Tea n VEGT
Teakettle n HOLW
Teapot n HOLW
Thirst n MOTV
Tight j PANG
Tipsy j PANG
Toast n FOND
Vermouth n VEGT
Vin n VEGT
Vodka n VEGT
Water n FLOW
Watered v FLOW
Watering v FLOW
Whiskey n VEGT
Wine n VEGT
Wining v VEGT
Zombie n VEGT

SOLE

Alone j SEP
Anchorite n SEP
Another p
Anybody p
Anyone p
Apiece d
Autism n SICK
Autobiography n PAST
Autocracy n LEAD
Autoerotic j SEX
Autohypnosis n REST
Autonomy n OPEN
Bachelor n MALE
Body n BODY
Case n SICK
Case n EVNT
Character n
Citizen n
Civilian n
Creature n
Customer n
Each j
Egg n
Ego n
Egocentric j MOTV
Egotism n MOTV
Everybody p WHOL
Everyman n WHOL
Everyone p WHOL

Existentialist n LIVE
Hermit n SEP
Hermitage n SEP
Hog v MOTV
Hogged v MOTV
Hogging v MOTV
I p WE
Identity n SHRP
Idiosyncrasy n AFAR
Idiosyncrasy n CRUX
Impersonal j LACK
Independence n OPEN
Individual n
Instance n EVNT
Isolate v SEP
Lone j SEP
Lonely j PANG
Lonesome j PANG
Masochism n DAMG
Masturbate v SEX
Me p WE
Mine p WE
Monolith n FORM
Monologue n TALK
Monomania n IDEA
Monopoly n HAVE
Monosyllable n TALK
My p WE
Myself p WE

Nobody n NO
Nobody n WEAK
Onanism n SEX
One n
Only j
Ontogeny n PAST
Other p
Others p
Parties n
Party n
Per b
Person n
Persona n
Personable j AGRE
Personal j
Personality n
Personify v SIML
Piece n
Private j SEP
Recluse j SEP
Self n
Selfassured j POWR
Selfconfidence n POWR
Selfconscious j IDEA
Selfconscious j PANG
Selfdefense n AID
Selfish j MOTV
Selfmade j POWR
Selfpity n WEAK

Selfpreservation n AID
Selfsame j SIML
Single j NUMR
Singlehanded d BODY
Singular j
Singular j AFAR
Sole j
Solely d
Soliloquy n TALK
Solitaire n PLAY
Solitary j SEP
Solitude n SEP
Solo j
Somebody p
Someone p
Soul n CRUX
Specimen n
Spinster n LADY
Subject n
Subjective j
Unaccompanied j SEP
Unicellular j SOMA
Unique j AFAR
Unit n GRUP
Unit n MSMT
Unit n
Waif n YNG
Whoever p

SOMA

Acid j FOOD
Acrid j AGGR
Adenoids n
Adrenalin n MTRL
Alimentary j FOOD
Ambrosia n GOOD

Anal j DIRT
Anatomy n IDEA
Anus n DIRT
Aorta n
Appendectomy n MEDC
Appendices n JOIN

Appendicitis n SICK
Aroma n VAPR
Artery n
Assimilate v SIML
Ate v FOOD
Auricle n

Autonomic j
Bawl v PANG
Belch v HEAR
Bellies n BODY
Belly n BODY
Bile n

Bile n AGGR
Bio f
Biochemist n IDEA
Biology n IDEA
Biopsy n MEDC
Bit v FOOD
Bite n FOOD
Biting v FOOD
Bitten v FOOD
Bitter j FOOD
Bled v OUT
Bleed v OUT
Blew v
Blood n
Bloodhound n ANML
Bloodied v DAMG
Bloods n
Bloodshed n DAMG
Bloodthirsty j DAMG
Bloody j
Bloody j DAMG
Bloody j BAD
Bloodying v DAMG
Blow v
Blubber n ANML
Bone n
Bone n MTRL
Bone v SEP
Bonier j
Boning v SEP
Bony j
Bowel n DIRT
Brain n IDEA
Brain v DAMG
Breadbasket n FOOD
Breath n VAPR
Breathe v VAPR
Breather n REST
Breathless j PANG
Breathtaking j PANG
Brokenhearted j PANG
Bronchial j
Bronchitis n SICK
Burp v HEAR
Capillary n HOLW
Cardiac j
Cardiograph n MECH
Cardiology n MEDC
Cartilage n
Cell n
Cellular j HOLW
Cerebral j IDEA
Charleyhorse n PANG
Chew v FOOD
Cholesterol n MTRL
Chromosome n
Chump v FOOD
Circulation n GO
Circulatory j GO
Clavicle n
Cloaca n DIRT
Clot n BLOK
Collarbone n BODY
Cologne n GOOD
Colon n DIRT

Congenital j BGIN
Constipate v BLOK
Constitution n
Consume v FOOD
Consumption n FOOD
Cord n
Cornea n VIEW
Corona n UP
Coronary j
Corpuscle n
Cortex n
Cortical j
Cortices n
Cough n HEAR
Cramp n BLOK
Cranial j
Craniology n MSMT
Cranium n
Crap n DIRT
Craps v DIRT
Crick n PANG
Cried v PANG
Cry n PANG
Cuspidor n HOLW
Cyst n HOLW
Cytology n IDEA
Cytoplasm n MTRL
Defecate v DIRT
Deodorant n CLEN
Deodorize v CLEN
Devour v FOOD
Diaphragm n BLOK
Digest v FOOD
Digestion n FOOD
Dine v FOOD
Diner n FOOD
Disc n
Disembowel v SEP
Disk n
Drank v SIP
Draw v IN
Drew v IN
Drink v SIP
Drool v FLOW
Drum n HEAR
Drunk v SIP
Dung n DIRT
Duodenum n
Eat v FOOD
Ectoplasm n
Ectoplasm n MYTH
Egg n BGIN
Ejaculate v OUT
Electrocardiogr n MSMT
Embryo n BGIN
Emetic n OUT
Entrail n
Enuresis n WEAK
Exhale v VAPR
Expire v VAPR
Extrasensory j AFAR
Faeces n DIRT
Fart n VAPR
Feces n DIRT
Fed v FOOD

Feed v FOOD
Femur n
Fenestra n HOLW
Fetal j BGIN
Fetid j DIRT
Fetus n BGIN
Flatus n VAPR
Flavor n FOOD
Foetus n BGIN
Foretaste n FORW
Fragrance n VAPR
Froth v FLOW
Gag v PANG
Gagged v PANG
Gagging v PANG
Gall n
Gallstone n SICK
Gamete n BGIN
Gammaglobulin n MEDC
Gasp v HEAR
Gastric j HOLW
Gastronomy n FOOD
Gene n BGIN
Genes n BGIN
Germ n BGIN
Gill n FLOW
Gizzard n ANML
Gland n
Gnaw v FOOD
Gobble v FOOD
Gonad n SEX
Goodhearted j GOOD
Gore n DAMG
Gorge n HOLW
Gorier j DAMG
Gory j DAMG
Gristle n
Gullet n HOLW
Gulp n FOOD
Gum n
Gum n VEGT
Gustation n FOOD
Gut n HOLW
Gut n POWR
Gut v OUT
Gutted v OUT
Guzzle v SIP
Hack n HEAR
Halitosis n DIRT
Hamstring n
Hamstring v BLOK
Hardhearted j AGGR
Hawk v HEAR
Hawked v HEAR
Hawking v HEAR
Heart n
Heartache n PANG
Heartbreak n PANG
Heartburn n SICK
Heartrending j PANG
Heartsick j PANG
Heartstring n MOTV
Heave v OUT
Hemal j
Hemic j

Hemoglobin n
Hiccup v HEAR
Histology n IDEA
Homeostasis n EVER
Hormone n
Huff v VAPR
Humor n FLOW
Huskily d POWR
Hyperventilate v LARG
Hysterectomy n MEDC
Imbibe v SIP
Incense n HEAT
Incontinence n WEAK
Ingest v FOOD
Inhale v VAPR
Innards n IN
Inspire v VAPR
Intestine n HOLW
Intramuscular j IN
Intravenous j IN
Itch n PANG
Kidney n
Lacrymose j PANG
Lactation n SIP
Lap v SIP
Lapped v SIP
Laryngitis n SICK
Larynx n TALK
Laxative j EASY
Laxative n MEDC
Lick n FOOD
Licked v FOOD
Licking v FOOD
Lifeblood n LIVE
Ligament n JOIN
Lighthearted j GLAD
Liver n
Lung n
Manure n DIRT
Marrow n CRUX
Masticate v FOOD
Membrane n
Menopause n LADY
Menstrual j LADY
Milt n MALE
Mitosis n SEP
Mucous n
Munch v FOOD
Musk n ANML
Myelin n
Nasal j
Nerve n
Nerves n
Nervous j
Neurology n MEDC
Nip v SIP
Nipped v SIP
Odor n VAPR
Olfactory j VAPR
Oocyte n BGIN
Oosperm n BGIN
Optic j VIEW
Optics n VIEW
Organic j LIVE
Orgasm n SEX

Osmosis n IN
Ovary n LADY
Overeat v FOOD
Overfeed v FOOD
Ovulate v LADY
Palatal j
Palate n
Palpitate v VARY
Pancreas n
Pant v VAPR
Patella n
Pectoral j
Pelvis n
Perfume n GOOD
Period n LADY
Peristalsis n VARY
Perspire v FLOW
Pharynx n
Phlegm n
Photosynthesis n VIEW
Physic n MEDC
Physiology n IDEA
Piquancy n AGRE
Pith n CRUX
Pituitary j
Placenta n LADY
Plasma n
Poignant j SHRP
Pore n OPEN
Potable j SIP
Potation n SIP
Pregnancy n BGIN
Proctology n MEDC
Prolapse n DOWN
Prostate j MALE
Protoplasm n MTRL
Psychosomatic j SICK

Puke v OUT
Pull v SIP
Pulled v SIP
Pulmonary j
Pulse n VARY
Pungent j SHRP
Pupil n VIEW
Pus n DIRT
Quaff v SIP
Rancid j DIRT
Rectal j DIRT
Rectum n DIRT
Reflex j EVNT
Regurgitate v OUT
Relish n FOND
Respiration n VAPR
Retina n VIEW
Rh n
Rhesus n
Rhinencephalon n
Rib n
Rod n VIEW
Root v OUT
Ruminate v FOOD
Sac n HOLW
Saliva n FLOW
Sanguine j COLR
Sanguine j MOTV
Sanguine j DAMG
Sap n VEGT
Sap n CRUX
Savor n GOOD
Scent n VAPR
Semen n MALE
Sensation n IDEA
Sense n IDEA
Sensing v IDEA

Sensory j IDEA
Serum n
Shit v DIRT
Sip v SIP
Skeleton n FORM
Skull n
Skull n IDEA
Smell n VAPR
Sneeze n OUT
Sniff n VAPR
Snore n HEAR
Somatic j
Sour j FOOD
Sour j DIRT
Soured v DIRT
Souring v DIRT
Spat v OUT
Spay v MEDC
Sperm n MALE
Sphincter n BLOK
Spice n FOOD
Spicy j FOOD
Spine n
Spineless j WEAK
Spit v OUT
Spleen n
Spleen n AGGR
Stomach n BODY
Stool n DIRT
Subcutaneous j BODY
Suck v SIP
Sucked v SIP
Sucker n SIP
Swallow n FOOD
Swallowed v FOOD
Swallowing v FOOD
Sweat v FLOW

Sweated v FLOW
Sweet j GOOD
Swig v SIP
Swill v SIP
Sympathetic j
Tang n
Tart j FOOD
Taste n FOOD
Tear n FLOW
Tearful j PANG
Tendon n
Tensor n
Throat n BODY
Tingle v
Tissue n
Tonsil n
Tonsilectomy n MEDC
Tract n
Unicellular j SOLE
Unsavory j AGGR
Unsweetened j FOOD
Urine n DIRT
Vasectomy n MEDC
Vein n
Vertebra n
Vertebrate j ANML
Vomit v OUT
Water n DIRT
Weep v PANG
Wept v PANG
Wheeze n HEAR
Whiff n VAPR
Womb n LADY
Zygote n BGIN

SOME

Allocate v AID
Allot v AID
Amount n
Any j
Apportion v AID
Aspect n VIEW
Balance n
Batch n
Bit n LITL
Branch n
Canto n WRIT
Chapter n WRIT
Chapter n GRUP
Chunk n LARG
Clip n
Cob n
Component n
Constituent n
Crumb n LITL
Dab n JOIN
Dabbed v JOIN
Dash n

Deal n
Degree n
Department n GRUP
Detachment n GRUP
Detail n
Detail n GRUP
Division n GRUP
Dose n
Draughts n
Element n CRUX
Elementary j CRUX
Elements n CRUX
Excerpt n WRIT
Facet n
Factor n
Few j LITL
Flake n
Flaking v
Flaky j
Fleck n DIRT
Fleck n
Fraction n NUMR

Fragment n
Frame n PLAY
Gob n
Grist n CRUX
Half n NUMR
Half n PLAY
Halfway j GO
Halve v SEP
Handful n BODY
Hemi f NUMR
Hemicycle n FORM
Hemisphere n FORM
Hint n IDEA
Hinted v IDEA
Hunk n
Incomplete j WEAK
Ingredient n
Inning n PLAY
Installment n MONY
Installment n
Leg n
Lick n LITL

Lock n BODY
Margin n
Maybe d
Measure n
Midway d GO
Modicum n LITL
Net j
Note n
Occasional j
Overdose n LARG
Panel n
Paragraph n WRIT
Parcel n
Parcel v SEP
Part n
Partial j
Partially d
Particle n LITL
Parttime j TIME
Passage n WRIT
Pat n
Patch n

Parts of speech; a article; b preposition; c conjunction; d adverb; f prefix; i interjection;
j adjective; n noun; p pronoun; r phrase; v verb.

Percent n NUMR
Perhaps d
Phase n
Phylum n GRUP
Piece n
Pieced v
Piecemeal j
Piecing v
Pinch n
Plat n ERTH
Plot n ERTH
Portion n
Portion n MONY
Possibility n
Potential n
Proportion n NUMR
Quantity n
Quarter n NUMR
Quarter n PLAY
Quarter v SEP
Quartered v NUMR
Quartered v SEP

Quartering v NUMR
Quartering v SEP
Quota n NUMR
Ration v
Remainder n
Remains v
Remnant n
Remnant n FABR
Residue n
Respect n
Rest n
Round n
Rounds n
Rubber n PLAY
Sample v
Scrap n
Seam n
Seams n
Section n
Section v SHRP
Segment n
Segment v SEP

Semi f
Several j
Shard n
Share v HAVE
Shot n
Shred n SEP
Slab n FORM
Slip n
Snip n SHRP
Some j
Sometimes d TIME
Somewhat d
Space n
Spaces n
Specimen n
Spot v
Stage n
Stanza n WRIT
Strain n
Strand n
Stratum n
Streak n

Streak v COLR
Streaked v COLR
Streaking v COLR
Strip n
Suggestion n
Supplied v AID
Supplied v
Supply n AID
Tinge n
Tinge n COLR
Touch n
Trace n
Tuft n
Twist n VARY
Unfinished j
Vein n
Vestige n
Wedge n FORM
Wisp n LITL

SUB

Accessory n AID
Adulate v FOND
Ancillary j AID
Apprentice n WORK
Auxiliary j AID
Below b DOWN
Beneath b DOWN
Bondage n BLOK
Bow v DOWN
Bowed v DOWN
Bowing v DOWN
Chattel n
Colonialism n GRUP
Colonize v GRUP
Colony n GRUP
Corporal n
Corporals n
Courtier n
Defer v AGRE
Deference n AGRE
Degrade v AGGR
Demote v
Depend v AID
Devil n
Disciple n HOLY
Disciple n
Docile j GLAD
Downgrade v DOWN
Downtrodden j DOWN

Enslave v BLOK
Fawn v FOND
Fawned v FOND
Fawning v FOND
Feudal j LEAD
Flunkies n
Flunky n
Follow v AGRE
Freshman n EDUC
Frosh n EDUC
Heeler n
Henchman n MALE
Henpeck v AGGR
Heteronomy n LAW
Hireling n MONY
Homage n
Inferior j DOWN
Jackal n ANML
Junior j EDUC
Junior j YNG
Kowtow v DOWN
Lackey n
Low j DOWN
Manservant n MALE
Marionette n PLAY
Menial j TRIV
Minion n
Minor j
Minor n EDUC

Minored v EDUC
Minoring v EDUC
Minority n GRUP
Novitiate n HOLY
Obedience n AGRE
Obeisance n
Obey v AGRE
Obsequious j FOND
Overdependent j AID
Parasite n BUG
Parasite n AID
Pawn n PLAY
Peon n WORK
Plebe n EDUC
Private n
Protege n AID
Puppet n PLAY
Puppet n
Retinue n GRUP
Satellite n ASTR
Scrub n PLAY
Scrubbed v PLAY
Second j
Secondary j
Secondclass j GRUP
Secondrate j TRIV
Servant n AID
Servile j
Sidekick n JOIN

Slave n
Sophomore n EDUC
Stooge n
Sub j
Subaltern n
Subcommittee n GRUP
Subject n
Subjected v
Subjecting v
Subjugate v LEAD
Submission n WEAK
Submissive j WEAK
Submit v WEAK
Subordinate j
Subservient j
Subsidiary j
Suite n GRUP
Sycophant n FOND
Tame j GLAD
Taming v GLAD
Tractable j
Train n GRUP
Truckle v
Under b DOWN
Undergraduate n EDUC
Underneath b DOWN
Understudy n EDUC
Vassal n

TALK

Abracadabra n FOOL
Accent n EMPH
Accost v
Accost v SEX
Adage n IDEA
Address n
Adjective n FORM
Adlib v EASY

Admonish v AGGR
Adverb n FORM
Aforementioned j FORW
Aforesaid j FORW
Ahoy i FLOW
Alias n FALS
Allegation n
Allege v

Alleging v
Alliterate v SIML
Allude v
Allusion n
Anecdote n
Animadversion n AGGR
Announce v
Anonymous j COVR

Answer n
Answer n IDEA
Antonym n OPPO
Aphasia n SICK
Aphorism n IDEA
Apostrophe n
Appellation n
Argot n CRIM

Argue v AGGR
Argue v OPPO
Article n FORM
Articulate v SHRP
Aside n SEP
Ask v
Asked v
Aspersion n AGGR
Aspirate v HEAR
Aspirating v HEAR
Aspiration n HEAR
Assert v
Aver v
Avers v
Avow v AGRE
Baa n ANML
Babble v HEAR
Bade v
Ballad n MUSC
Bandied v
Bandy v
Banter v FOOL
Bark n ANML
Barker n HEAR
Barnstorm v GO
Bay v ANML
Bayed v ANML
Baying v ANML
Bays v ANML
Beef v AGGR
Beefed v AGGR
Beefing v AGGR
Beefs v AGGR
Bellow v HEAR
Berate v AGGR
Bewail v PANG
Bicker v AGGR
Bid v
Bird n AGGR
Bitch v AGGR
Bitched v AGGR
Bitches v AGGR
Bitching v AGGR
Blab v OPEN
Blarney n FALS
Blasphemy n BAD
Blather n FOOL
Bleat v ANML
Blithering j FOOL
Blow v POWR
Blubber v PANG
Blurb n
Blurt v
Bluster v AGGR
Boast n POWR
Bombast n FOOL
Boo v AGGR
Boos n AGGR
Bowwow n ANML
Brag v POWR
Braggart n POWR
Bray n ANML
Brief n LITL
Brief v IDEA
Briefed v IDEA

Briefing v IDEA
Briefs n LITL
Briefs v IDEA
Broach v OPEN
Broadcast n LARG
Brogue n
Bull n FOOL
Burble v HEAR
Byword n
Cackle n ANML
Call n HEAR
Calling v HEAR
Calypso n MUSC
Cant n COVR
Cant n FALS
Cantata n MUSC
Canted v FALS
Cantor n HOLY
Carol n MUSC
Carp v AGGR
Carped v AGGR
Carping v AGGR
Carps v AGGR
Case n FORM
Catcall n ANML
Caw n ANML
Celtic n
Chaff n GLAD
Chanson n MUSC
Chant v MUSC
Chanting v MUSC
Chat n
Chatted v
Chatter v
Chatterbox n MUCH
Cheep n ANML
Cheer n AGRE
Cheering v AGRE
Chide v AGGR
Chirp v ANML
Chitchat n TRIV
Ciceronian j POWR
Circumlocution n VARY
Citation n
Cite v
Citing v
Clause n FORM
Cliche n TRIV
Cluck v ANML
Cognomen n
Colloquy n JOIN
Comeback n AGGR
Comment v
Commune v JOIN
Communed v JOIN
Communicant n
Communicate v
Communing v JOIN
Communion n JOIN
Communique n
Confab n
Confabulate v
Confabulate v FALS
Confer v JOIN
Conference n JOIN

Conjugate v FORM
Conjunction n FORM
Consonant n FORM
Contact v JOIN
Conversation n
Converse v
Conversed v
Converses v
Conversing v
Coo v FOND
Coo v ANML
Copulative n FORM
Couch v
Couched v
Couches v
Couching v
Crack n GLAD
Cracked v GLAD
Cried v HEAR
Crier n HEAR
Croak v ANML
Croaked v ANML
Croaker n ANML
Croon v MUSC
Crossexamine v BLUR
Crow v ANML
Crow v POWR
Cry n HEAR
Cuckoo n ANML
Curr v ANML
Curse n BAD
Cursing v BAD
Cuss n BAD
Dative j FORM
Deacon v HOLY
Debate n OPPO
Declaim v
Declamation n
Declare v
Declension n FORM
Decline v FORM
Decree n LEAD
Decried v AGGR
Decry v AGGR
Deliver v
Delivery n
Denomination n
Denounce v AGGR
Denunciation n AGGR
Depose v LAW
Deposing v LAW
Deposition n LAW
Descant v
Describe v SIML
Description n SIML
Dialect n
Dialogue n
Diatribe n AGGR
Dicker v MART
Dictaphone n MECH
Dictate v
Dictate v LEAD
Diction n
Dictum n IDEA
Digest n LITL

Digress v VARY
Diphthong n FORM
Disc n MUSC
Discourse n
Discuss v
Disk n MUSC
Disquisition n
Ditties n MUSC
Ditty n MUSC
Drawl n REST
Dress v AGGR
Dressed v AGGR
Dresses v AGGR
Dressing v AGGR
Drivel n FOOL
Dumb j LACK
Dutch n
Edict n LEAD
Ejaculate v QUIK
Elegy n PANG
Ellipsis n LACK
Elocution n
Eloquence n POWR
English n
Enquire v BLUR
Entitle v
Enunciate v
Epigram n IDEA
Epilogue n END
Epithet n BAD
Epitome n LITL
Etymology n BGIN
Eulogy n AGRE
Euphemism n GOOD
Exclaim v EMPH
Exclamation n EMPH
Excursive j VARY
Exordium n FORW
Expatiate v
Expletive n EMPH
Expound v IDEA
Express v
Expressed v
Expression n
Fable n MYTH
Fiat n LEAD
Filibuster v BLOK
Floor n DOWN
Fluent j EASY
Forecast n FORW
Forename n FORW
Foretell v FORW
Foretold v FORW
Foreword n FORW
Forum n OPEN
Gab n
Gabbed v
Gabble v ANML
Gabby j
Gag n BLOK
Gagged v BLOK
Gagging v BLOK
Gainsay v OPPO
Garrulous j TRIV
Gas v VAPR

Genitive j FORM
Gerund n FORM
Gibberish n FOOL
Gibe n AGGR
Gibing v AGGR
Gobble v ANML
Gossip n TRIV
Grace n HOLY
Grammar n FORM
Grandiloquence n POWR
Grapevine n COVR
Greek n BLUR
Grill v BLUR
Grilled v BLUR
Groan n PANG
Grouse v AGGR
Growl n AGGR
Grumble v AGGR
Grunt n HEAR
Guff n FALS
Haggle v AGGR
Hail v
Hail v AGRE
Hails v
Hails v AGRE
Harangue v BLUR
Harp v EVER
Harped v EVER
Harping v EVER
Hearsay n HEAR
Hebrew n
Heckle v AGGR
Heehaw n ANML
Hem v HEAR
Herald n FORW
Heteronym n OPPO
Hexameter n
Hiss n AGGR
Hiss n ANML
Holler n HEAR
Homily n HOLY
Homonym n SIML
Honk v ANML
Hoot n ANML
Howl n ANML
Hyperbole n LARG
Iambic j
Idiom n
Idyl n ERTH
Imperfect j FORM
Inarticulate j BLUR
Incantation n MYTH
Incommunicado j BLOK
Inexpressible j BLUR
Infinitive n FORM
Inflect v FORM
Inform v IDEA
Informant n IDEA
Informer n OPEN
Inquire v BLUR
Inquisitive j BLUR
Intercom n JOIN
Interjection n EMPH
Interlocutor n
Interrogate v BLUR

Interview n JOIN
Intone v MUSC
Intransitive j FORM
Invective n AGGR
Inveigh v AGGR
Iterate v SIML
Jabber v FOOL
Jargon n FOOL
Jaw v AGGR
Jawed v AGGR
Jawing v AGGR
Jeer v AGGR
Jingle n
Josh v GLAD
Keen v PANG
Keened v PANG
Keening v PANG
Keens v PANG
Kibitz v AGGR
Laconic j LITL
Lament n PANG
Language n
Larynx n SOMA
Latin n
Lecture n EDUC
Legend n MYTH
Liar n FALS
Lie v FALS
Lied v FALS
Lies v FALS
Limerick n GLAD
Line n
Lingo n
Linguistics n IDEA
Lisp n WEAK
Litany n HOLY
Locution n
Loquacious j MUCH
Loudspeaker n HEAR
Low v ANML
Lying v FALS
Madrigal n MUSC
Magniloquence n LARG
Magpie n MUCH
Malediction n BAD
Mass n HOLY
Maxim n IDEA
Media n WRIT
Mention v
Meow v ANML
Mercury n MYTH
Message n
Messenger n
Metaphor n SIML
Mew n ANML
Minstrel n MUSC
Misinform v FALS
Misquote v FALS
Misspell v FALS
Misstate v FALS
Moan v PANG
Moniker n
Monologue n SOLE
Monosyllable n SOLE
Moo v ANML

Moot j BLUR
Morpheme n FORM
Motto n IDEA
Mumble n BLUR
Murmur n HEAR
Mute j LACK
Mutter n BLUR
Nag v AGGR
Nagged v AGGR
Name n
Name n POWR
Named v
Names v
Namesake n SIML
Naming v
Narrate v
Neigh n ANML
Neologism n FOOL
News n NEW
Nickname n
Nomenclature n
Nominative j FORM
Noun n FORM
Oath n BAD
Oath n HOLY
Object n FORM
Objective j FORM
Obloquy n AGGR
Observation n
Observe v
Observing v
Ode n MUSC
Opera n MUSC
Operatic j MUSC
Operetta n MUSC
Oral j
Oration n
Orator n
Oratorical j
Oratorio n MUSC
Oratory n
Outspoken j OPEN
Page v
Paged v
Paging v
Palaver v
Parable n MYTH
Paraphrase v
Parlance n
Parley n JOIN
Parole n AGRE
Parrot v SIML
Parroted v SIML
Parroting v SIML
Parse v FORM
Parsing v FORM
Participial j FORM
Participle n FORM
Patter n HEAR
Peep n ANML
Pentameter n MSMT
Perfect j FORM
Peroration n END
Phone v MECH
Phoneme n FORM

Phonetic j FORM
Phonic j FORM
Phoning v MECH
Phrase n FORM
Pidgin n
Pip v ANML
Pipped v ANML
Pipping v ANML
Pips n ANML
Pitch n MOTV
Pluperfect n FORM
Poem n
Poet n
Poetaster n TRIV
Poetess n LADY
Polemic n AGGR
Polyglot j MUCH
Powwow n GRUP
Prate v TRIV
Prattle v TRIV
Prayer n HOLY
Preach v HOLY
Preamble n FORW
Precis n LITL
Predicate n FORM
Preface n FORW
Prefix n FORM
Preposition n FORM
Prevaricate v FALS
Proclamation n OPEN
Profess v AGRE
Profession n AGRE
Prolegomenon n FORW
Prologue n FORW
Pronoun n FORM
Pronounce v
Pronounced v
Pronunciation n
Propose v KIN
Proposition v SEX
Prose n
Prosody n
Proverb n IDEA
Psalm n HOLY
Pseudonym n FALS
Pulpit n HOLY
Pun v GLAD
Purr n ANML
Quack n ANML
Queries v BLUR
Query n BLUR
Question n BLUR
Quibble v TRIV
Quip n GLAD
Quiz v BLUR
Quizzed v BLUR
Quizzical j BLUR
Quizzing v BLUR
Quote v
Quoting v
Radio n HEAR
Rag v AGGR
Rail v AGGR
Ramble v BLUR
Rant v AGGR

Rap v JOIN
Rapped v JOIN
Rate v AGGR
Rating v AGGR
Rave v FOND
Rave v PANG
Raving v FOND
Raving v PANG
Razz v AGGR
Recall v BACK
Recant v OPPO
Recapitulate v SIML
Receive v HEAR
Receiver n HEAR
Reception n HEAR
Recital n
Recite v
Reciting v
Record n MUSC
Recorder n MECH
Recount v
Refer v
Reference n
Reflexive j FORM
Refrain n MUSC
Rehash v
Rehearse v
Reiterate v
Rejoin v
Rejoinder n
Relate v
Related v
Relating v
Remark n
Remonstrate v AGGR
Render v
Repartee n GLAD
Repeat v SIML
Rephrase v
Replies v
Reply n
Report n
Reporter n
Reprehend v AGGR
Reprimand n AGGR
Reproach n AGGR
Reproof n AGGR
Reprove v AGGR
Response n
Retort n AGGR
Retorted v AGGR
Retorting v AGGR
Revile v AGGR
Rhetoric n
Rhyme v SIML
Roar n ANML
Rondeau n MUSC

Rondeau n
Root v AGRE
Rostrum n FORM
Round n MUSC
Rounds n MUSC
Rumor n
Saga n MYTH
Said v
Sang v MUSC
Sanskrit n
Sass v AGGR
Saw n IDEA
Saxon n
Say v
Saying v
Saying n IDEA
Schmooze v
Scold v AGGR
Scream v HEAR
Screech v HEAR
Semitic j
Sentence n FORM
Sentence n LAW
Serenade n MUSC
Sermon n HOLY
Service n HOLY
Shout v HEAR
Shriek v HEAR
Simile n SIML
Sing v MUSC
Slang n
Slavic j
Slogan n
Slur n AGGR
Snarl v AGGR
Snivel v PANG
Sob v PANG
Socalled j
Soliloquy n SOLE
Song n MUSC
Sonnet n
Speak v
Speech n
Spell v
Spelled v
Spelling v
Spiel n
Splutter v BLUR
Spoke v
Spoken v
Spokesman n
Spout v OUT
Squall v AGGR
Squawk n ANML
Squawk v AGGR
Squeal v OPEN
Stammer v WEAK

State v
Stated v
Statement n
States v
Stating v
Storied j
Stories n
Story n
Stump v GO
Stumped v GO
Stumping v GO
Stutter v WEAK
Subject n FORM
Subjective j FORM
Subjunctive n FORM
Suffix n FORM
Surname n
Swear v HOLY
Swear v BAD
Switchboard n JOIN
Swore v HOLY
Swore v BAD
Syllable n FORM
Synonym n SIML
Synopsis n LITL
Syntax n FORM
Tabbies n LADY
Taciturn j LITL
Tale n MYTH
Talk n
Tattle v OPEN
Taunt v AGGR
Telepathy n MYTH
Telephone v MECH
Television n VIEW
Tell v
Tell v IDEA
Teller n
Teller n NUMR
Telltale j OPEN
Tense n FORM
Term n
Terming v
Testament n AGRE
Testify v TRUE
Testimony n TRUE
Teutonic j
Tidings n NEW
Tirade n AGGR
Title n
Told v
Tongue n BODY
Transitive j FORM
Translate v VARY
TV n VIEW
Tweet n ANML
Twit v FOOL

Twitted v FOOL
Twitter n ANML
Uncommunicative j OPPO
Undeclared j COVR
Undertone n BLUR
Unspeakably d EMPH
Unspoken j COVR
Untold j MUCH
Untold j COVR
Upbraid v AGGR
Utter v
Valedictorian n POWR
Vaunt v POWR
Verb n FORM
Verbal j
Verbatim d SIML
Verbiage n TRIV
Verbose j MUCH
Vernacular n
Verse n
Vituperate v AGGR
Vocabulary n
Vocal j
Vociferous j HEAR
Voice n
Voluble j MUCH
Vow v AGRE
Vowed v AGRE
Vowel n FORM
Wag n GLAD
Wail n PANG
Warble n ANML
Whimper v PANG
Whine v PANG
Whinny n ANML
Whisper n HEAR
Whoop v ANML
Wisecrack n GLAD
Woof n ANML
Word n
Word n AGRE
Wordy j MUCH
Wrangle v AGGR
Yak v
Yakked v
Yammer v
Yap n ANML
Yarn n MYTH
Yell v HEAR
Yelp n ANML
Yiddish n
Yip v ANML
Yodel n MUSC
Yowl n ANML

TIME

Aeon n EVER
Afternoon n
Age n
Ageless j EVER
Anniversary n

Annual j
Annual n WRIT
Annuity n MONY
April n
AshWednesday n HOLY

August n
Autumn n
Awhile d
Bedtime n REST
Bell n MUSC

Bicentennial n
Bimonthly d NUMR
Birthday n BGIN
By b NEAR
Calendar n WRIT

Centenaries n	Fulltime j WHOL	Month n	Space n
Centenary j	Future n FORW	Morning n	Span n
Centennial j	Goodnight n SEP	Morrow n FORW	Spell n
Centuries n	Halloween n PLAY	Night n	Spelled v
Century n	Hanukkah n HOLY	Nightcap n SIP	Spelling v
Childhood n YNG	Harbinger n FORW	Nightcap n END	Spring n
Christmas n HOLY	Hence d FORW	Nightfall n	Springtime n
Chronology n FORW	Henceforth d FORW	Nighttime n	Still d EVER
Chronometer n MSMT	Hereafter d FORW	Nocturnal j	Summer n HEAT
Circa b NEAR	Heyday n POWR	Noon n	Sunday n
Climacteric n CRUX	Hibernal j COLD	November n	Sundial n MSMT
Clock n MECH	Hibernate v REST	Oclock n	Teen j NUMR
Clockwise j FORW	Holiday n PLAY	October n	Tenure n HAVE
Clockwork n MECH	Hour n MSMT	Offing n FORW	Term n EVER
Coeval j SIML	Hourglass n MSMT	Overnight d	Term n EDUC
Contemporary j SIML	Imminence n NEAR	Pallet n MECH	Thanksgiving n AID
Curfew n BLOK	Impend v NEAR	Parttime j SOME	Thenceforth d FORW
Daily j EVER	Instant n	Passover n HOLY	Thereafter d FORW
Daily n WRIT	Interim n SEP	Pastime n PLAY	Thursday n
Date n	Interlude n SEP	Pending b EVER	Till c
Date n JOIN	Intermission n SEP	Pendulum n VARY	Time n
Dateless j BLUR	Interval n SEP	Pentecost n HOLY	Timepiece n MECH
Dating v	Isochronous j SIML	Period n	Times n
Dating v JOIN	January n	Perpetuity n EVER	Times n WRIT
Dawn v BGIN	Jiffy n QUIK	PM n	Timing v
Day n	Jubilee n GLAD	Presentday j NEW	Today n NEW
Daybreak n BGIN	July n	Presently d NEAR	Tomorrow d FORW
Daydream n MYTH	June n	Punctual j SHRP	Tonight n
Daylight n VIEW	Late j	Purim n HOLY	Tour n EVER
Daytime n	Lateness n	Quadrennial j NUMR	Tuesday n
Deadline n END	Later d	Quarterly j NUMR	Twilight n BLUR
Decade n	Latest j	Quarterly n WRIT	Undated j
December n	Lent n HOLY	Recess n SEP	Unseasonable j OPPO
Decennial n	Lifetime n LIVE	Recessing v SEP	Until b
Decennium n	Longterm j EVER	Sabbath n HOLY	Untimely j OPPO
Due j	March n	Sandglass n MSMT	Verge n MECH
Duration n EVER	Matinee n PLAY	Saturday n	Vintage j VEGT
During b EVER	May n	Season n	Wartime n DAMG
Dusk n BLUR	Mealtime n FOOD	Season v POWR	Watch n MECH
Earlier j FORW	Meantime n	Seasoned v POWR	Wednesday n
Early j FORW	Meanwhile d	Seasoning v POWR	Week n
Easter n HOLY	Meridian n ASTR	Second j MSMT	Weekend n END
Elapse v SEP	Metronome n MSMT	Semester n EDUC	When d
Epoch n	Middleaged j	September n	While c
Escapement n MECH	Midnight n	Session n GRUP	Winter n COLD
Eve n FORW	Midsummer j HEAT	Shortlived j LITL	Wristwatch n MECH
Even n	Midwinter j COLD	Shortly d LITL	Xmas n HOLY
Evening n	Millennium n NUMR	Simultaneous j SIML	Year n
Fall n	Millennium n FORW	Since d	Yearbook n WRIT
February n	Minute j MSMT	Snap n QUIK	Yearlong j EVER
Forenoon n	Minutes n MSMT	Someday d	Yearly d
Forthcoming j FORW	Moment n	Sometime d	YomKippur n HOLY
Fortnight n	Momentary j VARY	Sometimes d SOME	
Friday n	Monday n	Soon d NEAR	

TRIV

Accidental j	Bare j	Bored v PANG	Cavalier j
Adventitious j	Bargain n MART	Boredom n PANG	Cavil n AGGR
Alloy n JOIN	Bauble n	Boring v PANG	Chaff n
Anticlimax n	Bootless j WEAK	Bricabrac n FURN	Cheap j MONY
Arid j LACK	Bore n PANG	But d	Cheap j

Parts of speech: a article; b preposition; c conjunction; d adverb; f prefix; i interjection;
j adjective; n noun; p pronoun; r phrase; v verb.

Cheapskate n MONY
Chitchat n TALK
Cliche n TALK
Colorless j COLR
Common j
Commonplace j MUCH
Conventional j EVER
Coquetry n SEX
Corn n FOOL
Cornier j FOOL
Corny j FOOL
Cursory j QUIK
Dabble v
Dally v REST
Dally v SEX
Dawdle v REST
Dead j DEAD
Deaden v DEAD
Deadwood n DEAD
Diddle v
Dilettante n WEAK
Dinky j
Doggerel n WRIT
Doodad n MECH
Doodle v WRIT
Drab j COLR
Drudge v WORK
Dull j
Empty j
Ennui n PANG
Extraneous j OUT
Extrinsic j OUT
Fastidious j MOTV
Featherbed v WORK
Fifthwheel n
Fig n VEGT
Finicky j MOTV
Flip j GLAD
Flippancy n GLAD
Flirt v SEX
Flirt v
Florid j GOOD
Flotsam n FLOW
Flowery j GOOD
Fray v
Frazzle n
Frill n FORM
Fritter v

Frivolous j GLAD
Fry n YNG
Futile j WEAK
Garish j VIEW
Garrulous j TALK
Gaudy j VIEW
Gossip n TALK
Gratuitous j
Groundless j
Grub v WORK
Grubbed v WORK
Hackneyed j
Hardly d
Harmless j AID
Hollow j HOLW
Humdrum j
Idle j
Immaterial j
Impertinence n AGGR
Inane j FOOL
Incidental j
Inconsequent j
Indifference n LACK
Inessential j
Inexpensive j MONY
Innocuous j AID
Inoffensive j AID
Insignificant n
Insipid j
Insubstantial j WEAK
Irrelevance n
Junk n DIRT
Just d
Knickknack n FURN
Lifeless j DEAD
Light j GLAD
Lightly d GLAD
Listless j PANG
Lukewarm j MOTV
Lumber n FURN
Menial j SUB
Mere j
Minor j
Mongrel n ANML
Mundane j EVER
Mutt n ANML
Negligible j
Niggling j

Nominal j
Nondescript j
Nonentity n
Nonentity n
Notion n MART
Obsolete j PAST
Offhand j EASY
Only d
Ordinary j
Outmoded j PAST
Pall v PANG
Palled v PANG
Palling v PANG
Paltry j
Pedant n EDUC
Pedestrian j
Perfunctory j
Pettier j
Petty j
Philander v SEX
Picayune j
Piddle v
Piker n
Platitude n
Poetaster n TALK
Pointless j
Pooh i
Potboiler n MONY
Prate v TALK
Prattle v TALK
Precious j GOOD
Prissy j MOTV
Prosaic j
Quibble v TALK
Rag n FABR
Redundant j BULG
Rote n EVER
Rummage n
Scarcely d
Scrap n
Secondhand j
Secondrate j SUB
Shallow j
Shot j
Simply d
Slapdash j QUIK
Sop n AID
Squirt n YNG
Stereotype n SIML

Stickler n AGGR
Superficial j
Superfluous j
Tasteless j
Tatter v FABR
Tedious j PANG
Threadbare j FABR
Tinker v WORK
Token j
Trappings n GARB
Trifle n
Trinket n
Tripe n
Trite j
Trivial j
Truism n TRUE
Unconcern n
Unessential j
Uneventful j
Unimportant j
Uninspired j WEAK
Uninteresting j
Unnecessary j
Unoriginal j EVER
Unproductive j WEAK
Unprofitable j
Used j
Useless j
Vacuous j
Vain j WEAK
Valueless j
Vapid j
Verbiage n TALK
Void j END
Waste n LACK
Waste n DIRT
Waste n ERTH
Wear v
Wearing v
Whatnot n
Whippersnapper n
Whit n LITL
Wore v
Worn v
Wornout j
Worthless j

TRUE

Accurate j SHRP
Actual j
Affidavit n WRIT
Affirm v
Attest v
Authentic j
Axiom n IDEA
Bonafide j
Candid j OPEN
Candor n OPEN
Certificate n WRIT
Certify v
Check n
Checked v

Checker n
Cogent j IDEA
Confirm v AGRE
Correct v
Corrigible j
Corroborate v
Credential n WRIT
Credible j
Criterion n
Data n
Datum n
Defacto j
Demonstrate v IDEA
Document v WRIT

Documentary n WRIT
Establish v IDEA
Establishment n IDEA
Evidence n
Examination n OPEN
Experiment n
Fact n
Genuine j
Honest j GOOD
Impartial j
Incontestable j POWR
Incontrovertible j POWR
Indisputable j POWR
Indubitable j

Irrefutable j
Just j GOOD
Justice n GOOD
Justly d GOOD
Justness n GOOD
Legitimacy n LAW
Level v
Material j
Materialize v
Matteroffact j
Objective j
Objectivity n
Primafacie j OPEN
Probate n LAW

Probating v LAW
Probation n OPEN
Proof n
Prove v
Proving v
Real j
Real j EMPH
Reality n
Realize v IDEA
Really d EMPH
Rectify v
Right d GOOD
Right n MOTV
Righted v GOOD
Righteous j GOOD
Righting v GOOD

Rightly d GOOD
Rights n MOTV
Rights v GOOD
Rorschach n BLUR
Science n IDEA
Shakedown n
Sincere j GOOD
Square j GOOD
Squarely d GOOD
Substantiate v
Tangible j
Test n
Tested v
Testify v TALK
Testimony n TALK
Testing v

Trial n LAW
Trial n
Tried j
Tried v LAW
True j
Truism n TRIV
Truth n
Try v
Try v LAW
Unaffected j EASY
Unbiased j
Undeniable j
Undoubted j
Unfeigned j
Unimpeachable j GOOD
Unprejudiced j

Unquestionable j
Valid j
Veracity n
Verify v
Vindicate v OPEN
Vouch v
Vouched v
Voucher n WRIT
Warrant n AID
Warrant n
Warranted v AID
Warranted v
Warranting v AID
Warranting v
Warranty n AID
Wholehearted j WHOL

UP

Above b
Above b LEAD
Aboveboard j OPEN
Acme n
Aerial j VAPR
Aerial n BULG
Aerialist n PLAY
Aero j VEHC
Aeronaut n VEHC
Aeroplane n VEHC
Air n VAPR
Aircraft n VEHC
Airline n VEHC
Airplane n VEHC
Airport n HOME
Albatross n ANML
Aloft d
Altimeter n MSMT
Altitude n MSMT
Antenna n BULG
Apex n
Apices n
Apogee n
Aquiline j ANML
Arise v GO
Arise v BGIN
Arose v GO
Arose v BGIN
Ascend v GO
Ascendancy n LEAD
Ascension n GO
Atop d
Attic n HOME
Auk n ANML
Aviation n VEHC
Awning n COVR
Balcony n HOME
Barnstorm v GO
Bat n ANML
Bee n BUG
Beetle n BUG
Belfry n MUSC
Bird n ANML
Birds n ANML
Blackbird n ANML
Blimp n VEHC

Bluebird n ANML
Bluejay n ANML
Bobolink n ANML
Bobwhite n ANML
Brow n END
Bumblebee n BUG
Buoy v FLOW
Buoyant j FLOW
Butterflies n BUG
Butterfly n BUG
Buzzard n ANML
Canary n ANML
Canopy n COVR
Capital n FORM
Cardinal n ANML
Cardinals n ANML
Catbird n ANML
Ceiling n COVR
Celestial j ASTR
Chat n ANML
Chicken n ANML
Chopper n VEHC
Cicada n BUG
Clerestory n VIEW
Climactic j CRUX
Climax n CRUX
Climb v GO
Condor n ANML
Corona n SOMA
Courser n ANML
Cowbird n ANML
Crane n MECH
Crane n ANML
Creeper n ANML
Crest n
Cresting v
Crow n ANML
Crown n BODY
Crown n
Cuckoo n ANML
Darningneedle n BUG
Davit n MECH
Daw n ANML
Dirigible n VEHC
Dogfight n DAMG
Dome n COVR

Dove n ANML
Downstairs d DOWN
Dragonfly n BUG
Drake n ANML
Drone n BUG
Drone n VEHC
Drosophila n BUG
Duck n ANML
Eagle n ANML
Eave n FORM
Eaves n FORM
Egret n ANML
Elevate v GO
Elevate v POWR
Elevation n GO
Elevation n POWR
Elevation n MSMT
Elevator n DOWN
Eminence n BULG
Erect v FORM
Erect v
Erection n FORM
Escalate v GO
Falcon n ANML
Finch n ANML
Firefly n BUG
Firmament n ASTR
Flamingo n ANML
Flew v GO
Flicker n ANML
Flier n GO
Flies n BUG
Flies v GO
Float v GO
Floated v GO
Floating v GO
Flown v GO
Fly n BUG
Fly v GO
Flyer n GO
Fowl n ANML
Gable n FORM
Gander n ANML
Garret n HOME
Geese n ANML
Glider n VEHC

Gnat n BUG
Goose n ANML
Grackle n ANML
Grouse n ANML
Gull n ANML
Haggard n ANML
Halcyon n ANML
Hangbird n ANML
Harrier n ANML
Hawk n ANML
Heaven n ASTR
Heavenward d ASTR
Heft v GO
Height n
Height n MSMT
Heighten v LARG
Helicopter n VEHC
Heron n ANML
High j
High j GLAD
High j POWR
High j MSMT
High j GOOD
Highfalutin j FOOL
Highland n ERTH
Highness n
Hike v GO
Hoist n GO
Homer n ANML
Hornet n BUG
Hover v GO
Hummingbird n ANML
Hydroplane n VEHC
Ibis n ANML
Jack n MECH
Jacked v MECH
Jacking v MECH
Jay n ANML
Jet n VEHC
Jetliner n VEHC
Jetted v VEHC
Jetting v VEHC
Kite n PLAY
Kite n ANML
Kiting v PLAY
Ladder n DOWN

Lark n ANML
Lift n GO
Lift n AID
Locust n BUG
Loft n HOME
Loft v GO
Lofted v GO
Loftier j
Loftier j GOOD
Lofting v GO
Lofty j
Lofty j GOOD
Loon n ANML
Macaw n ANML
Magpie n ANML
Mallard n ANML
Mantis n BUG
Martin n ANML
Meridian n POWR
Mezzanine n HOME
Minaret n HOME
Monoplane n VEHC
Mosquito n BUG
Moth n BUG
Mount v GO
Mount n ANML
Mounted v GO
Mounting v GO
Mynah n ANML
Nightingale n ANML
Nutcracker n ANML
Oriole n ANML
Ornithology n ANML
Osprey n ANML
Over b
Overflew v GO
Overflight n GO
Overfly v GO
Overground j ERTH
Overhang n DOWN
Overhead j
Overlaid n
Overland j ERTH
Overlay n
Overleap v GO
Overlie v

Overlook v VIEW
Overlying n
Overpass n PATH
Owl n ANML
Parakeet n ANML
Parrot n ANML
Partridge n ANML
Peacock n ANML
Peak n ERTH
Peak n POWR
Peaked j ERTH
Pelican n ANML
Penthouse n HOME
Perch n REST
Perpendicular j FORM
Petrel n ANML
Pheasant n ANML
Phoebe n ANML
Pigeon n ANML
Pinion n BODY
Pinioned j BODY
Pinnacle n ERTH
Pinnacle n POWR
Pintail n ANML
Plane n VEHC
Plateau n ERTH
Plover n ANML
Quail n ANML
Rafter n FORM
Raise v GO
Raising v GO
Raven n ANML
Rear v
Reared v
Rearing v
Right v FORM
Righted v FORM
Righting v FORM
Rights v FORM
Rise v GO
Rise n BULG
Risen v GO
Robin n ANML
Rocket n VEHC
Rocket v GO
Roof n COVR

Rook n ANML
Rooster n ANML
Rose v GO
Rung n DOWN
Sail v GO
Sailed v GO
Sailing v GO
Sandpiper n ANML
Scale v GO
Skies n ASTR
Sky n ASTR
Skylight n VIEW
Skyscraper n FORM
Snipe n ANML
Soar v GO
Sparrow n ANML
Spire n FORM
Stair n DOWN
Stand v
Standing v
Starling n ANML
Stature n
Steeple n FORM
Step n DOWN
Stepladder n DOWN
Steps n DOWN
Stilt n FORM
Stood v
Summit n
Sunrise n ASTR
Superior j
Surface n FORM
Swallow n ANML
Swan n ANML
Top n
Top n COVR
Top v SHRP
Top v POWR
Topaz n ANML
Topless j LACK
Topmost j EMPH
Topped v
Topped v COVR
Topped v SHRP
Topped v POWR
Tops n

Tops n COVR
Tops v SHRP
Tops v POWR
Tower n HOME
Tower v
Towered v
Towering v
Trapeze n PLAY
Treetop n VEGT
Turkey n ANML
Turret n HOME
Up b
Up j END
Upbringing n AID
Uphill d BULG
Upper j
Upright j
Upright j GOOD
Upside n
Upstairs d
Upstanding j GOOD
Upstate j PLAC
Upstream d FLOW
Uptown d PLAC
Upward d
Vault v GO
Vaulted v GO
Vaulting v GO
Vertex n
Vulture n ANML
Wasp n BUG
Watchtower n VIEW
Weigh v FLOW
Wing n BODY
Wing n FORM
Wing v GO
Winged j BODY
Winged j FORM
Winged v GO
Winging v GO
Winnow v GO
Wren n ANML
Zenith n
Zeppelin n VEHC

VAPR

Aerate v CLEN
Aerial j UP
Aerodynamics n POWR
Aether n
Air n WEA
Air n UP
Air v OPEN
Aired v WEA
Aired v OPEN
Airing v WEA
Airing v OPEN
Airless j LACK
Airs n WEA
Airs n FALS
Airs v OPEN
Airy j WEA

Airy j EASY
Anemometer n MSMT
Aroma n SOMA
Aspirate v OUT
Aspirating v OUT
Aspiration n OUT
Atmosphere n ASTR
Atmosphere n HOLW
Atmosphere n MSMT
Atmospheric j ASTR
Atmospheric j HOLW
Atomizer n MECH
Aura n HOLW
Balloon n PLAY
Balloon n VEHC
Barometer n MSMT

Blew v GO
Blow v GO
Blower n MECH
Breath n SOMA
Breathe v SOMA
Breeze n WEA
Breeze n EASY
Butane n
Chlorinate v CLEN
Chlorine n
Chloroform n REST
Cloud n BLUR
Cloudless j WEA
Cumuli n WEA
Cumulus n WEA
Deflate v LITL

Draft n
Ether n
Ether n ASTR
Ethereal j MYTH
Etherize v
Evaporate v FLOW
Exhale v SOMA
Expire v SOMA
Fan n MECH
Fart n SOMA
Flatus n SOMA
Fog n BLUR
Fragrance n SOMA
Fume n DIRT
Gas n
Gas n DAMG

Gas v TALK
Gust n WEA
Halo n VIEW
Haze n BLUR
Hazier j BLUR
Hazy j BLUR
Helium n
Huff v SOMA
Hydrogen n
Inflate v BULG
Inflating v BULG
Inflation n BULG
Inhale v SOMA
Inspire v SOMA
Krypton n
Malodorous j DIRT
Mist n FLOW

Misted v FLOW
Nimbus n VIEW
Nitrogen n
Odor n SOMA
Olfactory j SOMA
Oxygen n
Ozone n
Pant v SOMA
Pneumatic j
Propane n MTRL
Puff n
Pump n MECH
Pumped v MECH
Pumping v MECH
Reek v DIRT
Respiration n SOMA
Respirator n MECH

Scent n SOMA
Scuba j MECH
Smell n SOMA
Smog n BLUR
Smoke n HEAT
Sniff n SOMA
Snorkel n MECH
Space n ASTR
Stank v DIRT
Steam n HEAT
Steam v GO
Steamed v HEAT
Steamed v GO
Steams v HEAT
Steams v GO
Stench n DIRT
Stink v DIRT

Stratosphere n ASTR
Stunk v DIRT
Suck v IN
Sucked v IN
Sucker n IN
Suction n IN
Vacuum n LACK
Vapor n BLUR
Waft v GO
Whiff n
Whiff n SOMA
Wind n WEA
Wind n IDEA
Winds n WEA
Windy j WEA
Xenon n
Zephyr n WEA

VARY

Aberrant j OPPO
Aberration n OPPO
Aberration n SICK
About b
Adapt v SIML
Adhoc j
Adjust v SIML
Agitate v
Akimbo j BODY
Alter v
Alternate v
Alternating v
Amend v
Anagram n WRIT
Angle v
Angling v
Antiphony n MUSC
Arabesque n FORM
Around b
Askance d AGGR
Askew d
Aslant d
Asymmetry n FORM
Aversion n
Avert v BLOK
Avert v
Avoid v
Awry j FALS
Bandied v
Bandy v
Bank v GO
Baroque j FORM
Bat v
Beat n MUSC
Beg v
Begged v
Bend n
Bend v WEAK
Bender n
Bends n
Bends n SICK
Bends v WEAK
Bent j
Bent v WEAK
Bevel v

Bias n
Blink v VIEW
Bob v
Bobbed v
Bobbing v
Bobs v
Boomerang v GO
Bounce v GO
Bow n DOWN
Bow n
Bowed v DOWN
Bowed v
Bower n
Bowing v DOWN
Bowing v
Buckle v WEAK
Cadence n MUSC
Cant n
Canted v
Caprice n MOTV
Capsize v DAMG
Careen v
Carom n GO
Cartwheel n GO
Change n
Chatter v HEAR
Checker v
Checkered j
Chop n
Choppy j
Churn n HOLW
Churn v
Circle v GO
Circuit n GO
Circulate v GO
Circulating v GO
Circulation n WRIT
Circulation n GO
Circumlocution n TALK
Circumnavigate v GO
Circumvent v FALS
Clot v FORM
Coagulate v FORM
Coarse j
Cock v

Cocked v
Cockeyed j BODY
Cocking v
Cocks v
Coil v FORM
Collapse v LITL
Collapsible j LITL
Comb v FLOW
Combed v FLOW
Comber n FLOW
Combing v FLOW
Commute v
Commuting v
Compass v GO
Compassed v GO
Compassing v GO
Condense v FLOW
Congeal v FORM
Contort v
Contorting v
Contortionist n BODY
Conversion n
Convert v
Convertible j
Convertible n VEHC
Convolute v
Convulse v PANG
Corkscrew n MECH
Corrugate v FORM
Covary v SIML
Crease n
Crimp v
Crinkle v
Crisp v
Crisscross v JOIN
Crisscross v GO
Crook n
Crooking v
Crouch v DOWN
Crumple v
Curl n
Curl n BODY
Curler n
Curlicue n
Curling v

Curvaceous j LADY
Curve n
Curving v
Cut v GO
Cutoff n PATH
Cutting v GO
Cycle n FORW
Cycle n GO
Cycled v GO
Cyclic j FORW
Cycling v GO
Decenter v SHRP
Decentralize v SHRP
Deciduous j BODY
Decompress v POWR
Deflect v GO
Deform v DIRT
Deform v BAD
Deform v FORM
Defrost v COLD
Deliquesce v FLOW
Denature v CRUX
Derail v GO
Derange v
Desultory j
Detour n GO
Develop v LARG
Develop v
Develop v AID
Deviate v
Deviate v OPPO
Devious j
Diffract v
Digress v TALK
Discursive j
Dislocate v
Displace v
Dissolve v FLOW
Dissuade v IDEA
Distort v FALS
Distract v IDEA
Diverge v OPPO
Diversion n
Diversion n IDEA
Divert v

Divert v IDEA	Flips v QUIK	Hunching v BULG	Molted v BODY
Dodge v GO	Flop v HEAR	Impermanence n	Momentary j TIME
Dogleg n ANML	Flounce v GO	Incline v	Mutate v
Double v GO	Flounder v WEAK	Inconstant j	Nod v REST
Drawn j PANG	Floundered v WEAK	Indirect j	Nuance n COLR
Duck v	Floundering v WEAK	Instability n WEAK	Oblique j
Ducked v	Fluctuate v	Interchange n SIML	Offset n
Ducking v	Flutter n HEAR	Interchange n PATH	Offsets v
Ductile j EASY	Flutter n QUIK	Intermittent j	Oscillate v
Eccentric j FORM	Fold n FORM	Introvert v IN	Overdevelop v LARG
Eddy n FLOW	Fold v WEAK	Invert v OPPO	Overdevelop v
Elastic j EASY	Folded v	Irregular j	Overturn v
Elastic n FABR	Folded v WEAK	Jackknife v	Palpitate v SOMA
Elude v OPEN	Folder n FORM	Jackknifed v	Paroxysm n PANG
Elusive j OPEN	Folding v	Jackknifes v	Parried v BLOK
Encode v WRIT	Folding v WEAK	Jackknifing v	Parry n BLOK
Ephemeral j SEP	Frizz v	Jag v SHRP	Pendulum n DOWN
Errant j FALS	Frizzle v	Jagged j SHRP	Pendulum n TIME
Errant j GO	Furl v	Jar v AGGR	Periodic j EVER
Erratic j	Gainer n DOWN	Jarred v AGGR	Peristalsis n SOMA
Erratic j AFAR	Gave v	Jell v FORM	Permutation n
Escape n	Genuflect v BODY	Jerk n QUIK	Pirouette n GO
Eschew v	Girdle v GO	Jerked v QUIK	Pitch n
Evade v	Give v	Jerking v QUIK	Pitched v
Evanesce v SEP	Glance v GO	Jig n MECH	Pitching v
Evasion n	Gnarl n VEGT	Jig v SHRP	Pivot n CRUX
Evolve v FORW	Gnarl v	Jigged v SHRP	Plait v FORM
Exchange n	Goggle v VIEW	Jigging v SHRP	Plastic j EASY
Excursive j TALK	Goggles v VIEW	Jiggle n	Plasticity n EASY
Falter v WEAK	Grade n PATH	Jog n	Play v
Fan v COLD	Grate v LITL	Jolt n DAMG	Pleat n
Fan v WEAK	Grating v LITL	Jostle v JOIN	Pliable j EASY
Fanned v COLD	Grew v LARG	Jounce v GO	Plied j FORM
Fanned v WEAK	Grew v	Juggle v FALS	Ply n FORM
Ferment n	Grind v LITL	Kaleidoscope n VIEW	Protean j FORM
Ferment n PANG	Grinder n LITL	Keel v DAMG	Provisional j
Fickle j	Grinds v LITL	Kink n	Pucker v
Fit n	Ground v DAMG	Knead v	Pull v
Fitful j	Ground v LITL	Knockkneed j BODY	Pulled v
Fitful j PANG	Grow v LARG	Lean v	Pulse n SOMA
Flank v GO	Grow v	Leaned v	Pulverize v LITL
Flanked v GO	Grown v LARG	Leaning v	Pulverize v DAMG
Flanking v GO	Grown v	Leans v	Purse v
Flap n HEAR	Growth n LARG	Leaven v EASY	Pursed v
Flap n FORM	Gyrate v GO	Lilt n EASY	Pursing v
Flapped v HEAR	Gyroscope n MECH	Limber j EASY	Quake n ERTH
Flapped v FORM	Heave v	List n	Quake v PANG
Flapper n HEAR	Heel v	Listed v	Quake v
Flection n	Heeled v	Lithe j EASY	Qualify v CRUX
Fleeting j QUIK	Heeling v	Lurch n	Quaver v HEAR
Flex v	Helical j FORM	Makeshift j	Quaver n MUSC
Flexible j EASY	Helicoid j FORM	Malleable j	Quicksilver n MTRL
Flexing v	Hitch n GO	Meander v GO	Quirk n
Flick n QUIK	Hitched v GO	Melt v EASY	Quiver n
Flicked v QUIK	Hobble v GO	Mercurial j	Quiver v PANG
Flicker n VIEW	Hobbled v GO	Miss v	Readjust v
Flicker n QUIK	Hook n	Missed v	Recline v REST
Flightier j FOOL	Hook n DAMG	Missing v	Reel v
Flighty j FOOL	Hover v	Mobile j EASY	Reel v WEAK
Flip n QUIK	Hunch n BULG	Modify v	Reform n GOOD
Flipped v QUIK	Hunchback n BODY	Modulate v	Refraction n VIEW
Flipping v QUIK	Hunched v BULG	Molt v BODY	Remodel v FORM

Parts of speech: a article; b preposition; c conjunction; d adverb; f prefix; i interjection;
j adjective; n noun; p pronoun; r phrase; v verb.

Render v
Replace v SIML
Resilient j EASY
Reverse n BACK
Reverse n OPPO
Revise v
Revolution n GO
Revolution n DAMG
Revolve v GO
Rheostat n ION
Rhythm n MUSC
Ricochet v GO
Rip n FLOW
Ripple n
Rock v
Rocked v
Rocker n
Rocking v
Rococo j FORM
Rotary n PATH
Rotate v GO
Rough j
Rough n ERTH
Roughed v
Roughing v
Round v GO
Roundabout j
Rounded v GO
Rounding v GO
Rounds n GO
Rub v JOIN
Rubbed v JOIN
Rubbing v JOIN
Ruffle v
Ruffle n GARB
Rumple v
Rustle v HEAR
Scramble v JOIN
Screwball n PLAY
Seesaw n
Shake n
Shake v PANG
Shake v JOIN
Shaking v
Shaking v PANG
Shaking v JOIN
Shaky j WEAK
Sheer v
Sheered v
Sheering v
Shied v WEAK
Shift n
Shimmer v VIEW
Shirk v FALS
Shiver v
Shook v
Shook v PANG
Shook v JOIN
Shrivel v LITL
Shrug v BODY
Shudder v PANG
Shuffle v JOIN

Shun v
Shunt v GO
Shy v PANG
Sidelong j
Sidestep v GO
Sidetrack v GO
Sinuous j
Skip v
Skip v GO
Skirt v GO
Skirting v GO
Slant n
Slew v
Slope n
Slue v
Soluble j FLOW
Somersault n GO
Spasm n QUIK
Spasmodic j QUIK
Spastic j
Spin v GO
Spiral j FORM
Sporadic j
Sport n
Spring n MECH
Spun v GO
Spur n PATH
Squint v VIEW
Stagger v
Stagger v GO
Stir v
Stirred v
Stoop v DOWN
Stroke n JOIN
Stroked v JOIN
Stroking v JOIN
Stumble v WEAK
Sub n SIML
Subbed v SIML
Subs v SIML
Substitute v SIML
Supersede v SIML
Supplant v SIML
Supple j EASY
Surf n FLOW
Sway v
Swerve v GO
Swing v GO
Switch n
Swivel v
Swung v GO
Syncopate v MUSC
Tack n GO
Tailor v FORM
Tamper v BAD
Tangent n JOIN
Temporary j
Tentative j
Thaw n FLOW
Thrash v AGGR
Throb n
Tilt n

Tip n
Tips v
Toe v
Torque n POWR
Tortuous j
Toss v
Totter v WEAK
Transform v
Transient j SEP
Transition n
Transitory j SEP
Translate v
Translate v TALK
Transplant v VEGT
Transplant v GO
Transpose v
Tremble n PANG
Tremor n
Tremulous j PANG
Trip v WEAK
Tuck n GARB
Tumble v GO
Tumbled v GO
Tumbledown j WEAK
Turn n GO
Turn n AID
Turn n PANG
Turnabout n PATH
Turncoat n AGGR
Turnover n
Twine v JOIN
Twining v JOIN
Twinkle n VIEW
Twirl v GO
Twist n
Twist n FOOD
Twist n SOME
Twisted v
Twisting v
Twitch n
Uncoil v FORM
Undid v
Undo v
Undulate v
Unequal j
Uneven j
Unfold v OPEN
Unfurl v OPEN
Unroll v FORM
Unsettled j
Unsettled j PANG
Unsettled j OPPO
Unstable j WEAK
Unsteady j WEAK
Unwind v
Upend v WEAK
Upheaval n DAMG
Upset v WEAK
Vacillate v BLUR
Variable j
Varied v
Varied v OPPO

Various j
Vary v
Vary v OPPO
Veer v
Verge v NEAR
Vibrate v
Viceversa r OPPO
Volatile j
Waddle n GO
Wag n
Wallow v BAD
Warp n FALS
Warp v FLOW
Warped v FALS
Warped v FLOW
Warping v FALS
Warping v FLOW
Wave n
Wave n BULG
Wave n FLOW
Waver v
Waver v WEAK
Wayward j GO
Weave v GO
Welter v BAD
Wheel v QUIK
Wheeled v QUIK
Wheeling v QUIK
Whim n MOTV
Whip v
Whir n HEAR
Whirl n QUIK
Whirl v GO
Whirlpool n FLOW
Whirlwind n WEA
Wiggle v
Wild j
Wind v
Wind v GO
Wind v END
Winds v
Winds v GO
Winds v END
Wink n VIEW
Wink n QUIK
Wobble v WEAK
Wound v
Wound v GO
Wound v END
Wove v GO
Wreathe v FORM
Wreathing v FORM
Wriggle v
Wrinkle v
Writhe v PANG
Wry j
Yaw v
Zigzag j
Zigzag v GO

Abloom j
Absinthe n SIP
Acorn n FOOD
Agrarian j ERTH
Agriculture n ERTH
Agronomy n ERTH
Alcohol n MTRL
Alcohol n SIP
Alcoholic j SIP
Ale n SIP
Alfalfa n
Algae n FLOW
Almond n FOOD
Anemone n
Anise n FOOD
Apple n FOOD
Applejack n SIP
Applesauce n FOOD
Apricot n FOOD
Arable j ERTH
Arbor n HOME
Arbor n
Artichoke n FOOD
Ash n MTRL
Ash n
Ashes n
Asparagus n FOOD
Aspen n
Aster n
Atropine n MEDC
Avocado n FOOD
Azalea n
Backwood j BACK
Balsa n
Balsa n MTRL
Balsam n
Balsam n MTRL
Banana n FOOD
Bark n BODY
Bay n
Bean n FOOD
Beech n
Beech n MTRL
Beer n SIP
Berry n FOOD
Birch n
Birch n MTRL
Birdseye n
Blackjack n COLR
Blade n BODY
Bloom v BODY
Bloomed v BODY
Blossom v BODY
Bluebell n
Blueberry n FOOD
Board n MTRL
Boards n MTRL
Booze n SIP
Botany n IDEA
Bough n BODY
Bouquet n GRUP
Bourbon n SIP
Boutonniere n GARB
Bower n HOME
Boxwood n

Branch n BODY
Brandies n SIP
Brandy n SIP
Bread n FOOD
Broccoli n FOOD
Browse v FOOD
Brush n
Bud v BGIN
Budded v BGIN
Budding v BGIN
Bulb n BGIN
Burgundy n SIP
Burlap n FABR
Bush n
Bush n ERTH
Bushes n
Bushes n ERTH
Bushier j
Bushwhacker n DAMG
Bushy j
Buttercup n
Cabbage n FOOD
Cactus n
Calico j FABR
Calyx n BODY
Cane n FOOD
Cane n MTRL
Caned v MTRL
Caning v MTRL
Cantaloupe n FOOD
Caper n FOOD
Caramel n FOOD
Carnation n
Carrot n FOOD
Cashew n FOOD
Castor n
Castoroil n MTRL
Cattail n
Cauliflower n FOOD
Cedar n
Cedar n MTRL
Celery n FOOD
Cereal n FOOD
Chaff n
Champagne n SIP
Cheesecloth n FABR
Cherry n FOOD
Cherry n MTRL
Chestnut n FOOD
Chestnut n MTRL
Chianti n SIP
Chicle n FOOD
Chicory n FOOD
Chili n FOOD
Chintz j FABR
Chive n FOOD
Chlorophyll n MTRL
Chlorophyll n COLR
Chocolate n FOOD
Chocolate n SIP
Chrysanthemum n
Cider n SIP
Cinnamon n FOOD
Citric j FOOD
Citron n FOOD

Citronella n
Citrus j FOOD
Clapboard n MTRL
Claret n SIP
Clove n FOOD
Clover n
Cloverleaf j FORM
Cob n BODY
Cobbler n SIP
Cobbler n FOOD
Cocaine n MEDC
Cockle n
Cockle n FOOD
Cocoa n SIP
Cocoa n
Cocoanut n FOOD
Coconut n FOOD
Coffee n SIP
Cognac n SIP
Coke n SIP
Cola n SIP
Coleslaw n FOOD
Collard n FOOD
Combine n MECH
Comfit n FOOD
Cone n BODY
Coniferous j BODY
Conservatories n HOME
Conservatory n HOME
Copra n FOOD
Cordial n SIP
Corduroy j FABR
Core n CRUX
Coring v CRUX
Cork n MTRL
Corn n FOOD
Cornstarch n FOOD
Corny j FOOD
Corsage n GARB
Cortex n BODY
Cortices n BODY
Cosmos n
Cotton n FABR
Crabapple n FOOD
Cranberry n FOOD
Crash n FABR
Creeper n GO
Cress n FOOD
Crop n
Cropper n WORK
Cucumber n FOOD
Currant n FOOD
Curried v FOOD
Curry n FOOD
Cypress n
Cypress n MTRL
Daffodil n
Dahlia n
Daisies n
Daisy n
Dandelion n
Daphne n
Darnel n
Date n FOOD
Deal n MTRL

Deflower v SEP
Defoliate v SEP
Delphinium n
Demitasse n SIP
Denim n FABR
Dill j FOOD
Dimity n FABR
Dogwood n
Dough n FOOD
Driftwood n FLOW
Duck n FABR
Ear n BODY
Ebony n MTRL
Ebony n
Eggplant n FOOD
Elderberry n
Elm n
Endive n FOOD
Escarole n FOOD
Eucalyptus n
Eucalyptus n MTRL
Evergreen n
Eye n BODY
Farina n FOOD
Fern n
Fig n FOOD
Fig n TRIV
Filbert n FOOD
Fir n
Fir n MTRL
Firewood n HEAT
Flip n SIP
Floral j
Florist n
Flour n FOOD
Flower n
Flower n POWR
Flowerpot n HOLW
Flowery j
Foliage n BODY
Follicle n
Forest n
Forsythia n
Foxglove n
Fritter n FOOD
Frond n BODY
Fruit n FOOD
Fruit n END
Fruit n SEX
Fruited j FOOD
Fruiter n VEHC
Fruiter n FOOD
Fruitful j FOOD
Fruitful j AID
Fruitless j WEAK
Fuchsia n
Fungus j SICK
Fungus n
Garden n ERTH
Gardenia n
Garland n FORM
Garlic n FOOD
Gentian n
Geranium n
Germ n BGIN

Gherkin n FOOD	Hull n BODY	Lumber n MTRL	Palm n
Gin n SIP	Hull v SEP	Magnolia n	Palm n POWR
Ginger n FOOD	Husk n BODY	Mahogany n MTRL	Palmetto n
Gingham n FABR	Hyacinth n	Maize n FOOD	Pansy n
Ginkgo n	Hydrangea n	Malt n SIP	Papaya n FOOD
Glade n	Indigo n COLR	Mandarin n FOOD	Paprika n FOOD
Gladiola n	Iris n	Mango n FOOD	Park n ERTH
Gnarl v VARY	Ivies n	Mangrove n	Parsley n FOOD
Gourd n BODY	Ivy n	Maple n	Parsnip n FOOD
Graft n JOIN	Jam n FOOD	Maple n MTRL	Pastoral j ERTH
Graham j	Jasmine n	Maraschino n	Pasture n FOOD
Grain n	Jonquil n	Margarine n FOOD	Pea n FOOD
Granary n HOLW	Juice n SIP	Marigold n	Peach n FOOD
Grape n FOOD	Juicier j SIP	Marijuana n MEDC	Peanut n FOOD
Grapefruit n FOOD	Juicy j SIP	Marjoram n FOOD	Pear n FOOD
Grapevine n FOOD	Jungle n	Marmalade n FOOD	Peas n FOOD
Grass n	Juniper n	Marshmallow n FOOD	Peat n ERTH
Graze v FOOD	Junket n FOOD	Martini n SIP	Pecan n FOOD
Green n COLR	Jute n FABR	Mash n SIP	Pekoe n SIP
Greenery n COLR	Kale n FOOD	Meadow n ERTH	Pepper n FOOD
Greenhouse n HOME	Kelp n FLOW	Meal n FOOD	Peppermint n FOOD
Grenadine n SIP	Kernel n BGIN	Mealy j FOOD	Persimmon n FOOD
Grist n	Ketchup n FOOD	Melon n FOOD	Petal n BODY
Grits n FOOD	Khaki n FABR	Mesquite n	Petunia n
Groats n FOOD	Knot n BODY	Millet n FOOD	Picalilly n FOOD
Grove n	Knothole n HOLW	Mimosa n	Pickle n FOOD
Guava n FOOD	Kohlrabi n FOOD	Mint n FOOD	Pimento n FOOD
Gum n FOOD	Kumquat n FOOD	Mistletoe n	Pimpernel n
Gum n SOMA	Landscape v ERTH	Mocha j FOOD	Pine n
Gumbo n	Laurel n	Molasses n FOOD	Pine n MTRL
Hammock n ERTH	Laurel n POWR	Mold n DIRT	Pineapple n FOOD
Harvest n HAVE	Lavender n	Moldy j DIRT	Pink n
Hawthorn n	Lawn n	Moss n	Pip n BGIN
Hay n	Leaf n BODY	Mulberry n	Pippin n FOOD
Hay n REST	Leaven v EASY	Mulberry n FOOD	Pips n BGIN
Haycock n BULG	Leaves n BODY	Mulch n AID	Pistachio n FOOD
Haymaker n WORK	Leek n FOOD	Muscatel n SIP	Pistil n BODY
Haymow n HOLW	Legume n FOOD	Mushroom n FOOD	Pit n
Haystack n BULG	Lei n FORM	Muskmelon n FOOD	Pitted v OUT
Hazel n	Leis n FORM	Must n SIP	Pitting v OUT
Header n MECH	Lemon n FOOD	Mustard n FOOD	Plane n
Heath n ERTH	Lemon n WEAK	Myrrh n MTRL	Plank n MTRL
Heath n	Lemonade n SIP	Myrtle n	Plankton n FLOW
Hedge n BLOK	Lentil n FOOD	Nasturtium n	Plant n ERTH
Hedgerow n FORW	Lettuce n FOOD	Nectar n SIP	Plantain n
Heliotrope n ASTR	Lichen n	Nectarine n FOOD	Plantation n ERTH
Hemlock n	Licorice n FOOD	Nettle n SHRP	Planted v ERTH
Hemp n FABR	Lilac n	Nursery n AID	Planting v ERTH
Hemp n MEDC	Lilies n	Nut n FOOD	Plug n FOOD
Herb n FOOD	Lily n	Nutmeg n FOOD	Plum n FOOD
Herb n MEDC	Limb n BODY	Nutshell n HOLW	Pod n HOLW
Herbivore n FOOD	Limbed j BODY	Oak n	Poinsettia n
Hermitage n SIP	Lime n FOOD	Oak n MTRL	Pollen n BGIN
Heroin n MEDC	Linden n	Oat n FOOD	Pollinate v BGIN
Hessian n FABR	Linen n FABR	Oil n FOOD	Pomegranate n FOOD
Hickory n	Linseed n MTRL	Oils n FOOD	Pompon n
Hickory n MTRL	Liqueur n SIP	Okra n FOOD	Poplar n
Hollies n	Liquor n SIP	Oleander n	Poppies n
Holly n	Litter n MTRL	Oleomargarine n FOOD	Poppy n
Honeysuckle n	Locust n	Olive n FOOD	Port n SIP
Hop n	Log n MTRL	Onion n FOOD	Porter n SIP
Horseradish n FOOD	Loganberry n FOOD	Opium n MEDC	Posies n
Horticulture n	Logged v MTRL	Orange n FOOD	Posy n
Hothouse n HOME	Logging v MTRL	Orchard n ERTH	Pot n MEDC
Huckleberry n FOOD	Lotus n	Orchid n	Potato n FOOD

Prairie n ERTH
Primrose n
Produce n
Prune n FOOD
Pumpernickel n FOOD
Pumpkin n FOOD
Punk n
Pussywillow n
Quince n FOOD
Quinine n MEDC
Radish n FOOD
Raisin n FOOD
Raspberry n FOOD
Reap v HAVE
Redwood n COLR
Redwood n MTRL
Reed n
Rhododendron n
Rhubarb n FOOD
Rice n FOOD
Rind n BODY
Roll n FOOD
Root n BGIN
Rose n
Rosy j
Rum n SIP
Rush n
Rushes n
Rust n SICK
Rye n FOOD
Rye n SIP
Sack n SIP
Saffron n
Sage n FOOD
Sagebrush n
Sake n SIP
Sallow n
Sandalwood n MTRL
Sandalwood n
Sanka n SIP

Sap n SOMA
Sapling n YNG
Sarsaparilla n
Sarsaparilla n SIP
Sassafras n
Sauerkraut n FOOD
Sauterne n SIP
Scallion n FOOD
Schnapps n SIP
Scotch n SIP
Scrub n
Seaweed n FLOW
Sedge n
Seed n BGIN
Shag n FOOD
Shagbark n
Sharecropper n WORK
Shell n BODY
Sherry n SIP
Shoot n BGIN
Shrub n
Snowball n
Sod n ERTH
Sodded v ERTH
Sodding v ERTH
Sow v BGIN
Sowed v BGIN
Sowing v BGIN
Spice n FOOD
Spinach n FOOD
Spray n GRUP
Sprout v BGIN
Spruce n
Spruce n MTRL
Squash n FOOD
Stalk n BODY
Stand n GRUP
Starch n MTRL
Stem n BODY
Stemmed j BODY

Stout n SIP
Straw n MTRL
Strawberry n FOOD
Stubble n
Sucker n
Sugar n FOOD
Sunflower n ASTR
Sycamore n
Tapioca n FOOD
Taproot n BGIN
Tartar n
Tea n SIP
Thistle n SHRP
Thorn n SHRP
Timber n MTRL
Toadstool n
Tobacco n FOOD
Tomato n FOOD
Tomato n LADY
Transplant v VARY
Tree n
Tree n FORM
Treetop n UP
Trunk n BODY
Trunks n BODY
Tuber n
Tulip n
Turf n ERTH
Turpentine n MTRL
Twig n BODY
Underbrush n
Unleavened j LACK
Vanilla j FOOD
Vegetable n FOOD
Vegetation n
Vermouth n SIP
Vin n SIP
Vine n
Vinegar n FOOD
Vineyard n ERTH

Vintage j TIME
Violet n
Vodka n SIP
Walnut n MTRL
Walnut n FOOD
Watercress n FOOD
Watermelon n FOOD
Weed n
Weed v CLEN
Wheat n FOOD
Whiskey n SIP
Wholewheat j WHOL
Wicker n MTRL
Wicker n HOLW
Wild n ERTH
Wilderness n ERTH
Willow n
Willow n MTRL
Willow n MECH
Willow v CLEN
Wine n SIP
Wining v SIP
Wistaria n
Wood n MTRL
Wood n
Wooded j
Woods n MTRL
Woods n
Wormwood n BUG
Wreath n FORM
Yam n FOOD
Yeast n FOOD
Yew n
Zinnia n
Zombie n SIP
Zoysia n
Zucchini n FOOD

VEHC

Aboard b IN
Aero j UP
Aeronaut n UP
Aeroplane n UP
Aircraft n UP
Airline n UP
Airplane n UP
Ambulance n MEDC
Argosy n FLOW
Ark n FLOW
Armada n DAMG
Astronaut n ASTR
Auto n
Auto v GO
Autobahn n PATH
Autoed v GO
Automobile n
Automotive j
Aviation n UP
Axle n MECH
Balloon n VAPR
Barge n FLOW

Barges n FLOW
Bark n FLOW
Bicycle n
Bicycle v GO
Bike n
Bike v GO
Biked v GO
Biking v GO
Blimp n UP
Board n
Board v IN
Boarded v IN
Boarder n IN
Boarding v IN
Boards v IN
Boat n FLOW
Bobsled n COLD
Bomber n DAMG
Boxcar n HOLW
Bridge n FLOW
Brig n FLOW
Buggies n

Buggy n
Bulldoze v WORK
Bulldozer n WORK
Bus n
Bus v GO
Busing v GO
Bussed v GO
Busses n
Busses v GO
Bussing v GO
Cab n
Cabbies n
Cabby n
Caboose n HOME
Caisson n DAMG
Camion n
Canoe n FLOW
Car n
Caravan n GRUP
Caravan n
Cargo n MART
Carhop n AID

Carload n BULG
Carport n HOME
Carriage n
Carrier n MART
Carrier n FLOW
Carryall n
Cart n
Cart v GO
Cartage n MONY
Cartage n GO
Carted v GO
Carter n GO
Carting v GO
Catamaran n FLOW
Chaise n
Chariot n
Chauffeur n AID
Chopper n UP
Clipper n FLOW
Coach n
Coaster n FLOW
Coaster n

Cockpit n HOME
Cockswain n LEAD
Collier n FLOW
Commute v GO
Commuter n GO
Commuting v GO
Conning n FLOW
Convertible n VARY
Conveyance n
Cosmonaut n ASTR
Coupe n
Coxswain n LEAD
Craft n
Cruise v GO
Cutter n FLOW
Cycle n
Cycle v GO
Cycled v GO
Cycling v GO
Cyclist n
Detrain v SEP
Dhow n FLOW
Dinghy n FLOW
Dirigible n UP
Disembark v SEP
Dollies n
Dolly n
Dories n FLOW
Dory n FLOW
Dozer n ERTH
Dray n
Drive v GO
Driver n LEAD
Driver n WORK
Drone n UP
Drove v GO
Dugout n FLOW
Engine n MECH
Engineer n LEAD
Express n QUIK
Fare n MONY
Fares n MONY
Ferried v GO
Ferries n FLOW
Ferries v GO
Ferry n FLOW
Ferry v GO
Flat n WEAK
Flatboat n FLOW
Flatcar n FORM
Flats n WEAK

Fleet n GRUP
Flivver n
Float n PLAY
Fly n
Flyer n QUIK
Freight n MONY
Freight n MART
Freighter n FLOW
Frigate n FLOW
Fruiter n VEGT
Fuselage n FORM
Galleon n FLOW
Galley n FLOW
Garage n HOME
Glider n UP
Gocart n
Gondola n FLOW
Hack n
Hackney n
Hangar n HOME
Hansom n
Hearse n DEAD
Helicopter n UP
Hotrod n QUIK
Hulk n FLOW
Hydroplane n UP
Jalopy n
Jeep n
Jet n UP
Jetliner n UP
Jetted v UP
Jetting v UP
Junk n FLOW
Kayak n FLOW
Ketch n FLOW
Launch n FLOW
Lifeboat n FLOW
Limousine n
Line n MART
Liner n FLOW
Local n REST
Locomotive n MECH
Lorry n
Monoplane n UP
Monorail n
Motor v GO
Motorboat n FLOW
Motorcade n
Motorcycle n
Motored v GO
Motoring v GO

Omnibus n
Overdrive n MECH
Packet n FLOW
Paddywagon n BLOK
Park v REST
Parked v REST
Parking v REST
Pedal n MECH
Pedal v GO
Perambulator n YNG
Phaeton n
Pickup n
Pilot n LEAD
Plane n UP
Pontoon n FLOW
Poop n FLOW
Pullman n REST
Punt n FLOW
Pushcart n
Raft n FLOW
Rail n
Railroad n
Railroad v FALS
Railroaded v FALS
Railroading v FALS
Railway n
Regatta n FLOW
Rig n
Rocket n UP
Rowboat n FLOW
Runabout n
Sailboat n FLOW
Sampan n FLOW
Schooner n FLOW
Scooter n
Scow n FLOW
Shell n FLOW
Ship n FLOW
Ship n
Ship v GO
Shipboard n FLOW
Skiff n FLOW
Sled n COLD
Sledge n COLD
Sleeper n REST
Sleigh n COLD
Sloop n FLOW
Smack n FLOW
Snowplow n COLD
Spacecraft n ASTR
Sputnik n ASTR

Stage n
Stagecoach n
Stateroom n HOME
Steamboat n FLOW
Steamer n FLOW
Steamship n FLOW
Sub n FLOW
Submarine n FLOW
Subs n FLOW
Subway n DOWN
Sulkies n
Sulky n
Tank n DAMG
Tartan n FLOW
Taxi n
Taxi v GO
Taxicab n
Tender n FLOW
Tire n
Tractor n
Traffic n GO
Trailer n
Train n
Transport n GO
Transportation n GO
Tricycle n
Troika n ANML
Truck n
Truck v GO
Trucked v GO
Trucking v GO
Trucks n
Trucks v GO
Tube n HOLW
Tug n FLOW
Underground n DOWN
Van n
Vehicle n
Vessel n FLOW
Vessel n
Wagon n
Wheel n
Wheel v GO
Wheelbarrow n WORK
Wheeled v GO
Wheeling v GO
Windjammer n FLOW
Yacht n FLOW
Yawl n FLOW
Zeppelin n UP

VIEW

Ablaze j HEAT
Afire j HEAT
Aflame j HEAT
Aglow j
Alight j
Alpha n ASTR
Apparition n MYTH
Appear v

Appear v IDEA
Appearance n
Armory n
Arms n
Aspect n
Aspect n SOME
Astigmatism n SICK
Aureole n HOLW

Aurora n ASTR
Badge n
Badge n POWR
Banner j POWR
Banner n
Beacon n
Beam n
Beheld v

Behold v
Beholder n
Beta n ASTR
Bifocal j AID
Binocular j BODY
Binoculars n MECH
Birdseye j LITL
Birthmark n BGIN

Parts of speech: a article; b preposition; c conjunction; d adverb; f prefix; i interjection;
j adjective; n noun; p pronoun; r phrase; v verb.

Blackjack n COLR	Disappear v SEP	Glance n QUIK	Lighten v
Blaze n HEAT	Discern v	Glare n	Lighthouse n HOME
Blaze n	Display v OPEN	Glare n AGGR	Lighting v
Blaze v BGIN	Ecce v	Glass n AID	Lighting v HEAT
Blazon n	Effulgent j	Glasses n AID	Lightning n WEA
Blind j SICK	Emblazon v COLR	Glaucoma n SICK	Lights v
Blind j COVR	Emblem n	Glaze n	Lights v HEAT
Blindfold n COVR	Enlargement n LARG	Glazier n MART	Limelight n POWR
Blink v VARY	Ensign n	Glazing v	Lit v HEAT
Blip n	Espionage n COVR	Gleam n	Lithograph n WRIT
Bloodshot j SICK	Etch v SHRP	Glimmer v	Look n
Blot v COVR	Evince v OPEN	Glimpse n QUIK	Lookout n
Blotted v COVR	Exhibit n OPEN	Glisten v	Loom v BLUR
Brand n HEAT	Exhibition n OPEN	Glitter n	Loomed v BLUR
Brand n MART	Exhibitionist n SEX	Gloss n EASY	Looming v BLUR
Branding v HEAT	Expose v OPEN	Gloss n FALS	Lorgnette n AID
Bright j	Exposing v OPEN	Glossy j EASY	Lucid j
Brilliant j	Exposition n OPEN	Glow n HEAT	Luminary n POWR
Browse v	Exposure n OPEN	Glowed v HEAT	Luminous j
Bulb n	Eye n BODY	Glower v AGGR	Lurid j
Buoy n FLOW	Eyeball n BODY	Goggle v VARY	Luster n
Burnish v CLEN	Eyebrow n BODY	Goggles n AID	Luster n GOOD
Camera n MECH	Eyeglass n BODY	Goggles v VARY	Lustrous j
Candelabrum n FORM	Eyelash n BODY	Graphic j SHRP	Macroscopic j LARG
Candescence n	Farsighted j AFAR	Graven j SHRP	Mark v
Candle n HEAT	Feature n CRUX	Halo n VAPR	Marked v
Candle n MSMT	Featuring v CRUX	Halo n GOOD	Marking v
Candlelight n HEAT	Film n	Headlight n FORW	Marquee n PLAY
Cartoon n FOOL	Film n PLAY	Heraldry n	Microscope n MECH
Casement n FORM	Fire n HEAT	Highlight v SHRP	Mirage n MYTH
Cataract n SICK	Fireball n HEAT	Ideogram n WRIT	Mirror n
Chandelier n FURN	Fired v HEAT	Illuminate v	Mobile n FORM
Channel n HEAR	Firelight n HEAT	Illuminate v IDEA	Monocle n AID
Cheesecake n LADY	Fires n HEAT	Illuminate v WRIT	Montage n JOIN
Chevron n	Fireworks n HEAT	Illustrate v	Moonbeam n ASTR
Clairvoyant j MYTH	Firing v HEAT	Illustrate v IDEA	Moonlight n ASTR
Clerestory n UP	Flag n	Image n	Moonshine n ASTR
Closeup n NEAR	Flags n	Imaging v	Movies n PLAY
Collimate v MECH	Flagstaff n FORM	Imperceptible j COVR	Myopia n SICK
Comb v OPEN	Flamboyant j POWR	Impress n	Negative n OPPO
Combed v OPEN	Flame n HEAT	Impression n	Newsreel n NEW
Comber n OPEN	Flamed v HEAT	Impressionism n	Nimbus n VAPR
Combing v OPEN	Flaming v HEAT	Incandescence n HEAT	Notice v
Conspicuous j OPEN	Flare v HEAT	Inconspicuous j BLUR	Observable j
Cornea n SOMA	Flash v QUIK	Insight n IDEA	Observation n
Corona n ASTR	Flashier j POWR	Insignia n	Observatory n ASTR
Corona n	Flashlight n	Inspect v OPEN	Observe v
Countersign n SIML	Flashy j POWR	Inspector n OPEN	Observing v
Crest n	Flaunt v POWR	Invisible j COVR	Oculist n MEDC
Crystal n MTRL	Flicker n PLAY	Iridescence n COLR	Ogle v
Daguerreotype n	Flicker n VARY	Iris n BODY	Onlooker n
Dash n MECH	Floodlight n	Irradiate v	Opacity n BLUR
Dashboard n MECH	Fluorescent j	Jack n	Opalescent j
Daylight n TIME	Footlight n DOWN	Kaleidoscope n VARY	Opaque j BLUR
Dazzle v BLUR	Foresee v FORW	Lambent j EASY	Ophthalmology n MEDC
Decal n JOIN	Foresight n FORW	Lamp n	Optic j SOMA
Demonstrate v	Frame n FORM	Landmark n ERTH	Optician n MEDC
Depict v	Frontispiece n FORW	Lantern n	Optics n SOMA
Descried v OPEN	Funnies n GLAD	Leer n AGGR	Oscilloscope n MECH
Descry v OPEN	Gape v	Leering v AGGR	Ostentation n OPEN
Device n	Gaping v	Lens n	Outlook n IDEA
Dial n FORM	Garish j TRIV	Light j	Outshine v POWR
Dialed v FORM	Gaudy j TRIV	Light n HEAT	Overlook v UP
Dialing v FORM	Gawk v FOOL	Lighted v	Overlook v FALS
Diaphanous j	Gaze v	Lighted v HEAT	Oversaw v LEAD

Oversee v LEAD
Overtone n
Overview n WHOL
Pan v
Pane n MTRL
Panned v
Panning v
Panorama n WHOL
Peek v
Peekaboo n
Peep n
Peer v
Peered v
Peering v
Pennant n
Perceive v IDEA
Percept n IDEA
Periscope n MECH
Perspective n
Peruse v WRIT
Phantasma n MYTH
Philately n WRIT
Phosphoresce v
Photo n
Photoelectric j ION
Photogenic j GOOD
Photograph n
Photogravure n MECH
Photostat n SIML
Photosynthesis n SOMA
Pictograph n WRIT
Pictorial j
Picture n
Pictures n
Picturesque j GOOD
Pincenez n AID
Pinkeye n SICK
Pinup n
Placard n WRIT
Plaque n
Plate n
Plexiglass n MTRL
Polaroid n MTRL
Portray v SIML
Posted v WRIT
Poster n WRIT
Posting v WRIT
Posts v WRIT
Preview n FORW
Print n WRIT
Prism n FORM
Projectionist n MECH

Prospect n
Pupil n SOMA
Pyrotechnic j HEAT
Radiance n GLAD
Radiant j GLAD
Radiate v
Ray n
Read v WRIT
Reading v WRIT
Reappear v
Reflect v SIML
Refraction n VARY
Regard n
Regarded v
Regarding v
Regards v
Register v
Registered v
Registering v
Relief n FORM
Retina n SOMA
Retrospect n BACK
Review n IDEA
Rhinestone n MTRL
Rod n SOMA
Sash n FORM
Saw v
Scan v
Scene n
Scenery n
Scenic j
Scintillate v
Scintillate v POWR
Screen v
Scrimshaw n SHRP
Scrutiny n IDEA
Sculpture n FORM
Seal n
See v
Seem v IDEA
Seen v
Sees v
Sheen n
Sheer j OPEN
Shield n
Shimmer v VARY
Shine n
Shine v CLEN
Shine v POWR
Shiner n
Shingle n FORM
Shone v

Shone v POWR
Shoot v
Shortsighted j LITL
Shot n
Show n
Showed v
Showing v
Shown v
Sight n
Sight n BODY
Sights n
Sightseeing n PLAY
Sign n
Signal n
Signet n
Sketch n SIML
Skylight n UP
Slide n
Snap n QUIK
Snapped v QUIK
Snaps v QUIK
Snapshot n
Snoop v OPEN
Spangle n MTRL
Spangle v
Spark v HEAT
Sparkle v
Spectacle n
Spectacles n AID
Spectacles n
Spectacular j POWR
Spectator n
Spectroscope n COLR
Spied v COVR
Spies v COVR
Spot v
Spotlight n SHRP
Spotted v
Spy n COVR
Spyglass n MECH
Squint v VARY
Stamp n WRIT
Stamped v WRIT
Standard n
Stare n
Staring v
Starlight n ASTR
Starspangled j FORM
Stereoscopy n MECH
Sties n SICK
Stigma n BAD
Still n REST

Stills n REST
Sty n SICK
Sunbeam n ASTR
Sunlight n ASTR
Survey n
Survey n IDEA
Tableau n
Taper n
Tattoo n
Telescope n MECH
Television n TALK
Tinsel n MTRL
Torch n
Torch n HEAT
Trademark n MART
Transit n MECH
Translucent j
Transparent j OPEN
TV n TALK
Twinkle n VARY
Unnoticed j COVR
Unperceived j COVR
Unseen j COVR
Unsightly j BAD
Vanish v SEP
Varnish n MTRL
View n
Vignette n
Visibility n
Vision n
Vision n FORW
Vision n MYTH
Visionary j FORW
Vista n
Visual j
Vivid j EMPH
Voyeur n SEX
Watch v
Watch v AID
Watchman n AID
Watchtower n UP
Wideeyed j BODY
Window n
Windows n
Windowsill n FORM
Windshield n AID
Wink n VARY
Witness n
Woodcut n SHRP
Xray n ION

WE

I p SOLE
Me p SOLE
Mine p SOLE

My p SOLE
Myself p SOLE
Our p

Ours p
Us p
We p

WEA

Air n VAPR
Aired v VAPR
Airing v VAPR
Airs n VAPR

Airy j VAPR
Blast n DAMG
Blizzard n DAMG
Bluster v AGGR

Breeze n VAPR
Climate n
Clime n
Cloud n BLUR

Cloudburst n FLOW
Cloudless j VAPR
Cumuli n VAPR
Cumulus n VAPR

Cyclone n DAMG
Downpour n FLOW
Drizzle n FLOW
Easterly n PLAC
Elements n
Fog n BLUR
Gale n DAMG
Gust n VAPR
Hail v FLOW
Hails v FLOW
Hailstone n FLOW
Haze n BLUR
Hazier j BLUR
Hazy j BLUR
Hurricane n DAMG
JackFrost n COLD

Lee n AID
Lightning n VIEW
Mist n BLUR
Misted v BLUR
Monsoon n DAMG
Nimbus n BLUR
Overcast j BLUR
Pluvial j FLOW
Pour v FLOW
Precipitate v FLOW
Rain n FLOW
Rainbow n COLR
Raincoat n GARB
Raindrop n FLOW
Rainfall n FLOW
Shower n FLOW

Sleet n COLD
Smog n BLUR
Snow n COLD
Snowball n COLD
Snowflake n COLD
Snows n COLD
Snowstorm n DAMG
Snowwhite j COLR
Squall n DAMG
Storm n DAMG
Temperate j EASY
Tempest n DAMG
Thunder n HEAR
Thunderbolt n DAMG
Thunders v HEAR
Thunderstorm n DAMG

Tornado n DAMG
Twister n DAMG
Umbrella n GARB
Vane n FORM
Weather n
Weather v POWR
Weathervane n FORM
Whirlwind n VARY
Wind n VAPR
Windbreaker n GARB
Windfall n AID
Windfall n DOWN
Windmill n WORK
Winds n VAPR
Windy j VAPR
Zephyr n VAPR

WEAK

Abase v BAD
Abject j
Alsoran n GO
Amateur j
Anaemic j
Anemic j
Artless j
Atrophy n LACK
Attenuate v LITL
Attrition n
Awkward j
Backward j BACK
Bashful j
Beard v POWR
Beat v POWR
Beat j
Beaten j POWR
Bend v VARY
Bends v VARY
Bent v VARY
Best v POWR
Bested v POWR
Besting v POWR
Better v POWR
Blunder n FALS
Bobble v
Boot v GARB
Booted v GARB
Bootless j TRIV
Botch v
Break v
Breakdown n
Brittle j
Broke v
Broken j
Buckle v VARY
Bum n BAD
Bumpkin n
Bungle v
Bushed j
Bust n
Busted v
Busting v
Butt n
Butterfinger n BODY
Callow j YNG

Capitulate v
Castoff j SEP
Cave v DAMG
Caving v DAMG
Cede v
Ceding v
Chicken n ANML
Chickened v ANML
Chickening v ANML
Clumsy j
Codger n AGGR
Collapse v
Comedown n GO
Commoner n GRUP
Compromise v
Concede v AGRE
Concession n AGRE
Conquer v POWR
Conquest n POWR
Cop v
Copped v
Copping v
Corrode v DIRT
Corrosion n DIRT
Cow v PANG
Coward n
Cowed v PANG
Cower v PANG
Cowing v PANG
Coy j
Crack v
Cracked v
Cracker n
Craven j
Cream v POWR
Creamed v POWR
Cringe v PANG
Cripple v SICK
Cripple v DAMG
Cropper n DOWN
Crude j
Crumble v SEP
Cub n YNG
Cumbersome n
Dastard n BAD
Daunt v

Deadbeat n DEAD
Debacle n DAMG
Debility n
Decay n DIRT
Decompensate v
Decrepit j DIRT
Decrepitude n DIRT
Decrescent j LITL
Default n
Defeat v POWR
Defeating v POWR
Defeatist n
Defect n
Defect v SEP
Defenseless j
Delicacy n
Delicate j
Delinquency n
Demoralize v
Demure j
Depose v SEP
Deposing v SEP
Derelict j BAD
Deteriorate v DIRT
Dethrone v SEP
Devaluate v LITL
Diffident j
Dilettante n TRIV
Dilute v
Disability n
Disadvantage n
Disarm v DAMG
Disqualify v
Dissipate v
Dogtired j EMPH
Down v POWR
Downed v POWR
Downfall n DOWN
Downing v POWR
Drawback n
Droop v DOWN
Dud n
Duffer n
Dysfunction n
Efface v
Effete j

Emasculate v SEX
Enervate v
Enuresis n SOMA
Erode v
Erosion n
Error n FALS
Exhaust v
Exhausting v
Exhaustion n
Fade v
Fading v
Fag v
Fagged v
Fail v
Faint j PANG
Fallible j
Falter v VARY
Fan v VARY
Fanned v VARY
Fatigue v
Fatigues v
Feeble j
Fiasco n
Fizzle n
Flabbier j EASY
Flabby j EASY
Flaccid j EASY
Flag v
Flags v
Flat j
Flat n VEHC
Flats n VEHC
Flatten v POWR
Flaw n FALS
Fledgling n YNG
Flimsy j
Flop v
Flounder v VARY
Floundered v VARY
Floundering v VARY
Fluff n
Flunk v
Foible n
Foil v BLOK
Foiled v BLOK
Foiling v BLOK

Fold v VARY	Ineligible j	Novice n	Sapped v LACK
Folded v VARY	Inept j	Overawe v PANG	Scapegoat n ANML
Folding v VARY	Inexperience n	Overcame v POWR	Selfpity n SOLE
Founder v	Inexpert j	Overcome v POWR	Setback n BACK
Foundered v	Infirm j	Overpower v POWR	Shaky j VARY
Foundering v	Infirmity n	Overthrow v POWR	Sheep n ANML
Fragile j	Ingenue n LADY	Overwhelm v POWR	Shellack v POWR
Frail j	Inglorious j BAD	Pale j COLR	Shied v VARY
Fruitless j VEGT	Inoperable j	Pallid j COLR	Shoddy j
Fumble v	Inoperative j	Pallor n COLR	Shortcoming n
Futile j TRIV	Insecure j	Pantywaist n YNG	Shrivel v
Game j SICK	Instability n VARY	Pariah n SEP	Shy j
Gangling j LARG	Insubstantial j TRIV	Passive j REST	Sissy n
Gauche j	Insufficient j LACK	Pathetic j PANG	Slip n EASY
Gave v	Intimidate v PANG	Peter v	Slipshod j DIRT
Gawk n FOOL	Invalid j SICK	Pipsqueak n LITL	Slouch n REST
Gawkier j FOOL	Involuntary j	Piteous j PANG	Slump n DOWN
Gawky j FOOL	Irresolute j	Pitiful j	Sorry j
Give v	Irresponsible j	Plug n ANML	Spineless j SOMA
Goat n ANML	Jade n ANML	Poltroon n	Stale j DIRT
Goof v FOOL	Jade v	Poop v	Stammer v TALK
Green j COLR	Jaded v	Pooped v	Stricken j DAMG
Greenhorn n	Jading v	Pooping v	Stumble v VARY
Groggy j PANG	Jellyfish n ANML	Poor j LACK	Stutter v TALK
Grovel v	Kaput j END	Poverty n LACK	Subdue v POWR
Gullible j	Kilter n	Powerless j LACK	Submission n SUB
Hack n ANML	Lame j SICK	Pregnability n	Submissive j SUB
Halfcocked j	Lame j	Premature j FORW	Submit v SUB
Halfhearted j	Laming v SICK	Prey n DAMG	Substandard j
Halt n SICK	Languish v REST	Primitive j	Subvert v DAMG
Ham n	Lapse v	Prostrate v DOWN	Succumb v
Ham v FOOL	Lax j EASY	Provincial j PLAC	Succumb v DEAD
Hammed v FOOL	Laxity n EASY	Puerile j YNG	Sucker n FALS
Handicap n BLOK	Lemon n VEGT	Pull v	Surrender n
Hapless j	Lick v POWR	Pulled v	Susceptible j MOTV
Helpless j	Licked v POWR	Punily d	Threw v POWR
Hick n	Licking v POWR	Punk j	Throw v POWR
Hillbilly n BULG	Limp j EASY	Puny j	Timid j
Hobble v GO	Limp n GO	Pushover n EASY	Tire v
Hobbled v GO	Limped v GO	Quail v PANG	Tired v
Hobbledehoy n YNG	Limping v GO	Quailed v PANG	Tiring v
Homelier j	Lisp n TALK	Quailing v PANG	Totter v VARY
Homely j	Lose v LACK	Quarry n DAMG	Trim v POWR
Humble j	Maladroit j	Quarries n DAMG	Trimmed v POWR
Humiliate v AGGR	Mean j	Ramshackle j FORM	Trip v VARY
Humility n	Mediocre j	Raw j	Trounce v POWR
Ignoble j BAD	Meek j	Recreant n	Tucker v
Immature j YNG	Mice n ANML	Reel v VARY	Tumbledown j VARY
Impair v DAMG	Mince v	Relapse n	Tyro n
Imperfect j	Mince v GO	Remiss j	Unable j
Impotence n	Miscarriage n FALS	Resign v	Unassuming j
Impotence n SEX	Miscarry v FALS	Reticent j	Underdeveloped j
Impoverish v LACK	Misfire v FALS	Rickety j	Underdog n ANML
Impractical j	Misfit n FALS	Rookie n	Undermine v DAMG
Inability n	Mistake n FALS	Rout n GO	Underprivileged j LACK
Inadequacy n	Mouse n ANML	Routed v GO	Undeveloped j
Incapable j	Muddle n BLUR	Routing v GO	Undid v
Incapacity n	Muff v	Rustic n ERTH	Undo v
Incompetence n	Muffed v	Rustier j	Unequal j OPPO
Incomplete j SOME	Muffing v	Rusty j	Unfit j
Incontinence n SOMA	Naive j	Sad j	Unfortunate j
Indefensible j	Nambypamby j	Sap n FOOL	Ungainly j
Ineffectual j	Neglect v	Sap v DAMG	Unguarded j OPEN
Inefficacy n	Neophyte n	Sap v LACK	Unimproved j
Inefficiency n	Nobody n SOLE	Sapped v DAMG	Uninspired j TRIV

Unlucky j	Unstable j VARY	Vain j TRIV	Wearing v PANG
Unobtrusive j	Unsteady j VARY	Vanquish v POWR	Weary j PANG
Unpolished j	Unsuccessful j	Victim n DAMG	Whip v POWR
Unprepared j	Unsure j BLUR	Vitiate v BAD	Wilt v
Unproductive j TRIV	Untactful j	Vulnerable j	Wishywashy j
Unprotected j	Untenable j	Wan j COLR	Wither v
Unqualified j	Untrained j EDUC	Wane v LITL	Wizen v
Unreliable j	Untrustworthy j AGGR	Waning v LITL	Wobble v VARY
Unripe j	Unwary j	Waterloo n PLAC	Wore v PANG
Unsafe j DAMG	Unwieldy j	Waver v VARY	Worn v PANG
Unsatisfactory j	Unworthy j	Weak j	Wornout j PANG
Unskilled j	Upend v VARY	Wear v PANG	Yellow j COLR
Unsophistocated j	Upset v VARY	Wearily d PANG	Yield v
Unsound j	Upset v POWR	Weariness n PANG	Yokel n

WHOL

Absolute j EMPH	Ecumenical j HOLY	Indivisible j JOIN	Summed v NUMR
Absolutism n LEAD	Endemic j NEAR	Intact j AID	Summed v
Aggregate j GRUP	Entire j	Integer n NUMR	Summing v NUMR
All j	Entities n	Integral j CRUX	Summing v
Almighty j POWR	Entity n	Integral j NUMR	Thorough j
Altogether d	Environment n HOLW	Integrate v JOIN	Thoroughgoing j
Amount n	Epidemic n SICK	Jackpot n HOLW	Throughout b
Catholic j	Every j	Man n GRUP	Total j
Clean j CLEN	Everybody p SOLE	Mankind n GRUP	Total n NUMR
Common j	Everyman n SOLE	Microcosm n LITL	Totaling v
Common n PLAC	Everyone p SOLE	Milieu n HOLW	Totaling v NUMR
Commoned v	Everything p	Natural j	Unabridged j
Commonweal n AID	Everywhere d PLAC	Nature n	Unanimous j AGRE
Communal j GRUP	Exhaustive j END	Omnipotence n POWR	Unconditional j
Community n GRUP	Full j BULG	Omnipresence n NEAR	Uncut j
Complement n	Fullfledged j POWR	Omniscient j IDEA	Underworld n DOWN
Complete v END	Fullgrown j LARG	Omnivorous j FOOD	Undivided j
Completely d EMPH	Fulllength j LARG	Overall j	Uniform j SIML
Comprehend v	Fulltime j TIME	Overview n VIEW	Universal j
Comprise v JOIN	General n	Pan f	Universe n
Consist v	Generic j	Pandemic j	Weltanschauung n IDEA
Consisted v	Globe n ERTH	Panorama n VIEW	Whole j
Corpora n	Gross j	Pantheism n HOLY	Wholehearted j TRUE
Corpus n	Gross v	Pervade v IN	Wholewheat j VEGT
Cosmic j FORM	Grossing v	Plenary j	Wholly d EMPH
Cosmology n IDEA	Human j GRUP	Solid j	World n
Cosmopolitan j PLAC	Humanity n GRUP	Solidarity n GRUP	Worldwide j LARG
Cosmos n FORM	Illimitable j LARG	Sum n NUMR	
Ecology n LIVE	Include v	Sum n	

WORK

Anvil n FORM	Beetle n MECH	Calisthenic j PLAY	Cooper n HOLW
Apprentice n SUB	Bit n SHRP	Calling n	Coppersmith n MTRL
Artifact n	Blacksmith n HEAT	Career n	Coworker n SIML
Artisan n POWR	Bluecollar j	Caretaker n AID	Craft n POWR
Auger n SHRP	Brace n	Carpenter n FORM	Craft n GRUP
Awl n SHRP	Breadwinner n MONY	Chimneysweep n CLEN	Crafted v POWR
Ax n SHRP	Bricklayer n FORM	Chisel v SHRP	Crafting v POWR
Axe n SHRP	Build v FORM	Chore n	Cropper n VEGT
Axed v SHRP	Building v FORM	Collier n ERTH	Crowbar n FORM
Axes n SHRP	Bulldoze v VEHC	Construct v FORM	Cultivate v ERTH
Axing v SHRP	Bulldozer n VEHC	Constructing v FORM	Custodian n AID
Barbell n FORM	Busier j	Contractor n AGRE	Distillery n SIP
Beaten j	Busy j	Coolie n	Drafthorse n ANML

Parts of speech: a article; b preposition; c conjunction; d adverb; f prefix; i interjection;
j adjective; n noun; p pronoun; r phrase; v verb.

Drill v SHRP
Driver n VEHC
Drudge v TRIV
Dumbbell n PLAY
Duties n MOTV
Duty n MOTV
Earn v MONY
Earned v MONY
Effort n
Electrician n ION
Employ v
Employed v
Employee n
Employer n LEAD
Exercise n
Exert v
Fabricate v
Factory n HOME
Farm n ERTH
Fashion v FORM
Fashioning v FORM
Fatigues n GARB
Featherbed v TRIV
File v
Filing v
Filings n MTRL
Foreman n LEAD
Forge v HEAT
Fork n
Foundry n HEAT
Function n
Functional j
Functioned v
Functioning v
Glassblower n MTRL
Grind v
Grinder n
Grinds v
Ground v
Grub v TRIV
Grubbed v TRIV
Hammer n
Hand n BODY
Handicraft n BODY

Handiwork n BODY
Hands n BODY
Handyman n AID
Hardware n MECH
Hatchet n SHRP
Haymaker n VEGT
Help n AID
Hind n
Hoe n
Housework n HOME
Implement n
Industrial j MART
Industries n MART
Industrious j EVER
Industry n EVER
Industry n MART
Janitor n AID
Job n
Journeyman n POWR
Kolkohz n ERTH
Labor n
Laboratory n HOME
Lever n
Line n
Mallet n
Malpractice n FALS
Manufacture v MART
Mason n FORM
Mechanic n MECH
Mill n MECH
Milled v MECH
Milling v MECH
Mine n ERTH
Mined v ERTH
Mines n ERTH
Mining v ERTH
Moonlight v CRIM
Occupation n
Occupied v
Occupy v
Operate v
Operating v
Opus n
Pallet n

Peasant n ERTH
Peon n SUB
Personnel n GRUP
Pestle n
Pickax n SHRP
Picket n BLOK
Pitchfork n SHRP
Plane n EASY
Planed v EASY
Planing v EASY
Plant n MART
Plebeian j GRUP
Plier n
Plow v ERTH
Plumber n FLOW
Position n
Post n
Posts n
Practice n EVER
Practitioner n EVER
Profession n
Profession n GRUP
Proletarian n GRUP
Pursuit n
Pushup n
Rake n
Ranch n ERTH
Rasp n HEAR
Rebuild v FORM
Reconstruct v FORM
Repairman n AID
Salary n MONY
Sandhog n HOLW
Saw n SHRP
Scab n AGGR
Scabbed v AGGR
Scabbing v AGGR
Screwdriver n JOIN
Scythe n SHRP
Sharecropper n VEGT
Shop n MART
Shovel n HOLW
Situation n
Sledge n

Smith n
Snake n ANML
Soldier v FALS
Spade n
Spin v FABR
Spun v FABR
Strenuous j
Strike v BLOK
Striking v BLOK
Struck v BLOK
Studio n HOME
Task n
Taskmaster n LEAD
Till v ERTH
Tilled v ERTH
Tilling v ERTH
Tills v ERTH
Tinker n MTRL
Tinker v TRIV
Toil v
Toiled v
Tool n
Trade n MART
Travail n PANG
Trowel n
Unemployment n LACK
Vocation n
Wage n MONY
Wheelbarrow n VEHC
Windmill n WEA
Work n
Work n FORM
Work v PANG
Worked v
Worked v PANG
Working v
Working v PANG
Workman n MALE
Works v
Works n FORM
Works v PANG
Workshop n HOME
Wrench n
Wrenches n

WRIT

A n
A n EDUC
A n MUSC
ABC n
ABC n CRUX
Acrostic n
Actuaries n MART
Actuary n MART
Address n PLAC
Affidavit n TRUE
Agate n
Agenda n
Alacarte j FOOD
Album n
Almanac n
Alpha n
Alphabet n FORW
Amanuensis n

Anagram n VARY
Annals n PAST
Annotate v
Annual n TIME
Anthology n GRUP
Apocalypse n HOLY
Apocrypha n HOLY
Apostrophe n
Appendices n JOIN
Application n MOTV
Archives n
Archives n HOME
Article n
Asterisk n EMPH
Author n
Authoring v
Autograph v
B n

B n EDUC
B n MUSC
Beta n
Bible n HOLY
Biblical j HOLY
Bibliography n
Bill n
Bill n LAW
Billboard n FORM
Billed v
Billing v
Biography n PAST
Blank n LACK
Blanked v LACK
Blotter n
Book n
Book v LAW
Bookcase n HOLW

Booked v LAW
Booking v LAW
Bookish j
Bookkeeper n MART
Booklet n
Books n
Books v LAW
Bookseller n MART
Bookstore n MART
Braille n
Brochure n
Bull n HOLY
Bulletin n
Bulls n HOLY
C n
C n EDUC
C n MUSC
Cable n

Cablegram n
Cahier n
Calendar n TIME
Canon n HOLY
Canonical j HOLY
Canto n SOME
Capital j LARG
Capitalize v LARG
Caption n
Carbon n SIML
Card n
Carded v
Carding v
Caret n
Catalogue n FORW
Catechism n HOLY
Certificate n TRUE
Chalk n MTRL
Chapter n SOME
Character n
Charter n LAW
Check n
Check n MONY
Checked v
Chirography n
Chit n MONY
Chronicle n PAST
Chronicle n
Cipher n COVR
Circular n
Circulation n VARY
Circumflex n EMPH
Circumscribe v HOLW
Clef n MUSC
Clerical j MART
Clerk n MART
Coauthor n JOIN
Colon n
Column n
Columnist n
Comics n GLAD
Comma n
Compendium n LITL
Composition n FORM
Concordance n FORW
Context n HOLW
Contract n AGRE
Cookbook n FOOD
Copied v SIML
Copy n SIML
Correspond v
Countersign v
Couplet n JOIN
Coupon n
Courier n GO
Cover n HOLW
Crayon n COLR
Credential n TRUE
Crib n CRIM
Cribbed v CRIM
Cribbing v CRIM
Cross v SEP
Crosshatch n FORM
Crossword j JOIN
Cryptogram n COVR

Cursive j EASY
Cypher n COVR
D n
D n EDUC
D n MUSC
Dactyl n
Daily n TIME
Dash n FORM
Decipher v OPEN
Decode v OPEN
Decretal n HOLY
Deed n LAW
Delta n
Desk n FURN
Deuteronomy n HOLY
Diacritic n EMPH
Diaries n
Diary n
Dictionary n FORW
Diploma n POWR
Directory n FORW
Dispatch n
Dissertation n IDEA
Ditto n SIML
Docket n LAW
Document n
Document v TRUE
Documentary n TRUE
Doggerel n TRIV
Doodle v TRIV
Dossier n
Dot n LITL
Draft n FORM
Draft n MONY
Drafted v FORM
Draughts n MONY
Draughtsman n FORM
Draw v
Drawn v
Drew v
Dummy n
Duplicator n MECH
E n
E n MUSC
E n EDUC
Ecclesiastes n HOLY
Edit v AID
Editing v AID
Edition n
Editor n AID
Elite j
Encode v VARY
Encyclopedia n FORW
Endorse v AGRE
Enroll v JOIN
Enter v IN
Entries n IN
Entry n IN
Epigraph n
Epistle n
Epistle n HOLY
Epitaph n DEAD
Essay n
Excerpt n SOME
Extra n MUCH

F n
F n MUSC
F n EDUC
File v FORW
Filing v FORW
Fingerprint n BODY
Flyer n
Flyleaf n
Folder n HOLW
Folio n
Font n
Footnote n DOWN
Footprint n BODY
Forge v FALS
Forgery n FALS
Form n FORM
G n
G n MUSC
Galley n
Gamma n
Gazette n
Gloss n IDEA
Glossary n FORW
Gospel n HOLY
Gothic j
Graphic j
Graphology n IDEA
Guidebook n AID
H n
Haggada n HOLY
Hagiology n HOLY
Hallmark n GOOD
Hand n BODY
Handbook n AID
Handwriting n BODY
Haphtarah n HOLY
Hatch n FORM
Matched v FORM
Heading n FORW
Headline n FORW
Hieroglyphic n
Hieroglyphic n BLUR
Hymnal n HOLY
Hyphen n SEP
I n
I n FORM
Ideogram n VIEW
Illegible j BLUR
Illiteracy n FOOL
Illuminate v VIEW
Imprimatur n AGRE
Index n
Initial n
Ink n COLR
Inscription n
Invoice n MART
Issue n
Italicize v EMPH
J n
Jot v
Journal n
Justify v SIML
K n
Kerygma n HOLY
Koran n HOLY

L n
L n FORM
Label n
Leaf n
Leaflet n
Lease n HAVE
Leaves n
Lectern n FURN
Ledger n
Legend n
Legible j SHRP
Letter n
Letterhead n FORW
Lexicon n FORW
Librarian n
Libraries n HOME
Library n HOME
Libretto n MUSC
License n AGRE
Line n
List n FORW
Listed v FORW
Literacy n EDUC
Literal j SIML
Literary j
Literate j EDUC
Literature n
Lithograph n VIEW
Lithograph n MECH
Log n
Logged v
Logging v
M n
Magazine n
Mail n GO
Mailing v GO
Mails v GO
Manifest n MART
Manual n
Manuscript n
Mark v
Marked v
Marking v
Media n TALK
Memo n
Memoir n PAST
Memorandum n
Menu n FOOD
Mimeograph v MECH
Minutes n
Misprint n FALS
Misread v FALS
Missive n
Monogram n
Ms n
N n
Newsboy n YNG
Newspaper n NEW
Notary n LAW
Notation n
Note n
Note n MONY
Notebook n
Noted v
Noting v

Novel n
Novels n
O n
O n FORM
Obituary n DEAD
Offset n MECH
Omnibus n MUCH
P n
Pad n
Page n
Pagination n FORW
Pamphlet n
Paper n MTRL
Paperback n
Papyrus n MTRL
Paragraph n SOME
Parchment n MTRL
Parenthesis n SEP
Pass n GO
Passage n SOME
Passes n GO
Passport n GO
Pastel n COLR
Pastoral n HOLY
Payroll n MONY
Pen n
Pencil n
Penmanship n
Penned v
Penning v
Pens v
Period n END
Periodical n
Permit n AGRE
Peruse v VIEW
Pharmacopoeia n MEDC
Philately n VIEW
Philology n IDEA
Phylactery n HOLY
Pi n NUMR
Pi n
Pica n MSMT
Pictograph n VIEW
Placard n VIEW
Plagiarism n CRIM
Playwright n PLAY
Polygraph n MECH
Pony n CRIM
Portfolio n HOLW

Post n GO
Post v
Postage n MONY
Postal j GO
Postcard n GO
Posted v GO
Posted v VIEW
Poster n VIEW
Posting v GO
Posting v VIEW
Postoffice n HOME
Posts v GO
Posts v VIEW
Postscript n BACK
Press n MECH
Primer n
Print v MECH
Print n VIEW
Process n LAW
Program n FORM
Prospectus n FORW
Protocol n
Publication n OPEN
Publish v OPEN
Punctuate v
Punctuation n
Q n
Quarterly n TIME
Quatrain n
Quill n
R n
Read v VIEW
Reading v VIEW
Receipt n HAVE
Record n
Recorder n
Register n
Registered v
Registering v
Registrar n
Registration n
Reporter n
Retrace v SIML
Review n IDEA
Roll n FORW
Roster n FORW
S n
S n FORM
Schedule v FORW

Scoop v POWR
Score n MUSC
Scrapbook n
Scratch n SHRP
Scrawl n
Scribble v
Scribe n
Script n
Scripture n HOLY
Scroll n
Scroll n FORM
Secretary n
Secretary n LEAD
Secretary n FURN
Semicolon n
Sheepskin n POWR
Shorthand n LITL
Sign v
Signature n
Signed v
Slate n
SOS n DAMG
Staff n MUSC
Stamp n
Stamp n VIEW
Stamped v
Stamped v VIEW
Stanza n SOME
Stationer n MART
Stationery n
Statute n LAW
Stencil v
Stenography n
Stereotype n MECH
Sticker n JOIN
Stub n LITL
Subscript n DOWN
Syllabus n
T n
T n FORM
Tab n MONY
Table n FORM
Tables n FORM
Tablet n
Tabular j FORM
Tabulate v FORM
Tag v JOIN
Telegram n
Testament n HOLY

Testament n MOTV
Text n
Textbook n EDUC
Textual j
Thesaurus n FORW
Theses n IDEA
Thesis n IDEA
Tick v
Ticked v
Ticket n
Ticking v
Times n TIME
Tome n
Trace v SIML
Traced v SIML
Tract n
Transcribe v SIML
Treatise n
Type n
Type v MECH
Typewrite v MECH
Typing v MECH
Typist n MECH
U n
U n FORM
Underwrite v AID
Unlisted j
Unmarked j BLUR
Unpublished j COVR
Unwritten j
V n
V n FORM
Visa n AID
Volume n
Voucher n TRUE
W n
Warrant n LAW
Wire n
Writ n LAW
Write v
Writing v
Written v
X n
X n FORM
Xerox v SIML
Y n
Y n FORM
Yearbook n TIME
Z n

YNG

Adolescent j
Aladdin n MYTH
Babied v AID
Babies n
Babies v AID
Baby n
Baby v AID
Babying v AID
Bassinet n REST
Bib n GARB
Bobbysox n GARB
Bootee n GARB
Boy n MALE

Brat n AGGR
Brood n GRUP
Brood j BGIN
Brownie n LADY
Cadet n MALE
Calf n ANML
Callow j WEAK
Calves n ANML
Chick n ANML
Chick n LADY
Child n
Child n KIN
Childbirth n BGIN

Childhood n TIME
Childish j FOOL
Childless j LACK
Childlike j SIML
Children n
Children n KIN
Chit n
Colleen n LADY
Colt n ANML
Conceive v BGIN
Conception n BGIN
Cradle n REST
Creche n AID

Crib n REST
Cribbed v REST
Cribbing v REST
Cub n ANML
Cub n WEAK
Cubbed v ANML
Diaper n GARB
Duckling n ANML
Enfant n
Fawn n ANML
Filial j KIN
Filly n ANML
Fledgling n WEAK

Foal n ANML

Foundling n SEP

Fry n TRIV

Fry n FLOW

Girl n LADY

Godchild n KIN

Gosling n ANML

Grandchild n KIN

Grub n BUG

Heifer n ANML

Highchair n REST

Hobbledehoy n WEAK

Immature j WEAK

Imp n BAD

Impish j BAD

Infancy n

Infant n

Infanticide n DEAD

Infantile j

Junior j SUB

Juvenile j

Kid n ANML

Kid n

Kindergarten n EDUC

Kitten n ANML

Kitties n ANML

Kitty n ANML

Lad n MALE

Lamb n ANML

Larva n BUG

Lass n LADY

Layette n GARB

Litter n ANML

Maiden n LADY

Master n MALE

Mongolian n SICK

Moppet n

Nestling n ANML

Newsboy n WRIT

Nurse v SIP

Nursery n HOME

Offspring n KIN

Page n AID

Pantywaist n WEAK

Papoose n

Parturition n BGIN

Pediatric j MEDC

Perambulator n VEHC

Playpen n PLAY

Posterity n FORW

Precocity.n POWR

Puberty n SEX

Pubescence n SEX

Puerile j WEAK

Pullet n ANML

Pup n ANML

Puppies n ANML

Puppies n FOOL

Puppy n ANML

Puppy n FOOL

Ragamuffin n DIRT

Sapling n VEGT

Schoolboy n EDUC

Schoolgirl n EDUC

Spawn v BGIN

Squirt n TRIV

Stepchild n KIN

Stripling n MALE

Suckling n SIP

Waif n SOLE

Yearling n ANML

Young j

Youngster n

Youth n

references

Bleuler, Eugen. *Dementia praecox*. New York: International Universities Press, 1950.

Boissière, Prudence. *Dictionnaire analogique de la langue française* (Fifth ed.). Paris: A. Boyer, 1882.

Bousfield, Weston A. The occurrence of clusters in the recall of randomly arranged associates. *The Journal of General Psychology,* 1953, *49*, 229-240.

Bousfield, Weston A., Cohen, Burton H. and Whitmarsh, Gerald A. Associative clustering in the recall of words of different taxonomic frequencies of occurrence. *Psychological Reports,* 1958, *4*, 39-44.

Bousfield, Weston A., Puff, C. Richard and Cowan, Thaddeus M. The development of constancies in sequential organization during repeated free recall. *Journal of Verbal Learning and Verbal Behavior,* 1964, *6*, 489-495.

Buck, Carl D. *A dictionary of selected synonyms in the principal Indo-European languages*. Chicago: The University of Chicago Press, 1949.

Casares, Julio. *Diccionario ideológico de la lengua Española* (1959). Barcelona: Editorial Gustavo Gili, S. A., 1963.

Cofer, Charles N. On some factors in the organizational characteristics of free recall. *American Psychologist*, 1965, *20*, 261-272.

Cofer, Charles N. Associative overlap and category membership as variables in paired-associate learning. *Journal of Verbal Learning and Verbal Behavior*, 1968, *7*, 230-235.

Dornseiff, Franz. *Der deutsche Wortschatz nach Sachgruppen*. Berlin: Walter d Gruyter & Co., 1954.

Fillenbaum, Samuel and Rapoport, Amnon. *Structures in the subjective lexicon*. New York: Academic Press, 1971.

Freud, Sigmund. Psycho-analytic notes upon an autobiographical account of a case of paranoia (dementia paranoides) (1911). *The standard edition of the complete psychological works of Sigmund Freud, Vol. XIII*. London: Hogarth Press, 1953.

Hallig, Rudolf and Wartburg, Walther von. *Begriffssystem als Grundlage für die Lexikographie. Versuch eines Ordnungsschemas*. Berlin: Akademie-Verlag, 1963.

Hartsough, Ross and Laffal, Julius. Content analysis of scientific writings. *The Journal of General Psychology*, 1970, *83*, 193-206.

Katz, Jerrold J. and Postal, Paul M. *An integrated theory of linguistic descriptions*. Cambridge, Massachusetts: The M.I.T. Press, 1964.

Laffal, Julius. The contextual associates of sun and God in Schreber's autobiography. *The Journal of Abnormal and Social Psychology*, 1960, *61*, 474-479.

Laffal, Julius. Changes in the language of a schizophrenic patient during psychotherapy. *The Journal of Abnormal and Social Psychology*, 1961, *63*, 422-427.

Laffal, Julius. *Pathological and normal language*. New York: Atherton Press, 1965.

Laffal, Julius. Characteristics of the three person conversation. *Journal of Verbal Learning and Verbal Behavior*, 1967, *6*, 555-559.

Laffal, Julius. An approach to the total content analysis of speech in psychotherapy. In John M. Shlein, Ed. *Research in psychotherapy, Vol. III*. Washington, D. C.: American Psychological Association, 1968.

Laffal, Julius. Contextual similarities as a basis for inference. In George Gerbner, Ole R. Holsti, Klaus Krippendorff, William J. Paisley and Philip J. Stone, Eds. *The analysis of communication content*. New York: John Wiley and Sons, 1969.

Laffal, Julius. Toward a conceptual grammar and lexicon. *Computers and the Humanities*, 1970, *4*, 173-186.

Laffal, Julius and Feldman, Sheldon. The structure of single word and continuous word associations. *Journal of Verbal Learning and Verbal Behavior*, 1962, *1*, 54-61.

Laffal, Julius and Feldman, Sheldon. The structure of free speech. *Journal of Verbal Learning and Verbal Behavior*, 1963, 2, 498-503.

Macalpine, Ida and Hunter, Richard A. Discussion of the Schreber case. In Daniel Paul Schreber. *Memoirs of my nervous illness*. Tr. by Ida Macalpine and Richard A. Hunter. Cambridge, Massachusetts: Robert Bentley, 1955.

Mandler, George. Organization and memory. In Kenneth W. Spence and Janet T. Spence, Eds. *The psychology of learning and motivation, Vol. I*. New York: Academic Press, 1967.

Miller, George A. English verbs of motion: a case study in semantics and lexical memory. In Arthur W. Melton and Edwin Martin, Eds. *Coding processes in human memory*. Washington, D. C.: V. H. Winston and Sons, 1972.

Naess, Arne. Synonymity as revealed by intuition. *Philosophical Review*, 1957, *66*, 87-93.

Ogden, Charles K. *Opposition, a linguistic and psychological analysis*. London: K. Paul, Trench, Trubner, 1932.

Roget, Peter Mark. *Roget's international thesaurus* (1852). New York: Thomas Y. Crowell, 1960.

Schreber, Daniel Paul. *Memoirs of my nervous illness* (1903). Tr. by Ida Macalpine and Richard A. Hunter. Cambridge, Massachusetts: Robert Bentley, 1955.

Spurgeon, Caroline F. E. *Shakespeare's imagery and what it tells us* (1935). Cambridge: University Press, 1958.

Trier, Jost. Das sprachliche Feld. *Neue Jahrbücher für Wissenschaft und Jugendbildung*, 1934, *10*, 428-449.

Tulving, Endel. Subjective organization in free recall of "unrelated" words. *Psychological Review*, 1962, *69*, 344-354.

Watson, David and Laffal, Julius. Sources of verbalizations of psychotherapists about patients. *The Journal of General Psychology*, 1963, *68*, 89-98.

Weisgerber, Leo. Sprache und Begriffsbildung. *Actes du quatrième congrès international de linguistes*. Copenhagen: Einar Munksgaard, 1938.

index